A History of Victorian Literature

BLACKWELL HISTORIES OF LITERATURE

General editor: Peter Brown, University of Kent, Canterbury

The books in this series renew and redefine a familiar form by recognizing that to write literary history involves more than placing texts in chronological sequence. Thus the emphasis within each volume falls both on plotting the significant literary developments of a given period, and on the wider cultural contexts within which they occurred. 'Cultural history' is construed in broad terms and authors address such issues as politics, society, the arts, ideologies, varieties of literary production and consumption, and dominant genres and modes. The effect of each volume is to give the reader a sense of possessing a crucial sector of literary terrain, of understanding the forces that give a period its distinctive cast, and of seeing how writing of a given period impacts on, and is shaped by, its cultural circumstances.

Published to date

Old English Literature	Robert Fulk
Seventeenth-Century English Literature	Thomas N. Corns
Victorian Literature	James Eli Adams

A History of
Victorian Literature

James Eli Adams

WILEY-BLACKWELL

A John Wiley & Sons, Ltd., Publication

Blackwell Publishing was acquired by John Wiley & Sons in February 2007. Blackwell's publishing program has been merged with Wiley's global Scientific, Technical, and Medical business to form Wiley-Blackwell.

Registered Office
John Wiley & Sons Ltd, The Atrium, Southern Gate, Chichester, West Sussex, PO19 8SQ, United Kingdom

Editorial Offices
350 Main Street, Malden, MA 02148-5020, USA
9600 Garsington Road, Oxford, OX4 2DQ, UK
The Atrium, Southern Gate, Chichester, West Sussex, PO19 8SQ, UK

For details of our global editorial offices, for customer services, and for information about how to apply for permission to reuse the copyright material in this book please see our website at www.wiley.com/wiley-blackwell.

Library of Congress Cataloging-in-Publication Data

Adams, James Eli.
  A history of Victorian literature / James Eli Adams.
    p. cm. – (Blackwell histories of literature)
  Includes bibliographical references and index.
  ISBN 978-0-631-22082-4 (alk. paper)
    1. English literature–19th century–History and criticism. 2. Literature and society–Great Britain–History–19th century. I. Title.
  PR461.A33 2009
  820.9'008–dc22

                                                    2008031713

A catalogue record for this book is available from the British Library.

Set in 10.5/13pt Galliard
by SPi Publisher Services, Pondicherry, India

1   2009

Contents

———

A signal work of literary historiography: broad and sound in its fabric, detail richly textured in its detail. Along the tensed warp of Victorian culture that emerged in a daze from Romantic premisses and plunged at last into a twentieth century it had inadvertently invented, Adams weaves through overlapping historical nodes – industrial-domestic, pious-scientific, democratic-imperial, class-blent and gender-bent – a steady weft of agile, expert readings of essays, poems, biographies, dramas, and especially novels. Shuttling among genres lets him season a diet of judiciously received readings with fresh discoveries about, say, the concurrent maturation of new kinds of prose fiction and long poem toward 1850, or the ideologically laden recourse to life-writing in the 1870s and 1880s. The sheer quantity of this comprehensive history is matched by the genial quality of the historian who comprehends it, and whose infectiously self-renewing enthusiasm makes great learning look like great fun. It has been many decades, and several major reorientations in critical scholarship, since we last saw a literary-historical synopsis on this scale. Rejoicing to imagine this book representing our generation's Victorianism to posterity, we must admit that to have Adams as our spokesman feels a little like boasting.

Herbert F. Tucker, University of Virginia

Preface

This is a narrative history addressed to students and general readers wishing to learn more about the world of Victorian literature. It naturally presumes an interest whetted by encounters with that body of writing, but it does not presume close prior acquaintance with particular authors or genres. The narrative is informed by a good deal of contemporary scholarship and criticism, but I offer little explicit engagement with academic criticism (although I have done my best to acknowledge general as well as specific forms of scholarly indebtedness). Instead, I have devoted the confining space to gathering in a broader range of texts and careers than otherwise would have been possible. I've tried to balance the claims of category and chronology, hoping to steer between chronicle ("The following works were published in 1843") and the "guide," organized around genre or critical theme. The volume has a strong chronological thrust, and hence the introduction will be a more rewarding point of entry than the index. At the same time, the history necessarily depends on analyses of particular episodes or developments whose significance can be elicited only through departures (sometimes extensive) from strict chronology. My aim is to sketch a complex, changing field of literary production and reception without surrendering the rich particularity of individual works and authors.

One emphasis to this end is a great deal of attention to Victorian reviews of major writers. The most obvious value of contemporary reception is its capacity to crystallize what seems distinctive, sometimes strange, in Victorian structures of feeling (in Raymond Williams's useful phrase). Reviewing also offers a means of decomposing, as it were, our existing conceptions of major authors and genres, and thereby revivifying them. We can see literary careers less as unbroken, fixed expanses and more as ongoing, changing constructions, within which Victorian readers confronted phenomena very different from what we encounter in our Penguins. From this vantage we're reminded, for example, that Dickens's career in the 1830s is not that of a novelist, but of an increasingly prolific and popular writer of magazine sketches, whose writing changes the very form of the novel. Reviews also remind us of how complexly literary form and value are bound up with a broad range of social norms – most obviously, the force of gender and class. Particularly in the early stages of a writer's career, a review can seem an exercise much like the sizing up of strangers that is such an important experience in Victorian novels. As they try to place new or emergent authors, reviewers are especially likely to reveal their tacit norms and expectations, and thus to give us a sense of the audiences that the author is trying to reach. In the process, they offer unusually suggestive responses to a central question in any literary history: what was "literature"? How did one recognize it, what was it for, and how did one measure its success or failure? Reviews, finally, also remind us that Victorian engagements with these questions need not be narrowly historical or parochial; they often reveal writers of extraordinary intelligence, wit, erudition, self-awareness, and passion – minds that should rebuke any inclination to patronize the past.

A glance at the 1,400 double-columned, densely printed pages of the *Cambridge Bibliography of English Literature* of 1800–1900 will underscore, if it should need emphasis, how much a history of this kind necessarily omits. (I particularly regret not having more space for journalism, the economics of publishing, history, literature by working-class authors, science writing, and writing from and about imperial dominions.) Carlyle pointedly summed up a more subtle, equally insoluble problem confronting historians: "Narrative is *linear*, action is *solid*." Even had we space enough and time, no history could interweave adequately the countless lines of character and event that constitute the "action" of Victorian literature. We can never reach consensus as to the shape of that world and its meanings. But I hope that this inevitably partial account not only is stimulating as a narrative in its own right, but also will suggest new significance in familiar texts (and in the world from which they emerged) while at the same time prompting readers to seek out the unfamiliar at first hand. I predictably have lingered over major figures such as Tennyson, Dickens, George Eliot, and Oscar Wilde, largely to explain why they have figured so centrally in our understandings of Victorian literature. But I also have tried to give sustained attention to lesser-known authors and forms – most obviously, sensation fiction and the "new woman" novel – not only because they change our understanding of more familiar land-marks, but because they offer neglected intrinsic pleasures. The analysis and description throughout is partly an exercise in enticement, hoping to allure readers into pursuing a closer knowledge of the works and figures mentioned here. Conrad in one of his critical prefaces urges that his "task" as a writer is "above all, to make you see." I would be very happy above all to make you read more Victorian literature.

A project of this sort brings home the extraordinary scope and richness of Victorian literature not only as a body of writing but also as a field of study. In concluding it, I am tempted to thank everyone who has ever taught or written about or discussed it. But I must confine myself to some particularly crucial sources of support and guidance. Andrew McNeillie first beguiled me into undertaking this work, and since then a number of editors at Blackwell – in particular, Al Bertrand and Emma Bennett – have been encouraging and (above all) patient: thanks to all of them. I owe a manifold debt to Cornell University and the Cornell Department of English: for extraordinary library resources, generous leave time, and financial support for our gifted graduate students, who not only have helped with research but have sustained many lively, stimulating conversations. Thanks in particular to Zubair Amir, Karen Bourrier, David Coombs, Katy Croghan-Alarcon, Meghan Freeman, Sarah Heidt, Esther Hu, Michael Klotz, Seph Murtagh, Andrea Rehn, Danielle St. Hilaire, Kim Snyder-Manganelli, and Robin Sowards. I benefited from the generosity and insight of Joseph Bizup, Andrew Miller, and Jonah Siegel, three very fine and very busy scholars who took the time to offer sympathetic readings of a large portion of the project at a particularly difficult juncture; I'm only sorry they could not save me from more lapses. Throughout this project I've been inspired by the example of Herbert F. Tucker, no stranger to large undertakings, with whom I've enjoyed ongoing discussion about the forms and possibilities of literary history, while enduring ongoing envy of his brilliant work. Among the many debts recorded in the citations, the scholarship of Michael Booth, Donald Gray, Dorothy Mermin, and John Sutherland was especially helpful in lifting the burdens of my ignorance. I also would like to thank the intellectual communities in which I have been fortunate to participate: the Victorian Division of the Modern Language Association; the Northeast Victorian Studies Association; the North American Victorian Studies Association; the Dickens Project at the University of California at Santa Cruz; the VICTORIA listserv (presided over by the redoubtable Patrick Leary); and *Victorian Studies.*

This work is dedicated to the two remarkable women with whom I share my life, Michele Moody-Adams and Katherine Claire Moody Adams. Both of them will be very glad that it is done, but it could never have been finished without them.

Note on Citations

Page references supplied for a single citation correlate with the sequence of passages as they are quoted and therefore may not be listed consecutively.

Introduction: Locating Victorian Literature

Byron is Dead

In 1824, a 14-year-old boy in Lincolnshire carved on a stone the words, "Byron is dead." For the young Alfred Tennyson, something rare and wonderful had vanished from the world. His sense of loss was echoed by innumerable contemporaries throughout Europe; it has shaped literary history ever since. But Byron's vivid afterlife also reflects a powerful cultural ambivalence in nineteenth-century Britain, which lies at the heart of what became Victorian literature.

Byron's death seemed and seems to mark the end of an era, which relegates the subsequent years before the ascent of Victoria – or at least before 1832, the date of the First Reform Bill – into an eerie twilight, mentioned largely as an interregnum, an awkward gap between the "Romantic" and "Victorian" epochs. That twilight obscures the many continuities between those two worlds. Thomas Carlyle, the single most influential "Victorian sage," may seem to belong to a world very different from that of John Keats, yet the two men were born only a month apart. Throughout the shaping of Victorian literature, moreover, the figure of Byron remained very much alive. He was an inescapable and many-faceted icon – of poetry, of imagination, of excess, of daring, of dissolution, of rebellion, the emblem of an old order, the herald of a new. When Carlyle in *Sartor Resartus* (1831–3) struggled to imagine a new era of belief, he exhorted, "Close thy Byron, open thy Goethe."

Of course, the familiar divisions of literary history are largely flags of convenience, and "Victorian" more than most derives its authority from an accident of political history and royal biology: the 64-year reign of the young woman who came to the throne in 1837 and presided over decades of unparalleled economic, social, and political transformation. Even before Victoria was crowned, however, a wide range of contemporaries echoed Carlyle's announcement of a new epoch, and shared his sense that "the times are unexampled." Whether with joy or foreboding – or, most often, a mixture of the two – 1830 witnessed a crescendo of agreement that Britain stood on the brink of a radical break with established institutions, habits, and ways of life. That sense of rupture was defined preeminently along class lines. John Stuart Mill put it trenchantly: "the spirit of the age" had confirmed the bankruptcy of government by a hereditary aristocracy. "The superior capacity of the higher ranks for the exercise of worldly power is now a broken spell" (Mill 1963–91: xxii.315). The remainder of the century would see not only a persistent expansion of middle-class political power, but also the corresponding ascendancy of a distinctly middle-class ethos, which was built around self-discipline, earnest struggle, and the hallowing of domestic life. Yet the enchantment of aristocracy would linger through much of the century – not only in persistent political influence, but in subtly pervasive norms of value, identity, and conduct. Even as the rising middle classes defined themselves against the aristocracy, their images of human fulfillment remained widely in thrall to aristocratic modes of style and possibility. This is the tension encapsulated in the afterlife of Byron, which was shaped by the history leading up to the coronation of Victoria.

Cultural Contexts

In the wake of the Napoleonic Wars, which ended in 1815, British political energies were redirected towards domestic issues. Although the reach of its empire was unparalleled and growing, empire had not become the focus of public attention that it would become in the latter half of the century. National chauvinism found its readiest expression in the victory over France and the growing economic might of British commerce and industry. The growth of industrialization, however, also exacerbated political unrest, repressed during the war years. Industrialization offered new opportunities for workers, but it also created new stresses. As traditional "cottage industries" such as handloom weaving were displaced by steam power, increasing numbers of workers lost their jobs, and their protests stirred fear among the propertied classes. Displaced laborers migrated to expanding industrial towns, where explosive growth opened up new forms of employment, but also subjected workers to newly volatile economic cycles, while frequent bouts of unemployment strained traditional (meager) resources of poor relief. Meanwhile, the so-called "Corn Laws," instituted following the Napoleonic Wars to protect agricultural interests, increased the pinch of hunger by subsidizing the price of grain at artificially high levels, thus creating a division of class interests that became a flash point of early Victorian politics.

Resentment over the Corn Laws helped to shape the political identity of an increasingly affluent middle class, which chafed at the exorbitant political influence of wealthy landowners. The growing economic leverage of middle-class citizens, many of whom remained disenfranchised by religion or lack of landed property, gradually was felt in politics. In 1829, Parliament ratified "Catholic Emancipation," which removed many of the long-standing restrictions on the political rights of Catholics. The repeal of statutes dating back to Henry VIII – and sustained in many quarters by virulent antipathy to "Popery" – struck many as a threat to the core of British identity, because it eroded the religious foundations of the state. The following year, the death of George IV aroused little sorrow but great anxiety; a month after the June 1830 prorogation of Parliament, revolution broke out in France, and subsequently elsewhere on the continent. Against these events, a proposed extension of the franchise in Britain – what would become known as the "Reform Bill" – quickly became the central topic of parliamentary election debate, fanned by widespread reports of industrial unrest. When cholera broke out in 1829, more than a few commentators read in it a sign of divine wrath: when a little-known Scotsman named Thomas Carlyle published an essay on the upheaval in 1829, he gave it a portentous biblical title: "Signs of the Times."

The early 1830s thus nurtured an unusual sense of historical self-consciousness, which centered on challenges to the traditional political order. In the midst of these events, John Stuart Mill claimed in a newspaper article that "the conviction is already not far from universal, that the times are pregnant with change; and that the nineteenth century will be known to posterity as the era of one of the greatest revolutions of which history has preserved the remembrance, in the human mind, and in the whole constitution of human society" (Mill 1963–91: xxii.228–9). The singularity of the moment was underscored in Mill's title, "The Spirit of the Age." The phrase, he noted, "is in some measure a novel expression. I do not believe it to be met with in any work exceeding fifty years in antiquity. The idea of comparing one's own age with former ages, or with our notion of those which are yet to come, had occurred to philosophers; but it never before was itself the dominant idea of any age" (228). The fiercely logical Mill envisioned the idea of aristocratic government as "a broken spell," but he did not appreciate the lingering enchantment of aristocratic life.

In 1830 Byron embodied aristocratic luxury and privilege at its most alluring, and most dangerous. That allure was writ large in contemporary fiction, which was largely divided between the towering presence of Sir Walter Scott and a new genre of "silver-fork" novels, so called because of their preoccupation with the (often imaginary) particulars of aristocratic opulence. A central figure in these works was the dandy, a figure vividly embodied in Edward Bulwer's *Pelham* (1828), the most popular novel of the later decade. The dandy incarnates a sardonic, detached elegance loosely derived from the model of Byron by way of "Beau" Brummel, whose energies were divided between dress and a withering disdain for the world. Byron's own memoirs were deemed too scandalous for publication, and were infamously burnt by his own publisher, John Murray (who stood to make a fortune by them, but feared the irreparable loss of both Byron's reputation and his own). When Thomas Moore's sympathetic *Life of Byron* was published in 1830, it occasioned widespread attacks on Byron's poetry and personal character, which frequently were generalized into sweeping claims about aristocratic excess, inanity, and disdain for common morality – attacks which in turn gathered in *Pelham* and much of the silver-fork school. In the midst of the debate, Carlyle was seized with the idea of "the dandiacal body" and the "satanic school" of poetry as leitmotifs in a satire of aristocratic self-absorption. What began as a squib grew into *Sartor Resartus*, one of the most influential celebrations of those virtues that we have come to think of as distinctly "Victorian": duty, faith, self-denial, earnestness, and "the gospel of work." Repudiation of the dandy thus helped to shape the Victorian sage.

Middle-class attacks on an aristocracy deemed unworthy of its power were focused in two broad, outwardly antithetical developments of late eighteenth-century thought that reached their zenith in the reign of Victoria. The first was Benthamism, or utilitarianism, of which John

Stuart Mill became the most influential exponent. Jeremy Bentham (1748–1832), "the father of English innovation," as Mill called him," the "great subversive" thinker of his age (Mill 1963–91: x.78), argued that the morality of an action was to be gauged, not by some intrinsic quality in the action or the agent, but by its consequences: its usefulness or utility, understood in the elemental terms of maximizing pleasure and minimizing pain. This outwardly simple conception organized a corrosively skeptical analysis of established legal, political, and social orders, which were grounded (Bentham pointed out) in accumulations of tradition predominantly shaped by the interests of a small elite. Bentham's analytic model helped to direct the reformist impulses of Victorian England, which gathered in a host of institutions, from Parliament to urban sanitation, and were chronicled in voluminous reports that form an important subgenre of Victorian literature. Many critics would attack the rationalistic emphasis of Benthamism as a highly brittle understanding of human psychology. Yet even his most vehement critics betray his influence: Dickens's *Hard Times* (1854) is the most famous literary attack on Bentham's alleged antipathy to imagination, yet *Hard Times* is bookended by two other novels, *Bleak House* (1851–3) and *Little Dorrit* (1856), that obsessively attack government incompetence and neglect of human needs.

A very different reformist emphasis derived from the broad, epochal religious movement loosely known as Evangelicalism. On its surface, the movement seemed antithetical to Benthamism. Bentham was an atheist of a consummately Enlightenment habit of mind, confident that the road to progress and happiness lay through unfettered human inquiry. evangelicals, by contrast, chastised such presumption, and insisted on the need for divine salvation that could be attained only through strenuous piety. Bentham located pleasure at the heart of his ethics, even formulating a "hedonic calculus"; evangelicals were notoriously suspicious of pleasure. As Leslie Stephen (Virginia Woolf's father) recalled of his father, "He once smoked a cigar, and found it so delicious that he never smoked again" (Houghton 1957: 236). Yet Evangelicalism also made its impact in large part through criticism of the aristocracy, in and out of government. Through the leadership of William Wilberforce (himself a wealthy landowner), Evangelicals within the Church of England from roughly the 1780s held up for the privileged classes the momentous example of John Wesley's preaching earlier in the century, which had led to the formation of Methodism. Wilberforce and his colleagues sought to reinvigorate Christian piety among the affluent, envisioning human life as an arena of constant moral struggle, resisting temptation and mastering desire. These imperatives had a profound impact on legislation – evangelicals spearheaded the abolition of the English slave trade and laws governing factory conditions – and more generally on the texture of both public and private life, as its deep suspicion of desire gave rise to an austerity often offended even by the reading of novels.

Such norms pointedly contested the example of the notoriously dissolute English Court during the Regency (1810–20) and subsequent reign of George IV (1820–30). And that contrast in turn reflected a crucial worldliness in Evangelical influence. Though Wilberforce's piety was unquestionably sincere, one major impetus for the spread of Evangelicalism was the horrific cautionary tale unfolding across the Channel in 1789. The specter of the French Revolution would haunt the privileged classes of Britain for much of the nineteenth century. (In 1872 the former Prime Minister, Earl Russell, on his deathbed heard the sound of breaking glass, and cried, "The Revolution has begun.") For Wilberforce, the revolution embodied the prospect not merely of working-class insurrection in pursuit of greater political power, but the still more unsettling anxiety that the aristocracy might indeed have forfeited its moral claim to that power. Ideals of moral, and particularly sexual, discipline thus became central forms of symbolic capital in Victorian political and social debate. While Wilberforce wanted to reform aristocratic governance, not overturn it, evangelical piety was in theory (if not always in practice) egalitarian. It offered a powerful symbolic weapon to subordinate classes, who could argue that aristocratic profligacy showed their unfitness to rule. Britain, they urged, would best be led by those who could best govern themselves.

Self-discipline thus became a crucial engine of social progress and individual stature. Conservative commentators had long explained the social order as a providential arrangement, in which every individual was born to a "place" or "station" ultimately sanctioned by God. Schemes of economic and political progress threatened this order, and provoked numerous countering appeals to older models of faith and value – most notably an imagined medieval world of harmonious social hierarchy. But a static hierarchy of rank could not withstand the dynamism of an industrial economy. Beginning with the development of steam power in the latter half of the eighteenth century, forms of mechanized production would transform not only the rhythms of daily life but also the very sense of human possibility. Steam, remarks a character in *Mill on the Floss* (1860), "drives on every wheel double pace and the wheel of Fortune along with 'em." The new economy offered unrivalled potential for amassing (and losing) wealth, as well as unprecedented opportunities to shape and fashion one's identity. As never before, "rags to riches" could seem more than a fairy-tale fantasy. At the same time, however, such dynamism encouraged a host of anxieties about identity and self-determination, memorably encapsulated in Pip's abrupt transformation in *Great Expectations*. "I was a blacksmith's boy but yesterday; I am – but what shall I say I am – today?" (Dickens 1996: 248). "Constantly shifting the boundaries of social intercourse," in the words of *Middlemarch* (Eliot 1995c: 95), such mobility made encounters with strangers and strange places an increasingly common but unsettling challenge. "Nothing being really fixed in our society," Edward Bulwer argued in 1833 (at least by comparison to nations on the continent), the English developed as defenses an increasingly guarded attitude that startled European visitors (Bulwer 1833). Much of the elaborate etiquette that we think of as distinctly Victorian – rituals of introduction, calling cards, the chaperoning of unmarried women, intricate decorums of dress – is at root a strategy for coping with social mobility, by affirming one's own claims to recognition while at the same time maintaining a distance that allows one to "place" new acquaintances (Davidoff 1973). The Victorian novel developed into a form uniquely suited to represent these dynamics, capturing the textures of social interaction, aspiration, and anxiety, within which social hierarchy could seem both a stimulus and a barrier to personal achievement.

The rise of industrial capitalism transformed the social fabric in a yet more profound way. The nascent science of political economy decreed that economic life was an incessant pursuit of self-interest, which led individuals to see themselves locked into conflict with those who occupied different or competing roles in the dynamics of production. Whereas apologists for a pre-industrial order could presume that social hierarchy was harmonized by bonds of reciprocal moral obligation, under industrial capitalism such bonds were increasingly subsumed by mere contract, within which every individual presumably sought to maximize his own interests. The seeming resolution of all human attachment into "the cash nexus" became an obsessive preoccupation of early Victorian critics. "We call it a Society," Carlyle wrote in 1843, "and go about professing openly the totalest separation, isolation. Our life is not a mutual helpfulness ... it is a mutual hostility" (Carlyle 1977: 148).

One powerful response to such strains was the Victorian cult of domesticity. This was another outgrowth of Evangelicalism, which enshrined the decorous, loving home as the emblem of a pious and well-ordered life. But, as the new century unfolded, the ideal developed into an increasingly insistent division of "separate spheres" rationalized primarily in terms of the burdens faced by men. Their perpetual struggle for "worldly aggrandizement," as Sarah Stickney Ellis put it, was "constantly misleading their steps, closing their ears against the voice of conscience, and beguiling them with the promise of peace, where peace was never found" (Chase and Levenson 2000: 45). Poised against the coarsening effect of this "warfare," the domestic woman – "woman in her highest moral capacity" – acted as both guidance and balm, a source of value outside the world of exchange. This led to the idea of a woman being associated with an instinctive, well-nigh angelic devotion to the needs of others, and thus a moral "influence" which elevated and refined those around her. So complete was her selflessness that some commentators were troubled by the very idea of feminine sexual desire. Thus it was that the home became, in one of the more delirious celebrations of the ideal, what John Ruskin in *Sesame and Lilies* called "the place of Peace; the shelter, not only from all injury, but from all terror, doubt, and division" (Ruskin 1903: xviii, 122).

Of course, "separate spheres" is profoundly misleading: not only is it impossible to seal off the two realms from one another, but also the attempt is logically incoherent. In Victorian celebrations of private life the home became an emphatically public place, called on to demonstrate varieties of moral and civic probity. (A similar dynamic has been reconstituted today under the slogan of "family values," in which a political candidate's ostensibly private life is blazoned on election posters.) Gender in this context became a powerful arena for articulating political conflict, which is one reason why domestic life became such a resonant preoccupation of Victorian literature. The celebration of selflessness and devotion as the keynotes of feminine character implicitly attacked an aristocratic model, under which women derived their value from beauty, kinship, and money. And masculinity was subjected to corresponding revision, particularly in pointed debates over the ideal of the gentleman. Revising a traditional norm founded on independent wealth – a gentleman never sullied his hands with "trade" – there emerged a more egalitarian model, which gave new stress to self-discipline, earnestness, and piety, along with older virtues of honesty, courage, and power.

Women who aspired to something more than domesticity naturally chafed at their exclusion from more direct participation in public affairs. Harriet Martineau, one of the most prominent liberal social critics of the first half of the period, rejected with contempt those who resisted civil rights for women on the grounds of "the virtual influence of woman; her swaying the judgment and will of man through the heart; and so forth." In arguing with such notions, she rejoined, "One might as well try to dissect the morning mist" (Martineau 1962: 152–3). From roughly the early 1840s, an increasingly vocal and diverse feminism would join Martineau in contesting these views. Yet versions of the domestic ideal held ground among women as well as men – in part because it offered women a dignity long denied them. Traditionally demeaned as daughters of Eve, creatures of undisciplined desire who lured men into temptation, women now were exalted as paragons of restraint, while men became the embodiment of sexual license. But the celebration of female purity also underwrote a host of stark and constricting dichotomies, which allowed little middle ground between angel and whore. The trappings of "fallen" sexuality – the prostitute and the seduction plot – thus became central features of Victorian narrative, in and out of novels. Related suspicions would come to shadow the careers of many women writers, who made their own claims to publicity and self-assertion. In 1837, Robert Southey, the Poet Laureate, famously rebuked the writerly aspirations of an unknown Charlotte Brontë: "Literature cannot be the business of a woman's life, and it ought not to be." A decade later, a male character in Geraldine Jewsbury's *The Half-Sisters* (1848) points up a suspicion widely attached to women writers: "A woman who makes her mind public in any way, or exhibits herself in any way, no matter how it may be dignified by the title of art, seems to me little better than a woman of a particular class" (Mermin 1993: 15, 17).

Poor women were always more readily exposed to sexual suspicion, for they lacked the forms of shelter – both literal and figurative – that domesticity provided the affluent. In theory egalitarian, the domestic ideal naturally was informed by economic power: the more comfortable one's surroundings and the more secure one's income, the more readily home could be imagined as a refuge from the world at large. Indeed, the very concept of "separate spheres" answers to a profound transformation in social geography. Pre-industrial labor and trade typically took place in or near one's residence – "above the shop" or "across the yard." The rise of machine power and factories, as well as broader networks of distribution, required more elaborate facilities separate from the home, and, as they created a great deal of noise and dirt, they also created a desire for more distant residence. The urban working classes, meanwhile, remained locked into frequently abysmal housing conditions, particularly in the burgeoning industrial towns of the north. By the middle of the century, the living conditions of the poor would become an urgent preoccupation of both novelists and "urban investigators," forerunners of modern sociologists and ethnographers, who voyaged into the slums of London as if into the lairs of alien tribes.

As the growing separation between home and business nurtured an imaginative topography in which "separate spheres" could flourish, it enforced an unprecedented segregation, both geographic and psychic, of rich and poor. Reviewers for the major journals – most of them middle class – frequently marveled at the cultural abyss separating affluence and poverty across mere blocks of central London, a gulf brought into view more often by literature than by direct observation. Thackeray in an 1838 review pointed to a burgeoning world of working-class literature largely unknown to the "respectable" classes. Ignorance was exacerbated by the frictions of economic life. The "mutual hostility" of contract crystallized in workers a growing class-consciousness, most obviously in efforts to organize trades unions, which were greeted by capitalists and most middle-class commentators as knots of conspiracy and violence. The gradual erosion of traditional forms of deference – though meager indeed by comparison with modern British life – exacerbated subtle frictions in daily encounters, and reinforced among the propertied classes the association of the poor with violence and danger.

In most Victorian literature – where most authors were of broadly middle-class standing – representations of the poor are tinged with exoticism, as well as a vague fear of beings so outwardly remote. In large part, novels addressed such anxieties by externalizing them, thereby transforming danger into something strangely fascinating. In the "Newgate" novel of criminal life and so-called "industrial" fiction dealing with working-class characters, the fascination takes on a quasi-ethnographic cast, as if charting the workings of a dangerous alien world. The anxiety is more subtly registered in the insistent celebration of sympathy in literature. Though sympathy became a byword of novel criticism in particular, an index of the novelist's insight into human character, the quality derived much of its urgency from the sense that it might overcome, or at least disarm, social tensions. Sympathy encouraged belief in the fundamental harmony of rich and poor, typically grounded in the Wordsworthian faith that "we have all of us one human heart." Praise of sympathy above other literary virtues reminds us of how powerfully Victorian literature is bound up with Victorian society.

The Literary Field

The technological revolutions of nineteenth-century life naturally had a profound effect on literature – not merely its availability, but the range of its forms and its changing audiences. At the outset of the century, the high cost of paper and printing, and the inflationary pressures of the Napoleonic Wars, made print an expensive commodity. The romantic popularity of poetry was in part a result of its relative brevity, and hence affordability. By 1820, the development of machine-made paper and the rotary steam press had begun to dramatically reduce the cost of printing, and monthly journals began to proliferate, the most notable before 1832 being *Blackwood's*, *The London Review*, *The Westminster Review*, *Colburn's New Monthly Magazine*, and *Fraser's*. As focal points of intellectual and political debate and a source of assured income from authorship (a rare security), periodical writing in the later 1820s commanded an authority that it has rarely enjoyed before or since (Marshall 1996). In 1825, the bravura style of an article on Milton in the *Edinburgh Review* caused a small sensation, and launched the momentous political and literary career of its 25-year-old author, Thomas Macaulay.

The literary field was further affected by a bank crisis of 1825, which led to the failure of several major publishing firms – most notably Constable, the publisher of the *Encyclopedia Britannica* and Sir Walter Scott – and left those who weathered the storm much less willing to take risks on new authors, particularly poets. John Murray, who had published Byron, gave up on nearly everything but travel writing and biography – and the *Quarterly Review*, which became his economic bedrock. Like its great Whig rival, the *Edinburgh*, the Tory *Quarterly* was founded at the beginning of the century principally as a party organ (priced accordingly, affordable primarily to the small number of Englishmen who possessed the right to vote). Although the older quarterlies took in a broad swath of contemporary intellectual life, and remained a cultural landmark for much of the century, they gradually were displaced by monthlies, which eventually combined essays and reviews with fiction published in serial installments.

With the increased affordability of print, reading became politically charged as never before. Various schemes of progress and reform became united under the banner of the "march of mind" grounded in the distribution of reading matter to an ever-wider audience. Radical journalists pressing for greater working-class political rights caused deep concern in the government. In an effort to regulate their writings, Parliament in 1820 passed the Seditious Publications Act, which imposed a tax of 4d on any publication that could be interpreted as news – the so-called "tax on knowledge" that became a rallying cry, and nurtured the slogan "Knowledge is Power." Working-class politics found another outlet, and another source of solidarity, in pirated printings of poetry aligned with radicalism, such as Shelley's *Queen Mab* and Byron's *Don Juan*. Partly in an effort to defuse this agitation, Henry Brougham spearheaded the founding of the Society for the Diffusion of Useful Knowledge (1826), which subsidized a host of publications designed to convey practical, "improving" education to the working classes. (Radicals complained that "Broughamism" also inculcated docility by deflecting attention from the sufferings of the poor.) Meanwhile, religious groups apprehensive of this emphasis on secular knowledge countered with their own organizations, most notably the Society for the Promotion of Christian Knowledge, which had been founded in 1698 but took advantage of new technology (and subsidies from wealthy patrons) to distribute tracts by the tens, even hundreds, of thousands. (A single tract, *The Dairyman's Daughter* by the Rev. Leigh Richmond, is believed to have sold some 2,000,000 copies in the 1830s and 1840s [L James 1963: 121].) New cheap serials also emerged to address and nurture this burgeoning market. Chambers' *Edinburgh Journal* (1831) within a few years reached a circulation of 80,000. In 1832 the SDUK supported the founding of the *Penny Magazine*, published by Charles Knight, which called on recent technology to incorporate newly efficient reproductions of wood engraving, which would come to be a staple of Victorian novels. The *Penny Magazine*, which quickly attained a circulation of more than 100,000, was soon joined by the SPCK's *Saturday Magazine*, whose circulation reached 80,000.

Scholars have debated how much of this circulation actually reached the intended working-class reader. What is clear is that these "improving" publications could not crowd aside a vigorous market of more demotic reading, which was solidified by increasing concentration of the poor in large towns and cities. Well into the Victorian period, the primary literature of the literate poor consisted of traditional chapbooks, ballads, broadsheets, and "penny dreadfuls" – cheaply printed narratives of violence and crime, often in a broadly gothic vein. A representative serial devoted to the form was *The Calendar of Horrors: A Series of Romantic Legends, Terrific Tales, Awful Narrations, and Supernatural Adventures* (1835–6). This was the market that Thackeray described in his 1838 *Fraser's* review, but it persisted well beyond his bemused condescension and other more forceful attacks. Surveys in 1840 recorded some 80 cheap magazines circulating in London – none costing more than twopence, most of them a penny or less. Only four of them were primarily political; nine were scientific (in the vein of the *Penny Magazine*), five were "licentious" (at least quasi-pornographic), four were devoted to drama, 16 to biographies and memoirs, and 22 exclusively to fiction. That proportion would increase markedly during the 1840s, when G. W. M. Reynolds scored a huge success with his long-running serials in the "dreadful" mode in the *London Journal* and subsequently *Reynolds's Miscellany* – one of which, *The Mysteries of the Court of London*, contains over 4 millions words (L. James 1963: 27).

This history can register only a tiny sampling of this flood of print, which swelled over the course of the century, as an expanding reading public and a gradual removal of the so-called knowledge taxes created ever-new markets for enterprising publishers, much to the consternation of the guardians of literary morality. In 1830, "literature" as we think of it today – forms of "imaginative" writing typically confined to fiction, poetry, and drama, with some allowance for memoir and critical writing – remained a far more indeterminate category, which was difficult to disentangle from journalism, and in which not only political writing, but also history, science, and religion figured prominently. Indeed, religious titles remained for much of the period the single largest category of publication. Of some 45,000 books announced in the London Catalogue between 1816 and 1851, fully one-fourth were works of divinity (Dodds 1952: 23).

A further distortion of the literary field is bound up with the very idea of a national literature. Over the course of the century, even as American literature begin to assume its own separate identity, the Atlantic Ocean became a less imposing barrier to literary exchange, and increasingly the two countries came to resemble a single transatlantic market for literature in the English language. In part this stemmed from the lack of international copyright until 1891, which allowed American publishers to pirate English bestsellers in huge quantities. But the exchange was two-way. It has been argued that the American Longfellow was the single most popular Victorian poet (St. Clair 2004: 391), and later Walt Whitman would have a powerful, if more narrowly circumscribed, influence. The most popular novels increasingly were international bestsellers. The most famous was Stowe's *Uncle Tom's Cabin*, which sold some one and a half million copies in the 1850s. A the outset of the period, Fenimore Cooper's frontier tales were extremely popular, and helped to shape the late-Victorian adventure vogue, as did Melville's more sexually daring early tales of South Sea life. In the latter half of the century, Henry James built much of his career around the probing of cultural boundaries, analyzing putatively distinctive qualities of the American character from his base in London, where he also figured centrally in debate over the novel as a form, and helped to shape "modernism" as a markedly Anglo-American movement. A similarly complex exchange emerged early in the period when Ralph Waldo Emerson arranged for the American publication of Carlyle's *Sartor Resartus* (its first appearance in book form), which initiated a lifelong correspondence, in which "transcendentalism" took shape as a transatlantic phenomenon. When Emerson came to England in 1848, his lectures were eagerly attended by writers who found his individualism a heady, sometimes dangerous, contribution to contemporary religious skepticism, while Emerson in turn memorialized the visit in *England and the English* – one of many hundreds of travel volumes over the course of the century devoted to analyzing what in the next century would become known as the "special relationship."

An Age of Prose

Amid the great debates prompted by Catholic Emancipation and the prospect of a Reform Bill, many commentators in 1830 noted that political commentary in journals and newspapers had displaced nearly every other form of literary exchange. Even by 1828, John Stuart Mill (himself a vigorous participant in the debates) expressed a widely echoed worry that the predominance of periodicals was contributing to the "degradation" of literature generally (Mill 1963–91: 12–13). Thought, it seemed, was being transformed into a commodity.

This concern points to a momentous logic in developing literary institutions. Over against a view of literature as one more product generated by market demand, Mill and other critics would shape an ideal of literature – poetry in particular – as a locus of value beyond exchange, a deeply personal form of expression and responsiveness to the world that elicited intimate forms of understanding between author and reader. This notion developed into an ideal of "culture," a source of value nurtured primarily through aesthetic experience, which could be set against utilitarianism and other schemes that would reduce all forms of value to material interests. This development gave unusual prominence to periodical writing and other literary forms that have survived their original context under the awkward academic rubric, "non-fiction prose."

In the romantic era the prose essay (particularly in the hands of Lamb, Hazlitt, and DeQuincey) became an unusually supple vehicle for varieties of introspection as well as social and literary comment. The dislocations of the early Victorian decades created an audience eager for writing that addressed new social prospects and perplexities. These worries were focused most pointedly in religious doubt, but in a world of greatly expanding literacy, where, to adapt Marx's phrase, all that is solid seemed to be melting into air, the craving for new sources of value was unusually pervasive. This hunger is registered in the expanding popularity of lectures and public readings, along with the remarkable tolerance among Victorian audiences for sometimes excoriating attacks on their character and values. As many commentators have noted, Victorian social critics often seem rivals of the preacher or prophet, "elegant Jeremiahs," to adopt a tag bestowed on Matthew Arnold. Drawing on rhetorical traditions of sermon and prophecy as well as earlier traditions of essayistic writing, authors such as Carlyle, Ruskin, and Arnold developed highly distinctive styles, which endeavor not merely to convince but also, more fundamentally, to jolt to attention readers lulled by fatigue, complacency, or a superabundance of print. Many readers in pursuit of new social and intellectual possibility were bewildered by the new vistas, and were glad to embrace writers as guides to the perplexed. Hence the increasing association of great literature with the wisdom of a sage – a title first and most influentially attached to Carlyle, "the sage of Chelsea." *Sartor Resartus* (1831) was a harbinger of the extraordinary generic innovation associated with Victorian prose. This well-nigh unclassifiable work clearly draws on traditional religious exhortation, but combines it with elements of biography, German romance, prose satire, philosophy, and social polemic, stirring up a heady concoction whose influence readers were still celebrating a half-century later.

For Carlyle, as for many Victorians, biography was a particularly satisfying form. Though its popularity gave rise to many dreary monuments of familial piety (heavily redacted *Lives and Letters* became an object of scorn later in the century), biography figured centrally as a model of moral struggle, of figures who triumphed over – or, occasionally, were paralyzed by – the distinctive social and spiritual challenges of the age. Life writing was an especially resonant vehicle for probing relations between individuals and the social order; Samuel Smiles's best-selling *Self-Help* (1859), which helped to inaugurate a genre still popular today, is in essence a series of brief lives. In Victorian religious debate, lives of the saints, or of renowned dissenters, or of Jesus himself (as in Strauss's scandalous *Das Leben Jesu*, translated by George Eliot) frequently were enlisted as crucial exhibits. Autobiography and memoir had a similar power, but it was a somewhat more unsettling genre, bound up as it was with what struck many Victorian as overweening self-regard and erosion of privacy. Yet the genre became increasingly central to cultural debate in the latter half of the century. Works such as Newman's *Apologia Pro Vita Sua*, Mill's *Autobiography*, and Froude's *Life of Carlyle* captured not only the shapes of particular lives but also the formation of distinctive modes of belief. Carlyle's entire career was an extended engagement with biography, pivoting as it did on the idea of heroism, from his early accounts of German literature, in which Goethe was the central exemplar, through the parodic biographical dimensions of *Sartor Resartus*, his lectures on *Heroes and Hero-Worship*, and his increasingly eccentric preoccupation with multi-volume chronicles of Cromwell and Frederick the Great. The biographical impulse also found its way into the novel, with the rise of the *Bildungsroman* or "novel of development," from *Jane Eyre* to *Great Expectations*. It also was an important force in poetry, not merely in the lyric, but in long poems such as Tennyson's *In Memoriam* and Elizabeth Barrett Browning's *Aurora Leigh*. More subtly, biography informed the rise of the dramatic monologue, in which distinctive historical epochs or intellectual movements were frequently condensed in the evocation of a single and singular speaker.

In focusing on "representative men," in Emerson's phrase, biography was bound up with the newly acute awareness of history reflected in the notion of a "spirit of the age." Over the course of the century, this perception would develop into a thoroughgoing historicism, which presumed that forms of belief and value could be fully understood only in terms of the historical context that shaped them – a point of view that would prove particularly unsettling to traditional religious beliefs. In the early part of the period, however, history frequently was invoked to rationalize present courses of action. Macaulay's *History of England* (1849–59) became the prime exemplar of a "Whig view of history" as a chronicle of unending progress driven by political and economic liberalism, while religious conservatives, most influentially the Tractarians, looked to history to recover forms of contact and continuity with the early Christian epoch. Newman would develop an unusually sophisticated theory of religious development that allowed for historical continuity amid doctrinal change, while more skeptical scholars such as W. E. H Lecky (*History of the Rise and Spirit of Rationalism* [1865]) and H. T. Buckle (*The History of Civilization in England* [1857–61]) found in history a fitful but triumphal advance of reason over superstition. Over the course of the century, however, writers became increasingly engaged by the sheer strangeness of the past. The sense of the past as "a foreign country," as the twentieth-century novelist L. P. Hartley put it, recognizes an aestheticizing power in historical distance, and a capacity to unsettle or disarm moral preconceptions. This effect is registered in literary forms as varied as the historical novel, the dramatic monologue, and a wide range of late-Victorian criticism. At the same time, the past could be felt at work in the present as a means of explaining otherwise baffling forms of thought – as in the pioneering anthropologist E. B. Tylor's theory of cultural "survivals."

Preoccupation with history created an environment well-equipped to grasp the momentous significance of Darwin, whose work was in turn nurtured by it. T. H. Huxley in "Science and Culture" pointed out a striking congruence between the two realms of thought. "When a biologist meets with an anomaly, he instinctively turns to the study of development to clear it up. The rationale of contradictory opinions may with equal confidence be sought in history" (Huxley 1905: 128). "Development" gathered in speculations across a wide range of science, from geology to embryology to natural history to astrophysical speculations on the origins of the cosmos, and from these realms it also spread into emergent discourses of anthropology and sociology. The great divide that we have come to call "the two cultures" of science and the humanities only began to make itself felt in the latter half of the period. Well into the 1870s, science generally – and natural science in particular – engaged the attention of a broadly literate public, whose interests are reflected in the enormous popularity of both natural history and authors such as Tennyson, whose *In Memoriam* ponders the impact of proto-evolutionary speculation a decade before *The Origin of Species* was published. Stunning advances in a wide range of technology offered an especially fitting theme for triumphalist history, crowning the Baconian dream of mastery over the natural world. Samuel Smiles's *The Lives of the Engineers* found in its subjects the stuff of romantic heroism. Biology and engineering joined hands in a host of Victorian reformist impulses, such as public health campaigns addressing epidemic disease and the lack of adequate sanitation and housing. Those campaigns in turn generated a literature of their own, from parliamentary "blue books" to the "social problem" novel to polemical social criticism to a broad array of journalism.

As it opened up new avenues of transport and communication – most notably, railways from the early 1830s and, soon after, the telegraph – technological innovation also opened new literary frontiers. Foreign travel, in particular, which had been a bastion of privilege epitomized in the continental "Grand Tour," became accessible to an increasingly broad public, which in turn formed a market for a burgeoning literature describing distant lands. The reach of the British Empire added special allure to Asia, Africa, South America, and the Middle East, while North America offered particularly resonant comparisons to Britain and its institutions. Readier access to France, Italy, and Greece made possible a newly vivid and extensive acquaintance with the history of Western art and architecture – a development reinforced at home by the expansion of public collections (the National Gallery was funded in 1824) and increased access to the treasures of great estates. The new prominence of the visual arts in English life called out new forms of critical writing, in which aesthetic concerns were increasingly linked to social diagnoses, most notably in the hugely influential writing of John Ruskin. With the large-scale rebuilding and expansion of urban England, architecture became an especially fierce arena of debate. As the choice of style came to seem an index of national character (typically fought out in relation to a similarly moralized account of architectural traditions) once again an outwardly minor literary form took on great social resonance.

The Situation of Poetry

For many commentators in 1830, poetry seemed in a desperate state, despite its cultural cachet. The extraordinary popularity of their immediate predecessors – Byron and Scott, above all, although pirated editions of Shelley were popular among working-class readers – indicated that poetry retained its long-standing centrality in English culture. Throughout the early decades of the era, many readers still composed verse to commemorate public or private events of special moment, suggesting that poetry retained a distinctly elevating and solemnizing force. In the 1830s and 1840s, critics frequently measured aspiring poets against a demand not only for emotional engagement but also for moral vision, and slapped down pretenders with a correspondingly fierce condescension. The combativeness, typically captured in archly gendered terms, reflected the eminence of the office – which admitted women and working-class men only on special suffrage. The most enduringly popular volume of the latter half of the 1820s was John Keble's *The Christian Year* (1827), which owed much of its prominence to its immersion in Anglican worship and belief.

At the same time, the achievement of the great Romantics – a daunting act to follow under any circumstances – was countered by a new impatience associated with the rise of utilitarianism and the "march of mind," which increasingly relegated poetry to the realm of the trivial or childish. Bentham famously averred that when it came to giving pleasure, poetry amounted to no more than pushpin. Even Macaulay in his essay on Milton declared that poetry was an achievement that civilization simply would outgrow. Macaulay loved poetry – his *Lays of Ancient Rome* (1842) would be one of the best-selling poetry volumes of the age – but he loved his progress more.

More immediately disabling for aspiring poets, however, was the financial crisis of 1825, which left publishers feeling that poetry from unfamiliar writers was too risky a speculation. As a rule, unknown poets could be published in volume form only if they underwrote the costs, which naturally narrowed the social spectrum of potential authors. Some of the slack was taken up by the literary annuals, expensive and elaborately illustrated volumes akin to ladies' keepsake albums, designed principally as holiday gifts, in which poems typically were paired with finely wrought steel engravings. From the founding of *Forget Me Not* in 1823, annuals quickly came to dominate the poetry market over the next decade. The major annuals – *Forget Me Not* was joined by *The Literary Souvenir* and *The Keepsake* – cost 12 shillings apiece versus five for a typical volume of poetry, but they sold in the thousands (as compared to the typical edition of 200 for a new volume of poetry), through an adroit marketing that in turn allowed editors to pay exorbitant fees to well-known contributors. Male poets in particular disparaged the genre – "There is no other reading. They haunt me. I die of Albophobia," Charles Lamb wrote in 1827 – but nearly all succumbed to the fees on offer (Adburgham 1983). The form allowed unusual prominence to women poets, most notably Felicia Hemans and Letitia Landon (or L. E. L.), who in 1830 were two of the most prominent voices in English poetry.

Unsurprisingly, the affiliation of poetry with the feminized world of the annuals further exasperated critical frustration at the dearth of new poetry generally. "The reign of poesy is over, at least for half a century," declared the hero of Disraeli's *Vivian Grey* (1827). That verdict proved premature, but poets – particularly male poets – would be increasingly fearful that cultural authority had passed to other literary forms. "Poetry having ceased to be read, or published, or written," Carlyle remarked in 1832, "how can it continue to be reviewed?" In fact, however, poetry reviews capture some of the epoch's most provocative and far-reaching reflection on the cultural contexts and moral burdens of art generally. The reception of Tennyson's *Poems* of 1830 encapsulates a host of conflicting demands that would confront the poet through much of the century: a cult of intimate expression clashed with demands for a poetry of public life and wisdom; the seeming tension between fidelity to beauty and moral obligation; the place of religious faith in a poetry attentive to the particulars of daily experience. These concerns recur throughout major critical debates of the age – the challenge of the novel as an epic of modern life; the rise of aestheticism and the "fleshly" school; the poetry of decadence – and they invigorate the major formal innovations of the era, the dramatic monologue and the so-called "novel-in-verse." But even after Swinburne's outrages on popular taste in the 1860s, the cultural situation of poetry remained precarious, responsive to a dilemma articulated in the earliest Victorian criticism. Does poetry have a function beyond that of emotional anodyne, of therapy for jangled nerves and intellectual confusion? Is the poet destined to become, as William Morris put it, "the idle singer of an empty day"?

Victorian Theater

While the institutions of poetry were under pressure in 1830, the decline of the drama had become a cliché. "Everywhere throughout Europe," Bulwer wrote in *England and the English* (1833), "the glory of the theater is beginning to grow dim," its former blaze certain to "die off in silence and darkness, like an extinct volcano" (Bulwer 1833: 135). There was similar consensus about the cause of the decline, in Britain at least: lack of financial reward even for successful playwrights, and the theater-going public's pleasure in elaborate spectacle. Before the 1860s, playwrights were paid at a flat rate, which was unaffected by the length of a run. One of the great successes of the 1860s, *Our American Cousin*, netted the manager of the Haymarket Theatre the fabulous sum of 20,000 pounds (the annual income of Britain's wealthiest nobility); its author, Tom Taylor, received 150 pounds. In the 1830s the standard fee for a first-run drama at minor theaters was between 50 and 70 pounds – which put great pressure on dramatists to be prolific (and to borrow heavily from foreign sources) but made it almost impossible for them to live comfortably through playwriting alone.

Meanwhile, playwrights confronted an audience accustomed to increasingly spectacular staging, a development nourished by the peculiar history of the British stage. In a backhanded tribute to the political power of the theater, the Licensing Act of 1737 had granted a monopoly on "legitimate" drama to only two London theaters, Covent Garden and Drury Lane. "At present the English, instead of finding politics on the stage, find their stage in politics," quipped Bulwer (Bulwer 1833: 237). Unlicensed theaters were barred from staging productions with speaking parts; hence they resorted to forms of mime, dumbshow, and musical accompaniment, along with increasingly elaborate stage technology, nurturing a taste for spectacle that spread in turn to the legitimate theaters. As R. H. Horne put it, in his *New Spirit of the Age* (1844), the stature of playwrights has declined "because the public taste has been perverted, and cannot improve of itself, and because managers, without a single exception, persist in pandering to that perversion, viz., addressing gaudy and expensive shows to the external senses." (Horne 1844: ii.93). Even after the Theatre Regulation Act of 1843 abolished the patent theater privileges, these trends persisted, creating the enduring image of the Victorian playhouse as an immense space in which performers were dwarfed by their surroundings, and the primary mode of engagement was visual, with actors warring against their backdrops by means of elaborately stylized movement and speech delivered in hectoring, stentorian register. The conditions nurtured a particular conception of the actor as virtuoso – even if it also tended to coarsen the spectacle into histrionics accessible to thousands of spectators. Only gradually did actresses come more into the foreground, and begin to slip free of the taint that associated their profession with prostitution. Indeed, not until the 1890s, with the "new drama" of Ibsen and Shaw – or so the traditional history runs – did the stage became a central locus of cultural innovation and debate.

But these verdicts say as much about an elitist hierarchy of dramatic forms as they do of the power of drama. Drama has always been an arena for battles over the puritanism of British culture. In 1830, when many dissenters and evangelicals shuddered at the idea of setting foot in a playhouse (a thrilling transgression memorably recorded in the best-selling *John Halifax, Gentleman* [1856]) a visitor to London might have been struck more than anything by the sheer variety of theatrical forms on exhibit: farce, pantomime, burlesque, melodrama, opera, drawing-room comedy, Shakespeare. This is the age, moreover, in which "private theatricals" took a central place in affluent domestic life. In the major theaters, tragedy gradually turned into "drama," an amalgam of intrigue, sensation, idealism, and domestic sentiment that would endure throughout the remainder of the century, and on into the next in different media, notably cinema and television (Booth 1991). The dominant form was melodrama, which was mainly popular and proletarian in theme and sentiment, frequently preoccupied with the exploitation of the poor by aristocratic or wealthy villains (many of the theaters devoted to melodrama were in working-class neighborhoods). More generally, its representation of stark moral conflict and highly wrought emotion also made it a compelling vehicle for dramatizing contemporary social problems, which remained largely absent in other literary forms. By the end of the century, comic melodrama had fused with burlesque in the world of the music hall, which became the central cultural arena for testing the emergent boundaries of "high" and "low", mass and elite cultural distinctions.

The Novel After Scott

The most profound impact of early Victorian drama arguably came in another genre altogether, the novel, where it helped to shape the single most important literary career of the Victorian era, that of Dickens. The novel in 1830 was the youngest and least established of the major genres, still widely suspect as at best a shallow amusement or distraction, frequently indistinguishable from "romance," and thus for many conservative religious readers a dangerous indulgence in daydreams and lying. Yet the stature of the form had been transfigured by the career of a single writer, Sir Walter Scott. Scott's Waverly novels, which began to appear anonymously in 1812, were hugely popular, not least because the traditional domestic interests of the form were developed within richly detailed accounts of British history, particularly the relations between England and Scotland, from medieval times to the present. In effect, Scott rescued romance from its feminine associations, and pointed towards the subsequent development of the novel as the dominant literary form of the century. From the moment that Scott's novels began to claim the public's interest, the *Athenaeum* proclaimed in 1828, "we think we can trace a decline of the interest which was taken in poetry" (Chittick 1990: 22).

Scott's career reshaped the fortunes of the novel in a further manner, which again reflects the financial upheavals of the mid-1820s. In the wake of Constable's bankruptcy, Scott himself was financially ruined, but he and the publisher both labored to honorably repay their debts. In the process, Scott probably hastened his death in 1832, but Constable's enterprising partner Cassell evolved a new format for publishing novels. The success of Scott's fiction had established a standard format and price for a novel – three volumes sold for a price of 31s 6d – that persisted until the 1890s. This largely arbitrary figure priced new fiction beyond the reach of even many middle-class readers – it represented more than a week's income for most working-class families – but its resilience reflects its economic benefits to those who published and distributed fiction (to an audience that in the late 1820s was probably no more than 50,000 [Sutherland 1976: 17]). The price gave an effective monopoly to circulating libraries, which purchased new novels in large numbers from publishers and then rented them, thereby gaining great influence over the content of fiction. The system thus allowed publishers to see much of an edition sold even before publication, and enabled them to turn a profit on small press runs (Sutherland 1976: 13–17). *Constable's Miscellany*, however, initiated the reprinting of novels in a one-volume edition for the price of 10 shillings. The gesture was of a piece with many other schemes of the period for distributing literature to wider audiences, all of them in keeping with the growing cultural democratization and the celebration of "useful knowledge." But the reprinting of novels not only reinforced Scott's popularity; it also put back into circulation older works, thereby reinforcing the prominence and popularity of the form. More broadly, Scott's popularity underwrote a new conception of the author. He had published anonymously, because gentlemen did not wish to be engaged in trade, but by his death he had become the exemplar of professional authorship, which developed in close relationship with the ongoing expansion of publishing and audiences.

The novel was especially well adapted to explore and even to define central aspects of Victorian experience and belief. Formally, it developed as an interplay of romance and realism, of fantasy both shaped and obstructed by the imperatives of social and material life. The very construction of realistic "character" is grounded in forms of alienation; it presupposes minds able to withdraw into a psychic space free from, or at least resistant to, social determination. Of course, that same withdrawal may come to seem imprisoning, and nurture a yearning for fuller sense of contact with other (similarly withdrawn) minds; the illusion of such contact is an experience that novelistic representation – particularly through what becomes known as "free indirect discourse" – is uniquely able to offer. As this emphasis on interiority also might encourage a faith in personal autonomy, more recent critics have seen in the work of the Victorian novel a "discipline" that buttressed the premises of classical liberalism. The Victorians themselves saw that regimen less as a gesture of political freedom than as a submission to higher powers, whether duty or God. Thus Thomas Arnold suggests how powerfully introspection was part of the legacy of evangelicalism: "What I feel daily more and more to need," he confided to a friend, "is to have intercourse with those who take life in earnest. It is very painful to be to be always on the surface of things ... I want a sign, which one catches by a sort of masonry, that a man knows what he is about in life ..." (Stanley 1844: 275). Here is a longing for communion that might well be gratified by the rich sense of interiority developed in realistic characterization. Certainly the experience of novel-reading reinforced Victorian structures of private life, not only in its thematic content but as the experience of reading organized that life. This effect became especially marked with the explosive growth of serial publishing ushered in by the early success of Dickens, within which the reception of the latest installment might be a highlight of weekly or monthly domestic routine.

The domestic interests of the English novel – given newly sophisticated embodiment in the work of Edgeworth and Austen – seemed an especially apt vehicle for probing the interrelations of public and private realms. The marriage plot, long seen to be a defining convention of the English novel, took on new resonance in this context – so much so that the formal development of the novel might be charted largely in terms of the various stresses to which the marriage plot is subjected. That structure gradually came to seem less plausible as a means of reconciling varieties of social and formal conflict, particularly as the novel developed into what Henry James decried as "baggy monsters," sprawling works that juggled multiple plots and many dozens of characters in their efforts to evoke an ever-richer texture of social and psychological representation. Moreover, realism frequently drew on the persistent, potentially discordant energies of gothic, which are especially marked in the works of the Brontës. The gothic would resurface throughout the century in generic innovation – in the "sensation novels" of the 1860s, and again in increasingly bold psychological speculation in the romance revival of the 1880s and 1890s (*Jekyll and Hyde*, *The Turn of the Screw*, *The Picture of Dorian Gray*), as well as in what has been called "imperial gothic," in the novels of H. Rider Haggard and Bram Stoker. But British realism remained powerfully bound to domestic interests – so much so that the "New Woman" fiction that emerged in the 1890s could shock audiences simply by resisting the forms of closure typically provided by marriage.

By mid-century the novel had become the dominant cultural form in Britain, and it retained that authority at the death of Victoria, just as the genre itself had become far more manifold, even protean, and its audiences far more fragmented. In an age before electronic entertainments, the novel gave literature a centrality in English culture unequaled before or since. More than any other genre it has come to define what it meant to be "Victorian." Its influence in this regard has only been strengthened by the medium that has usurped its cultural dominance, film, whose artists have found in Victorian narrative irresistible incitements to adaptation and new ambitions to capture the workings of human consciousness and social life.

1

"The Times are Unexampled": Literature in the Age of Machinery, 1830–1850

Constructing the Man of Letters

"The whole world here is doing a Tarantula Dance of Political Reform, and has no ear left for literature." So Carlyle complained to Goethe in August of 1831 (Carlyle 1970–2006: v.327). He was not alone: the great stir surrounding prospects for electoral reform seemed for the moment to crowd aside all other literary interests. The agitation, however, helped to shape a model of critical reflection that gave new weight to literature. The sense of historical rupture announced on all sides was on this view fundamentally a crisis of belief – what a later generation would call an ideological crisis. Traditional forms of faith that undergirded both the English state and personal selfhood were giving way; the times required not merely new political arrangements, but new grounds of identity and belief. Of course, that very designation reflected a skeptical cast of mind. New myths, it seemed, could no longer be found in sacred texts and revelations. They would be derived from secular writings and experience – something that came to be called "literature" in our modern sense of the term. And the best guide to that trove of possibility would be a figure known as "the man of letters."

The most resonant versions of this story were honed through an unlikely literary exchange. In 1831 Carlyle (1795–1881), struggling to eke out a living as an author in the remote Scottish hamlet of Craigenputtoch, came upon "The Spirit of the Age," a series of articles in the London *Examiner* by John Stuart Mill (1806–73). Carlyle wrote to Mill, praising his analysis (in mocking echo of Voltaire's Pangloss) as "the first ... which he had ever seen in a newspaper, hinting that the age was not the best of all possible ages" (Mill 1963–91: xii. 241). Both men understood the political crisis in historical terms, but Carlyle recognized in Mill's analysis of the situation more psychological complexity than the young Mill himself was yet able to appreciate. The present age, Mill pronounced, was above all "an age of transition. Mankind have outgrown old institutions and old doctrines, and have not yet acquired new ones" (Mill 1963–91: xxii. 230). But Mill's analysis allows for little sense of ambivalence or self-division: "Mankind are then divided into those who are still what they were, and those who have changed: into the men of the present age, and the men of the past" (xxii.228). Such was Mill's faith in the irresistible logic of reform – "The superior capacity of the higher ranks for the exercise of worldly power is now a broken spell" (xxii. 231) – that he overlooked a third category in his partition of mankind: those men at home in neither the present nor the past, who are themselves in a state of transition.

Carlyle's diagnosis emphasized precisely this middle state. "The Old has passed away," he wrote in "Characteristics" (1831), "but alas, the new appears not in its stead; the time is still in pangs of travail with the New" (Carlyle 1869: ii.373). This burden of baffled self-consciousness and suspended allegiance – "wandering between two worlds, one dead, / The other powerless to be born" as Matthew Arnold put it a generation later ("Stanzas from the Grande Chartreuse") – would echo throughout the period. Mill's faith in the power of logic afforded him a relatively secure ground of value, but Carlyle understood the moment as a more inchoate crisis of belief. Benthamism and its affiliated ideologies – most notably, laissez-faire economics – offered no source of value outside the self, save the various forms of "machinery" designed to further competing self-interests. In pressing this point, Carlyle launched a searching critique of liberal individualism, and ultimately of Enlightenment rationality. The goal was an ethical ground apart from material rewards, a source of value beyond contract and exchange, which Carlyle associated with deeply personal, intuitive modes of understanding. In this emphasis Carlyle is an heir to Burke and Coleridge, and aligned in important respects with more conventional religious thinkers. His position would be echoed by, among others, the theologian John Henry Newman, who in a riposte to secular schemes of progress ("The Tamworth Reading Room") attacked their spiritual impoverishment: "Wonder is not religion, or we should be worshipping our railroads" (Newman 1965: 106). But whereas Newman resisted "liberalism" by urging the reassertion of clerical power and a return to a purer, more primitive Christianity, Carlyle was convinced that traditional modes of faith had lost their hold.

Carlyle's personal history made him better prepared than Mill to appreciate the struggle for new belief, which became the focus of his greatest work. Mill was born into a radical, free-thinking, middle-class intellectual community in London, and from his father he secured comfortable employment at the East India Company, a position that provided him a steady income and abundant time for writing. Carlyle, the son of a stonemason, had to struggle for nearly two decades to make a living by his writing, and to hammer out a faith to replace the strenuous Calvinism of his parents, who had hoped he would become a minister in the Scottish Kirk. The barbed irony so distinctive of his mature writings emerged in his early letters, largely as mockery of his own sense of failure, which led him to see the very fact of self-consciousness as an index of corrosive doubt. Even after his lapse from orthodox belief, Carlyle envied the preacher's authority, both spiritual and social, and he aspired to endow the author's career with its own "sacredness": "Authors are martyrs – witnesses for truth, – or else nothing. Money cannot make or unmake them" (Froude 1882: ii.264). Yet his own circumstances made this an unusually strenuous demand. "We have no Men of Letters now, but only Literary Gentlemen," he complained (Carlyle 1869: iii.104). Unlike literary gentlemen, however, men of letters had to live by their writing.

This burden had been a recurrent theme of Samuel Johnson (on whom Carlyle wrote an early, admiring essay), but Johnson at least possessed a firm Christian faith. Carlyle in his years of struggle came to envision himself as a latter-day prophet of a new dispensation, straddling Jewish and Christian Testaments. At once Jeremiah and John the Baptist, he excoriated the failings of England and foretold its imminent collapse, while at the same time heralding "a new mythus" that would rescue the country from its bewilderment – although the form of that redeeming faith remained elusive. Hence the appeal of figures of radical alienation: St John the Baptist, Ahab, Ishmael. Yet Carlyle's growing audience ultimately embraced such estrangement as a warrant of integrity. As his admiring biographer J. A. Froude put it, "He called himself a Bedouin, and a Bedouin he was, owing no allegiance save to his Maker and his own conscience" (Froude 1882: ii.402). The "free-lance" writer, in other contexts vilified as an unprincipled hack, became a model of detachment from party, tradition, and unreflective "allegiance" of all kinds. Here was the realm of the man of letters – a space that would come to be associated with the work of "culture" and criticism generally. In the meantime, Carlyle's prophetic mantle offered a consolation to many over the century who shared his large ambitions: the prophet is always unappreciated in his own country.

The struggle towards new forms of belief could best be understood within an emblematic personal history. Carlyle derived this insight from Goethe, whose work he translated and would influentially celebrate. In 1831 Carlyle undertook a work of his own in the broad vein of Goethe's *Wilhelm Meister*, a central example of the German *Bildungsroman*, or novel of development. But that was not quite how Carlyle put it: "I am writing nonsense," he wrote in his notebook; "a book about clothes" (Carlyle 1970–2006: 5.174). The book began as an attack on the dandy, the icon of an enervated aristocracy oblivious to the suffering around it. But Carlyle also saw in the trope of clothing and fashion a figure for the force of history, in particular, the incessant transformation of human beliefs and institutions. Humankind is always struggling to find adequate vesture, in Carlyle's terms, for its beliefs – vesture which culminates in their conception of divinity. "The thing Visible, nay the thing Imagined, the thing in any way conceived as Visible, what is it but a Garment, a Clothing of the higher, celestial Invisible?" (Carlyle 1908: 49). The trope has a long literary history – witness *King Lear* – but it took on added topicality through the revolutionary *sans-culottes* in France, a precedent still haunting England in 1832. Here was a radical questioning of the existing fabric of belief gone horribly wrong. How could present-day England envision a new set of clothing nobler, more truly spiritual, than that of the dandy? Hence the enigmatic title of Carlyle's volume: *Sartor Resartus*, the tailor retailored.

Sartor Resartus is a rare amalgam of genres: sentimental romance, autobiography, sermon, *Bildungsroman*, theological treatise, all subjected to withering parody yet cohering into a deeply felt, multi-layered narrative of spiritual crisis and resolution. The struggle for belief is refracted through two embedded narratives, whose depictions of intellectual life still can sting. The peripatetic career of the late Diogenes Teufelsdrockh ("God-born Devils'-dung"), Professor of Things in General at the University of Weissnichtwo ("Who knows where?"), is being reconstructed from random scraps of writing, contained in a dozen large bags bequeathed to the bewildered editor, Sauerteig. The interplay of these two narratives generates dizzying ironic play captured in the radical dualisms of Carlyle's language (God and Devil, spirit and dung): "The grand unparalleled peculiarity of Teufelsdröckh is, that with all this Descendentalism, he combines a Transcendentalism, no less superlative; whereby if on the one hand he degrades man below most animals ... he, on the other, exalts him beyond the visible Heavens" (Carlyle 1908: 48). As Carlyle sends up both Goethe's *The Sorrows of Werther* and his own early efforts as a reverent biographer of Goethe, he also locates in Teufelsdröckh an archetypal struggle for belief. The most frequently excerpted section of the book is a conversion narrative – or "Baphometic Fire-baptism," in Teufelsdröck's eccentric idiom (128) – in which Teufelsdröckh moves from "The Everlasting Nay" through "The Center of Indifference" to "The Everlasting Yea." He must overcome an "unbelief" epitomized in utilitarianism, which for Carlyle exemplifies the reduction of human experience to mere appetite, a notion that he mocks incessantly: "what, in these dull unimaginative days, are the terrors of Conscience to the diseases of the Liver! Not on Morality, but on Cookery, let us build our stronghold: there brandishing our frying-pan, as censer" (123). Only by rediscovering the "higher, celestial Invisible" can Teufelsdröckh recognize that the universe is not a godless mechanism but a divine organism, within which he can realize a genuinely moral existence.

The result was too much even for the wits at *Fraser's Magazine*, where *Sartor* was first published in installments in 1833–4. Mill was puzzled; even Ralph Waldo Emerson, who came to know Carlyle through the work and arranged for its American publication as a book, complained of the willfully obscure style (Carlyle 1970–2006: 5.196, 8.135). It was published as a book in England only after the success of Carlyle's next major work, *The French Revolution*, in 1837. Yet within a generation *Sartor Resartus* had become something like a guide to the perplexed. In keeping with its skeptical historicist treatment of religious doctrine, the book shies away from a specifically religious credo. But its special appeal lay in a consoling vagueness. As T. H. Huxley put it in a letter some 30 years later, "*Sartor Resartus* taught me that a fervent belief is compatible with an entire absence of theology" (Irvine 1972: 131). In effect, Carlyle conjured up a divinity shorn of doctrinal specifics, a sense of indwelling spiritual presence evoked most suggestively in what he called "Natural Supernaturalism." Over against what Max Weber would later call "the disenchantment of the world," Carlyle struggled to evoke a world of all-encompassing mystery, and a correspondent awe and reverence in the beholder who can recognize this as the index of a spiritual dimension in mankind. Carlyle thus offered a sanctification of the everyday, in which sheer self-denying devotion to one's labor became a form of worship – and a means of putting down the gnawing pangs of doubt. "Doubt of any sort cannot be removed except by Action" (Carlyle 1908: 147). Hence Carlyle transforms the Platonic injunction, "Know thyself" into the more palpable, "Know what thou canst work at," and proceeds to generalize the imperative from John 9:4: "Work while it is called Today; for the Night cometh, wherein no man can work" (149). The "gospel of work," as it become known, was perhaps Carlyle's most influential contribution to Victorian thought – along with his celebration of those heroic individuals who most fully embody it. In this way *Sartor* pays symphonic tribute to the power of sublimation: one escapes from the burdens of doubt, even self-consciousness, through utter immersion in duty. The nature of that duty remained vague, as innumerable commentators pointed out, and when conjoined with the deification of heroic will, Carlyle's exhortations opened the way to a cult of great men. But for at least a generation this hint of authoritarianism was obscured by the hunger for authority itself.

Mill and Carlyle would later part company in bitter political disagreement, but Mill took to heart the example of *Sartor*. When in the 1850s Mill believed he was dying, he felt impelled – much against the instincts of his own reticence – to set down the development of his thought in the form of an autobiography. Within that volume (published posthumously in 1874) the pivot of Mill's narrative became "A Crisis in My Mental History," an event he located in the late 1820s. The analytic habit of mind inculcated by the example of Bentham and his father's rigorous training (Mill began learning Greek at the age of three) had eroded his capacity to feel – so much that he could not find pleasure even in the imagined triumph of Benthamite reflection. In effect, he had come to Carlyle's conclusion that Logic is always saying No. His emergence from the depression, Mill recalls, gave him a new appreciation for what he calls Carlyle's "anti-self-consciousness theory": "Ask yourself whether you are happy, and you cease to be so. The only chance is to treat, not happiness, but some end external to it, as the purpose of life" (Mill 1963–92: i.145–7). Mill drew from this ordeal a new appreciation for "the internal culture of the individual," which Bentham had failed to recognize. Later in the 1830s, Mill would incorporate his new attention to emotional life in a revisionist view of Benthamism, which he most fully developed in pendant essays on Bentham and Coleridge. What had seemed a sharp antagonism became a more subtly modulated dialectic, pointing to a synthesis that Mill would pursue in his own writings. Stereotyped as a model of unfeeling rationality, Mill in fact would provide especially resonant understandings of anxiety and emotional need. And he paid fulsome tribute to the influence of Carlyle, "the mystic," in guiding him towards a newly exacting analysis of human feeling and education.

The Burdens of Poetry

Mill's mental crisis led him to an unusually suggestive account of the situation of poetry in 1830. Poetry tended to be disparaged by both evangelicals and Benthamites; the former as part of a more inclusive suspicion of imagination; the latter as a source of pleasure no more exalted than pushpin, in Bentham's dismissive phrase. Mill, however, had discovered during his mental crisis "a medicine for my state of mind" in reading Wordsworth. His poetry "seemed to be the very culture of the feelings, which I was in quest of" (Mill 1963–92: 1:151). In rethinking his utilitarian inheritance, Mill came to emphasize the imagination that Bentham had neglected, "the power by which one human being enters into the mind and circumstances of another" (Mill 1963–92: x.92). For much of the century, the power to arouse sympathetic understanding was the special virtue of literature generally, and of poetry in particular. And critics came to define the work of culture along the lines of Mill's "culture of the feelings," as a force which guided and constrained instrumental reason, the logic of means and ends, the mental "machinery" associated with an increasingly mechanized world.

When Mill described the work of poetry, however, it seemed at once terribly fragile and deeply anti-social. In an essay of 1833, he defined poetry in sharp contrast to eloquence: "both alike the expression or utterance of feeling," but "eloquence is *heard*; poetry is *overheard*." Poetry is distinguished above all by "utter unconsciousness of a listener": in true poetry, there will be "no trace of consciousness that any eyes are upon us" (Mill 1960–93: i.348–9). In this ideal of pure effusion, awareness of an audience necessarily subverts the integrity of feeling. This striking antagonism (reminiscent of Carlyle's wrestling with self-consciousness) suggests a deep anxiety about selfhood and subjectivity. True poetry is not merely a warrant of emotional authenticity, it also suggests that such integrity can exist only in resistance or oblivion to society at large. Mill's individualism made this fear of social mediation an unusually vexing issue, one that he would engage most fully in *On Liberty*. But the tension resonates throughout early Victorian poetry, in which the poet's relation to an audience becomes a standing problem. Inherent in this emphasis, moreover, is the possibility that poetry will be reduced to an emotional balm, and will lose its purchase on a wider world of thought and value that had traditionally been the burden of the epic. This became a recurrent burden in Victorian quarrels with romanticism, such as Henry Taylor's Preface to his historical drama *Philip van Artevelde* (1834), which complains that "the popular poetry of the times" (Byron in particular) valued feeling and "external embellishments" at the expense of reflection and understanding, the poet's obligation of "seeing all things, to infer and to instruct" (Taylor 1894: xi). Carlyle offered a more radical criticism: the age was devoid of wisdom for the poet to express. "All art is but a reminiscence now," he wrote in 1833, "for us in these days *Prophecy* (well understood) not Poetry is the thing wanted; how can we *sing* and *paint* when we do not yet *believe* and *see*?" (Carlyle 1970–2006: vii.9).

Such impatience reflected in part the increasing association of poetry with women and femininity. Literary histories typically date Victorian poetry from the appearance of Tennyson's *Poems* in 1830. But when Tennyson made his debut, the two most popular contemporary poets (beyond the elderly Scott) were Felicia Hemans and Letitia Landon (who wrote under the initials L. E. L.). Hemans (1790–1835) passed most of her adult life in a small Welsh village, yet she became one of the most popular English poets of the nineteenth century, above all during the years between 1830 and 1850. One of the rare women able to support a family through her writing, by 1831 Hemans was earning two guineas per page for her poetry from *Blackwood's Edinburgh Magazine*, more than even Scott commanded (Feldman 1999: 72–4). The keynote of her lyrics – and of her popularity – is an outwardly unlikely conjunction of domestic affections and patriotic fervor.

Hemans was the most prominent voice in the marked domestication of English verse that developed in the wake of Byron's death in 1824. Over against Byron's deracinated exiles, for whom domestic happiness was at best a memory, at worst a delusion, Hemans's poetry dwelt insistently on the spaces – physical and psychic – of home. Most often, the emotional texture of home (particularly maternal devotion) is evoked through loss; death shadows nearly all of her lyrics, whether her ostensible subject be a troubadour, a conqueror, or, as one title has it, "The forsaken Hearth": "The Hearth, the Hearth is desolate, the fire is quench'd and gone /That into happy children's eyes once brightly laughing shone" (ll. 1–2; Hemans 2002).

"Home" readily extended beyond the hearth, however, to embrace England itself, whose distinction could be evoked in turn through juxtaposition with a much wider world, not merely as a space of difference, but as a realm increasingly under English dominion. In this light, home in Hemans's poetry could be more than the cozy nest of so much later Victorian fantasy; it was a realm within which the obscure, seemingly self-abnegating lives of women – their love, their devotion, and the grief that underscored those – resonated with larger political struggles. Thus "The Homes of England" (1827) is prefaced with an epigraph from Scott's *Marmion*, "Where's the coward who would not dare /To fight for such a land?," and moves from "gladsome looks of household love" to a concluding exhortation,

> The free, fair homes of England!
> Long, long in hut and hall,
> May hearts of native proof be rear'd
> To guard each hallow'd wall!
> And green for ever be the groves,
> And bright the flowery sod,
> Where first the child's glad spirit loves
> Its country and its God!
> (ll. 33–40; Hemans 2002)

In such lyrics, patriotism and familial affection are fused in a single, all-encompassing devotion. (As those virtues came to seem less compelling, so did Hemans's lyrics.) The effect is notable even in Hemans's most famous poem, "Casabianca" of 1829 ("The boy stood on the burning deck ..."), which would remain a staple of school recitation more than a century after her death. The setting is far removed from domesticity, yet the heroism it celebrates is not that of a traditional warrior. It is the unflinching loyalty of "a young faithful heart," who refuses to abandon his dying father even as their ship is consumed by fire. In this apotheosis of devotion ("wreathing fires ...wrapped the ship in splendour wild" [ll. 28–9]; Hemans 2002) Hemans discovers heroism in traditionally feminine virtues – to such an extent that the self-immolation seems eerily akin to suttee. But that echo, unsettling as it may be, hints at some of the stresses increasingly associated with the demands facing Victorian woman, who were likewise expected to wait on voices that might never reply.

This plangent note was widely observed, and meant much to Letitia Landon or "L. E. L" (1802–38). "No emotion is more truly, or more often pictured in her song, than that craving for affection ... which answers not unto the call" (Landon 1997: 177), she wrote in a tribute after Hemans's death in 1835. L. E. L's lyrics rehearsed similar dramas of thwarted affection, but in a manner more extravagant and unguarded, in a career as meteoric as Hemans's was withdrawn. Whereas Hemans remained securely removed from the London literary scene, the "Mrs." a warrant of respectable domesticity (ironically, her husband had abandoned her when she was pregnant with their fifth child), Landon almost from her first publication, when she was just out of her teens, plunged into literary society, and walked a moral tightrope before a public alternately enraptured and punishing. Her poems quickly became objects of curiosity as well as admiration. Bulwer Lytton, in a review of L. E. L.'s 1831 novel, *Romance and Reality*, recalled during his Cambridge days "a rush every Saturday afternoon for 'The Literary Gazette'" in pursuit of "the three magical letters of 'L. E. L.'" "And all of us praised the verse, and all of us guessed at the author. We soon learned it was a female, and our admiration was doubled, and our conjectures tripled. Was she young? Was she pretty? And ... was she rich?" (Landon 1997: 331). With her growing visibility in the literary world, particularly after the success of *The Improvisatrice* in 1824, such speculation soon spilled into gossip that dogged her for the remaining decade of her brief life – a wounding version of the suspicions aroused by women bold enough to lay claim to public notice. (Only a century and a half after her death did it become known that Landon in fact gave birth to several children fathered by her most vocal advocate, the editor William Jerdan [Leary 2005: 72].)

In her poetry, meanwhile, the tears of unrequited love (a preoccupation that wearied even her admirers) mingled with dismay at the alienation experienced by literary women. As she wrote in her eulogy of Hemans, "Genius places a woman in an unnatural position; notoriety frightens away affection; and superiority has for its attendant fear, not love" (Landon 1997: 183) – a sentiment she discovered in the ending of Hemans's "Corinne at the Capitol":

> Happier, happier far than thou
> With the laurel on thy brow,
> She that makes the humblest hearth
> Lovely but to one on earth.
>
> (Landon 1997: 184)

The tangled relations of love and laurel frequently perplexed her own poetry. From early works largely content to rehearse the paradoxical pleasures of grief, L. E. L. moved to more complex meditations on poetry and feeling. In "Memory" (1837), one of her last poems, love disrupts a life in which "to dream and to create has been my fate, / Alone, apart from life's more busy scheming," and prompts the memory of an earlier day in which the depiction of love had not been complicated by experience:

> Oh! Give me back the past that took no part
>   In the existence it was but surveying:
> That knew not then of the awaken'd heart
>   Amid the life of other lives delaying.
>
> Why should such be mine own? I sought it not:
>   More than content to live apart and lonely,
> The feverish tumult of a loving lot,
>   Is what I wish'd and thought to picture only.
>
> (ll. 21–8; Landon 1997)

Such expressions could seem meretricious, merely "pictured," and thus well suited to the illustrated annuals to which L. E. L. devoted so large an amount of her time (her main source of income after 1831 was editing and producing much of the copy for *Fisher's Drawing Room Scrap Book*). But it may also suggest that her poems found so large an audience through focusing on the sheer power of feeling – enacting the very response they aimed to arouse in their readers.

Unrequited longing figured centrally in the reception of another poet a few years younger than Landon. When *Poems, Chiefly Lyrical*, by A. Tennyson, was published in 1830, nearly all reviewers praised a lyric entitled "Mariana." Inspired by a brief allusion in Shakespeare's *Measure for Measure* to the neglected fiancée of Angelo – "There, at

the moated grange, resides this dejected Mariana," (III.1) – the young
Tennyson evoked a world of haunting abandonment:

> With blackest moss the flower-pots
>   Were thickly crusted, one and all;
> The rusted nails fell from the knots
>   That held the pear to the gable-wall.
> The broken sheds look'd sad and strange:
>   Unlifted was the clinking latch;
>   Weeded and worn the ancient thatch
> Upon the lonely moated grange.
>   She only said, "My life is dreary,
>   He cometh not, she said;
>   She said, "I am aweary, aweary,
>   I would that I were dead!"
>
>   (ll. 1–12; Tennyson 1969)

Prolonged over seven stanzas, each with a variation of the opening
refrain ("I am aweary, aweary ..."), the poem elaborates a sense of
desolation unrivaled even in Hemans: domesticity is emptied of all
solace. In this baffled longing, as in its markedly pictorial cast, this is a
poem deeply indebted to the much-derided annuals. But critics found
it mesmerizing: "Words surely never excited a more vivid feeling of
physical and spiritual dreariness," Mill commented, and he went on to
praise Tennyson's capacity for "scene-painting ... the power of creating scenery, in keeping with some state of human feeling; so fitted as
to be the embodied subject of it, and to summon up the state of feeling
itself, with a force not to be surpassed by anything but reality." W. J.
Fox in the *Westminster* similarly applauded the sympathetic power,
marveling that "our author has the secret of the transmigration of the
soul. He can cast his spirit into any living thing, real or imaginary"
(Jump 1971: 87, 27).

The reception of *Poems, Chiefly Lyrical* has to some degree overshadowed the poems themselves. The work gained unusual notice for
a first volume of lyrics, largely because the poet had won the Chancellor's
medal for English verse at Cambridge in 1829 for a poem entitled
"Timbuctoo," which was widely applauded by Tennyson's well-
connected friends (even those who confessed they found this Shelleyan
dream-vision profoundly obscure). But supporters felt obliged to
defend *Poems* by distinguishing it from the poetry of the annuals.
Women poets evoking such bereavement were liable to be chastised for

unreflective self-absorption; Tennyson was praised for his powers of sympathy. An array of lyrics celebrating women – or at least their names: Oriana, Claribel, Lilian, Isabel, Madeline, Adeline – called forth similar enthusiasm, even from critics who recognized their affinities to the portrait galleries of the annuals. "A considerable number of the poems are amatory," W. J. Fox rather guardedly acknowledged; but "they are the expression not of heartless sensuality, nor of a sickly refinement, nor of fantastic devotion, but of manly love; and they illustrate the philosophy of the passion while they exhibit the various phases of its existence, and embody its power" (Jump 1971: 29). The defensive undercurrent – not heartless and sickly but "manly," not mere passion but "the philosophy of the passion" – was a preemptive strike against a suspicion that would dog much of Tennyson's early career, and eventually would come to shadow poetry itself.

The romantic celebration of fidelity to personal experience readily clashed with a demand for collective and public forms of moral affirmation, such as the "Prophecy" Carlyle sought. "Mariana," offering no scope for action or change, was perfectly suited to provoke Carlyle: "If Alfred Tennyson could only make that long wail, like the winter wind, about Mariana in the Moated Grange, and could not get her to throw herself into the ditch, or could not bring her another man to relieve her ennui, he had much better have left her alone altogether" (Tennyson 1969: 49). The tension between public enlightenment and private, sometimes hermetic, introspection is inscribed within Tennyson's 1830 volume in the pendant poems, "The Poet" and "The Poet's Mind." The former, with its concluding personification of Freedom – "No sword /Of wrath her right arm whirl'd, /But one poor poet's scroll, and with *his* word /She shook the world" (ll.53–6; Tennyson 1969) – is a Shelleyan tribute to the poet as unacknowledged legislator. But "The Poet's Mind" locates poetry in an isolated sanctuary, a "holy ground" of beautiful song secure from intrusions of "the sophist," who could never fathom the poet's mind (ll. 8–9).

This conflict became the focal point of a review of *Poems, Chiefly Lyrical* by Tennyson's close friend A. H. Hallam, which would prove a landmark in nineteenth-century understandings of poetry. With all the confidence of his 21 years, Hallam urged that people who failed to appreciate Tennyson were expecting the wrong kind of poetry. They were looking for poetry of reflection, which Hallam associated preeminently with Wordsworth, and they presumed that profound thoughts make for beautiful poetry. But the predominant motive of great poetry, he rejoined, must be "the desire of beauty"; otherwise, "the result is false in art." Tennyson, like Shelley and Keats before him, is a poet of sensation; theirs is a life "of immediate sympathy with the external universe" rather than a disposition to "purely intellectual contemplation." Hallam's sympathies are clear enough – and he gave them added edge with his claim that "the cockney school ... contained more genuine inspiration, and adhered more speedily to that portion of the truth which it embraced, than any *form* of art that has existed in this country since the day of Milton." This gauntlet ("the Cockney School" attacks on Keats and Hunt were little more than a decade old) raised a further dilemma. If the poetry of sensation emanates from an innate poetic *constitution* different from that of other beings, if such poets "constantly felt, sentiments of exquisite pleasure or pain, which most men were not permitted to experience," then their appreciation requires special effort from readers, a patient attentiveness that most don't bother to exert (Jump 1969: 35–8).

Here was the dilemma that Wordsworth had discovered a generation earlier, when his optimistic pronouncements in the Preface to *Lyrical Ballads* gave way to the view, in the "Essay Supplementary" (1815), that a poet must create the taste by which he is to be enjoyed. This view was a harbinger of the avant-garde, but Hallam, like Wordsworth before him, had to explain this neglect by falling back on a theory of cultural decline. Whereas "[i]n youthful periods of any literature there is an expansive and communicative tendency in mind, which produces unreservedness of communion, and reciprocity of vigour between different orders of intelligence," since the time of Shakespeare "we have undergone a period of degradation" which has given rise to "that return of the mind upon itself, and the habit of seeking relief in idiosyncrasies rather than community of interest" (Jump 1969: 41). This diagnosis of a disabling self-consciousness, which undermines poetry's power as a vehicle of general sympathy, would echo throughout Victorian reflection on poetry – indeed, it points forward to T. S Eliot's pronouncement a century later that literary history had witnessed a "dissociation of sensibility" after the Renaissance, "from which we have never recovered" (Eliot 1932: 288). Even those who celebrate poetry are shadowed by a sense of its decline.

Hallam's most inflammatory gesture, however, was his invocation of Keats and Shelley. This incited a series of critical reactions that underscores the fiercely political character of early Victorian reviewing.

The radical associations of the *Westminster*, where Fox's encomiums had appeared, and Hallam's cheeky praise of the cockney school brought out from John Wilson (writing as "Christopher North" in *Blackwood's*) an echo of the fierce attacks on Keats. Fox's praise in the *Westminster*, North pronounced, is "a perfect specimen of the super-hyperbolical ultra-extravagance of outrageous Cockney eulogistic foolishness ... the purest mere matter of moonshine ever mouthed by an idiot-lunatic, slavering in the palsied dotage of the extremest super-annuation ever inflicted on a being." As in the attacks on Keats, failed poetic pretensions are nothing less than a failure of manhood (against which Fox had so carefully defended him): "Mr. Tennyson should speak of the sea so as to rouse the souls of sailors, rather than the soles of tailors ... Unfortunately, he seems never to have seen a ship" (Jump 1969: 54–6). For the remainder of the century Tennyson's admirers would defend him against such suspicions – in the process effacing the profound continuities between his early work and that of his female contemporaries.

North's invective had little impact on Tennyson's next volume, which was largely written, and would be published just a few months later. But it did sting him into responding (against the advice of Hallam) with a squib of his own against "crusty Christopher," and this misguided gesture set none other than J. W. Croker, author of the famous attacks on Keats, to sharpening his critical knives: "I undertake Tennyson," he wrote to the son of John Murray, publisher of the *Quarterly*, "and hope to make another Keats of him" (Jump 1969: 2). The subsequent review became one of the most infamous hatchet jobs of the nineteenth century, an exercise in heavy, unremitting sarcasm that attempted to demolish Tennyson's poetic pretensions. The review clearly was a great blow to a man easily stung – bafflingly so to his friends – by hostile criticism. Indeed, it was long read as a turning point in Tennyson's career, which shocked him into what would become known as the "ten years' silence." But the major redirection of Tennyson's early work had already begun in the 1832 volume, which contained the first versions of half a dozen of Tennyson's best-known lyrics.

The emotional focus of the 1832 *Poems* is narrower than that of the earlier volume. With remarkable, even obsessive tenacity, Tennyson returns to images of a feminine or feminized being longing for release from isolation or abandonment: "The Lady of Shalott," "Oenone," "The Palace of Art," "The Lotos-Eaters." Yet in each of these works, the same longing is chastened through some form of distancing, which ironically or dramatically frames the expression of desire – and the lyric impulse itself. Thus the predicament of the central figure, caught between her desires and a world that thwarts or discredits them, comes to resemble the situation of the poet himself. This structure is most emphatic, even schematic, in "The Palace of Art" – an elaborate response to suspicions that Tennyson wished, as a Cambridge contemporary objected, to "live in art" (Tennyson 1969: 400). The poet's feminine soul inhabits "a lordly pleasure-house" (l. 1), contemplating in solitude the world and its artistic treasures as a many-faceted aesthetic spectacle. Likened to Lucretius's Epicurean gods – a favorite early-Victorian emblem of indifference to human struggle – this hubristic soul is clearly set up for a fall. But her ordeal does not begin until 54 of 74 stanzas have passed in the evocation of aesthetic pleasure – a disproportion that suggests Tennyson's own deep attraction to that "God-like isolation" (l. 197). Once thrown down from her loftiness, moreover, the soul experiences no reconciliation with a wider world; instead she remains "Shut up as in a crumbling tomb, girt round / With blackness as a solid wall" (ll. 273–4), rather as if Mariana were imprisoned in the British Museum, wistfully looking forward to a return to her treasures "when I have purged my guilt" (l. 296; Tennyson 1969).

"The Palace of Art" captures a preoccupation with the morality of art that leads from Keats's "Eve of St. Agnes" to Wilde's *The Picture of Dorian Gray*, by way of the monologues of Browning, the art criticism of Ruskin, and the rise of aestheticism. As visual art became available to an ever larger public, the pleasures of beauty were more widely celebrated, but its power seemed to many observers something disturbing, even tyrannical, confounding moral restraint. Art itself could thus seem a form of temptation, to be resisted or indulged, but rarely to be contemplated with the serenity that so many Victorians would locate in classical Greece. Already in Tennyson's poetry art seems the mastery of contradictory allegiances. This predicament is most vividly rendered in another evocation of feminine solitude, "The Lady of Shalott" – a poem that would captivate generations of Victorian artists. The image of a woman in a tower, working on a tapestry that cannot fully embody her desires, caught between the demands of her weaving and the wider world she glimpses from her window, has long seemed a self-reflexive evocation of Tennyson's own sense of vocation. The "curse" under which the Lady labors also seems to capture tensions inherent in the very institution of poetry, as critics simultaneously demand both fidelity to inner life and insight into a more impersonal world of action.

Poets increasingly responded to this tension not only thematically, but through formal innovation, particularly the dramatic framing of lyric. This tactic allows Tennyson to enrich the sense of interiority in the speaker's voice even as it disavows identification with it. Of course the very titling of "Mariana" effects a version of this; the effusion is placed as the utterance of a character other than the poet, and thereby in turn solicits not merely identification with the feeling, but analysis of it as a revelation of character. The device is greatly enriched in "Oenone," the first of Tennyson's brilliant lyric appropriations of Greek mythology. Here the character's situation echoes that of Mariana, with Oenone – the deserted wife of Paris – recounting her sufferings to "mother Ida," but the poem is entirely given to the lament, which builds out a far more elaborate narrative and far more resonant emotions captured in a newly supple blank verse. It concludes:

> I will rise and go
> Down into Troy, and ere the stars come forth
> Talk with the wild Cassandra, for she says
> A fire dances before her, and a sound
> Rings ever in her ears of armèd men.
> What this may be I know not, but I know
> That, whereso'er I am by night or day,
> All earth and air seem only burning fire.
>   (ll. 257–64; Tennyson 1969)

The reader's awareness of what Oenone does not comprehend – that Cassandra's prophecy foretells the imminent Trojan Wars – creates an ironic frame that underscores her bewilderment, which in turn appeals to the reader's sympathy.

Elsewhere, Tennyson uses a similar allusive frame to chasten sympathy, and to create the peculiar forms of cognitive dissonance that would come to characterize the dramatic monologue. His procedure in "The Lotos-Eaters" is formally that of "Oenone": he finds a moment of baffled longing, and thus the lyrical impulse, at the margins of Greek epic – in this instance, imagining Odysseus's crew clinging to the island of the Lotos as a respite from their years of voyaging. Once again, an evocative landscape introduces the lyrical utterance proper. But the overall effect is to underscore the ironic discrepancy between the mariners' desires and the burdens of duty – not to mention the fate known to the reader, that their longing to remain on the island is doomed to be frustrated. In many respects the poem recalls "The Palace of Art," most obviously as the mariners also long for the detachment of Epicurean gods. But here the tension is pressed to a radical ambivalence – against the lure of the island, captured in hypnotic, trance-like verse, comes a recognition of the exorbitance of the mariners' desire:

> All things have rest: why should we toil alone,
> We only toil, who are the first of things,
> And make perpetual moan,
> Still from one sorrow to another thrown …
>
> (ll. 60–3; Tennyson 1969)

Their longing for "dreamful ease" is ultimately a yearning for oblivion: "death is the end of life," they sing (l. 86) – not only its cessation but its goal. Indeed, the longing for death is so powerful that Tennyson himself introduced cautionary revisions in subsequent editions, in an effort (again recalling "The Palace of Art") to underscore the failure of discipline. But the lure of annihilation clearly answers to a central impulse of his imagination – which makes Tennyson's subsequent eminence in Victorian literature all the more striking. This culture fabled for its dedication to earnest struggle was enraptured by laments of the abandoned or bereft, figures who can imagine satisfaction only as a release from their agony, often in death.

Tennyson's early poetry underscores a radically anti-social dimension in lyric desire – all the more evident when the expression of longing is framed (as in "The Lotos Eaters") by the social imperatives it resists. In this regard, it seems to reinforce Mill's contrast between poetry and oratory. But Mill's formulation was confounded by the development of a new genre foreshadowed by "The Lotos Eaters." The dramatic monologue is built on the interplay of voice and an implied audience; it is a genre in which identity is not merely social but is quite insistently a rhetorical effect. There are many precedents for the form – perhaps most notably the feminine figure of "the Improvisatrice" that Landon had derived from the example of Mme. de Staël's novel *Corinne* (1807). But in Landon's usage the dramatic framing is less markedly ironic; even when the "I" of the poem is located in a character other than the poet, the poem does not evoke an irony of moral distance. The contrast, critics have suggested, reflects the insistent gendering of poetry; women poets "could not afford irony, since their first work was to show their right to a place in poetry, not their discordance with it" (Mermin 1993: 65).

Robert Browning, the greatest virtuoso of the dramatic monologue, did not begin to develop the form until later in the decade. His poetic debut was famously inauspicious. *Pauline: A Fragment of a Confession* appeared in March of 1833 (its costs underwritten by the poet's father) and not a single copy was sold. Reviews were in fact mixed: although the wags at *Fraser's* professed to believe it the work of a madman, or the current Whig ministry, others praised it and predicted great success for the anonymous author. But this divided response was overshadowed by one review – which was never published, but which found its way back to Browning in a closely annotated copy, with a summary judgment on the flyleaf:

> With considerable poetic powers, the writer seems to me possessed with a more intense and morbid self-consciousness than I ever knew in any sane human being. I should think it a sincere confession ... if the "Pauline" were not evidently a mere phantasm. All about her is full of inconsistency – he neither loves her nor fancies he loves her, yet he insists upon *talking* love to her. If she existed and loved him, he treats her most ungenerously. (Irvine and Honan 1974: 40)

Thus John Stuart Mill, who with characteristic acuity lays open a tension that would shape much of Browning's career. *Pauline* is nominally dramatic, an impassioned outpouring to a loved one whose physical presence is evoked in the opening lines: "Pauline, mine own, bend o'er me – thy soft breast /Shall pant to mine – bend o'er me ..." (ll. 1–2; Browning 1970). Yet in the more than one thousand lines of blank verse that follow, this interlocutor fades into a colossal self-absorption as the speaker rehearses his poetic aspirations and anxieties. The true beloved is the poet Shelley, the "Sun-treader" who by the poem's conclusion has entirely displaced Pauline as both guide and protector:

> Thou must be ever with me, most in gloom
> If such must come, but chiefly when I die,
> For I seem, dying, as one going in the dark
> To fight a giant; but live thou for ever
> And be to all what thou hast been to me!
>
>   (ll. 1024–8)

Browning recorded in the same copy his bitterness at Mill's verdict. But he shaped a more enduring response in the following year. Invited on a trip to St Petersburg, Browning during the journey produced "Porphyria's Lover," a poem that in 60 lines achieves a drama alien to *Pauline*, and does so precisely by ironizing the lyricism of another self-absorbed speaker. What opens as the recollection of a romantic tryst in a cottage, abruptly veers into pathology:

> That moment she was mine, mine, fair,
> Perfectly pure and good: I found
> A thing to do, and all her hair
> In one long yellow string I wound
> Three times her little throat around
> And strangled her.
>
> (ll. 36–41; Browning 1970)

With this jarring revelation, an identification with the speaker's passion is checked by bewilderment at the enormity of his act. Sympathy is abruptly alienated – far more thoroughly than in Tennyson's monologues, where (as in "The Lotos Eaters") the seductive lyricism so often overwhelms the implied interdictions.

Browning's mastery of this dissonance is epitomized in "My Last Duchess," where the seemingly effortless urbanity of the Duke of Ferrara gradually discloses a monomaniacal, ultimately murderous obsession with his own authority. Even his young wife's innocent heart, "too soon made glad, /Too easily impressed" (ll. 22–3; Browning 1970) is a challenge to his supremacy that must be punished by death:

> Oh sir, she smiled, no doubt,
> Whene'er I passed her; but who passed without
> Much the same smile? This grew; I gave commands;
> Then all smiles stopped together. There she stands
> As if alive.
>
> (ll. 42–7)

In his deranged connoisseurship, the Duke conflates morality and aesthetics, judging human beings as objects designed to give him pleasure. The logic is clinched by the painting of his late wife that he proudly points out in the opening line of the poem: only thus, reduced to an artifact, can "my last duchess" be fully possessed. Yet the work of the painting is radically ambiguous: it captures her in the sense that it imprisons her, and yet it also is faithful to her. In an important sense she lives on in that image (as in the Duke's own self-betraying words), in "the depth and passion of its earnest glance" (l. 8). This powerfully equivocal view of art – a gesture of fidelity to the world, but also a means to shape the world to one's desires – will be a recurrent preoccupation not only of Browning's monologues but of Victorian critical reflection.

It is a self-reflexive theme, of course, which bears on Browning's representation of voice, and the sometimes tense interplay between his own sense of authorial mastery and a genuine delight in the varieties of the human psyche. Browning's monologues rarely stage a problem in order to resolve it; "My Last Duchess" evokes a sense of the speaker's mind as a world unto itself, creating a striking illusion of psychic depth. At the same time, the form prompts us to recognize that the illusion of a perfect self-absorption depends on an audience. The Duke's presence is emphatically histrionic, a performance for an implied listener; his psychology is inescapably social. Over against Mill and other celebrants of the perfectly autonomous poetic self, Browning evokes selves anxiously, utterly dependent on the regard of other eyes and ears, selves (it seems) that are fundamentally rhetorical performances. And virtuoso performances they are; the greatest wonder of Browning's own pieces may be the illusion of such an array of disparate voices. From the interplay of Browning's largely contemporary idiom and the barest of historical context we conjure up the speech of an Italian Renaissance noble, whose language seems so powerfully colloquial that first-time readers almost never notice that he speaks in rhymed couplets.

It would be some time before Browning would sound all these possibilities; he remained smitten with the theater, and turned his attention to a more conventional form, the verse-drama. *Paracelsus*, published in 1835, is very much in the tradition of the romantic "closet drama," its hero a Shelleyan quester in the image of Prometheus – or Frankenstein. Though the poem captures Browning's perennial interest in the forms of ambition and the fine line between visionary and crank, the treatment is for the most part sympathetic – perhaps because the protagonist's aspirations and anxieties are very much those of a young poet envisioning his own pursuit of "sacred knowledge" (1.786) and not averse to being acknowledged as "one /Of higher order, under other laws /Than bind us" (11.696–8; Browning 1970). (This antinomian streak – a sure sign of vaulting ambition – characterizes a host of

Browning's speakers.) Indeed, the very idea of a "career" – its possible trajectories and informing values – is a recurrent theme of the poem. John Forster in *The Examiner* obligingly predicted "a brilliant career," and in another review conjoined him "without the slightest hesitation" with "Shelley, Coleridge, Wordsworth" (Litzinger and Smalley 1970: 41, 45). But Browning would remember mostly the detractors. He continued to envision success – like so many of his contemporaries – in the theater.

Theater in the 1830s

The persistent lure of theatrical glory in the 1830s is perplexing. The decline of the stage was one of the sturdiest clichés of the era. The cavernous surroundings and the machinery of spectacle created a physical environment hostile to psychological nuance, and as a result aspiring playwrights (with ample precedent among the romantics) often produced dramatic verse that made no pretensions to being fitted for staging. Certainly performance conditions hastened the long decline of English classical tragedy. A rare success in this vein was *Ion* by Thomas Talfourd (better known today for his subsequent advocacy of international copyright), which debuted at Covent Garden in May of 1836. Though to modern ears its blank verse is cold and inert, and its moral conflicts a clash of Christian ethos with a "principle of inexorable fate" more appropriate to its classical Greek setting (Horne 1844: 254–6), it became one of the most widely admired tragedies of the time. Some of this may be a by-product of the self-conscious austerity of the verse and construction, which chimes with the recommendations of Taylor's Preface to *Philip van Artevelde*. More likely it reflected a virtuoso performance by William Macready, the renowned actor-manager of Covent Garden. Browning jumped at the chance to make his formal debut as a playwright with Macready in the starring role of *Strafford*, a drama of the English Civil War that opened at Covent Garden later in the same year. But not even Macready's talents could secure a warm reception.

Despite Talfourd's success, critics increasingly complained of a debilitating self-consciousness in efforts to imitate an older dramatic form. The most successful dramatists of the day, G. W. Lewes would argue in 1850, were "precisely those who do *not* imitate the Elizabethan form" (Booth 1991: 149). One compromise was a vogue for historical drama, such as *Strafford*, which clung to some traditional decorums of classical theater while affording greater romantic intrigue, whose often predictable structure might be submerged in exotic settings and characters. Fanny Kemble, the leading actress of the age, testified to the vogue with two verse dramas, *Francis the First* (1832) and *The Star of Seville* (1837). The greatest successes in this line came from Edward Bulwer (later Bulwer-Lytton, 1803–73) who along with Sheridan Knowles was the most successful dramatist of the 1830s, and the most versatile and visible English writer of the decade. *The Lady of Lyons* (1838) and *Richelieu; or The Conspiracy* (1839) were both staged by Macready at Covent Garden, and remained in repertory for the rest of the century; the title role in the latter offered an especially appealing part for virtuoso actors such as Edwin Booth and Irving. Bulwer has been called "the only example in nineteenth-century England of an established man of letters turning successfully to the stage" (Booth 1969–76: i.239) – a verdict that suggests the peculiar demands facing Victorian playwrights. (Knowles, in telling contrast, by 1846 was a bankrupt.)

Far and away the leading force in the transformation of Victorian theater was melodrama, whose presence in Victorian culture it is hard to overstate. Unlike historical drama, melodrama was mainly popular and proletarian in theme and sentiment, its preoccupation with stark moral conflict easily adapted to staging the exploitation of the poor by aristocratic or wealthy villains (many of the theaters devoted to melodrama were in working-class neighborhoods). Through such materials melodrama frequently engaged, however crudely, contemporary social problems markedly absent in the likes of *Ion*. One popular strand of the genre, the nautical melodrama, emerged in the 1820s out of earlier patriotic entertainments about British naval victories in the French wars. Douglas Jerrold's *Black-Eyed Susan*, first produced in 1829, was an especially popular and durable example of the form, which nurtured one of the most enduring Victorian stereotypes, the rough yet loyal and fearless British "tar," paragon of unpretentious patriotism, whose vogue endured long enough to be parodied by Gilbert and Sullivan.

Increasingly, however, in the drama as in the lyric, the sea yielded to more domestic preoccupations. Sheridan Knowles, Horne argued, personifies the age in his "truly domestic feeling. The age is domestic, and so is he. Comfort – not passionate imaginings, – is the aim of every body" (Horne 1844: ii.86). Melodrama gathered in an increasingly wide swath of everyday working-class life, and was ahead of the novel in representing the poor as figures of sympathy, not just comic material. Jerrold's *The Rent Day* (1832) is exemplary of melodrama dealing with rural settings, which presumably appealed in part to a newly urbanized population that within memory had emigrated from the countryside. The many versions of Sweeney Todd, "the demon barber of Fleet Street," reflect a widespread preoccupation with urban danger and squalor, as do a host of related crime melodramas, such as Dibdin Pitt's *Simon Lee* (1839) and *Susan Hopley* (1841), as well as clusters of works devoted to gambling, drink, and other vices. New forms of social conflict were registered with special force in factory melodramas, a by-product of "the factory question," fierce debates about the working conditions of emergent industrial labor, which anticipate the preoccupations of the so-called "industrial novel" that emerged in the 1840s. *The Factory Lad* by the otherwise obscure John Walker, which premiered at the Surrey in October of 1832, presses the social engagement of the genre to unusual extremes, foregoing both comic relief and the usually obligatory happy ending.

Fiction in the Early 1830s

If melodrama looks forward to the world of silent film, a medium strikingly akin to the early Victorian stage, it also became a shaping presence in the Victorian novel, where it helped to form the single most important literary career of the Victorian era. In 1830, however, novelists tended to be divided between two often discordant forms of writing: the historical fiction associated with Scott and the "silver-fork" novel of contemporary life. The onslaught against Byron orchestrated by *Fraser's* in 1830 also gathered in much of the silver-fork school, particularly Bulwer, who had scored a huge success with his 1828 novel *Pelham*. *Pelham* is a consummate example of the silver-fork school, but it draws its hero away from the rarefied precincts of the *bon ton* into the criminal underworld, as Pelham struggles to solve the murder of an acquaintance. The novel points to the sociological investments of the genre, offering its broadly middle-class readership vantages into opposite extremes of English society, neither of which they were ever likely to experience in person. But Bulwer, unlike most writers in this genre, also fancied himself a philosophical radical, and his treatment of the poor is energized by political as well as novelistic interests. As in Godwin's *Caleb Williams* (1794), the gothic device of obsessive pursuit exposes the harrowing of innocence by unjust power (Mary Shelley had worked a unique variation on this structure in *Frankenstein*).

Unsympathetic readers, however, saw no moral design in *Pelham*. They were repelled by what seemed a self-indulgent dandyism, expressed alike in lavish evocations of "the best circles" and their world of glittering mirrors, and in a seemingly indiscriminate delight in low company, where morality was submerged in slumming. This criticism (naturally inflamed by the success of the novel) was heightened by Bulwer's further triumph in 1830 with *Paul Clifford*, a novel wholly given over to the world of eighteenth-century highwaymen, and relying extensively on the "flash" criminal slang that became popular with novelists throughout the thirties. With the 1832 publication of *Eugene Aram*, which recounted the career of a historical murderer, Bulwer provoked *Fraser's* into one of the most aggressive literary vendettas of the age, which continued over nearly 15 years. (As if this were not enough, when Bulwer separated from his wife Rosina a few years later, she turned her considerable talents to writing a series of scabrous *romans-à-clef* such as *Cleveley* [1839].)

Envy aside, the ferocity of these attacks reflects broader social dynamics that influenced the subject matter of the novel, the course of individual careers, and the general prestige of the genre. The attack on dandyism was first and foremost an attack on social presumption. Though the dandy may seem an aristocratic figure, the pursuit of an elegant, refined detachment was most often the paradoxical badge of a young man on the make. The dandy's fastidiousness ostensibly set him apart from society at large, but it also solicited the collective attention it seemed to disdain. This dynamic shaped the early social careers of a striking number of important novelists in the 1830s – not merely Bulwer, but also Disraeli, Ainsworth, and Dickens, all of whom were widely characterized as dandies. (Dickens, perhaps in expiation, filled the pages of his later novels with dandies grown old.) The early career of Benjamin Disraeli (1804–81) closely paralleled Bulwer's. A sequence of novels, from *Vivian Grey* (1826), which was puffed as "a sort of *Don Juan* in prose," through *Venetia* (1837), all were deeply responsive to the silver-fork mode (in some respects Disraeli never outgrew it), and many observers mocked him for confusing himself with his protagonists. "That egregious young coxcomb Disraeli was there, too," wrote Lady Morgan in 1833, "outraging the privilege a young man has of being absurd" (Adburgham 1983: 195). As the label of "dandy" or "coxcomb" chastened the pretensions of young men of letters, it also pointed to the increasing preoccupation of novelists with precisely such dynamics of social mobility and resistance. But the fervor of attacks on dandyism also reflected the increasing social and cultural authority of the novel as a genre. As Horne put it in 1844, "Prose fiction has acquired a more respectable status within the last half century than it held at any previous period in English literature ...the novel itself has undergone a complete revolution. It is no longer a mere fantasy of the imagination .... but a sensible book, insinuating in an exceedingly agreeable form ... a great deal of useful knowledge, historical, social, and moral" (Horne 1844: i.215). This growing dignity and influence in turn would become an increasingly self-reflexive element of the novelist's craft. The attacks on Bulwer thus suggest how readily the dandy could figure a standing challenge to decorums extending well beyond fashion. As in early attacks on Tennyson, literary and social polemics were complexly intertwined.

Such a twofold attack is enshrined in the very phrase "the silver-fork novel." In Hazlitt's withering 1827 review (of a forgotten work by Theodore Hook), the fixation on affluence betrays children with their faces at the candy-shop window, writers fantasizing about a world from which they remain excluded. The author, as Hazlitt put it, "informs you that the quality eat fish with silver forks." The novelists themselves naturally resisted this characterization. Catherine Gore, who was the most popular and prolific writer of the school, announced in her preface to *Pin Money* (1831) that she aimed to bring "the familiar narrative of Miss Austen to a higher sphere of society." Other readers, however, recognized in Gore's work (as in the genre generally) a preoccupation with "trade" markedly different from that of Austen's novels: "A novel like *Pin Money*," the *Westminster Review* remarked, "is, in fact, a sort of London Directory ... it has sometimes occurred to us, that the persons who are really at the bottom of these singular productions [novels of fashionable life], are no other than a certain set of dealers in articles of luxury, who know the value of getting notoriety" (Adburgham 1983: 211). The reviewer's gibe glances at the silver-fork novel as itself a merchandising phenomenon. Henry Colburn, the leading publisher of the school, was notoriously adept at arranging favorable advance reviews, or "puffs," of his authors. Gore, ironically, would veil her own prolific output in anonymity, lest she seem to be debasing her currency: two of her novels, *Greville* and *Cecil*, were published in the same week in 1841. The reviewer also captured a more far-reaching social logic, by which pretensions to higher status are reflected in unusually conspicuous consumption (a concept Theodore Veblen formulated only 60 years later). As silver-fork novels set this dynamic into sharp relief, they call attention to a central impulse of realism in the Victorian novel, whereby fictional authority is established through closely detailed rendering of everyday life – "the presence of the present" (Altick 1991). In this regard the silver-fork school is at one with Bulwer's pursuit of "flash" language: the social antithesis veils a shared aim to document a particular milieu, in a manner that points to the emergence of something akin to anthropological observation.

Bulwer himself followed out this logic with *Paul Clifford*, which created a sensation. Though best known today for its often-parodied opening sentence, "It was a dark and stormy night," it was said to have the largest first printing of any English novel to that time, which nonetheless sold out on publication day. Like *Pelham*, the novel straddles elite and outcast worlds, but with more overt satiric and political design. The eponymous hero's dual life as highwayman and West End dandy undermines any moral hierarchy between the two, and Bulwer's characteristic attacks on abuses of power (Paul is drawn into criminality through unjust imprisonment) gain further edge from the thinly disguised portraits of contemporary politicians as Fieldingesque thieves (the Duke of Wellington, for example, appears as "Fighting Attie") This is the work that established Bulwer as the leading novelist of the early 1830s. Though its satiric humor largely disarmed criticism of sometimes slack prose – beyond attacks in *Fraser's*, that is, whose editor Maginn was lampooned in the character of MacGrawler – many readers were unsettled by a highwayman hero. This reservation blew into a firestorm with the publication of *Eugene Aram* in 1832, which took as its protagonist not merely a criminal but a historical murderer, and presented him in a manner largely free of moralism. Aram in Bulwer's treatment is the victim less of injustice than of his own mind: he is a romantic quester, something akin to Browning's Paracelsus in Newgate, likewise brought down by an intellectual pride that shades into antinomian faith in his immunity to ordinary laws. As the Preface puts it, Bulwer aimed "to impart to this Romance something of the nature of Tragedy." But many critics, led by *Fraser's*, found only indulgence. Maginn accused Bulwer of "awakening sympathy with interesting criminals, and wasting sensibilities on the scaffold and the gaol" (Hollingsworth 1963: 93).

Though the fascination of the criminal-hero persisted throughout the 1830s, the "Newgate School" did not acquire its label until the end of the decade, in the wake of *Oliver Twist* (1838) and William Ainsworth's *Jack Sheppard* (1839). Earlier in the decade, social outcasts were associated more with historical fiction – a further extension of fictional frontiers identified with Scott, whose Waverley novels were launched by imagining a middle-class hero plunged into an alien, sometimes bewildering, outlaw world. Thus Ainsworth's *Rookwood* (1834), which recounted the life of Dick Turpin, hanged in 1739, prompted many comparisons to Scott – the height of praise for a novelist in the early 1830s – and Ainsworth (1805–82) would become the most popular historical novelist of the nineteenth century after Scott (Sutherland 1989: 13). From 1836–45, he collaborated with the great illustrator Cruickshank, which both reflected and reinforced his stature. Ainsworth's prolific career was shadowed by the still more abundant historical romances of G. P. R. James (1799?–1860), which have eluded attempts even to catalogue them. James's career began in 1829 with *Richelieu*, a novel clearly modeled on Scott's *Quentin Durward* (Scott returned the compliment by praising the novel), and continued with unflagging productivity. Long before the career ended, however, James would be derided for his "irresistible tendency to pile up circumstantial particulars," a quality which Horne called "fatal to those forms of art which demand intensity of passion" (Horne 1844: 1.231). Such criticism, along with Thackeray's devastating 1847 *Punch* parody, "Barbazure," suggests an emergent standard of novelistic craft that would undermine the stature of many earlier Victorian novelists.

A further popular novelist of proletarian life was Frederick Marryat (1792–1848), a distinguished naval veteran, usually styled "Captain," who took up novel-writing after resigning his commission in 1828. His first novel, *Frank Mildmay*, appeared in 1829, and he scored his first large success with *Peter Simple* in 1834. For *Mr Midshipman Easy* (1836) he received 1,000 pounds, inaugurating an income that would make him "one of the consistently best-paid novelists of the nineteenth century" (Sutherland 1989: 414). Marryat had the good luck to coincide with a vogue for melodramatic and ballad renderings of sailing life, which flourished as Trafalgar and other epic Napoleonic battles were beginning to recede in memory. As novelists further contributed to the romance of the British "tar," their attention to the often-brutal character of life at sea – whether in the Navy or among merchant sailors – chimed with the contemporary popularity of novels of low life. (Marryat's *Jacob Faithful* [1834] shares many preoccupations with Ainsworth's *Rookwood*, published in the same year.) Rather quickly, however, the nautical novels – in common with the adventure tale generally, which gathered in much of Scott's work – came to be associated with juvenile readers. Marryat's *Masterman Ready* (1842) was an especially momentous stage in the development of what would come to be called "boys' adventure."

In the early 1830s Bulwer seemed the major successor to Scott. Born into a wealthy, aristocratic family, educated at Cambridge (where he won the Chancellor's Medal in 1825, four years before Tennyson), Bulwer moved with distinctive ease between the silver-fork genre and historical romances. His first historical novel, *Devereux* (1829), was not a success (although the 1,500 pounds he received from Colburn for the copyright testifies to the popularity of *Pelham*). But his return to the form, with *The Last Days of Pompeii* (1834) and *Rienzi* (1835), produced two further best-sellers. *Rienzi* offers a more serious and substantial analysis of history, focusing as it does on the hero's rise to power within political conflict in fourteenth-century Italy – a treatment that anticipated Carlyle's understanding of history as largely the biography of great men. *The Last Days* lacks any sustained analysis of historical forces – it relies heavily on the foreboding and sensation inherent in its title, a backdrop against which Bulwer focused on the "ordinary incidents of life," in a self-conscious swerve away from the more elevated themes that might be expected of its historical setting. The novel also draws liberally on stage melodrama, as when the exposure of Apaecides's murderer coincides with the eruption of Vesuvius. It has been repeatedly adopted for stage and screen – filmed as early as 1898 – and remains Bulwer's most popular novel.

Dickens and the Forms of Fiction

The single work that more than any other shaped the Victorian novel as a literary form was one that early readers found hard to classify. One reviewer in 1836 called it "a magazine consisting of only one article"; six months later it was "a series of monthly pamphlets," "a monthly produced of popular entertainments" (Chittick 1990: 65, 75). The new work hardly seemed a novel, since it was emerging in monthly parts, a format only rarely used for anything but cheap reprints – which led another reviewer to remark on "a plan … so altogether anomalous, that it is no easy matter to determine in what class of composition to place them" (P. Collins 1971: 57). But all agreed, in the words of the

Quarterly Review in October 1837, that "the popularity of this writer is one of the most remarkable literary phenomena of recent times" (Chittick 1990: 88). The writer, as the English-speaking world quickly learned, was a 24-year-old court reporter named Charles Dickens (1812–70).

The Pickwick Papers, as the work soon became known, was not Dickens's literary debut. In 1833, the 21-year-old reporter enlarged his journalistic profile by submitting a sketch to the *Morning Chronicle* entitled "A Dinner at Poplar Walk," an anonymous publication that earned him only the pleasure of seeing it in print. It was little more than a competent beginning in a well-established form, the urban sketch, a more anecdotal and picturesque (and less insistently moralized) offshoot of the eighteenth-century periodical essay. But Dickens's piece was soon reprinted, the young author produced more, and in August of 1834 he took up the pseudonym Boz, a gesture that suggests a new authorial self-consciousness, the record of a distinctive sensibility rather than the transcriptions of a mere reporter. Reviewers began to single out the attentiveness of the observation, and that distinction was confirmed when *Sketches by Boz* was published in volume form on February 7, 1836 – the author's twenty-fourth birthday. Three days later, an enterprising publisher, eager to cash in on the vogue of sporting comedy popularized by the fiction of Robert Surtees in his *New Sporting Magazine* (1831), approached Boz to provide text for a series of comic illustrations depicting a "Nimrod Club" of cockney sportsmen. The young author rather presumptuously resisted the rural sporting format, and asked for more balance between text and plates. By the time William Hall had left Dickens's flat, he had agreed to publish monthly parts of about 12,000 words each, a total of 20 issues selling for a shilling apiece. And then, as Dickens would famously recall, "I thought of Mr. Pickwick." Dickens became the dominant partner in the venture after the suicide of the illustrator, Robert Seymour, just a few months later, but the first several numbers of the series sold only about 400 copies apiece. The great stir began with the appearance of the September number introducing Sam Weller, a cockney groom who became Mr. Pickwick's servant. With his comic soliloquies frequently reprinted, sales swelled, until they reached 40,000 per number, and reviewers everywhere began commenting on Dickens's dizzying rise to fame.

Why such success? Critics typically pointed to cultural geography. Dickens, most agreed, captured a part of London unknown to many of his readers, who at the outset were relatively affluent. Thus the *Quarterly* commended "his felicity in working up the genuine mother-wit and unadulterated vernacular idioms of the lower classes of London – for he grows comparatively common-place and tame the moment his foot is off the stones, and betrays infallible symptoms of Cockneyism in all his aspirations at rurality" (P. Collins 1971: 60). At times such response passed into the idiom of scientific discovery: "the regions about Saffron Hill are less known to our great world than the Oxford Tracts, the inhabitants are still less; they are as human, at least to all appearances, as are the Esquimaux or the Russians, and probably (though the Zoological society will not vouch for it) endowed with souls" (P. Collins 1971: 81). Here is the quasi-ethnographic pleasure of contact with exotic worlds that a middle-class audience also enjoyed in both the silver-fork and the criminal novel (as well as, half a century later, *National Geographic* magazine). But Dickens did not provoke the hostility aroused by those other forms. To be sure, "Cockneydom" was a niche at once literary and social, and unsympathetic readers throughout his career would decry Dickens's eccentric style and lapses into vulgarity (a preoccupation that Dickens himself would frequently satirize). At the same time, however, Dickens's early novels – unlike *Pelham* or *Paul Clifford* – represent social division without making it threatening.

Dickens himself had encouraged this benign view from his earliest sketches, which were in large part a demotic counterpart of "silver-fork" writing, often seizing upon "groups of people," as the narrator of "Seven Dials" puts it, "whose appearance and dwellings would fill any mind but a regular Londoner's with astonishment" (92). The phrasing captures the distinctive vantage of Dickens's narration: a "regular Londoner" is one well-versed in the arcane passageways of the city – frequently likened to a maze – yet able to evoke its scenes with a stranger's detachment. This is a decidedly liminal perspective, straddling boundaries of social membership, of inside and outside, in a manner that anticipates (like so much of Victorian urban writing) the stance of the anthropological "participant observer," as well as journalistic "feature" writing. This structure notably distinguishes *Sketches by Boz* from earlier urban sketches like Pierce Egan's best-selling *Life in London* (1820), which relies consistently on the comic perspective of a tourist.

"Astonishment," however, is a limiting response to urban life, and Dickens's great success was in leavening it with sympathy, whether of comedy or pathos. Both derive from an insistent nostalgia. In a world where, as he mockingly puts it in "The Last Cab-Driver," " 'Improvement' has penetrated to the very innermost recesses of our omnibuses" (Dickens 1995: 181), Dickens is drawn to scenes of loss and dispossession, or to the vulnerable beings teetering on the verge. Sometimes the pattern is one of large-scale cultural displacement wrought by slum clearance and related "Improvement"; elsewhere he is drawn to arcs of individual decline, as in the host of lives that converge in "The Pawnbroker's Shop." This sketch culminates in the image of a prostitute with a "sunken face, where a daub of rouge serves only as an index to the ravages of squandered health never to be regained, and lost happiness never to be restored." Yet even this degraded creature remains susceptible to sympathy, in which the heart vibrates "to some slight circumstance apparently trivial in itself, but connected by some undefined and indistinct association, with past days that can never be recalled" (Dickens 1995: 228). Humanity is redeemed by the integrity of memory. Here Dickens is clearly drawing on – perhaps helping to form – a nostalgic cultural imaginary that would echo through Victorian literature, as in Tennysonian melancholy, likewise preoccupied by "the days that are no more."

Such encounters are not far removed from those of Baudelaire's Paris, where modernity is experienced as the insistent shock of the new. But Dickens's appeal to sympathy softens the experience of change, recalling in this regard Charles Lamb's *Essays of Elia*, a model that Dickens developed into a more crowded canvas, with greater topicality and more intricate social detail. The tug of sympathy is especially strong in what would become Dickens's special métier, the world of "shabby-genteel people," as a sketch of that title puts it: "that depressed face, and timorous air of conscious poverty ... will make your heart ache – always supposing that you are neither a philosopher, nor a political economist"; "the miserable poor man ... who feels his poverty and vainly tries to conceal it, is one of the most pitiable objects in human nature" (Dickens 1995: 305–7). The pathos derives from these characters' consciousness of their own degradation – which also signals a kind of redemption. This complex of feeling lies at the heart of melodrama, but Dickens put it into especially influential circulation. It is unmistakable, for example, in Victorian preoccupation with "fallen" women, who are most threatening precisely when they lack this sense of shame. Yet Dickens also discovers in even the most marginal lives the sustaining power of fantasy. His delight in public and private theatricals extends to a keen eye for the theatricality of everyday life, the highly elaborated vanities in which self-dramatization may be at once comic and deeply pathetic, a delirium of self-importance, a pitiable retreat from reality, or simply a necessary psychic crutch. Throughout the early fiction, melodramatic theatricality may be alternately a damning stigma and a life force.

Domestic comedy may be as old as Aristophanes, but it takes on new energy among Dickens's shabby-genteel, where the mundane decorums of "respectability" become surprisingly complex and anxious claims to social recognition. The central concerns of *The Pickwick Papers* are securely in place as early as "The Boarding House" of 1834 – the second part of which was the first sketch published over the name "Boz." The humor shows unsteadiness in its over-emphasis: " 'Money isn't no object whatsoever to me,' said the *lady*, 'so much as living in a state of retirement and obtrusion' " (*Sketches* 341; Dickens's italics). But *The Pickwick Papers* often creates the illusion of transpiring in a single enormous boarding-house – or in an England that seems very small indeed, a country in which Pickwick and his cronies seem unable to escape from familiar faces. The coziness of this world is of a piece with the extravagantly loose narrative structure: "If you leave me to suggest our destination," Pickwick remarks at one point, "I say Bath. I think none of us has ever been there" (Dickens 1987: 578). While this waywardness enables a good deal of topical improvisation – the satire of the Eatandswill election campaign was a special favorite of early audiences – it is threaded by a preoccupation with domestic intrigue, which in turn calls out a well-nigh obsessive delight in storytelling. Pickwick envisions himself as a natural historian, "an observer of human nature, sir," but the objects of his scrutiny are compulsive informants, delighting in narration of all kinds, from hastily improvised falsehoods to somber recountings of family decline. The characters' performances are most insistently directed to romance, where the resilience of human vanity, and Dickens's virtuoso manipulation of the conventions for narrating desire, sustain the comedy. Thus domestic melodrama is skewered in Mr. Jingle's effort to thwart his rival Tupman's pursuit of Miss Wardle:

> "Stay, Mr Jingle!" said the spinster aunt emphatically. "You have made an allusion to Mr Tupman – explain it!"
> "Never!" exclaimed Jingle, with a professional (i.e. theatrical) air. "Never!" And, by way of showing that he had no desire to be questioned further, he drew a chair close to that of the spinster aunt and sat down.

"Mr. Jingle," said the aunt, "I entreat – I implore you, if there is any dreadful mystery connected with Mr. Tupman, reveal it."

"Can I," said Mr. Jingle, "can I see – lovely creature – sacrificed at the shrine – heartless avarice!" He appeared to be struggling with various conflicting sensations for a few seconds, then said in a low deep voice –

"Tupman only wants your money."

"The wretch!" exclaimed the spinster, with energetic indignation. (Mr. Jingle's doubts were resolved. She *had* money.) (Dickens 1987: 182–3)

As Jingle's ostensible fervor is punctured by his venality, so Tupman's declarations of affection jostle with petty calculations of income. Yet the entire episode is suffused with desire, which crystallizes grotesquely in "the fat boy," who shadows the lovers amid "the quiet seclusion of Dingley Dell," and discloses their tryst to the spinster aunt with the leering preface, "I wants to make your flesh creep" (180).

This comic evocation of desire again suggests the force of melodrama, which resists the forms of "deep" selfhood that will become associated with novelistic realism (including Dickens's own) later in the century. Throughout early Dickens, psychic depths are the province of villainous or inept schemers – epitomized by Sergeant Buzfuz in his delirious interrogation of Mr. Pickwick's shopping lists to his landlady: " 'Chops and Tomata sauce. Yours, Pickwick' [...] Gentlemen, is the happiness of a sensitive and confiding female to be trifled away by such shallow artifices as these?" (562–3). The comedy conjures up a deep design pointedly absent in Pickwick's character. At the same time, the travesty is the harbinger of a mode of suspicious reading that will become increasingly prominent over the course of the century, particularly in the arena of sexuality. It is this aspect of Dickens's genius that begins to suggest why he was deeply admired by Kafka – and why, in turn, Kafka's own bleak works could provoke uproarious laughter among his inner circle. The widow Bardell's delusory pursuit of Pickwick (which is sustained over virtually the entire series) often takes us to the brink of paranoia, or an imagined world of radically abridged freedom. "Is it not a wonderful circumstance," Pickwick remarks at another episode of jealous delusion, "that we seem destined to enter no man's house without involving him in some degree of trouble?" (324). Such fantasies lead to the threshold of a dream world, of submission to psychic forces that overwhelm waking rationality. Yet the possibility is almost invariably defused. "It's like a dream … a hideous dream," Pickwick remarks early on, "the idea of a man's walking around all day, with a horse he can't get rid of" (137). The comic deflation of the "hideous" captures the fundamentally benign tenor of the action. There is little place for nightmare in the world of Pickwick.

Sam Weller is an especially important agent in disarming aggression, in part by making it comically explicit. Initially exempt from the domestic intrigue, Weller offers a running choric commentary on the violent energies informing it. "He's the wictim of connubiality, as Blue Beard's domestic chaplain said" (353) – a wisdom clearly derived from his jaded father. "If ever you gets to up'ards o' fifty, and feels disposed to go a marryin' anybody – no matter who – jist set yourself up in your own room, if you've got one, and pison yourself off hand. Hangin's wulgar, so don't you have nothin' to say to that. Pison yourself, Samivel, my boy, pison yourself, and you'll be glad on it arterwards" (398). Reviewers give little hint of the violence energizing such comedy, and instead turned the Wellers into homespun philosophers. But this softening may reflect the emblematic force attached to Sam and his father as servants. In a world in which human relations seemed increasingly reduced to what Carlyle was soon to call "the cash nexus," the master–servant relationship could evoke an older order, in which social hierarchy might be imagined in terms of reciprocal obligation and dependence. In this regard, the novel's comedy seemed to harmonize disparate classes. "The tendency of his writings," in the words of T. H. Lister (himself a minor novelist of the silver-fork school), "is to make us practically benevolent – to excite our sympathy on behalf of the aggrieved and suffering in all classes; and especially in those who are most removed from observation" (P. Collins 1971: 71). Literature served to defuse middle-class anxieties about the poor – anxieties that became increasingly pressing in the late thirties. Such praise also suggests how readily the reader's experience of "sympathy" could come to displace and defer more concrete responses to human suffering.

The avoidance of class frictions in *Pickwick Papers* was thrown into sharp relief by Dickens's next work. As the conservative *Quarterly Review* put it, "Boz so rarely mixes up in politics, or panders to vulgar prejudices about serious things, we regret to see him joining an outcry which is partly factious, partly sentimental, partly interested" (P. Collins 1971: 84). *Oliver Twist, or the Parish Boy's Progress* centrally engaged the "serious things" of contemporary politics; it began life as a satire aimed at the New Poor Law. The Poor Law Amendment Act of 1834, a central mechanism of the sweeping "improvement" that Dickens regarded so skeptically, transformed a system of charity dating back to the reign of Elizabeth. For local parish relief it substituted a centralized administration designed to guarantee uniform relief, but also remolded that relief into a harsh deterrent. Able-bodied paupers were required to live in workhouses, under a regimen of subsistence diet, numbing labor, and separation from other family members – an existence designed to make relief a last resort for the utterly desperate.

The New Poor Law was a shock to traditional humanitarian sentiments, but a boon to the novelist. In its concern with abstract, deracinated "individuals," the law provoked a countervailing appeal to concrete persons inhabiting particular communities, which were bound together by personal attachment, shared history, and common needs, rather than systematizing rationality. Here was a realm of expertise that the novel could claim as its own. As early as 1836, Dickens prefaced "A Visit to Newgate" with the words, "We have only to premise, that we do not intend to fatigue the reader with any statistical accounts of the prison; they will be found at length in numerous reports of various committees ... We saw the prison, and saw the prisoners; and what we did see, and what we thought, we will tell at once in our own way" (Dickens 1995: 235). "Our own way" – a particularized appeal to sympathy – resists the universalizing claims of statistics or "system," and thereby stakes out what will become a central impulse of the Victorian novel generally. Young Oliver's famous request, "More, please," asks not merely for nourishment but for fuller recognition of his humanity.

Against the self-absorbed bureaucracy lampooned in the figure of Bumble, familial bonds of love and mutual concern are reaffirmed by appeals to melodrama. This feature of *Oliver Twist* has made the novel immensely popular in theatrical representation since its first appearance. It also offends the expectations that we have come to associate with the Victorian novel. An account of perfect, unwavering innocence triumphing over a world of ravening evil: what could be less *realistic?* But a novelistic realism that depends on the evocation of private psychology necessarily emphasizes forms of alienation, weakening the social and moral bonds on which Dickens wishes to insist. In melodrama, by contrast, moral order is manifested through the performance of clear-cut public identities, in shared communal structures – a world in which everyone is related socially, but in a public sphere that doesn't accommodate "deep" self-consciousness. In its very form, then, as well as its theme, the novel laments a lost social order. Within melodrama, psychic depth becomes a mark of criminality, a sign that someone has something to hide. The alienation bound up in psychological realism is reserved for criminals and other threats to moral order. The form thus adds a peculiar imaginative torque to a familiar moral conundrum of storytelling: the aesthetic appeal of complex character works against the association of virtue with transparency. The dramatic monologue, especially in Robert Browning's work, is built on this tension. Dickens's early novels, however, are more keenly concerned with locating a secure moral lodestar, which is liable to make virtue seem insipid.

These tensions became even more palpable in *Nicholas Nickleby* (1838–9), which Dickens took up while he was still in the midst of writing *Oliver Twist*, and before he had even completed *Pickwick*. Like *Oliver Twist*, the novel is centrally concerned with persecuted virtue, but here evil is identified with more familiar villains: figures of wealth and power set against a stainless hero defending the innocence of both his sister and young Smyke, an abused orphan whom Nicholas has rescued from a horrific boys' school in remote Yorkshire. *Nicholas Nickleby* is the most melodramatic of all Dickens's novels, and fulsome in wry tributes to the form, most notably through an extensive plot line taking Nicholas into the theatrical troupe of Mr. Crummles, where he triumphs as both an actor and an adapter of plays. At the same time, theatricality is tainted by association with villains who depend on a disjunction between surface and substance. Even the more comic (because relatively inept) parasites, such as Squeers the one-eyed schoolmaster and the profligate Mantalini, are stigmatized by their performances. As a foil to such scheming, the well-nigh defining attribute of integrity – and feminine virtue in particular – is resistance to theatricality. Hence Kate Nickleby's vigorous repudiation of "show," with her "guileless thoughts" set against her uncle Ralph's "wily plots and calculations" (Dickens 1978: 182). Yet these pressures tend in turn to make the hero something of a cipher. Over against the predatory aristocrats of the novel, led by Sir Mulberry Hawk, Nicholas is distinguished above all by chivalric concern for the weak. His virtues embody an ideal of the gentleman as a moral standing, rather than (as in Hawk's view) a matter of social rank. Melodrama in this light is clearly linked to an emergent middle-class self-assertion. But this contrast brings to light the limits of melodrama in the representation of both psychic and social complexity. Nicholas in effect performs his own virtue, but his melodramatic selfhood does not allow for change – only the revelation of an essential being.

In *Oliver Twist*, the one character who breaks free of melodrama is Fagin. Though inflected by a long tradition of anti-Semitic stereotyping, he develops into a complex, at moments charismatic power, whose captivating displays of avuncular kindness veil a ruthless pursuit of gain, which ultimately crumbles into terror at his own helplessness. The startling ferocity of Dickens's moral rhetoric – as when Fagin is likened to a reptile in offal (Dickens 1982: 116) – also insinuates a coy paradox: Fagin, ostensible enemy of the established order, only amplifies the principles energizing the New Poor Law. He is a much more formidable threat than the inane officialdom epitomized by Bumble, precisely because he is so much better at looking out for "number one" (275) – a self-interest that aligns the criminal underworld with utilitarian reformers devoted to Bentham's "hedonic calculus." Yet Fagin's powers are facilitated by his capacity for an alluring tenderness – as in the moment when his deft handkerchief tricks elicit from young Oliver (almost for the first time) a self-forgetful delight. So prominent is this feature of Fagin's character, and so fragile does he seem after his final capture, that his ultimate fate seems exorbitant retribution for his crimes as a fence. But the more damning, unstated indictment is Fagin's corruption of youth. His criminal alliances contain a powerful sexual undercurrent that surfaces most clearly in the recriminations of Nancy, who insinuates that Fagin had procured her for Sikes, and is more subtly suggested in Fagin's dealings with his boys (246). It is his association with illicit sexuality that more than anything damns Fagin.

The power to discipline that sexuality is a further dimension of the allure of melodrama. Nancy herself may be an utterly implausible character – Thackeray wrote an entire novel, *Catherine*, mocking the stereotype of the virtuous whore – but Nancy is crucial to the novel as more than a plot device; she embodies the social death that Oliver escapes. She also affirms the resilient humanity that she outwardly has forfeited. The novel never explains why Oliver is not more brutalized by his experience – why, when he is "in a fair way of being reduced, for life, to a state of brutal stupidity and sullenness by the ill-usage he had received" (Dickens 1982: 23), he remains untainted by the surrounding depravity. But his enduring purity is that of melodrama: he is a pawn, a focus of contention between two worlds, the criminal gang and middle-class respectability, which for much of the novel literally fight for possession of him. "[L]et him feel that he is one of us," Fagin exhorts Sikes (120), as if he were adopting Oliver into a surrogate family. As so often in Dickens, the virtues of domesticity are markedly defensive in impetus – as if the heaven that is the drawing room of young Rose Maylie ("earth seemed not her element" [180]) crystallized in response to its diabolical counterparts lingering out of doors. One of the novel's most haunting moments comes when Oliver awakens from sleep to the dream-like apparition of Fagin at the window of that sanctuary (217). Even Nancy will reproduce a version of Rose's unwavering and self-forgetful affection in her fidelity to Sikes, whom she refuses to give up even when she knows herself in mortal danger. At the same time, the sense of threat associated with her sexuality is never quite expelled. Years later, Nancy's death became a centerpiece of Dickens's public readings, which he performed with a ferocity that probably hastened his own death, as if in obscure responsiveness to the very energies he was casting out: "There is a passion *for hunting something* deeply implanted in the human breast" (61; Dickens's emphasis). All of which may suggest how important melodrama was to the shaping of Victorian domesticity, and to coping with desires that unsettle that ideal.

Dickens's spectacular early success revolutionized the very form of the novel, and with it the dynamics of both publishing and reading. The high fixed costs of serial publication made it suited to a relatively small number of popular novelists. But the price of a shilling per monthly number brought new novels within the means of the middle class; the serial format encouraged more reviews, and thus more sales, enlarging the profits of both authors and publishers. The format also provided a ready vehicle for advertising, which knitted the novel itself more tightly to a burgeoning commodity culture. The expansion of printing formats and profits created the need for newly intricate legal arrangements between author and publisher (Patten 55–60). Serial publication also made novel-reading a more emphatically social experience. Dickens's novels were richly suited to public reading, which enabled them to reach even an illiterate audience, but beyond this the regular anticipation and discussion of each new number enriched the sense of an emphatically communal experience, which was readily woven into other forms of daily life. In a manifold sense, Dickens was the first novelist truly *to belong* to the English people (Patten 1978: 60). To a remarkable extent, he also shaped their sense of themselves as a people.

Poetry after the Annuals

Dickens's rise to fame coincided with a marked decline in the popularity of the poetry annuals – a development encouraged by a chorus of parody. Thackeray in 1837 bemoaned their preoccupation with "water-lily, chilly, stilly, shivering beside a streamlet, plight, blighted, love-benighted, falsehood sharper than a gimlet." (Thackeray n.d.: 19). Mrs. Leo Hunter in *Pickwick Papers* chimed in with "Ode to an Expiring Frog":

> Can I view thee panting, lying
> On thy stomach, without sighing;
> Can I unmoved see thee dying
> > On a log
> > Expiring frog!
> > (Dickens 1987: 275)

A potent sense of rivalry animates such mockery, which responds to criticism of Dickens's own art as a demotic, uncouth form: his early novels repeatedly deflate pompous arbiters of taste, for whom drama and poetry remained the summit of literary decorum. (In *The Old Curiosity Shop* Mrs. Jarley finds her model of the "calm and classical" in a waxwork [Dickens 1998: 207].) More broadly, however, one can see in such barbs a battle for cultural ascendancy that would play out across the century. By the 1850s many critics were claiming that the novel had displaced poetry as the preeminent modern literary form, and well into the 1870s a novelistic character given to citing poetry often thereby types himself (or more often, herself) as a self-absorbed dreamer, at odds with the more worldly ethos of the novel.

In 1838, the decline of the annuals was punctuated by the untimely death of L. E. L., which struck more than a few readers as the end of an era in poetry – recalling the dramatic curtailment of an earlier generation:

> We have not forgotten the electric shock which the death of Byron, falling in his prime and in a noble cause, sent through Europe: nor the more expected, but not less solemn and strongly recognized departure of Sir Walter Scott; but neither of these exceeded that with which the news was received of the sudden decease of this still young and popular poetess. (Landon 1997: 346)

The mysterious circumstances of her death – she died in Africa, just four months after her marriage to the English governor of the Cape

Coast Castle (in contemporary Ghana), with an empty bottle of prussic acid in her hand – were weirdly in keeping with the mystique that had surrounded her career. Even after death L. E. L. remained an object of mesmerizing, scandalous fascination. "What is poetry, and what is a poetical career?" she had asked three years earlier. "The first is to have an organization of extreme sensibility, which the second exposes bare-headed to the rudest weather. The original impulse is irresistible ... But never can success repay its cost" (Landon 1997: 184).

Ironically, L. E. L. had applied these comments to another poet to whom they seemed far less apt. They appeared in "On the Character of Mrs. Hemans' Writings," published shortly after Hemans's death in 1835 – a death which, like her poetic career, was far more decorous. Despite their differences, L. E. L.'s "Stanzas on the Death of Mrs. Hemans" found common cause not only in their womanhood, but also in what she had identified as the dominant emotion of Hemans's poetry, "that craving for affection which answers not unto the call":

> Wound to a pitch too exquisite
>   The souls' fine chords are wrung;
> With misery and melody
>   They are too highly strung.
> The heart is made too sensitive
>   Life's daily pain to bear;
> It beats in music, but it beats
>   Beneath a deep despair.
>
>   (ll. 57–64; Landon 1997)

A third poet, however, offered a tribute to Hemans that rather brusquely quarreled with L. E. L.'s emphasis on suffering. "Felicia Hemans (To L. E. L., Referring to her Monody on that Poetess)" by Elizabeth Barrett (1806–61) rejected L. E. L.'s exhortation to bring flowers, urging a more austere tribute:

> But bring not near her solemn corse, the type of human seeming!
> Lay only dust's stern verity upon her dust undreaming.
>
> Nor mourn, O living One, because her part in life was mourning.
> Would she have lost the poet's fire, for anguish of the burning ...
>
> Perhaps she shuddered, while the world's cold hand her brow was
>   wreathing.

But never wronged that mystic breath, which breathed in all her breathing;

Which drew from rocky earth and man, abstractions high and moving –
Beauty, if not the beautiful, and love, if not the loving.

(ll. 15–24)

This richly equivocal elegy applauds Hemans's discovery of solace in the midst of suffering, but also hints at the limitations of "abstractions" set against a concrete sense of lived experience. It chimes with Barrett's sense that Hemans was finally "a lady rather than a woman" (a note of rivalry that would be echoed in Charlotte Brontë's view of Jane Austen).

Certainly Barrett's own poetry aimed to express more of the woman. In this regard, L. E. L. was the more formidable model, who had captivated Barrett's attention from her first reading of Landon in the mid-1820s. But Barrett recoiled from L. E. L.'s exposure to gossip and scandal, and from the narrowly insistent refrain of frustrated desire, which ultimately seemed a form of narcissism. This was the subtle burden of Barrett's elegy for L. E. L., which appeared three weeks after news of her death, and responds to a poem by L. E. L. published about the same time, "Night at Sea," written on the voyage to Africa, with a refrain, "My friends, my absent friends! Do you think of me as I think of you?" "It seemed not much to ask," Barrett answers, but ultimately it is presumptuous: the pathos of the unanswered question blends "with ocean's sound, /Which dashed its mocking infinite around /One thirsty for a little love" (ll. 37–9). "Not much, and yet too much," the poet concludes, and turns instead to imagine the same question being posed by God. Barrett's *The Seraphim and Other Poems* (1838), the first volume published over her name, was centrally concerned with religious faith, but joined this to another source of comfort, Wordsworthian romanticism. Still, Barrett was more engaged by the romantic poet's sense of estrangement from childhood than by the forms of redemption his poetry evokes. Romantic nature remained a dubious consolation for Barrett, as redolent of Byronic subjectivism and a pantheism alien to her evangelical upbringing, but also because it was so insistently shaped by masculine desire – as in Wordsworth's credo in "Tintern Abbey," "Nature never did betray the heart that loved her."

Wordsworth in November of 1835 composed his own moving tribute to the passing of an age. After reading of the death of James Hogg, "the Ettrick Shepherd," he composed an "extempore effusion," which also noted the deaths in the previous year of his old friends Coleridge and

Charles Lamb and of Sir Walter Scott two years before; when reprinted for his 1837 collection, he added a stanza alluding to Hemans. The litany of deaths not only underscored Wordsworth's own survival, it ushered in an unprecedented appreciation of his poetry. Though he had long abandoned his early radicalism (when *The Prelude* was published posthumously in 1850 Macaulay was startled to discover it "to the last degree Jacobitical" [Gill 1998: 29]), Wordsworth had remained something of a coterie poet, stigmatized by early attacks on "the Lake school." But *Yarrow Revisited, and Other Poems*, published in 1835, was the first of his volumes to sell widely (new editions followed in 1836 and 1839) and in 1837 Moxon paid him 1,000 pounds for the right to publish his complete works – which was more than Wordsworth had earned in his entire career (Marshall 2002: 348). Six years later he would be rewarded with the Laureateship, on the death of Robert Southey. Increasingly, readers extracted even from Wordsworth's early poetry a humanitarianism divorced from politics, which offered consoling images of reconciliation in the midst of social turmoil. Much like the early Dickens, Wordsworth was praised for removing barriers between rich and poor, and insisting "we have all of us one human heart" – a sentiment that was to feel increasingly urgent in the "hungry forties." Even Wordsworth's solitude in the Lake District, once seen as a mark of eccentricity, became a warrant of contemplative power and emotional integrity that transcended political conflict – something of the therapeutic effect which Mill recalled deriving from Wordsworth in the late 1820s. The political radical turned apostate was enshrined as a version of the Victorian sage.

Wordsworth's growing popularity also reflected in part, however, the dearth of younger poets claiming anything like the popularity of Byron and Scott. On the basis of sales and circulation, "Victorian poetry" in the 1830s is primarily Romantic poetry. The most popular volume to appear in the latter part of the decade was Martin Tupper's *Proverbial Philosophy*, the first series of which appeared in 1838. It became a stunning success, which prompted Tupper to compose three more volumes under the same title, the last in 1876; the first volume alone would go through more than 50 editions in the next 50 years, and the group of titles sold more than 250,000 copies in England alone (Gray 1976: 386). Nearly bereft of formal distinction, the volume's popularity suggests the pleasure Victorian readers derived from a confident didacticism:

> By culture man may do all things, short of the miracle, – Creation:
> Here is the limit of thy power, – here let thy pride be stayed:

The soil may be rich, and the mind may be active, but neither yield
   unsown
The eye cannot make light, nor the mind make spirit:
Therefore it is wise in man to name all novelty invention:
For it is to find out things that are, not to create the unexisting:
It is to cling to contiguities, to be keen in catching likeness,
And with energetic elasticity to leap the gulfs of contrast.

(ll. 31–8; Gray 1976)

With the deaths of L. E. L. and Hemans, Browning still obscure, and
Tennyson silent since his 1832 volume, the scene for poetry in 1838
was not a hopeful one. Amid a growing sense of political unrest, readers increasingly turned to other genres.

Literature of Travel

The rapid development of transportation technology over the course
of the nineteenth century – most notably the railway and steam-powered
shipping – made travel accessible to a much wider range of the public
than ever before, and brought a corresponding expansion of the
literature of travel. Much of this writing held an interest akin to that
of romance, the representation of unusual people and customs in
exotic settings, but the pleasures of anecdote and vivid description
were bound up with (more or less self-conscious) forms of national
self-definition. Travel literature insists on the construction of difference: to mark a place or a people as distinctive necessarily implies a
culture or national character different from one's own. To declare that
something is peculiarly French entails something about what it means
to be English. In this regard, travel writing participates in an impulse
central to the Victorian novel, which scholars have come to call
"autoethnography": in discovering a distinctive coherence or identity
in an alien culture, one is implicitly delineating the contours of one's
own (Buzard 2005).

In the wake of the Napoleonic Wars, the French were the most
powerful cultural "other" in the British imagination, and over the
course of the century they would remain a crucial foil in defining varieties of Englishness, whether in celebration or lament. In the early
1830s, however, America became a newly compelling destination,
despite the manifold difficulties of travel to and within the young
republic. Part of the allure was of course the cultural proximity, but

the shared language and heritage grounded a sense that America was the future – one version of it, anyway, which was crucially divided from Europe by the rise of democracy. That prospect, which had taken on new urgency with the passage of the Reform Bill, was complicated by the discordant, disturbing persistence of slavery. It was the novel phenomenon of democratic society that drew Alexis DeTocqueville to America in the 1830s. English engagements rarely aimed at such system or sweep as his *Democracy in America* (1836), but even the most anecdotal sense of daily life tended to be animated by a spirit of rivalry, in which the relative superiority of two ways of life hangs in the balance.

The literary appeal of American travel was first brought home by Frances Trollope's *Domestic Manners of the Americans* (1832), which caused a great stir on both sides of the Atlantic, and started Trollope on her writing career. Trollope (1779–1863) had emigrated to America in 1829 and settled in Cincinnati, on the Ohio River, at that point the westernmost major city in the country, intending to set up as a shop-keeper. When the business failed, Trollope thought to recoup some of her losses with her pen, recording a journey from New Orleans up the Mississippi and the Ohio rivers, and then on by coach across the Alleghenies to the East Coast. Trollope inflamed American sentiments, and stoked the self-satisfaction of her readers at home, by insistently pointing up "the want of refinement" in daily American life. She was particularly incensed by what would become a leitmotif of travel narratives, the American habit of profuse spitting, and was bemused by the lack of class hierarchy in everyday encounters, smiling at being "introduced in form to a milliner" (Trollope 1949: 13). (Trollope was writing barely 15 years after Austen had recorded the blunders of Mr. Collins addressing himself to Darcy.) The title emphasis on "domestic manners" disclaims any interest in large political questions – the conservative Trollope adopted a conventionally feminine posture in this regard – but her observations point to the growing importance of domesticity as an ideal that perplexed the boundaries of public and private. If domestic conditions reflected a disorder in "the moral and religious conditions of the people," then they spoke to a fundamental flaw in the state.

A more concerted reflection on American social structures came from *Society in America* (1837) by Harriet Martineau (1802–76), an economic radical who rose to fame in the early 1830s with her *Illustrations of Political Economy*, fictional tales designed to bring home the imperatives of laissez-faire economics to a broad readership. Martineau, a fearless commentator on social issues (Barrett Browning called her "the most manlike woman in the three kingdoms" [Mermin 1989: 100]), emphatically rejected the self-imposed constraints of Trollope, and offered a sweeping analysis of the social dynamics of both American and Britain. While pointing out the moral evasions of slaveholders (which failed to trouble Trollope), Martineau also saw in the American devotion to industry grounds for a critique of the British aristocracy, in which she notes a disdain for labor that Carlyle soon would lampoon as the "Gospel of Dilettantism." She also offered a particularly searching account of the American cult of domestic womanhood, anticipating a growing feminist chorus that the ostensible worship of femininity actually constrains and enfeebles the lives of women by denying them a wider sphere of education and activity.

A host of other writers during the thirties contributed to establishing a regular American itinerary, which in addition to Niagara Falls – a destination prompting almost unfailing raptures over its sublimity – included travels to the major American cities from Boston as far south as Baltimore and Washington, and frequently a journey out to the frontier of the Ohio. Many travelers visited a round of sights that spoke to reformist energies in both America and England – prisons, schools for the poor, factories, asylums – and nearly all grappled with that disturbing phenomenon of encountering a slave, which called out frequently baffled and contradictory responses. The journey that aroused the most comment was that of Charles Dickens in 1842. The 30-year-old Dickens, already famous in America, was eagerly awaited and rapturously greeted. Dickens for his part was animated partly by the quest for international copyright, since wholesale American piracy of his work was costing him dearly, but he also was deeply drawn to the egalitarianism of American life, and applauded much that he found in institutions of public health and education. Yet he was quickly shocked by the sheer vehemence of his reception, and by the unflagging demands for his time and attention, above all by the aggressive newspapermen. The first-hand encounter with slavery further appalled him, and he incorporated in his finished volume, *American Notes* (1843), a withering critique of the institution borrowed from Theodore Weld, who had printed a collection of reward advertisements for escaped slaves, frequently identified by scars from whips, knives, or gunshots – a standing catalogue of the violence that slaveholders typically claimed had no place in their benign governance. The Americans, Dickens claimed, were a people resistant to criticism, and response to the book bore that out. It was some while before the wounds healed.

British travel to Europe naturally was more frequent, and offered more immediate pleasures – warmer climes, beautiful cities, elegant goods, and (for some) sexual license. The expansion of cross-Channel travel after the Napoleonic Wars nurtured an entirely new genre, travel handbooks, most famously those of Baedeker in Germany and John Murray in London (the phrase itself was coined by John Murray II in 1834). In these books, one can see the eighteenth-century Grand Tour, a leisurely survey of major capitals and historical sites designed to burnish the worldliness of young aristocrats, metamorphosing into a more egalitarian pursuit. Over the course of the century European travel for many would be closely bound up with an ideal of "culture," at once a body of experience and a state of mind increasingly associated with responsiveness to great art, above all in Italy. But the sheer proliferation of travel nurtured increasingly varied subgenres of travel literature. On the one hand, the prototype of Byron's Childe Harold had a continued allure for single young gentlemen of means, who with increasing frequency bemoaned the crowds of tourists, and over the course of the century would seek out ever more remote and solitary destinations, first in the Middle East, and subsequently in Africa, where travel was increasingly drawn into the orbit of empire. The increasing affordability of tourism for the middle class also nourished what has been called the "tourist abroad" plot, often in the vein of Trollope in America, in which the glories of St. Peter's in Rome jostled with laments over Italian manners, beggars, and bedding: Dickens's *Travels in Italy* is in this regard characteristic. At the same time, travel abroad could encourage more concerted self-reflection, prompting a newly sustained grappling with personal and national identity: thus Brontë's Lucy Snowe in Brussels, Eliot's Dorothea Brooke in Rome, Henry James's Americans across Europe. In all of these writers, the knowingness associated with extensive travel becomes a claim to authority closely akin to that of the novelist.

History and Heroism

In early Victorian historiography, the past remained preeminently a moral mirror in which to contemplate the present, whether in Macaulay's triumphalist schemes of progress or (less often) in answering laments of national decline. Only later in the century does history come to seem a truly estranging force, a source and embodiment of more radical clashes of value, which frequently exerts a powerfully aestheticizing power – as, for example, in the monologues of Browning. For early Victorians, the bearing of the past on the present seemed most urgent in accounts of recent working-class uprisings, fear of which reached a new pitch in 1839.

Hard on the heels of the final installment of *Oliver Twist* in April there appeared another novel of criminal life whose popularity outstripped even that of *Twist*. William Ainsworth's *Jack Sheppard* became one of the sensations of the era; by the autumn of 1839, eight different theatrical versions were being staged in London. *Sheppard* pushed the moral boundaries farther than anything in "respectable" fiction. Not only did the novel celebrate criminal life (rather than an innocent's rescue from it) but it gave more explicit attention to sexuality than Dickens had risked. Its dubious celebrity was sealed in 1840, when the valet of Sir William Russell slit his employer's throat, and later claimed to have been inspired by *Jack Sheppard*. In the ensuing controversy, critics condemned the subject matter by calling the work a "Newgate novel," and extended the label retroactively to *Twist*. Dickens angrily rejected the association, insisting in his 1841 Preface that the novel had a strenuous moral design, including an effort "to banish from the lips of the lowest character I introduced, any expression that could by possibility offend" (Dickens 1982: xxvii). But the label stuck.

The "Newgate novel" controversy, like most attacks on immoral literature, registered a larger social unease. The eager reception of *Pickwick* was shaped by insistent reference to the gulf between rich and poor, which Dickens was praised for rendering so benignly. Even as *Pickwick* was appearing, however, the rise of Chartism was challenging the harmonies Dickens evoked. The First Reform Bill, ironically, had exacerbated long-standing working-class discontent over their disenfranchisement. Although it excluded wage-earners from suffrage – and more clearly than any previous legislation vested political rights in property – Reform initially encouraged working-class optimism. It was (in theory) the death-knell of patronage and corruption, the herald of a new age of more egalitarian politics. Yet the propertied classes were predictably reluctant to dilute their own privilege, and even writers sympathetic to workers tended to urge upon them an uneasy blend of "improvement" and self-denial. The publications of the SDUK and SPCK were at one in celebrating self-discipline and self-restraint, virtues eminently suited to an emergent industrial capitalism and the material progress it promised. But while political economy promised energetic strivers the reward of palpable social advance, workers often were struggling for mere sustenance, and they were exposed to increasingly volatile economic cycles that threatened destitution.

The working poor confronting such hardships found the New Poor Law of 1834 an especially egregious affront. Moreover, working-class efforts to enhance their economic leverage were blocked by legislation and fierce capitalist resistance. Few early Victorian social bodies were more demonized than trades unions, which typically were represented as diabolical conspiracies against social and political order. It was within this context that the propertied classes were haunted by the threat of civil insurrection. And those fears took especially palpable form with the rise of Chartism. Though its name derived from a specific political program, a six-point "Charter" of demands made to Parliament in a formal mass petition, the term quickly came to stand for a more inchoate, and thus more threatening, body of resentment among the poor and disenfranchised. "Chartism means the bitter discontent grown fierce and mad," as Carlyle put it in his lengthy 1839 pamphlet on the movement (Carlyle 1971: 151).

Against this backdrop, the French Revolution of 1789 (with aftershocks in numerous continental revolutions in 1830) loomed large in the minds of the propertied classes. Within early Victorian social polemic, it bodied forth a nightmare of absolute rupture with the past – a leveling of social hierarchy that brought cataclysmic violence and suffering in its wake. As the ultimate cautionary tale against a rush to democracy, the revolution seemed an event in domestic as well as French history. "A revolt of the oppressed lower classes against the oppressing or neglecting upper classes," Carlyle wrote in *Chartism*, was "not a French event only; no, a European one; full of stern monition to all countries of Europe." "These Chartisms, Radicalism, Reform Bill, Tithe Bill ... are our French Revolution" (Carlyle 1971: 181). Even amid the appalling disorder of the Terror, however, Carlyle discovered a struggle, however groping and destructive, toward some form of spiritual renewal. The *sans-culottes* had been a powerful emblem for the author of *Sartor Resartus*, who was captivated by the vision of an entire nation freed of "old garnitures and social vestures" living for a time in an emblematic nakedness, a social state of pure possibility. Once *Sartor* was completed, and sank nearly without a trace, Carlyle turned to history to press home this larger significance.

When Carlyle's *French Revolution* appeared in 1837, stunned reviewers evoked loftier genres. John Stuart Mill likened it to an epic poem, recalling Aristotle's tribute to poetry as a narrative more philosophical than history because less bound by probability. J. A. Froude rejoined, "It is rather an Aeschylean drama, composed of facts literally true, in which the Furies are once more walking on the prosaic earth and shaking their serpent hair" (Froude 1904: i.76). Froude's assessment hints at what most impressed contemporaries in the work of this still-obscure writer: the dazzling style. Carlyle himself called it "a wild savage Book, itself a kind of French Revolution" (Carlyle 1970–2006: ix.115), and for some readers that savagery underscores an aestheticizing impulse in Carlyle's history, in which the revolution as spectacle displaces reflection on its causes. But Carlyle's language is of a piece with his analysis in pressing to the very thresholds of reason:

> What a Paris, when the darkness fell! A European metropolitan City hurled suddenly forth from its old combinations and arrangements; to crash tumultuously together, seeking new ... Seven hundred thousand individuals, on the sudden, find all their old paths, old ways of thinking and acting, vanish from under their feet. And so there go they, with clangour and terror, they know not as yet whether running, swimming or flying, – headlong into the New Era. (Carlyle 1989: i.187)

As Carlyle summons up elemental fury – one chapter is entitled "the gods are athirst" – he turns most often to the female figures of Greek mythology that struck Froude: "they lie always, those subterranean Eumenides (fabulous and yet so true), in the dullest existence of man" (i.186). Figures of maenadic frenzy would have a curiously potent afterlife in Victorian England, where no violence seemed more fearful than that of women possessed by murderous rage. "Alas then, is man's civilization only a wrappage, through which the savage nature of him can still burst, infernal as ever!" (ii.370). The bewildering effects of such "savage nature" are reinforced by Carlyle's canny manipulation of perspective, which develops out of his long meditation on the peculiar narrative challenges history poses. "Narrative is *linear*, action is *solid*," he had declared in an early essay, "On History" (Carlyle 1971: 55). Thus the narrative shifts abruptly between various points of view – the French Revolution took place in the heart of every participant, he urges at one point – and between highly particular description and reflection on the difficulty of making sense of the confusion. At moments Carlyle seems to throw up his hands: History cannot fully explain the turmoil, but can only "*look* honestly at it, and name what she can of it!" (Carlyle 1989: ii.333). Even that challenge is amplified by shifts between past tense and historical present, which pursue a dramatic effect that would thrust the reader into the midst of the action, and frequently create something akin to cinematic jump-cutting between simultaneous events. As that technique would influence the later novels of Dickens, it would reverberate even in the rise of twentieth-century film, in the work of such admirers of Victorian narrative as Sergei Eisenstein.

A few individuals stand out from this sea of anonymity, appearing (for a time at least) to redirect the current by intimating the basis of new social order. Mirabeau is the first of Carlyle's political heroes, a prime exemplar of the antinomian defiance that fascinated Carlyle even more than it did Browning. "Moralities not a few must shriek condemningly over this Mirabeau; the Morality by which he could be judged has not yet got uttered in the speech of men. We will say this of him again: That he is a Reality and no Simulacrum; a living son of Nature our general Mother; not a hollow Artifice, and mechanism of Conventionalities, son of nothing, *brother* to nothing" (i.451–2). Carlyle's view of history focused on the lives of great men, the solitary heroes who, in their power to rally the devotion of others less gifted, also manifested a divine order at work in the world. Increasingly, this was the only mark of divinity that could command Carlyle's own faith. In 1840, he gave a series of public lectures entitled *On Heroes, Hero-Worship, and the Heroic in History*, in which he startled his (generally appreciative) audience by devoting a chapter to Mohammed, his example of "the Hero as Prophet." Compared to "Benthamee Utility, virtue by Profit and Loss; reducing this God's-world to a dead brute Steam-engine," Mohammed's faith, grounded in earnest struggle and stern recognition of "the Infinite Nature of Duty," seemed much the nobler view of life (Carlyle 1908: 309–10). Carlyle's celebration of the hero became an object of deep suspicion in the twentieth century, and some have argued that it was one current in the rise of modern totalitarianism. But the view of history as an archive of individual greatness was a central Victorian axiom, which vindicated the power of human agency itself – a concern that would gradually come to figure centrally in the novel as well. History, Carlyle insisted, is "an infinite conjugation of the verb *to do*"; in an era when action had given way to inertia, history became "the grand Poem of our Time" (Carlyle 1970–2006: vi.466).

Carlylean heroism thus responded to growing worry that modern life undermined individual freedom, whether through social conformism, technology, sheer numbers, or the constraints of one's own psychology. The tension animates Carlyle's figure of the critic as prophet, who must keep society at a distance to maintain his integrity, but thereby courts his own neglect. The writer of a book, Carlyle claims, "is an accident in society. He wanders like a wild Ishmaelite, in a world in which he is as the spiritual light." This self-conception propels the rhetorical high-wire act that bewildered so many readers: a prophet readily understood was suspect of "quackery," as Carlyle put it, yet fidelity to a truth that was ultimately ineffable was liable to reduce him to mere silence. The insistence that his own writing is "wild, " "savage," "uncouth," is one means of declaring a sincerity that confounds all decorum.

Victorian audiences ultimately embraced Carlyle, and largely on his own terms, as "the sage of Chelsea," whose stern iconoclasm was the best warrant of his integrity. It is hard to over-state Carlyle's influence on the intellectual generation that came of age in the 1840s. With the publication of his *Critical and Miscellaneous Essays* in 1840, he became (as Eliza Lynn Linton would recall a generation later) "the yeast plant, fermenting the whole literary brew" (Ray 1955: 224), and virtually every writer of the next two decades left testimony to his impact. Much of the allure stemmed from the fact that he seemed, as one commentator put it, a "sect of one." Whereas his intellectual rivals – Mill and Macaulay, preeminently – could easily be affiliated with "sects" both religious and political, Carlyle seemed to confound categorization. And yet he seemed to incarnate a distinctive and charismatic form of belief, and as such ministered to the intellectual anxiety that a broad readership came to experience as a crisis of faith.

Another influential, if narrower, circle of devoted followers gathered around Carlyle's exact contemporary, Thomas Arnold. Arnold's achievements were impressive – he was an influential liberal historian of Ancient Rome, a theologian in the movement dubbed "Broad Church" (urging a more inclusive interpretation of Anglican doctrine), and the reforming headmaster of Rugby School – but this was not the stuff of traditional heroism. After his early death in 1842, however, Arnold was enshrined in a biography by his pupil A. P. Stanley, *Life and Correspondence of Thomas Arnold, D.D.* (1844), which became one of the best-selling biographies ever published in Britain. Biography, both historical and fictional, gained popularity in concert with the search for heroism; the form summoned up especially vivid moral exemplars. Stanley managed to capture for a large audience the extraordinary devotion that Arnold commanded among his students. Although Rugby – like all the most prestigious Victorian public schools – was profoundly elitist (Arnold refused to admit sons of "tradesmen," since they were not gentlemen), and Arnold himself was suspect in many circles for his liberal politics, Stanley presented him as a moral exemplar who transcended politics and class. Stanley's Arnold was a consummate model of earnestness, fervent and rigorous yet humble in his piety and devoted to the intellectual and spiritual welfare of his young charges. His image loomed so large that he became one of the four "eminent Victorians" that Lytton Strachey tried to cut down to size in 1918.

The hunger for guidance from heroes fastened onto yet another figure coming to national prominence at the same time. Like Carlyle, John Henry Newman (1801–90) derided hymns to secular "improvement," which, as he saw it, "does not contemplate raising man above himself," and whose rationalistic psychology was deeply impoverished in its understanding of human value and motivation. "First shoot round corners, and you may not despair of converting by a syllogism," as Newman put it in a lengthy attack on secular education, "The Tamworth Reading Room," first published in a series of letters to *The Times* in 1840. "After all, man is not a reasoning animal; he is a seeing, feeling, contemplating, acting animal" (Newman 1965: 101–2). This view chimes with Carlyle's celebration of heroism, and even has a more muted echo in Mill's contemporaneous rethinking of Benthamism as a stance that too little accommodated the power of feeling. The search for values beyond self-interest and calculation would resonate throughout the critique of industrial society made on behalf of "culture." But Newman wrote out of fierce devotion to, and from the innermost bastion of, the Christianity that both Mill and Carlyle had abandoned. He was an Anglican clergyman and tutor at Oxford, where he had gained widespread attention for his role in a religious movement called Tractarianism – so much so that his admirers soon became known as "Newmanites."

The Tractarian movement derived its name from a series of "Tracts for the Times," which began in September of 1833, prompted by John Keble's sermon a few months earlier on "National Apostasy." Unlike the vast majority of Victorian religious tracts, these were addressed not to the poor, or even to parishioners generally, but to the clergy themselves, "brothers in Christ," arguing that the integrity of the Church of England was being compromised by increasing state control. They urged renewed recognition of the authority of the clergy as a priesthood, whose powers were derived by "apostolical succession" from St. Peter, "the Vicar of Christ." In this broad sense, the Tracts chimed with numerous conservative attacks on "the spirit of the age" as a rupture with fundamental British traditions. But the Tracts had a special force because they emanated from Oxford, and they evolved into a social formation deeply unsettling to Protestant Britain. The appeal to tradition and the ineffable power of personal influence was especially alluring at Oxford, which was still something of an Anglican seminary: all degree candidates were required to formally subscribe to the Thirty-nine Articles of the Church of England, and all tutors were Anglican clergymen, who understood their teaching roles to be closely bound up with pastoral guidance. Newman, a brilliant rhetorician and a charismatic personal presence, became rector of the University Church, St. Mary's, in 1837, and exerted a mesmerizing influence over many students. The fascination he aroused would be conjured up in numerous personal memoirs, such as that of Matthew Arnold, who decades later evoked Newman preaching in St. Mary's, undeterred by the fact that he never witnessed it. Newman's later writings on the history of Christian doctrine would have a large impact on historical reflection generally. Those who resisted Newman's appeal, however, denounced the "Puseyites," as they also were known (after the influential and well-connected E. B. Pusey), as a standing danger to the Church of England. In appealing to apostolic succession and unbroken connection with the early Church, Newman and his allies were urging what seemed like a return to Roman Catholicism – a drift reinforced by association with vows of celibacy and more formal liturgy. Thomas Arnold leveled the charge in especially pointed manner, in an 1836 *Edinburgh Review* article, "The Oxford Malignants."

The sense of intellectual daring was part of Newman's appeal to the many young men who experienced it. Despite the marked divergence in their beliefs, both Newman and Carlyle epitomized the outsider punished for his integrity, alienated from the establishment by his stern truth-telling. Newman, speaking for a collective priesthood in frequently anonymous address, and seemingly at the opposite end of the theological spectrum from Carlyle – the cloistered monk versus the ascetic prophet – would by the early 1840s become another charismatic solitary, and a spiritual icon whose authority rivaled that of

Carlyle. By the mid-1840s Carlyle, Newman, and Arnold almost seemed to lead distinct political parties at Oxford and Cambridge, where earnest undergraduates were characterized by their divergent loyalties – a sense of mingled rivalry and emulation that figures centrally in novels and memoirs of the period.

Social Crisis and the Novel

Newman's threatening affiliation with Catholicism led popular caricatures to link Tractarianism to Chartism and the threat of working-class insurrection. The vividness of Catholicism in the Victorian imagination far exceeded its actual social prominence and power, but like Chartism and trades unions, Roman clergy in Britain (formally disestablished for nearly three centuries) could be seen as a secret society bent on overthrowing the social order – and closely aligned with the restive, disenfranchised Irish. Growing controversy over the substance of the Tracts fueled a conspiratorial imagination already boiling in 1839, in the wake of the "Newport Uprising" and other portents (so it seemed) of working-class revolt.

Those anxieties were inflamed by yet another literary work that polemically engaged recent social debate. Throughout the 1830s, "the factory question" had been a locus of intense debate in literary journals and on the floor of Parliament, which was debating the "Ten Hours Bill," an act that (among other things) would ban the employment of children under 12 in factories and mines for more than 10 hours a day, six days a week. These debates underscored both the novelty and the momentousness of industrial labor, which would seem to make it an obvious subject for novelists. But though John Walker had addressed factory labor in his 1832 melodrama, *The Factory Lad* throughout the thirties novelistic interest was overwhelmed by polemical fervor. Harriet Martineau's *Principles of Political Economy* in 1834 offered a fictional account of factory labor, "A Manchester Strike," but the narrative was a straightforward didactic tale enforcing the lessons of political economy by warning against the follies of trades unions and strikes. Only in 1839 did Frances Trollope show how well Dickensian romance could represent the child laborer as a victim of political economy.

The hero of Trollope's *The Life and Adventures of Michael Armstrong, The Factory Boy* is an Oliver Twist deported to the industrial north of England. Unleavened by Dickens's humor, however, and in many ways bolder in its representation of working-class desperation (one episode, with accompanying illustration, describes small boys competing with pigs for scraps of food), Trollope's novel aroused even more antipathy from reviewers when it began appearing in monthly parts in March of 1839. The *Athenaeum* accused her of "scattering firebrands among the people" and implored her to remember "that the most probable immediate effect of her pennings and her pencillings will be the burning of factories ... [and] the plunder of property of all kinds"; a reviewer in Bolton accordingly urged that she receive the same jail sentences passed on radical agitators for using "violent language against the 'monster cotton-mills.'" "I don't think anyone cares much for Michael Armstrong," the staunchly Tory novelist remarked, "except the Chartists. A new kind of patrons for me!" (Heineman 1979: 184, 171).

Throughout the late thirties, novels were lightning rods for political anxiety. The *Athenaeum* review of Trollope on 16 October 1839 linked political incendiarism and debased literary appetite; the *Examiner* of 3 November 1839 declared that the Newgate novels and silver-fork were "complementary aspects of a society's continued cringing to St James"; the *Monthly Review* of February 1840 declared, "The times are out of joint, and Chartism rages while Jack Sheppard *reads*" (Chittick 1990: 158). Such responses also reflect the increasing cultural authority of the novel. As Mary Mitford wrote to Elizabeth Barrett, "What things these are – the Jack Sheppards, and Squeers, and Oliver Twists, and Michael Armstrongs – All the worse because of their power to move men's souls" (Heineman 1979: 171).

Novelists, however, would not develop a more sustained engagement with industrialism and class division until the mid-1840s. (Charlotte Tonna's *Helen Fleetwood* [1841] is a partial exception, but it primarily exhorts factory workers to embrace Christianity in order to save themselves from the moral dangers of their workplace.) Some of this silence may represent a shrinking from the hostility Trollope aroused. But it also seems to reflect the disorienting novelty of large-scale factory labor, which at this stage remained a phenomenon of the north, above all of Yorkshire and Lancashire, where Manchester was dubbed "the workshop of the world." When Dickens visited Manchester in 1838 and 1839, conducted on the latter visit by the evangelical social reformer, Lord Ashley, he vowed "to strike the heaviest blow in my power for these unfortunate creatures," but it would be 15 years before he took up the topic more directly (Johnson 1952: 225). In a passage in *The Old Curiosity Shop* (Dickens 1998: 329–43), written soon after his visit to Manchester, Nell and her grandfather on their journey approach an industrial landscape whose smoke and glare seem nightmarish – but they tellingly skirt direct contact with it, as would Dickens himself until 1854, when he set to work on *Hard Times.*

Novelists like Dickens who drew their subjects from London or rural settings – which in the late 1830s meant nearly all novelists – were depicting a very different social order. There was ample precedent in eighteenth-century fiction for the social dynamics of Dickens's early fiction, but an industrial order, to adapt Carlyle's phrase, was "unexampled." Nonetheless, Dickens by the end of the decade was growing restive with his own achievement. When *Nickleby* began appearing in April 1838, reviewers were still identifying Dickens not as a novelist, but as a writer of "entertainments." The benchmark for serious novel-writing continued to be Scott, whose achievement took on renewed authority with the appearance of a massive *Life of Scott* by his son-in-law John Lockhart, which appeared in a series of seven volumes between March 1837 and March 1838 (dwarfing in size Boswell's *Life of Johnson*). Dickens tacitly conceded the distance between himself and the master in a letter of January 1839, envisioning a work to be published "as a Novel, and not in portions" (Chittick 1990: 130). This was the long-deferred *Barnaby Rudge*, a historical novel set in London in the 1780s, and centered on the anti-Catholic "Gordon riots." Having envisioned the work in Scott's traditional three-volume format, however, Dickens soon was blocked; already the serial form was providing an energizing sense of contact with an audience (and regular deadlines) that seemed a necessary spur. Having stepped down from editing *Bentley's Magazine,* he undertook a new weekly series for Chapman and Hall entitled *Master Humphrey's Clock,* for which he produced *The Old Curiosity Shop* (1841).

The Old Curiosity Shop would turn out to be Dickens's greatest success to date, owing partly to the weekly format, partly to its relentless presentation of persecuted virtue – virtue not only enduring, but positively flowering under neglect. Stories of crowds gathering on the docks in New York to await the latest installment may be exaggerated, but they reflect the gripping appeal of the mysteriously ailing heroine, Little Nell, who would outlive the book as a paragon of Victorian sentimentality. Even Ruskin's disdainful opinion more than 40 years later (in "Fiction Fair and Foul"), that Dickens had butchered Nell like a lamb for the market, suggests the bitterness of a frustrated lover. It is difficult to explain this hold, in which the redemptive force of innocence – associated with both domesticity and the countryside – blurs into the ritual purgation offered by a scapegoat. Nell's decline is set against a London bleaker than in any of Dickens's previous works, full of danger and foreboding mystery, centered around the demonic figure of Quilp – the most volatile to date in Dickens's gallery of villains lusting for absolute domination, a well of energy on which he would draw throughout his career. The elemental contraries of the book's moral typology are at war with both plot and character development. "With gradually failing strength and heightening resolution, there had sprung up a purified and altered mind" in Nell, the narrator remarks (Dickens 1998: 391) – but it is hard for a reader to see any impurities requiring alteration in the first place.

The Domestic Ideal

In *Barnaby Rudge* (1842), Dickens's long-standing fascination with motiveless malignity found a resonant embodiment in mob violence – a motif that clearly registered contemporary political insecurity. Yet the historical setting also enabled Dickens to frame a newly insistent celebration of domesticity as a distinctly middle-class virtue. The energies of the novel remain powerfully melodramatic, with yet another aristocratic rake harrowing a vulnerable young woman, Dolly Varden. But the main villain, John Chester, is arraigned for more subtle corruption. Modeled on Chesterfield, whose *Letters to his Son* would become a favorite butt of Victorian earnestness, Chester is most dangerous not in his brutishness, but in a social ethos that values elegance and calculated self-interest over selfless devotion. A Victorian ideal of domesticity is solidified through his suave disdain for it: "Marriage is a civil contract," he chastens his ardent son, "people marry to better their worldly condition and improve appearances; it is an affair of house and furniture, of liveries, servants, equipage, and so forth" (Dickens 1997: 309). Chester's contempt for the heart seems a graver threat to social order than the riots fomented by Lord George Gordon, who is a mere cipher.

A series of events in the late 1830s gave new prominence to an ideal of domestic life centered on feminine influence. First among them, of course, was the ascension in 1837 of a young female monarch, who placed the division of public and private realms into newly urgent, and sometimes perplexing, prominence. In that same year, public attention was riveted by a marriage gone horribly wrong, after George Norton accused the Prime Minister, Lord Melbourne, of an adulterous affair with his wife, Caroline Norton – a famous beauty, granddaughter of the Irish dramatist Sheridan, and a poet of some note. The lawsuit inspired Dickens's travesty in "Bardell vs. Pickwick," but it had more somber ramifications for Caroline Norton: although her husband's suit was thrown out and Melbourne continued in his post, she was turned into a pariah barred from contact with her own children, who under English law were entirely subject to the will of their father. When the sympathetic MP Thomas Talfourd introduced an "Infant Custody Bill" that would offer women greater rights, Norton published a series of supporting pamphlets and articles – which excited new excoriations of her character, in part because the sheer exposure of her private misery seemed scandalous. Against such abuse, often insinuating that Norton wished to license female profligacy, she insisted on the chastening example of feminine devotion: "Did this author never see that very usual and customary sight, a modest and affectionate wife? Did he never see a woman watching the cradle of her sick child? Did he never see a mother teaching her little one to pray?" (Chase and Levenson 2000: 43).

Female tenderness and modesty thus became an emphatically political issue, and a rebuke to men who would presume less of women. The power of those virtues assumed even greater scope in the polemics of Sarah Stickney Ellis, who in 1839 launched a series of publications that perhaps more than any other codified the notion of "separate spheres" for men and women. In *The Women of England, The Wives of England, The Daughters of England* – the titles themselves suggest the single-mindedness of her commitment – Ellis insisted on the crucial importance of women confining themselves to home and family life, where their influence created an essential refuge from and counterweight to the increasingly combative and coarsening public realm. The notoriety of these writings as monuments to sexual inequality has overshadowed much of their cutting political critique, under which the sustaining and purifying influence of women is necessary to counteract the brutality of *homo economicus*:

There is no union in the great field of action in which he is engaged; but envy, and hatred, and opposition, to the close of day – every man's hand against his brother, and each struggling to exalt himself, not merely by trampling upon the fallen foe, but by usurping the place of his weaker brother, who faints by his side. (Chase and Levenson 2000: 78)

In opposition to this struggle, Ellis invested women with extraordinary power, but power that could be exerted only by embracing a perpetual confinement to domestic affairs, and to the needs of others. Woman, she wrote, "whose whole life, from the cradle to the grave, is one of feeling, rather than of action; whose highest duty is often to suffer and be still; whose deepest enjoyments are all nothing, and is nothing, of herself; whose experience, if unanticipated, is a total blank," nonetheless possesses a "world of interest ... wide as the realm of humanity, boundless as the ocean of life, and enduring as eternity" (Chase and Levenson 2000: 80). Woman embodied and conveyed the "poetry" of human nature, and without her distinctive "influence," it seemed, human affairs would soon revert to savage aggression.

Such idealizing became a long-standing impediment to women's rights, but it also would reinforce the association of art and aesthetic experience with femininity. Women's influence, as Ellis describes it, is strikingly akin to that which critics increasingly assigned to literature and culture. In the meantime, however, the doctrine of separate spheres made representations of middle-class daily life seem a matter of great social urgency – and threats to it a kind of a desecration. Thus the narrator of *Barnaby Rudge* reflects on a ruined house:

> The ashes of the commonest fire are melancholy things ... How much more sad the crumbled embers of a home: the casting down of that great altar, where the worst among us sometimes perform the worship of the heart; and where the best have offered up such sacrifices, and done such deeds of heroism, as, chronicled, would put the proudest temples of old Time, with all their vaunting annals, to the Blush! (Dickens 1997: 725)

The image subtly conflates domestic strife and social catastrophe: both forces tumble "that great altar" at which so many Victorians came to worship.

From Silver-Fork to Farce

Middle-class domestic life rapidly came to the foreground of novels in the 1840s – a development widely remarked at the time. In 1837, Harriet Martineau recalled, John Murray refused her novel *Deerbrook* (1837) because its subject was drawn from "middle life": "People liked high life in novels, and low life, and ancient life; and people of any rank presented by Dickens, in his peculiar artistic light ... but it was not supposed that they would bear a presentment of the familiar life of every day" (Adburgham 1983: 294). By 1840 the situation seemed to be rapidly changing. In 1841 E. C. Grey would complain (in his novel *The Little Wife*), "Novel-writing has completely changed its character. From its high-flown, elaborate style, it is now fallen into its opposite extreme; from improbabilities, always impalpable, sometimes gross, now, in their place, we find nothing but the hum-drummeries of reality" (L. James 1963: 96). Although the prolific Catherine Gore scored successes with *Cecil, or The Adventures of a Coxcomb* (1841) and *The Banker's Wife, Or Court and City* (1843), the "fashionable" vogue was greatly diminished, and *Jack Sheppard* was the zenith of the Newgate novel. Ainsworth himself was unsettled by the controversy he provoked, and increasingly withdrew into safer historical precincts, in works like *The Tower of London* (1840), *Old Saint Paul's* (1841), and *Saint James's* (1844). Bentley gave him 2,000 pounds for the first of these, but he descended to 100 pounds per title for the 25 novels that Ainsworth ground out between 1860 and his death in 1882. And by the end of the decade, an exasperated publisher would tell Anthony Trollope, "Your historical novel is not worth a damn" (Sutherland 1989: 298).

The turn to more modest forms of domesticity drew on both the popularity of Dickens and parody of the silver-fork mode (a recurrent feature of Dickens's early fiction). Samuel Warren's *Ten Thousand A-Year*, for example, began appearing in *Blackwood's* in October of 1839, and on publication in volume form in 1841 became one of the best-selling comic novels of the century. It recounts the rags to riches story of a downtrodden young draper's assistant, Tittlebat Titmouse, who unexpectedly inherits a magnificent fortune and estate through the legal forgeries of Quirk, Gammon, and Snap. The ironies surrounding the rapacious vulgarity of the hero are not subtle – "How the reptile propensities of his mean nature had thriven beneath the sudden sunshine of unexpected prosperity!" (Warren 1832: 23) – but the work offers rollicking satire of social ambition and conspicuous consumption, as well as an insider's view of unscrupulous legal machinations (Warren [1807–77] was a successful barrister). As Warren's novel deflates the pretensions of the silver-fork school, it also depicts a comic type increasingly prominent in novels at mid-century. Titmouse is a consummate example of "the gent" – a label that gained wide currency with the publication of Albert Smith's *The Natural History of the Gent*

(1847). The gent is an awkward, callow young man of slender means and family standing who aspires to the gentleman's stature. Eager to distinguish himself from the working class by mimicking the address and behavior of his social superiors, the gent is comically inept in his struggles, typically reduced to comic externals: the over-formal yet shabby dress of the failed dandy, diminutive size and surname (Titmouse, Titmarsh, Tittlebat), which signal his lack of power, and his eager awkwardness, so pointedly at odds with the ease of the true gentleman.

The prominence of the gent owes much to contemporary social anxiety. As novelists increasingly turned their attention to middle-class life, a natural focus was the often elusive boundaries that delineated social membership and exclusion. One of the most acute students of these anxieties was William Makepeace Thackeray (1811–63), a prolific reviewer, sketch-writer, and illustrator who signed on as a regular contributor to *Fraser's* in 1837. Thackeray's first series of sketches, *The Yellowplush Papers* (1837–8), originated as the mocking review of a guide to "silver-fork" etiquette, seen through the eyes of one Charles James Yellowplush, a liveried footman: "to describ fashnabble life, ONE OF US must do the thing, to do it well" (Ray 1955: 198). At about the same time, he constructed for his art reviews the persona of Michael Angelo Titmarsh – a typical bit of self-ironization. Thackeray's next serial, *Catherine* (1839–40), was a more sustained parody of the "Newgate" genre based on the life of Catherine Hayes, who was burnt at Tyburn in 1726 for murdering her husband. From the outset, Thackeray's comedy drew on a more jaundiced view of class relations than Dickens's, derived in part from his own bitter sense of dispossession. Born into a wealthy Anglo-Indian family and educated at Charterhouse and Cambridge (among major Victorian novelists only Bulwer came from similar privilege, perhaps one reason for Thackeray's lifelong rivalry with him), Thackeray stood to inherit a comfortable fortune that was lost through bad investments, and he spent much of his life worrying over fine lines of class division and exposure to the waywardness of modern economic life. At this stage of his career, though a year older than Dickens, he remained very much a sketch-writer; *The Paris Sketch Book* (1840), his first published volume, appeared well after Dickens's rise to fame.

Sketch-writers gained an especially appealing venue with the founding of *Punch* in 1841, which recognized the growing audience for comic literature and topical humor, both literary and visual. Although the magazine did not publish extended fiction, it offered regular space

to a number of fiction writers. Thackeray would become its most
famous contributor, particularly after the publication of *A Book of Snobs*
(1847), but initially the leading figure on the journal (beyond its
editor, Mark Lemon) was Douglas Jerrold, whose *Story of a Feather*
(1843) and *Mrs. Caudle's Curtain Lectures* (1845) were great successes. *The Story of a Feather* is a "thing story," a series of sketches
linked by the device of an ostrich feather passed through a broad array
of English society, in the process evoking connections between the
most exalted and the most vulnerable, such as a poor featherdresser
named Patty Butler. Even in this work Jerrold – known for his slashing
political squibs and vigorous radicalism – anchored his comedy in a
special sympathy for the poor. *Mrs. Caudle* offers a more traditional –
but perhaps for that reason, ultimately more popular – series of domestic sketches, recounting the ordeals of the henpecked Job Caudle, a toy
and doll merchant, who must endure his wife's nightly scoldings on
quotidian topics.

The 1840s, like every decade of the period, were full of ephemeral
comic fiction, such as *The Greatest Plague of Life* (1847), by Henry and
Augustus Mayhew. Meanwhile, Robert Surtees (1805–64) produced a
trilogy of popular but more durable comic novels featuring a character
that he had first created for the *New Monthly Magazine* (and which
became a central impetus behind *The Pickwick Papers*): Jorrocks, the
rich, bloated huntsman who had earned his fortune as a Cockney
grocer. In *Jorrocks's Jaunts and Jollities* (1838), *Handley Cross, Or the
Spa Hunt* (1843) and *Hillingdon Hall, Or the Cockney Squire* (1845),
Surtees spins variations on the seemingly inexhaustible comedy of class,
as the vulgar, bacchanalian tradesman cuts a swath through the world
of landed squires. Surtees himself belonged to the latter realm: he
wrote as an amateur, and knew from the inside the world he chronicled in the likes of *Mr. Sponge's Sporting Tour* (1853). Most of his
novels were serialized by Bradbury and Evans, the publishers of *Punch*,
and illustrated by John Leech, one of the magazine's most eminent
contributors.

Poetry in the Early 1840s

The future of English poetry, gloomy in 1838, hardly seemed brighter
in 1842. In 1839 Philip James Bailey (1816–1902) had a success with
Festus, which suggests the enduring appeal of Romantic closet drama,

notably Goethe's *Faust* and even Browning's *Paracelsus* – with which it shares an antinomian hero who takes as his subject the cosmos. But Bailey made Browning's poem seem positively austere; initially a poem of 8,000 lines, by its seventh and final edition *Festus* had expanded to 40,000 lines. These successes notwithstanding, Richard Hengist Horne (1803–84) in 1843 protested the modest sales of contemporary poetry by publishing his epic *Orion* at a farthing a copy. Whether owing to the price or the subject, a vaguely Keatsian treatment of Greek myth, the volume proved immensely popular, emboldening Horne to produce his *New Spirit of the Age* in the following year.

But 1842 would turn out to be one of the more momentous years for Victorian poetry. The most popular volume published that year was Macaulay's *Lays of Ancient Rome*, whose title suggests its debt to Scott's *Lays of the Last Minstrel*. Macaulay deftly appropriated Scott's ballad style to the treatment of classical themes, and the result was one of the best-selling poetry volumes of the age; it sold 18,000 copies over the next decade, and 100,000 by 1875. Its images of heroic fidelity (much like Hemans's "Casabianca") would become a staple of schoolroom declamation:

> Then out spake brave Horatius
>   The Captain of the gate:
> "To every man upon this earth
>   Death cometh soon or late.
> And how can man die better
>   Than facing fearful odds,
> For the ashes of his father
>   And the temple of his Gods."
>   ("Horatius" ll. 201–8; Gray 1976)

Less widely noted, but eagerly greeted by critics, was the two-volume *Poems* of Tennyson. It ended the poet's "Ten Year's Silence," a lapse that most commentators have attributed to the shock of his friend Arthur Henry Hallam's death at 21, in October of 1833. On this reading of his career, which Tennyson encouraged, the touchstone poem was "Ulysses," another of his brilliant monologues drawn from the margins of Homeric legend (refracted through Dante), which evokes the aged Ulysses setting out on new voyages after his disappointing return to life in Ithaca. As Tennyson described it, "The poem was written soon after Arthur Hallam's death, and it gives the feeling about the need of going forward and braving the struggle of life perhaps more simply than anything in *In Memoriam*" (Tennyson 1969: 560). But the shock was embraced by an imagination already well versed in fantasies of surrender and desolation, so hauntingly evoked in the likes of "Mariana." Even Ulysses's affirmation of enduring struggle is a surprisingly enervated one:

> My purpose holds
> To sail beyond the sunset, and the baths
> Of all the western stars, until I die.
> It may be that the gulfs will wash us down:
> It may be we shall touch the Happy Isles
> And see the brave Achilles, whom we knew.
>   (ll. 59–64; Tennyson 1969)

This Ulysses would be more at home with his mariners on the island of the Lotos. Few 23-year-olds have written more eloquently of decrepitude and broken will.

Volume One of the new *Poems* largely reprinted the 1832 edition (with occasionally extensive revisions, notably of "The Lady of Shalott"), adding six new poems, most of them political poems written in 1833, expressing anxiety over the Reform Bill. Volume Two was entirely new work, which moved in two broad directions: more narrative poetry, much of it in blank verse (rare in 1832), and more venturesome experiments in the monologue, along the lines of "Ulysses." The volume opens with six poems later categorized as "English Idyls," largely derived from Greek pastoral, in settings mostly drawn from English country houses and their grounds, backdrop to the familiar clash between money and desire: "They wedded her to sixty thousand pounds /To lands in Kent and messuages in York" ("Edwin Morris," ll. 126–7). In their evocations of romance, often through its frustration, the poems look forward to Tennyson's greatest popular success, *Enoch Arden* (1864). The one exception is the haunting "Morte D'Arthur," drawn from Thomas Malory's fifteenth-century prose epic of the same title, which recounts the final collapse of Arthur's "old order," and his departure to an unknown world "Among new men, strange faces, other minds" (l. 238). In both setting and emotional resonance, "Morte" is strikingly at odds with the other Idyls (as well as with other poems in the volume in medieval dress), and owes its place in the "Idyls" to a characteristically self-mistrustful narrative frame. "The Epic" introduces the poem as the fragment of an aborted epic by one Everard Hall, who recites it for his friends as a Christmas Eve entertainment, but only after disparaging it as a misguided effort to write about "heroic times": "For Nature brings not back the Mastodon, / Nor we those times" (ll. 36–7). With this seemingly offhand gesture, Tennyson anticipated a heated debate a decade later over the subject matter of contemporary poetry. But not for another 15 years did he plunge into medieval legend in earnest.

Narrative and monologue, and the future direction of Tennyson's career, were most suggestively evoked in "Locksley Hall." This was the 1842 poem most widely cited by contemporaries, and has been a favorite ever since of historians looking for a banner of Victorian optimism:

> Not in vain the distance beckons. Forward, forward let us range,
> Let the great world spin forever down the ringing grooves of change.
>
> (ll.181–2)

Yet this famous hymn to progress is typically wrenched from its context. It is uttered within a dramatic monologue, in which the speaker rages over a thwarted romance and indulges a fantasy of escaping from "this march of mind" into life on a tropical island:

> There the passions cramped no longer shall have scope and breathing
>   space;
> I will take some dusky woman, she shall rear my dusky race.
>
> (ll. 167–8)

This fantasy and its subsequent repudiation – "I, to herd with narrow foreheads, vacant of our glorious gains, /Like a beast with lower pleasures, like a beast with lower pains!" (ll. 175–6) – capture not only the racial hierarchies informing Victorian schemes of progress, but also the asceticism undergirding the "march of mind." Progress is grounded in self-discipline, in the power to renounce. Within such austere regimens, tropic margins become an increasingly prominent realm of fantasy, as a space at the very edge of sovereignty, both political domination and self-control. ("It is all right," Charles Kingsley murmured on his deathbed, "All under rule.") Even as Britain was conquering such spaces, the victory rarely seemed unequivocal, for the tropics always beckoned as an escape from the work of self-conquest: like "The Lotos-Eaters," "Locksley Hall" pivots on the dream of "going native." As the poem also enacts a struggle against this fantasy, it was praised by Charles Kingsley in 1850 as "the poem which, as we think deservedly, has had most influence on the minds of the young men of our day" (Kingsley 1890: 114). The monologue form itself here performs the work of discipline that Kingsley praises: the skittish disavowal of "The Epic" gives way to a structure that subdues fantasy through dramatized rehearsal and repudiation. Tennysonian speakers repeatedly enact versions of "that stern monodrama," as Carlyle called it in *Sartor*, "*No Object and No Rest*" (Carlyle 1908: 93).

Robert Browning was developing the dramatic monologue along different lines, which crystallized in his own volume of 1842, *Dramatic Lyrics*. Although he had arrived at a prototype of the form in 1835, with "Porphyria's Lover" and "Johannes Agricola in Meditation," Browning in the interval had been devoting his main energies to the theater, with *Strafford* in 1837 followed by *King Victor and King Charles* (which failed to please Macready) and subsequently *A Blot in the Scutcheon*, which received three performances in 1843, and finally *Colombe's Birthday*, the last play Browning wrote for the stage, which was published in 1844 but not performed until 1853. In March 1840 he published a work whose infamy has overshadowed the obscurity of his dramas, his long-pondered and heavily revised *Sordello*, which had occupied him through much of the decade (it had been advertised as "nearly ready" in 1837), a narrative in six books set amidst the conflict between Guelphs and Ghibellines in thirteenth-century Italy. The hero's conflict of loyalty plays out a familiar tension between the claims of action and poetry, power and sympathy, yet the poem quickly became a byword for obscurity – Mrs. Carlyle remarked that she could not discover whether Sordello was a man, a city, or a book. It has been argued that Browning was working in a dramatic vein akin to that of Carlyle in *The French Revolution*, subordinating narrative structure to something like dramatic immediacy. But not even Carlyle's prose approached Browning's punishing syntax.

After this fiasco, Browning felt that he no longer could call on his father to subsidize his publications. In April 1841 the publisher Edward Moxon brought out a new work as the first of what would become eight inexpensive pamphlets, *Bells and Pomegranates*. *Pippa Passes* is a lyrical drama structured around a young mill girl's passage through the town of Asolo. She picks out the four most prominent families in town and sets out to "see their happiness" (l. 204; Browning 1970), but as she passes by she only brings to light varieties of misery to which she remains oblivious, while her songs break in on these troubled lives as a prod to, if not their redemption, at least greater self-awareness. Though critical response was still overshadowed by the reception of *Sordello*, most readers praised the work – although then as now they tended to separate lyric utterance from its dramatic context. The untroubled faith of Pippa's famous refrain, "God's in his heaven, all's right with the world" (ll. 228–9), has too often been identified as Browning's own. Still, the impact of these snatches of lyric on the characters who overhear them clearly reflects a central ambition of Browning's own more artful songs.

Browning's greatest achievement to date appeared in November of 1842, when Moxon published *Dramatic Lyrics*, a slender pamphlet reprinting "Porphyria's Lover" and "Johannes Agricola in Meditation" (still entitled "Madhouse Cells" I and II) and adding a dozen unpublished monologues. Some of the novelty of the volume may have been obscured by its organization: eight of the 14 poems appeared in pendant structure, which called attention to anecdotal interest and picturesque setting. Thus what we now know as "My Last Duchess" and "Count Gismond" appeared as "Italy and France," and were followed by "Incident of the French Camp" and "Soliloquy of the Spanish Cloister." But the opening Advertisement pointed to a more distinctive aspiration (less in pride than defensiveness, perhaps), calling the poems "though for the most part Lyric in expression, always Dramatic in principle, and so many utterances of so many imaginary persons, not mine" (Browning 1970: 365). Presumably few readers would have mistaken the poet for the Duke of Ferrara, but Browning's uneasiness on the point suggests something of the rhetorical confusion that would dog reception of his work for another two decades. Browning's monologues increasingly evoked "imaginary persons" through subtle resistance to an imagined audience, shaping individuality by confounding moral stereotype:

> Our interest's on the dangerous edge of things.
> The tender murderer, the honest thief,
> The superstitious atheist ...
> We watch while these in equilibrium keep
> The giddy line midway: one step aside,
> They're classed and done with.
>
> (ll. 395–401; Browning 1970)

This oxymoronic catalogue from "Bishop Blougram's Apology" (1855) holds for most of Browning's best monologues, whose moral "equilibrium" creates a psychological complexity unrivaled by the early Victorian novel.

Browning's series of pamphlets found an especially enthusiastic reader in Elizabeth Barrett. In "Lady Geraldine's Courtship," the most popular poem of her 1844 *Poems*, the poet Bertram reads aloud from modern poets, including "from Browning some 'Pomegranate,' which, if cut deep down the middle, /Shows a heart within blood-tinctured, of a veined humanity" (ll. 163–4; E. B. B.). Her two-volume *Poems* enjoyed far greater success than Browning's fruit, in part because it did not require such penetration to reveal its heart. She was especially successful with the ballads, which had much of the appeal of Macaulay's *Lays*: they offered a narrative that captured relatively straightforward, impersonal appeal to familiar emotions. The most popular lyric of the collection, "Catarina to Camoens," outwardly resembles Browning's historical monologues. It imagines the deathbed reflections of a lady of the Portuguese court recalling the swashbuckling soldier-poet whose suit had been forbidden by her family, but whose poetry recorded both his love and her beauty – although not her words. But whereas Browning's lyrics encourage a skeptical detachment from the speaker, Barrett invites an unwavering sympathy with Catarina's wistful thought of her vanished beauty and the love it had evoked. "Lady Geraldine's Courtship," the final piece written for the two volumes (to balance out their length) returns to the ballad form, but with two innovations: it is set in modern life, recounting a poet's love for a young aristocrat, and it has a happy ending, as the lady overcomes the barriers of rank to love not only the poem but the poet. In this regard, it is a telling contrast to "Locksley Hall," which it recalls not only thematically but rhythmically: in Tennyson thwarted love conjures up the psychic fragility of the speaker, who finds solace only in strenuous sublimation.

The Literature of Labor

"Lady Geraldine's Courtship" evokes a world far removed from the economic volatility and recurrent famine of the 1840s – a decade that came to be known as "the Hungry Forties." Carlyle's impatient rebuke, "how can we *sing* and *paint* when we do not yet *believe* and *see*?" had rarely seemed more topical. But many of the most vivid responses to revelations about appalling working conditions in factories and mines came from poets. Song is especially suited to capture the sheer repetitiveness of most human labor, whether manual or industrial – a feature that would bedevil the so-called "industrial novel," which captures very little of industry itself. Lyric is also traditionally a vehicle of pathos, readily adapted to evoking sympathy with those who seemed most vulnerable and abused, women and children. Caroline Norton's *A Voice from the Factories* (1836) took up the theme, although her Spenserian stanza, redolent of "Eve of St. Agnes" and "The Lotos Eaters," was not ideal to conveying the sorrow "these little pent-up wretches feel" (l. 83; T. Collins 1999). Many writers were galvanized by the *First Report of the Commission for Inquiry into the Employment and Condition of Children in Mines and Manufactories*, released in May of 1842. The details chastened all but the most callous advocates of laissez-faire, and frequently beggared literary decorum. Poets rarely conjured up the particulars of seven-year-olds working 13-hour days in mines, crawling half-naked through dank, narrow shafts pulling coal in carts chained to their waists, as if they were draft animals. But Barrett's lyric "The Cry of the Children," published the following summer, conjured up the outrages in evocatively general terms, shining a beam of Victorian sentimentality on the subversion of a cherished ideal:

> And well may the children weep before you
>   They are weary ere they run;
> They have never seen the sunshine, nor the glory
>   Which is brighter than the sun.
> They know the grief of man, without its wisdom;
>   They sink in man's despair, without its calm;
> Are slaves, without the liberty in Christendom,
>   Are martyrs, by the pang without the palm …
>   (ll.125–32; E. B. B.)

The pointed reference to slavery in the land of the free – itself a legacy of the early labor movement – would echo throughout the decade.

    The power of lyric repetition was turned to even more forceful social polemic in Thomas Hood's "The Song of the Shirt," published to great acclaim in *Punch* at Christmas of 1843:

> With fingers weary and worn,
>   With eyelids heavy and red,
> A woman sat in unwomanly rags,
>   Plying her needle and thread –
>   Stitch! Stitch! Stitch!

> In poverty, hunger, and dirt,
> And still with a voice of dolorous pitch, –
> Would that its tone could reach the Rich! –
> She sang this "Song of the Shirt!"
> (ll. 81–9; T. Collins 1999)

The plight of seamstresses was a recurrent subject of early Victorian literature, not only because of the grueling nature of ill-paid "close work" under bad lighting (which frequently led to premature blindness) but also because the situation was so clearly a travesty of Victorian platitudes about womanhood. As the more forceful critics pointed out – in the teeth of ongoing appeals to providential ordering – "womanhood" seemed to be reserved for women who could afford not to work.

Working-class writers had a special interest in the conditions of labor, yet they produced a relatively small amount of poetry addressing the topic – save for anonymous ballads and chants, which in their affiliation with a collective oral tradition are largely alien to modern notions of authorship. A six-day, 70-hour work week left little time or energy for literary composition – hence the dearth of novels by writers actually employed in factory or manual labor. Even laborers able to produce poetry in their fleeting spare time tended to address their work to a predominantly middle-class readership, which might experience pangs of sympathy at the thought of suffering children, but did not readily turn to lyric evocations of often brutal, demoralizing labor – or to the expression of radical politics. An exception was Ebeneezer Elliott's *Corn-Law Rhymes* (1831), which captivated Carlyle among others, but Elliott could afford to ignore middle-class tastes, since he had married into a family able to support him as the master of his own iron factory (Cross 1985: 148). Edwin Waugh, "the Lancashire Burns," became famous for his dialect poetry, and Thomas Cooper gained wide notice as the most famous "Chartist poet," particularly for *The Purgatory of Suicides* (1845). J. C. Prince gained some renown as a poet of Manchester life, but Prince's career exemplifies a further challenge confronting working-class poets. Insofar as the poet continued to be thought of as a being of special refinement, those aspiring to that office tended to envision themselves as set apart from fellow laborers – or at least as poets first, workers second. They accordingly resisted working-class politics, instead expressing (like Prince) sentiments much dearer to middle-class sensibilities: progress would come, he exhorted, "Not from without, from Charters and Republics, but from within, from the Spirit working in each, not by wrath and haste, but by patience, made perfect through suffering" (Cross 1985: 144). This quietistic stance would be echoed throughout the so-called "industrial novel" – an emphatically middle-class genre. It was further enforced by middle-class editors and publishers, who frequently reshaped both sentiment and diction to fit respectable tastes. Such mediation most famously bedeviled John Clare, but it continued into the much later career of Gerald Massey, whose first volume, *Voices of Freedom, Lyrics of Love* (1850) on republication in 1854 was re-titled *The Ballad of Babe Christabel, with other Lyrical Poems* (Cross 1985: 156).

Working-class poetry did give rise to a genre of broader readership, the working-man's autobiography. Early in the period such poetry still was sufficiently novel that it typically was prefaced by a memoir of the poet, such as Southey's "Introductory Essay on the Lives and Works of Our Uneducated Poets," prefixed to *Attempts in Verse of John Jones* (1831). After Samuel Bamford's *Passages in the Life of a Radical* appeared in 1844, it was followed by a host of other autobiographies, including James Carter's *Memoirs of a Working Man* (1845), Alexander Somerville's *Autobiography of a Working Man* (1848), and James Born's *Autobiography of a Beggar Boy* (1855). Most distinctive was *Geoffrey Malvern* (1843) by Thomas Miller, the only novel of a working-class writer's literary career, and a very rich guide to the London literary world of the 1830s (Cross 1985: 128, 138). The impact of these works would be felt not only in the industrial novel, but in the rise of the English *Bildungsroman*, most importantly Thackeray's *Pendennis* and Dickens's *David Copperfield*.

Medievalism

For many writers working-class suffering was a symptom of more fundamental social disorder, and a remarkable variety of them shared, at least in broad outline, an alternative social vision. They looked to an imagined medieval order as a rebuke to the variety of evils they saw besetting the present: hunger, brutal working conditions, social division, lack of faith, the degradation of the physical world, a general coarsening of human behavior, a lack of confidence in individual action. Medievalism first took hold in the realm of architecture in the late eighteenth century, when a renewal of interest in Gothic soon was invigorated by the belief that architecture epitomized the society that produced it. In this way, critics revitalized the understanding of aesthetic taste as an index of moral values and faith. The view received especially trenchant expression in an 1836 work by the architect Augustus Welby Pugin, *Contrasts: or, a Parallel between the Noble Edifices of the Middle Ages and the Corresponding Buildings of the Present Day; showing the Present Decay of Taste*. Pugin, who influenced the reconstruction of the Houses of Parliament in the Gothic style, offered 19 plates juxtaposing medieval and contemporary cites and towns, to underscore a "decay of taste" more encompassing than the phrase might suggest. In *Contrasts*, the submergence of Gothic (or "Christian," as Pugin would have it) in broadly "classical" architecture was inseparable from a landscape increasingly given over to jails and workhouses. Pugin's contrasts recast a clash articulated throughout debate over the Reform Bill, perhaps most sharply in Macaulay's review of Robert Southey's *Sir Thomas More; or, Colloquies on the Progress and Prospects of Society* (1829). Southey, a voice of Romantic Toryism, repudiated reform by evoking an earlier, pastoral England in which the happiness and morality of the people were grounded in the wise governance of Christian rulers. Macaulay rejoined that religion was a treacherous foundation for civil government, and that human happiness was best secured "not by the omniscient and omnipotent State, but by the untrammeled prudence and energy of the people" (Macaulay 1873: ii.187). For Macaulay, echoing Mill and other Victorian liberals, the dramatic advances in human comfort and religious tolerance since the age of More pointed to a wholly secular ground of civilization. Macaulay would offer his own encapsulation of this progress in the third chapter of Volume One of his *History of England*, "England in 1685." The historical re-framing of this clash would reverberate throughout the century – above all in the work of the art critic John Ruskin.

The emblematic juxtaposition of modern and medieval orders took on new immediacy in 1843, when Carlyle published a searing jeremiad, *Past and Present*, one of the great works of Victorian social criticism. Carlyle faced a rhetorical challenge grown all too familiar since: how does one prompt readers to feel outraged by suffering – poverty, homelessness, hunger – when it has come to seem part of a natural order? Carlyle unleashed all his rhetorical pyrotechnics, struggling to transfigure the spectacle of able-bodied, skilled men sitting idle or confined in workhouses. To political economists they were merely the by-product of stern economic laws. To Carlyle they were victims of the curse of Midas, starving in the midst of plenty, in a world in which all moral bonds were dissolved in the worship of luxury and profit, and all human relations were reduced to the "cash nexus." Bewildered workers seeking redress could find only the competing "gospels" of "dilettantism" and "mammonism" – Carlyle's slogans for an idle aristocracy and rapacious manufacturing interests, which he personified in a host of grotesque, almost Dantean caricatures, from Quacks to "dead-sea apes" to "Bucaniers" to "Byronic meat-hooks" creaking in the wind. "We call it a Society; and go about professing openly the totalest separation, isolation. Our life is not a mutual helpfulness ... it is a mutual hostility" (Carlyle 1977: 148).

The diagnosis, if not the rhetoric, would become even more familiar with the rise of socialism: human beings cannot be left wholly at the mercy of economic exchange, their worth valued solely in terms of contract. But Carlyle's solution is more of his time. The answer is not greater democracy – democracy, for Carlyle, is part of the problem, because it reinforces the reduction of human relations to political and legal formulas. Instead, Carlyle exhorts industrialists to transform their own self-conceptions and become "Captains of Industry," inspiring and leading an army of loyal workers. Carlyle's coinage, its figurative force long worn away, captures the paternalistic character of so much early Victorian social criticism. Victorian workers are less in need of freedom than of guidance and a sense of purpose. Men in battle do not fight for profit or a contractual obligation; they risk their lives out of brotherhood and loyalty to a cause. Workers can hardly find that inspiration in an ethos that grounds human worth and connection on the vacillations of the market.

At its core, then, Carlyle's medievalism is a reconfiguration of chivalry, which would redeem contemporary society through a model of heroism. Similar appeals are widespread throughout the century (Girouard 1981). But Carlyle's hero is a far cry from Chaucer's "verry parfit knighte." Tellingly, there are no women in Carlyle's medieval order, and his models of heroism pay little heed to the tenderness or concern for the weak that became a central component in Victorian ideals of the gentleman. What Carlyle does share with early-Victorian medievalism is an unabashed celebration of social hierarchy, an imaginary feudal order (largely derived from the novels of Scott) in which the rationalizing "march of mind" yields to romantic visions of tradition, and freedom matters less than the sense of deep and reciprocal moral obligation. *Past and Present* is organized around an emblematic contrast (recalling Pugin) between the St Ives workhouse and the medieval abbey of St Edmundsbury, but the faith that most engages Carlyle is that which the monks invest in their Abbot Samson. Like most emblems of Victorian medievalism, Samson is at best nominally Catholic (Pugin was Catholic, but most Victorians envisioned the epoch through decidedly Protestant eyes). Samson is, however, a model of manhood, whose wise and decisive action secures unwavering loyalty and resolves all social conflicts. Carlyle's is a medievalism distinguished above all by charismatic masculinity.

Aristocratic interests in the early forties embraced more overtly self-serving versions of medievalism. At times the dream was difficult to distinguish from a fancy-dress ball, as in the laughable "Eglintoun tournament" of 1839, in which a re-enactment of jousting combat was foiled by torrential rains, and amused bystanders could enjoy the spectacle of knights in armor carrying umbrellas. Equally picturesque was "Young England," a faction within the Tory party whose title is further evidence of an emergent generational consciousness responsive to accelerating social change. Young England, however, was devoted mainly to reinvigorating aristocratic political dominance. Their early figurehead was Lord John Manners, the glamorous son of the Duke of Rutland, who in 1841 published a volume of verse, *England's Trust*, which unblushingly idealized a lost feudal order, an age in which

> Each knew his place – king, peasant, peer or priest,
> The greatest owed connection with the least
>
> Let wealth and commerce, laws and learning die
> But leave us still our old nobility!
>
> (Girouard 1981: 83)

Carlyle certainly could appreciate this insistence on "connection," but not Manners's fatuous suggestion that the noblest cause was aristocracy itself.

"The Two Nations"

"Young England" might have remained a footnote in political history were it not for another young Tory MP, who in 1841 was angling for a more influential role in the party. In May of 1844 Benjamin Disraeli published the first of three novels that would become known as the

"Young England" trilogy. *Conigsby; or The New Generation*, often called the first English political novel, is at one level a party manifesto in three volumes, intricately working out Disraeli's view that the Whigs had transformed England into an oligarchy on the model of medieval Venice, and that only a rejuvenated Tory party could restore to England a proper balance of powers – which is to say, a more direct contact with its own medieval institutions. But the excitement aroused by the novel had less to do with its tendentious analyses than with its unmistakable allusions to contemporary political intrigue, which Disraeli encouraged by publishing a key linking dozens of characters to their historical counterparts. The silver-fork impulse lingers: imagination seems to count for less than the illusion of an insider's perspective, which offers vicarious access to elite social circles.

Looking back, Disraeli would characterize the trilogy in highly schematic terms: *Coningsby* dealt with "the origin and condition of political parties," and *Tancred; or The New Crusade* (1847) with "the duties of the Church as a main remedial agency in our present state" (Disraeli 1983: 15–16). But the most influential and enduringly popular of the trilogy, and of all Disraeli's novels, was its central volume, *Sybil, or The Two Nations* (1845), which addressed "the condition of the people." It was a topic of growing urgency in the midst of the hungry forties, even before the worst of the famine in Ireland. Just the previous year, a young German manufacturer visiting Manchester to study its achievement as "the workshop of the world" was so appalled by the physical environment that he penned an impassioned exposeé of *The Condition of the English Working Class* (1845). Like Friedrich Engels, Disraeli worked hard to capture the details of working-class hardship, relying on parliamentary reports into factory conditions. The focal point of the novel, however, became less the conditions of labor than a more inchoate "social problem": the danger lurking in an "impassable gulf" between rich and poor, "the two nations" of the novel's subtitle, which by 1845 in fact was a well-worn trope. In presenting the factory as a microcosm of class conflict – underscored by setting the novel within the rise of Chartism in the late 1830s – *Sybil* establishes many of the conventions of what would become known as "the industrial novel." Dire social conditions – here focused in the slum of Wodgate, also known as "Hell-house Yard" – create an environment in which sincerely aggrieved laborers, who wish merely to support their families, are exploited by demonic "political agitators," who whip resentment into mob violence that culminates in a frenzy of destruction (often out of seeming pleasure in sheer anarchy). Meanwhile, the integrity of the disciplined worker is embodied in a single man – here the factory inspector Walter Gerard – who attempts to resist the mob, and suffers for his independence. Ultimately, however, the social conflicts are ascribed to simple ignorance, which allows them to be resolved not through any large social transformation, such as a change in the nature of factory labor, but through the enlargement of individual moral sympathies – above all through cross-class romance.

What makes Disraeli's engagement more distinctive – and what gave his novels their popularity then and now – was his conjunction of social sympathy with a fantasy of aristocratic glamor, which extends to the very style of the novel. The effect is something like a parliamentary Blue Book rewritten as the libretto of an Italian opera – a note struck in Disraeli's summary of his aims: "In an age of political infidelity, of mean passions and petty thoughts, I would have impressed upon the rising race not to despair, but to seek in a right understanding of the history of their country and in the energies of heroic youth – the elements of national welfare" (Disraeli 1980: 496). In addressing contemporary social conflict through the lens of history, the novel is clearly indebted to Carlyle, both as it evokes a falling away from an earlier paternalism, and as it envisions redress through the emergence of a hero who might, in Sybil's words, "protect the people" (210). It also shares with the Oxford movement (then at the very zenith of its notoriety, with Newman's imminent secession to Rome) a claim to spiritual authority through the restoration of historical continuity, a return to origins somehow lost sight of or betrayed. But neither Carlyle nor Newman conjured up so debonair a hero as Charles Egremont, the younger brother of the Earl of Marney, who breaks with his family to address the urgent social divisions they ignore. ("The people do not want employment," pronounces Egremont's brother, with coarse Malthusian logic, "all this employment is a stimulus to population" [161].) Like Disraeli's earliest novels, *Sybil* is raptly ambivalent towards the aristocracy, heaping disdain on its shallowness and self-absorption while at the same time reveling in its elegance. Much of Egremont's appeal lies precisely in his effortless urbanity, a distinctly English *sprezzatura*. In effect, the novel refracts aristocratic life through the lens of bourgeois values – celebrating domestic womanhood and, above all, earnestness – while at the same time largely erasing the middle classes, and conveying Disraeli's deep suspicion of an ethos that would choose Cabinet ministers on the basis of private virtue rather than public policy.

With the middle class confined largely to shabby political operatives, rich and poor are placed into insistent juxtaposition, parliamentary salons opening onto trade union meetings. Such contrasts, however, also elicit unexpected affinities, particularly in Disraeli's fascination with secrecy and the social dynamics of the coterie. Disraeli was keenly sensitive to dynamics of membership and exclusion: he was the son of Isaac D'Israeli, a distinguished man of letters and a Jew who had his children baptized and raised as Christians. The pervasive anti-Semitism of Victorian Britain nurtured in Disraeli a paranoid imagination that was brilliantly suited to the times. He divides his novelistic world into insiders and outsiders, for whom the fundamental event is "initiation" into secret knowledge, whether it be the identity of the next Prime Minister or the details of a Chartist conspiracy. (Disraeli readily acknowledges the comic parallels between parliamentary intrigue and the meetings of trade unions.) The most overt link between the two worlds, however, lies in romance, as the culminating marriage of Egremont and Sybil bridges the "gulf" between the two nations. The resolution also crowns the intrigue surrounding Sybil's own ancestry: the "daughter of the people" turns out to be the rightful Lady Marney, heiress to one of the oldest – and thus, in Disraeli's eyes, most legitimate – titles in England. Personal genealogy thereby reaffirms Disraeli's political designs, but it also hints at the persistence of the gulf: the Hon. Charles Egremont could hardly be expected to marry a seamstress.

A very different engagement with the lives of the working classes emerged in the mid-forties in the fiction of Elizabeth Gaskell (1810–1865). Unlike Disraeli, Gaskell had first-hand acquaintance with the lives of the poor, particularly in Manchester, of which she is as important a chronicler as Engels. Born Elizabeth Stevenson in London, she grew up in the small town of Knutsford, some 16 miles from Manchester, to which she moved after her marriage in 1832 to the Unitarian clergyman William Gaskell, whose position brought him into close contact with a broad section of Manchester life. She brought that knowledge to a series of magazine sketches throughout the 1840s, followed by the appearance of *Mary Barton* (anonymously) in October 1848. Like *Sybil*, the novel casts back to the events of the late 1830s, and Gaskell also focuses on a radical social division between rich and poor: "we are to live as separate as if we were in two worlds; ay as separate as Dives and Lazarus," says John Barton (Gaskell 1970: 45). But Gaskell offers a more substantive cultural geography. The subtitle, "A Tale of Manchester Life," suggests an understanding of Manchester as a distinctive social order shaped by industrial labor. The heroine's father, John Barton, is "a through specimen of a Manchester man, born of factory workers, and himself bred up in youth, and living in manhood, among the mills" (41); when the heroine travels to the docks of Liverpool, sailors seem "a new race of men" (352). Like Mayhew and other "urban investigators" in London, Gaskell writes for an audience of outsiders, and her documentary impulse similarly functions as a kind of ethnography – particularly in her attention to local idiom (which is frequently glossed in footnotes). The novel incorporates a good deal of anonymous dialect poetry, such as "Th' Owdham Weaver," which typically circulated in broadsides or as oral tradition, capturing working-class travails in a form that middle-class readers would rarely encounter. Such details further a broadly Wordsworthian effort to imagine "the romance in the lives of some of those who elbowed me daily" (37).

The main emphasis, however, falls on the sufferings – physical and psychological – of workers at the mercy of a newly volatile economy, which leaves them recurrently unemployed and desperately vulnerable to hunger and sickness. Inasmuch as it attempts to explain working-class unrest, this emphasis works to humanize a struggle that had been widely demonized among the affluent classes. What might seem an attack on the social fabric is at root, the novel suggests, a claim to common humanity. And yet Gaskell's sympathy for the working classes jostles uneasily with efforts to resolve their moral grievances into mere resentment, and thus to disarm them. The rhetorical balancing-act emerges early in the novel, when Gaskell vividly evokes the exasperation of the unemployed worker who witnesses untroubled luxury among the mill-owners:

> The contrast is too great. Why should he alone suffer from bad times?
>
> I know that this is not really the case: but what I wish to impress is what the workman thinks and feels. True, that with child-like improvidence, good times will often dissipate his grumbling, and make him forget all prudence and foresight.
>
> But there are earnest men among these people, men who have endured wrongs without complaining, but without ever forgetting or forgiving those whom (they believe) have caused all the woe. (Gaskell 1970: 60)

With the second paragraph, the worker's experience is transformed into illusion, albeit one that should enlist our sympathy – at least when entertained by the honorable, "earnest" poor. Although Gaskell's preface disclaims any knowledge of political economy, her emphasis here is in keeping with its tenets: if a free market is indeed self-regulating, then conflict can originate only in ignorance. Under the pressure of this individualism, trade unions and Chartists can only be a desperate, misguided threat to economic and social order, which feeds on "hoards of vengeance" (61) rather than principled resistance to the worker's lack of power.

A subsequent allusion to *Frankenstein* reinforces the dilemma: "The actions of the uneducated man seem to me typified in those of Frankenstein, that monster of many human qualities ... Why have we made them what they are; a powerful monster, yet without inner means for peace and happiness?" (Gaskell 1970: 219–20). Shelley's novel brings home the challenges of securing mutual recognition between master and "monster." Ultimately, that recognition is brought about through another act of desperate working-class violence – the murder of a mill-owner's son. The bridge achieved in *Sybil* through marriage is effected here through the reconciliation of the owner and the murderer, both consumed with the lust for revenge, yet ultimately brought to feel themselves "brothers in the deep suffering of the heart" (435). Once again, the social structure is displaced and transcended through the power of individual sympathy: "The mourner before him was no longer the employer, a being of another race ... no longer the enemy, the oppressor, but a very poor, and desolate old man" (435). Romance, meanwhile, functions primarily to chasten Mary Barton's own social aspirations, as her affections are redirected from George Carson, the mill-owner's son, to the worker whose status matches her own.

"The two nations" assumed importantly different forms, with social conflicts less amenable even to fictional resolution, in Anglo-Irish fiction. At the beginning of the nineteenth century, Ireland itself represented a very small literary market, which naturally encouraged Irish writers to look to London. That focus was reinforced by the formal Union of Britain and Ireland in 1800 – "a union of the shark with its prey," as Byron sardonically noted, passed in the wake of a 1798 uprising against British rule – which naturally encouraged English interest in a country ostensibly part of the "United Kingdom" yet so different in language, religion, and history. Catholic Emancipation in 1829, prompted largely by Irish protest, only fanned apprehension in England of a newly empowered alien presence so close at hand. Such tensions did not affect the huge success of Thomas Moore's *Irish Melodies* (1808–34), which reinforced a long-standing association of Ireland with the harp and the bard. Although Moore's celebration of Ireland's past glory hints at the stirring of nationalist sentiment, little in Moore's lyrics gave much hint of contemporary Irish life. Maria Edgeworth was the first influential novelist to treat that life in a broadly realistic (albeit comic) vein; her *Castle Rackrent* (1800) and *The Absentee* (1812) would have a large impact on the growth of regionalist fiction generally. But she abandoned Irish settings after 1817; as she explained to her brother in 1834, "it is impossible to draw Ireland as she now is in a book of fiction; realities are too strong, party passions are too violent, to bear to see, or to look at their faces in the looking-glass" (Hare 1894: ii.150).

The surge of interest in Irish subjects in the 1820s diverted attention from party passions, focusing instead on descriptions of the Irish peasantry and oral tradition, written or collected by both Irish and English writers. The travel writer Anna Maria Hall produced such volumes as *Sketches of Irish Character* (1829), while other Irish writers produced a host of first-hand accounts: Mary Leadbeater's *Collection of Lives of the Irish Peasantry* (1822), Michael James Whitty's *Tales of Irish Life* (1824), T. C. Croker's *Researches in the South of Ireland* (1824), Mrs. Samuel Carter's *Sketches of Irish Character* (1829), W. H. Maxwell's *Wild Sports in the West of Ireland* (1832) (Jeffares and van den Kemp 2005: 11). In such works, the grinding poverty of agrarian Ireland had little to do with politics; it was a mere fact of life typically leavened by the imaginative resourcefulness and resilience of the Irish peasantry. T. C. Croker's *Legends and Traditions of the South of Ireland* (1825) inaugurated a number of similar collections, which variously navigated a dual audience: an English or conservative Anglo-Irish readership pleased to see a picturesque Irish peasantry given over to dreams and revelry, and an Irish audience that could look to such tales as a foundation of national identity – much as the Grimms collected their "Märchen" as ostensible repositories of a collective German *volk*.

Anglo-Irish literature thus became increasingly associated with varieties of comedy, epitomized in the creation of what later generations would attack as the "stage Irishman." That development emerges in the career of Samuel Lover (1797–1868). Lover began as a song-writer in the style of Moore, then entered into the vogue for folktale with *Legends and Stories of Ireland* (1831 and 1834), before turning to the novel, where his best-known work is *Handy Andy* (1842), an "Irish Tale" serialized in *Bentley's* with Lover's own illustrations, and thus competing for attention with the comic serials in *Punch*. The adventures of the hapless hero with a host of familiar types – most of them bound up with drink – invite readers to laugh at the squalor of his mother and cousin in rags living off potatoes in a hovel shared with a pig, and to sympathize when Andy turns out to be the lost son of an aristocrat who is rescued from Ireland for proper society in London.

Even more successful as a comic writer was Charles Lever (1806–72), the best-selling Irish novelist of the century. Lever, educated at Trinity College Dublin and trained as a surgeon, took up writing for the *Dublin University Magazine*, the leading journal of the Tory Protestant establishment, which in 1839 serialized Lever's first novel, *The Confessions of Harry Lorrequeur*. The headlong pace and general spirit of the work, a rollicking, disjointed picturesque tale of a young Irish soldier who finds himself drawn into adventures all over Europe, are summed up in its conclusion: "The next day I got married. The End" (Lever 1899: ii.285). The novel was a huge success, republished in both monthly serial and book form (with illustrations by Phiz, Dickens's illustrator). Lever followed it up with *Charles O'Malley, The Irish Dragoon* (1841), a more substantial and slightly more serious work in the same vein (its hero returns from the Peninsular Wars to life as a reforming landlord), which was just as successful. The novels (with a new one almost annually) brought Lever money, fame, an offer to edit the *Dublin University Magazine*, and friendship with many British literary lights (Thackeray paid fulsome tribute to Lever's conviviality, though he parodied his prose). But though Lever continued to produce novels, he quickly found himself ground down by political conflicts – inflamed by his editorship and his famously volatile temper (he was known as "Doctor Quicksilver") – and in 1845 he left Ireland, to spend the rest of his life principally in Florence and Trieste.

Lever's departure coincided with an event that forever changed Ireland and its literature, the Famine. In 1845 the failure of the potato crop – long the staple food of the Irish peasantry – inaugurated a series of disastrous harvests that led to massive hunger and death from starvation and disease, and that continued until 1851. Eyewitness accounts of the suffering are horrifying: the barely living surrounded by the bodies of their families, corpses devoured by starving dogs, even survivors reduced to living skeletons, "ghouls." Ireland, in 1845 the most densely populated country in Europe, over the next decade lost nearly half its population to death and emigration. The catastrophe – exacerbated by the reluctance of the British government to intervene – abruptly undermined the comedy of Handy Andy and his ilk. But it also nearly defied novelistic representation. One exception was the work of William Carleton (1794–1869), who, unlike the middle-class Dublin Protestants Lover and Lever, was the son of a Catholic tenant farmer, the youngest of 14 children in a family whose mother spoke only Irish. Carleton's early career certainly participated in the work of stereotyping; he first came to notice with his *Traits and Stories of the Irish Peasantry* (1830 and 1833) which helped to popularize the image of the brawling, boozing Paddy. But Carleton wrote from much closer acquaintance with peasant life, and with less eye to the British public than Lover and Lever – the latter of whom he frequently attacked for his coziness with British interests. Beginning with *Fardorougha, The Miser* (1839), Carleton produced a series of works that earned him the label "the peasant's novelist." The most harrowing of these is *The Black Prophet, A Tale of the Irish Famine* (1847), serialized in the *Dublin University Magazine* in the second year of the disaster but drawing on Carleton's experience of earlier famines in 1817 and 1822. Few other novelists could master the horrifying material, and the shadow of the Famine inhibited the production of Irish fiction for several decades, as the old comic types seemed abruptly desiccated and the staples of the romance plot insubstantial.

The gulf between rich and poor, which became the most encompassing "problem" of the early Victorian social novel, took on added resonance in 1848. With famine gripping Ireland, the continent was roiled by widespread insurrection and revolution, and fears of similar violence loomed large in England itself, especially in large rallies of Chartists exasperated by the failure of Parliament even to acknowledge their petitions. On the eve of a planned monster procession from Kennington Common to Westminster on April 10, anxiety reached such a pitch that military forces were mobilized under the elderly Duke of Wellington. In the event, the rally was dampened by both weather and the restraint of its organizers, and it turned out to mark the beginning of the end of Chartism. But it also marked the emergence of an important literary career. As a young clergyman in the rural parish of Eversley in Berkshire, Charles Kingsley (1819–75) had ventured to London to observe the rally; what he saw solidified his belief that the Church of England had to defuse the most radical political demands by answering at least some working-class economic grievances. That aim informed *The People's Friend; or Politics for the People*, a periodical in which Kingsley joined with the liberal theologian F. D. Maurice and others interested in working-class conciliation. Writing under the pseudonym "Parson Lot," Kingsley helped to define what would become known as "Christian Socialism," proclaiming a fundamental Christian sympathy across classes, which might be turned to improving working-class lives.

Later in 1848 Kingsley began a serial novel, *Yeast: A Problem*, published in *Fraser's*, which called attention to the sufferings of agricultural workers – an aim that proved too radical for the journal's editors, who suspended the serial. In the following year he began a more substantial project. When Henry Mayhew's series of articles in *The Morning Chronicle*, "London Labour and the London Poor," called attention to (among other things) deplorable working conditions among clothes-makers in London, Kingsley responded with a pamphlet, "Cheap Clothes and Nasty," denouncing the "sweating" system among London tailors, and urging the formation of independent associations among working men. "Why should we not work and live together in our own workshops, or our own houses, for our own profit?" he asked, adopting a fictive identification with the urban artisan (Kingsley 1902: vii.76). It seems a modest enough political program, but such organization of labor defied contemporary political economy (J. S. Mill's two-volume treatise on the subject, which held the field for a quarter-century, was published in that same year). In the *Edinburgh Review*, W. R. Greg (a spokesman for "the Manchester school" of free-trade advocates) rejoined that Kingsley wished to cocoon men with "artificial environments which shall make subsistence certain, enterprise superfluous, and virtue easy, low-pitched, and monotonous" (Greg 1851: 17). The objection points up the crucial place of willpower and self-discipline in mid-Victorian representations of labor, and those figured centrally as Kingsley developed his pamphlet into a novel, *Alton Locke: Tailor and Poet* (1850).

Alton Locke, as its subtitle suggests, brings the divide of rich and poor into focus through the literary aspirations of a working man, who is largely based on Thomas Cooper (with whom Kingsley corresponded about the Kennington rally). The novel captures the exhausting working conditions that left so little time or energy for literary achievement, but it is more attentive to another theme of working-class memoirs, the effort to win middle-class recognition without surrendering one's self-respect – more pointedly, to distinguish genuine respect from mere condescension. For Locke, the sense of thwarted intellectual possibility is sharpened by contact with an affluent cousin, in whose company he witnesses a series of glaring contrasts: between pastoral landscapes and London slums, between wealth and grinding poverty, between the effortless grace of Lord Lynedale and Locke's own awkward, eager ambition. As Locke's poetry wins acknowledgment from young aristocrats, the novel becomes increasingly preoccupied with nuances of social rank – particularly the distinction between patronage and friendship, and whether, and in what ways, the working man can earn the status of a gentleman. Tellingly, romance figures here only in Locke's hopeless passion for an upper-class beauty, "a queen, rather to be feared than loved" (Kingsley 1902: vii.268): social divisions are negotiated almost entirely by reflections on the working man's conduct, particularly the attainment of physical vitality and self-discipline that distinguish the true gentleman (and would also restrain Locke's social ambition). When Locke, like so many protagonists of the industrial novel, is lured into a compromising affiliation with Chartism and unreflectively incites a riot, he places the blame on his "maddening desire of influence" (viii: 130). Once again, the industrial novel defines an arena for the regulation of desire, but here that struggle is inflected by Kingsley's own anxieties about class standing and manhood: the yearning to secure recognition as a gentleman was fundamentally a middle-class concern. By the middle of the century it would become an urgent theme for a host of novelists.

"What's Money After All?"

The turn of the novel towards contemporary social issues was most notable in the work of Dickens. For a time, in the early 1840s, Dickens's own novels lagged behind more venturesome engagements with topical issues. Though *Oliver Twist* is sometimes categorized as a "social problem" novel, the focal point of its satire is not the disjunction between rich and poor, but the New Poor Law, and its representation of psychology remained predominantly melodramatic. Dickens's early fiction was generally praised for representing rich and poor in relative harmony, typically through pre-industrial economic relations (most notably master–servant), but after the immense success of *Old Curiosity Shop* the formula grew tired. After his foray into historical fiction with *Barnaby Rudge*, Dickens had his first major disappointment with *Martin Chuzzlewit*. He signed a contract for it in 1841, but did not begin writing until the following autumn; in the meantime he visited America and produced *American Notes*, which would have an important impact on the new novel. *Chuzzlewit* contains some of Dickens's most famous characters – most notably Pecksniff, the quintessence of hypocritical propriety (" 'the very sight of skittles,' Mr Pecksniff eloquently pursued, 'is far from being congenial to a delicate mind' " [Dickens 1999: 453]), and Sairey Gamp, the drunken private nurse who is one of Dickens's most memorable figures of misrule: "Wishin' you lots of sickness, my darling creetur," she tells her fellow nurse, Betsy Prig (444). But their very prominence hints at the unusually loose construction of the book. The central action is a familiar wrangling over inheritance, with Martin Chuzzlewit the younger unjustly disowned by his grandfather Martin, and Pecksniff working to solidify the breach in order to secure his own profit. The oedipal energies informing this quarrel are a staple of Dickens's early novels, as is the shabby-genteel milieu of Todgers' lodging house, around which much of the action orbits. But the development is unsteady in tone and unusually static, and Dickens himself seems to have grown tired of it: a quarter of the way through serialization he abruptly shifted the setting to America, where Martin's travels allow Dickens to rehearse some of his excoriating commentary from *American Notes*. When Martin returns to England and is restored to his rightful inheritance, old Martin sums up the action with the rather feeble maxim, "the curse of our house ... has been the love of self" (752).

The love of self became an increasingly somber preoccupation in Dickens's works during the 1840s. On a visit to Manchester in 1843, he was especially moved by the so-called "ragged schools," volunteer institutes giving free instruction to poor children otherwise bereft of formal education; when he returned to London he began a one-volume story describing the triumph of love over greed. *A Christmas Carol* (1843) became the first of Dickens's annual "Christmas books," an onslaught against *homo economicus* aimed at the lucrative holiday market, and fueled by the disappointing financial returns of *Chuzzelwit* (to maximize his profit, Dickens arranged for Chapman and Hall to publish the work on commission, with Dickens bearing all costs). As so often in Dickens, the relations between sympathy and self-interest took surprising turns, but his association of Christmas with the triumph of feeling captured a growing audience. In the following year, *The Chimes* took on the complacency of the London aldermen who would deny the reality of suffering. "There's a certain amount of cant in vogue about starvation," one remarks, "and I intend to put it down," but the spirit of the holiday conquers even such callousness (Dickens 2006: 103).

In Dickens's next serial novel, love of self verges on the truly mon-strous. More importantly, following the hints of the Christmas stories, it is something more than an individual failing, or even a family curse; it is a symptom of disorder in society at large. This emphasis has led many critics to see *Dombey and Son* as a watershed in Dickens's career, even the pivotal moment between "early" and "late" Dickens. But the newly acerbic social scrutiny was not what most impressed contempo-raries. They were instead riveted by the pathos of another dying child, Paul Dombey, whose deathbed aroused a tumult equaled only by that of Little Nell. "Oh, my dear, dear Dickens!" wrote one reader, "what a no. 5 you have now given us! I have so cried and sobbed over it last night, and again this morning; and felt my heart purified by those tears, and blessed and loved you for making me shed them; and I never can bless and love you enough" (P. Collins 1971: 217). Few effusions so memorably capture the power of sentiment in Victorian culture. These were the words of Francis Jeffrey, the Lord Chancellor, a famously acerbic *Edinburgh* reviewer who had excoriated a host of romantic poets, memorably opening a review of Wordsworth's *Excursion* (1815) with the words, "This will never do." What had become of the hanging judge of Romantic reviewing?

With all allowance for the mellowing of age, Jeffrey's effusion cap-tures a shift in emotional climate that helps to explain why Dickens was so cherished by early Victorians. His readers seem to have found in tears (whether of grief or joy) an obscure vindication of their very power to feel, and thus by extension a hope that the world at large might be capable of extending a like sympathy to others – including themselves. Tears, that is, seemed to confirm the presence of emotional warmth in an increasingly cold and dangerous world. They extended the domestic realm to a larger imagined community. No one rivaled Dickens in his power to arouse tears; as Thackeray memorably exclaimed of *Dombey* (while in the midst of composing *Vanity Fair*), "There's no writing against such power as this – one has no chance! Read that chap-ter describing young Paul's death; it is unsurpassed! – it is stupendous!" (P. Collins 1971: 219).

Such responses suggest the risk Dickens took when he juxtaposed pathos with jaundiced portraits of English institutions and their repre-sentatives, locating evil not merely in melodramatic villains, but in society itself. As Dickens's novels assumed an increasing burden of social criticism, they were liable to forfeit precisely that cathartic relief that Jeffrey and others cherished. And we see this disappointment in the reception of *Dombey*. Audiences were moved by young Florence Dombey's unwavering affection for her father in the face of his chilling neglect; although some reviewers complained that her devotion was unbelievable, Macaulay, among others, wept as if his heart would break. But they were perplexed by the novel's interest in a countervailing world of emotional dearth and rigidity, centered on Dombey's second marriage, to the imperious Edith Granger, and the machinations of his suavely devious Manager, John Carker. For most readers today, Dickens's anatomy of Dombey's marriage represents the more ambitious portion of the book, in which the derangement of romance comes to embody a corrupt social order. When the young Paul asks, "What is money after all?" "I mean, Papa, what can it do?" his father responds, "Money, Paul, can do anything" (Dickens 1970: 152). Like Carlyle's invocation of Midas, the answer points to a growing idolatry in English life. Dombey's unyielding will and obsession with appearances summon up a world that sacrifices affection at the altar of power, while Edith's resistance brings home (as she insists) the predicament of a woman who is effectively bought and sold by the men who value her as a social ornament – a predicament daringly if awkwardly underscored by her affiliation with a prostitute, as well as her own quietly audacious conduct as a wife. The larger designs are further underscored by a newly sustained pursuit of unifying motifs such as the flowing river, whose prominence puzzled a number of reviewers, and above all the railroad, which was reshaping the material fabric of London, but also was reorienting the very experience of distance, mobility, and leisure – so much so that it became an emblem of modern life. Though we tend to imagine the railways primarily as a physical phenomenon, memorably evoked in the leveling of "Stagg's Gardens" to make space for a new terminal, Dickens also captures their economic allure, both as an avenue of mobility for working men (here young Tootles) and as they sparked a speculative stock boom that would resound through novels of the later 1840s and 1850s.

Most broadly, *Dombey* confirms the significance of domesticity as an arena of far-reaching social and political conflict. This was borne out by the greatest of all skeptical mid-Victorian representations of domestic life, Thackeray's *Vanity Fair*, which began serial publication as *Dombey* was appearing. The original title seemed to disclaim any large ambition: "Pen and Pencil Sketches of English Society" suggests a direct extension of Thackeray's earlier career as a sketch-writer and humorist. But the novel quickly expanded beyond anything Dickens had attempted to this point. Though "English Society" is that of the upper classes, Thackeray probes its reliance on extended networks of servants, dependants, and tradesmen, people whose livelihood hangs on the solvency of the affluent – and who (accordingly) are especially acute observers of financial affairs. The novel is particularly engaged by the interplay between old and new money, the landed gentry and the city merchant, the aristocratic disdain for "trade" screening an eager desire to marry into mercantile fortunes, the proud independence of the honest English merchant jostling with a groveling snobbery, which constantly solicits aristocratic regard and envisions nothing greater than raising one's child to a title.

The two worlds are interwoven above all through the machinations of one of the great heroines of English literature, Becky Sharp, whose extraordinary skill as a social actress – she truly is the star of the Fair – is the focal point of a more penetrating, albeit more cynical, scrutiny of social mobility (both upward and downward) than Dickens would undertake until *Great Expectations*. The orphaned daughter of a penniless artist (memories of her childhood recall Thackeray's bohemian days in the early thirties), Becky eventually climbs almost to the summit of English society, on her way making plain, and increasingly exploiting, the gaps between moral and social eminence. Becky's economic leverage, Thackeray cuttingly points out, grows with each new compromise of her virtue. So long as tradesmen believe she is the mistress of Lord Steyne, they will continue to extend her credit; should that connection be ruptured, or should she turn out to be in reality virtuous, she would be financially ruined. In negotiating this play of appearances, Becky recalls the agility of Defoe's Moll Flanders, but Thackeray's novel more thoroughly undercuts faith in providential design. In the stunning close of chapter 32, for example, describing the aftermath of Waterloo, the ever-keen Ruskin recognized "blasphemy of the most fatal and subtle kind": "Darkness came down on the field and city, and Amelia was praying for George, who was lying on his face, dead, with a bullet through his heart" (Thackeray 2001: 375). Both Moll and Becky incarnate the economic energies of their times – with the implication that everything (including themselves) is for sale – but Becky, along with her age, depends far more on the dangerous wonders of credit. Much of the suspense of the novel hangs on Thackeray's manipulation of the pun in that term (from the Latin *credere*), whereby financial commitment depends on a more encompassing yet unsteady belief in appearances – a belief often rudely dispelled. "Living on nothing a year," in one of Thackeray's memorable chapter titles, thus becomes a feat of extraordinary social dexterity and moral callousness, a life of ongoing performance in which social identity is resolved into theater. Therein lies what may be the most corrosive insight of Thackeray's novel: in the world of obsessive concern with social appearance and "getting on," almost no one is what she seems.

Bankruptcy thus resonates more profoundly in *Vanity Fair* than in *Dombey and Son*. Dombey's fall is punishment for his pride, his deluded belief that "money can do anything," but in Thackeray's world bankruptcy hints at a more comprehensive moral derangement – bearing out Carlyle's sardonic remark that "the Hell of the English" is "the terror of 'Not succeeding'" (Carlyle 1977: 148). Thackeray's example would influence a host of subsequent narratives in which financial catastrophe opens onto a more inclusive moral bankruptcy: Dickens's *Little Dorritt* (1856) and *Our Mutual Friend* (1865), Tennyson's *Maud* (1855), and Trollope's *The Way We Live Now* (1875), among many others. Yet admiration for the range and acuity of *Vanity Fair* was tempered by worry that its criticism was at base cynical. Certainly that suspicion was enhanced by Thackeray's audacious narrator, a garrulous, thrusting presence whose shifting persona is most often that of a stage manager overseeing a street fair or puppet show, and who at nearly every turn intervenes to restrain, or even obstruct, sympathetic identification with the main characters. The contrast with Dickens was glaring: if the early Dickensian narrator seemed a benevolent neighbor, Thackeray's is the acquaintance who raises awkward questions about one's bank account. Readers, then as now, found it difficult to reconcile affection for two such different talents; they tended to praise one by contrast with the other. That division would shape discussion of the novel for nearly two decades.

Romance and Religion

Two other works published in that remarkable year of 1847 would leave an even more enduring mark on the history of the English novel. They marked the emergence of the most famous literary family in British history – at first appearance the Bells: Acton, Currer, and Ellis, authors of *Anne Grey*, *The Professor*, and *Wuthering Heights*, respectively. The choice of pseudonyms reflected their anxiety to fend off stereotypes surrounding women novelists, and the forms of criticism incited by Mrs. Trollope's choice of "unfeminine" topics – although such images have only been strengthened, ironically, by their enduring popularity. Particularly through film adaptation, the works of the Brontës (Anne, 1820–49; Charlotte, 1816–55; Emily, 1818–48) in their different ways have worn into archetypal expressions of women's romantic longing and fulfillment, an association that has often relegated them to the realm of adolescent fiction. This image makes it hard to understand their initial reception, which found them very much more daunting, even dangerous.

After declining *The Professor*, Smith and Elder brought out Currer Bell's other novel, *Jane Eyre*, to immediate success, which prompted eager speculation as to the author's identity. Although reviewers compared it to earlier works of domestic fiction, particularly those of Austen and Edgeworth, many presumed the author was indeed a man (George Smith was astonished when Currer and Anne Bell presented themselves at his London offices) – perhaps because, in a word many reviewers invoked, the book evinced such "power." That honorific joined two achievements, psychological acuity and emotional intensity, in which romantic passion was linked to an unusually fervent assertion of feminine dignity and independence. The passion was so forceful that it struck some readers as strident and threatening. In the most famous attack on the novel, in the *Quarterly* in 1848, Elizabeth Rigby (later Lady Eastlake) declared:

> Altogether the autobiography of *Jane Eyre* is pre-eminently an anti-Christian composition. There is throughout it a murmuring against the comforts of the rich and against the privation of the poor, which, as far as each individual is concerned, is a murmuring against God's appointment ... We do not hesitate to say that the tone of mind and thought which has overthrown authority and violated every code human and divine abroad, and fostered Chartism and rebellion at home, is the same which has also written *Jane Eyre*. (M. Allott 1974: 109–10)

Rigby's animus seems exorbitant, but it captures a central impulse of the novel. Jane's self-assertion is a standing challenge to the world that would relegate her to stereotyped insignificance, as, in her own words, "a Governess – disconnected, poor, and plain" (C. Brontë 1996: 183). Like Thackeray's heroine, Brontë's heroine exposes the prejudices of the upper-class world in which she comes to reside, but whereas Becky exploits prejudice to become a part of that world, Jane challenges it, thereby reaffirming a different social order.

In all of Victorian literature, *Jane Eyre* offers perhaps the most vivid example of the reconfiguring of social authority through gender – particularly through contrasting models of femininity. As a governess, Jane occupies a notoriously difficult, even paradoxical, social space, which reflects the burdens of domesticity for unmarried women lacking independent income. Although a governess had to be "respectable" – affluent families would not hire working-class women to oversee their children's education – the governess was haunted by the stigma attached to wage labor: respectable women did not work for a living. This dilemma could be finessed by women writers, but a governess within the household frequently was isolated from family and servants alike. In underscoring this dilemma, Brontë takes aim at an aristocratic order contemptuous of Jane's very existence, and thereby extends the early Victorian critique of aristocracy in works as diverse as *The Women of England* and *Barnaby Rudge*. Blanche Ingram, beautiful, elegant, theatrical, disdainful of all outside her sphere, incarnates aristocratic luxury and display in her very body, which is doubled in the more overt, and explicitly erotic, pathology of Bertha Rochester – who in effect brings the sexual license of empire and the tropics home to England. In the "Quakerish" Jane, by contrast, Blanche's ornamental being is countered by an ideal of inner worth, of moral character located in earnestness, independence, and self-discipline. (Emblematically, Blanche delights in playing charades, whereas Jane has never heard of the activity.) The aristocrat and the madwoman thus become parallel foils to a fundamentally middle-class ethos – which ultimately is embraced by Rochester as well.

The transformation of gender necessarily affects men as well as women. Rochester's eventual humbling places Jane in relation to two different models of masculinity, broadly parallel to those that Thackeray evokes in *Vanity Fair*. (Brontë dedicated the second edition of *Jane Eyre* to Thackeray.) Whereas George Osborne envisions himself as a throwback to the traditional, aristocratic gentleman, compounded of martial valor, dashing presence, and unlimited credit, William Dobbin incarnates a humbler ideal, more suited to an emergent middle class. He is physically awkward and self-effacing – it seems programmatic than Dobbin doesn't dance – but he finds his fulfillment in duty (military and domestic) and kindness to the weak. Thackeray characteristically undercuts easy sympathy: Dobbin's judgment is called into question by his devotion to George's widow, Amelia Sedley, a paragon of domestic femininity reduced to helpless, inane passivity, oblivious to

Dobbin's attentions, absorbed in daydreams and a fiercely protective spoiling of her child. In *Jane Eyre*, by contrast, the humbling of Rochester represents a chastening of the Byronic hero, but Byronic energies are transferred to Jane herself, whose fierce independence is worlds removed from Amelia's parasitic existence. Virginia Woolf would complain that Brontë has no trace of "speculative curiosity"; "all her force, and it is the more tremendous for being constricted, goes into the assertion, 'I live,' 'I hate,' 'I feel'" (Woolf 1953: 161–2). Woolf exaggerates, but she points to the stress that Brontëan passion exerts on the romance plot. The aspiration to a communion that transcends social identity – "it is my spirit that addresses your spirit," Jane tells Rochester, "just as if both had passed through the grave" (C. Brontë 1996: 284) – is felt not only in the elements of gothic convention (mysterious voices, ghostly presences in the attic) but also in the novel's conclusion. In a work so mistrustful of "the medium of custom, conventionalities," marriage itself tends to seem a brittle consolation.

The turbulence of *Jane Eyre* echoes in Anne Brontë's *The Tenant of Wildfell Hall* (1848), which disturbed many readers with its vivid account of a woman trapped in marriage to an alcoholic. (The subject drew closely on the decline of the Brontës' dissolute brother, Bramwell, although it was also the recurrent theme of so-called temperance fiction.) But the violent emotional oscillation of *Jane Eyre*, its incessant movement between rebellion and self-repression – "I know no medium," Jane remarks, in dealing with antipathetic characters, "between absolute submission and determined revolt" (C. Brontë: 446) – is even more boldly rendered in *Wuthering Heights*. Emily Brontë's novel represents a world in which passion explodes the bounds of middle-class gentility, and presses against the very limits of realistic representation. Marriage is not the fulfillment of desire but the containment of a longing that can never be satisfied – and whose intensity vexes personal identity itself. "Nelly, I *am* Heathcliff," Catherine famously exclaims (E. Brontë 1995: 64). And Heathcliff's desire in turn is channeled into revenge against the family that had "rescued" him from his orphaned state. His mysterious disappearance and return in the midst of the novel as a man of fortune aligns economic success with thwarted erotic longing. Far from being vindicated by middle-class refinement, Heathcliff incarnates an image of ambition laying waste that ideal.

From its first publication, readers have found *Wuthering Heights* disturbing, sometimes bewildering, yet riveting – "a strange sort of book," declared one early reviewer, "baffling all regular criticism; yet, it is impossible to begin and not to finish it." "The general effect is inexpressibly painful" yet "the reality of unreality has never been so aptly illustrated." As the young D. G. Rossetti wrote to a friend, "it is a fiend of a book, an incredible monster ... The action is laid in Hell, – only it seems places and people have English names there" (M. Allott 1974: 298, 300). Film adaptations of the book tend to efface its idiosyncratic narrative structure. The novel's action is framed by the journal of one Lockwood, the new tenant of Thrushcross Grange, who gathers the history of its mysteriously savage owner, Heathcliff, through the recollections of the housekeeper, Nelly Dean, whose memories range back over a quarter of a century, to encompass two generations of the intertwined central families. The uncertain reliability of this narration creates a form of perspectivalism, underscored by the play of visual description throughout the novel, which emphasizes passing glimpses through windows or doors left ajar. The recurrent effect is of an unsettling voyeurism into a domestic realm that, far from being a refuge from struggle, papers over unfathomable reservoirs of longing and rage. Thackeray's eavesdropping seems in comparison merely jaunty. The volcanic passion of Heathcliff draws on both gothic romance and Byronic drama: "I have lost the faculty of enjoying their destruction," he laments at one point (E. Brontë 1995: 248), leading Nelly to wonder, "Is he a ghoul, or a vampire?" (250). And Yorkshire itself comes to seem a remote planet, alien to more civilized precincts (48) – an emphasis that would be taken up in Gaskell's 1856 *Life of Charlotte Brontë*, the opening chapters of which evoke her Yorkshire environs less as an English county than as the site of an anthropological expedition.

The singular fury of *Wuthering Heights* underscores by contrast a more direct engagement with social and political conflict in many domestic novels of the decade. Throughout the forties, religious conflict was a central theme of the novel, particularly in the wake of the Oxford movement and a number of well-publicized conversions to Catholicism. Religious faith is a well-nigh inescapable dimension of Victorian experience, where even non-belief typically is felt as resistance to orthodoxy rather than its mere absence. But doctrinal conflicts were especially sharp in the forties and early fifties, when dramas of conversion expressed in outwardly small quarrels very large social tensions. Even for unsympathetic observers, these experiences were full of pathos: religious converts exposed themselves to widespread dismay and derision, which frequently strained or even sundered the most intimate bonds of friendship and family. But the anxiety aroused by the likes of Newman, who "went over" to Rome in 1845, resonated widely in a social order that was still felt to rest on Protestant faith, and it could flare into deeply paranoid responses, particularly after the re-establishment of the Roman Catholic hierarchy in Britain in 1850, a gesture quickly dubbed the "Papal Aggression."

Even before that event, the revival of sisterhoods within the Anglican Church had conjured up fantasies of vulnerable young women deluded by scheming priests – a scenario straight from the pages of Radcliffe and other gothic novelists, whose work would be echoed in many mid-Victorian narratives. Catherine Sinclair's *Beatrice* (1850) dwells on just this fantasy – "The object of Romanism is entirely to subjugate the will and the intellect" (Sinclair n.d.: xiv) – as does *Father Eustace* (1847) by Mrs. Trollope, always quick to seize on topical subjects. The subtitle of William Sewell's *Hawkstone: A Tale of and for England* (1845) captures the sense of fanatical urgency in a host of anti-Catholic fictions. Sewell (1804–74) represents a Catholic "stranger" preying on the town of Hawkestone, fanning industrial revolt, kidnapping Anglican clergy, and murdering children – only to find his rightful fate when he is eaten alive by rats in the basement of Hawkestone Priory. This from an Anglican clergyman and Fellow of Exeter College, Oxford, who was himself a Tractarian, outraged by what he saw as Newman's apostasy. Sewell's sister Elizabeth (1815–1906), although also a High Church controversialist, had a more temperate but more durable career as a novelist, which focused on the role of faith in the lives of women, particularly the unmarried. *Margaret Perceval* (1847), for example, explores the protagonist's wrestling with the rival claims of Anglican and Catholic faith, while *The Experience of Life* (1853), set before the rise of Tractarianism, focuses on the allure of Dissent.

Though Sewell might seem worlds removed from the Brontës in denying her heroines romantic fulfillment, her work in fact underscores a persistent concern in Charlotte's fiction and many domestic novels of the time. Both writers explored the potential clash between faith and domestic fulfillment, under which love may come to seem, as Jane reflects of Rochester, a form of idolatry. "My future husband was becoming to me my own world; and more than the world: almost my hope of heaven. He stood between me and every thought of religion, as an eclipse intervenes between man and the broad sun. I could not, in those days, see God for his creature" (C. Brontë 196: 307). Emily Brontë's characters embrace this eclipse: "I have nearly attained my heaven" (E. Brontë 1995: 233), Heathcliff breathes on his deathbed, and the novel does not dispute this. But Charlotte Brontë's heroines typically struggle with a worry that romance is a falling-off from a higher calling. Not for nothing are the final words of *Jane Eyre* given over to the ascetic missionary, St John Rivers. Lady Georgiana Fullerton (1812–85) pursued a similar theme from a Catholic vantage, focusing on the burdens of piety in aristocratic life. In her first and most popular novel, *Ellen Middleton* (1844), the heroine spends much of her life agonizing over a fit of temper at the age of 15, which caused the death of a young cousin; tortured by both guilt and blackmail, Ellen escapes her ordeal only when she is able to confess the truth and die absolved. Fullerton's next novel, *Grantley Manor* (1847), focuses on a romance agonizingly concealed and thwarted by religious differences – a tension "somewhat too remorselessly protracted," as the *Athenaeum* reviewer complained (Sutherland 1989: 259).

Newman himself turned to the novel to explore his own controversial history in *Loss and Gain, The Story of a Convert* (1848), which recounts the religious doubts and subsequent conversion of an Oxford student named Charles Reding, and offers a vivid portrait of Oxford undergraduate life in the 1830s and 1840s. A more turbulent record, which has been called "the most notorious religious novel of the century" (Sutherland 1989: 458), was produced by one of Newman's more embattled admirers, the Oxford don James Anthony Froude (1818–94), younger brother of one of Newman's early allies (and later Carlyle's biographer). Like the protagonist of *The Nemesis of Faith* (1849), Froude found that neither Newman's charisma nor Carlyle's quest for a new mythus could quell his youthful skepticism. In the figure of Markham Sutherland he imagined a young clergyman whose "honest doubt," as Tennyson would put it, obliges him to surrender his religious offices and to drift in agonizing confusion to the brink of suicide, from which he is rescued only to die with his doubts still unresolved. Froude was scripting his own early career; his outraged superior at Exeter College, none other than William Sewell, publicly burned the novel, and Froude was forced to resign his fellowship.

These topical engagements brought distinctive formal challenges, inasmuch as they resisted the authority of the marriage plot. Newman's *Loss and Gain* in this regard is not far removed from the world of *Jane Eyre*: each explores the potential dissonance between a sense of spiritual calling – whether the priesthood or a woman's personal dignity – and married life. To these concerns, religious experience offered alternative narratives of conflict, suspense, and closure – not merely conversion but martyrdom (which for many Victorians included the fate of the spinster). These possibilities blossomed in a host of domestic fiction indebted to Tractarianism, including Felicia Skene's *Use and Abuse* (1849), a distinctive amalgam of gothic fantasy and Tractarian piety, and a broad swath of the work of the prolific Charlotte Yonge (1823–1901), most notably her 1853 best-seller *The Heir of Redclyffe*. Religious polemics even gave rise to a distinct subgenre of historical fiction set in the age of early Christianity, which seemed an especially vivid mirror of contemporary religious controversy. Kingsley's *Hypatia* (1853) presented the Alexandrian philosopher of its title as a martyr to a religious fanaticism that sounds strangely like first-century Tractarianism (the subtitle, "Old Foes with New Faces," gives the game away). Nicholas Wiseman, recently named Cardinal of Westminster, responded with *Fabiola* (1854), which dwells in some-times excruciating detail on fourth-century martyrdom, and Newman himself pursued similar interests in *Callista* (1856), set in third-cen-tury North Africa. In every instance the setting licensed often grue-some violence, a feature of the subgenre that would persist at least until Walter Pater's *Marius the Epicurean* (1885), and hints at the powerfully masochistic energies undergirding mid-Victorian religious discipline.

The Novel of Development

In representing a struggle towards a more assured sense of identity grounded in new forms of belief, all of these narratives recall the model of *Sartor Resartus*, and, more distantly, Goethe's *Wilhelm Meister*, the founding example of the *Bildungsroman*, the novel of development or education. (Richard Monckton-Milnes saw in *The Nemesis of Faith* "a sort of religious anti-religious *Wilhelm Meister*" [Howe 1966: 234].) The form obviously draws on the energies of autobiography and the sense of individual distinction so crucial to romanticism, a view with which Rousseau memorably opened his *Confessions* (1770): "I may not be better than other men," Rousseau averred, "but at least I am different: *au moins, je suis autre*" (Rousseau 1953: 17). In the *Bildungsroman*, the self-discovery and self-definition of the protagonist tend to be more emphatically social, conjured up in large part by new prospects of social mobility, a world of possibility at once exhilarating and fearful. The challenge is memorably evoked in the bewilderment of Pip in *Great Expectations*, who undergoes something we've learned to call an identity crisis: "I was a blacksmith's boy but yesterday; I am – what shall I say I am – to-day?" (Dickens 1996: 248). The same interest in the fluidity of identity is registered by the sheer prominence of orphans in Victorian fiction. In a world where birth does not so predictably determine one's social prospects, identity itself is at once more malleable and less secure.

Of course, identity remained powerfully constrained by social class and, even more, by gender. The *Bildungsroman* has an inherent self-reflexivity that naturally appealed to novelists: the challenge of constructing a coherent narrative was the challenge of finding a satisfying shape and purpose in a life or career – which might well be one's own. But the shapes available to men and women remained profoundly different. For a male protagonist, the main line of fulfillment comes in the public sphere, and marriage and domestic life are important principally as they support or obstruct the hero's endeavors there. For heroines, the most consequential choice is invariably who, or whether, to marry. Thus *Jane Eyre*, the greatest female *Bildungsroman* in English, offers Jane the choice between religious service and a truly companionate marriage. We may hear in the background Carlyle's imperative, "know what thou canst work at," but that command typically pressures only those female characters who, through accident or choice, pursue a life outside of marriage.

For novelists, writing itself naturally had special resonance as a vocation, but to convey the allure of the writer's life one needed an audience willing to believe that it was a worthy calling, a career in which success or failure was a matter of some moment. The construction of "the man of letters" in the 1830s of course spoke to precisely this concern, and novels about the development of a novelist first appear in England in that decade, in conjunction with the consolidation of "literature" as a source of something more than amusement. Bulwer's *Ernest Maltravers* (1837) is the earliest example of the genre (with a pun on its hero's first name that would resonate for the rest of the century). G. H. Lewes's more earnest *Ranthorpe*, about the struggles of an aspiring poet, appeared in 1847, and along with Thomas Miller's *Geoffrey Malvern* (1843) seems to have influenced Kingsley's *Alton Locke*. But the *Bildungsroman* really came to prominence in England with the epochal pendant of Thackeray's *Pendennis* and Dickens's *David Copperfield*, both published in 1850 (Thackeray's began appearing in serial form six months before Dickens's novel, in November 1848).

The fame of Dickens's "favorite child," as he called *David Copperfield*, has overshadowed Thackeray's exactly contemporary novel of a writer's life. For all their differences, both works locate the protagonist's central challenge less in writing itself – an activity that Dickens evokes only very obliquely – than in a moral struggle towards self-mastery. Pendennis's "greatest enemy," the novel announces, is himself; and David similarly diagnoses at the root of his unhappiness an "undisciplined heart." Both failings are elicited above all in relations with women, both doting mothers and prospective wives. But the imaginative foci of the two novels are otherwise crucially divergent in both social milieu and narrative arc, which were avidly explored in the many reviews that considered the two works together.

Most notably, Dickens's novel is an autobiographical fiction, written in the first person. "The Personal History and Experience of David Copperfield the Younger" dwells at great length on childhood trauma – tapping into personal reminiscence so intimate that Dickens was unable to confess to anyone save his close friend and biographer, John Forster, that David's humiliating time at Warren's blacking factory was drawn from his own life. Thackeray's third-person narration, by contrast, opens with Pendennis already 18, and being tempted by compromising infatuation with an actress 10 years his senior. Pen's first 16 years are passed over in a single chapter and a few subsequent retrospects, whereas it is not until the fourth number that the 10-year-old David begins his famous ordeal in the blacking factory, and his schooldays do not come to an end until the seventh. Pen's reminiscences are most energetic and voluminous – and, for many readers, most alluring – in recounting the bohemian life of literary London in the 1830s: as Andrew Lang later remembered, *Pendennis* made him want to "run away to literature" (Cross 1985: 110). In this socially marginal sphere, moral waywardness is measured, as so often in Thackeray, by the idea of the gentleman, here incarnated by Pen's bachelor uncle, Colonel Pendennis. All of this reflects the investments of Thackeray "the university man," a status that set him apart from most of his fellow novelists, and informed his famous complaint in the Preface that contemporary prudishness inhibited more open depictions of "what moves in the real world":

> Since the author of Tom Jones was buried, no writer of fiction among us has been permitted to depict to his utmost power a MAN. We must

drape him, and give him a certain conventional simper. Society will not tolerate the Natural in our Art. (Thackeray 1991: xvi)

In Dickens, by contrast, the gentleman's urbanity is a suspect virtue, the norm itself more often travestied than realized, in keeping with a focus towards the shabby-genteel end of the social spectrum, which is epitomized by the hapless Micawber. The one prominent character of more distinguished descent, Steerforth, harks back to the aristocratic rakes of Dickens's early novels, though he is invested with a more substantial psychology, which anticipates a host of deracinated, cynical idlers that figure prominently in the later novels. Steerforth is a particularly seductive model to the younger Davy – or "Daisy," as he calls him – whose lapse of discipline he doubles in more destructive fashion, and their homoerotically charged friendship echoes David's entanglement with the grasping Uriah Heep, a predator drawn from the lower rungs of the social ladder.

Thackeray's novel, in short, draws identity in more emphatically social terms, from the more pronounced influence of an extended family to the greater attention to nuances of social form. The Dickensian self depends on a more pronounced interiority, with sexuality in particular generating a more feverish sense of danger than in Thackeray, and with a corresponding sense of guilt more powerful than the shameful lapses of honorable conduct that afflict Pendennis. Reviews of the two works registered this different emphasis in formal as well as social terms. Dickens's greater range was that of an "ideal" art that readily lapsed into the "extravagant" or "grotesque," Thackeray's was an art more devoted to "the real," more attentive to outward form, but in its greater detachment more liable to cynicism. That distinction would be more broadly elaborated in the 1850s, with the rise of "realism" as a central concern in discussion of the novel generally. But the reception of these two works confirmed the new cultural stature that the novel had achieved over the course of the 1840s. David Masson, one of the most astute mid-Victorian critics, concluded his review by complaining of a lack of effort toward "artistic perfection" among contemporary novelists, who "candidly own that they write to make money and amuse people" (Tillotson and Hawes 1968: 126). This may seem a familiar refrain, but prior to the 1840s few critics would have envisioned the novel as anything but a popular amusement. The bar of "artistic perfection" suggests the new authority of the form.

Art, Politics, and Faith

Poetry in the latter half of the 1840s reflected the currency of both domestic narrative and religious crisis. Browning in 1850 published a volume entitled *Christmas Eve and Easter-Day*, which contained two lengthy personal narratives meditating on contemporary challenges to Christian belief. But his more powerful engagements with the topic came in the monologue form, which offered an extremely supple vehicle for exploring psychologies of faith and doubt. "An Epistle of Karshish" (1855), for example, transposes to the first century CE a recognizably contemporary conflict between a scientific habit of mind and religious experience. Browning imagines an Arab doctor confronting in his travels the story of "a Nazarene physician" who allegedly revived a man from the dead – a story Karshish tries to dismiss as sheer delusion, but which leaves his skeptical materialism deeply shaken. He has been listening to the strangely riveting first-hand account of a man named Lazarus. "How can he give his neighbour the real ground /His own conviction?" the fascinated Karshish asks (ll. 216–17; Browning 1970). Browning's monologues increasingly seek to evoke just such grounds, anchoring varieties of "conviction" – religious, aesthetic, moral, of more or less plausible content – in the evocation of a distinctive psychology, albeit a psychology unusually responsive to a skeptical implied audience. Much of the power lies in Browning's ability to evoke a sense of unresolved ambivalence. Thus "Bishop Blougram's Apology," from his 1855 volume *Men and Women*, has left critics to this day debating how to respond to the Bishop's reflections on his office and faith, an eminently suave, worldly, unruffled self-portrait from a character clearly modeled on the widely demonized bishops of the newly restored Roman Catholic hierarchy. The example of Browning's monologues would be developed less equivocally in memoir and autobiography, supremely John Henry Newman's *Apologia pro Vita Sua* of 1864, which takes up in dead earnest and at great length precisely the challenge that Karshish ponders: how can he give his neighbor the real ground of a faith and a life that so deeply affronts most Englishmen?

Victorian poetry also increasingly engaged the domestic interests central to the novel. The success of "Lady Geraldine's Courtship" planted in Elizabeth Barrett's mind the idea of a long poem set in contemporary times, which eventually culminated in *Aurora Leigh* (1856).

More immediately, however, it provided an uncanny model for a strange turn of events in Barrett's highly sheltered life. In January of 1845 she received an extraordinary letter from the young poet whose work she had commended in her own poetry, but to whom she was otherwise a complete stranger: "I love your verses with all my heart, dear Miss Barrett," wrote Robert Browning, " … into me it has gone, and part of me it become, this great living poetry of yours … I do, as I say, love these books with all my heart – and I love you too" (Browning and Barrett 1969: 3). The famous courtship would be enshrined in two literary memorials. The first was the continuation of a project already underway, which would draw its title from Robert's affection for "Catarina to Camoens." *Sonnets from the Portuguese* is a sequence of 44 Petrarchan sonnets recounting a courtship that culminates in a confident and enduring love. The conjunction of nakedly personal expression – Barrett Browning did not show it to Robert until they had been married for three years – and the sheer popularity of the poem (is there a love poem in English quoted more often than the penultimate sonnet, "How do I love thee? Let me count the ways …"?) has struck many critics as a hallmark of sentimentalism. Yet the poem inaugurated a mid-century revival of the love sonnet sequence, and (more broadly) helped to shape a major Victorian poetic innovation, the long poem telling a story through a lyrical sequence in a modern setting. The appearance of *Sonnets from the Portuguese* in 1850, a few months after *In Memoriam*, would soon be followed by Arnold's *Switzerland*, Clough's *Amours de Voyage*, Patmore's *The Angel in the House*, and Tennyson's *Maud*, and would continue to resonate into the 1890s.

The second great monument to the Brownings' courtship was their correspondence. Although it would not be published for nearly 50 years, it captures the extraordinary energies that mid-Victorian writers invested in letters, and the peculiar satisfactions that letter-writing afforded. Letters of course offered forms of contact across distances that remained difficult to travel. But even between neighbors they also enabled forms of intimacy that would have felt more awkward in face-to-face encounters, and sometimes offered a semblance of conversation by means of an extraordinary postal service that, following the introduction of the penny post in 1839, provided up to five deliveries per day. Letter-writing was particularly valuable to middle-class women, whose mobility and intellectual opportunity were in various ways circumscribed. The sheer volume of correspondence between the two poets suggests that it must have been written with a good deal of spontaneity – albeit one that had been honed by years of practice. This exchange offers the further pleasure of unrivaled insight into the minds of two important English poets, each writing for an unusually sympathetic audience (something for which their poetic careers had taught them to be deeply grateful).

Such revelations were a source of increasing fascination across the century, which is reflected in the upsurge of memoirs and biographies of writers, which typically incorporated large swaths of correspondence, sometimes of unsettling frankness. (Richard Monckton-Milnes's *Life and Letters of John Keats* (1848) provoked considerable controversy for including Keats's passionate letters to his lover Fanny Brawne.) The Brownings, however, offer the fantasy of an epistolary courtship brought to life. It was a fairy tale – most obviously, an awakening of Sleeping Beauty. But that parallel ceded an unsettling amount of control to the male rescuer. Much of the emotional complexity of the letters derives from Barrett's discomfort, despite her powerful yearning to escape from her isolation, with Browning's eagerness to assume the role of chivalric hero rescuing the damsel in distress – or, in the particular form that haunted Browning's imagination, Perseus rescuing Andromeda from a monster, a role that Barrett's tyrannical father was born to play. The correspondence breaks off on September 17, 1846; the next day, Elizabeth Barrett left 50 Wimpole Street to be married. Her father, who had forbidden all of his children to marry, lived up to his threats: he never again communicated with his daughter.

After their marriage, the Brownings made their way to Italy, eventually settling in Florence, where they joined a sizeable community of British expatriates. Italy loomed large in the Victorian imagination – in part simply as a haven of warmth and sunlight, which had a special allure for Britons fleeing a harsh climate (particularly invalids like Barrett Browning). Long a central destination on the aristocratic "Grand Tour," Italy also resonated for an expanding audience of travelers as a primary origin and site of culture, and thus for the forms of education and refinement associated above all with the experience of visual art. Historically a secondary presence in British culture, painting and sculpture assumed much greater public significance over the course of the nineteenth century through enhanced access to great collections, both through the founding of municipal galleries – the National Gallery in London was funded in 1824 – and the increasing hospitality of private collectors to public exhibition. Browning's monologues frequently explore the mingled allure and unease aroused by closer contact with unfamiliar color and form, particularly that of religious painting, an art often boldly sensual in its representation of sacred history. Even by the early 1830s, in the fictional chronology of George Eliot's *Middlemarch*, the great collections of the Vatican represent a new "language" that overwhelms Dorothea Casaubon, who thereby epitomizes the response of a puritanical culture newly exposed to the sometimes unsettling glories of Renaissance painting.

A large body of writing developed to address this challenge, ranging from travel guides, in which art galleries and collections occupied a large place, to more systematic treatments, typically organized thematically. The prolific writings of Anna Jameson (1794–1860) encompass the spectrum, ranging from exhibition reviews and a handbook to the public galleries of London (1845) to a series of book-length studies gathered as *Sacred and Legendary Art* (1857), as well as a host of memoirs of artists. (She also produced a number of works exploring the lives of women, including an early novel, *Diary of an Ennuyée*, a study of the Madonna in art, and collective biographies of famous queens, society women, and "loves of the poets.") The most influential Victorian guide to the world of visual art was John Ruskin (1819–1900), whose idiosyncratic childhood (memorably described in his unfinished autobiography, *Praeterita*) encapsulated the larger tensions besetting much contemporary response to the arts. Ruskin was the only child of a wealthy and deeply conservative Scottish couple, who brought John up in highly protective isolation and strict piety (much of his childhood was passed in reading and re-reading aloud with his mother the entire Bible). His father, a sherry merchant, also was an art collector, who especially prized the works of J. M. W. Turner (whom the young Ruskin visited in his studio), and who took the family on extensive travel in Italy. From this experience Ruskin came to regard art and architecture not only as sources of ravishing pleasure, but as the crowning embodiments of human value – and human corruption. "To see clearly," he would declare, "is poetry, prophecy, and religion, all in one" (*Works* 5: 333) – a credo that suggests his deep indebtedness to Carlyle.

With such a foundation, art criticism became a criticism of life itself, a comprehensive engagement with human experience, and Ruskin's writing is among the most varied and voluminous of any Victorian writer. The sheer range of his interests is encapsulated (if that is the word) in *Modern Painters*, "Dedicated to the Landscape Artists of England," which appeared in five volumes published over 17 years. Ruskin began in 1843 with a defense of the painting of Turner against contemporary derision ("By a Graduate of Oxford" – the wealthy Ruskin still upheld a model of the author as an anonymous gentleman) and concluded in 1860 with two increasingly digressive volumes full of extravagantly fanciful allegorical readings of favorite images. Throughout the project an outwardly logical, synoptical structure – the work opens "I. Of General Principles. Of the Nature of the Ideas Conveyable by Art" – is at war with immersion in the sheer proliferation of beautiful particulars. While the early work concentrated on art's fidelity to nature – answering criticism that Turner's art was merely muddy – the later works expanded in their social engagement, in effect gathering in the lives of the figures in the landscape, and of the painters and the societies from which they emerged. Noticed initially for the sheer force of his descriptive power and his distinctive style, by turns clinically precise, slashing, lyrical, and hortatory (with a deeply biblical allusiveness), Ruskin was increasingly recognized as one of the most powerful and idiosyncratic of Victorian social critics, who perpetually confounded party labels (such as "Radical Tory"). At the outset of his career, English art criticism was largely confined to exhibit reviews. By 1860, Ruskin had so transfigured the genre that "art criticism" seemed inadequate to describe his work, which had become a thoroughgoing engagement with social and political history, and Ruskin in his ferocious self-confidence had become one of the most admired and reviled of Victorian sages.

Ruskin was drawn to Italy preeminently for its landscapes and its art; he spent much of the latter part of the 1840s in Venice, the city that most captivated him, working on *The Stones of Venice* (1851). To different travelers, Italy offered seductions beyond architecture. It was a locus of freedom, traditionally of the erotic pleasures that had so captivated Byron and other sexual adventurers, but more recently of movements for political liberty, as various Italian leaders struggled to consolidate an Italian nation freed from subjugation by foreign powers. Barrett Browning of course had been drawn to political engagement in her earlier lyrics, and the first poem she wrote in Italy was apparently "The Runaway Slave at Pilgrim's Point," composed at the request of the Anti-Slavery Bazaar of Boston. She referred to it as a ballad, but it is a long dramatic monologue, motivated by a deeply personal sense of guilt: "I belong to a family of West Indian slaveholders," she wrote to Ruskin ten years later, "and if I believed in curses, I should be afraid"

(Mermin 1989: 156–7). Her first long poem written in Italy was *Casa Guidi Windows* (1851), a poem built around the vexing contrast between Tuscany's glorious cultural past and its dismal political present. The title refers to the view from the Brownings' apartment, where Elizabeth in 1847 watched crowds who seemed to be heralding the Risorgimento, the "resurgence" and reunification of Italy under Grand Duke Leopold II, but later pondered the collapse of those hopes in the wake of revolutions across the continent in 1848. The poem, organized in two parts recording these separate responses, aroused little enthusiasm, in part because readers did not much care for poetry immersed in the intricacies of foreign politics – particularly when it came from a woman.

A more oblique response to a different political struggle (albeit one set in an indeterminate southern clime) came from Tennyson, who in *The Princess* (1847) managed to fuse his familiar bent for romantic frustration with attention to growing calls for women's rights. An emergent feminism was a natural by-product of the importance attached to domestic womanhood, but much of Tennyson's immediate impetus seems to have come from America. To be sure, British novelists were devoting increasing attention to women who resisted their standing as "relative creatures." Before *Jane Eyre* appeared, Geraldine Jewsbury's *Zoe* (1845), one of the earliest Victorian novels dealing with religious doubt, recounted the life of a highly educated woman in the later eighteenth century, who moves through literary society in London and France, undermines the vocation of a Jesuit priest, and (after the death of her elderly husband) becomes passionately involved with Mirabeau. "At last," Bulwer-Lytton commented, "an honest woman speaks out, right or wrong, to the world" (Sutherland 1989: 689). But while Jewsbury was influenced by the example of George Sand in France, Tennyson was especially attentive to the emergence of an American social type. Although the Seneca Falls Convention would not take place until the following year, he evidently had absorbed from recent writings about radical thought and social experiments in America – even outwardly parodic treatments such as *Martin Chuzzlewit* – an image of the "strong-minded" woman. He recast this image in his title character, a woman who renounces marriage in order to found a university for women – to the predictable amazement and outrage of the men around her.

A poem about a women's university might seem the very cutting-edge of topicality in 1847, but even Barrett Browning, who had heard about it as "The University of Women," remarked, "isn't the world too old & fond of steam, for blank verse poems, in ever so many books, to be written on the fairies?" (Tennyson 1969: 741). The sheer iconoclasm of the topic helps to explain Tennyson's characteristic recourse to defensive ironic framing (as in "The Epic"). The poem struck most readers as a bewildering amalgam of daring social speculation, Persian romance, and domestic farce, with male undergraduates cross-dressing in order to sneak into the women's sanctuary. When Princess Ida rejects the nameless Prince, to whom she had been pledged in infancy, her affront to traditional femininity staggers the young man and arouses a chorus of male denunciation, in which the most vehement voice is the Prince's father: "Man is the hunter; woman is his game" (l. 5.147; Tennyson 1969). Over against this hoary model of sexual domination, the Prince is allowed to seem deeply sympathetic to Ida's aims, the herald of a new kind of masculinity: "Henceforth thou hast a helper, me, that knows /The woman's cause is man's" (ll. 7.242–3). But this declaration comes only after Ida has renounced her project as a selfish corruption of her "cause" and acknowledges instead the more pressing claims of the Prince's love (brought out by his striking passivity through much of the poem, in which Ida's resistance seems to have undermined any secure ground of action). The psychology is unusually brittle, and Tennyson hedged his bets from the outset. He titled the poem *The Princess: A Medley*, and framed the poem with a narrative in which Princess Ida is the collective fantasy of a group of undergraduates on a summer holiday, on the grounds of a country estate hosting a meeting of the local Mechanics' Institute. Tennyson was evidently deeply captivated by the topic; he tinkered with the poem through seven editions, most notably adding a feature that until recently has been the only part of the poem frequently reprinted: a set of ravishing lyrics interpolated between the seven parts of the poem, including "The splendour falls on castle walls," "Sweet and low, sweet and low," and "Ask me no more." Ultimately, however, he pronounced it "only a medley."

"I gave up all hope of Tennyson after *The Princess*," recalled his friend Edward Fitzgerald, but by the end of the decade Tennyson had become the benchmark against which young poets were measured. In November of 1848 appeared *The Bothie of Toper- na-Fuosich: A Long-Vacation Pastoral*, recounting the adventures of a "reading party" of Oxford undergraduates in the Scottish Highlands. Written in rough approximation of classical hexameters, the poem explores with a mostly deft comic touch the ironies announced in the title: that of a group of university men encountering Highland society through the lens of Theocritus, and in the process coming to reconsider both Greek poetry and their own privilege. The poem rather gingerly broaches contemporary radical politics in the figure of Hewson, clearly the closest thing to an authorial surrogate:

> Philip Hewson the poet,
> Hewson, the radical hot, hating lords and scorning ladies,
> Silent mostly, but often reviling in fire and fury
> Feudal tenures, mercantile lords, competitions, and bishops ...
> (ll. 1.131–4; Clough 1951)

The poem echoes many of the concerns of *The Princess* – Hewson also is hot against the constricting model of modern womanhood – but the romance is inflected with more assured irony and social realism than Tennyson's poem. When Hewson meets in Elspie of the Highlands the girl of his dreams, he sees no future for them together except in emigration to New Zealand. The free-wheeling political discussion offended some reviewers, others sniffed at the poem as too much for "the initiated" (so *The Spectator* complained), while some fellow initiates paraded their erudition in objecting to false quantity in the hexameters. But many readers were delighted by the poem's interweaving of evocative landscape and novelistic social portraiture: "It is a noble poem. Tennyson must look to his laurels" was the verdict of Emerson, in a letter to the author, Arthur Hugh Clough (Thorpe 1972: 33).

For the relatively few contemporaries acquainted with his poetry, Clough became the emblem of a debilitating struggle with religious doubt, and for some a paragon of failed genius, almost a Victorian Coleridge. At his early death in 1862 he was widely seen as never having lived up to his early promise. Born in England but raised in the United States, Clough enjoyed great success at Rugby School (where he became a close friend of the schoolmaster's son, Matthew Arnold) and later at Oxford. But he resigned his fellowship at Oriel College soon after publication of the *Bothie*, because he felt unable to subscribe to the Thirty-Nine Articles of the Church of England, as required of all Oxford fellows. The strenuous moralism of Arnold's Rugby nurtured a sometimes tormented religious scrupulosity, but also a keenly satiric observation of English society, both of which found their way into his poetry and discouraged him from publishing it. Little of the buoyancy in *The Bothie* informs Clough's later work, save in a more pointedly, sometimes savagely ironic vein. Clough's lyrics are largely divided between stern anatomies of his own skepticism (much influenced by the German biblical scholar Strauss, who also would have a large impact on George Eliot) and often fierce attacks on smug religiosity. "Qui Laborat, Orat" rehearses the tenuous consolations of Carlyle; in the more wrackingly skeptical "Easter Day," written in Naples in 1849, Clough evokes in an irregular ode (reminiscent of Wordsworth's "Intimations" Ode) a lacerating skepticism clinched by the refrain, "He is not risen." A much briefer (perhaps incomplete) second part seems to temper this with the refrain, "He is risen," but more arresting is the cancelled opening of this section:

> So while the blear-eyed pimp beside me walked,
> And talked,
> For instance, of the beautiful danseuse,
> And 'Eccellenza sure must see, if he would choose'
>
> (Clough 1953: 479)

The sharp worldly observation – daring in both subject and idiom – characterizes Clough's greatest works, in which the aims of poetry clearly are converging with those of the novel, particularly French realists such as Balzac. "The Latest Decalogue" offers a withering evocation of English hypocrisy in a travesty of the Ten Commandments:

> Though shalt have one God only; who
> Would be at the expense of two?
> No graven images may be
> Worshipped, except the currency ...
> Honour thy parents; that is, all
> From whom advancement may befall;
> Thou shalt not kill; but need'st not strive
> Officiously to keep alive ...
>
> (ll. 1–4, 11–14)

The affinities of poetry and the novel are even more striking in *Amours de Voyage*, a testament to the allure of Italy more equivocal than *Casa Guidi Windows*. A gently satiric narrative in epistolary form, following affluent English travelers in Rome during the revolutions of 1848, the poem conjoins keen social description with subtle mockery of its focal consciousness, a young man abroad and adrift, mulling over the possibility of heroic action while listening to the roar of nearby cannon. Written in the early 1850s but published only in 1858 (in America), the poem sums up a good deal of Clough's own self-division in its central character, Claude: "So through the city I wander, unsatisfied ever, /Reverent so I accept, doubtful because I revere" (ll. 1.283–4; Clough 1953). More audacious still is "Dipsychus," which develops from an opening citation of "Easter Day" a series of 13 scenes loosely modeled on Goethe's *Faust* crossed with the satiric edge of late Byron (but with more formal variety). The protagonist, whose name ("Two-Souled") captures Clough's familiar vacillation, is another young man on the Grand Tour, this time in Venice, where he is attended by a raffish "Spirit" whose cynicism points up the struggles of the title character, earnestly wrestling with the worldly wisdom Clough so often satirized:

> Where are the great, whom thou would'st wish to praise thee?
> Where are the pure, whom thou would'st choose to love thee?
> Where are the brave, to stand supreme above thee,
> Whose high commands would rouse, whose chidings raise thee?
>
> (iv.122–5)

This introspection is answered by the Spirit:

> As I sat at the café, I said to myself,
> They may talk all they please about what they call pelf,
> They may sneer as they like about eating and drinking,
> But help it I cannot, I cannot help thinking,
> How pleasant it is to have money, heigh ho!
> How pleasant it is to have money.
>
> (iv.130–5)

The ironic verve of *Dipsychus* has led many to regard it as Clough's greatest achievement, but the satire was too difficult to disentangle from cynicism, and the poem was never published in his lifetime.

As he dramatized a young poet's self-doubt, Clough also raised provocative questions about the value and decorums of poetry. Who was it addressing, what purpose did it serve, what subjects were appropriate, did criteria of "dignity" still obtain? Those issues would grow increasingly explicit in critical debate over the next two decades, but they emerged in the reception of an 1849 volume entitled *The Strayed Reveller*, by "A". The keenest readers recognized a profound conflict at the heart of the slender volume, which was reflected in the two longest poems. The title poem looked to Book X of *The Odyssey* to evoke a fundamentally romantic conception of poetry as a joy won at the cost of suffering: "such a price /The Gods exact for song: /To become what we sing" (ll. 232–4; Arnold 1979). Yet "Resignation" celebrates freedom as a conquest of emotion, an amalgam of Wordsworthian detachment and ancient stoicism yielding an insight "whose secret is not joy, but peace." Critics generally praised the various figures of displacement or helplessness – the strayed reveler, a gipsy child by the seashore, "The Abandoned Merman," "The Sick King in Bokhara" ("And what I would, I cannot do") – in which the influence of Wordsworth and Tennyson is especially marked. But nearly all reviewers expressed some impatience with the recurrent appeal to classical forms and subject matter. In a generally favorable review, Kingsley put the objection with his usual bluntness: "What does the age want with fragments of an Antigone?" (Dawson 1973: 43). The subsequent career of the volume's author, Matthew Arnold, might be thought of as a sustained meditation on just that question. Kingsley's desire for a poetry engaging contemporary life may have been unusually vehement: "Life unrolling *before* him! As if it could unroll to purpose anywhere but in him; as if the poet, or any one else, could know aught of life except by living it, and that in bitter, painful earnest" (44). But many reviewers found the erudite melancholy remote and recherché, a kind of escapism. Their reactions hint at anxiety that poetry itself could come to seem ephemeral, a view that soon would be openly embraced in Morris's "idle singer of an empty day."

In Memoriam

Events of 1850 dispelled such a worry, at least for the time being. On June 1, Moxon published a volume-length poem entitled *In Memoriam AHH Obit MDCCCXXXIII*. Praise for the work was immediate, widespread, fervent, and lasting, and it secured the unnamed author, Tennyson, not only the Laureateship but also consensus that the Laureate was (for once) truly the major poet of his time. When *The Prelude* was published a few months later, following Wordsworth's death in April, the edition of 2,000 required a year to sell; *In Memoriam* went through five editions and roughly 25,000 copies in a year and a half. After Prince Albert's death from cholera in 1861, Queen Victoria confided to Tennyson, "Next to the Bible, my comfort is *In Memoriam*."

Later admirers have been more skeptical: in T. S. Eliot's influential account, "Its faith is a poor thing, but its doubt is a very intense experience" (Eliot 1932: 336). The power of Tennysonian doubt, however, may suggest why Victorians found its faith so consoling, and why it has remained a central document of Victorian culture.

In Memoriam is often called one of the three great English elegies, joining Milton's *Lycidas* and Shelley's *Adonais*. Unlike those poems, however, it only rarely evokes pastoral convention, and then principally to address an anxiety about both the design and the audience of the poem. In section 21, for example, "I sing to him that rests below," the trope of piping to his dead friend conjures up a profound unease about audience, as each passing "traveler" derides the poet. One complains that the poet "would make weakness weak," effeminizing himself and his hearers; another remarks, "He loves to make parade of pain," affirming his own sensibility more than any respect for the dead; yet another objects that "private sorrow's barren song" has no place in a world of momentous political struggle and scientific advance. The feebleness of the poet's response – "I do but sing because I must, / And pipe but as the linnets sing" – appeals to a Millian understanding of absolute emotional integrity, suggesting how powerfully Tennyson feels these objections – which are challenges, ultimately, to lyric poetry itself.

Tennyson not merely risks but to a degree incites such response through resolute commitment to the particulars of mourning. For most of the nearly 17 years of composition, Tennyson did not think of himself as writing a single poem. Not long before publication, he was still referring to a "book of elegies," a phrase that does justice not only to the separate integrity of each section, but also to the difficulty of reconciling the ragged grief with some larger design. The poem offers landmarks by which to chart a chronological progression, which unfolds over roughly three years: sections 28, 78, and 104 are set at Christmas, and sections 72 and 98 mark the anniversary of the death. But the narrative structure is tenuous, inasmuch as the large emotional arc – from numbing grief through moral questioning and rage through acquiescence into something like celebration – is not clearly tethered to anything like a plot. The sonnet sequence offers a formal precedent, and Shakespeare's sonnets clearly were especially resonant for Tennyson in their celebration of intense male friendship. Indeed, some early readers, including Hallam's father, were unsettled by this affiliation, which has been developed in recent criticism that elicits the powerful homoeroticism in Tennyson's grief. But structurally the poem more closely resembles a private journal or diary. The diary typically is divided between ongoing chronology and fixation on certain recurrent themes, and the entries may seem highly disjunctive, moving without explanation to new attitudes or concerns. Much occurs in the interstices, as it were, whether through genuine resolution of conflict or sheer exhaustion, which may be registered in highly oblique fashion, through subtle shifts of attention or tone. A diary, moreover, raises questions of audience akin to those that trouble Tennyson. At times poetry feels a wholly private exercise, whose value may be anchored less in self-understanding than in sheer routine – "that sad mechanic exercise /Like dull narcotics, numbing pain" (5.7–8; Tennyson 1969)

At the same time, however, the design of the poem works to give a larger shape, and thus an emblematic force, to the central crisis. In this regard, it resembles the central episodes of *Sartor Resartus* and Mill's *Autobiography*. As in those works, the appeal is to something more particular than the universality of suffering. Tennyson struggles to articulate through personal grief a host of more topical anxieties, appealing to forms of awareness and perplexity that made his suffering seem distinctly modern, because it could be gathered into a theme of progress, both personal and collective. Unlike most autobiographies – but in keeping with Wordsworth's example – the body of the poem opens with its central crisis:

> I held it truth, with him who sings
> 　　To one clear harp in diver tones
> 　　That men may rise on stepping-stones
> Of their dead selves to higher things.
>
> But who shall so forecast the years
> 　　And find in loss a gain to match?
> 　　Or reach a hand through time to catch
> The far-off interest of tears?
>
> 　　　　　　　　　　　　　　　　(1.1–8)

The poet casts the rupture in his personal history in terms that evoke a host of grand Victorian narratives. His language conjures up "loss and gain" both personal and economic; one's "rise" in the world, or towards the more inclusive awareness charted in Goethean *Bildung* and other nineteenth-century narratives of personal development;

"progress" conceived in collective terms, as "the march of mind"; even – in some ways the most vivid figurative cluster of the poem – in terms of the development of humankind as a species moving towards "higher things." Might all of these other narratives turn out to reflect groundless faiths, to be records more of rupture than continuity? Tennyson thus frames his dilemma in a manner that unites emotional, formal, and intellectual challenges. The recuperation of his dead friend Arthur Hallam – the sense that Hallam is not irrevocably lost, that his death was not senseless – may restore a larger faith that all is "toil cooperant to an end," both in the world at large and in the structure of the poem.

Tennyson's doubt is most sweepingly phrased in wrestling with modern science. Though Tennyson's proto-evolutionary speculations notably antedate Darwin's *Origin of Species*, he had been deeply impressed by Charles Lyell's writings on geology and especially by Robert Chambers's *Vestiges of the Natural History of Creation*, which caused a sensation when it was published anonymously in 1844. Haunted by the findings of modern geology, so starkly at odds with the consoling image of "Mother Nature," the poet contemplates in the fossils of extinct species an image of history as recurrent catastrophe. What evidence of a beneficent Being could one find in this record of continual, seemingly implacable destruction? And what of "Man, her last work,"

> Who trusted God was love indeed
> And love Creation's final law –
> Tho' Nature, red in tooth and claw
> With ravine, shrieked against his creed ...
>
> (56.13–16)

If Man, too, is destined to share the fate of "Dragons of the prime," his life and hopes are "a dream, /A discord." "Nature, red in tooth and claw" is a phrase that has drifted free of its context to sum up nothing less than modern evolutionary thought. For Tennyson, however, it speaks a far more intimate betrayal, rather like that afflicting the hero in *The Princess*: a man bereft of love cries for the attention of a maternal being, who answers his pleas with the peremptory "I care for nothing, all shall go" (56.4).

Tellingly, the poem offers no solution to this most harrowing of doubts. "Peace; come away" the next section opens, as if this perplexity never can be laid to rest. It is relegated to a realm of mystery eased by more immediate forms of solace in the visible world, and in the growing, visceral sense that Hallam is not wholly absent. Tennysonian doubt is so powerful in part because even his most sweeping affirmations of faith give away so much to the worldview of modern science. The Prologue that introduces the poem with an address to "Strong Son of God, immortal Love," already concedes that religion is a world beyond "knowledge":

> We have but faith; we cannot know,
>   For knowledge is of things we see;
>   And yet we trust it comes from thee,
> A beam in darkness: let it grow.
>
> (Prologue 21–4)

As throughout the poem, the drama of absence and doubt is reinforced by the distinctive stanza form. The nested rhymes create a potent sense of enclosure and containment that underscores the balance or tension of opposing forces: here, for instance, it may seem that "let it grow" is resisted by "we cannot know." By the same token, the breach of this closure creates striking effects, which suggest an abrupt expansion or acceleration of the argument – at times, a dizzying exhilaration, as in section 86, "Sweet after showers, ambrosial air ..." in which a single sentence unfolds across four stanzas and eleven enjambed lines to culminate in the imagination beckoning

> From belt to belt of crimson seas
>   On leagues of odor streaming far,
>   To where in yonder orient star,
> A thousand spirits whisper 'Peace.'
>
> (86.13–16)

It is in some ways a microcosm of the latter half of the poem: the ebbing of grief is reflected in newly vivid responsiveness to the landscape, whose evocative power in turn evokes an increasing assurance that Hallam remains present to him, that like the evening star, "Sweet Hesper-Phosphor,"

> Thou, like my present and my past,
> Thy place is changed, thou art the same.
>
> (121.19–20)

Rupture is repaired, and harmony reaffirmed in an epithalamion, which forms the poem's Epilogue. Though the poet remains a mere witness of the marriage, the ceremony displays here its extraordinary power as an emblem not only of elemental desire but of the very fabric of civilization – and for Tennyson the warrant of an overarching progress of humankind toward higher forms of being.

2

Crystal Palace and *Bleak House*: Expansion and Anomie, 1851–1873

The 1850s typically have been regarded as the very zenith of Victorian energy and self-confidence. "Of all decades in our history," G. M. Young remarked, "a wise man would choose the eighteen-fifties to be young in" (Young 1964: 77). The labor unrest, famine, and economic volatility that marked the "Hungry Forties" seemed to have been left behind, reform movements were underway on all fronts, and Britain's world markets were rapidly expanding. Literary markets also were expanding; advances in technology, such as power binding, made possible new economies of scale, which supported a host of cheap reprint editions of popular authors ("cheap" itself remained an honorific, meaning "affordable" rather than "shoddy"). From the late 1840s railways alone created an entirely new market for such editions, as travelers looked for novels to read over increasingly distant journeys – a demand that publishers were quick to meet, driving down prices as low as 1 1/2d per reprinted serial part and one shilling per volume. (Routledge astonished competitors of their "Railway Library" in 1854 by purchasing 19 of Bulwer-Lytton's copyrights for 20,000 pounds and still turning a long-term profit with reprints of his novels.) Repeal of the Stamp Duty (1855) and Paper Duty (1861), last of the so-called "taxes on knowledge," encouraged the formation of widely distributed penny newspapers – most influentially *The Daily Telegraph* (1855) – as well as monthly and weekly periodicals, such as the *Saturday Review* (1855), which offered new outlets for writers in all forms. The novel was rapidly becoming the dominant literary form, a development that in turn prompted newly exacting criticism of the genre.

The intellectual monument to this energy and confidence is often taken to be Macaulay's *History of England* (volumes 3 and 4 published in 1855), which chronicles a steady march of progress leading toward the expansive present, and pointing toward the future with seemingly boundless faith in the continued "march of mind" – a narrative that became known as "the Whig view of history." The emblematic embodiment of this confidence, so the story runs, was the Great Exhibition that opened in Hyde Park in 1851. The "Crystal Palace" incarnated a faith that "all sort of problems will vanish in a twinkling" – so mocked the acerbic narrator of Dostoevsky's *Notes from Underground* (Dostoevsky 1968: 283), mulling over its significance a decade later and half a continent away.

Yet the major literary currents of the decade also register a growing unease with the state of England – at least the swelling chorus of what Matthew Arnold would call "a self-satisfaction which is retarding and vulgarising" (Arnold 1960–77: iii.271). As public confidence shaded into complacency and smugness, it would be questioned and contested not only in a burgeoning social criticism, but also in the novel, narrative poetry, history, and even the lyric. To a remarkable extent work across these genres became a form of social criticism, writing with a "mission" or addressing a "problem" – to the dismay of readers who looked to literature for simpler pleasures. A related scrutiny was prompted by newly intense and uneasy consciousness of Britain's place in a wider world. Even the dazzling products within the Crystal Palace were arranged by national rather than technological affiliation, as if to acknowledge the extent to which England and Englishness were enmeshed in other nations and cultures, whether through economic trade, traditional dynastic politics in Europe, or its far-flung colonial dominions, where in 1857 the uprising of Indian troops against their British commanders became one of the greatest national traumas of the century.

The most famous literary riposte to mid-Victorian smugness may be the character of Podsnap in Dickens's *Our Mutual Friend* (1865), who incarnates Englishness as a triumphant insularity. Any challenges to social and moral decorum are measured against the sensibility of an adolescent girl – "would it bring a blush into the cheek of the young person?" – and all challenges to existing social arrangements are dismissed as "Not English" (Dickens 1971: 175). Much of the best-known literature produced over the next two decades would press against such constraints, prompting almost continual debate over the nature of the reading public – or publics, as the audiences became increasingly diverse – and what constituted acceptable subject matter for their reading. Meanwhile, political orthodoxies would be challenged by appeals for a Second Reform Bill and a rising tide of democratic sentiment, which no longer was easily contained by traditional appeals to social deference and divine order. Indeed, divinity itself was exposed to unparalleled challenge with the publication of Darwin's *Origin of Species* (1859), whose aftershocks would continue throughout the century. Macaulay's optimism thus jostled with a more equivocal view, which the increasingly skeptical Dickens projected onto an earlier epoch in *A Tale of Two Cities* (1859): "It was the best of times, it was the worst of times."

The Novel and Society

Even as the Great Exhibition was just underway, Dickens offered a dissenting response: while the public marveled at the Crystal Palace, he constructed *Bleak House* (serialized from November 1851 through August 1853). Coming off the triumphant success of *Copperfield*, which would remain the favorite of most readers (as of Dickens himself), many were perplexed by the new novel. Reviewers complained of a lack of plot, and seemed overwhelmed by the vast array of secondary characters, which were frequently singled out as mere grotesques, with no place in a larger design. The confusion is in keeping with the famous opening paragraph, which begins in the syntax of a reporter's dispatch ("London. Michaelmas term lately over ..."), then unfolds into a panorama of central London "gone into mourning ... for the death of the sun," shrouded in such mud and fog that "it would not be wonderful to meet a Megalosaurus, forty feet long or so, wandering like an elephantine lizard up Holborn Hill" (Dickens 1993: 49). The atmosphere introduces a newly ambitious design; more than any of Dickens's earlier novels, *Bleak House* links narrative and social order. "What connection can there be," asks the narrator, between the aristocratic world of Sir Leicester Dedlock and an orphaned, illiterate London streetsweeper known only as Jo, who "lives – that is to say, Jo has not yet died – in a ruinous place called Tom-all-Alone's?" (272). In the answer lies both an enigma that drives the plot and a fundamental moral bond between the highest and lowest reaches of the social order: connection to social ruin underscores complicity in it.

This emphasis was not new to either fiction or social criticism. Carlyle's *Past and Present*, for example, also dwells on contagious disease as the demonic emblem of a neglected "sisterhood" that transcends class, while Gaskell in *Mary Barton* had evoked a similar structure in Manchester life. In *Dombey and Son* Dickens himself had insistently worked to connect high and low, but there the design was accomplished principally through metaphor, by linking the wealthy bride with the prostitute as emblems of a single alienated womanhood; metonymic structures, which would bring such characters into plausible physical proximity, were far less forceful. In *Bleak House*, Dickens more thoroughly interweaves high and low, most boldly through an innovative structure that divides the story between two narrators. An anonymous, omniscient narrator witnesses events in the present tense and comments on them with worldly outrage; his record alternates with the retrospective, first-person account of an orphaned teenager, Esther Summerson, an innocent who is plunged into the maze of London through her unwitting involvement in the infamous Chancery suit of Jarndyce versus Jarndyce. As the third-person narrator tacitly frames Esther's "progress" from a privileged distance, he captures connections that elude her inexperienced eye, but her very innocence (recalling that of Browning's Pippa) radiates an instinctive sympathy and warmth that, in its ability to restore severed bonds, has a redemptive force on all she encounters. (Tellingly, Esther is represented only through her own eyes and the comments of those she meets, never through the worldly lens of the omniscient narrator.) Dickens's incorrigible faith in the power of young womanhood in this case tried even his admirers, not to mention John Stuart Mill, who was infuriated (he wrote of "that creature Dickens") that the celebration of Esther's energies was set against the mockery of public engagement by women, such as the charitable work of Mrs. Pardiggle and Mrs. Jellyby. But the novel's incessant preoccupation with neglected or abandoned children, and Esther's emblematic housekeeping, revivifies a cliché: charity begins at home.

One impetus for *Bleak House* was a growing body of reporting on the often appalling living conditions among the urban poor. In 1849, the *Morning Chronicle* published an article by Henry Mayhew, "A Visit to the Cholera Districts of Bermondsey," which recorded horrifying images of slum-dwellers gleaning their only drinking water from open drains contaminated with human waste. Similar conditions had been reported in Edwin Chadwick's 1842 *Report on the Sanitary Condition of the Labouring Population of Great Britain* (Engels's writings on Manchester had not yet appeared in English), but Mayhew's newspaper report had much wider circulation, and created a great stir – even prompting a former Lord Mayor to deny the very existence of Jacob's Island, the focus of Mayhew's report (he insisted that the place had been invented by Dickens in *Oliver Twist*). The response encouraged Mayhew to pursue further investigations, which grew into his massive *London Labour and the London Poor* (1861–2), a pioneering work of sociological investigation published in four volumes. These were structured by a trope that shaped representations of poverty throughout the period: Mayhew called himself "a traveler in the undiscovered country of the poor," "of whom the public has less knowledge than of the most distant tribes of the earth" (Mayhew 1968: 1.xv). This figure, recalling the early reception of Dickens, underscored for middle-class readers a fascinating exoticism in poverty, like that conjured up in travel writing from abroad – twin appeals that would be conjoined in contemporary fascination with gypsies, most notably in George Borrow's *Lavengro* (1851). For Mayhew, the poor were likewise nomadic "tribes" – a notion that, for all his avowals of sympathy, readily suggested that they also were "savages." Dickens's satire of Mrs. Jellyby's visions for distant "Borrioboola-Gha" is grounded in this congruence, and while it urged that the savage at home had a prior claim on readers' attention, the same trope could disable sympathy. Over the coming decades, as constructions of national identity became more concertedly and violently racialized, descriptions of the poor as "savage" would magnify social divisions within Britain. The poor – like indigenous peoples abroad – were a race apart from middle-class Britons, inherently resistant to civilizing influence, and thus a standing danger to social order. The fascination of exoticism shaded into a plea for stern control.

Even those who were disappointed by *Bleak House* conceded there was nothing like it (were it from an unknown author, the refrain went, it would be thought "astonishing"). So distinctive was Dickens's achievement that reviewers tended to map the literary landscape in terms of "the inimitable" and everyone else, although Thackeray was the most formidable rival. (Bulwer-Lytton, frequently a point of comparison in the late 1840s and still immensely popular, as Routledge's Railway Library would prove, followed up the success of *The Caxtons*

(1849) with a sequel, *My Novel: Or Varieties of English Life* (1853), a provincial novel as sprawling as its subtitle suggests, but he had returned to Parliament in 1852, and published little full-length fiction afterwards.) The fortuitous conjunction of *Copperfield* and *Pendennis* initiated a habit among reviewers of discovering in Dickens and Thackeray a host of complementary strengths. Dickens was the more fanciful, extravagant, sympathetic genius, who found his special métier in the lives of the poor and shabby genteel, while Thackeray was the more descriptive, "easy," but penetrating and ironic commentator, whose worldliness was displayed in a special intimacy with more elite circles of social and literary life. Indeed, from the time of *Vanity Fair*, Thackeray's novels were inevitably greeted by debates over the boundary between irony and cynicism.

The powerful satiric bent of Thackeray's writings, as many commentators pointed out, showed deep affinities with eighteenth-century writers, whom he made the topic of a lecture series on "the English humourists" in 1851 (published as a book in 1853) and with whom he undertook a more startling act of imaginative sympathy the following year, with the publication of *The History of Henry Esmond* (1852). The novel, autobiographical in form but predominantly third-person narration, not only is set in the reign of Queen Anne (much of the action surrounds the Jacobite uprising of 1714), but also is written in a voice recalling the essayistic prose of Addison and Steele, and was even published in type fonts of the earlier period. Reviewers generally applauded the stylistic dexterity and plot management, but the subject matter renewed suspicion of the "tone of social feeling" in his work, as John Forster put it. Readers were unsettled by the conjunction of Esmond's hopeless passion for the flirtatious Beatrix Esmond (a more refined version of Becky Sharp, reviewers noted) with the suggestion that his true happiness resided in the arms of the woman he had long treated as a quasi-maternal confidante – Beatrix's own mother. Many readers squirmed at the hint of incest – "the most uncomfortable book you can imagine," wrote Marian Evans, likening it to the more overtly daring fictions of George Sand. Even admirers suggested that its appeal would be constrained by its boldness. "All educated readers ... will enjoy Edmond heartily," wrote Forster; "though how far the circulating libraries may approve of the shadowy impression left by it as a story of life, we cannot undertake to say" (Tillotson and Hawes 1969: 146, 150, 151).

Thackeray's next novel, *The Newcomes* (which began appearing in parts in October 1853, just as *Bleak House* wound up), garnered more confident praise. Focusing (as its title suggests) on several generations of an arriviste family of bankers, this very long novel lacks much narrative drive, but its richly textured evocation of upper-middle-class life and the more raffish art world is energized by a frustrated idealism (the young bohemian in Thackeray died hard), which dwells on the manifold corruption of marriage through social ambition. For Thackeray, the allure of money and power was always hedged by the burden of keeping up appearances – captured in the novel's subtitle, "Memoirs of a Most Respectable Family" – and he continued to associate wealth with the lingering notion of marriage as a merely prudential arrangement, which serves as a foil to the celebration of romantic desire and domestic happiness. The nominal protagonist of the novel, young Clive Newsome, longs (like Thackeray himself) for the socially dubious career of an artist, and his love for his wealthy cousin Ethel Newcome is thwarted by her family's resistance. The real hero of the story is Clive's father, Colonel Thomas Newsome, a veteran of the British army in India who returns home to oversee the education of his only child, and who is recognized in London as a consummate gentleman. One of the novel's great achievements is to make this paragon seem at once plausible and humanly engaging – primarily through the innocence that informs the Colonel's devotion, and the resignation with which he bears financial ruin, dying (in a famous scene, frequently evoked by later novelists) as a humble pensioner at Greyfriars. A more assured and generally acknowledged moral arbiter than Dobbin of *Vanity Fair*, the Colonel also casts back to the eighteenth-century paragon, Richardson's Sir Charles Grandison, and more distantly to Don Quixote. The Colonel's nobility and the unswerving decency of Ethel (in this regard a departure from the Becky Sharp model) went a long way to redeem Thackeray from the suspicion of cynicism, while preserving, in his more subtly drawn social canvas, the important divergence from Dickens.

Victorians celebrated domesticity in a world where nearly a third of women were not married, and novelists devoted increasing attention to women who resisted or were marginalized by the ideal. Spinsters became increasingly prominent figures in novels of the late 1840s and 1850s. Caroline Helstone in Brontë's *Shirley* (1849) dwells at length over the single life that she fears awaits her. "Where is my place in the world?" she wonders, shrinking from what seems one of the few prospects open to her, work as a governess (C. Brontë 1974: 190). Mild as this may seem, it impressed many readers as rather daring self-assertion; Margaret Oliphant 20 years later recalled young girls being taught that such worries "should be religiously kept to themselves" (Oliphant 1867: 263). Caroline is paired with the brash, assertive Shirley Keeldar, an heiress whose financial security enables her to contemplate single life with the nonchalance of many a Victorian bachelor (Shirley was a traditionally masculine forename; Brontë's character helped to shift its gender). A more complex treatment of the topic informs *Villette* (1853), Brontë's final novel. The action follows the outlines of Brontë's own early life, as the orphaned Lucy Snowe makes her way to the city of Villette (Brussels), where she finds employment as an English teacher. Like *Jane Eyre*, the novel is written in the first person, but Lucy is a more consummate outsider even than Jane, and more given to acerbic comment on the various models of womanhood she confronts. Her alienation and psychic interiority become even more pronounced in the claustrophobic world of Madame Beck's *pensionnat*, where constant surveillance and the shadowy presence of Catholic conspiracies in the city at large reproduce something of Radcliffe's gothic. (As throughout Brontë's work, English identity is sharpened through contrast with a French-speaking world.) Lucy's resignation is shaken by her attraction to Monsieur Paul, the French master with whom she develops a tortuous flirtation, but she punishes herself with a masochistic zeal unsurpassed in Brontë's writing. Whereas Jane repeatedly invokes "Reason" to chastise "Fancy" in an inner agony that sometimes borders on the bipolar, Lucy embraces erotic rejection with the fervor of martyrdom: "I invoked Conviction to nail upon me the certainty, abhorred while embraced, to fix it with the strongest spikes her strongest strokes could drive; and when the iron entered my soul, I stood up, as I thought, renovated" (C. Brontë 1979: 426). The teasingly inconclusive ending – "leave sunny imaginations hope" – conveys an almost paralyzing ambivalence toward married life. (Sadly, Brontë had good reason to feel uneasy. In the following year she was engaged to one of her father's curates, soon after the marriage became pregnant, and died of complications at the age of 38.)

Gaskell represented spinsterhood with greater equanimity, publishing in 1853 a volume entitled *Cranford*, which treats with gentle comedy a country town in which all the property owners are elderly spinsters or widows – the Amazons, as the opening sentence wryly dubs them. The book is unusually loose in structure, retaining its origin as a series of sketches in Dickens's recently founded periodical *Household*

Words, where it began to appear in the final number of 1851. But it keenly represents the social dynamics of this highly conservative community, the muted pleasures and more potent anxieties of "general but unacknowledged poverty" – unacknowledged "because that subject savoured of commerce and trade" (Gaskell 1976: 41). Gaskell cultivates an insider's perspective by means of a first-person narrator (identified only near the end of the book), who registers both the affections and subtle rivalries that sustain this world of women. Amid the steady pressure of managing both private finances and public image, the characters are troubled less by romantic deprivation than by their economic vulnerability, which culminates in the all-too-familiar trauma of early Victorian life, a bank failure.

As she was writing *Cranford*, Gaskell was working on a more daring project, too disturbing in its subject matter to be published in *Household Words* or any other family journal. *Ruth* (1853) explores a different departure from domestic life, the history of an unwed mother. In its outlines, the story is a sustained cliché of romance gone wrong. An orphaned seamstress, Ruth Hilton is seduced by a feckless young gentleman who abandons her on discovering that she is pregnant. Taken in by an elderly dissenting minister and his spinster sister, she proves a paragon of feminine virtue, not only as a mother but as a sick nurse to the poor; when fever rages, she ventures "right into the very jaws of the fierce disease" (Gaskell 2001: 360) only to die from it after selflessly nursing the very man who had abandoned her. It is a measure of the stigma attached to illegitimacy that Gaskell felt Ruth had to become a saint in order to claim readers' sympathy – though even this did not disarm many scolding reviewers. The more durable interest of the novel lies in Gaskell's attention to the burgeoning rhetoric of feminine purity, and the psychic and moral energies sustaining it. The book dwells at length on the familiar clash between Christian charity and the demonizing of the "fallen" woman, and more subtly – but more probingly – on the shock of discovering that such a woman might be hard to distinguish from the most virtuous. "Who was true? Who was not? Who was good and pure? Who was not? The very foundations of Jemima's belief in her mind were shaken" (272). (The response would resonate later in the decade, unexpectedly, in Tennyson's *Idylls of the King*.) Most broadly, the novel elicits Gaskell's characteristic preoccupation with the moral rigidity informing worldly success – the complacency of the Pharisees, the biblical model that shaped many novelistic treatments of the same concern.

Gaskell extended this preoccupation in *North and South*, which solidifies the crucial association in the industrial novel between social order and self-discipline. The novel was originally entitled "Margaret Hale," after its main character, and the change in title underscores a larger ambition. Though set in Manchester, like *Mary Barton*, it undertakes a more comprehensive social portrait, which sets the more tranquil, agrarian south against the frenetic energy and social dynamism of the industrial north. The two worlds are bought together in the experience of Margaret, whose clergyman father resigns his living in a gesture of conscience and moves his family from the village of Helstone to the bustling factory town of Milton-Northern (Manchester). The social descent of the Hales, like that of so many families in Victorian fiction, is accentuated by a mother clinging to rural gentility, an allegiance predictably overwhelmed by the spectacle of Milton, where Mr. Hale finds "something dazzling" in the spectacle of so much energy and power. Margaret, characteristically, finds herself wondering whether "in the triumph of the crowded procession ... the helpless have been trampled on" (Gaskell 1970a: 108). Her outsider's perspective underscores "the rough independent way" of Milton girls and "the open, fearless manner" of the workmen Margaret encounters in the streets (110), and that new distance also enforces a more benign view of manufacturing interests than in *Mary Barton*. Thornton, a young manufacturer, repeatedly claims that labor relations have become more just as "the power of masters and men became more evenly balanced," and the workers have come to recognize the power of self-discipline as a lever of social mobility. The novel is filled with Tennysonian visions of progress – "every man has it within him to mount, step by step, on each wonder he achieves to higher marvels still" (122) – which are sustained by the power of self-regulation in all spheres of life. Margaret constantly works to restrain her emotions – "vexed and ashamed at the difficulty of keeping her right place, and her calm unconsciousness of heart" (303) – but in the process wrestles with "that most difficult problem for women, how much was to be utterly merged in obedience to authority, and how much might be set apart for freedom in working" (508). The collapse of discipline is epitomized, as in so much Victorian fiction, by a mob, whose cry "was as the demoniac desire of some terrible wild beast for the food that is withheld from his ravening" (232). But Thornton's faith in political economy must be chastened by greater sympathy for those who suffer under the iron hand of the market. Through his contact with a single upright working man, he comes to experience the quintessential recognition of Victorian social fiction – "that 'we have all of us one human heart' " (511) – and he ultimately seeks out "some intercourse with hands beyond the mere 'cash nexus' " (525). Marriage to Margaret predictably crowns this new awareness, but it cannot come about until Thornton himself has been humbled by the failure of his business, and Margaret in turn gains an unexpected inheritance – a leveling of fortunes that novelists increasingly made a prerequisite of domestic happiness.

The serialization of *North and South* in *Household Words* had been preceded by Dickens's long-deferred engagement with the industrial north, *Hard Times* (1854), whose germ was Dickens's observation of a bitter textile strike at Preston. The view of modern industry in *Hard Times* is a good deal bleaker than Gaskell's. In Thornton's "idea of merchant-life," the fantasy of economic power at least is bound to an ideal of personal integrity: "Far away, in the East and the West, where his person would never be known, his name was to be regarded, and his wishes to be fulfilled, and his word pass like gold" (Gaskell 1970a: 511). In the world of *Hard Times*, ambition has curdled into mechanical routine, emotional numbness, and brute domination. Its famous caricature of Benthamite rationality – "Now, what I want is, Facts," the novel begins, "Teach these boys and girls nothing but Facts" (Dickens 1966: 5) – links failure of sympathy to a more thoroughgoing alienation, which is suspicious of any form of mental life not obviously "useful." From Parliament to Coketown to the Gradgrind family, England is afflicted by an obsession with means and ends that has cast out the pleasures of imagination and simple human affection. "Hard times" have descended as more than an economic burden. Following a by-now conventional gesture of the "social problem" novel, class conflict is focused in the inner struggle of a single working-class character, here Stephen Blackpool, who is caught between the warring claims of labor and capital. Stephen stands out because of his resistance to a planned strike, but the experience of the workers is more peripheral than in Gaskell. While the narrator urges his middle-class readers to appreciate that the workers were "gravely, deeply, faithfully in earnest," and "through their very delusions, showed great qualities," in fact the demonized union organizers receive almost as much voice as Blackpool, whose stoic forbearance is summed up in his feeble conclusion, "aw's a muddle" (207).

The novel seems more engaged by another injustice, Stephen's inability to divorce a drunken and dissolute wife who long since had abandoned him. Debate over English divorce laws would take on increasing prominence in the nation at large, and in Dickens's personal life, later in the decade. In *Hard Times*, Stephen's predicament echoes in a derangement of more affluent domestic life, which Dickens also lays at the door of Gradgrind, whose mistrust of imagination and feeling drives his daughter Louisa into a mercenary marriage to Bounderby, and leaves her vulnerable to the predatory Harthouse. As "Harthouse" conjures up a supercilious aristocratic idleness for which the hothouse became an increasingly prominent emblem, "Bounderby" underscores the self-absorbed pomposity and deception of a character who travesties the ideal of the self-made man. In this world of moral and emotional bankruptcy, the only agent of redemption is tellingly located outside the main action, in the grotesque community of Sleary's circus, the last vestige of a world held together by bonds of mutual affection and respect.

Dickens dedicated *Hard Times* to Carlyle, and attacks on the book frequently linked Dickens with Carlyle and another harsh social critic, Ruskin. Carlyle's ferocious *Latter-Day Pamphlets* (1850), particularly its inflammatory "Occasional Discourse on the Nigger Question," had alienated many readers, and, although he recovered some favor with his memoir of John Sterling (1851), over the course of the 1850s Carlyle became more an eminence than a productive writer, as he immersed himself in a long-pondered life of Frederick the Great (1858–65). Ruskin, however, gained new prominence when he published *The Stones of Venice* in 1853. Although his topic seemed far removed from the Great Exhibition, the history of Venetian architecture became in his treatment a withering critique of Victorian complacency, including a representation of industrial labor more probing than anything to be found in the industrial novel. Paxton's sleekly utilitarian Crystal Palace, often celebrated as a harbinger of Modernist architecture, was to Ruskin an outrage, because it curtailed the profuse ornament and coloration that in his view most fully expressed the imagination of both architect and craftsman. Venetian gothic offered a treasure house of these features, and in *Stones* Ruskin made an early plea for the preservation of historic architecture, while railing against the Venetians' neglect of the buildings that were crumbling around them. At the same time, however, Ruskin urged that the value of those structures was ultimately ethical: in them one could read the changing moral temper of a society, which had impelled the rise and decline of a once-great mercantile and maritime power.

Ruskin clearly wanted the English to see themselves in this mirror, and the bearings of his analysis on contemporary society were nowhere more vivid than in "The Nature of Gothic." This frequently excerpted chapter turns on the emblematic contrast of past and present that structures so much of Victorian medievalism, in Carlyle, in Pugin's architectural polemics of the 1830s, and in the reconfiguration of chivalry beginning with Digby's *The Broad Sword of Honour* in 1824. Ruskin himself would return to the motif in 1860, in the fifth and final volume of *Modern Painters*, where a chapter called "The Two Boyhoods" juxtaposes the formative years of Giorgione and Turner. "The Nature of Gothic" has largely transcended the medievalist tradition, however, because the crucial sense of dispossession it elicits is not a loss of traditional faith, but a loss of freedom. In Ruskin's extraordinary evocation of alienated labor, "Gothic" comes to embody familiar Victorian virtues: restless energy, aspiring spirit, truth, earnestness, humility, but above all freedom of expression. The roughness and imperfection of Gothic ornament are, paradoxically, a virtue of the tradition, because they bear witness to the power of imagination, which always exceeds the worker's capacity to realize it concretely. Industrial production, on the other hand, with its "engine-turned precision" has encouraged a misplaced desire for perfection that can only be won through imaginative enslavement of the laborer. "Men may be beaten, chained, tormented, yoked like cattle, slaughtered like summer flies, and yet remain in one sense, and the best sense, free. But to smother their souls with them ... to make the flesh and skin which, after the worm's work is on it, is to see God, into leathern thongs to yoke machinery with, – this is to be slave-masters indeed" (Ruskin 1903–12: x.193).

The fierce rhetoric makes even Dickens seem timid; few middle-class novelists ever risked so bold an analysis of class relations. The "degradation of the operative into a machine" has turned class differences into "a precipice between upper and lower grounds in the field of humanity" (x.194). "The division of labour," Ruskin continues, is "a false name. It is not truly speaking, the labour that is divided, but the men – Divided into mere segments of men – broken into small fragments and crumbs of life; so that all the little piece of intelligence that is left in a man is not enough to make a pin, or a nail, but exhausts itself in making the point of a pin or the head of a nail" (x.196). Men who make glass beads, for example, sit at their work all day, their hands vibrating with a perpetual and exquisitely timed palsy, and the beads dropping beneath their vibration like hail. Neither they, nor the men who draw out the rods or fuse the fragments, have the smallest occasion for the use of any single human faculty; and every young lady, therefore, who buys glass beads is engaged in the slave trade. (x.197)

The breathtaking leap of the final sentence typifies Ruskin's offhand provocations, which worked on multiple fronts. By proponents of political economy he was denounced as a mere crank (or worse). But his celebration of handicraft would have a profound influence on the work of William Morris and the arts and crafts movement, and more broadly in the articulation of culture as a mode of freedom, in which untrammeled imagination was increasingly invoked to resist stultifying convention.

Crimea and the Forms of Heroism

A further blow to British complacency came from the Crimean War with Russia, which was declared in March of 1854. The first European war involving Britain since the defeat of Napoleon (and the last until World War I), Crimea provoked an outpouring of patriotic fervor that soon gave way to disillusionment: incompetent planning by military leaders led to battlefield stalemate, while leaving British troops woefully undersupplied and ravaged by the agonies of climate and disease. The failings were vividly reported by *The Times* correspondent, W. E. Russell, whose dispatches would become a prototype of modern journalism, both in their eyewitness detail and in their relay by telegraph. In Russell's accounts, Crimea became one more emblem of aristocratic incompetence, which needed to be rectified by middle-class efficiency and commitment. The most vivid emblem of that intervention became "the lady with the lamp," Florence Nightingale, who helped to reorganize military hospital facilities at Scutari by relying on women as nurses, a project unparalleled in a military theater of operations), but one clearly nurtured in part by novelistic celebrations of domestic womanhood, such as *Ruth*. In the figure of Nightingale a decidedly mid-Victorian heroism supplanted the martial virtues. In an exemplary tribute by Mary Seacole, another woman who made her way to the Crimea, Nightingale became "that Englishwoman whose name shall never die, but sound like music on the lips of British men until the hour of doom" (Peck 1988: 34).

As Crimea became a byword for administrative incompetence, the war resonated even in works that never mention it. *Little Dorrit*, which Dickens began in 1855, is one of his most ambitious novels, developing the social engagements of *Hard Times* through an inheritance plot so labyrinthine that many editions of the novel offer a brief synopsis of it. Gradgrind's utilitarian rationality is eerily doubled in the rigidity and gloom of evangelicalism, the "stern religion" that has broken the will of Dickens's hero, Arthur Clennam, and is blazoned forth in the "penitential garb" of English Sundays, when all public amusement is banished (Dickens 1967: 67). The social mobility embodied in Bounderby becomes a pervasive, at times disorienting, motion, as a surprising array of characters traverse the gulf evoked by the two halves of the novel, entitled "Poverty" and "Riches." The Dorrit family, most obviously, moves from imprisonment for debt at Marshalsea Prison – as a fellow inmate remarks, "we have got to the bottom, we can't fall, and what have we found? Peace" (103) – to the heights of British society, and back again. As a figure of self-invention, the provincial Bounderby pales alongside the mysterious financier Merdle, a man who seems to have the whole country in his pocket: "nobody knew with the least precision what Mr. Merdle's business was, except that it was to coin money" (445; his meteoric rise and fall were modeled on the scandalous career of the railway entrepreneur Sir John Sadleir). The dilettantish Harthouse has a counterpart in Henry Gowan, a painter whose social ambitions far exceed his artistic commitments. Throughout *Little Dorrit*, characters' ongoing invocations of "savagery" as foils to English life predictably turn out to level the distinction. This is a society founded on naked aggression, in which wealth seems tainted by *merdre*. Perhaps for this reason, it was Dickens's least popular novel to date. Not even the long sufferings of its title character – another of Dickens's abject child-women in the mold of Little Nell – provided sufficient cathartic relief from the gloom.

The most furious criticism of the novel, however, was aimed at Dickens's satire of government bureaucracy under the guise of "the Circumlocution office," whose overriding concern is "HOW NOT TO DO IT" (Dickens 1967: 143). The attack pointedly echoed parliamentary revelations about Crimea, but it infuriated middle-class government officials, who throughout the decade had been working to reduce the force of patronage by opening up the civil service through competitive examinations. Dickens portrayed government office as a sinecure for aristocratic parasites such as Sir Tite Barnacle, "a politic-diplomatic hocus pocus piece of machinery ... for the assistance of the nobs in keeping off the snobs" (157–8) – "snobs" still referring to the upwardly aspiring rather than to those who looked down from above. James Fitzjames Stephen, a barrister and prolific writer for the *Saturday Review*, offered a characteristic response, livid but also confounded. He professed Dickens beneath contempt as a social critic: an answer to his novel, Stephen suggests, is akin to "a refutation of the jokes of the clown in a Christmas pantomime." Yet his angry reviews are a measure of the exasperation that Dickens, a man "utterly destitute of any kind of solid acquirements" (P. Collins 1971: 348), should have so far-reaching an influence.

The appeal to "solid acquirements" marshals the ethos of the Victorian professional man, in whose eyes the novelist panders to "the vast majority of mankind" who "think little, and cultivate themselves still less":

> Freedom, law, established rules, have their difficulties. They are possible only to men who will be patient, quiet, moderate, and tolerant of difference in opinion; and therefore their results are intolerable to a feminine, irritable, noisy mind, which is always clamouring and shrieking for protection and guidance. (P. Collins 1971: 349)

Once again, artistic failure is construed as a lapse of manhood. But here manliness ratifies the distinctive virtues of mid-Victorian liberalism, of "men who will be patient, quiet, moderate, and tolerant of difference in opinion." As liberals have discovered (then and now), this is not a very alluring ideal of manhood; indeed, it is largely an effort to disable the forms of impulsive, unqualified self-assertion and aggression so often dubbed heroic. That dilemma posed a challenge taken up in a great deal of literature at mid-century: re-imagining heroism in an age that seemed to have little place for it.

Crimea, for all its association with official incompetence, did offer occasions to celebrate an older model of martial valor. Reading one of Russell's dispatches in December of 1854, recounting a cavalry assault against a battery of artillery, Tennyson composed "The Charge of the Light Brigade," which appeared in *The Examiner* on 9 December. Unlike Carlyle's association of heroism with charismatic power, Tennyson's poem celebrates something bordering on absurdity. "Some hideous blunder," the newspaper reported, had sent a brigade of cavalry, their sabers glinting in the sun, into a suicidal charge against a battery of cannon ringing what Tennyson christened "the valley of Death." With the poem's dactyllic meter brilliantly evoking the steady gallop toward catastrophe – "Half a league, half a league, half a league onward …" – Tennyson evokes a field of glory that merges the tableaux of heroic painting with the inexorable doom of classical tragedy. "*C'est magnifique, mais c'est ne pas la guerre,*" murmured a bewildered French observer of the scene, but for Tennyson that was the point. He was commemorating magnificence nobler than warfare, an utterly self-less, courageous devotion to duty in the face of death: "Their's not to make reply, Their's not to reason why, Their's but to do and die" (13–15; Tennyson 1969). Across the gulf of a century and a half of increasingly efficient and mechanized slaughter, such sentiments echo strangely. Indeed, the poem was in some respects an anachronism in its own time, an elegy to a waning aristocratic code epitomized by the cavalry (McGann 1982). But the poem also represents one of the most memorable Victorian affirmations of heroism in modern society, as a commitment to value beyond the world of exchange. It has resonated on battlefields since.

A different model of heroism suffused a more bellicose response to Crimea, Charles Kingsley's *Westward Ho!* (1855), which would become one of the best-selling novels of the period (and was the first novel to be published by Macmillan). Set in the Elizabethan age, Kingsley's novel follows the exploits of a group of mariners loosely affiliated with Sir Francis Drake's voyages of conquest and exploration to the Americas. Its celebration of often-brutal English power clearly addressed anxieties affiliated with Crimea – as Kingsley himself acknowledged when he called it "a most ruthless, bloodthirsty book (just what the times want, I think)" (Kingsley 1902: ii.179). Dedicated to the English Rajah Brooke of Sarawak, who had recently been censured in Parliament for his brutal suppression of the indigenous population, the novel aligns the march of civilization with frenzies of combat. Its hero, Amyas Leigh, has been brought up in his Devon village under the austere warrior ethos of "the old Persians, 'to speak the truth and to draw the bow,'" yet he also believes it "the finest thing in the world to be a gentleman." He delights in being "the most terrible fighter" in his village, yet also is devoted to the weak, and avoids causing needless pain to anyone; "for the rest, he never thought about thinking, or felt about feeling" (Kingsley 1902: v.65).

The instinctive, unreflective assurance evoked by that last line shows the influence of the Carlylean hero.

Three other best-sellers of the mid-1850s celebrated related versions of contemporary heroism. Charlotte Yonge's *The Heir of Redclyffe* (1853) evokes a latter-day chivalry within the confines of domestic romance. The book focuses on the rivalry of two cousins, Guy Morville and Philip Edmonstone, successive heirs to the great estate of Redclyffe, each of whom must struggle towards self-mastery and humility, while at the same time learning to reconcile that self-discipline with the duties of social life. As this summary may suggest, it is a novel curiously lacking in major incident. In the one episode of traditional heroism, Guy hurls himself into a raging sea to save shipwrecked sailors, but caps his ordeal with a characteristic gloss: "I was glad to have been out on such a night, if only for the magnificent sensation it gives to realize one's own powerlessness and His might" (Yonge 1997: 311). The model for such humility was Tractarianism (Yonge was a parishioner of John Keble, and devoted the proceeds of her very successful career to various church interests) but much of the novel's popularity derived from Yonge's ability to discover in Tractarian piety a hint of the Byronic. Sir Guy, sensitive and high-strung, deeply responsive to poetry, ever-conscious of the "doom" of an ancestry renowned for violence and bloodshed, has an especially difficult time mastering his passions. His "mystery, reserve, and defiance" (230) markedly recall the allure of Byron's "brooding and lowering heroes" (399). But by the time he dies at the ripe age of 21, Guy is celebrated as an exemplary knight (likened to Sir Galahad) whose great conquest is that of his own passions, an example that serves to redeem the very man who has made his life miserable, his cousin Philip. The book was hugely popular, with testimonies to its impact coming from readers as diverse as William Morris and soldiers in the Crimea. Yonge (1823–1901) went on to a prolific career as "the Author of *The Heir of Redclyffe*."

Diana Mulock's *John Halifax, Gentleman*, another best-seller published three years later, locates heroism in a more distinctively modern struggle, that of the self-made man. Mulock herself (later Mulock Craik, 1826–77) was an eldest child who at 19 was left to support her younger siblings, and had early successes with *The Ogilvies* (1849) and *The Head of the Family* (1853), a domestic saga in the vein of *The Newcomes* and *The Caxtons*. With *John Halifax* she turned to a different social milieu, the world of a Quaker tannery owner in the early part of the century. But, for all its distance from Yonge's High Anglican landed gentry, Mulock's work underscores the asceticism that was central to both evangelical faith and Tractarianism, as well as their common appeal to medieval chivalry. "Like a young knight of the middle ages" (Mulock 2005: 175), John Halifax is a paragon of self-discipline more assured than Guy Morville. When the 14-year-old orphan presents himself at the home of Phineas Fletcher, the tannery owner's son and narrator of the novel, he announces himself as "a person of independent property, which consists of my head and my two hands" (40). Here, stated with rare concision, is the fantasy of social transformation that had been gaining ground among the upwardly aspiring since the late eighteenth century: even without inherited wealth, an energetic, disciplined resourcefulness could challenge and supplant the parasitic idleness of the ruling class. (The novel's historical frame underscores this resonance, placing Halifax's birth in 1780 so that his personal history is interwoven with the rise of steam power and industrial unrest, as well as the more sweeping social transformations he comes to epitomize.)

The ideal of the self-made man marks one horizon of liberal reflection, in a dream of perfect autonomy and self-determination. As the dazzled Phineas phrases it, Halifax "was indebted to no forefathers for a family history; the chronicle commenced with himself, and was altogether of his own making" (Mulock 2005: 41). The chronicle of noble ancestors gives way to the steady, inexorable triumph of discipline over economic disadvantage and aristocratic contempt. But that triumph depends on reshaping the ideal of the gentleman along middle-class lines, and opposing Halifax's virtues to those of mere rank and inherited privilege. The real victory, Halifax insists, is one of character: when he is asked, "Why cannot thee keep in thy own rank?," he responds that "honest tradesman" is "only my calling, not me. I – John Halifax, – am just the same, whether in the tan-yard or Dr. Jessup's drawing room" (198). Here is the hallmark of the Victorian gentleman, a frank and principled independence of mind (memorably evoked in the same year in Newman's *Idea of a University*). At every stage the plot reinforces this ideal, which is crowned when the son of the dissolute landowner who had insulted Halifax as a young man renounces his earldom in order to prove himself worthy of marrying John Halifax's daughter. Halifax's death on August 1, 1834, the date of the abolition of slavery in the British colonies, is the final pointing of the egalitarian ideal informing Halifax's ascent.

Guy Livingstone (1857), by G. A. Lawrence (1827–76), returns to an aristocratic milieu, where it pushes the violent oscillations of manly aggression and self-discipline to a pitch that outstrips even *Westward Ho!*, evoking a masculinity so violent that it came to be dubbed "berserker." Yet even Lawrence's novel pays tribute to the chivalric heroism most influentially evoked by Yonge. Livingstone is an upper-class paragon, a Rugby and Oxford man who liberally quotes from Homer and classical drama, the heir to a large estate, and a dashing, brutally strong and decisive cavalry officer in the Life Guards, given over to hard riding, hunting, gambling, and drinking; he is frequently termed "savage." (At one point in the novel he shows a new temperance when he picks an offender up by the throat and holds him against a wall, but refrains from smashing him to the ground [Lawrence 1860: 250].) For all his worldliness and cynicism towards women and courtship – preoccupations he feels obliged to attend to in intervals between more engrossing concerns – Livingstone is a model of honor, courtesy, and sheer resilience, able to drink all night and appear bright-eyed for duty in the morning. Much as in Kingsley's novels, however, the narrative abruptly turns on itself with "a humbling of the strong, self-reliant nature," on the familiar model of the medieval knight (the novel is full of references to Malory). As Livingstone undergoes a painful process of expiation for infidelity to his virtuous fiancée, the man of rippled muscles ends his life providing one more example of stoic humility. Most heroic when helpless in the face of death, Livingstone underscores an emergent literary model of strong but sensitive masculinity: men are moved, the narrator remarks, by "the simple and quiet sorrows ... we yawn over the wailings of Werther and Raphael; but we ponder gravely over the last chapters of the *Heir of Redclyffe*; and feel a curious sensation in the throat – perhaps the slightest dimness of vision – when reading *The Newcomes*, how that noble old soldier [Col. Newcome] crowned the chivalry of a stainless life, dying in the Grey Brother's gown" (276). A more effusive early Victorian piety is giving way to the stiff upper lip.

The preoccupation with heroism clearly reflects pressure on the very idea of manhood. The vogue of "muscular" manhood, stressing sheer physical vigor on the model of an older martial ethos, was reflected in an efflorescence of markedly weak or physically disabled male characters in fiction, which set into relief more hardy protagonists. In *John Halifax*, an unspecified "hereditary disease" bars Phineas Fletcher from both matrimony and economic struggle, while Guy's disabled cousin Charles in *The Heir of Redclyffe* elicits both his tenderness and his strength; even Guy Livingstone is paired with a weak friend who underscores his power but also his forbearance. This emphasis on physical strength gained widest currency in what became known as "muscular Christianity" – a term described in J. F. Stephen's *Saturday Review* account of Kingsley's *Two Years Ago* (1857): "His ideal is a man who fears God and can walk a thousand miles in a thousand hours, who, in the language which Mr. Kingsley has made popular, breathes God's free air on God's rich earth, and at the same time can hit a woodcock, doctor a horse, and twist a poker around his fingers" (Bevington 1941: 188). As a young man during the height of the Oxford movement, Kingsley was unnerved by the charismatic Newman, whose strenuous piety (which celebrated chastity among the priesthood) seemed to undermine the virility of his own calling. Out of these deeply personal anxieties, Kingsley transmuted Carlylean heroism into an aggressively masculine Christianity, a piety not merely combined with, but to a large extent expressed through, unflinching physical hardiness – an ideal that would find unexpected resonance in the wake of Crimea and imperial expansion.

Although "muscular Christianity" is most often associated with Kingsley, the ideal was put into broadest circulation in a groundbreaking novel by another writer, *Tom Brown's Schooldays* (1857) by Thomas Hughes (1822–96). Based on his own experiences at Rugby under the headmastership of Thomas Arnold, Hughes's novel inaugurated the genre of "the school story" (revitalized in the Harry Potter novels of J. K. Rowling). The work found a surprisingly large audience, not only of the nostalgic "old boys" whom Hughes explicitly addressed, but also among a wider public increasingly alert to the forms of social mobility associated with public school education, which was rapidly expanding at the time. (The French translation had a profound impact on Pierre Coubertin, founder of the modern Olympics movement.) Hughes, a barrister, knew Kingsley well, and shared his allegiance to the Christian Socialism of F. D. Maurice. But Hughes himself disliked the "muscular Christian" tag, and in a subsequent novel, *Tom Brown at Oxford* (1860), worked to distance his protagonist from the suspicious informing Stephen's phrase – most notably, that as it celebrated masculine energy the new "muscularity" tacitly licensed male sensuality. (An enthusiastic *Saturday Review* account of Kingsley's poetry in Andromeda [1858], called him "the great Apostle of the Flesh" ["Kingsley's Andromeda," 594].)

Certainly, Tom Brown's Schooldays chastens Tom's animal sprits by juxtaposing them with the piety of his sickly friend, Arthur, another physically weak foil to a strong protagonist. But Hughes's Rugby (like Lawrence's) differs markedly from that of Stanley's famous *Life* of Arnold, published just 13 years earlier, where organized sports have little place. On its face, the novel urges a balance of strength and tenderness, athleticism and piety, in a manner that closely parallels the emphases of *The Heir of Redclyffe* and *John Halifax, Gentleman*. All the energy of the novel, however, derives from the headlong pugnacity and high spirits of Tom; Arthur's physical weakness seems unwitting testimony to the waning of Arnoldian spiritual discipline. Despite its moral design, Hughes's novel would solidify the popular association of public school achievement with athletic prowess (to the extent that many scholars have attributed the cult of athleticism to Arnold himself, who had little interest in sports). As the expanding public schools over the latter half of the century increasingly prepared young men to become colonial administrators, games-playing became a model for nothing less than imperial manhood. "If asked what our muscular Christianity has done," one late-Victorian headmaster pronounced, "we point to the British Empire" (Mangan 1986: 148).

Empire

The close association of athleticism and martial heroism would flourish through the remainder of the century, culminating in the lines of Henry Newbolt in "Vitai Lampada":

> The sand of the desert is sodden red –
>   Red with the wreck of the square that broke
> The gatling's jammed and the colonel dead,
>   And the regiment blind with dust and smoke.
> The river of death has brimmed its banks,
>   And England's far and Honor a name,
> But the voice of a schoolboy rallies the ranks –
>   "Play up! Play up! And play the game!"
>   (ll. 9–16; Newbolt 1898)

Tom Brown's Schooldays thus points to an epochal development, in which "muscular" and adventure fiction for boys would profoundly shape the imagination of empire. For the first two decades of Victoria's reign, the most important cultural "other" in the British imagination was located immediately across the Channel. Things French in novels from Bulwer to Brontë to Dickens are foils to an increasingly keen sense of Englishness, while anxious reviewers of a host of cultural phenomena were vigilant to censure all that smacked of Gallic licentiousness or delusion. The maintenance of empire, by contrast, remained in the early Victorian years a relatively peripheral presence in British literature. It made itself felt most directly in narratives of missionary work – the most famous, David Livingstone's *Missionary Travels* (1857) – which extended through much of the empire, and in the occasional novel holding forth the prospect of that vocation (*Jane Eyre* most notably), although novelists rarely followed missionaries to their remote destinations. The memoirs of various travelers, such as Harriet Ward's *Five Years in Kaffirland* (1848), underscored the reach of British influence, as did (more directly) earlier narratives of naval engagement and exploration, such as those of Cook in the South Pacific. But at mid-century British sea power was mostly identified with triumphs of the Napoleonic Wars, as was Britain's military prowess generally. After Waterloo, moreover, the army occupied a much less prominent place in English life – marginalized in large part by the increasing sway of middle-class, domestic norms that had less place for traditionally aristocratic, martial virtues. Early Victorian literature offers few treatments of imperial campaigns outside of Europe, such as the First Afghan War (1839–41), First Opium War (1840–2), or the Maori Wars of 1843–8. Instead the army figures largely in historical contexts – as in *Vanity Fair* and *Henry Esmond* – or as a shadowy background to the present life of retired soldiers. The exception is a cluster of novels of military life written in the 1830s and 1840s by W. H. Maxwell, G. R. Gleig, and (most notably) Charles Lever, but even these works tend to look back to the Napoleonic Wars, and devote much of their attention to an ideal of aristocratic manhood whose appeal is in large part nostalgic. (The ebbing of the ideal is fairly explicit in Thackeray's treatment of George Osborne, more subtly at work in Tennyson's "Charge of the Light Brigade," and much less notable in the novels of Lever.) By the time of Tennyson's *Maud* (1855), the yearning for a military career could seem a marker of radical alienation from middle-class life (Peck 1988).

Although romantic poetry is suffused with fantasies of exotic lands, specifically imperial possessions came into public consciousness more directly in campaigns against slavery, which focused on the West Indies. The abolition of slavery in British dominions in 1834 did not dampen the resonance of slavery as a figure for other forms of oppression, as in

Jane Eyre and "The Nature of Gothic." Thus a range of social issues in and out of novels – most notably industrial labor and "the woman question" – continued to evoke forms of domination associated with empire. The West Indies had a further resonance as the source of many British fortunes (including that of Elizabeth Barrett's father) and as a site of sexual license. The woman of mixed race, a surprisingly pervasive figure in early Victorian literature, was an especially tense emblem of the islands as a space of sexual domination, reflected most notably in the frightening Bertha Mason in *Jane Eyre*, but also in comic figures such as Miss Schwartz in *Vanity Fair*, where the unsettling reality of miscegenation is dampened by racist mockery. But distant islands also could seem alluring spaces of freedom from Victorian discipline, as in the poetry of Tennyson, where the fantasy of "going native" is resisted with a fervor that betrays its deep appeal.

India in the first half of the century was a less vivid literary presence. Certainly it was central to the large ambitions of social and political reformers, and works such as James Mill's *History of British India* (1817) and Macaulay's "Minute on Indian Education" (1836) have become crucial documents in the study of British imperialism. But India figured far less prominently in early Victorian fiction. Although it appears in some romantic poetry as a vaguely tropical space of fantasy, in novels its presence is felt principally in retired military officers or Anglo-Indian officials, such as Jos Sedley in *Vanity Fair*, and in a variety of commodities, particularly clothing, which mark the growing importance of trade with South Asia (as well as the purchasing power of their owners). Such characters and articles are especially prominent in Thackeray, who was born in Bombay to an Anglo-Indian family. The earliest successful novel to deal extensively with Indian life was Philip Meadows Taylor's *The Confessions of a Thug* (1839), which drew on Taylor's service with the Nixam of Hyderabad in describing the cult of Thuggee, which resorted to robbery and assassination in its devotion to the goddess Kali. The novel was an immense success – it introduced the word "thug" into the language – and Taylor followed it with *Tippoo Sultaun* (1840), a tale of the Mysore War in the late eighteenth century. This proved much less successful, and was Taylor's last effort in this vein until the 1860s. A less sensational view of Indian life, and one more focused on the British presence there, was *Oakfield, or Fellowship in the East* (1853), by William Delafield Arnold, Matthew's younger brother. Although the work contains a vivid account of the Sikh Wars of 1846, *Oakfield* is principally a novel of reform, which in the spirit of

Arnold's Rugby arraigns the moral laxity of the East India Company's army, bringing to bear on an older military ethos an ideal of Christian manliness much in the vein of *The Heir of Redclyffe*, published the same year.

Empire became a newly vivid reality in the national consciousness in 1857, when Britons were jolted by news of "the Indian Mutiny" or Sepoy Rebellion. Beginning in May, revolts by Indian troops ("Sepoys") against their British officers spread to a number of garrisons across the north of India, where scores of Britons – some of them non-combatants – were killed, and others suffered horribly under long sieges, most notoriously at Cawnpore. British reaction was fierce, and frightening in its extremity – fueled above all by accounts, since largely discredited, of British women being raped by the rebels, or killing themselves to escape that fate. Dickens wrote to a friend that he would like "to exterminate the Race upon whom the stain of the late cruelties rested ... to blot it out of mankind and raze it off the face of the earth" (Peck 1988: 82). He recast those sentiments in a short story, "The Perils of Certain English Prisoners," published in the Christmas number of *Household Words* in 1857. Here was combat that seemed to violate the British home itself. Such trauma was difficult to assimilate to novelistic treatment, although Dickens's rage clearly informs *A Tale of Two Cities* (1859), where the French revolutionaries are "tigers," and the hero, Sidney Carton, shares his surname with the main character of "Perils." The earliest direct literary responses were eyewitness accounts, such as *The Story of Cawnpore* (1859) by Mowbray Thompson, a British soldier who was one of the very few survivors of the siege and massacre there, and melodrama, such as Boucicault's *Jessie Brown, or The Relief of Lucknow* (a favorite theme), which was well suited to capture the stark moral oppositions informing most accounts. The first novel to treat the rebellion directly, Edward Money's *The Wife and the Ward* (1859), resembles eyewitness accounts in its abrupt truncation of events with the deaths of all the English characters. It was apparently too difficult to imagine a renewed order more durable than that of sheer revenge. Only gradually did more hopeful versions of an Anglo-Indian social order emerge; novels about the Mutiny began to proliferate only several decades later, culminating in the 1890s.

By that time, however, Britain's imperial mission had become even more expansive and more volatile, and attitudes towards the subjugated populations had hardened. In the wake of the Mutiny, earlier rationales for empire appealing to a civilizing process increasingly gave way to appeals for the subjugation of "savage" peoples. Those appeals were buttressed by increasingly rigid and quasi-scientific systems of racial hierarchy, most notably those sponsored by the "Anthropological Society" of London, founded by John Hunt in 1864. In the process, models of masculinity that initially had been cruxes of social ambition, or even something like personal therapy, came to seem a linchpin of empire. With this development, adventure narratives, whose archetype was *Robinson Crusoe*, took on new popularity and significance. Their celebration of courage, resourcefulness, and physical resilience, although often addressed specifically to an adolescent audience, seemed just what Britain in general required. A best-selling example, R. M. Ballantyne's *Coral Island* (1857), was published in the year of the Mutiny. Though replete with pirates and cannibals, the story of three young sailors marooned in the South Pacific suggests the close link between missionary narratives, adventure stories, and chronicles of empire. Not only does the narrator, Ralph Rover, frequently invoke "the great and kind Creator of this beautiful world" (Ballantyne 1949: 31), but the boys' adventure ultimately merges with the work of an English missionary, whose conversion of one group of native island-ers leads them to forsake cannibalism, and to rescue the young casta-ways from their bloodthirsty fellows. The boys' triumphant hardiness thus merges with the broader civilizing mission, whereby "the false gods of Mango were reduced to ashes!" (334). Although *Coral Island* is far less bellicose than many subsequent adventures – the boys are exempted from killing anyone – it is one harbinger of a world increas-ingly subjected to imperial rule. The island of the Lotos Eaters had become a space to be conquered.

Spasmodics and Other Poets

Muscular manhood might seem to leave little place for poetry, but in 1857 Kingsley himself produced a novel that conjoined the Crimean War with an emblematic poet. *Two Years Ago* is a topical grab-bag, even by Kingsley's notoriously loose standards of construction: vari-ous plot strands gather in Crimea, American slavery (in a bow to *Uncle Tom's Cabin*, which had a huge impact in England, one character is an escaped mulatta posing as an Italian opera singer), modern sanita-tion (a cholera epidemic looms), and a crisis of vocation in its central character, Tom Thurnival, a physician who doubles as something like an international man of mystery. But the most vigorous of Kingsley's hobby-horses, masculinity, undergoes a separate crisis in the figure of Elsley Vavasour, a fashionable poet whose name turns out to be an alias disguising his working-class origins as John Briggs. The effete and high-strung Vavasour, who relies on opium to calm his nerves, was clearly aimed at the recent vogue for the work of several working-class poets, who had been grouped in jest as the "Spasmodic" school. Yet some commentators took the character to be a hit at Tennyson, and that confusion suggests some of the anxieties informing British poetry in the 1850s. A generation earlier, Macaulay had been unruffled by the prospect (as he saw it) that poetry would simply be left behind by the march of mind, but now a number of poets themselves expressed anxiety that poetry was cutting itself adrift from modern life.

That fear seems perplexing after the immense success of *In Memoriam* in 1850, and Tennyson's appointment later that year as Poet Laureate. Soon after, however, critics were hailing the appearance of a "new poet," whose meteoric rise and fall prompted energetic debate over the state of poetry. In 1853, David Bogue published *Poems* by Alexander Smith (1830–67), which garnered wide critical attention for its distinctive style. Though distinctive, it was not singular. As embodied in his most lengthy poem, "A Life-Drama," Smith's verse recalled Browning's early dramatic poetry (notably *Pauline* and *Paracelsus*) in its celebration of antinomian struggle, which also had resonated in Philip Bailey's *Festus*, T. H. Horne's *Orion*, and J. Weston Marston's *Gerald* (1842), and would be echoed in Sydney Dobell's *Balder* (1853). Smith's poetry represents a zenith of Victorian subjectivism, in which the impulse to capture the inward life almost entirely overwhelms the worldly engagement that an outwardly dramatic form seems to promise. The pursuit of emotional intensity impels long, often tortuous meditations in blank verse grappling with the speaker's desires and perplexities, which frequently are expressed in wildly inflated style, particularly a hypertrophy of metaphor that is sometimes daringly erotic, but frequently turgid:

> Like a wild lover, who has found his love
> Worthless and foul, our friend, the sea, has left
> His paramour the shore; naked she lies,
> Ugly and black and bare. Hark how he moans!
>
> (Smith 1853: 97)

Critics unsurprisingly attacked such boldness, but the peculiar ferocity of the criticism seemed bound up with Smith's humble social origins: this distinctive poetic idiom was the product of a Glasgow "mechanic," following in his father's craft as a designer of lace patterns. For all of its subjectivism, moreover, Smith's poetry – like that of earlier poets in the "Spasmodic School" – claimed its protagonists were representative men of the age, typically poets struggling to give expression to its distinctive spirit. Their very confusion, it was suggested, their often strained and bewildered groping towards psychic equilibrium, was a decidedly contemporary habit of mind, which in Smith's poetry was aligned with working-class aspirations and radical politics. With Sydney Dobell he published sonnets on Crimea in *England in Time of War* (1856), in which longing for glory jostled with lament for the suffering. Such ambitions called out much of the same polemic that had greeted Keats and the "Cockney School" 35 years earlier. As Kingsley's Vavasour makes plain, poetry remained closely bound to social pretension. Accordingly, the most devastating attack took the form of ridicule. A parody in *Punch* by W. E. Aytoun entitled *Firmilian: A Spasmodic Poem* (1853) cut short Smith's vogue, and that of the poetry he came to represent, in the very act of christening it. Far more than Keats, this new "fiery particle" did indeed seem to have been snuffed out by an article.

But the comet left a marked afterglow. Smith's poetry triggered one of the most important critical exchanges of the era, when in July of 1853 the *North American Review* offered an account of "Recent English Poetry" comparing Smith's *Poems* with Arnold's two volumes, *Empedocles on Etna, and other Poems*, and *The Strayed Reveler and Other Poems*. For this reviewer, Smith's humble background was more than picturesque; it seemed integral to a distinctive poetry sharply opposed to "the ordinary languid collectanea published by young men of literary habits." Over against the fervid, sometimes incoherent, but recognizably contemporary poetry of Smith, the reviewer turns a withering disdain against the poetry of "A," which he identifies with an educated elite (hence "collectanea") that appreciates poetry only in the guise of earlier ages. Insiders could appreciate a still sharper edge to this conflict: they knew that the anonymous reviewer was Arnold's close friend, Arthur Hugh Clough (Clough 1999: 1263).

In his review, Clough reverses the terms of the Cockney School attack: it is elite culture that is enervating modern poetry, whose rejuvenation lies more with "the latest disciple of the school of Keats" than with Arnold's deeply learned appropriations of classical styles and themes. His achievements, Clough wearily concedes, "have undoubtedly a great literary value," yet "people much prefer 'Vanity Fair' and 'Bleak House.'" The familiar emphasis on sympathy as a binding social force, articulated in a conflict between general and particular, common and eccentric, Clough recasts along generic lines. The novel has come to address "general wants, ordinary feelings, the obvious rather than the rare facts of human nature" and to give form and shape to "the actual, palpable things with which our everyday life is concerned," and it is this emphasis that Smith's poetry likewise takes up (Clough 1999: 1255). Arnold's poetry, by contrast, finds pleasure in wire-drawn refinements of ancient motifs, as in his treatment of Arthurian legend in "Tristram and Iseult": "We listen, indeed, not quite unpleased, to a sort of faint musical mumble, conveying at times a kind of subdued half-sense, or intimating, perhaps a three-quarters-implied question; is anything real? – is love anything? – What is anything? – is there substance enough even in sorrow to mark the lapse of time? – is not passion a diseased unrest ...?" (1263). The qualities, Clough continues (in a vein that suggests how widespread the Carlylean diagnosis had become) "exemplify something certainly of an overeducated weakness of purpose in Western Europe ... a disposition to press too far the finer and subtler intellectual and moral susceptibilities." In order to balance "ascetic and timid self-culture," the world must press toward the opposite extreme of "unquestioning, unhesitating confidence," which can find poetry in "the busy seats of industry," even "in the blank and desolate streets and upon the solitary bridges of the midnight city" ([1265–6; 1256]).

The self-doubt reflected in Clough's own poetry gave a special edge to his mockery of Arnold. But the temperamental affinity also gave him special insight into Arnold's audience and, more pointedly, into the peculiar way in which Arnold freights romantic love with large questions of belief. Arnoldian longing typically conjures up a sweeping history in which some earlier, lost epoch is imagined as a time of untroubled faith. "Dover Beach," his best-known lyric, famously couches its appeal for love against "the melancholy, long withdrawing roar" of "the Sea of Faith" (an eccentric seduction deftly parodied in Anthony Hecht's "Dover Bitch," which reworks the poem from the unnamed woman's vantage). In "Stanzas from the Grande Chartreuse," Arnold fused personal and historical crisis even more suggestively, imagining himself "wandering between two worlds, one dead /The other powerless to be born ..." (ll. 84–5; Arnold 1979). Throughout Arnold's career, poetry registers this crisis with special urgency, but it cannot supply a new "mythus," in Carlyle's term, to compensate for the loss. In his later critical essays, Arnold will suggest that poetry's sheer fidelity to feeling will be a bulwark against the ruins of traditional faith. But "Stanzas," like all his early poetry, is haunted by the prospect that feeling itself has no place in modern life, that the poet's "melancholy" is as much "an outworn theme" as the worship of the Carthusian monks who have prompted the meditation. The "last of the race of them who grieve" join hands with "Last of the people who believe!" (ll. 110, 112). "What helps it," he asks, that Shelley uttered his "lovely wail" or Byron staged "the pageant of his bleeding heart"? Poetry survives in the valley of its saying, Auden will conclude nearly a century later, but Arnold already concedes much to the utilitarian ethos against which he struggles.

The intellectual fatigue is most fully evoked in *Empedocles on Etna*, the title poem of Arnold's 1852 volume, which develops the emblematic landscape of Arnold's earlier lyrics. Repeatedly the Arnoldian lyric speaker ascends from "a darkling plain" ("Dover Beach") of mundane confusion into a lofty vantage associated with detached contemplation (on the model of Lucretius's Epicurean gods) as well as with a journey back in time, both personal and historical. In the figure of Empedocles, a Greek philosopher of the fifth century BCE, Arnold found a stoic quester after truth – a man who "sees things as they are," as he put it in his reading notes – disdained by the world at large. "The world is all against him, and incredulous of the truth; his mind is overtasked by the effort to hold fast so great and severe a truth in solitude." After ascending Etna, he is unable to turn back to the plains below, and leaps into the volcano – seeking to be "reunited with the universe," but suggesting that this consummately romantic aspiration can be only a Pyrrhic victory (Arnold 1979: 154–5).

The poem was especially vulnerable to Clough's disdain, and his criticism apparently struck home, for when Arnold republished the volume later that year, he withdrew the poem. But he added a Preface, explaining that he had withdrawn the poem "not because the subject of it was a Sicilian Greek born between two and three thousand years ago," but because the poem was *too* modern. Steeped as it was in "the doubts, the discouragement, of Hamlet and of Faust," the poem represented a situation in which "suffering finds no vent in action" and therefore failed to "inspirit and rejoice the reader" (Arnold 1960–77:

i.1–3). It must give pleasure, as the American poet Wallace Stevens would later put it, but the current state of English poetry, Arnold continued, conspired against that aim. Poets had abandoned the Aristotelian devotion to human action as the foundation of poetry, and with it coherent poetic structure, what Arnold (echoing Goethe) calls *Architechtonice*. "With us the expression predominates over the action," as critics encourage poets to "gratify them with occasional bursts of fine writing, and with a shower of isolated thoughts and images" (i.7). Clough had made much the same objection to Smith's poems, but Arnold was stalking bigger game, ultimately romanticism itself. Responding to a recent defender of the Spasmodics, who had declared "a true allegory of the state of one's own mind" was the summit of poetry, Arnold exclaimed, "No assuredly, it is not, it never can be so: no great poetical work has ever been produced with such an aim" (i.8).

History has not been kind to Arnold's verdict, published just three years after Wordsworth's *Prelude*. But this rallying cry for a renewed classicism (echoing that of Sir Henry Taylor in 1834) bears witness to the confusion Arnold likewise evokes in his lyrics. "An age wanting in moral grandeur" will supply few actions worthy of poetry, but can find some compensation in classical Greece: "in the endeavour to learn and practice, amid the bewildering confusion of our times, what is sound and true in poetical art, I seemed to find the only sure guidance, the only solid footing, among the ancients" (Arnold 1960–77: i.14). We are once again ascending the mountain, scrambling up the trail and trying not to slip into the abyss. Arnold was already at work on a long narrative, *Sohrab and Rustum* (1853), which embodied his prescriptions. But neither this nor a subsequent effort at classical tragedy, *Merope* (1857), has ever captured much enthusiasm. Instead, they reinforce Clough's advice: "The only safe course" for the modern poet, he had enjoined (taking up Arnold's own trope), would come "not by turning and twisting his eyes, in the hopes of seeing things as Homer, Sophocles, Virgil, or Milton saw them, but by seeing them, by accepting them as he sees them, and faithfully depicting them accordingly" (Clough 1999: 1264). In October of 1857, Arnold was elected Professor of Poetry at Oxford, and he turned his energies towards criticism – producing what would be the most influential literary criticism of the latter half of the century.

If the rise of Spasmodic poetry thus helped to redirect Arnold's career, its influence is more vivid and immediate in Tennyson's *Maud*

(1855), which returns us to the Crimea. *Maud* was a shock to many readers who had been moved by the elegiac consolations of *In Memoriam*. The subject matter is vintage Tennyson: the poem germinated from an expression of unrequited longing, "Oh, that 'twere possible," and develops a lament over social dispossession and erotic frustration associated with lost family fortunes, which clearly draws on Tennyson's own early adulthood, even to the characterization of his speaker as the "heir of madness." But the lyric impulse is diffused through a dramatic monologue of more than 1,200 lines, opening with the cry "I hate," and developing radical disjunctions of perspective and mood through widely varied meters and stanza structures. Preternaturally vivid observation is often difficult to disentangle from fantasy and moments of sheer delirium:

> Oh, why have they not buried me deep enough?
> Is it kind to have made me a grave so rough,
> Me, that was once a quiet sleeper?
> Maybe still I am but half-dead;
> Then I cannot be wholly dumb ...
>
> (ii. 334–8; Tennyson 1969)

For a public still unaccustomed to the dramatic monologue (Robert Browning remained largely unrecognized) Tennyson's poem was especially disorienting, lacking even the clearly delineated dramatic situation and character that typically distinguishes Browning's monologues. Tennyson's speaker evokes a more brittle psyche, anticipating the more thoroughgoing dispersal of the lyric self in T. S. Eliot's "The Love Song of J. Alfred Prufrock." And yet this very fluidity enabled astonishing technical brilliance. It also allowed for splenetic diatribes against contemporary social abuses, which at moments veer into the suggestion that violence itself might be therapeutic:

> Ah, for a man to arise in me,
> That the man I am may cease to be.
>
> (i.396–7)

Such fantasies of rejuvenated manhood take up the burden of "Locksley Hall." Here, too, the speaker closes by vowing to recover from despair and to embrace war as a redemptive rebuke to both individual and national degradation. He will "wake to the higher aims" of a country at war,

And many a darkness into the light shall leap,
And shine in the sudden making of splendid names,
And noble thought be freer under the sun,
And the heart of a people beat with one desire;
For the peace, that I deemed no peace, is over and done,
And now by the side of the Black and the Baltic deep,
And deathful-grinning mouths of the fortress, flames
The blood-red blossom of war with a heart of fire.

(iii.46–53)

To the reader confident of the poem's dramatic frame, this pointedly ironizes a patriotism that has passed into pathology – even to the "blood-red blossom" of the final line, which hints at a powerful current of sublimated aggression, taking up a cluster of references to blood that from the opening lines conjoin desire and death. Tennyson's contemporaries, however, for whom the Spasmodics were still fresh, could not so confidently separate speaker and poet. A reviewer in Tait's *Edinburgh Magazine* memorably arraigned the phrase "long, long canker of peace" as if it were Tennyson's own sentiment: " If any man comes forward to say or sing that the slaughter of 30,000 Englishmen in the Crimea tends to prevent women poisoning their babies, for the sake of burial fees, in Birmingham, he is bound to show cause ..." (Tennyson 1969: 1092). Even readers who grasped the monologue form were unsettled by the sympathy with a figure so profoundly morbid (an epithet frequently applied to Browning's speakers). It seemed to pervert the sympathetic power of imagination that resounds through so many Victorian tributes to literature. Perhaps Tennyson was responding to such concerns in the following year, when he added a new ending, which concluded:

It is better to fight for the good than to rail at the ill;
I have felt with my native land, I am one with my kind,
I embrace the purpose of God, and the doom assigned.

(iii.57–9)

But as this seemed to crown the speaker's recovery, it also further eroded the ironic frame of the monologue – dampening the speaker's eccentricity, but also reining in some of the sheer audacity of Tennyson's lyricism. Tennyson himself would later call the poem "a little *Hamlet,*" which is revealing not only in its hint of self-congratulation, but as it suggests the sometimes fine line between heroism and madness.

Though *Maud* may suggest that love and war are disjunctive worlds, in Victorian poetry as in the novel courtship and romance frequently figure a larger social and political order, even when the work lacks the explicit topicality of *The Princess* or an industrial novel. One telling example is a poem by a young librarian at the British Museum, Coventry Patmore (1823–96), whose title would become a byword of the age. *The Angel in the House*, originally published in two parts as *The Betrothal* (1854) and *The Espousals* (1856), each in 12 cantos and comprising some 4,000 lines, has become shorthand for all that is most sentimental and confining in Victorian views of womanhood and domestic life. Certainly it can be ransacked for such attitudes:

> A rapture of submission lifts
>   Her life into celestial rest;
> There's nothing left of that she was;
>   Back to the babe the woman dies,
> And all the wisdom that she has
>   Is to love him for being wise.
>   (2. viii. Prelude 1; Patmore 1949)

Such excerpting has doomed *The Angel in the House* to be one of the great unread monuments of mid-Victorian culture. But few poems could withstand such selective attention (the sentiment Patmore evokes here derives fairly directly from *Paradise Lost*) and the neglect has obscured a very distinctive achievement. The poem is, most obviously, a narrative of domestic life, something it shares with *In Memoriam*, *Amours de Voyage*, and *Aurora Leigh*, all of which thereby register the growing ascendancy of the novel. But Patmore's idealization of love (the "angel" of the title) owes much to earlier lyric, most notably the metaphysical poets, and the narrative of the poem unfolds through an unusual structure. Each canto opens with two to five lyric "Preludes" developing aspects of the leading themes informing the narrative section, a lengthier "idyll" given the same title as the Canto proper. Within the Preludes, Patmore rings changes on the idea of love as itself a form of sovereignty, but also as a many-faceted "paradox" that cultivates mutuality in subordination, and strength in weakness. Patmore recalls Donne's love poetry in particular by evoking not only a power beyond the material present, but the all too palpable travails of its pursuit:

> With her, as with a desperate town,
>   Too weak to stand, too proud to treat,

> The conqueror, though the walls are down,
>   Has still to capture street by street ...
>
> (II.2. i)

Building stanzas of variable length out of relatively simple tetrameter quatrains, Patmore evolved a markedly supple form, but also one of relative figurative austerity. The juxtaposition of lyric and narrative often is jarring, as when an epigrammatic tribute to "constancy rewarded" celebrating "variety /which men who change can never know" gives way to ham-fisted efforts to capture colloquial speech:

> "How long she's tarrying! Green's Hotel
>   I'm sure you'll like. The charge is fair,
> "The wines good. I remember well
>   I stay'd once, with her mother, there."
>
> (II.ix)

Ultimately, however, the poem evokes a very distinctive sense of ethereal refinement in everyday life, a subdued elegance, even courtliness, that struck a powerful chord. The poem went through five editions in nine years, and sold some 250,000 copies by the time of the poet's death in 1896.

Virginia Woolf in the following century declared that in order to write, she had to kill the angel in the house (Woolf 1974: 237–8). A more immediate rejoinder to Patmore appeared in 1856, when Elizabeth Barrett Browning brought out a book-length narrative in blank verse that she had been pondering for a decade. Encouraged by the reception of "Lady Geraldine's Courtship," she wrote to Robert Browning during their courtship in 1845 of "a sort of novel-poem ... running into the midst of our conventions, and rushing into drawing-rooms and the like ... meeting face to face and without mask the Humanity of the age, and speaking the truth of it plainly" (Mermin 1989: 186). The result, *Aurora Leigh*, became one of the best-selling poems of the century.

Though the poem has become best known in association with "the woman question," Barrett Browning later professed surprise at this. In her mind that concern was "collateral" to the aim of reaffirming the value of poetry itself:

> Nay, if there's room for poets in this world
> A little overgrown, (I think there is)

> Their sole work is to represent the age,
> Their age, not Charlemagne's, – this live, throbbing age,
> That brawls, cheats, maddens, calculates, aspires,
> And spends more passion, more heroic heat,
> Betwixt the mirrors of its drawing-rooms,
> Than Roland with his knights at Roncesvalles.
> To flinch from modern varnish, coat or flounce,
> Cry out for togas and the picturesque,
> Is fatal, – foolish too.
>
> (v.200–10; Barrett Browning 1996)

Like Clough, Barrett Browning worries that poetry may be losing its relevance to contemporary life through a facile idealizing of the past, which blinds it to the richness of the present. It is within this large debate that she situates the autobiography of an aspiring woman poet, and acerbically depicts the domestic obstacles to women's intellectual aspirations.

With a heroine who is half-Italian, born and raised in Florence, the poem approaches English life from a suggestively liminal perspective, with a privileged distance closely akin to that commanded by first-person narrators in the novel. After the deaths of her parents, Aurora is sent to live in England with her father's sister, whose insular, tightly wound obsession with decorum is evoked with bleak concision. She lived "a quiet life, which was not life at all" – indeed, "life" ("O life, O poetry, which means life in life! [i.915–16] – the term echoes throughout the poem) seems to be precisely what England represses: "There seemed more true life in my father's grave /Than in all of England" (i.375–6). The focus of the attack is the model of womanhood celebrated by Sarah Stickney Ellis and others:

> their angelic reach
> Of virtue, chiefly used to sit and darn,
> And fatten household sinners, – their, in brief,
> Potential faculty in everything
> Of abdicating power in it ...
>
> (i.430–43)

Within this scheme, Aurora's aunt seems a feminine Podsnap – "She liked a Woman to be womanly, /And English women, she thanked God and sighed ... /Were models to the universe" (i.444–7). Such discipline enforces domestic routine to keep down the "quickening inner life" (i.1027) that is redolent of Italy, and that Aurora strives in vain to repress. It was

> As if she said, "I know there's something wrong;
> I know I have not ground you down enough
> To flatten and bake you to a wholesome crust
> For household uses and proprieties ..."
>
> (i.1039–42)

This excruciating oppression animates what now seems Aurora's rather jejune ideal of poets as transcendent beings, set apart from ordinary mortals, "called to stand up straight as demi-gods, /Support the intolerable strain and stress /Of the universal" (ii.385–6). Her fervent, remarkably unmodulated ideal of romantic autonomy recalls the spasmodics, as does the poem's often turgid figurative language:

> Never flinch,
> But still, unscrupulously epic, catch
> Upon the burning lava of a song
> The full-veined, heaving, double-breasted Age
>
> (v.236)

Although commentators have tried to disentangle Aurora's views from those of Barrett Browning herself, such operatic claims clearly respond to skepticism about the value of poetry in general. Answering the condescension of Carlyle and others, Aurora insists that the true poet is a creature of absolute integrity:

> He will not suffer the best critic known
> To step into the sunshine of free thought
> And self-absorbed conception and exact
> An inch-long swerving of the holy lines.
>
> (v. 251–7)

Over against such confidence, Aurora's cousin, Romney Leigh, incarnates two popular suspicions of her vocation. He believes that poetry cannot address contemporary needs, and that in any event it is beyond the capacity of women. The objections gather force from being interwoven with an outwardly iconoclastic and progressive politics.

Romney exemplifies that surprisingly prominent mid-century type, the aristocratic radical: he is a Christian Socialist who has turned his ancient country home into a "phalanstery" housing the poor. But he is also a seductive erotic presence, which brings the romance plot into Aurora's *Bildungsroman*. As in contemporary novels, the heroine's initial resistance affirms her independence of mind – which extends to refusing any form of inheritance that might compromise her sense of autonomy. Like Brontë's Rochester (parallels between the two narratives were widely noted), Romney must come to recognize the independence and dignity of the woman he loves; unlike Rochester, he must also concede the power of poetry, which entails confessing the inadequacy of his own schemes for social reform. So much for the tidy divisions of "separate spheres": as throughout mid-Victorian literature, the reconciliation of divergent perspectives in marriage becomes a paradigm for resolving a host of social conflicts.

The poem is not terribly solicitous of the poor in general, who seem to Aurora more in need of spiritual redemption than food. The one poor character singled out for attention is the preternaturally virtuous Marian Erle, whom Romney proposes to marry, less out of love than as a symbol of social harmony. When Marian, egged on by Lady Waldemar, concludes that she is unfit to be Romney's wife, this paragon of selfless virtue flees to France, where she is raped and gives birth to an illegitimate child. The theme was provocative, but in the wake of Gaskell's *Ruth* became an increasingly prominent means of urging sympathy with the plight of women subjected to sexual exploitation and violence. Marian's fate echoes in the poem's repeated attacks on prostitution, but she is redeemed by what seems her enduring stigma, her child, whose "infant eyes," Aurora remarks, "have set me praying" (i.335–6). Yet a hard moralism persists beneath this tolerance. Marian fiercely resists Aurora's unreflective use of the word "seduced" to describe her predicament. "I was murdered," she insists, but while this underscores the violence she has suffered, it also rescues her from the anathema of enjoying sexual pleasure outside of marriage. For that freedom, *Aurora Leigh* has no place.

Mrs. Browning's husband, as he still was largely known, had published a new volume of his own in the previous year. Robert was less sanguine than his wife about Italy as a realm of political freedom, but in *Men and Women* (1855) it enabled an extraordinary poetic exuberance. The volume, one of the greatest of the century, contains many widely anthologized poems, evoking a broad range of experience in a startling variety of stanza forms, which are rarely repeated – as Browning proudly notes in his concluding poem, "One Word More," where he tots up his "fifty men and women." This closing exhortation, which professes a directness and sincerity of utterance not to be found in the 50 poems preceding it, encourages a view of the volume as a collection of dramatic monologues – a view sustained by anthologies, where the most cited tend to be monologues with clear and emphatic historical (and thus ironic) frames: "Fra Lippo Lippi," "Andrea del Sarto," "A Tocatta of Galuppi's," even the nightmarish "Childe Roland to the Dark Tower Came." As a whole, however, the volume is more lyrical than this distribution would suggest, more in keeping with two other of its most-anthologized poems, "Love Among the Ruins" and "Two in the Campagna." The majority of the poems conform to the title not in variety of characterization, but in exploring the force of the conjunction: they are expressions and explorations of romantic love, the yearning for it, the obstacles to it, and the rare (and fleeting) moments in which it is realized. The titles alone suggest a swerve from the specificity of the monologue: "A Lovers' Quarrel," "A Woman's Last Word," "By the Fire-Side," "Any Wife to Any Husband," "A Serenade at the Villla," "My Star," "A Pretty Woman," "Respectability," "Love in a Life," "Life in a Love," "One Way of Love," "Another Way of Love" (the various pendants also reinforce the power of the binary), "The Last Ride Together," "In Three Days," "In a Year," "Women and Roses." In all these works the historical framing that shapes Browning's most famous monologues drops away – and, with it, much of the incitement to read the poems dramatically or ironically.

The opening poem, "Love Among the Ruins," sets the pattern, and in a form that suggests an embrace of both love and lyric as a withdrawal from larger ambitions and traditionally elevated themes. Its seven stanzas are organized by the contrast between an epic past – a world impelled by "lust of glory" in all its forms – and the ruins of that world, reduced to a carpet of grass that "embeds /Every vestige of the city," and on which the poet now awaits his lover.

> In one year they sent a million fighters forth
>   South and North,
> And they built their gods a brazen pillar high
>   As the sky,
> Yet reserved a thousand chariots in full force –
>   Gold, of course.
> Oh heart! Oh blood that freezes, blood that burns!
>   Earth's returns

For whole centuries of folly, noise and sin!
        Shut them in,
With their triumphs and their glories and the rest!
        Love is best!
                                        (ll. 73–84; Browning 1970)

Here, it seems, is a quintessence of the sentimentalism that energizes Victorian domesticity: not only is Love "best," but its value is starkly opposed to a public life literally reduced to ruins. To modern readers, this might solicit a profound sense of diminishment, but it answered to something very powerful in Browning and Victorian audiences.

"Love is best," but not easily realized, and the lyrics frequently explore tensions within romantic longing itself. "Two in the Campagna" expresses a yearning for more complete communion – "I would that you were all to me, /You that are just so much, no more" (ll. 36–7) – but ultimately surrenders the dream associated with the "good minute" of a romantic epiphany. Linked to the ideal of the perfect moment is "The Last Ride Together," which celebrates "the instant made eternity" – couched, tellingly, as a question: "What if. …. " such an experience were possible? (ll. 101–8). Instead of securely fulfilled desire, the speaker of "Two in the Campagna" is left pondering "Infinite passion, and the pain / Of finite hearts that yearn" (ll. 59–60). This is a pointed reflection on the titanic longing of Browning's early poetry, and on romanticism at large, but it does not repudiate romantic passion so much as it reconfigures it. Only pain can confirm one's capacity to feel. Contentment bespeaks a more tepid spirit, or a willingness to compromise, whereas disappointment measures the power of longing. Longing in turn intimates the possibility of transcendence, of a sphere of human experience extending beyond the finite, as "Andrea del Sarto" famously puts it: "a man's reach should exceed his grasp /Or what's a heaven for?" (ll. 97–8). Not "heaven," but "a heaven," as if each man harbors his own image of redemption, at once the goal of longing and also, more unpredictably, a spur to the intrinsic pleasures of striving. It is as if passion itself were sanctified.

The Power of Art

The most famous poems in *Men and Women* explore the psychology of intellectual commitment, in the worlds of art, science, and faith. Gone are the moral monsters of "My Last Duchess" or "Porphyria's Lover." The great monologues of the volume are interested less in pathology than in the ways in which private desire shapes public engagement – whether works of art or modes of belief. In the two great "painter poems," "Fra Lippo Lippi" and "Andrea del Sarto," Browning explores the psychological wellsprings of art, and an important ambivalence about art's means and ends. Like Ruskin in *Modern Painters* (volumes 3 and 4 of which were published in the same year as *Men and Women*), Browning in "Fra Lippo Lippi" explores the moral bearings of art's sensuality, so often invoked as a paragon of human vanity. The tension is thrown into especially bold relief in Renaissance painting, where Christian motifs ostensibly signifying otherworldly devotion are realized in deeply alluring sensuous form. The bravura opening of the poem evokes this tension with brilliant economy, as Fra Lippo addresses the night watch that has cornered the holy father by torchlight "at alley's end / Where sportive ladies leave their doors ajar" (ll. 5–6). A monk caught outside a brothel is an unlikely spokesman for an artistic program, but what emerges is a compelling defense of naturalism in painting – and, by implication, in art generally. "Zooks, sir, flesh and blood, /That's all I'm made of" (ll. 60–1), Lippo exclaims, and those forces animate his best painting. His delight in the visible, tactile world is guided not by formal training, but by powers of observation honed by deprivation, "my lesson learned, the value and significance of flesh" (l. 268). That lesson wins ready assent from the untutored public, who savor "the life" in Lippo's painting, but it unsettles the religious authorities, who demand a painting that would "lift them over" the "perishable clay," make viewers "forget there's such a thing as flesh" (ll. 180–2). The opposition – clearly recasting some of the bewildered contemporary response to Browning's poetry – elicits from Fra Lippo one of the most audacious Victorian proclamations of the power of art

> Or say there's beauty with no soul at all –
> (I never saw it – put the case the same –)
> If you get simple beauty and naught else
> You get about the best thing God invents;
> That's somewhat; and you'll find the soul you have missed,
> Within yourself, when you return him thanks.
>
> (ll. 215–20)

Aristotelian mimesis is invested with redemptive power:

> we're made so that we love
> First when we see them painted, things we have passed
> Perhaps a hundred times nor cared to see;

> And so they are better, painted – better to us,
> Which is the same thing. Art was given for that;
> God uses us to help each other so ...
> If I drew higher things with the same truth!
> That were to take the Prior's pulpit place,
> Interpret God to all of you!
>
> (ll. 300–11)

And yet this redemptive energy remains tethered to the sensuality of a monk "out of bounds."

Fra Lippo thus becomes an unlikely harbinger of the Modernist conjunction of artistic genius and swaggering virility, which energizes the cults of such painters as Picasso and Pollock. Of course the monk also enables Browning to hedge his bets both morally, by distancing the painter's sentiments from the poet's, and aesthetically, by rehearsing a program to which Browning's own poetry doesn't wholly subscribe. His other famous painter poem, "Andrea del Sarto," in fact turns on an importantly different conception of the art. It is overtly concerned with the clash between two schemes of value, beauty and money. The painter laments having sacrificed his quest for excellence to satisfy the desires of his wife, Lucrezia, to whom the monologue is addressed – and who, he suggests, fails to appreciate either form of devotion, even to the extent of conducting an affair with an unnamed "cousin." The ostensibly celibate monk is a figure of sexual potency, the painter married to his beautiful model is emasculated: such are the ironies of Browning's monologues. But Andrea's great defeat, as he recounts it, was the surrender of his artistic ambition. More assured in technique than even Raphael, the mechanical perfection of his work condemns him, for it bespeaks a failure of aspiration, of artistic passion. "Less is more":

> There burns a truer light of God in them,
> In their vexed beating stuffed and stopped-up brain,
> Heart, or whate'er else, than goes on to prompt
> This low-pulsed forthright craftsman's hand of mine ...
> Ah, but a man's reach should exceed his grasp,
> Or what's a heaven for? All is silver-grey
> Placid and perfect with my art; the worse!
>
> (ll. 79–82; 97–9)

Andrea's famous exhortation recalls Ruskin's "Nature of Gothic": imperfection is the signature of soul. At the same time, the poem is psychologically more complex than "Fra Lippo Lippi," evoking as it does a more radical ambiguity. Did Andrea knowingly surrender his larger aims out of devotion to Lucrezia – and thus, in response to a moral dilemma, a clash of public and private imperatives – or does his failure stem from some more fundamental weakness of will, for which Lucrezia serves as a scapegoat? In either case, Andrea's view of art is not Lippo's. Whereas Lippo would have the meaning of art, as of the world itself, fully manifest in the image, Andrea locates genius in the intimation of a fulfillment beyond the material present. He sees in Raphael's work a

> Reaching, that heaven might so replenish him,
> Above and through his art – for it gives way;
> That arm is wrongly put – and there again –
> A fault to pardon in the drawing's lines,
> Its body, so to speak: its soul is right,
> He means right ...
>
> (ll. 109–14)

Andrea thus reopens the rift between body and soul that Lippo attempts to fuse.

The world of art, and the relations between painting and poetry, gained wider currency not only through Ruskin's pugnacious criticism but also through a movement of which he became an influential defender, the Pre-Raphaelites. Pre-Raphaelitism, one of the most durable of Victorian medievalisms, took shape in 1848 when three young painters, John Everett Millais, William Holman Hunt, and Dante Gabriel Rossetti, formed the nucleus of a group declaring itself a "Brotherhood" in rebellion against the British art establishment. They invoked as their model the work of Italian painters prior to Raphael, from whose titanic achievement so much subsequent painting derived. Like many nineteenth-century aesthetic programs, Pre-Raphaelitism proclaimed a return to nature, which as embodied in the (widely varied) canvases of the Brotherhood became associated with sharp outline, intense coloration, an avoidance of shadow, and vivid detail. Although the early work of the Pre-Raphaelites was frequently attacked for distortion and exaggeration, the movement soon gained a prominence beyond the world of painting. As their subject matter tended to be literary and historical ("The First Translation of the Bible into English," "The Girlhood of Mary Virgin," "Christ in the Carpenter's Shop"), Pre-Raphaelitism came to seem itself a mode of narration, and "Pre-Raphaelite" became shorthand for painstaking attention to detail. As the movement became associated above all with Rossetti and his distinctive portraits of women in apparent trances, with exaggerated mouths and unbound hair signaling a profound sensuality, "Pre-Raphaelite" also came to label a particular kind of boldly erotic femininity that soon would figure centrally in debates over the morality of art.

The Pre-Raphaelites left a more direct mark on English literature at mid-century in a body of poetry written not only by D. G. Rossetti and his sister Christina, but also by Patmore and (later) George Meredith, William Morris, and Algernon Swinburne. The congruence between painting and poetry is tellingly suggested by attacks on the Pre-Raphaelite painting, which echo Arnold's criticism of fragmentation in modern poetry. In both cases, what seemed missing was the power of composition, a structure that would modulate and harmonize vivid particulars, and thus soften the visual or cognitive impact of the work. The early lyrics of D. G. Rossetti in particular tend to rebuke this expectation. "The Blessed Damozel," published in 1850 in the short-lived PRB periodical *The Germ*, describes a woman who "leaned out /From the gold bar of heaven" (ll. 1–2; Rossetti 1901) dreaming of the earthly lover she has left behind. The lyric is replete with Christian symbolism, drawn most notably from the poetry of Dante Gabriel's namesake, but the situation ultimately shares more with "The Lady of Shalott" than with the *Vita Nuova*. The poem offers no religious consolation, and the damozel herself seems only partially abstracted from an earthly, physical existence: she leans out over the gold bar "Until her bosom must have made /The bar she leaned on warm" (ll. 45–6). The effect recalls the world of *Wuthering Heights*, where the communion between heaven and earth feels similarly direct yet wrenchingly obstructed. In "The Woodspurge," written a few years later (but not published, along with most of Rosssetti's poetry, until 1870), Rossetti more explicitly empties out a traditional symbolic register, and with it any sense of transcendent meaning. In a manner reminiscent of Wordsworth's "I Wandered Lonely," the peripatetic poet finds himself contemplating a woodspurge in bloom, "three cups in one". Then comes the final stanza:

> From perfect grief there need not be
> Wisdom or even memory

> One thing then learnt remains to me
> The woodspurge has a cup of three.
>
> (ll. 13–16)

The reader of Wordsworth would expect some form of epiphanic awareness – if not of a spiritual presence in nature, at least of the restorative power of apprehending the natural world. Rossetti offers only the bare physical detail – all the more arresting for its lack of emblematic force.

Realisms

The Pre-Raphaelite proclamation of a return to nature constituted one influential mid-century defense of realism in art. Another even more influential understanding of the concept came to wide notice with the career of George Eliot (1819–81). The appearance of *Adam Bede* in 1859 was one of the great success stories of Victorian publishing. Within four months of its publication by Blackwood, this three-volume work by an unknown novelist had gone through three printings, and a cheaper one-volume edition sold 10,000 copies by year's end. "Its author takes rank at once among the masters of the art," wrote the often acerbic critic of the London *Times*, E. S. Dallas, one voice in a chorus of praise (D. Carroll 1971: 77). Success intensified the mystery surrounding "George Eliot." Evidently he was well acquainted with rural life in the English Midlands near Coventry; as the guessing game began, local readers were quick to see historical prototypes for characters in Eliot's earlier fiction, a collection of three novellas entitled *Scenes of Clerical Life*, which had appeared in *Blackwoods* in 1857. But the pseudonym in fact concealed a life that genuinely merited the over-used tag, "scandalous."

The protagonist of *Adam Bede* was modeled on Robert Evans, a carpenter who had risen to be an estate agent for the wealthy Newdigate family in Warwickshire, and whose wife gave birth to a daughter, Mary Ann, in 1819. The novel's imaginative germ was the story of Mary Ann's Methodist aunt comforting a condemned woman in her jail cell, and the unlettered faith of rural laborers figures centrally in the novel, set against the struggles of those less secure in their belief. Mary Ann herself experienced an intense but short-lived evangelical fervor in her late teens; her subsequent decision to withdraw from church attendance was the most traumatic event of her early life. As she became acquainted with other skeptics and "advanced" thinkers, Evans became immersed in the so-called "Higher Criticism" in Germany, which treated the Bible not as literal truth but as profound yet artful storytelling. She subsequently translated a monument of that thought, Strauss's *Das Leben Jesu* (1846), and then Feuerbach's *Des Wesen des Christentums* (1854), which offered something like an anthropology of Christianity, treating it as an allegory of human moral development, in which suffering itself becomes a form of baptism that brings the sufferer to fuller awareness, and to the recognition of those higher human powers – mercy, sympathy, love – that are incarnated in the Christian God. In 1850 Marian Evans (as she now called herself) moved to London and began work as the managing editor of the *Westminster Review*, for which she also wrote reviews on a broad range of books. All of this amounted to a bold and highly unconventional career for an unmarried woman, which in itself would have left Marian Evans an important place in the history of continental thought in England. Even more daring, however, was her decision in 1853 to live with George Henry Lewes, an influential journalist and editor, who was married but unable to divorce his wife. It was Lewes who in 1856 suggested that she try her hand at fiction – within which a recurrent theme became the social pressures besetting unconventional women, women of intense passion and intellectual ambition. One response to those pressures was her decision to publish under a male pseudonym, George Eliot.

Uniquely among Victorian writers, George Eliot had staked out a program for the novel even before she turned to fiction. In her review of the third volume of Ruskin's *Modern Painters*, in the spring of 1856, she praised Ruskin's criticism in terms that would capture her own aspirations as a novelist:

> The truth of infinite value that he teaches is realism – the doctrine that all truth and beauty are to be attained by a humble and faithful study of nature, not by substituting vague forms, bred by imagination on the mists of feeling, in place of definite, substantial reality. The thorough acceptance of this doctrine would remould our life; and he who teaches its application to any one department of human activity with such power as Mr. Ruskin is a prophet for his generation. (Eliot 1856: 626)

"Realism" was a charged word in literary discussion of the 1850s, inasmuch as it was associated primarily with French writing, particularly the novels of Balzac and George Sand, and frequently connoted not a particular manner of treatment so much as morally provocative subject matter. (The association was strengthened by the 1857 publication of Flaubert's *Madame Bovary* and its subsequent prosecution for obscenity.) But Eliot's usage exemplifies a characteristic English appeal to the concept as an instrument of moral education. Eliot's realism, like Ruskin's, is an exercise in humility and austerity – even renunciation – which enlarges a reader's powers of sympathy. Realism rebukes the visions of "imagination" – or at least tests them against "definite, substantial" reality, which presumably will dispel the merely visionary, and enhance one's appreciation of the everyday. Throughout her career, but particularly in her early novels, Eliot celebrates the capacity to find value in unprepossessing subject matter – ignoble, vulgar, even repugnant – as the hallmark of realism. The world of the Tulliver family in *Mill on the Floss* (1860), the narrator guesses, will seem one of "oppressive narrowness," but "it is necessary that we should feel it, if we care to understand how it acted on the lives of Tom and Maggie ..." (Eliot 1979: 362–3). Similar apologies inform the work of many Victorian novelists, but Eliot formalizes the dynamic. Realism enlarges the reader's understanding by nurturing sympathy, which is confirmed above all in the power to feel a common humanity at work in humble modes of life, petty aspirations, thwarted desires. "It is only the very largest souls," the narrator comments on the hero of her earliest story, "Amos Barton," "who will be able to appreciate and pity him – who will discern and love sincerity of purpose amid all the bungling feebleness of achievement" (Eliot 1973: 61).

Like an increasing number of writers and critics in the 1850s, Eliot defined her view of the novel by contrast with Dickens. "Art is the nearest thing to life," she exhorts in an 1856 review of Riehl's *Natural History of German Life*: "it is a mode of amplifying experience and extending our contact with our fellow-men beyond the bounds of our personal lot. All the more sacred is the task of the artist when he undertakes to paint the life of the People. Falsification here is far more pernicious than in the more artificial aspects of life" (Eliot 1963: 271). And it is here that Dickens fails. For all his fidelity to "the external traits of our town population," "he scarcely ever passes from the humorous and external to the emotional and tragic, without becoming as transcendent in his unreality as he was a moment before in his artistic truthfulness" (271). Eliot stakes out for her own art the "psychological character" that she claims Dickens neglects. "Realism" thus aims not only for plausibility, but for the suggestion of psychic depth in characters, and our illusion of vicarious participation in their innermost life. This emphasis would come to be widely shared among novelists in the second half of the century, and as developed in the novels of Henry James in particular, it became a paradigmatic structure in the Modernist novel – the great achievements of Conrad, Joyce, and Woolf, among others.

Realism also would nurture an increasingly self-conscious narrative stance. As realism is defined in resistance to fantasy or projection, as a submission to external reality, it tacitly appeals to an ideal of objectivity, and thereby raises questions as to whether such an ideal is attainable. Thus in *Middlemarch*, Eliot's narrator will famously suggest that the coherence of any narrative is necessarily a projection of the perceiving mind, whose consciousnesses organizes an outwardly chaotic world the way a beam of light orders the random scratches on a pier glass. Such optical tropes tether realism to epistemological concerns about our ways of knowing. These would become especially prominent in the Modernist novel – notably Conrad and Woolf – but the issues are at play in Rossetti's "Woodspurge," with its refusal of familiar modes of poetic meaning. In the third volume of *Modern Painters* (1856), Ruskin pointed to a similar crisis of representation when he analyzed varieties of personification – "the cruel, crawling form" – as examples of what he called "pathetic fallacy." Such projections, he argued, betray a "falseness" in the representation of "external things," and "reflect a mind and body in some sort too weak to deal fully with what is before them or upon them." The diagnosis chimes with Eliot's account of realism (and the Carlylean celebration of "Fact"): adequate understanding, perception that resists distorting emotions and fantasies, is not merely difficult, it is a kind of heroic struggle.

Eliot's celebration of self-consciousness as a path to moral redemption resonates in Dallas's glowing appreciation of *Adam Bede*; it underscores, he wrote, "that we are all alike – that the human heart is one" (D. Carroll 1971: 77). This is the soothing note that we have heard throughout praise of Victorian poetry and fiction; even in the pastoral community of Hayslope, we glimpse those fears of social division that were more explicitly assuaged in the industrial novel. Some of this emphasis also grows out of Eliot's religious reflection, particularly the example of Feuerbach. But the novel also bears witness to a broader secularizing force, a Wordsworthian romanticism that informs all of Eliot's early novels. As Eliot resists traditional literary decorums in pursuit of a truer, more elemental image of humanity, her realism echoes Wordsworth's Preface to *Lyrical Ballads*. Like Wordsworth, Eliot locates this humanity preeminently in rural life: "It will be a country story – full of the breath of cows and the scent of hay," as she described her first novel. In such settings, Eliot was better able to explore the conjoint influence of landscape and history on human experience, and to represent society itself, as she put in her review of Riehl, as "*incarnate history*" (D. Carroll 1971: 287; Eliot's emphasis). At the same time, however, her romanticism was supplemented by contemporary moral philosophy, which she had found deeply consoling in her own early religious struggles. It is hard to imagine that a work called "The Philosophy of Necessity" could be liberating, but Richard Congreve's speculations offered the young Mary Ann Evans a sense of universal moral order compatible with deep religious skepticism. In the novels of George Eliot, this influence echoes in repeated stress on the inexorability of human action, the notion that (as *Adam Bede* puts it) "consequences are unpitying" (Eliot 1980: 217). The effect resembles a secular nemesis, whose effects fall most harshly on characters who succumb to egoism, the cardinal failing in Eliot's fiction. Sympathy provides insight into this moral law, but also cushions its blow.

The year before George Eliot turned to fiction with *Scenes of Clerical Life*, another novel about clerical life brought Anthony Trollope (1815–83) his first wide notice. Trollope, son of Frances, was already 40 in 1855, and had been publishing novels since 1847, writing in the free hours of his career as a clerk with the Post Office. His first two novels, *The Macdermots of Ballycoran* (1847) and *The Kellys and the O'Kellys* (1848), were set in Ireland, where he was stationed at the time, and depict courtship and financial intrigue within the landed gentry (the Macdermots) and aristocracy (the Kellys). Although Trollope steered clear of the bleak distress of the Famine, their generally genial tone went largely unnoticed, the same fate that met a novel set during the French Revolution, *The Vendée* (1850). Transferred back to England, Trollope in 1855 published *The Warden*, a slender novel set in the cathedral town of Barchester (a thinly-veiled Salisbury), dealing with ecclesiastical infighting over the terms of a charitable bequest. The reception of this less-than-enticing subject reveals a good deal about both Trollope's art and the state of the novel in the mid-1850s.

For all the attacks on Dickens's social satire, fiction during the 1850s became increasingly aligned with social reform. Humphrey House's well-known comment on Dickens's career has in this light a larger resonance: in the early Victorian novel a bad smell is a bad smell, but by the 1850s, a bad smell is a problem (House 1941: 135). Eliot's early novels do not fit the mold of "social problem" fiction (though alcoholism in *The Scenes of Clerical Life* does glance at so-called "temperance fiction"), but her celebration of realism chimes with this association, inasmuch as it makes the novel an instrument that might "remould the world." *The Warden* was greeted in this context, but with some puzzlement, for Trollope's attention to the putative social abuse – "that vexed question, the administration of the charitable trusts in England," as the *Athenaeum* put it – seemed not wholly in earnest. "Everything is left in disorder and ruin, as though the design of the writer was to teach the folly of rectifying abuses," complained the *Eclectic Review* (Smalley 1969: 39). Others concluded that Trollope was satirizing the very genre of the "problem novel" – with some reason, given his characterization of John Bold, whose passion is "the reform of all abuses," the parodies of Carlyle (as "Dr. Pessimist Anticant"), Dickens ("Mr. Popular Sentiment"), and *The Times*, here the *Jupiter*, with its thundering, know-nothing leaders on topics of the day. But the comedy ultimately has little to do with doctrinal and political allegiances, save as the clash between divergent views might elicit the characters of those who hold them. More precisely, Trollope focuses on figures whose beliefs are not "held" so much as they are unreflectively followed, as automatically as breathing, until some minor figure of misrule suddenly challenges the routine, and characters are jolted into defending – or, in rarer cases, questioning – the established forms of everyday life.

A decade earlier it would have been hard to imagine such comedy wrung from religion. Sectarian debate had been so fierce from the time of Catholic emancipation through the rise of Tractarianism and the spread of evangelical fervor that in novels dealing centrally with religious life, doctrinal conflict tended to overwhelm all else. But in Trollope's fiction, as in Eliot's *Scenes of Clerical Life*, religion is treated with a distance that feels almost like nostalgia. The main interest no longer resides in the spiritual integrity of the clergyman and his establishment – typically defined in opposition to the state, whether among High Anglicans or evangelical "Low Church" and dissenting believers. Instead, conflict pivots on the moral choices informing everyday life within religious institutions. The aristocratic authority once attached to those institutions has been largely trivialized, appropriated to the aims of bourgeois self-definition and social ambition (Kucich 1994: 41–74).

As Trollope's art seems so thoroughly aligned with middle-class interests, it has been an object of great suspicion to many recent critics, who have arraigned Trollope for heavy-handed didacticism or unreflective complicity in coercive social discipline (Miller 1988: 107–45). But Trollope offers a more canny and incisive social anatomy than this suggests. In *The Warden*, the title character is a still point of meek resignation surrounded by fierce ambition and in-fighting. The Reverend Harding's quiet devotion to his duties makes a mockery of the reformers' caricatures, but his exorbitant sense of integrity in the face of their attacks (he imagines himself "gibbeted before ferocious multitudes" [Trollope 1980:127]) at the same time emasculates him in the eyes of his fellow clergy. How could he bow to an argument for reform that would undermine his own livelihood? His post is "an arrangement which everyone knows is essentially just and serviceable to the church," as Archdeacon Grantly puts it, in a telling conflation of justice and self-interest (115), and even the Warden's daughter calls his decision to resign "madness" (243). The reactions underscore both the Warden's otherworldliness – he shudders at an argument that has "so much practical, but odious common sense in it" (123) – and the insularity of Barchester. The often inflated self-importance of the clerical world makes it a ready source of comedy, but its very narrowness also allows certain moral touchstones to persist with special clarity and resonance – most notably, the idea of the gentleman. When the Warden imagines himself exposed before "every gentleman in the land" (172), we are encouraged to smile at his exaggerated delicacy and yet also to appreciate the gravity of the imagined tribunal.

The Warden became the first of six novels dealing with the world of Barchester. *Barchester Towers*, published in 1857, offers a more inclusive social portrait, which gathers in an array of landed families around which county life revolves (and whose roles are developed in subsequent novels), as well as divisions within the Church. From the opening page, the action turns on the connections between two different ministries – the offices of the Church of England depend on the favor of Her Majesty's Government – and the rivalry between the evangelical Slope and the Tractarian Arabin, both recent arrivals in Barchester who compete for preferment in the Church and the hand of the Warden's now-widowed daughter. But the Reverend Harding remains the moral center, the man who wins by not competing. The narrator of the novel, meanwhile, serves as a different foil to the intrigue he chronicles, embodying an urbane moderation that forswears all emotional extravagance: "let me ever remember my living friends, but forget them as soon as dead!" (Trollope 1980a: 1.16). These perspectives serve as foils to the often hilarious eccentricities of the various families in the novel, such as the arch-conservative Thornes of Ullathorne – Miss Thorne is "a pure Druidess" who "had adopted the Christian religion as a milder form of the religion of her ancestors" (1.217) – and the bohemian Stanhopes, decayed gentry largely resident in Italy, whose feckless son Ethelbert amuses himself by taking up various religions – "I was a Jew once myself," he nonchalantly remarks to the Bishop (1.103) – and whose sister, Signora Neroni, a mysteriously crippled femme fatale, devotes herself to captivating men young and old. Meanwhile, Mrs. Proudie, the Bishop's wife, is so adept at manipulating her husband that Church politics at times seem an extension of their bedtime conversations. The almost irresistible impulse to catalogue Trollope's characters says much about his art.

Barchester Towers would remain for most critics the benchmark achievement of Trollope's early career, but readers had much to choose from. From this juncture, Trollope became a byword for prolific output; *The Three Clerks* and *Doctor Thorne* both followed within twelve months, and by 1865 he had published within the space of ten years a dozen novels, two volumes of travel, and two collections of stories. "I quite admit that I crowded my wares into the market too quickly," he later acknowledged (Trollope 1980: 173), but Trollope's compulsive working habits, famously chronicled in his *Autobiography*, were a standing rebuke to any muse. The novelist's work was just that, a craft more akin to carpentry than that of the Wordsworthian poet, whereby one turned out so many words per morning, every morning, without fail. To Trollope's detractors this industrial regimen reflected a disdain for novel-writing as an art, likewise reflected in his intrusive narrators, who frequently dispel any illusion of reality by interrupting the action to comment on the challenges of writing itself: "a difficulty begins to make itself manifest in the necessity of disposing of all our friends in the small remainder of this one volume. Oh, that Mr. Longman would allow me a fourth!" (Trollope 1980a: 2.178) But though this habit would exasperate the young Henry James, most readers were engaged by the lack of pretension. Within a few years, Trollope became a central point of reference in reviews of contemporary fiction.

Two Guineveres

Trollope became celebrated for his portraits of young women, typically vivacious and independent-minded but still ready to find fulfillment in marriage. The appeal of these heroines may have reflected worries that middle-class women were becoming less ready to find satisfaction so closely tethered to domesticity. In *The Mill on the Floss* (1860), George Eliot portrayed a heroine whose intellectual hunger is but one facet of a deep alienation from her family and provincial community. With a dark complexion and coarse hair that are an affront to both family tradition and feminine ideals, Maggie Tulliver feels herself an outsider from birth, and that estrangement nurtures her longing for an array of possibilities denied to girls, most notably the formal education that is wasted on her stolid, unimaginative brother. The novel develops an extraordinarily rich portrait of repression, in which Maggie attempts to renounce her frustrated longings – intellectual, social, and erotic – only to experience them with redoubled force. Such an ordeal, the novel suggests, awaits any young woman who questions the moral grounds of power that she cannot directly challenge, and who seeks an identity of her own, apart from family and kinship. "We don't ask what a woman does – we ask whom she belongs to" (G. Eliot 1979: 542–3): the traditional notion of woman as a "relative creature" rebukes Maggie's effort to seek her own path.

Of course domestic womanhood had been challenged in *Aurora Leigh*, and it was coming under increasing pressure as Eliot was writing. The situation of women is a crux even in a contemporary poetic landmark seemingly worlds removed from *Mill on the Floss*. In the late 1850s, Tennyson began composing what would become *Idylls of the King*. The poem we now know by that title, however, came into the world in very different form. The 1859 edition contained only four parts, each of them titled with a woman's name: "Enid," "Vivien," "Elaine," and "Guinevere." The earliest readers of the poem did not follow the rise and fall of a kingdom. Instead, they read a poem preoccupied with varieties of feminine character, which (predictably enough) worried over the sexual discipline of its heroines, leaving male characters agitated far more by questions of feminine purity and fidelity than by knightly combat. But that worry underscores the crucial importance of marriage in Victorian understandings of civic life. Tennyson's insistence on the affiliation of "truth" and "troth" lays bare one of the foundations of Victorian domestic ideology, and subjects it to an acid bath.

The most harrowing moment of the poem comes in "Guinevere," when Arthur denounces the infidelity of his Queen, who lies at his feet. After pronouncing his enduring love, he continues:

> Yet must I leave thee, woman, to thy shame.
> I hold that man the worst of public foes

Who either for his own or children's sake
To save his blood from scandal, lets the wife
Whom he knows false, abide and rule the house:
For being through his cowardice allowed
Her station, taken everywhere for pure,
She like a new disease, unknown to me,
Creeps, no precaution used, among the crowd.
(ll. 508–16; Tennyson 1969)

The treachery of the "false" woman is as devastating as venereal disease to the body politic. It is a stunning trope; just as stunning were the reactions of Tennyson's contemporaries to this melodramatic tableau. "It is the resplendent top of human excellence," wrote the future Prime Minister, Gladstone. "It made me blubber, bucketsful," confided the poet and watercolorist Edward Lear (H. Tennyson 1897: 2.130). We cannot fully fathom such exorbitant responses, but they suggest that the passage tapped into very powerful anxieties. One need not presume bad faith – that these readers were not genuinely moved by Tennyson's insistence on Arthur's godlike magnanimity and self-control. Yet the comments also suggest a more inchoate relief at the containment of an especially unsettling treachery. Sexual betrayal may bite deeply into any psyche, and Tennyson had rehearsed the fantasy in a number of earlier poems, such as *Maud* and "Locksley Hall." Here, however, he makes wayward sexuality nothing less than the downfall of Camelot. Hyperbolic as that may be, the fantasy is central to Victorian culture; it is hard to overstate the power of domesticity as an ideal of perfect understanding and fidelity, and of feminine devotion to the needs of men and children.

The ideal was always a fragile one, but it seemed under particular strain in the later 1850s. Widespread discussion of the legal forms of divorce and marriage culminated in fierce parliamentary debate surrounding the Matrimonial Causes Act of 1857, which made divorce more readily accessible, along with legislation to allow married women more control over property (not enacted until 1870). Although the Divorce Bill ratified the double standard – husbands required only one ground, women two; even desertion was not sufficient basis for a woman to divorce if not compounded by physical cruelty – its passage troubled many husbands, and more than a few wives, because it allowed women a new degree of autonomy, and thereby seemed to unsettle the harmony of wills that underwrote domestic peace. The debate also called

attention to the most sordid private facts of respectable English domesticity, in the avidly followed divorce proceedings published in London
newspapers, which exposed not only brutality, betrayal, and sexual deviance, but mutual allegations of fabrication, slander, and suborned testimony. *Idylls of the King* from its earliest conception is surprisingly
redolent of this world. The poem is structured not simply by contrasting
models of female sexuality – the faithful Enid and Elaine juxtaposed
with the wayward Vivien and Guinevere – but also by networks of
rumor, gossip, slander, and scandal, within which characters are
constantly demanding "proof" not only of individual fidelity but of
the stories that characters tell about one another. An early title of the
Idylls, "The True and the False," had in this light an inescapable social
as well as moral bearing. And contemporaries grasped the connection:
a review in *Blackwood*'s aligned *Idylls* with the Divorce Bill and
"La Traviata" as evidence of contemporary moral decay. Hence, too,
an unexpected point in Swinburne's sneer: "treated as he has treated it,
the story is rather a case for the divorce-court than for poetry" (Jump
1971: 319–21).

Guinevere was an especially unsettling heroine, who confounded
the stereotype of the fallen woman as an outcast broken by poverty
and exploitation or seduced by social ambition. In the lives of Hetty
Sorrel, Ruth, Marian Erle, and a host of Dickensian fallen women,
sexuality is bound up with social marginality, which tempers their
status with poignancy. Guinevere, by contrast, seems merely bored.
Lancelot enlivens a gray, monotonous cocoon of privilege through
sheer erotic energy. Even in her remorse, just before Arthur
denounces her, her thoughts drift back to her first sight of the King,
when she

> thought him cold,
> High, self-contain'd, and passionless, not like him,
> 'Not like my Lancelot' ...
>   ("Guinevere" ll. 402–4; Tennyson 1969)

What unsettled Victorian readers was not the fact of Guinevere's
desire – Tennyson is not invoking the shibboleth of anesthetized
Victorian women being told to "lie back and think of England." The
crux is that Guinevere fails to control her desire, and thereby ruptures
the most fundamental social bonds; hence Arthur's claim that the
disintegration of his kingdom was "all thro' thee!" (l. 490).

Guinevere's wayward desire seems tepid, however, by comparison with an exactly contemporary treatment by William Morris (1839–96), "The Defence of Guenevere," the title poem of an 1858 volume. Other writers, particularly historical romancers in the vein of Scott, had been drawn to medieval settings as stages for violence as well as chivalric devotion, but Morris's medievalism conjures up extraordinarily raw passion. "The Haystack in the Floods," for example, offers an eerily laconic account of a woman who refuses to submit to her captor, and thus is forced to watch her lover beheaded by his frustrated rival and his henchmen, who "beat /His head to pieces at their feet" (ll. 150–1). In "The Defence" Morris returns to Malory's account of Guenevere's trial, but his heroine, unlike Tennyson's, answers her accuser with fierce defiance:

> Nevertheless you, O Sir Gauwaine, lie.
> Whatever may have happened through these years,
> God knows I speak truth, knowing that you lie.
>> (ll. 86–8; Morris 1883)

The bewildering logic – whatever happened, I am telling the truth – is bound up with an equally startling erotic candor:

> I scarce dare talk of the remembered bliss
>
> When both our mouths went wandering in one way.
> And aching sorely, met among the leaves;
> Our hands being left behind strained far away.
>> (ll. 135–8)

Although the dramatic format of the poem encourages us to read it as a monologue – Morris's early poetry owes much to Browning – the moral frame is more elusive than in Browning's work. Initially, Guenevere affirms that the law itself is a mystery: imagine seeing an angel, she exhorts her tribunal, holding up a red cloth and a blue, asking you to choose between one, and after choosing "heaven's colour, the blue," being condemned to hell. When she then claims that Gawain "nonetheless" lies, she seems to shift the ground from outward events – "Whatever may have happened" – to some moral ground in the quality of the passion itself. Yet Guenevere soon appeals to a more conventional norm, whose authority she unsettles in the very act of invoking it:

"Being such a lady could I weep these tears
If this were true? A great queen such as I
Having sinn'd this way, straight her conscience sears ..."

(ll. 145–7)

As she raises the possibility that "a great queen" might be a consummate actress, or simply untroubled by conscience, she anticipates yet a further appeal: "say no rash word /Against me, being so beautiful ... will you dare, /When you have looked a little on my brow, /To say this thing is vile?" (ll. 224–5, 236–8). With this final defense, Morris's adulterous queen poses a question that would agitate artists and their audiences for the remainder of the century: does the power of beauty confound morality?

Morris's volume would have an important influence in the formation of aestheticism in the following decade, particularly through the work of Walter Pater, whose famous conclusion to *The Renaissance* originated in an 1868 review of Morris's poetry. That poetry also prods readers to ponder the fantasies that beauty may arouse – and the dynamics of what we have since come to call objectification. This emphasis teases out a thread implicit in Browning's painter poems, and indeed throughout the contemporary art world: the intricate, often vexed relations between art, sexuality, and commerce, which frequently crystallize in the figure of the artist's model, but more overtly in the fallen woman. This association is rather jauntily treated in D. G. Rossetti's "Jenny" (written in the 1850s, but not published until 1870), perhaps the best-known Victorian poetic rendering of a prostitute. The speaker's swagger doesn't quite conceal a more pointed self-reflection in pondering the sleeping woman he has hired. On the one hand, she is an epitome of commodified sexuality (he strews coins in her hair). But the poem also unsettles easy divisions between respectable and fallen women – in large part by drawing out the power of male projection, which figured so powerfully in the reception of Rossetti's own painting:

Yet Jenny, looking long at you,
The woman almost fades from view.
A cipher of man's changeless sum
Of lust, past, present, and to come
Is left. A riddle that one shrinks
To challenge from the scornful sphinx.

(ll. 276–81; D. G. Rossetti 1901)

Anticipating the most evocative of Victorian femme fatales, Pater's Mona Lisa, the poem performs the slippage it analyzes: how do we distinguish between genuine sympathy for a woman's objectification and a re-enactment of it? But the proliferation of the femme fatale in later Victorian literature would incorporate another image of disturbing femininity, which was drawn from a new kind of novel.

Sensation

In April 1859, Charles Dickens started a new weekly periodical, *All the Year Round*, leading off with a serialization of his latest novel, *A Tale of Two Cities*. The gambit paid off with sales far outstripping those of his older weekly, *Household Words*, but it left Dickens to find another serial that could sustain his readership. He turned to the 35- year-old Wilkie Collins (1824–89). Collins, the son of a successful painter, had met Dickens in 1851, when he was the little-known author of a single published novel, *Antonina, or the Fall of Rome* (1850), a modest entry in the burgeoning subgenre of historical novels depicting imperial decadence. In 1852 Bentley published *Basil: A Story of Modern Life*, whose subtitle hints at Collins's provocative account of cross-class romance and domestic treachery (the surname of Basil, the wronged husband who narrates the novel, is withheld "for reasons of honour"). Although the novel was widely attacked for its "revolting details" of adultery (which naturally helped to increase sales), Dickens was impressed by its construction, and soon became Collins's mentor and collaborator. They co-authored a number of stories for Dickens's weeklies, which also would serialize four of Collins's novels, and traveled together on the continent, where Dickens apparently appreciated Collins's louche attitude towards sexual propriety (Collins maintained separate households and fathered all of his children out of wedlock). After two further novels reflecting Collins's fascination with class boundaries and detection plots, *Hide and Seek* (1854) and *The Dead Secret* (1857), his new serial opened in *All the Year Round* on November 24, 1859, under the title *The Woman in White*. It marked the beginning of a phenomenon that became known as the sensation novel.

Within a few months Collins's serial had generated a frenzy of commercial appropriation: Woman in White perfume, Woman in White cloaks and bonnets, Woman in White waltzes and quadrilles, along with a host of stage versions (Page 1974: 13). Though for a time the work seemed *sui generis*, it is fundamentally a reframing of the gothic novel in a contemporary setting. The young Henry James recognized as much in reviewing Mary Elizabeth Braddon's works: whereas the harrowing ordeals of "the horror novel," as he called it, typically were relegated to an exotic setting (usually where villainous priests ran riot), Collins introduced "the most mysterious of mysteries, the mysteries which are at our own doors" (Page 1974: 122). As the psychic harrowing of gothic was re-framed within contemporary domestic life, sensation fiction drew on the traditions of melodrama, both dramatic and novelistic, in order to represent the torment of innocence, or (where innocence was dubious) at least startling revelations of what lay beneath. When Thackeray ends chapter 14 of *Vanity Fair* with the brilliant curtain of Becky Sharp exclaiming, "But Sir Pitt, I'm married already," he might be preemptively satirizing the bigamy plots of sensation fiction.

The new form drew its name from an elemental appeal distilled early in Collins's novel, in a scene to which reviewers constantly returned. When Walter Hartright, strolling down a dark road in the middle of the night, feels a mysterious touch on his shoulder, "few readers" (remarked the eminently cool and skeptical Margaret Oliphant) "will be able to resist the mysterious thrill of this sudden touch. The sensation is distinct and indisputable ... the shock is as sudden, as startling, as unexpected and incomprehensible to us as it is to the hero of the tale ... The reader's nerves are affected like the hero's ... He, too, is chilled by a confused and unexplainable alarm ... The effect is pure sensation" (Page 1974: 118–19) "[T]hrill ... shock ... startling ... nerves ... chilled ... alarm": this cluster of associations grounded "sensation" in visceral experience, but also made the shudder a premonition of moral outrage. "Sensation" thus linked the intimately private with a public realm of scandal, particularly scandal intruding on the realm ostensibly most immune to it, domestic life. Sensation fiction became the genre of the home under siege.

Although Collins's novel was almost universally applauded, the proliferation of similar novels soon caused alarm. The popularity of a genre appealing to "sensation" aroused fears that it was a degrading stimulant gratifying a debased appetite – like the longing for "a dram or a dose," as Henry Mansel put it (Mansel 1863: 485). But some of the shift in opinion reflected a shift in the gendering of villainy. In *Woman in White* treachery is emphatically a masculine province; Count Fosco, the main architect, is the consummate gothic villain of mid-Victorian fiction, and was roundly praised as a character. In later works – most notably, *Lady Audley's Secret* (1862) and *Aurora Floyd* (1862) by Mary Elizabeth Braddon (1835–1915), *East Lynne* (1861) by Mrs. Henry Wood (1814–87), and Collins's own *No Name* (1862) and *Armadale* (1866) – transgression is woman's work. The most fearsome threat to domesticity came from those presumed to be its bulwark. And with an increasingly audacious elaboration of feminine treachery, marriage became a realm of brute oppression or cunning deception, exploited by villains so ruthlessly ambitious that their "pleasing outsides," as Mansel put it, concealed "some demon in human shape" (489).

In its preoccupation with adulterous, bigamous, even murderous, women, sensation fiction clearly drew on the preoccupations that animated contemporary poetic treatments of female transgression. The mixture of exorbitant desire and cunning crystallized the most exaggerated anxieties provoked by the Married Woman's Property Act and "strong-minded" women of an emergent feminism. Mansel even invoked Mary Wollstonecraft as a model for sensation heroines. Unlike Guinevere, however, the fallen women of sensation fiction were unmistakably modern. As Mansel put it, "proximity" was a crucial element of the appeal: "It is necessary to be near a mine to be blown up by its explosion" (488). The "beautiful fiend" of *Lady Audley's Secret* is a distinctive amalgam of two independent modern women, the literary governess and the Pre-Raphaelite model. When two men discover a hidden "pre-Raphaelite" portrait of Lady Audley, lending "a strange, sinister light to the deep blue eyes," they glimpse an inner being disguised by her outward beauty (Braddon 1998: 72). Such images quickly gained wide circulation.

Much sensation fiction might be summed up under the sardonic phrase *Modern Love*, which is the title George Meredith (1828–1909) chose for a sonnet sequence published in 1862. The son of a failed tailor – a fact that shaped a good deal of his fiction – Meredith had published an early volume of poetry in 1851, shortly after marrying the widowed daughter of the satiric novelist Thomas Love Peacock (whose fiction clearly influenced Meredith's own). The marriage collapsed in 1858, when his wife left him and their son for another man, who then deserted her; she died in 1861, unreconciled with Meredith. This grueling experience was the basis of *Modern Love*, which draws ironically on the Elizabethan sonnet sequence to present what Meredith takes to be a distinctly modern version of frustrated desire, the challenge of enduring erotic betrayal without troubling the decorum of middle-class society:

> With sparkling surface-eyes we ply the ball;
> It is in truth a most contagious game:
> HIDING THE SKELETON shall be its name.
> Such play as this the devils might appal!
>
> (xviii.5–8; Meredith 1976)

The frequently unsteady tone and shifting, glancing point of view reflects the challenge of finding a poetic idiom adequate to an action better suited to "that French novel"; "in England we'll not hear of it," the poet archly comments, we think it "quite unnatural" (xxv.1–5). But the ironic formal juxtaposition also provides a means to contain the poet's rage. Meredith struggles to make his speaker seem less self-righteous than Tennyson's Arthur, gesturing in conclusion toward a reciprocal failing, over-reliance on that old Carlylean bugbear of self-consciousness: "the fatal knife, /Deep questioning, which probes to endless dole" (l.9–10). But such efforts at even-handedness, and the broader appeals to realism, could not staunch the predictable disgust even among reviewers who greatly admired other poems in the volume. Hutton complained of "confusion between 'fast' taste and what Mr. Meredith mistakes for courageous realism – poetic pre-Raphaelitism." The *Spectator* reviewer called the poem a "sickly little peccadillo," and tellingly prescribed a remedy in Tennyson's "Guinevere" (Williams 1971: 95–7).

The power of melodrama in sensation fiction underscored the very close connection between the novel and the stage. Ellen Wood's *East Lynne* (1861) was probably the most frequently adapted sensation novel. Its debt to melodrama is extravagant: the heroine abandons her husband and children for another man, who abandons her in turn, leaving her with an illegitimate child; disfigured in a train crash, she returns East Lynne to serve as governess to her own children, who do not recognize her. By January of 1863 (the serial had concluded in September of 1861) two different productions had opened in New York, two more had opened in London by February of 1866, and by 1899 there had been an estimated 20 different adaptations in England alone (of which only three exist in printed form, underscoring the ephemerality of so much Victorian theater). The novel, meanwhile, sold 400,000 copies by the end of the century. Collins himself wrote for the stage, often in collaboration with Dickens (who met his future mistress Ellen Ternan while acting in Collins's melodrama *The Frozen Deep* [1857]). In his Letter of Dedication to *Basil*, Collins described the novel and the play as "twin-sisters in the family of Fiction …. one is a drama narrated, as the other is a drama acted" (Pykett 2005: 94). Another novelist soon to become associated with sensation fiction, Charles Reade (1814–80), began his career in 1849 by adapting French farces for the English stage, and first gained wide notice with a comedy, *Masks and Faces* (1852), co-written with Tom Taylor, which he then adapted into his first novel, *Meg Woffington* (1853). Throughout his career Reade would alternate between fiction and playwriting – often attracting complaints from fellow novelists whose works he plundered for material. The novel as a form, however, offered far more lucrative financial prospects; a successful novelist might earn 3,000 pounds or more from a serial and subsequent re-publication, whereas playwrights rarely received more than 150 pounds for a script; the vast bulk of profits remained for the theater manager. But those profits could be enormous, and the demand for melodrama offered constant employment, although only a few writers were sufficiently prolific to make a decent living from playwriting alone.

Improving prospects for theatrical melodrama emerged in the career of Dion Boucicault (1822–90), whose rise tellingly coincided with that of sensation fiction. Boucicault, an Irishman whose heritage is almost as shadowy as a sensation heroine's (both his birth date and his actual father are uncertain), got his start in the professional theater when he was only about 17, as the author of one of many provincial stage adaptations of *Jack Sheppard*. Less than two years later, in 1841, his play *London Assurance* was produced at Covent Garden. Although the work was markedly derivative, a comedy full of familiar eighteenth-century stereotypes in the mode of Sheridan, it was a huge success, remaining in the repertory for the rest of the century, and earning the young playwright an unusually large fee of 300 pounds. But that reward proved unique, and Boucicault reverted to the familiar routine of grinding out adaptations and the occasional original melodrama. As managers invariably reminded him, they could easily enough pay 50 pounds for the quick makeover of a French melodrama or farce. Boucicault accordingly signed on in 1850 as literary adviser to Charles Kean at the Princess Theater, where his adaptation of *The Corsican Brothers*, a French play derived from a story by Dumas, earned Kean a small fortune, but added nothing to Boucicault's salary.

Realizing a playwright's earnings could never rival those of a manager or even a lead actor, Boucicault in 1853 organized a company headed by his wife, the Scottish actress Agnes Robertson, on a tour of North America, where he remained for the rest of the decade. His output there reflects his extraordinary resourcefulness in recycling plots, as well as popular hunger for increasingly elaborate spectacle, in which domestic melodrama turned into "sensation" drama. *The Poor of New York, The Streets of New York, The Poor of Liverpool, The Streets of London, The Streets of Dublin, The Streets of Philadelphia*, and *The Money Panic of '57* are all in essence the same play, crowned by a scene in which the villain emerges from a burning house whose flames are being doused by an actual fire engine (Hogan 1969: 66). *The Octoroon* (1859), which reflects a fascination with American slavery sharpened by *Uncle Tom's Cabin*, features an exploding steamboat – and two different endings; in English performances the heroine survived, whereas the American version ended with her suicide, apparently the only fate imaginable for a woman of mixed race abandoned by her white protector. Boucicault's greatest success came with *The Colleen Bawn*, a loose adaptation of an Irish novel about a genial poacher and the fair-haired girl of the title. After opening the play in New York in March 1860, Boucicault and Robertson returned to London in July, where Boucicault was able to drive a momentous bargain. The manager of the Adelphi, desperate for a hit, agreed to pay him not only his fee for playing the lead – a role that culminated in a scene of him diving into the ocean to rescue the colleen bawn from drowning – but also a royalty of one pound per act for each performance. The play ran for a record 278 performances (Queen Victoria saw it three times), netting Boucicault a huge return and setting a precedent that would transform the English stage, though it would be another 20 years before stage managers fully capitulated to the idea of paying a playwright royalties.

An even more popular and versatile writer for the stage was Tom Taylor (1817–80) – unusual among his fellow playwrights not only for the range of his plays but as a scion of wealth educated at Trinity College, Cambridge. In 1844, he gave up a Fellowship at Trinity to read law in London, where he began a long connection with the recently founded *Punch*, and contributed short plays – mostly farces and burlesques – to the Lyceum Theatre. His reputation as a writer of comedies began with his collaboration with Charles Reade (another part-time barrister and university man), *Masks and Faces* (1852), produced at the Haymarket, which creates a comedy of stage illusion centered on an eighteenth-century actress famed for her "breeches parts." Critics were impressed by an unusually sophisticated play of dramatic irony in keeping with the title. In 1855 the Olympic Theatre staged *Still Waters Run Deep*, a domestic melodrama focusing on a placid husband whose frictions with his new wife have been exacerbated by meddling relatives, who have turned over her fortune to a con artist – who of course is exposed in the end by the suddenly heroic and resourceful husband. *Our American Cousin* (the play Lincoln was watching when he was assassinated), first staged in New York in 1858, returned to broad comedy, centering on a Vermont backwoodsman who inherits an English fortune. Although the play sends up American idiosyncrasies, the loud and often boorish Asa Trenchard is balanced by a buffoonish English aristocrat, Lord Dundreary, whose first appearance evokes from the American protagonist the words, "Concentrated essence of baboons, what on earth is that?" The play ran for more than 800 performances in New York before opening at the Haymarket in November of 1861, and Dundreary became one of the great comic turns of the latter half of the century. In 1860 (which began with the staging of his adaptation of *A Tale of Two Cities*), Taylor had become so popular that he was commissioned to write plays for three different managements. In 1863, he returned to melodrama to create what would become his most famous work, *The Ticket of Leave Man*. Staged at the Olympic, a theater associated with affluent audiences, the new play found its subject in unexpectedly sordid material, the struggles of a naïf from Lancashire who is falsely arrested for forgery (after a furious first-act struggle in which the real villains escape). After prison, he must struggle to make a new life while evading the taint of his conviction (a ticket of leave man is a discharged convict) and helping to capture the true criminals, in concert with what scholars have called the first fully realized stage representation of a British policeman. The play was another sensation, evoking the environment of urban poverty – typically a marginal presence in fashionable melodrama – with the abundantly detailed staging and careful construction usually reserved for dramas of the more privileged. It was revived throughout the century, and at least as recently as the mid-1970s.

Drama throughout the remainder of the 1860s was dominated by melodrama – most notably in the figure of the actor-manager Henry Irving at the Lyceum, who enjoyed a huge success in *The Bells* by Leopold Lewis (1870), which depicts the haunting of a murderer whose psychology is disclosed through dazzling stage effects. The major exception to the predominance of melodrama was the work of

Thomas William Robertson (1829–71), which offered an unusual melding of broad comedy with more intricate, vernacular realism reminiscent of domestic fiction – William Archer would call him "a pre-Raphaelite of the theatre" (Emeljanow 1987: 105) – and a form of counterpoint recalling the multi-plot structures of Victorian novels. He came to notice with *Society* (1865), which was quickly followed by a series of the trademark one-word titles, which hint at a larger thematic ambition than most of his contemporaries: *Ours* (1866), *Caste* (1867), *Play* (1868), and (all in 1869) *Home, Dreams,* and *School.* The last, a society fairy tale, ran for 800 performances under the Bancrofts, who offered unusually detailed, naturalistic staging of his works, and whose management of the Prince of Wales theater helped draw more affluent audiences. *Caste,* his most durable success, was one of the first plays sent on a national tour by its London company. But, for all their innovations in stagecraft, Robertson's representation of social conflict could not rival that of the novel.

Dreams of Self-Fashioning

Another distinctly modern element in Collins's transfiguration of gothic was a multi-faceted legal discourse. Sensation novelists clearly learned much from divorce cases reported in the daily paper – indeed, some critics referred to the new form as "the Newspaper novel." More generally, law enforcement and legal proceedings offered models for the detection and exposure of transgression, and for narrative as a means of discovering, or constructing, social and moral truth. For all the audacity of his subject matter, Collins was most proud of his novel as "an experiment," whereby the narration was divided among the various characters of the novel, each offering his or her own records of events bearing on the mystery of the title character. While some reviewers objected that this feature merely recast the epistolary form, Collins's paradigm was emphatically legal. The story is told "by more than one pen, as the story of an offense against the laws is told by more than one witness" (Collins 1999: 9). From the late 1830s onwards, novelists had tacitly challenged the traditional authority of the legal advocate, both through direct mockery (as in *Pickwick Papers*) and, more subtly, by usurping legal authority to argue in behalf of the dispossessed and voiceless (Schramm 2000). But the mimicry of legal proceedings obviously complicates more direct advocacy. Collins may rationalize his narrative structure as a means of presenting the truth "in its most direct and intelligible aspect," but the limited and shifting focalizations and consequent dramatic ironies tend to amplify characters' bewilderment and frailty – and to heighten the reader's suspense. In essence, the technique works to thicken the aura of mystery that ultimately will be dispelled.

Some readers objected to this manipulation as an obstacle to sympathetic response; reviewers frequently used the word "riddle." The more appreciative, such as Oliphant, suggested that mystery worked as something like a secular version of the sacred; in an increasingly skeptical age mystery could charge even the most mundane details with a sense of indwelling moral significance. But secrets had a special resonance for mid-Victorian audiences as they bear on human identity. The central mysteries of sensation fiction are less a question of "who did it?" than of "who is she?" And how did she become what she appears to be? One by-product of social mobility was an increasing fascination with the ways in which human identity may be manipulated: discarded, exchanged, invented, reshaped as an individual makes her way through new walks of life. Such malleability arouses a good deal of popular unease in early Victorian narratives of social ascent, as in the suspicion of performance aroused by parvenus like Becky Sharp. The anxiety becomes more acute as identity comes to be less securely bound to actual acquaintance, and instead devolves into a parcel of disembodied information, an array of external facts and features – name, historical records, handwriting, physical descriptions – existing apart from the person they ostensibly describe. As identity becomes something akin to a commodity, it enables new modes of self-invention, but it also creates new possibilities of self-estrangement. In a world of increasingly intricate record-keeping, one's true or previous identity has a life of its own, which others may discover and manipulate to their own ends. This is one reason (beyond the sheer pleasure of suspense) for the startling proliferation of blackmail plots in mid-Victorian literature, which appear even in novels that seem far removed from sensation fiction – such as *Middlemarch* (Welsh 1985). In an emergent information culture, identity frequently seems resolved into labels, scraps of paper, stray signatures, records in a church registry. When the restoration of moral order turns on the exposure of false identity or a concealed past, the observable world becomes a field of evidence.

The novels of Collins, Braddon, and other sensation writers thus help to shape the world of detective fiction. The literary detective first emerges in the stories of Edgar Allan Poe in the early 1840s. What for

Poe is a formal and psychological experiment – an attempt to narrate pure ratiocination – assumes in British fiction a more emphatically social character. In *Bleak House*, for example, detective Sergeant Bucket's criminal investigation has the more elemental function of disclosing hidden connections among the outwardly divergent characters and the various realms of society they represent. In sensation fiction social disorder takes on a more lurid moral coloring, and detection becomes a more urgent challenge. When the drawing rooms of England are occupied by beautiful fiends, something clearly is rotten, and exposure of the impostor comes to seem (as in *Hamlet*) a higher calling. Thus as Robert Audley investigates the disappearance of his friend George Talboys, which requires him to pry into the background of his uncle's beautiful young wife, he overcomes his own self-revulsion (a gentleman is not a spy) by insisting "a hand that is stronger than my own is beckoning me onward" (Braddon 1998: 255). In suggesting that transgression may be exposed and punished through an inexorable "chain" of evidence or events, a tightly woven narrative of cause and effect, sensation fiction unexpectedly converges with Tennyson's account of Guinevere's fatal transgression, and with the moral energies of George Eliot's early fiction, with their insistence that "consequences are unpitying." The discovery of irresistible causality in human affairs – a structure the novelist is preeminently suited to represent – assumes the traditional role of providence. Over against the skepticism raised by the likes of Morris's "Defence of Guenevere," these novels offer patterns of indwelling moral order in a secular world.

Detection alone, however, cannot contain energies as disruptive as those of Lady Audley. Robert Audley must draw further support from the world of medicine. The Victorian insistence that purity and submission are innate, "natural" attributes of women created a quandary in explaining women who failed to display those virtues. An emergent Victorian psychiatry filled the breach: Lady Audley and her like must be mad, and their proper home is an asylum. Yet Braddon's novel is tantalizingly ambiguous on this point. When Robert summons an eminent specialist, the physician after his initial interview with Lady Audley concludes:

> there is no evidence of madness in anything that she had done. She ran away from her home, because her home was not a pleasant one. There is no madness in that. She committed the crime of bigamy, because by that crime she obtained fortune and position. There is no madness in that. (Braddon 1998: 370)

The passage suggests that science has been coopted to constrain feminine ambition, and that the novel's conclusion captures a grim irony in the situation of women. In any case, the concluding diagnosis of insanity is a harbinger of an increasing "normalization" of literary character, which is grounded in the expanding authority of medicine and psychology – a development that becomes especially prominent in the 1880s.

Sensation novels more readily accommodate male ambition and self-fashioning. Hartright in *Woman in White* occupies the uneasy position of a drawing master in a wealthy household, a place whose liminality resembles that of a governess: he is nominally a gentleman, but is constantly made to feel that he is a servant. Robert Audley, by contrast, exemplifies the indolent aristocratic dilettante of vaguely bohemian inclinations who is a familiar type of mid-Victorian fiction, most notably in Dickens's later novels. Despite their different social positions, both men are effeminate, lacking the conventional markers of masculinity derived from erotic and social power. Sir Percival taunts his wife with threats to horsewhip her drawing master, while the thought of Robert Audley as a lover prompts incredulity from other men in the novel: "it can't be the cousin, sir" (Braddon 1998: 131). Both men gain virility by rescuing others from oppressive mystery: as they assume the role of detectives, their wayward energies gain focus and force. Robert is elevated, ironically, by becoming an accomplished lawyer, the scion of the landed gentry displaying the eminently bourgeois virtue of earnestness; Hartright overcomes his social inferiority by being absorbed into the gentry, as father of the heir to Limmeridge.

The fantasy of social ascent was captured most profoundly in Dickens's *Great Expectations*, which appeared in weekly parts in *All the Year Round* beginning in December of 1860 – just four months after the wind-up of *A Woman in White*. The novel was widely reviewed as Dickens's try at the new "sensation" rage, which is less perverse than it might sound. The novel is steeped in physical gloom: from its opening scenes on the Essex marshes to the interior of Miss Havisham's house to the filth of London. The novel's young hero-narrator, Pip, finds himself at every turn brushing against crime and criminality, from the invective of his fierce older sister and guardian, Mrs. Jo Gargery, to his harrowing encounter with escaped convicts on the marshes, to his life in London, which pivots around contact with the defense attorney Jaggers and his highly dubious clientele, to the ultimate discovery of his mysterious benefactor and even the identity of his beloved Estella. It is also a novel of great suspense, and full of jarring sensation from its famous opening scene onward. The pressure of publishing in weekly numbers seems to have encouraged a plot structure markedly tighter than in any of Dickens's monthly serials.

In *Great Expectations*, however, "incident" does not trump character – a familiar complaint of sensation fiction. Instead, Pip is Dickens's most fully realized narrator, even more than David Copperfield, and arguably the richest character in all of his fiction. Pip's experience to a remarkable extent crystallizes the large aspirations and anxieties of mid-Victorian culture, in which the dream of social ascent is dogged by the confusion of virtue and wealth. In a world in which "rags to riches" was no longer simply the stuff of fairy tale, Pip is hardly alone in registering "the stupendous power of money." With his abrupt transformation into a young gentleman, the world around him is similarly transfigured. Newly obsequious shopkeepers call out an answering hauteur in Pip, which is hilariously travestied by Trabb's boy: "Don't know yah! 'pon my soul don't know yah!" he mocks, in a more pithy comment on snobbery than anything in *Dombey* (Dickens 1996: 246). Yet the first thing to which wealth introduces Pip is a sense of shame, the class-consciousness instilled by Estella's taunts that he is merely "common." The desire to rise, the novel suggests, is fueled by and in turn reinforces the poisonous notion that poverty is a crime. In this light, one might read the entire book as a further reworking of the memory of the blacking factory, which had formed a pivotal episode in *David Copperfield*. What there triggered a fear of abandonment becomes here the origin of false consciousness, which Pip must exorcise in order to understand the gentleman as a moral achievement quite distinct from the possession of wealth. As in so much of Dickens, one must be materially dispossessed in order to discover true value, in the human bonds that have been ruptured.

At the same time, the novel offers a newly self-reflexive preoccupation with human agency. Early Victorian schemes of progress and political economy are founded on a bedrock of individual autonomy, a deeply held faith that individuals are free to shape their own worldly destinies. Over the course of the century this faith begins to fray, and gradually yields to an emergent psychology attentive to a host of forces – social, biological, and more elusively psychological – that constrain human self-determination. In *Great Expectations* questions of freedom are most obviously thematic: Pip believes that he is a gentleman, and thus distinguished above all by independence, but that identity turns out to be a role scripted by another character. Pip's experience is the very antithesis of self-determination. His predicament, which he compares to that of Frankenstein's monster, is doubled in the subplot involving Estella, whose social privilege likewise turns out to be the expression of someone's else's revenge. Her offhand remark, "We are not free to follow our own devices, you and I," resonates throughout the novel (Dickens 1996: 265). This awareness is more subtly reinforced in the narrative form, particularly in repeated references to "chains." This figure always brings to mind Pip's childhood in the blacksmith's shop, and also constitutes an enduring link to the taint of criminality he struggles to escape, but at the same time the trope underscores the "chains of circumstance" that become central in the construction of action and character – an emphasis the novel shares with the detection plots of sensation fiction. The formal dynamic links narrative structure and social determination in rich and suggestive ways, pointing to what would become a constitutive paradox of novelistic realism. In reading novels we indulge the fantasy of encountering "real people" that we know to be the figments of an author's imagination. More subtly, however, the celebration of realistic character as a representation of moral selfhood – which depends on the sense that characters make choices freely, and are to be judged accordingly – is countered by a criterion of plausibility, which seems to abridge precisely that autonomy. We are encouraged to find a character persuasive or compelling insofar as it is responsive to the pressure of circumstances. (Pip in this sense is a far more realistic character than Oliver Twist.) Realism is thus deeply bound up with the representation of causality, and realistic character is not a solitary, self-directed particle, but an ongoing transaction with the world at large, which always constrains one's power to choose – perhaps even one's very self-possession. There is thus a radical ambiguity in the notion of acting "out of character": behavior may seem at once caused by, and yet potentially defiant of, an existing self. It is a paradox akin to that in Miltonic predestination: even though Pip's character seems plausible insofar as it seems largely determined by his environment, we judge Pip as if he is making independent moral choices.

In its power to dramatize this tension, the Victorian novel became an unusually rich vehicle for the exploration of personal and social identity. In particular, novelistic realism strains the faith in personal autonomy that was so crucial to Victorian liberalism, and was epitomized in the ideal of the self-made man. That ideal was defined in stark opposition to an aristocratic model of identity evoked in, for example, the allure of Tennyson's lotos-eaters, paragons of a life of enervated ease. That allure persisted over the period, but novelists at mid-century typically disavowed it more vehemently. Characters who enjoy or aspire to such a life frequently suffer an emblematic humbling, often to the point of physical assault. Pip's self-chastisement fits a surprisingly insistent pattern, typically articulated by types more securely aristocratic in origin and mien: Braddon's Robert Audley, along with Dickens's more hard-edged characters, Steerforth in *David Copperfield*, Harthouse in *Hard Times*, Sydney Carton in *Tale of Two Cities*, and Eugene Wrayburn in *Our Mutual Friend*. Harthouse epitomizes the suspect qualities: a "certain air of exhaustion ... in part arising from excessive summer, and in part from excessive gentility. For it was to be seen with half an eye that he was a thorough gentleman, made to the model of the time; weary of everything, and putting no more faith in anything than Lucifer" (Dickens 1966: 91).

The self-made man is the antithesis of this type, a figure of unbounded energy, purposefulness, and faith in his own talents. Yet this ideal also unsettled many, as a fantasy in which ambition might trample every other human commitment, anything that might constrain one's power of self-fashioning. Over against the traditional conception of the gentleman as an inherited rank, the self-made man seemed to be literally self-begotten – the fantasy of perfect autonomy celebrated in *John Halifax, Gentleman*. Even before Mulock's novel appeared, the ideal had been mocked by a novelist unusually well placed to appreciate the titanic energies of self-creation. Josiah Bounderby in *Hard Times* bullies everyone with his self-admiring humility. "You are a man of family," he tells Harthouse; "Don't you deceive yourself for a moment by supposing I am a man of family. I am a bit of dirty riff-raff, and a genuine scrap of rag, tag, and bobtail" who knows "the exact depth of the gutter I have lifted myself out of" (Dickens 1966: 97). Bounderby's egoism even leads him to proclaim himself abandoned by a dissolute mother, whose existence (a loving and eminently respectable one, we discover) compromises his dream of immaculate self-conception.

The most famous tribute to the self-made man appeared in 1859, in one of the best-selling works of the century, Samuel Smiles's *Self-Help*. Although Smiles borrowed his title from Emerson, his individualism is not nearly so iconoclastic, and certainly is more nuanced than Dickens's parody. In particular, Smiles stresses indebtedness to past example: the work is in essence a collection of capsule biographies, much in the spirit of Carlyle. Moreover, Smiles takes great pains to align his ideal with that of the middle-class gentleman; the work concludes with a chapter entitled "Character – The True Gentleman," citing as an epigraph "the grand old name of Gentleman" from *In Memoriam*, and contending that "all of Self-Help is essentially about the gentleman" (Smiles 2002: 334). This was a familiar emphasis in visions of working-class social ascent, where the ideal of the gentleman had a two-pronged appeal: to the working man, as a badge of status, and to the propertied classes, as a constraint of unbridled ambition. Nonetheless, in the work's sometimes strident opposition to government regulation, it captures (as Smiles's editor points out) a libertarian strain that would resurface in Margaret Thatcher's Britain, with her 1987 remark that there is "no such thing as society" (Smiles 2002: 29).

In a conjunction beloved of historians, the single most influential monument of mid-Victorian liberalism also appeared in 1859. John Stuart Mill's *On Liberty* is a good deal less sanguine than Smiles about the prospects for self-determination. To the contrary, many observers remarked an "altogether melancholy" tone, as the *Saturday Review* put it, which seemed strangely discordant with prevailing optimism about the state of England (Pyle 1994: 15). For Mill, the great obstacle to progress was not government regulation, but a growing conformism, an abject deference to public opinion, which was stultifying individual thought and action. We live, Mill urged, "as under the eye of a hostile and dreaded censorship" (Mill 196–91: xviii. 264). Behind this pressure one could discern many sources of unease: the censoriousness of evangelical morality; the pressures of economic life, in which "character" had become a newly crucial norm in both business and social exchange; a fear of radical politics, still reverberating from revolutions on the continent and domestic unrest in the 1840s; a fear of sensuality, particularly as a force that might undermine family life; and a fear of challenges to religious faith, which for most observers still sustained the very fabric of social order.

In response to these pressures, Mill constructed a twofold appeal to heroic individualism, which invoked subtly divergent models of humanity – in effect, two different understandings of "character." In the first, freedom nurtured character in the sense of vital, focused energy. The world requires "strong natures," Mill urged, but under the tyranny of public opinion "human capacities are withered or starved" (264–5). This is a familiar utilitarian emphasis: progress depends on the power to generate new ideas and to withstand resistance to them. But this ideal readily shaded into a celebration of individuality as an intrinsic

rather than instrumental good, a harmonious, untrammeled development of one's innate capacities. Character in this sense is something
akin to culture, and is best evoked in aesthetic terms, as in the figure of
a tree allowed to grow without pruning. In a trope that would echo
throughout Victorian cultural criticism, Mill complained that under
popular morality, the "ideal of character is to be without any marked
character; to maim by compression, like a Chinese lady's foot, every
part of human nature which stands out prominently" (271–2). In this
emphasis, Mill's argument shares more with novelistic representations
of character, such as *Jane Eyre*, than with classical political economy.
"Individuality is the same thing with development" might serve as an
epigraph to any number of mid-Victorian novels (267). It is precisely
through the freedom to cultivate their distinctive qualities, Mill urges,
that "human beings become a noble and beautiful object of contemplation" (266). This is an image at odds with most conceptions of
Mill, the austere intellectual gladiator, always on trial, braced for
combat, prodding opponents to debate. But it is a different form of
heroism, one that in later criticism will come to embody the authority
of culture: the heroism of commitment to thought and aesthetic experience as ends in themselves, set against the "machinery" of unreflective or purely instrumental activity. In the discourse of culture, beauty
not only is its own reward, but has its own utility, as it stimulates in
others a more energetic and varied experience and reflection. This
emphasis reflects the persistent influence of German *Bildung*, which
Mill underscores with a quote from Humboldt: "the end of man ... is
the highest and most harmonious development of his powers to a
complete and consistent whole" (261). *On Liberty* thus marks a crucial
juncture in mid-Victorian thought: Mill infuses liberalism with a discourse of heroism that departs both from the cautious forbearance of a
J. F. Stephen and from the energetic assertion of the self-made man.

Narrating Nature: Darwin

Even as Mill was inveighing against intellectual cowardice and the
decline of individual genius, a country squire was putting the final
touches on arguably the most daring and unsettling book of the century. Charles Darwin's *On the Origin of Species By Means of Natural
Selection, or Preservation of Favoured Races in the Struggle for Life* (1859)
has had an impact so far-ranging and many-faceted that it confounds

brief summary. Darwin's theory did not constitute a radical break with prevailing science; evolution had been "in the air" for decades, so much so that Tennyson's *In Memoriam* (much influenced by Chambers's *Vestiges of Creation*) seemed to be arguing with Darwin a decade before the *Origin* appeared. Indeed, Darwin was spurred to write up his long-pondered theory (the main ideas were in place as early as 1839) only after a fellow naturalist, A. R. Wallace, presented a paper anticipating some of its central claims. Darwin's theory also was far from the first to undermine the idea of divine creation most influentially set forth in *Genesis*. The geologist Charles Lyell, on whom Darwin drew heavily, during the 1830s had argued that natural forces acted uniformly over time, constantly reshaping the face of the planet, and left an ongoing history of its power in "the evidence of the rocks" – a record which included those fossils of extinct species that so haunted Tennyson. As John Tyndall in his 1874 Belfast address would put it, "the strength of the doctrine of Evolution consists, not in an experimental demonstration … but in its general harmony with scientific thought" (Tyndall 1905: ii.206). Indeed, Darwin lacked any concept of genetics, and thus any plausible account of why variations occurred (as distinct from how they might establish new species). Thus at the heart of this theory, as critics pointed out, there was something of a black box. But Darwin nonetheless provided the most intricate, persuasive, and lucid account to date not only of extinction but also of the emergence of new species over time. The Newtonian world did not change; Darwinian nature was inherently, emphatically historical.

Darwin, then, tells a compelling story, a narrative at once expansive and intricately detailed, which reached all of educated Britain, and was appropriated to many, often conflicting ends. The idea of "struggle" between different species and their environment seemed to some commentators readily transferable to the analysis of society. This was a superficially plausible gesture (and one encouraged by Darwin's own subtitle). Darwin's theory resembles an extension to the animal and vegetable world of laissez-faire economics, or the intellectual marketplace of Millian liberalism. Thus Herbert Spencer, most influentially, coined the phrase "survival of the fittest" in order to describe social competition – with the clear implication that class hierarchies were underwritten by nature itself. In *The Principles of Sociology* (1876), Spenser (1820–1903) argued that societies are themselves organisms that evolve from "primitive" to more complex forms. This view would have an enormous impact in emergent sciences of anthropology and sociology, which typically formulated schemes of racial and cultural development grounded on a similar logic. But Spencer, like many commentators since, smuggled into his evolutionary scheme a sense of direction that Darwinian evolution does not provide. Spencer's "social Darwinism" (which persists in some forms of "evolutionary psychology") is closer to earlier Lamarckian schemes, whereby (for example) giraffes develop long necks in order to reach more food. This suggestion that evolutionary changes arise to meet a pre-existent need obscures one of the most disconcerting aspects of Darwin's theory: evolution offers no overarching direction, no governing telos. The present moment is not the culmination of the past, but one moment in an endless process of change. An animal happened to appear with a longer neck than its fellows, which in a particular milieu made it better adapted to survival; the same variation in another environment might prove fatal. The new species is "better" only in a strenuously relativist sense: the word that Darwin uses is not "progress" but "adaptation." As T. H. Huxley would insist in a famous 1893 essay, evolution provides no ethics.

Clearly this randomness was as much a blow to traditional faith as was the more obvious conflict with biblical schemes of creation. Yet Darwin's theory also provided a narrative model, as recent commentators have pointed out, that had much in common with those engaging a more familiar storyteller, the novelist. Not only does Darwinian theory incorporate history, it takes up familiar mythic themes of transformation and metamorphosis; it foregrounds the idea of kinship; it puts great stress (unlike, say, classical mechanics) on the particularity of the world, its sheer abundance and variety, as well as its subtle gradations and modulations (Beer 2000). Perhaps most suggestively, Darwinism discovers unifying structure without teleology. Victorian novelists likewise began with the assumption that the world they described was intelligible and coherent. But the efforts to embody that coherence in novelistic form – most obviously through coincidence and other residues of the so-called "providential plot" – were increasingly liable to seem either unrealistic, too obvious a simplification of the flux of experience, or to seem a deadening abridgement of human agency, in which the power of choice was thoroughly circumscribed by external forces. Thus Darwin leads back to another version of Mill's worry, which is also Estella's: we are not free, you and I. It would be some while before this impact was fully grasped by poets and novelists, but in the latter decades of the century, the impact would be immense.

Novels and their Audiences

As sensation fiction brought newly daring subject matter into representations of domestic life, it also prompted censure that recalled out-
cries over the "Newgate novel" in the late 1830s. The political situation
in 1860 certainly was more tranquil than that of 1839, when Chartism
had seemed a dire threat. But novels had become far more central to
English life, and were reaching a far broader audience. Whereas in
1839 the novel was still shadowed by widespread condescension and
religious mistrust of fiction, by the 1860s it was securely installed
within the middle-class household, a development facilitated by the
circulating library and the monthly magazine. These twin institutions
wielded immense influence over novelistic subject matter, which
prompted increasing complaints that literature was in danger of being
infantilized, its acceptability measured by its impact on Podsnap's
"young person." At the same time, the guardians of literary decorum
had to deal with novelists increasingly engaged by challenges to social
propriety. That friction chimed with Mill's analysis. In response to his
gloomy vision of conformism in *On Liberty*, many reviewers objected
that society was not a "mere *arbiter* between individuals," as R. H.
Hutton put it, but "an organised body, in the common life of which all
its members participate," and which would make freedom itself seem a
more substantially collective achievement (Pyle 1994: 100). In the
Victorian novel, however, ever-richer evocations of society as an
"organized body" were bound up with ever more complex accounts of
estrangement from it. George Eliot's *Mill on the Floss* explores precisely
this tension, showing how oppressive the "common life" could seem
to a young woman who found herself at odds with its norms of femininity. Women writers naturally had a special appreciation of the
abridgement of liberty, but novelists generally were increasingly fascinated by forms of alienation.

   These tensions were pointedly borne out in both the substance and
the reception of George Meredith's *The Ordeal of Richard Feverel*
(1859), a novel that might serve as a case study for *On Liberty*. Like
Modern Love, the novel was deeply affected by Meredith's personal history, and was in this regard a marked departure from his earlier novels.
Like those efforts, however, it resisted easy generic placement. *The
Shaving of Shagpat* (1855), "an Arabian entertainment," represents
something like a whimsical reworking of Middle Eastern folklore, while

Farina: A Legend of Cologne (1857) is a similarly comic, at times grotesque, reworking of medieval romance. *Feverel*, "A History of Father and Son," takes up the subject matter of the domestic novel, but treats the material through the lens of something like an eighteenth-century philosophic tale, with an expansive ironic commentary that many reviewers likened to Sterne's *Tristram Shandy*. The story describes a wealthy baronet who has been deserted by his wife, and in response attempts to raise his son in accord with "the System," which would guard young Richard from the allure of womankind. In the eccentric mannerism of Meredith's prose (which here hovers in free indirect discourse between the baronet's smug self-reflection and the narrator's acerbic commentary), "by hedging round the Youth from corruptness, and at the same time promoting his animal health, by helping him to Grow as he would, like a Tree of Eden; by advancing him to a certain moral fortitude ere the Apple-Disease was spontaneously developed, there would be seen something approaching to a perfect man" (Meredith 1971: 9). "The System," ringing changes on Mill's trope of development, predictably ends in shambles, as Richard's upbringing leaves him woefully unprepared to deal with the first experience of passion. Less predictable are the somber and ultimately violent repercussions of his unworldliness, which leads him into seduction by a prostitute (one of the "demimonde," as reviewers delicately put it) who has been hired by an aristocrat trying to seduce Feverel's virtuous young wife, and ultimately secures his ruin.

Reviewers were impressed by the originality of *Feverel*, but the book was a financial failure, because its subject matter proved too daring for Mudie's Library, which refused to order any copies. Mudie's had been founded in 1842 in response to the high cost of novels published in three-volume form. For an annual fee of one guinea per year, a subscriber could check out individual volumes of recent publications, an immense saving over the cost of purchasing "triple-deckers" that retailed for the long-standard price of 31s 6d (more than a weekly wage even for many middle-class readers). In 1858–9 alone, Mudie added nearly 400,000 volumes to its stock (two fifths of which was fiction) – a scale that enabled the firm to command steep discounts from publishers, to influence the size and date of an edition, and to effectively suppress subject matter it found objectionable. When W. H. Smith entered the business in the early 1860s, the two companies became known as "the twin tyrants of literature," and their sway would continue until the abrupt disintegration of the three-volume format in the early 1890s.

The circulation of fiction was further enlarged in 1859, when Macmillan founded the first one-shilling monthly aimed at a middle-class audience, principally as a house organ for its authors, whose novels could appear in serial before publication in volume form. *Macmillan's Magazine* began publication with Hughes's *Tom Brown at Oxford*, and subsequently serialized work by (among others) Kingsley, Oliphant, Hardy, Hodgson Burnett, Yonge, and R. D. Blackmore. Just a few months later, with Thackeray as its initial editor (at 2,000 pounds a year), Smith, Elder launched the *Cornhill Magazine*, which became the first journal aimed at a middle-class audience to sell 100,000 copies per number. It would earn renown as "the premier fiction-carrying magazine of the century" (Sutherland 1989: 150), publishing serials by Trollope, Reade, Collins, Gaskell, George Eliot, and later Thomas Hardy, as well as Thackeray himself. The success gave rise to a host of less successful imitators likewise echoing London geography – *Temple Bar*, *St. Paul's*, *Belgravia*, *St. James's* – as well as more raffish journals, such as the *Argosy*, edited by Mary Elizabeth Braddon, which specialized in sensation. The natural effect was to drive down demand for the free-standing serial novel pioneered by Dickens; for the same amount of money, a reader could get monthly installments of one novel (often two) with poetry and articles on a wide range of topics.

Thackeray's own career declined after *The Newcomes*. That work, though still prompting the familiar suspicions of cynicism (the *Christian Examiner* pronounced it "utterly devoid of earnestness" [Tillotson and Hawes 1969: 262]) was widely applauded as triumph of realism – a foil, as ever, to Dickens's treatment. Thackeray was "the greatest painter of manners who ever lived," although even this critic was slightly dismayed that "he manages to exist so entirely on the surface of things" – a disappointment gaining prominence in novel reviewing generally, as characters were measured against an emergent ideal of psychological depth (Tillotson and Hawes 1969: 266, 268). In *The Virginians*, which appeared in 24 numbers from 1857–9, Thackeray offered a sequel to Esmond set in Revolutionary America. Though the work sold nearly as well as *The Newcomes* (13,000 per number), it was not nearly so well received; critics were particularly frustrated by the lack of plot. In 1860 the invitation to edit the *Cornhill* bolstered Thackeray's spirits and bank account – though his correspondence reveals the sometimes amusing difficulties of the former bohemian serving as moral arbiter for middle-class drawing rooms. Beginning in 1861 he serialized in *Cornhill* his own new novel, *The Adventures of*

Philip, which returned to the milieu of *Pendennis*. Arthur Pendennis narrates Philip's financial and romantic struggles, which center around the vicissitudes of inheritance. After resigning from the *Cornhill* in 1862, he began a new serial for the journal, *Denis Duval*, another historical narrative in autobiographical form centered on the descendant of French Huguenots growing up in the 1760s. It was cut short by Thackeray's death on Christmas Eve 1863.

The *Cornhill* proved an especially valuable launching pad to Trollope, whose popularity and prolific output made him the most widely discussed novelist of the early 1860s. Although he had enjoyed a critical success with *Barchester Towers* in 1857, his readership expanded dramatically when *Framley Parsonage* (Trollope's first novel to be illustrated by John Everett Millais) appeared as the opening serial in the *Cornhill*. Trollope's laconic account of the novel in his *Autobiography* evokes qualities widely appreciated throughout the Barchester series: "The story was thoroughly English. There was a little fox-hunting and a little tuft-hunting, some Christian virtue and some Christian cant. There was no heroism and no villainy. There was much Church, but more love-making" (Trollope 1980: 143). *Framley Parsonage* was followed by an even greater success, *The Small House at Allington*, which began its run in September 1862. Trollope's heroine, Lily Dale, so captivated readers that they deluged the author with letters pleading that she marry her admirer, Johnny Eames. The novel brought Trollope 3,000 pounds, three times his earnings from *Framley Parsonage*; even before it appeared in book form, Trollope had become "almost a national institution," his works "the novels of the day" (Smalley 1969: 169).

Praise for Trollope, however, was qualified with remarkable and revealing consistency. He was applauded for his success at fulfilling modest aims, centering on the attentive observation of everyday life, but offering little in the way of narrative design or deep sympathies. As one enthusiastic review pronounced, "as far as it is possible for a novelist to be without invention he is without it …His sketches of character on which they depend for their value are the result of shrewd observation cleverly expressed in every-day phrase; never of any subtle or particular insight into character" (Smalley 1969: 118).

Repeatedly critics compared his novels to photography (which gained new prominence in the 1850s through personal *cartes de visites*). They offered distinctive pleasures, particularly as a foil to Dickens: readers comparing Trollope's characters in *The Three Clerks* with the Barnacles of *Little Dorrit* "will see at once the difference between a funny sketch and a genuine photograph" (Smalley 1969: 107). At the same time, the photograph offered many critics frustratingly little sense of inner being. As the young Henry James put it, Trollope's virtues "are all virtues of detail: the virtues of the photograph. The photograph lacks the supreme virtue of possessing a character" (Smalley 1969: 236). The wish for richer character was frequently expressed by comparisons to Charlotte Brontë. The woman who 15 years earlier had unsettled many readers now was a model of the passion and psychological complexity that critics missed in Trollope.

Critics frequently associated Trollope's appeal with the influence of the circulating libraries and the monthlies. In a jocular but generally sympathetic review of his career prior to the launch of the *Cornhill*, E. S. Dallas in *The Times* stressed Trollope's appeal to Mudie, "the mighty monarch of books that are good enough to be read, but not good enough or not cheap enough to be bought ... he is the Apollo of the circulating library." From this vantage, Trollope is "paramount above all others ... the most fertile, the most popular, the most successful author – that is to say, of the circulating library sort" (Smalley 1969: 103–4). "The circulating library sort" could be regarded with more or less condescension, but was acknowledged as a crucial power in contemporary literature, and critics generally were pleased to see its desires gratified by works both reliably entertaining and "manly." A similar note informs reviews of the magazine serials. One compares Trollope to the painter Frith as "the very best of second-rate reputations. Both are universally popular, and their popularity arises from the same cause. Everybody has read 'Framley Parsonage,' just as everybody has been to see the 'Derby Day' or the 'Railway Station'; and no London diner-out would imperil his reputation by venturing into society without being thoroughly posted up in the latest details of Sir Peregrine Orme's courtship" (Smalley 1969: 152). Again the condescension captures the allure of the literary institution: a quarter-century after *Pickwick*, serial publication remained a more emphatically social experience than reading the novel in volume form. The reading experience seemed itself a stimulus to, even an extension of, forms of social exchange being represented in the serials. And they were praised accordingly, in terms that might describe a welcome dinner guest. "We regard this work ...as matchless in its way, being so perfectly pure and yet so manly, such fitting food for men, but with no odour and no savour that shall hurt the tenderest maiden ... One feels in eminently good society with Mr Trollope. Not in the flashy, fashionable society of May Fair ... but your steady, safe-going, port-wine, and country-family society." As Dallas himself would conclude, "These novels are healthy and manly, and so long as Mr Anthony Trollope is the prince of the circulating library our readers may rest assured that it is a very useful, very pleasant, and very honorable institution" (Smalley 1969: 126, 104).

The epithet "manly" – a recurrent honorific in these discussions – is a particularly telling gauge of reviewers' concerns (which Dickens soon would skewer in his portrait of Podsnap). On the one hand, Trollope frequently suffered by comparison with two women writers, Charlotte Brontë and George Eliot (Dallas's 1859 encomium was published just weeks before the appearance of *Adam Bede*). But for most male reviewers these two authors were exceptions to an unsettling feminization of the novel as an institution, whose putative failings has been slashingly attacked by Eliot herself in an 1857 review, "Silly Novels by Lady Novelists." By 1862 the anxiety had been aggravated by the rage for melodrama and sensation, to which "manly" attributes were opposed: "a manly aversion to melodramatic art"; "plain and straightforward, utterly devoid of clap-trap"; "disdains all clap-trap or stage trickery"; "the most healthy and most masculine book that has been published in these later times" (Smalley 1969: 105, 164, 127).

As such defensive praise suggests, in 1862 the dominant fictional mode was sensation. "A book without a murder, a divorce, a seduction, or a bigamy," claimed a reviewer in *Fraser's* in 1863, "is not apparently considered either worth writing or reading; and a mystery and a secret are the chief qualifications of the modern novel" (Pykett 2005: 87). Collins followed up *The Woman in White* with *No Name*, also serialized in *All The Year Round*, which concerns the disinheritance of two young women after it is discovered that their parents were never legally married. In an effort to revenge themselves on the man who has displaced them and to regain the family name, the heroine, Magdalen Vanstone, assumes the identity of her former governess. In 1864, Collins launched another novel centering on a woman who marries under a false identity, although the audacious Lydia Gwilt (her surname signals her moral standing) does so to gain a new fortune, not to recover one lost. *Armadale*, which recounts her career, was serialized in the *Cornhill* – a measure of Collins's stature at the time. Meanwhile, Charles Reade (1814–80) took up the private asylums that figured so largely in sensation, making their abuses the focal point of *Hard Cash*, which was serialized in Dickens's *All the Year Round*

(1863). Though presented as a novel of reform, Reade characteristically took no half measures, relegating his hero to an asylum as part of a plot to steal the fortune of the title, and lingering over his nightmarish scenes of torment, "chained sane among the mad; on his wedding day; expecting with tied hands the sinister acts of the soul-murderers who had the power to make their lie a truth!" (Burns 1961: 217).

Reade's success marks an intriguing intersection of sensation and gothic within the "novel with a purpose," a form he had taken up with his first success, *It Is Never Too Late to Mend* (1856), which centers on English prison brutality and work in the Australian gold fields. The sensation vogue also nurtured evocations of something akin to pure terror, most notably from the Irish writer, Sheridan LeFanu (1816–73). This aspect of gothic had been kept alive throughout the period in penny serial and other cheap formats; the best known in this vein are James Rymer's *Varney the Vampire* (1847) and T. P. Prest's *String of Pearls* (1846), whose plot resembles a version of the melodrama *Sweeney Todd*. LeFanu began his writing career in the late 1830s with stories in various genres, from the comic to the supernatural and the thriller, most of which were published in the *Dublin University Magazine*, which was unusually receptive to the ghostly. In 1861 LeFanu took over editorship of the journal, which over the next decade serialized seven of his own novels. The most famous is *Uncle Silas* (1864), where Le Fanu comes closer than any Victorian to reviving the gothic of Radcliffe. After the death of her father, young Maud Ruthyn finds herself confined to the isolated Derbyshire country house of her widowed Uncle Silas, to whom she has been entrusted so that he might clear his name of earlier scandal – he is rumored to have killed a man in this very house – but who also stands to inherit Maud's fortune should she die before her twenty-first birthday. His "wild and piercing eye" and long white hair make him seem a kind of specter, and his cool, urbane detachment from all around him only compounds his fearful aura. When Maud complains of a field hand who routinely bloodies his own daughter, he responds, "To be sure it is brutality; but you must remember they are brutes, and it suits them" (LeFanu 1966: 213). Like the world of *Wuthering Heights*, LeFanu's is a hell in which the people speak English, but Emily Brontë's titanic battle of wills here gives way to a more familiar harrowing of helpless femininity.

The influence of sensation may be most telling in outwardly realistic novels, such as Margaret Oliphant's *Salem Chapel*, which began appearing in *Blackwood's* in February 1862. Oliphant (1828–97) was a paragon of the indefatigable Victorian author, soldiering on from project to project after her husband's death in 1859, heavily in debt to her generous publisher, struggling to win sufficient income to support three young children. Throughout the 1850s she had turned out more than a novel a year, of widely varied sorts – rural novels set in her native Scotland, historical fiction, "problem" novels, children's fiction – as well as translations, reviews, and a biography of Edward Irving, the charismatic Scottish preacher and one-time mentor of Carlyle who had enjoyed a meteoric rise and fall in the 1820s. Yet she was still only eking by in 1861, when she published in *Blackwood's* a sequence of long stories set in the fictional town of Carlingford. *Salem Chapel*, the first novel-length installment in what became *The Chronicles of Carlingford*, follows a newly minted Dissenting minister, Arthur Vincent, as he struggles to reconcile his pride and "painful gentility" (Oliphant 1986: 15) with the demands of his first congregation, Salem Chapel, whose social elite is comprised of "greengrocers, dealers in cheese and Bacon, milkmen, with some dress-makers of inferior pretensions, and teacher of day-schools of similar humble character" (2). Novelists had rarely offered sympathetic portraits of Dissenters, who retained a decided suspicion of fiction, and Oliphant was widely praised for her account of the Chapel community (a triumph of imagination, since Oliphant had no first-hand experience of anything like it). But Oliphant grafted onto that portrait a plot straight out of sensation fiction, full of hidden pasts, falsified names, abduction, and attempted murder. (Oliphant knew the genre well; in May 1862, as the novel was appearing, *Blackwood's* published her widely cited omnibus review of sensation fiction.) The result is a structural hodge-podge, but it succeeded in bringing Oliphant new prominence; she not only was able to pay her bills, but also managed to secure 1,500 pounds for her next novel, *The Perpetual Curate* (1864).

Such rewards paled before those of George Eliot. After the success of *Silas Marner* (1861), Smith, Elder lured her away from Blackwood with the unprecedented offer of 7,000 pounds to serialize her next novel in the *Cornhill*, where it ran from July 1862 through August 1863. (Blackwood offered 10,000 pounds for the entire copyright.) In a marked departure from the provincial English settings of her previous fiction, *Romola* is set in late-fifteenth-century Florence, tracing the spiritual development of its title character through the tumult of the religious and social upheaval surrounding the ascendancy of Savanarola. The devoted daughter of a blind scholar, Romola marries a charismatic but unscrupulous Greek adventurer, Tito, then falls under the spell of Savanarola – whose fanatical piety seems a distant mirror of the evangelicalism that the young Mary Ann Evans had for a time embraced – only to finally shake off his influence and discover fulfillment in a self-effacing maternal devotion, caring for the common-law wife and children whom Tito had abandoned. Romola's personal history is in many ways an archetype for Eliot's heroines – as for the author herself – particularly when she is struggling with the consequences of her own illusions. Thus, for example, after discovering Tito's treachery she removes her wedding ring:

> It brought a vague but arresting sense that she was somehow violently rending her life in two: a presentiment that the strong impulse which had seemed to exclude doubt and make her path clear might after all be blindness, and that there was something in human bonds which must prevent them from being broken with the breaking of illusions. (G. Eliot 1980: 391)

As it evokes a rupture with the past that turns on the death of an illusion, this moment of crisis resonates in a host of nineteenth-century life stories: the "Everlasting Nay" of Carlyle's Teufelsdröckh; the young John Stuart Mill recognizing the limits of Bentham's world; the young Mary Ann Evans renouncing her own evangelical faith. But for many readers, then as now, the emotional dynamics seem occluded by the preoccupation with historical verisimilitude. For readers who shared the interest in Renaissance Italy – Browning, Henry James, Walter Pater – the setting helped to make the novel Eliot's finest. For others, including most readers today, the massively detailed research too often lapses into antiquarianism. Certainly it took a toll on the author; she began the novel a young woman, she remarked, and ended it an old one.

The *Cornhill* also serialized Elizabeth Gaskell's fiction, which during the 1850s had come out primarily in Dickens's magazines. After *Sylvia's Lovers* (1863), set during the Napoleonic Wars, Gaskell produced a lengthy story entitled *Cousin Phyllis*, which ran in four numbers of the journal from November 1863 to February 1864. Her next (and final) novel, *Wives and Daughters*, began appearing in August 1864; after her sudden death in November 1865, Thackeray's successor, Frederick Greenwood, provided a concluding chapter drawn from Gaskell's remarks to her family about the resolution of the action. As the title suggests, *Wives and Daughters* is remote from the settings and reformist energies of Gaskell's earlier fiction, and recalls instead the comedy of Austen. The novel focuses on the challenges of courtship facing Molly Gibson, who must make her way through social minefields when her father, a widowed country physician, marries a widowed former governess obsessed with her own precarious social standing, and with a daughter of her own to marry off. In Gaskell's industrial novels social class figures principally as a stark and dangerous divide between capitalist and worker, but in *Wives and Daughters* the challenges inhere in navigating subtler, more elusive but still weighty distinctions, of a kind signaled by the contrast between old silks and new satins. The imperatives of class are felt in a host of mortifications, as when Molly's new stepmother, in a vein reminiscent of Pecksniff and foreshadowing Rosamond Vincy, objects to Molly's use of the phrase, "the apple of his eye": "Molly! Molly pray don't let me hear you using such vulgar expressions ... Proverbs and idioms are never used by people of education" (Gaskell 1969: 695). In Gaskell's comedy of social anxiety, one glimpses an arc linking Austen's world to that of Oscar Wilde.

A characteristically fierce engagement with social mobility came from Dickens. Following the publication of *Great Expectations*, Dickens devoted most of the early 1860s to his editorial work and to increasingly lucrative public readings from his novels. After the longest silence of his career, a new novel, *Our Mutual Friend*, began appearing in monthly parts in May of 1864. It is Dickens's single most complex narrative, sometimes bewildering in its turns and doublings, which pivot on the mistaken identity of a drowned man, a rightful heir living in disguise, and an elaborate ruse involving the fate of his inheritance. Amid this world of lost or disguised identity, Dickens arraigns an obsession with status blazoned forth in the pointedly named Veneerings, a young couple entertaining in a hall of mirrors who conjure up the appearance of fabulous wealth, derived from sources unknown. As the narrator acidly exhorts, "Have no antecedents, no established character, no cultivation, no ideas, no manners, have shares" (Dickens 1971: 159–60). The dominant leitmotifs of the novel are the polluted Thames, from which scavengers plunder dead bodies, and massive heaps of "dust," valuable sweepings gleaned from the notoriously filthy streets of London. There could hardly be a more insistent association of money with waste. More subtle is the gripping rivalry between a young working-class schoolmaster, Bradley Headstone, and another of Dickens's aristocratic idlers, Eugene Wrayburn, who are brought into conflict by their shared interest in Lizzie Hexam, daughter of Rogue

Riderhood, who makes his living scavenging the Thames. The character of Headstone develops the treatment of emotional repression in *Little Dorrit* and *Hard Times*, but here the anguish centers on the wounds of social class, as Headstone, struggling to make his way in the world, is tortured by Wrayburn's insouciant self-assurance. It is as if Dickens had set two halves of himself at war with one another. Critics, however, were for the most part unable to appreciate Dickens's power to externalize psychic conflict, continuing the refrain that, as Henry James put it, "it is one of the chief conditions of his genius not to see beneath the surface of things" (P. Collins 1971: 472).

Literature for Children

The new monthly magazines also provided an expanding medium for fiction aimed principally at children. *Macmillan* published in the 1860s two works that have become classics of children's literature: Kingsley's *The Water-Babies*, which was serialized in 1862–3, and *The Adventures of Alice in Wonderland*, by Lewis Carroll (Charles Dodgson, 1832–98), which appeared in 1865. These works often have been taken to inaugurate a "golden age" of children's literature in English, a belated flowering of romantic conceptions of childhood fertilized by a growing literary marketplace. The very notion of "children's literature" is a relatively recent historical development; only in the late seventeenth century does it come to be widely held that children have imaginative needs importantly different from those of adults. The works first enlisted to meet this presumed demand, the transcriptions of oral tradition that became known as folk tale and fairy tale, were in their origins emphatically communal entertainments, and efforts to delimit children's literature are bedeviled by the elusiveness of the implied audience. Adventure narratives in particular perplexed the boundaries. *Robinson Crusoe* was among the most popular works of children's literature in the nineteenth century, but it certainly was not written for children. Over the course of the century an increasing amount of domestic fiction was enjoyed by adolescent girls; Charlotte Yonge's works, particularly *The Daisy Chain* (1856), were especially notable in this regard. (More cynical readers – then as now – have seen in this broad appeal an arrested development in much of Victorian fiction, which contrasts with the much greater urbanity and sexual freedom of continental realism; their objections, in essence, would identify Dickens with Podsnap.) Even in works clearly addressed to younger readers, however, such as the fantasies of Carroll and Kingsley, many of the allusions and the arcane wordplay clearly appeal to adults.

Children's literature was more sharply demarcated early in the century, when it was largely divided between collections of simple lyrics – the chants and catches most influentially gathered by Newbery in the mid-eighteenth century – and didactic prose and verse setting forth models of proper behavior. Under the influence of evangelicalism, such instruction could be draconian. The very popular *History of the Fairchild Family* (1818) by Mary Martha Sherwood, for example, assumes that "All children are by nature evil, and ... pious and prudent persons must check their naughty passions in any way they have in their power," which for Sherwood includes descriptions of a father taking his children to view a rotting corpse on a gibbet, and a child burnt to death when she disobeys her parents (Hunt 1994: 48). Wordsworth and other romantic writers of course resisted such views, and associated childhood with untrammeled imagination, a position seconded in such works as the Lambs' *Tales from Shakespeare* (1808). But only in the 1830s did there emerge a broad resistance to prescriptive moralism, and with it a body of literature blurring the boundaries of child and adult readership. In 1839, *Holiday House* by Catherine Sinclair (no stranger to fierce moralizing in her own anti-Catholic fiction) attacked puritanical children's literature as monotonous and unreal. Translations of fairy- tale collections by Perrault (1826) and the Grimms (1829), and of Andersen's literary tales (from 1846 onwards) as well as Hoffman's parody of moralistic tales, *Struwwelpeter* (1848), contributed to an outpouring of fantasy, such as Ruskin's *King of the Golden River* (1851) and Thackeray's *Rose and the Ring* (1855). Fantasy expanded to novelistic length in the work of George MacDonald (1824–1905), a prolific Scottish writer who frequently mingled realistic and fantastic modes, and wrote fantasies aimed at both children (*At the Back of the North Wind* [1871], published in *Good Words for the Young*, which MacDonald edited) and adults, such as *Phantastes* (1858) and *Lilith* (1895). Dickens's attack on Gradgrindian education in *Hard Times* participates in this development; it was provoked in part when Dickens's former illustrator Cruikshank revised four classic fairy tales as teetotaller tracts – a gesture Dickens denounced in *Household Words* in 1853 as "Frauds on the Fairies." Though Dickens' attack was a rearguard engagement in a battle largely won, it brings home the polemical force frequently attached to fantasy as a mode of imaginative freedom, which resisted the burdens of practicality and common sense.

The cultivation of that freedom figures centrally in mid-Victorian children's literature. From the 1850s onwards the moral burden is rarely mere prohibition. Whereas early evangelical fiction tended to feature deathbed conversions, increasingly writers offered models of virtuous conduct and incitements to charity. The most notable writer in this vein was Hesba Stretton (Sarah Smith, 1832–1911) whose *Jessica's First Prayer* (1867), the tale of a homeless street waif, sold over a million copies. The resurgence of adventure fiction that began with Marryat in the 1830s offered more resistance to Christian piety, as it celebrated a hardy and resilient self-assertion; the rise of the "school story" with the advent of *Tom Brown's School Days* in effect refines that spirit. Like tales of life at sea, the school story depicts an all-male realm cordoned off from the world at large, but Hughes attempted to revise the popular view of the public school as little more than a test of hardiness, in part by allowing readier movement between school and family life. (William Golding famously reversed the development a century later with *The Lord of the Flies*.) As it inculcates piety alongside pugilism, Hughes's novel draws on the evangelical tradition – which is why it became a butt of mockery in later celebrations of more violent hardiness, such as Kipling's *Stalky And Co.* (1899). The evangelical temper was more pronounced in another famous school story, F. W. Farrar's *Eric, Or Little by Little* (1858). Farrar's strenuous didacticism – the subtitle points the road to ruin – was widely applauded (the story went through 24 editions in 31 years), but it also quickly became a byword for excessive rigor, in which discipline turned into prurient fixation on adolescent sexuality. (Even Yonge called it a "morbid dismal tale" [Wolff 1977: 220].) The effort to balance discipline and daring figures centrally in the juvenile magazines that began to flourish from about 1860. The inaugural issue of *The Boys of England* in 1866, edited by Edward John Brett, declared "Our tales and authors do not contain 'sermons in disguise,' which are always distasteful to boys, but a moral and healthy tone which may be maintained in conjunction with the boldest fiction" (Hunt 1994: 63). The claim steers a course between explicitly didactic fiction and the world of "penny dreadfuls," more sensational narratives aimed principally at a working-class audience (for whom six shillings, the original price of *Alice* in book form, represented several days' wages). *The Boy's Own Paper*, founded in 1879 by the Religious Tract Association, reached as many as 500,000 readers, with regular contributors including

Ballantyne and G. A. Henty (1832–1902), whose prodigious career as an author of boys' adventures began with *Out of the Pampas* (1868).

The Water Babies and *Alice in Wonderland* depict more fantastic realms, both explicitly modeled on dream states and accordingly episodic and meandering in structure: "fantasy" seems a more accurate generic label than "novel." Kingsley's reads like a fusion of Linnaeus and Rabelais (one of his avowed inspirations), or the opium reverie of a natural history buff fresh from reading *The Origin of Species.* The work is saturated in close observation of the English countryside, both Kingsley's own Eversley and the more far-flung sites of his many fishing and walking expeditions. That observation is loosely organized by the experience of Tom, an orphan chimney sweep transformed into the tiny amphibious creature of the title, as he floats downriver to the sea along with other children similarly abandoned. From the sea he makes his way back to the land world through a host of Swiftian landscapes, such as the land of the "Doasyoulikes," whose indolence has caused them to devolve from humans into apes (the work is haunted by the recent discovery of the gorilla), and finally to "the Other-end-of-Nowhere." For all of its topical allusions, whether to contemporary natural history or to Kingsley's increasingly reactionary politics (crows who peck to death a wounded fellow are "true republicans ... who do every one just what he likes" [Kingsley 1995: 141]), the work resists confident ascriptions of meaning. It is frequently described as a protest in behalf of chimney sweeps, but the narrative never circles back to Tom's original state, and Tom himself mentions it only in passing after his transformation. The more resonant conceit seems that of the begrimed young boy washed clean, a purification given new inflections within muscular Christianity. That cult of physical vigor is evoked in Kingsley's closing address to his five-year-old son: "do you learn your lessons, and thank God that you have plenty of cold water to wash in; and wash in it too, like a true English man" (183).

Alice in Wonderland engages in a more throughgoing frustration of moralism; few works have ever been more subversive of the pieties of childhood. The effect is encapsulated in its parodies of sententious poetry, whereby Watts's "How doth the little busy bee /Preserve each shining hour" turns into "How doth the little crocodile / Improve his shining tail." The effect is "nonsense" not as sheer gibberish, but as a concerted comic disruption of ordinary sense. In Wonderland, Alice experiences the power of rules in everyday life – the rules of language, social conduct, legal institutions – precisely through their subversion, which makes her experience akin to trying to play a game whose rules have been withheld, or are constantly changing in unpredictable ways. But children very often experience the adult world as just such a trial. That is one insight of a logician (Carroll was an Oxford mathematics don) who appreciates the limits of his own specialty. When the characters at the mad tea party demand that Alice speak in logically rigorous language, they absurdly fail to appreciate that the conventions governing everyday social life are fundamentally arbitrary. When logic is applied outside its proper sphere, it can seem mere bullying – which is what Alice encounters in most of her attempts at conversation. Language in Wonderland is less communicative than forensic, less a means of seeking mutual understanding than an instrument of domination – proving the point, winning the game, securing the verdict. Of course the very phrase "make fun of" reminds us that aggression is an integral part of humor. It was Carroll's genius to discover this impulse in the heart of Victorian domesticity. Illogical as social rules may be, one ignores them at one's peril. While Kingsley rings changes on the world of exploration, *Alice* recounts a derangement of domestic life, the crucible for a young girl of privilege, who is groomed from an early age to preside over social rules, and who finds herself instinctively grasping for proper etiquette even as she is falling down a bottomless shaft, or addressing a talking mouse. *Alice in Wonderland* has been a great favorite of artists engaged by altered states of consciousness, from the Surrealists in France to psychedelic rock bands in 1960s America, all of whom suggest that the work's dream-like character gives us access to timeless psychic states. But it gives us readier insight into the highly rule-bound society of mid-Victorian Oxford, a world in which being late for an appointment could upset even a white rabbit.

Poetry in the Early 1860s

Carroll's poetic parodies open onto the immense range and popularity of Victorian comic verse, which was a staple not only of the likes of *Punch* but of many collections by single authors. Despite the impact of political lyrics and ballads in the 1840s, lyric remained associated with emotional generality, inasmuch as it solicited a broad range of sympathy, and poetry engaging current affairs (as every issue of *Punch* bears out) was often assumed to be comic by virtue of its very topicality. Much of the most popular comic poetry drew that topicality from mimicry of contemporary poets and idioms. *The Bon Gaultier Ballads*, a collaboration by William Aytoun and Theodore Martin initiated in *Blackwood's*, collected in a number of editions (beginning in 1845) parodies of popular contemporary poems. "Locksley Hall," for example, returns as "Lay of the Lovelorn": "There the passions cramped no longer, shall have space to breathe, my cousin /I will take some savage woman–nay, I'll take at least a dozen." In the 1860s C. S. Calverley, a noted Latinist, began publishing more subtle burlesques of contemporary poets and their forms, such as "Ballad," a hit at D. G. Rossetti, in which the parenthetical refrain is *"Butter and eggs and a pound of cheese."* The *Ingoldsby Legends* of Richard Harris Barham, collected in three series in 1840, 1842, and 1847, offers a comic reworking of medievalism, retelling various legends and folk tales in wildly varied and rollicking stanzas, which remained popular through the century. (By 1895 Bentley had sold some 400,000 copies; Barham earned only the 100 pounds for which he sold the copyright.) Such poetry often confounds boundaries between child and adult audiences. The ever-popular limericks of Edward Lear's *Book of Nonsense* (1846), for example, with their audacious punning rhymes and neologisms, are typically reprinted in anthologies of children's poetry. But Lear's deadpan evocations of an anonymous "old man" besieged by a hostile world clearly have a further layer of appeal for readers approaching that sad condition. W. S. Gilbert first came to wide notice with *The Bab Ballads* (1869), originally published in Punch's rival *Fun* (founded 1861), and later collected with the lyrics from his collaboration with Arthur Sullivan. Like Lear, Gilbert illustrated his poems, which created a twofold burlesque of a wide range of institutions and attitudes, from imperial pride to the rituals of courtship, though the *Ballads* tend to be more acerbic than the operetta lyrics:

> The warrior whose ennobled name
> Is woven with his country's fame,
>   Triumphant over all,
> I found weak, palsied, bloated, blear,
> His province seemed to be, to leer
>   At bonnets in Pall Mall.
>   ("Disillusioned," ll 43–8; Gilbert 1924)

The popularity of comic verse – from a child's "counting-out" songs through literary parody and burlesque to highly sophisticated political satire – reflects a still-avid readership for poetry generally. That audience supported the rise to prominence of a number of women poets in the 1860s, their paths in large part blazed by the career of Barrett Browning. At the beginning of that career some 40 years earlier, the subject matter of women's poetry had been largely confined to effusive sentiment, romantic and domestic, and to the picturesque description that would become the mainstay of the Annuals. L. E. L.'s career served as cautionary emblem of the pitfalls attending too much public exposure, and reinforced the close tethering of women writers to domestic concerns. By 1860, Barrett Browning in particular had pushed back the frontiers of women's poetry by incorporating sharp and sustained social criticism and political engagement. The publication of *Aurora Leigh* confirmed her stature as the most admired woman poet not only of her generation, but in British history. The "poetess" remained a potent critical category: her achievement was understood in emphatically gendered terms. Nearly every review of Barrett Browning wrestled to capture the leavening of femininity with "masculine" strengths – "intellectual discipline," "vigour" – while frequently decrying transgression of the properly feminine. The *Dublin University Review*, for example, while commending language and thoughts that offered "surprise and delight everywhere," also urged that the poet's subject and "coarse" language in *Aurora Leigh* created "a book which is almost a closed volume for her own sex" (Donaldson 1993: 70).

Even admirers were tested, however, by Barrett Browning's *Songs Before Congress* (1860), a slender volume of nine emphatically political poems. It infuriated most reviewers, including many admirers, who were particularly exercised by "A Curse for a Nation." Directed against American slavery, many reviewers took it to be aimed at England, and denounced it as, in the words of the *Saturday Review*, "a delirium of imbecile one-sidedness." "To bless and not to curse is woman's function," pronounced Aytoun in *Blackwood's* (Donaldson 1993: 83). But Barrett Browning's death the following year prompted fervent eulogy, which continued in reviews of her *Last Poems* and a new (fifth) edition of the *Poems*, both published in 1862. "Her place among the immortals is secure," pronounced the usually temperate G. H. Lewes in *Blackwood's*. "The greatest of English poetesses of any time," judged Chorley in the *Athenaeum*, proving that "Genius has no sex" (though his review belied this claim). Even for dissenting voices, she remained the benchmark of women's poetic power: the *Saturday Review* attacked nearly all of her work, conceding that she was a "genuine poetess" but that *Aurora Leigh* provides "the most conclusive proof that no woman can hope to achieve what Mrs. B. failed to accomplish" (Donaldson 1993: 102, 90, 95).

The new climate for women writers in the late 1850s was closely bound up with an emergent feminism. Caroline Norton's lonely battle of the 1830s was more broadly engaged in the 1850s through parliamentary debates over women's property rights (themselves responsive in part to the more sweeping ambitions of the Seneca Falls Convention in America in 1848). In 1858, Barbara Leigh Bodichon and Bessie Rayner Parkes, who had been galvanized by those debates, founded the *English Women's Journal*, and generated a web of affiliation dubbed the Langham Place group. In 1860, they set up the Portfolio Society, as a forum in which women might share their work in both poetry and painting. Among those whose paths crossed there were Dora Greenwell, Jean Ingelow, Adelaide Procter, and Christina Rossetti.

Much of poetry by women in the 1860s speaks to the disjunction that had burdened poets since the early 1830s, and which clearly persists in a lyric by Rayner Parkes:

> Who is the Poet? He who sings,
> Of high, abstruse, and hidden things?
> Or rather he who with a liberal voice
> Does with the glad hearts of all earth rejoice?"
> ("For Adelaide," ll. 1–4; Leighton and Reynolds 1995)

Better poets rarely expressed the challenge so schematically, but a good deal of their work might be thought of as an effort to elicit shared, "liberal" significance in a world of hidden or unprepossessing experience. Dora Greenwell's *Poems* (1861), which followed a volume of the same title published in 1850, reveal an outspoken writer on theological and political issues, but the most traditional poet among these women. "The Singer" is squarely in the mold of L. E. L., grounding the poet's power in her suffering: "they who love and listen best /Can little guess or know /The wounds that from the singer's breast /Have let such sweetness flow" (ll. 93–6; Greenwell 1867). "The Railway Station" of 1850 might seem to anticipate Barrett Browning's plea for a poetry of contemporary life: "For not with Baron bold, with Minstrel tender" did romance die. But the idiom remains this hackneyed medievalism, and the scene does not evoke a distinct modernity; instead, the station is merely a new arena for human encounters in which love and memory "still" – a tellingly insistent adjective – exert their hold. "For here are Meetings ...And here are partings ... And here Time holds his steady pace unbroken" (ll. 41 ff). "A Song to Call to Remembrance: A Plea for the Coventry Ribbon-Weavers" (1867) reflects the vitality of this subgenre a generation after "Cry of the Children" but lacks the bitter irony of the most robust avowals of sympathy for the poor. Released from explicit moral burdens, however, Greenwell can display a lyric playfulness, as in "A Scherzo (A Shy Person's Wishes)" – which delicately evokes the burdens of domestic life that Nightingale and others decried more vehemently:

> With things that are hidden, and safe, and bold:
> With things that are timid, and shy, and free,
> Wishing to be;
> With the nut in its shell, with the seed in its pod,
> With the corn as it sprouts in the kindly clod ...
> To be couched with the beast in its torrid lair,
> Or drifting on ice with the polar bear,
> With the weaver at work at his quiet loom:
> Anywhere, anywhere, out of this room!
>
> (ll. 8–11; 26–9)

Jean Ingelow by the mid-1860s was celebrated as one of the major poets of her time; her *Poems* (1863) went into 20 editions, and was even more popular in America, where 100,000 copies were sold. It was followed by *A Poem of Doom* (1867) and *Poems, Second Series* (1874) The first volume is almost entirely narrative, in ballad, sequence, dialogue, and blank verse. At its best, as in the opening poem, "Divided," Ingelow's poetry shares the appeal of Tennyson's domestic idylls, evoking baffled desire amid picturesque landscapes, although it lacks the Tennyson's venturesome rhythm and figurative richness:

> The beck grows wider, the hands must sever.
>   On either margin, our songs all done,
> We move apart, while she singeth ever,
>   Taking the course of the stooping sun.
>
> (ll. 45–8)

More than most, Ingelow's reputation suffered with the reaction against sentimental verse; few poets have undergone more precipitous declines in esteem.

Adelaide Anne Procter also enjoyed great popularity, with a much briefer career but a more durable achievement. In 1861 she published *Legends and Lyrics*, the first series of which had appeared in 1858. Her career began in 1853 when she submitted poems to Dickens's *Household Words* – under a pseudonym, an expedient adopted to conceal not her gender, but her father, the minor romantic poet and playwright Bryan Procter ("Barry Cornwall"), who was one of Dickens's good friends. The title hints at an abundance of narrative, which was enjoying a great vogue; in the decade before her early death in 1864, Procter enjoyed sales that for a time among contemporaries trailed only those of Tennyson, who was an important influence. "My Picture Gallery" rewrites "The Palace of Art" as a series of more innocent pleasures enjoyed by the tired city clerk who at the end of day finds beauty in the skies:

> Skies strewn with rose fading, fading slowly,
> While one star trembling watched the sunset die;
> Or deep in gloom a sunset, hidden wholly,
> Save through gold rents torn in a violet sky.
>
> (ll. 33–6; Procter 1871)

In "Philip and Mildred" the hexameters of "Locksley Hall" convey a quieter tale of romantic disappointment, of love withering during a long separation while the young man seeks success away from the village where his betrothed waits, so that their long-deferred marriage ultimately crowns an emotional void:

> Darker grew the clouds above her, and the slow conviction clearer,
>   That he gave her home and pity, but that heart, and soul, and mind
> Were beyond her now; he loved her, and in youth he had been
>   near her,
> But he now had gone far onward, and had left her there behind.
>
> (ll. 153–6)

As so often in Procter, consolation lies in another world, where "Heaven unites again the links that Earth has broken." Much of this today seems fairly saccharine piety: her 1858 volume opens with "The Angel's Story," of the guardian watching over a "little sickly orphan," and her volumes are full of angelic presences and dreamy, melancholic retrospects – most famously in "A Lost Chord," later set to music by Sir Arthur Sullivan. But Procter's was an activist faith; she converted to Roman Catholicism in 1851, and her final volume, *A Chaplet of Verses*

(1863), is almost entirely religious in theme, offering polemic as well as piety. "The Jubilee of 1850" bemoans a country that "knows the names no longer /Of her own sainted dead, /Denies the faith they held, /And the cause for which they bled" (l. 17–20). It seems strange that such verse could be popular in the wake of the "Papal Aggression" of 1850, but it meshed with sternly Protestant denunciations of British moral decline, such as Ruskin's *Stones of Venice*. Procter's faith also animates her unusually vigorous lyrics evoking the distress of the poor, such as "The Cradle Song of the Poor" and "Homeless."

A younger poet who first came to note in the 1860s was Augusta Webster (1837–94), whose lengthy dramatic monologues offer unusually subtle, sometimes provocative soundings of what one reviewer called "the pain that lies hidden in our modern social life," most particularly the burdens of domestic womanhood (Webster 2000: 410). Two early volumes, *Blanche Lisle and Other Poems* (1860) and *Lilian Gray* (1864) appeared under the pseudonym Cecil Home, but Webster gained wider notice with *Dramatic Studies* (1866), *A Woman Sold and Other Poems* (1867), and *Portraits* (1870), as well as her translations of *Prometheus Unbound* (1866) and Euripides's *Medea* (1868). The title poem of *A Woman Sold* develops the familiar clash between love and money through the unfamiliar device of pendant dialogues, in which the title character wrestles with the choice as a young woman, and then in widowhood reflects on what she surrendered for comfort. *Portraits* is an especially arresting gallery of 11 blank-verse monologues, whose characters range from Medea and Circe through "A Preacher," "A Painter," "An Inventor," and "A Dilettante" – all of them showing the marked influence of Robert Browning. They are more diffuse than Browning's best monologues, more tenuous in dramatic occasion and more apt to drift into versified social commentary, but their social burden is often grounded in finely drawn psychology, especially of women wrestling with the momentous question of marriage. "The Happiest Girl on the World," for example, evokes the quiet perplexities of a girl recently engaged, who wonders if her feelings live up to the role: "oh to think he should be loving me /And I no more moved out of myself!" (ll. 80–1; Webster 2000). (The ambivalence was largely lost on reviewers, who read the poem as an endearing vow to live up to wifely duties.) The longest and most provocative poem of the volume, "A Castaway," rings distinctive changes on the figure of the fallen woman, as an elegant prostitute reviews her life, divided between defiance – "Fancy me /Infallible nursery saint, live code of law!" (ll. 419–20) – and regret: "No help, /No

help. No help. Some ways can be trodden back, /But never our way."
(ll. 438–40). The counterpoise of these conflicting impulses suggests
Webster's distinctive achievement: the speaker's clear-eyed scrutiny of
social hypocrisy and the pressures that drive women into prostitution,
along with her contempt for the cloistered virtue that condemns her –
"What right have they to scorn us – glass-case saints, / Dianas under lock
and key ..." (ll. 128–9) – never quite dispels the hint of self-loathing she
has absorbed from the world around her. Thus she dismisses the thought
of being a mother, only to reflect on her dead infant:

> Had he come before,
> And lived, come to me in the doubtful days
> When shame and boldness had not grown one sense,
> For his sake, with the courage come of him,
> I might have struggled back.
>
> (ll. 427–31)

Webster's poetry, which attracted a good deal of praise in her lifetime,
was largely neglected for nearly a century – perhaps because her characteristic form, the lengthy monologue, resists anthologizing. But the
sustained ambivalence captured in her best work is both a rich poetic
achievement and a revealing vantage on the burdens of gender in the
lives of mid-Victorian women.

The appearance of *Goblin Market and Other Poems* in 1862 inaugurated the public career of the most important Victorian woman poet
after Barrett Browning, Christina Rossetti. Rossetti's is one of the most
distinctive lyric styles of the latter half of the century, and one of the
most difficult to capture, employing as it does generally quite simple
and colloquial diction, but with remarkable rhythmic suppleness,
formal variety, and subdued but evocative imagery. Tonally, her work
is perhaps closest to Emily Dickinson (whose affinities Rossetti would
discover late in her life), but it is more modulated in its movement of
thought and feeling. The famous title poem of her first volume is a
partial exception, which builds a tale of wayward desire from the
elemental cadences of a nursery chant,

> Morning and evening
> Maids heard the goblins cry:
> "Come buy our orchard fruits
> Come buy, come buy ..."
>
> (ll. 1–4)

The poem evokes wild vacillations of temptation, resistance, and surrender in constantly varying meter, in lines ranging from two to five feet. Such rollicking form eludes ready analysis, and the voluminous commentary on the poem is mostly thematic. Critics have discovered in its narrative of seduction and redemption a host of conflicts: of sexual temptation, Victorian exchange, commodity fetishism, advertising, xenophobia, lesbian desire. In this susceptibility to allegorical reading, "Goblin's Market" might seem to stand apart from the lyrics, in which the predominant emotional note is resignation. Rossetti's poetry has often been folded into a model of "spinsterly" self-abnegation or reflection on human vanity, in which life is a perpetual surrender or chastening of longing. But the poetry frequently expresses a faint bemusement at the power of desire, and hints its shape and force through a detachment that often seems weird in the traditional sense of otherworldly, or faintly comic, even when the occasion is outwardly a haunting or harrowing.

> When I was dead, my spirit turned
>   To seek the much-frequented house:
> I passed the door, and saw my friends
>   Feasting beneath green orange boughs ...
>   ("At Home" ll. 1–4)

When Tennyson indulges similar fantasies of displacement, he emphasizes the pathos of exclusion; for Rossetti the chill of the "all-forgotten" also underscores the placid self-absorption of those for whom "life stood full at blessed noon," as if the contours of life were fully appreciable only from beyond the grave. Resignation on this view is not the submission to authority or surrender of womanly possibility that has troubled so many feminist critics of Rossetti's poetry; it seems instead a cultivation of heightened awareness, emotional intensity, and linguistic clarity. It resembles in this regard the quality of "reserve" celebrated in Tractarian theology, in which a conspicuous self-restraint could intimate the grasp of ineffable truth. Increasingly in Rossetti's poetry this stance takes an explicitly religious turn, as a preparation for life beyond the grave. And yet throughout her poetry she continues to frame the interplay of life and death – and even oblivion itself – in an arresting, paradoxical physicality:

> Yet come to me in dreams, that I may live
>   My very life again tho' cold in death:
> Come back to me in dreams, that I may give

Pulse for pulse, breath for breath:
Speak low, lean low,
As long ago, my love, how long ago.
("Echo" ll. 13–18)

The most popular poetry volume of the first half of the decade was Tennyson's *Enoch Arden and Other Poems* (1864), which quickly sold out a staggering initial printing of 60,000 copies. It is a slender volume, whose appeal centered on three blank-verse narratives (the longest the title poem, at 911 lines). While "Aylmer's Field" develops Tennyson's old concern with "filthy marriage-hindering mammon" (1. 374; Tennyson 1969), "Enoch Arden" is the quintessence of sentimental domestic narrative, as well as the culmination of another long-standing Tennysonian fantasy, of the paterfamilias displaced by a stranger – "him, that other, reigning in his place" (1. 759). Enoch is a fisherman, "a brave God-fearing man" who is driven by financial hardship to voyage to China; after nothing is heard from him for 11 years, his wife Annie finally marries the wealthy Philip (already "Father Philip" to Enoch's children, whose education he has supported). When Enoch, who has been shipwrecked alone on a remote island, finally returns – unrecognizable – and beholds the new domestic comfort, he creeps away to die, pausing only to confide his secret to a stranger: "tell her that I died /Blessing her, praying for her, loving her ..." (ll. 874–6). This pious self-abnegation was infused with Tennyson's abiding gift for the picturesque – the "word painting" so valued by contemporaries – and the volume enjoyed further success in an 1866 edition illustrated by Arthur Hughes.

Enoch Arden marked the zenith of Tennyson's popularity, but also offered a critical target to a new generation of poets restive under the constraints of poetic decorum. A hint of this shift was registered in the changing reception of Robert Browning. Despite Browning's pursuit of a wider audience with *Men and Women*, most of the reviews were at best grudging. One of the few exceptions was a notice in the *Westminster Review*, by Marian Evans, which conceded that Browning's poetry was challenging, but urged perseverance: if the reader "has to dive deep, 'he rises with the pearl'" (Smalley 1969: 174). The notice was a harbinger of new habits of reading, in which "difficulty" in poetry would come to seem not a stumbling-block but an honorific. In 1863, still in the shadow of his wife's fame, Browning gained wider recognition when his publisher brought out *Selections from the Poetry of Robert*

Browning, edited by John Forster and Barry Procter, as well as a one-volume *Poetical Works*. Critical reaction marked a newly vigorous appreciation of work so long dismissed as recondite, gnomic, or grotesque. "It is about time that we began to do justice to Robert Browning," declared *Fraser's* (Smalley 1969: 206). The turn was confirmed with the 1864 publication of *Dramatis Personae*, reviews of which were nearly uniformly enthusiastic.

Ironically, *Dramatis Personae* is markedly less substantial than *Men and Women*. It is roughly divided between poems of romantic disappointment and reflections on religious faith – two concerns obviously energized by the death of Barrett Browning – but it is only half the length of *Men and Women*, with a third of the volume taken up by a single monologue, "Mr. Sludge, 'The Medium.'" "Sludge," which is most obviously an attack on the spiritualist vogue that had captivated Barrett Browning, also offers a surprisingly supple reflection on human belief generally. The speaker's very name proclaims his debasement, yet his rambling apologia probes the social dynamics of faith, the pleasure and craft of performance, and ultimately of imagination – including that of poets: "I'm ready to believe my very self – /That every cheat's inspired, and every lie /Quick with a germ of truth" (ll. 1323–5; Browning 1970). In his insistently rhetorical concerns, as the speaker tries to turn the wrath of the patron who has exposed him, "Sludge" is very much in the vein of Browning's earlier, similarly self-reflexive monologues. It shares this rhetorical emphasis with "A Death in the Desert," another excursus on belief in which a dying Saint John, last of the apostles, imagines what will become of his faith once eye-witness testimony to the life of Jesus has gone out of the world.

For the most part, however, the monologues of *Dramatis Personae* are less dependent on a fully realized dramatic context. The speakers are on the whole more solitary, their sentiments less subject to ironic qualification. This is particularly notable of the cluster of poems dealing with romantic disappointment – "James Lee's Wife," "The Worst of It," "Dis Aliter Visum." "Too Late," "Youth and Art" – each of which summon up what Henry James would call "the unlived life":

> Each life unfulfilled, you see;
>   It hangs still, patchy and scrappy;
> We have not sighed deep, laughed free,
>   Starved, feasted, despaired, – been happy.
> ("Youth and Art," ll. 61–4)

"Rabbi Ben Ezra" offers an emotional pendant to such bitter retrospects – and to a very distinctive poem, *The Rubaiyyat of Omar Khayyam*, translated from the Persian by Edward Fitzgerald in 1859 but largely ignored until it was discovered and talked up by D. G. Rossetti in 1861. Fitzgerald (1809–83), a scholar of independent means who is best known for his correspondence with more famous writers (he was a contemporary of Tennyson at Cambridge), was drawn to the mixture of exotic setting and witty but melancholy injunction to seize the day:

> A Book of Verse underneath the Bough,
> A Jug of Wine, a Loaf of Bread – and Thou
>   Beside me singing in the Wilderness –
> Oh, Wilderness were Paradise enow!
>
> Some for the Glories of This World; and some
> Sigh for the Prophet's Paradise to come;
>   Ah, take the Cash, and let the Credit go,
> Nor heed the rumble of a distant Drum!
>
> (ll. 45–52; Fitzgerald 1999)

Though the celebration of pleasure in the moment is not far removed from "Two in the Campagna," Fitzgerald's languid, pessimistic tribute to "the fruitful Grape" challenged Browning's characteristic association of fulfillment with bracing struggle. Rabbi ben Ezra accordingly refuses a notion of age as a time of lassitude or resignation, and celebrates instead the continuing pursuit of wisdom through ever-widening experience: "Grow old along with me! / The best is yet to be, / The last of life, for which the first was made ..." (ll. 1–3). This heartiness bears little hint of ironic framing, and its hortatory register helped to make it a staple of school declamation well into the twentieth century – a fate hard to imagine for the likes of "My Last Duchess." After his wife's death, however, such optimism was for Browning a more precarious and hard-won stance than it may seem to later readers.

A subtler rhetorical context is evoked by "Caliban upon Setebos; or, Natural Theology in the Island," the most widely noted poem in the volume. The monologue is a striking contribution to post-Darwinian religious debate, a satirical treatment of the argument from design, whereby Caliban conjures up a divine order in his own image. But the satirical reading is complicated by the poem's bearings on the psychology of creation generally – a recurrent preoccupation of Browning's poetry, as of so much Victorian reflection on religion and art. Caliban's acute consciousness of his own suffering and weakness – he utters his musings in imagined shelter from "that other, whom his dam called God," wishing "to vex" but fearful of punishment – makes him unusually attentive to imagination as a mode of aggression, a pleasure well known to the creator of the Duke of Ferrara and the Bishop of St. Praxed's:

> Oh, He hath made things worthier than Himself,
> And envieth that, so helped, such things do more
> Than He who made them! What consoles but this?
> That they, unless through Him, do nought at all,
> And must submit: what other use in things?
>
> (ll. 112–16)

Criticism and Belief

Browning's monologues throw an arresting light on another major literary event of 1864, which underscored the enduring vitality of pamphlet warfare, and gave rise to one of the great autobiographies in the English language. John Henry Newman had for some time been living "out of the world" (Newman 1968: 301), as he put it, removed from the glare of publicity that had surrounded his conversion 20 years before. He had been a prolific writer on theology (*Essay on the Development of Christian Doctrine* [1845]), while the *Idea of a University* (1855), written during his seven years as Rector of the Catholic University in Ireland, contains one of the most influential defenses of the idea of a liberal education. But for most casual observers he remained a byword of disloyalty, even treachery – at best an enigmatic sophist like Browning's Bishop Blougram. That suspicion was given new currency on a most unlikely occasion, a review of J. A. Froude's *History of England* in the January 1864 number of *Macmillan's*, in which the reviewer remarked in passing that "Truth, for its own sake, had never been a virtue with the Roman clergy. Father Newman informs us that it need not, and on the whole ought not to be; that cunning is the weapon which Heaven has given to the saints wherewith to withstand the brute male force of the wicked world which marries and is given in marriage." The slur, which turned out to be Kingsley's – the insinuating appeal to "brute male force" is characteristic – naturally angered Newman, who wrote to the publishers to complain of "a grave and gratuitous slander" (Newman 1968: 299). When Kingsley responded with evasive geniality, professing to accept Newman's word that he did not mean what Kingsley had claimed, Newman refused to let it pass: "My *word*! I am struck dumb. Somehow I thought that it was my *word* that happened to be on trial." And when Kingsley rejoined by appealing to that universal solvent, "We are both gentlemen," Newman turned the knife: "I begin to see: he thought me a gentleman at the same time that he said that I taught lying on system. After all, it is not I but it is Mr. Kingsley who did not mean what he said" (309). Newman then published the exchange in a pamphlet, goading Kingsley into responding with a pamphlet of his own, "What, Then, Does Dr. Newman Mean?"

Newman had long been awaiting an opportunity of, as he put it, "pleading my cause before the world," and Kingsley, in his bluff and impulsive way, had provided an ideal occasion. "He asks what I mean; not about my words, not about my argument, not about my actions, as his ultimate point, but about that living intelligence, by which I write, and argue, and act" (Newman 1968: 11). The answer would require nothing less than "a history of my mind," which Newman accordingly poured out in seven pamphlets published over a mere six weeks (with an appendix on June 16), under the title *Apologia pro Vita Sua*. The challenge was in essence that which Browning's Karshish had recognized in Lazarus: "How can he give his neighbour the real ground, /His own conviction?" Unlike Lazarus, however, Newman was fully cognizant of his audience, which was suspicious not only of his belief but of his own conduct in coming to declare it. Even if he could not bring readers to share his faith, he might persuade them that his change of allegiance at Oxford grew out of an honest, deeply felt pursuit of truth, a quest in which he grappled with questions and imaginative needs felt even in childhood. This required rhetoric far different from the slashing forensic prose of his exchanges with Kingsley and other adversaries. While attempting to convey complex theological debates, the goal was a narrative "simply personal and historical," a concerted self-exposure that to the reticent Newman was profoundly unsettling. But his efforts gained a great deal of sympathy and praise, and helped to stimulate an outpouring of memoirs recalling the great religious struggles of the 1830s and 1840s.

Theological resistance naturally clouded nearly all reviews by Protestants, and some could concede Newman's sincerity only at the expense of his sanity (Newman 1968: 415). But for most readers he had gained the main point of vindicating his personal integrity – and with it, by implication, that of scores of fellow converts and priests of his "un-English" faith. Much of the suasive force lies in Newman's extraordinary power to make esoteric theological dispute, often grounded in episodes from the early Church, seem a matter of visceral anxiety and recognition in the present moment – almost a sort of haunting. In 1839, for example, as Newman was reading of an obscure fifth-century heretical sect called the Monophysites, he found his faith severely shaken: "I saw my face in that mirror and I was a Monophysite" (96). Rarely is intellectual history brought home with such vividness, as the well-worn trope hovers on the threshold of a literal, gothic uncanny: Newman looks into a mirror to see an alien visage – which turns out to be his own. Throughout the *Apologia* he summons similar "ghosts" of recognition, and the memories of momentous phrases that ring in his mind with the force of a revelation not quite understood – as if bearing out the boyhood yearning, evoked on the opening page of the work, that the Arabian Nights were true: "my imagination ran on unknown influences, on magical powers, and talismans" (98). Such confession offered aid and comfort to his enemies, but it was harnessed to Newman's keen analytic intelligence. Once "the vivid impression on my imagination faded away," he continues, "I had to determine its logical value, and its bearing upon my duty" (99). Disdainful as he might be of the "religion of feeling" nurtured by Liberalism, Newman remained deeply attuned to the psychological complexities of faith – a point of contact with many of Browning's monologues, which he would develop most fully in *An Essay In Aid of a Grammar of Assent* (1871).

Sectarian conflict had been dulled in part by a growing sense among readers attuned to those quarrels that a more immediate challenge was the sheer decline of religious faith. Though England in 1864 remained a fervently religious nation, elite thought was increasingly preoccupied with the impact of Darwin, and with a subtler but equally corrosive force, which had been at work a good deal longer. Early in the century in Germany, in an outgrowth of classical philology, traditionally sacred texts began to be interpreted as the products of human invention, the conjoint outgrowth of imagination and historical context. This so-called "Higher Criticism" led to Strauss's *Das Leben Jesu*, which recounted the life of Jesus as that of a human being, as well as to the work of Feuerbach, both of which had a profound impact on George Eliot (as well as the young Karl Marx). Though "the threat from Germany," as it became known – a quintessence of the Liberalism against which Newman had warred – had made its way to England as early as the 1820s (Thomas Arnold had been a student of the German critic Niebuhr), its impact came to be more widely felt in the 1850s, in the wake of Marian Evans's translations. (A. P. Stanley memorably wondered how Victorian religious history might have differed had the young Newman known German.) The force of the Higher Criticism was registered in a number of Browning's monologues exploring early Christian faith, such as "A Death in the Desert," but more momentously in a volume of studies by prominent scholars (including Benjamin Jowett, Professor of Greek at Oxford, and Frederick Temple, Headmaster of Rugby and a future Archbishop of Canterbury). *Essays and Reviews* (1860) deeply alarmed the Anglican hierarchy, stirring controversy that for a time eclipsed even Darwin; two of the clergymen involved were prosecuted and condemned by the ecclesiastical Court of Arches for "denying the inspiration of Holy Scripture," a verdict later overturned on appeal ("Hell dismissed with costs," one wag remarked). Two years later, the Anglican Bishop of Natal, John William Colenso, provoked further controversy when he argued that the Pentateuch contained numerous inconsistencies and factual errors, and therefore the Mosaic scriptures could not have been divinely inspired. From the 1820s, Broughamism and the "march of mind" had celebrated books as agents of secular enlightenment. Forty years on, questions of how to interpret those books had become newly urgent.

The most influential reader of the latter half of Victoria's reign was Matthew Arnold, who also was deeply inspired by continental criticism. Almost simultaneously with Dickens's satire of Podsnap, Arnold offered his own attack on English insularity, *Essays in Criticism*, published by *Macmillan's* in February 1865. The work grew out of a curious mesh of literary institutions old and new – the monthly periodical and the Professorship of Poetry at Oxford, founded in 1708. Elected to the Chair in 1857, Arnold was the first Professor of Poetry to lecture in English rather than Latin, but the change initially did little to win an audience. After several years of presenting his quarterly lecture to half-empty halls, he began to gain wider attention with a series of lectures on translating Homer – lectures applauded perhaps less for their insight into Homer than for their barbed criticism of particular translations, most notably that of Francis Newman, John Henry's brother. The three lectures were published in February of 1861; when a wounded Newman responded with a pamphlet of his own, Arnold offered a final lecture, "Last Words," which set out a newly confident sense of his aims as a critic: "The critic of poetry should have the finest tact, the nicest moderation, the most free, flexible, and elastic spirit imaginable; he should be indeed ... the *undulating* and *diverse* being of Montaigne" (Arnold 1960–77: i.174). Such "poise" was above all a function of style, and Arnold would develop one of the most distinctive critical voices of the century.

It is a measure of Homer's cultural standing in mid-Victorian Britain that Arnold's volume garnered several dozen reviews, and though many readers objected to his strikingly personal and often acerbic style, the volume made him a critic to be reckoned with. That reception energized his sense of an audience, and his mission to combat what he saw as the provincialism of English reflection. He found ready outlets for his reflection in the monthlies, particularly *Macmillan's*; periodical editors were increasingly receptive to literary essays that were not tethered to a review format, as they had been in the quarterlies. By 1864 Arnold had assembled nine essays – six derived from Oxford lectures, all of them previously published – for publication as *Essays in Criticism*. The title, Arnold wrote to his publisher, was meant to evoke "the old sense of the word *Essay – attempt – specimen*" – suggesting an unconventional project, which was emphatically comparative (Arnold 1960–77: iii.400). The cosmopolitan perspective had been encouraged by his work as a government schools inspector, which took him on tours of France and Germany, which he developed into several book-length studies comparing different educational systems. None of the essays in the new volume – on subjects from Marcus Aurelius to Heinrich Heine, Spinoza to the little-known French writers Maurice and Eugenie de Guerin – directly addresses English topics, but the introduction, "The Function of Criticism at the Present Time," pointedly underscores the bearing of the topic on English life. And it does so in terms still echoed in university catalogues throughout the English-speaking world. Criticism, Arnold declared, is "a disinterested endeavour to learn and propagate the best that is known and thought in the world" – "irrespective of practice, politics, and everything of the kind."

Many are skeptical nowadays of a criticism that claims to be beyond politics; it seems an impossible ideal, a vantage point that philosophers have called "the view from nowhere." But Arnold's stance grew out of sustained engagement with contemporary politics, and responds in part to the often absurdly partial, unreflective, sometimes vicious character of much mid-Victorian reviewing. The very title of the essay marks a shift from the Preface to *Poems* a decade earlier. Arnold still is seeking a sense of order and grounds of belief, but "the present time" signals a new historical specificity, no longer a trans-historical "modern" but the situation of contemporary England. Moreover, the subject matter of poetry itself has changed. Whereas the earlier essay put an Aristotelian emphasis on action, Arnold now laments a paucity of ideas. The Romantic poets, he insists, "did not know enough"; their very epoch lacked the "current of ideas" required to nourish the greatest poetry (Arnold 1960–77: iii.262). And England at the present continues to suffer the affliction: instead of valuing thought and ideas for their own sake, it suffers "the mania for giving an immediate political and practical application" to ideas (iii.265). The rational gives way to the mechanical, as Arnold puts it, invoking the pejorative epithet that pervades Victorian social criticism, and is epitomized in the steam engine – emblem both of "our passionate material progress" and its "absorbing and brutalizing influence" (iii.269). Hence Arnold's prescription that criticism cultivate "disinterestedness," that it resist "the practical view of things" by "resolutely following the law of its own nature, which is to be a free play of the mind on all subjects which it touches" (iii.270).

This emphasis shares much with Newman's plea for liberal education, and with Mill's evocation of "many-sidedness" in *On Liberty*. Like Mill, Arnold is dismayed by a pervasive anti-intellectualism in English life, in which curiosity itself is mistrusted as an idle or treacherous habit of mind – a condition that at moments makes the English seem akin to automata. Arnold's main animus is the smugness of contemporary political discourse, a "self-satisfaction which is retarding and vulgarizing," which he evokes through a host of political catchphrases drawn from newspaper reports that he then deflates with jarring contrasts. Thus, most pointedly, after quoting the Benthamite MP J. A. Roebuck celebrating the "unrivalled happiness" of England, Arnold quotes a brief newspaper item:

> A shocking child murder has just been committed at Nottingham. A girl named Wragg left the workhouse there on Saturday morning with her young illegitimate child. The child was soon afterwards found dead on the Malvern Hills, having been strangled. Wragg is in custody. (Arnold 1960–77: iii.273)

"There is profit for the spirit in such contrasts as this," Arnold continues, and he presents that contrast, again, in terms of style. "Mr Roebuck will have a poor opinion of an adversary who replies to his defiant songs of triumph by murmuring under his breath, *Wragg is in custody*, but in no other way will these songs of triumph be induced gradually to moderate themselves … and to fall into a softer and truer key" (iii.274). Against the bluster of Roebuck and his ilk, true criticism will be "serene," "quiet," "patient," "sincere, simple, flexible, ardent." Throughout his mature prose Arnold works to inculcate a persona with these qualities: genial, temperate, unruffled, self-possessed, always trying to rein in aggression with irony. He contrasts this stance with those of Ruskin and Carlyle. They might agree that the British Constitution seems "a colossal machine for the manufacture of Philistines," but "how is Mr. Carlyle to say this and not be misunderstood after his furious raid into the field with his Latter-Day Pamphlets? how is Mr. Ruskin, after his pugnacious political economy?" (iii.275) The "rush and roar" of practical life again is registered in failures of intellectual poise, in prose that is "furious" and "pugnacious" rather than serene, quiet, patient. The contrast recalls J. F. Stephen's attack on Dickens, but Arnold's liberal virtues are even more stoic, and that was why they proved so inflammatory: they seemed a standing affront to the pursuit of concrete improvement. That adversarial stance has become a persistent feature of academic reflection in the humanities, often to the exasperation of the practical-minded. In "The Function of Criticism" we already are on the high road to attacks on modern academics as "nattering nabobs of negativism" (William Safire's script for the US Vice President Spiro Agnew in the late 1960s). For Arnold, however, criticism as principled resistance was an essential prerequisite of literary and social transformation – and, more broadly, the pursuit of perfection.

The Pleasures of the Difficult

"The Function of Criticism" ends on an elegiac note, suggesting that in some epochs the only form of creation possible will be criticism. In fact, English poetry was at this moment undergoing a major generational shift, which was registered in two interlinked developments: a new appreciation for poetry that was difficult or obscure, and the increasing turn to subject matter that defied traditional decorums. The two were conjoined in the changing reception of Browning. While *The Times* in 1865 still complained that "poetry is with him an occult science," which asks too much of his readers (Smalley 1969: 268), more often those same attributes were praised (often by contrast with

Tennyson). "Browning is at once a more masculine, and a more intricate and subtle, thinker than Tennyson" (207). His meaning "has to be sought with diligence and close attention." If he is not understood, that is less a failure of Browning than of his audience: "Mr. Browning anticipates much too often that his readers will be not only as cultivated, but as intelligent as himself, and has never aimed at mass-popularity" (265). The emphasis also informs an important review that is less sympathetic, but which nonetheless confirms a new pairing of Tennyson and Browning as colossi of the poetic landscape. Walter Bagehot, in a joint review of *Enoch Arden* and *Dramatis Personae*, presented them as respective examples of the "ornate" and the "grotesque" in English poetry, both of which depart from a norm of "pure" poetry – three categories recalling the more familiar division of romantic, medieval, and classical. Tennyson's ornate art is a flashy, even tawdry, appeal to the reader that lacks the clarity and economy of pure art. Like flirtation, it thrills but does not satisfy: "though the *rouge* of ornate literature excites our eye, it also impairs our confidence" (Bagehot 1999: 1315; Bagehot's emphasis). For Bagehot ornate art appeals to a debased audience, who are taken in by "showy art": "We live in the realm of the half educated" (1318). Grotesque art, by contrast, represents its subject "in difficulties," in a sustained distortion of and resistance to the perfect type of pure art. For Bagehot the failing of this type of art is not its lack of beauty, but its inaccessibility: Browning's works "make a demand upon the reader's zeal and sense of duty to which the nature of most readers is unequal" (1318).

In its outlines, Bagehot's review recalls the classicism of Arnold's 1853 Preface, but his diagnosis places more responsibility on the reading public. This emphasis clearly reflects growing concern with an emergent mass culture, a concern animated in the 1860s by debate over a second Reform Bill and a correspondent concern with working-class education. A very similar note was sounded in the following year by Ruskin, in *Sesame and Lilies*. Of course Ruskin had long been excoriating readers for their failings – on the model of both the Calvinist ministers of his childhood and the man he addressed as his "master," Carlyle. In the early 1860s, however, Ruskin carried out his attacks with a newly secular emphasis. In 1858 he had undergone what he called an "unconversion" in Turin, as the clash between the piety of his parents and the lust of his eye finally grew too much to bear. After winding up *Modern Painters* in 1860, Ruskin produced *Unto this Last*, that "pugnacious" onslaught on contemporary political economy that

Arnold had criticized. Initially serialized in the first year of the *Cornhill*, the work bewildered many readers, and outraged more than a few, but it would prove extremely influential in the formation of British socialism, particularly in its refrain, "There is no wealth but Life."

In 1864 Ruskin developed his criticism in several memorable public addresses. The first, entitled "Traffic," marked the opening of the Corn Exchange in Bradford, where Ruskin began by blithely announcing that he cared not at all about the Exchange, because his audience did not. It was merely a temple to greed, which ought to be decorated with a frieze of "pendant purses" (Ruskin 1903–12: xviii.450). He grounded his attack, and his career, in the maxim, "Taste is not only a part and index of morality;–it is the ONLY morality ... Tell me what you like, and I'll tell you what you are" (xviii.434–5). He also lectured twice at Manchester, on books and on women's education, and those lectures were published the following year in *Sesame and Lilies*. "Of Queen's Gardens" has become so famous as the *ne plus ultra* of "separate spheres" ideology that it has overshadowed its companion piece, "Of King's Treasuries," which addresses the nature and value of reading. Ruskin offers a bravura close analysis of a passage from Milton's "Lycidas," which strikingly anticipates the "new criticism" of the following century, but he does so to illustrate a broader insistence on the difficulty of grasping "men's best wisdom," which is akin to mining for precious ore. One cannot get at even "one grain of the metal" without proper tools and strenuous labor. Only by penetrating the "cruel reticence in the breasts of wise men" can a reader enter into "aristocracy of companionship" with them (Ruskin 1903–12: xviii. 62–4).

This rhetoric of arcane significance became a focal point of controversy over the poetry of Algernon Charles Swinburne (1837–1909). Swinburne was born into the affluent landed gentry and schooled at Eton and Oxford, where he came under the influence of Rossetti and Morris, and dazzled audiences many years his senior with his irrepressible flow of erudite, acerbic, passionate, bawdy, often shocking talk – a monologue, as the young Henry Adams recalled, that left his listeners "astonished." At 22, Swinburne began his literary career on the well-worn path of verse drama – two of them published in a single volume, *The Queen-Mother* and *Rosamond* (1860), much indebted to Morris. "Of all still-born works, the stillest," Swinburne later recalled, but in 1865 he gained wider renown with *Atalanta in Calydon*, a 2,300-line drama drawn from ancient Greek models, particularly Aeschylus. The small audience able to appreciate such adaptation – anyone, as one review began, "who has tried, whether by way of a school or college exercise or for his own pleasure, to compose a poem or an essay in an ancient language" (Hyder 1970: 9) – was greatly impressed. While conceding that such efforts could never be faithful to their models – Arnold's *Merope* resonated as one among many cautionary examples – reviewers nonetheless found Swinburne's attempt, as the *Saturday Review* put it, "one of the most brilliant that our literature contains." This same critic's complaints would echo throughout Swinburne's career: his verse was prolix, over-insistent in its rather narrow range of imagery, trusting too much to "melody" to carry him along at the expense of thought. Nearly all agreed, however, on the sheer formal virtuosity – the *London Review* greeted him as a potential successor to Tennyson – and the "Choruses" remain frequently excerpted as examples of Swinburne's lyric gifts:

> Where shall we find her, how shall we sing to her,
>   Fold our hands round her knees and cling?
> O that man's heart were as fire and could spring to her,
>   Fire, or the strength of the streams that spring!
> For the stars and the winds are unto her
> As raiment, as songs of the harp player;
> For the risen stars and the fallen cling to her,
>   And the southwest wind and the west wind sing.
>   (ll. 17–24; Swinburne 1925)

But Swinburne turned esteem to notoriety with *Poems and Ballads* (1866), which became one of the great poetic scandals of the century. The volume is a triumph of technique, incorporating a broad range of forms and Swinburne's distinctive sonic virtuosity, with pulsing rhythms reinforcing extensive assonance and alliteration in an effect so pronounced that it quickly became an object of parody. But the strongest poems in the volume are often quite subtle in their rhythmic dexterity. "The Triumph of Time," for example, offers an expansive Browningesque meditation on love that might have been:

> We had stood as the sure stars stand, and moved
>   As the moon moves, loving the world; and seen
> Grief collapse as a thing disproved,
>   Death consume as a thing unclean,
> Twin halves of a perfect soul, made fast
>   Soul to soul while the years fell past;
> Had you loved me once, as you have not loved;
>   Had the chance been with us that has not been.
>   (ll. 41–8; Swinburne 1925)

This movement is a far cry from the headlong chime of rhyme so often invoked in parodies of Swinburne (including his own). Even Swinburne's pointed anti-theism is generally constrained by dramatic framing. In "The Garden of Proserpine," for example, Swinburne re-imagines Tennyson's "Lotos-Eaters" from the perspective of a pagan Roman of the fourth century, "after the proclamation in Rome of the Christian faith," as the subtitle puts it:

> Nay, for a little we live, and life hath mutable wings,
> A little while and we die; shall not life thrive as it may?
> For no man under the sky lives twice, outliving his day.
> And grief is a grievous thing, and a man hath enough of his tears;
> Why should he labour, and bring fresh grief to blacken his years?
> Thou hast conquered, O pale Galilean; the world has grown grey from
>   thy breath;
> We have drunken on things Lethean, and fed on the fullness of death.
>
> (ll. 30–6)

Much of the drama inheres in the speaker's effort to persuade himself of what Tennyson's mariners could take for granted: that death is indeed "a sleep."

But the monologue form could not disarm the fierce sensuality infusing a cluster of poems, particularly those evoking three dangerous women: "Faustine," "Dolores," and "Anactoria." The last, the bitter plaint of Sappho to a lover who deserted her, is unparalleled in the vehemence of its sadomasochistic eroticism, as she longs to recover a pleasure for which she would give up even poetry:

> Ah that my lips were tuneless lips, but pressed
> To the bruised blossom of thy scourged white breast!
> Ah that my mouth for Muse's milk were fed
> On the sweet blood thy sweet small wounds had bled!
> That with my tongue I felt them, and could taste
> The faint flakes from thy bosom to the waist!
> That I could drink thy veins as wine, and eat
> Thy breasts like honey!
>
> (ll. 105–12)

Just four years earlier, Meredith's *Modern Love* had been attacked for its sensuality, but it aroused nothing like the firestorm that broke over *Poems and Ballads*. Much of the outrage responded to the programmatic character of the affronts; it was not a lapse of taste, but a concerted effort to push back the limits of poetic decorum (a design that had been encouraged by Swinburne's acquaintance with contemporary French poetry, particularly Baudelaire's *Fleurs du Mal* of 1857). In the wake of *Enoch Arden*, more than a few progressive critics might have been sympathetic to the expansion of poetic subject matter, but Swinburne's extremity alienated even potential allies. John Morley, for example, an important free-thinking journalist (soon to edit the new *Fortnightly Review*) and admirer of John Stuart Mill, wrote in the *Saturday Review*,

> If he were a rebel against the fat-headed Philistines and poor-blooded Puritans who insist that all poetry should be such as may be widely placed in the hands of girls of eighteen, and is fit for the use of Sunday schools, he would have all wise and enlarged readers on his side. But there is an enormous difference between an attempt to revivify among us the grand old pagan conceptions of Joy, and an attempt to glorify all the bestial delights that the subtleness of Greek depravity was able to contrive. (Hyder 1970: 23)

Punch was more succinct, licensing Swinburne "to change his name to what is evidently its true form – SWINE-BORN" (Hyder 1970: xxii)

Combative as he was, even Swinburne seemed stunned by the outcry (several of the offending poems had been previously published in journals, without inciting controversy), and he published a defense, *Notes on Poems and Reviews*, whose main tack was to align the volume with the dramatic monologue. "[T]he book is dramatic, many-faced, multifarious; and no utterance of enjoyment or despair, belief or unbelief, can properly be assumed as the assertion of its author's personal feeling or faith" (Hyder 1970: 49). But this Browningesque apology was conjoined with a more tendentious appeal to a select readership, offering "man's food" to a reading public apparently tolerant only of "moral milkmen," a public with esteem "only for such as are content to write for children and girls" (54). Morley's preemptive attack had undermined this appeal, but it was developed in another defense of Swinburne published later in 1866. In *Notes on Poems and Ballads*, William Michael Rossetti (brother of Dante and Christina) locates in Swinburne a "strictly artistic power" that can be appreciated only by an elite readership:

> If Shelley is 'the poet for poets,' Swinburne might not unaptly be termed 'the poet for poetic students.' His writings exercise a great

fascination over qualified readers, and excite a very real enthusiasm for them: but these readers are not of that wide, popular, indiscriminate class who come to a poet to be moved by the subject matter, the affectingly told story ... Mr. Swinburne's readers are of another and a more restricted order ...[who prize] the beauty of execution. (Hyder 1970: 71–2)

Rossetti thus located in Swinburne's poetry not merely an eccentric temperament, but a gulf within the audience for poetry. Swinburne's poetry comes to stand for a body of achievement beyond the appreciation of most readers. It appeals "only to artistically constituted minds; to others, it is alien, even antipathetic." And the reason for the antipathy is not far to seek: under this conception of poetry, "art cannot be approached from the side of morals" (73–4).

With this defense, Rossetti offers one of the earliest apologies in English for what would soon be called "art-for-art's sake" – the notion that poetry is dedicated to formal perfection, not to moral improvement. "The direct function of the work" is "to enlarge the mental energy, add delicacy to the perceptions, stimulate and refine the emotions, satisfy the sense of beauty"; a poem may thereby also exert a moral influence, but this is not part of the poet's aim (Hyder 1970: 75). The argument hearkens back to Hallam's 1830 review of Tennyson, and to the tensions dramatized in some of Tennyson's early poetry, most obviously "The Palace of Art." But Hallam's "poetry of sensation" did not so clearly threaten poetry's crucial appeal to broad sympathy. Swinburne's "literary poetry," by contrast, is in Rossetti's account emphatically exclusionary; to appreciate it requires "study" that can be mastered only by "qualified" readers. The new appreciation of obliquity and difficulty informing the reception of *Dramatis Personae* is here amplified into something bordering on the arcane, as if the appreciation of certain forms of art entailed initiation into a secret society.

In the literature of art for art's sake – and, more broadly, the cultural movement that would become known as "aestheticism" – the defense of morally provocative subject matter was frequently couched in this rhetoric of arcane significance, as an appeal to an elite audience able to grasp depths of meaning unavailable to a larger public. Swinburne himself would develop this appeal in his pioneering study of William Blake, published in 1867, which introduced "art for art's sake" into English. Blake "had a faith of his own, made out of art for art's sake" (Swinburne 1925–7: xiv.147), and his obscurity was further evidence for Swinburne that "the sacramental elements of art and poetry are in no wise given for the sustenance or salvation of men in general, but reserved mainly for the sublime profit and intense pleasure of an elect body or church" (Swinburne 1925–7: xiv. 86).

The most influential celebration of aesthetic devotion would come from Walter Pater (1839–94). In 1868 Pater, a Fellow of Brasenose College, Oxford, reviewed for the *Westminster* two recent volumes of poetry by William Morris, *The Life and Death of Jason* (1867) and *The Earthly Paradise* (1868). Conjoining these with Morris's first volume, *The Defence of Guenevere* (1858), Pater found occasion for what became the most famous aestheticist manifesto in English. He recognized in Morris's poetry a twofold provocation. The first, in *Guenevere*, was an affront not merely to poetic decorum but to prevailing medievalisms. "The poem which gives its name to the volume is a thing tormented and awry with passion, like the body of Guenevere defending herself from the charge of adultery, and the accent falls in strange, unwonted places with the effect of a great cry" (Pater 1974: 106). (The power of this convulsive eroticism is underscored by Pater's recurrent use of "strange" – a Swinburnean emphasis that throughout his writings will suggest thresholds of new and dangerous experience.) Yet the poem, Pater argues, is faithful to medieval worship, not only the baffled longing of courtly love but also "the whole religion of the middle age," which in Pater's subversive phrasing becomes "but a beautiful disease or disorder of the senses" (107). "A passion of which the outlets are sealed, begets a tension of nerve, in which the sensible world comes to one with a reinforced brilliance and relief – all redness is turned into blood, all water into tears. Hence a wild, convulsed sensuousness in the poetry of the middle age" (108). With subtle audacity, Pater thus aligns the world of Morris and Swinburne with that of the troubadours.

Morris's recent poetry turns to more classical themes and treatment, "from dreamlight to daylight," as Pater puts it, but Pater wrings more overt provocation from *The Earthly Paradise*, which opens with an "Apology":

> Of Heaven or Hell I have no power to sing
> I cannot ease the burden of your fears,
> Or make quick-coming death a little thing,
> Or bring again the pleasure of past years,
> Nor for my words shall you forget your fears,

Or hope again for aught that I can say,
The idle singer of an empty day.

(ll. 1–7)

To such disdain for moral or intellectual utility, Pater imagines the objection, "The modern world is in possession of truths; what but a passing smile can it have for a kind of poetry which, assuming artistic beauty of form to be an end in itself, passes by those living interests which are connected with them" in order to choose between "a more and a less beautiful shadow" (Pater 1974: 113)? Pater rejoins that the pursuit of beauty as its own end is not merely compatible with "modern thought," but is positively enjoined by it. Drawing on the skeptical epistemology of Hume, Pater evokes a world of "experience" contracted to a flux of "impressions" registered by "an individual in his isolation, each mind keeping as a solitary prisoner its own dream of a world." The only solace for such radical solipsism, Pater urges, lies in cultivating the intensity of each passing moment, struggling to "be present always at the point where the greatest number of vital forces unite in their purest energy." "To burn always with this hard gem-like flame, to maintain this ecstasy, is success in life." Modern skepticism thus rejuvenates the ancient injunction, *carpe diem*. "Success in life" lies in "expanding the interval, in getting as many pulsations as possible into the given time," and that can best be achieved through "the desire of beauty, the love of art for art's sake: for art comes to you professing frankly to give nothing but the highest quality to your moments as they pass, and simply for those moments' sake" (115–16).

Pater's tour de force manifesto in behalf of aesthetic pleasure, later reprinted as the "Conclusion" to *Studies in the History of The Renaissance* (1873), would become one of the most influential critical documents of the remainder of the century. Unlike the apologies of Swinburne and Rossetti, it focuses exclusively on the spectator rather than the artist. Indeed, it might seem to displace the artist altogether, since the reward it urges is premised on the observer's power to find aesthetic stimulus wherever he turns: "any stirring of the senses, strange dyes, strange flowers and curious odours, or work of the artist's hands, or the face of one's friend" (Pater 1974: 115–16). But this emphasis made it all the more threatening: Pater offers an ethical program – not "success in art" but "success in life" (a phrase clearly designed to puncture more worldly notions of "success") – cut free of traditional ethical imperatives, a form of philosophical hedonism with no obligation beyond the cultivation of exquisite pleasure. The prospect became especially threatening to contemporaries as it was associated with the pleasures of ancient Greece.

The Hellenic Tradition

It is hard to overstate the authority of classical Greece in the intellectual life of Victorian Britain – from poetry, art, and architecture through social and political debate. Of course Greek had been a staple of elite education since the Renaissance, and some of its authority came from its power to mark that privilege (as in the reception of Arnold's writings). But throughout the century the allure of Greece was broader – as, for example, in the poetry of Keats. The riveting visual appeal of Greek sculpture had come into wide circulation with eighteenth-century excavations at Pompeii and elsewhere, and gained its greatest prominence with Lord Elgin's seizure of the Parthenon marbles. Beginning with the writings of the German critic Johan-Joachim Winckelmann in the middle of the eighteenth century, Greek art came to be understood as the supreme embodiment of a habit of mind opposed to the modern temper, associated with what Winckelmann called *Allgemeinheit* and *Heiterkeit*, breadth and calm. This was a rather wishful inference from the frenzied conflicts of Greek tragedy or the violence often depicted in Greek sculpture. But this emphasis would serve as a crucial foil to the nascent romanticism of Germany, the *Sturm und Drang* ("storm and stress") of the young Goethe, and it was through this association that classical Greece entered into British aesthetic and moral reflection. There the ideal of Greece exercised two related functions. First, Greek art embodied a principle of discipline or restraint of romantic energies. This appeal had little relevance to the novel, which was at once too young and too protean a form to be thus constrained; hence Dickens's mockery of the "classical" as something epitomized in a wax museum. But Arnold's "Preface" to his *Poems* of 1853 exemplifies the appeal of Greece at mid-century as a model of poetic order. The context of Arnold's Preface, in the wake of the spasmodic vogue, suggests that Greece took on new urgency as a critical touchstone in response to the expansion of both higher education and the literary marketplace; here was a decidedly elite ground for literary judgment, a function borne out in both the erudite barbs of "On Translating Homer" and the success of *Atalanta in Calydon*.

The second function of Greece, derived more directly from Winckelmann via Goethe, was to exemplify the ideal of harmonious, "many-sided" responsiveness to the world, that model of psychic integration and critical understanding that became central to Victorian social reflection through Carlyle and later Mill and mid-Victorian liberalism. But this widespread appeal carried within it a profound cultural dissonance. How could citizens of a professedly Christian country find a comprehensive source of value in a pagan world two thousand years old? Ruskin's criticism is saturated with this tension, frequently decrying Greek "perfection" as the expression of a godless pride. Indeed, Ruskin's celebration of Gothic rebukes the ascendancy of classical architecture by locating in Gothic an earnest, humble struggle to express the "soul" absent in Greek art. The atheist Mill was not ruffled by such concerns, and *On Liberty* underscored the cultural clash, aligning Christianity with a crabbed, repressive deformation of human energies, against which ancient Greece offered models of their harmonious development. Benjamin Jowett's influential translation of Plato in the 1860s implicitly addressed this division by construing the Greek in a manner that seemed compatible with Christian ethics. But Pater's Hellenism subtly underscores a more disturbing feature of Greek life, typically passed over in silence: its sanction of male homoeroticism.

The groundbreaking essay in this regard is "Winckelmann," published in the *Westminster Review* in 1867 and later incorporated in *The Renaissance*. Here Pater represents Winckelmann as a mysterious anachronism, a belated pagan who grasps the achievement of Greek art through an intuitive response "not merely intellectual," as Pater delicately phrases it. Drawing heavily on Plato's *Phaedrus*, with its evocation of pederastic structures of education between older and younger men, Pater locates Winckelman's "divinatory power over the Hellenic world" in an "enthusiasm ... dependent to a great degree on bodily temperament" (Pater 1980: 152), which is borne out by his response to the beautiful male forms of Greek sculpture. In his apology for Swinburne the previous year, Rossetti had declared that "we proceed to handle – and, if need be, to burn our fingers at – this somewhat scorching and explosive production" (Hyder 1970: 61). Winckelemann, by contrast, "fingers these pagan marbles with unsinged hands, with no sense of shame or loss" (Pater 1980: 177); he experiences no conflict between morality and "genuine artistic interests." As Winckelmann thereby confirms the authority of "the Hellenic tradition," he also lends its authority to the transgressive desires exemplified in his writings, and in Pater's.

Of course this apology was not readily available to most readers – even, apparently, to those of the radical *Westminster*, the bulk of whom presumably would have been shocked by it. Pater's argument, like most of his writing, proceeds with characteristic obliquity, implicitly addressing a divided audience: the educated reader interested in the study of Greece, and that much smaller circle which not only can grasp the excerpts from the *Phaedrus* in the original, but can catch the drift of Pater's never-quite-explicit identification with Winckelmann's desires. The surprising influence of Pater's muted, labyrinthine prose resided largely in this double-voicing; it may be the fullest flowering before high Modernism of the new appreciation of obliquity informing the reception of Browning (whose "Dis Aliter Visum" from *Dramatis Personae* Pater tellingly cites in "Winckelmann"). But Pater in 1867 remained largely unknown; his impact lay in the future. A more influential appeal to Hellenism was being mounted at the same time in response to another, more manifest dissonance in contemporary life: the apprehensions surrounding a Second Reform Bill.

Although debates surrounding the extension of suffrage in the 1860s turned on familiar class frictions, they also were bound up with the identity of a "Greater Britain" that extended around the globe, and with an increasingly complex stratification of society at home. In 1866 the Radical baronet Sir Charles Dilke "followed England round the world" by visiting English-speaking lands, particularly the United States and Australia, and recorded his experience in *Greater Britain* (1868), where he urged that the common "Anglo-Saxon" race formed a natural bond of unity that overrode local customs: "In essentials the race was always one" (Dilke 1968: i.v). Such imagined unity had been strained by the American Civil War, which was closely followed in Britain, both as a test case for democracy, and as a lightning rod of conflicting allegiances and economic interests within Britain. For many propertied Britons, the agrarian South seemed a more companionable social order than the industrial North, and when war broke out that sense of affinity often overrode a professed abhorrence of slavery. The working classes, who had frequently aligned their own situation with forms of slavery, supported the North – many in stoic disregard of their own economic interests, since the curtailment of cotton imports severely affected the textile industries. Late in 1865, race became a flashpoint within the empire, when a disturbance at Morant Bay in Jamaica led to a declaration of martial law by the Governor, Edward John Eyre, and the killing of several hundred unarmed people, including the execution without trial of a mixed-race member of the Jamaican House of Assembly. News of Eyre's actions sharply polarized intellectual life in England, with Mill and other radicals calling for an inquiry, and later moving that Eyre be brought to trial for murder, while another group (including Kingsley and Carlyle) formed in vigorous defense of his conduct, frequently contending that former slaves were incapable of full citizenship. Meanwhile, in Ireland the Fenian movement for independence, founded in 1858 with a declared willingness to resort to violence, had launched a series of increasingly unnerving disturbances, which provoked newly energetic stereotyping of "the Celt" as another being unfit for self-government.

Amidst this stir the Reform League, organized in 1865, was advocating manhood suffrage for all workers over 21 with stable residence (excluding paupers and criminals). Although the actual passage of the bill in 1867 would increase the number of eligible voters by only about 75 percent, they were concentrated in the urban boroughs rather than the counties, and the prospect generated immense fear among most of the existing electorate. Even Lord Derby, the Conservative Prime Minister at the time, described it as "a leap in the dark." One upshot of the fear was a new enthusiasm for popular education: Robert Lowe famously urged Parliament to "prevail on our future masters to learn their letters" (Read 1994: 94). A long-standing fear of working-class literacy had given way to fear of being governed by the uneducated. In answer to fears that electoral reform would amount to a "Swarmocracy," in Carlyle's derisive term, reformers invoked a Smilesian ideal of "character." Whereas Chartists in the 1840s had grounded working-class political claims simply in a man's property in his own labor, reform advocates now drew moral divisions distinguishing sober, responsible, "respectable" working men from those who lacked these virtues. An ideal of domesticity thus once again figured centrally in public debate, as respectability was increasingly vested in the head of a family. This association, however, worked against a growing feminist movement for female suffrage, whose most visible representative was John Stuart Mill, author of *The Subjection of Women* (1869), and the MP who on 20 May 1867 moved that in Clause Four of the Reform Bill, "man" be replaced with "person," which would have extended suffrage to women.

One of the most direct responses to the agitation was George Eliot's *Felix Holt, The Radical* (1866), which was written over a space of 14 months beginning in March 1865, as reform agitation grew. Centering on an election campaign on the eve of the First Reform Bill, the novel recasts the myth of the changeling to mount a cautionary reflection on social mobility. Young Esther Lyon, the adopted child of a poor dissenting minister, turns out to be the rightful heir of the Transome estate (a discovery secured through a famously tortuous account of inheritance law). The revelation gratifies Esther's dream of being a great lady (the natural flowering, it seems, of her innate refinement, compounded by her long-suppressed French ancestry), but her fantasy is checked by the novel's hero, a hard-working, iconoclastic, painfully austere watchmaker who scorns social ambition: "Why should I want to get into the middle class because I have some learning?" (Eliot 1995b: 145). This view reinforces long-standing Victorian criticism of social climbers caught up in "the push and scramble for money and position" (362), but Felix registers the more particular pressures of the 1860s. He is distinguished, first of all, not merely by personal integrity but by "the habitual meditative abstraction from objects of mere personal vanity or desire, which is the peculiar stamp of culture" – in a word, Arnoldian disinterestedness. Moreover, Felix offers not merely a critique of social mobility, but an outright rejection of it as something akin to class treason, an affront to "my heritage – an order I belong to ... I have the blood of a line of handicraftsmen in my veins" (366). Such Burkean fealty to tradition clashes with unregulated working-class desire, whose dangers are brought home when Felix is caught up in an election riot and charged with manslaughter. This well-worn device largely accounts for the novel's reputation as the last major industrial novel; modern industry is almost non-existent in the market town of Treby Magna, but Eliot's plot confirms the ongoing resonance of the working-class mob as an emblem of middle-class fears.

The polemical design of the novel was almost risibly underscored after the actual passage of the Reform Bill, when her publisher, Blackwood, asked Eliot to write "An Address to Working Men, by Felix Holt" for *Blackwood's Magazine* – a most unlikely forum for working-class readers. Eliot's appeal to self-discipline and education rather than political agitation, a direct extrapolation from the novel, clearly was directed at the anxieties of the affluent classes. But *Felix Holt* has interests beyond contemporary politics. As it interweaves the lives of landed gentry and town inhabitants across the social spectrum, it represents Eliot's most ambitious social panorama to date, one that looks forward to *Middlemarch* (which actually is narrower in its treatment of social class). The novel is most acute in its portrait of the

Transome family, whose matriarch lives in perpetual fear of the revelation of her own past, struggling to maintain her aristocratic dignity – she would have been "an object of hatred and reviling by a revolutionary mob" (Eliot 1995b: 104) – in a world which offers her neither purpose nor freedom, a world of "silken bondage" in which she is wholly at the mercy of the men she has loved. "God was cruel when he made women" (488), she reflects. Mrs. Transome's ordeal – which looks forward to that of Gwendolen in *Daniel Deronda* – is indebted to sensation fiction, turning as it does on intricate plot twists enabled by hidden identities, compromising documents, and the constant threat of scandal. But the melodramatic structures are modulated by Eliot's characteristic preoccupation with the irrevocability of moral error, which (as in *Romola*) can seem to divide a life in two. As it depicts the harrowing of Mrs. Transome, the novel almost lives up to its insistent invocation of tragic nemesis.

The most enduring literary engagement with domestic politics in the 1860s came from Matthew Arnold. *Essays in Criticism* was greeted with general enthusiasm, although the further Arnold ventured from strictly literary criticism – the essays on Joubert, the Guerins, and Heine – the more guarded reactions tended to become. "The Function of Criticism at the Present Time" had a predictably polarizing effect, as it seemed to invite something like an up-or-down vote on England itself. (The *Daily Telegraph*, the most widely read newspaper in Britain, stuck Arnold with the enduring label, "elegant Jeremiah.") Critics who demurred from Arnold's attack on English criticism were especially irritated by his disdain for practical considerations, and attacked him as effete and elitist: the ever-pugnacious J. F. Stephen likened him to the perfumed courtier in *Henry IV* whose sensibilities were offended by Hotspur's bloodied prisoners, while the Liberal politician John Bright sneered at "culture" as "a smattering of the two dead languages of Greek and Latin" (Dawson and Pfordresher 1979: 126, 203).

Arnold, always delighted to take up thrown gauntlets, made them the point of departure for his final Oxford lecture, "Culture and Its Enemies," which he delivered in May of 1867. The essay develops the main emphases of "The Function of Criticism," taking up a phrase from Swift, "sweetness and light," as his byword for "complete harmonious human perfection," an ideal that Arnold found rebuked on all sides by British philistinism. His attacks on the worship of "machinery" – the externals of wealth, social standing, sectarian allegiance – recall the criticism of Carlyle, Mill, and Ruskin, but his critique of "liberalism" is particularly indebted to Newman, to whom Arnold pays fulsome tribute. Arnold's is a more embattled position, however, in trying to redirect liberalism from within, and the essay takes particular pains to answer charges that "culture" is both elitist and mere quietism. Culture, he rejoins, "seeks to do away with classes." "The men of culture are the true apostles of equality," he urges, "who have laboured to divest knowledge of all that was harsh, uncouth, difficult, abstract, professional, exclusive." Its passion for sweetness and light is subordinate to "the passion for making them *prevail*" (Arnold 1960–77: v.113).

Political events gave this project new urgency, when the mob that had long haunted novelists' imaginations materialized in London. On 22 June 1866, when a large procession of Reform League marchers was denied admission to Hyde Park, an angry crowd knocked down a thousand yards of park railings. In retrospect it seems a rather tame byproduct of momentous political change, but to many it was a harrowing omen of revolution. Carlyle quickly penned a pamphlet, published in *Macmillan's*, "Shooting Niagara: And After?" which took the incident as the quintessence of "Swarmery," whose rule would be oealed by the Reform Act. It was the end of England, whose only hope lay in a reinvigorated aristocracy turning aside the fatal descent into democracy. Arnold had been even closer to the violence – he and his wife watched from their balcony in Chester Square as demonstrators stoned the nearby house of the Commissioner of Police – and what seemed to him a tepid police response galvanized a more sustained reflection on the state of England. He undertook a series of five further essays, and the six were published in volume form in January 1869, as *Culture and Anarchy: An Essay in Political and Social Criticism.*

In *Culture and Anarchy*, the trauma of Hyde Park is still fresh: Arnold worries over an ideal of individual liberty degraded into an Englishman's "right to march where he likes, meet where he likes, enter where he likes, hoot as he likes, threaten as he likes, smash as he likes" (Arnold 1960–77: v.119). Under this pressure, Arnold's familiar quest for an authority to guide and direct the aspiring poet resurfaces as the pursuit of a more comprehensive imperative, "the idea of public duty and of discipline, superior to the individual's self-will" (v.118). This, Arnold urges, is what culture provides; it is culture *or* anarchy. Against those who would align this authority with a particular social class – Arnold re-names the familiar trio Barbarians, Philistines, and Populace – he appeals instead to a "best self" that transcends class-consciousness, and will find expression in a group of "aliens" within each class, who are moved by "a general human spirit" (v.146–7). To Mill's emphases on many-sidedness Arnold thus conjoins a Burkean model of organic society that likewise appealed to George Eliot. Like the resolutions of the industrial novel, this diagnosis discovers the solution in "a frame of mind" (v.221), and thereby dodges more thorny issues of power. But Arnold's principal animus remains the English celebration of practical action, "our preference of doing to thinking," a tendency which he now ascribes to an imbalance of two ongoing, complementary forces, Hellenism and Hebraism. The choice of terms reflects both the authority of ancient Greece and the ongoing racializing of British social theory and British life – "the great and pregnant elements of difference which lie in race" (v.173), an emphasis to which Arnold contributed most notably in *The Study of Celtic Literature* (1867). Ultimately, the sloganeering weakens the coherence of the argument. Both forces, Arnold explains, are devoted to the pursuit of perfection, but Hellenism pursues it through reflection, the effort "to see things as they really are," Hebraism through moral discipline, "conduct and obedience" (v.165), "spontaneity of consciousness" versus "strictness of conscience." Arnold insists that the two must be balanced, but the balance clearly is skewed towards Hellenism – it is "the thinking side" versus "the acting side" – and ancient Greece, which "arrived ... at the idea of a comprehensive adjustment of the claims of both the sides in man, the moral as well as the intellectual, of a full estimate of both, of a reconciliation of both," though they failed to fully give it "adequate practical satisfaction" (v.179). Moreover, after insisting on "the great and pregnant elements of difference which lie in race," distinctions which "science has now made visible to everybody," Arnold then works to efface the distinction by insisting on "the essential unity of man" (v.173), in which ostensibly diverse racial attributes are redescribed as complementary "sides" of humankind.

Arnold's crucial contribution to later criticism was precisely what most irritated his contemporaries, his efforts to free criticism from the claims of practicality, to suggest that it followed its own ends, in which one of the central concerns was pleasure itself. That stance invited the objection that his enterprise was somehow unmanly, as Arnold himself notes in smiling at "the effeminate horror which, it is alleged, I have of practical reforms" (Arnold 1960–7: v.200). We have heard echoes of this polemic across the period, from the early attacks on Tennyson to the denunciations of Swinburne. But the consolidation of "culture" in the late 1860s came to be associated with a feminizing of criticism itself. Ruskin in "Traffic" had caustically referred to himself as a "man-milliner" in the eyes of the public, and such insinuations of compromised manhood intensified as Arnold's enterprise seemed to contract into a narrower, more hedonistic "self-culture" associated above all with Pater and later Wilde. Even Carlyle, ironically, become tainted by effeminacy, as W. J. Courthope ascribed to him a "gospel of inaction" that had shaped the "culture" of Arnold and Pater (Courthope 1874: 207). Arnold himself remained emphatic that culture aimed at "a general perfection" (Arnold 1960–7: v.192) and struggled to disarm its association with elitism or mere self-indulgence. But the feminizing of criticism became increasingly pronounced in the latter third of the century, and has reverberated ever since in the academic study of literature. When the early proponents of English as an academic discipline modeled the enterprise on classical philology, they were in part trying to ensure that literature could be a subject fit for real men.

Domesticity, Politics, Empire, and the Novel

The political ferment of the Reform Bill was a more muted but nonetheless palpable presence in domestic novels of the late 1860s. Election campaigns had been a staple of Victorian fiction from the time of Dickens's Eatanswill. Topicality aside, they were fields for vaulting ambition and intrigue, and for an array of venal or disruptive behavior (from bribery to drunkenness to riot), which might be depicted with gravity or hilarity (or both). Above all, election day drew together a microcosm of the social order (the ballot was public until 1874), a gathering across classes that was much rarer in everyday affairs. With further electoral reform, a parliamentary career seemed open to a broader range of men – including successful novelists – and the business of politics became more prominent. It held a special fascination for Trollope, who in 1864 began *Can You Forgive Her?*, which became the first of his parliamentary or Palliser novels, after their leading character. Initially he was recasting an unsuccessful effort at playwriting, *The Noble Jilt*, which depicted a young woman whose engagement with a beautiful, kind, but dull man of wealth and integrity is derailed by infatuation with her charming but dangerous cousin. In the novel, the ordeal of Alice Vavasor is doubled by that of Lady Glencora Palliser, a vivacious heiress whose marriage to Plantegenet Palliser, MP and heir to the Duke of Omnium, had been recorded near the end of *The Small House at Allingham*. Offered the very pinnacle of worldly status and comfort, Lady Glencora (recalling Tennyson's Guinevere) finds her passion stifled by the devoted but placid politician, whom she initially detests because he has no vices. *Can You Forgive Her?* thus magnifies the frictions between desire and prudence that are a staple of the Barsetshire novels. Trollopean routine is repeatedly energized by the challenge of "wild" behavior, which abounds not merely in caddish men but in reckless women; Alice is drawn to the brink of financial ruin and Lady Glencora to the verge of deserting her husband for her "utterly worthless" first love.

The Palliser marriage became for Trollope the focal interest of the novel, and subsequently the thread that linked five further novels, concluding with *The Duke's Children* (1880). Trollope attributed that long narrative arc to his interest in capturing subtle changes in character over "a life so stirring as theirs." The change is most notable in Glencora, who comes to sacrifice, as Trollope put it in his *Autobiography*, "the romance of her life" for "a rich reality" within which she comes to savor the pleasures of social and political eminence (183). Her happiness is never quite unalloyed, but that is part of her fascination; her energy and independence resist entire submission to conventional femininity. "I do not know that she was at all points a lady," the narrator remarks, "but had Fate so willed it she would have been a thorough gentleman" (Trollope 1973: 2.91). The tinge of bitterness in Glencora's vivacity is one facet of a worldliness in the Palliser novels that strains against the marriage plot. Yet the series affirms an idealism centered in politics itself – or in the dedication to political life epitomized by Palliser, who believes "the British House of Commons is everything" (2.417). This avowal – on the final page of the novel – may enhance our sympathy for Lady Glencora, but Trollope himself shared the passion. Aesthetically, he found in parliamentary intrigue "all the keen interest of a sensational novel" (2.10), but Palliser epitomized an integrity beyond intrigue. Trollope thought him the most substantial of all his characters, and called him "a very noble gentleman – such a one as justifies to the nation the seeming anomaly of an hereditary peerage and of primogeniture" (Trollope 1980: 181).

"It is the highest and most legitimate pride of an Englishman to have the letters M.P. written after his name," remarks the narrator of *Can You Forgive Her?*, and in 1867 Trollope began his fullest account of that standing. *Phineas Finn*, published serially in Trollope's own *St. Paul's* magazine, imagines pre-Reform Parliament from a neophyte's perspective, following the 25-year-old son of a rural Irish doctor who becomes an MP through distant connections and soon finds himself a junior Minister. Finn is in many ways an idealized image of Trollope himself, who while he was writing the novel stood unsuccessfully as a Liberal candidate in the post-Reform election of 1868. The novel offers a richly-textured account of the daily business of politics (Trollope did a good deal of research in the House of Commons), which is more revealing than anything to be found in Disraeli's more glamorous accounts, against which Trollope emphasizes the humdrum aspects of parliamentary life. Such texture is in keeping with the two central conflicts of the work, which shape much of the Palliser series. The most prominent is the familiar Trollopean competition between love and money – here magnified by the expectation than an MP possess independent wealth, a demand which puts Phineas's provincial Irish fiancée in the shade as he is tempted by various worldly women of fortune. The more pointed challenge, however, comes within Parliament itself, where Phineas finds himself asserting an independence of mind that estranges him from his own party leaders, and rebukes the cynical assumption that all politics is merely a screen for personal ambition.

Phineas Finn followed closely on Trollope's conclusion to the Barsetshire series, *The Last Chronicle of Barset*, published in the unusual format of 32 sixpence weekly parts appearing between December 1866 and July 1867, and then in two volumes later that year. Although this lengthy novel (Trollope's longest to date) gathers in a good deal of parvenu London society, which centers on a London stockbroker of dubious wealth ("City money is always chancy," as one character remarks [Trollope 1981: 259]) and his wife's relationship with a society painter, the focal point is Josiah Crawley, a pious but poor and embittered Barsetshire minister who is accused of stealing a twenty-pound check. On this slender thread Trollope hangs an extraordinary study of what William James would come to call accidie, a sick soul. Crawley is so consumed with his own failings that he cannot even remember how he came by the check, yet he refuses to assist in defending himself. Meanwhile, Barsetshire at large (the scandal mesmerizes the county) cannot decide whether Crawley's "odd," "queer" behavior is madness or a form of saintliness. They unite in admiration of his piety, but recoil from his single-mindedness as something profoundly unnatural: "the world wouldn't go on if there were many like that"

(795). As it confounds the self-interested calculation of all around him –
most notably the ever-imperious Mrs. Proudie – Crawley's abjection
unexpectedly parallels the geniality of Reverend Harding, whose death
in the volume marks a far more resonant close to the Barchester series
than the various marriages announced in the final chapter.

Reviewers frequently applauded Trollope's representation of young
women, whose vivacity tested the bounds of "wildness" but rarely
crossed it. Indeed, much of the comedy of courtship in his work deflates
a romantic energy still epitomized by Byron. After quoting from *The
Giaour*, a lawyer's daughter in the *Last Chronicle* remarks, "But that is
all over now, you know, and young people take houses in Woburn
Place, instead of being locked up, or drowned, or married to a hideous
monster behind a veil" (Trollope 1981: 406). The dig at Byronic heroism, however, reminded readers that such possibilities still loomed in
sensation fiction; one might find hideous monsters even in Woburn
Place. Sensation reverberated in a wide range of fiction in the form of
increasingly audacious heroines, who concertedly pressed against, or
seemed entirely oblivious to, the decorums of polite society. Charles
Reade's *Griffith Gaunt*, serialized in the *Argosy in* 1865–6, called
down a new round of attacks on sensation proper, but in 1868, Eliza
Lynn Linton suggested an even wider sphere of influence, with a series
of articles in the *Saturday Review* attacking "The Girl of the Period,"
an image largely drawn from the pages of contemporary fiction.

> The Girl of the Period envies the queens of the demi-monde far more
> than she abhors them ... Love in a cottage – that seductive dream
> which used to vex the heart and disturb the calculations of the prudent
> mother – is now a myth of past ages. The legal barter of herself for so
> much money, representing so much dash, so much luxury and pleasure –
> that is her idea of marriage; the only idea worth entertaining. For all
> seriousness of thought respecting the duties or the consequences of
> marriage, she has not a trace. (Linton 1884: 12–13)

Linton might well have had in mind the heroines of Rhoda Broughton,
who burst on the scene with two best-sellers in 1867. *Not Wisely but
too Well*, the second of the two novels, is the more conventional.
Though it quarrels with "the world's arithmetic," the mercenary calculations informing modern marriage, it is most striking as it evokes
Kate Chester's struggle to repress her passion for the married man who
urges her to come away with him. In *Cometh Up a Flower*, the bold
Nell Le Strange narrates her sacrifice of love for money, as she reluctantly

marries an affluent, middle-aged squire in order to repair the family fortunes: "the most matter-of-fact piece of barter in the world; so much young flesh and blood for so much current coin of the realm." There is little plot; the appeal resides in such concerted affronts to domestic piety, which is even more thoroughly outraged by Nell's sister Dolly, who readily agrees that she would sell her soul for gold. "Dolly," her sister blithely remarks, "is the sort of woman upon whom Mr. Algernon Swinburne would write pages of magnificent uncleanness" (Broughton 1993: 173).

A different form of novelistic boldness emerged with the career of Marie Louise de la Ramée (1839–1908), who wrote under the name Ouida. Ouida first came to notice with *Held in Bondage* (1863), which reads something like *Guy Livingstone* crossed with sensation fiction. Like most of Ouida's heroes, Granville De Vigne (whose name provided the title of the serial version) is a wealthy young man who moves effortlessly in "fast" society, but finds the most fitting outlet for his nonchalant, effete elegance as a calvary officer. That career leads him to far-flung settings, including the Charge of the Light Brigade in the Crimea, and into a number of romantic entanglements with women who are singular enough to unsettle his detachment. Ouida's best-known novel, *Under Two Flags* (1867), centers on the Hon. Bertie Cecil ("Beauty" to his acquaintances), another aristocratic paragon (son of a viscount, officer in the Life Guards, famous horseman and gambler) who fakes his death to save the honor of a young woman and his feckless brother, then ends up incognito fighting with the French in Algeria. He finds himself the object of hopeless devotion from one Cigarette – "I am no kitten, *bon zig*: take care of my talons" (Ouida 1890: 193) – an audacious camp follower (the name reflects one of her pleasures) who saves his life in battle, but who is unable to win his passion, even after she saves him yet again by throwing herself in front of the firing squad about to execute him. Ouida notably captures a powerful homoeroticism informing the mid-Victorian revival of aristocratic manhood – her heroes tend to be deeply resistant to the feminine allure surrounding them – but the audacious plotting and array of exotic setting and characters made her novels immensely popular.

Margaret Oliphant offered a strikingly different image of young femininity, but also a more subtle probing of prevailing gender norms, in *Miss Marjoribanks*, a further installment in the Chronicles of Carlingford published in 1866 after being serialized in *Blackwood's*. Lucilla Marjoribanks has been aptly called a Victorian Emma: an only child, imperious, meddling, unflappably confident, blithely self-absorbed – never more than when professing her interest in other people. When she loses her mother at 15, she finds her mission in life: under the guise of devoting herself to her father, she undertakes to transform "the lamentable condition" of Carlingford society; "all that was wanting was a master-hand to blend these different elements" (Oliphant 1870: 1.32). The domestic "queen" of Ruskin's celebration turns into a young social reformer, or a female Napoleon, as Oliphant insistently parodies the language of domestic sovereignty, a rhetoric most fully developed in Isabella Beeton's highly popular *Book of Household Management* (1859–61). "The beginning of the revolution" is the redecoration of the house (1.73), and its opening to the public is "the real beginning of her great work in Carlingford"; like all true revolutionaries, Lucilla is also an evangelist. Oliphant's narrator is unusually cutting – "she was not in the least 'viewy' in her own person, having been brought up in the old-fashioned orthodox way of having a great respect for religion, and as little to do with it as possible" (1.200). But Lucilla's sublime egotism makes the comedy more complex than such epigrammatic crackle suggests, because no one can quite fathom her. Complaining that her "evenings" lacked "any man who could flirt," "she lamented it with such sincerity that all the world thought her the most perfect actress in existence" (1.199) – but she is not acting. Ultimately her single-mindedness, which culminates in engineering an unlikely election of her candidate for Parliament, turns out to bring genuine comfort and happiness to others – though it does put pressure on the closure of the novel, since a woman so deeply satisfied by party-planning feels little want of a husband. But the seeming condescension of the narrator's tribute to "the pleasure of exercising a great faculty, and the natural confidence of genius in its own powers" (1.313) is countered by more than a little sympathy. Though less popular with contemporaries than Oliphant's other Carlingford novels, perhaps because of its frequently acerbic tone, it is a distinctive and undervalued achievement.

Sensation fiction typically captures domesticity under siege, but the home was vulnerable to dangers besides crazed women and ruthless social climbers, and in the latter 1860s gothic was increasingly the vehicle of anxieties associated with Britain's imperial engagements. These resonated in Collins's *The Moonstone* (1868), which was serialized in *All the Year Round*. Frequently described as the first detective novel, the novel recalls *A Woman in White* with a detection plot narrated by multiple characters, although it is more intricately plotted, and more richly characterizes its various narrators. But though the narrative presses towards an answer to a single question – who stole a famous diamond, "the moonstone," from the bedroom of Rachel Verinder? – the fearfulness evoked in the novel is centered less in that crime than in the diamond itself. Or rather, the true crime is the diamond's presence in England in the first place. Gabriel Betteredge, the Verinder steward, puts it best: "here was our quiet English home suddenly invaded by a devilish Indian Diamond – bringing after it a conspiracy of living rogues, set loose on us by the vengeance of a dead man ... Who ever heard the like of it – in the nineteenth century, mind; in an age of progress, and in a country which rejoices in the blessings of the British constitution?" (W. Collins 1966: 67). Betteridge's comic faith in the British constitution points to a more somber irony, in which the diamond itself seems eerily possessed of agency, and has "invaded" the domestic sanctuary, as if reversing the tide of British conquest. That peculiar reframing of the imperial frontier is brought home by the Indians sent to track down the jewel plundered at the siege of Seringapatam. Their presence outside the Verinder home tellingly echoes Fagin lingering outside the Maylie drawing room in *Oliver Twist*; the threat to domestic peace now comes from abroad rather than from an underclass at home. But the clash assumes a more complex hybridity in the character of Ezra Jennings, the man who will solve the mystery. He is a figure of mixed ancestry, with a complexion "of a gypsy darkness" and nose of "the ancient people of the East," his hair a striking amalgam of black and white; his "physiological experiment," which Collins underscores in his preface, aligns him with contemporary medical science, yet he is studying the effects of opium, which (echoing DeQuincey's "Opium Eater") is redolent of a timeless East that has become deeply lodged within an English psyche.

Such fantasies of "reverse colonization" would multiply over the remainder of the century, as Britain's imperial reach became at once more extensive and more precarious, and helped to shape a distinct subgenre that would become known as "imperial gothic." Dickens offered a gesture in that direction with a new novel that he began in 1869. Four years had passed since *Our Mutual Friend* – the longest such interval of his career. The years had been filled with increasingly lucrative but exhausting lecture tours, which he finally gave up on the advice of his doctor in April 1869. The new novel bore suggestive resemblances to *The Moonstone*, particularly in its gothic atmosphere and the evocation of violence associated with empire. *The Mystery of Edwin Drood* is set, uncharacteristically, in "an ancient English cathedral town" – the opening words of the novel – called Cloisterham (modeled on Rochester, where Dickens had lived as a child). Though the pervasive gloom of the setting recalls *Bleak House* in particular, the withdrawal from Dickens's familiar London setting enabled a sparer and more deliberate action, focused relatively narrowly on John Jasper, a cathedral music master, his young nephew Edwin Drood, and young Rosa Bud, reluctantly engaged to the equally reluctant Drood but the object of Jasper's fierce, undeclared passion.

The mystery, quite simply, is the abrupt disappearance of young Drood, and though the town does not suspect his outwardly adoring uncle, Jasper in fact leads a double life, which turns on his addiction to opium. From the novel's opening scene, in which a stupefied Jasper awakens in an opium den with "a Chinaman, a Lascar, and a haggard woman," his addiction discloses a repressed violence associated with empire, a presence so insistently evoked that even the "ancient" fabric of Cloisterham seems at times an imperial outpost (Dickens 1974: 37). Young Drood is an engineer who is setting out for the Middle East "to wake up Egypt a little" (96); Neville Landless and his sister resemble "beautiful barbaric captives brought from some wild tropical dominion" (85); the dark-skinned Neville, a hot-tempered young rival of Drood's "brought up among abject and servile dependents, of an inferior race" in Ceylon, fears he may have been tainted by "a drop of what is tigerish in their blood" (90). Even the Reverend Septimus Crisparkle, whose Trollopean surname and Kingsleyan regimen of early morning runs and cold baths seem to mark him as a moral paragon – "simply and staunchly true to his duty" – lashes out at Mr. Honeythunder and his fellow philanthropists as "run amuck like so many mad Malays" (207). In such a context, "savage" – a familiar epithet in Dickens's earlier, more comic renderings of male rivalry – becomes thoroughly racialized. Empire once again seems something "devilish" which has invaded not only a quiet English home but something like the collective unconscious of England.

The mystery of Edwin Drood remains unsolved. On June 8, 1870, after only six of a planned 12 numbers of the novel had been completed, Dickens suffered a massive stroke and died the following day. The notes of exasperation and even outright hostility that had greeted his more recent novels dropped away in a chorus of praise and lamentation. "It is an event world-wide," the irascible Carlyle wrote to

Dickens's friend John Forster, who would soon undertake the author-ized biography, "A *unique* of talents suddenly extinct, and has 'eclipsed' (we too may say) 'the harmless gaiety of nations.'" From America Longfellow wrote, "I never knew an author's death to cause such gen-eral mourning. It is no exaggeration to say that this whole country is stricken with grief." A leader in *The Times*, which had often attacked Dickens, urged that "Statesmen, men of science, philanthropists, the acknowledged benefactors of their race, might pass away, and yet not leave the void which will be caused by the death of Dickens" (E. Johnson 1952: 1155). He was buried in Westminster Abbey on the morning of June 14; tens of thousands of mourners filed past the grave before the Abbey was closed two days later. *Punch* offered an unchar-acteristically somber epitaph:

> He sleeps as he should sleep – among the great
>   In the old Abbey: sleep amid the few
> Of England's famous thousands whose high state
>   Is to lie with monarchs – monarchs too.
>   (Johnson 1952: 1157)

After Dickens

The death of Dickens marked the end of an era in the novel. Throughout the 1850s and 1860s, even with the emergence of George Eliot, Trollope, and sensation fiction, the complement of Dickens and Thackeray in their respective blue and yellow wrappers had remained the dominant frame of reference in assessing contemporary fiction. With their passing, George Eliot attained an unparalleled eminence, but her very distinction made it more difficult to map the literary land-scape. Two elderly novelists who had been famous even longer than Dickens were still publishing, but their careers were winding down. Disraeli, out of office following the passage of the Reform Bill, in 1870 published *Lothair*, a romance of typically lavish setting and garish intrigue, but with very little reference to parliamentary politics. In the following year, that other aging romancer, Bulwer-Lytton, published a single-volume utopian fantasy, *The Coming Race*, about the discovery of an underground civilization, the Vril-ya, which is sustained by "vril," an infinitely renewable source of electricity. The plot hangs on the romance between an alien priestess and the American mining engineer who has discovered her people, but the novel is best known as a pioneering work of science fiction – although its most enduring impact may be its commemoration in the beef extract known as Bovril, created soon afterwards and still in production. In 1873 Bulwer-Lytton completed a final three-volume novel, *Kenelm Chillingly*, which one might call a modern, bohemian picaresque, recounting the adventures of a young heir who after graduation from Cambridge drifts around the world incognito. The novel, which resembles a cross between a *Bildungsroman* and one of Bulwer-Lytton's early novels of criminal life, is in keeping with the sheer eclecticism of his prolific career, which ended with his death later that year.

Although Trollope's journal *St. Paul's* proved unsuccessful, in 1872 he enjoyed success with *The Eustace Diamonds*, serialized in the *Fortnightly*. The third in the Palliser series, although only peripherally related to the main line of action, the novel represents Trollope's quirky engagement with sensation fiction. Given Trollope's resistance to the axioms of that genre – not merely its extravagant passions, but its dependence on omnipresent mystery and secrets – the novel is in some ways almost a parody of the form. But Lizzie Eustace, parvenu widow of an immensely wealthy baronet, proves a resourceful spinner of tales in her own right, and her brief social buoyancy reflects the power of gossip to render fascinating that which it would ostracize. Trollope's narrative to this degree enters into the spirit of the sensation novel, and for a time Lizzie resembles a less socially agile Becky Sharp, although Trollopean society offers less field for self-invention than Thackeray's. Despite this success, *The Last Chronicle of Barset* remained the highwater mark of Trollope's popularity, which about this time began to wane – partly out of sheer fatigue at his prolific output.

Collins remained extremely popular in the 1870s, although more for his earlier works and stage adaptations of them than for more recent novels, which after the success of *The Moonstone* became increasingly polemical attacks on what he perceived as social abuses. *Man and Wife*, serialized in *Cassell's Magazine* in 1870, harnesses the machinery of gothic to an attack on marriage laws and the cult of athleticism. In this novel, it is the law itself that effectively imprisons married women, both by depriving them of property rights and (in Scotland) by forcing them into marriage solely on the grounds of a sexual relationship – here with a young aristocrat who cares for nothing but athletics. Collins followed this novel with *The New Magdalen*, serialized in 1872–3 in Bentley's *Temple Bar*. As the title suggests, the novel offers a defense of women forced into prostitution, but sets it within the just-concluded Franco–Prussian War, which enables Collins to inveigh against the barbarism of the European powers. The polemical designs persisted through most of his works over the next two decades, which are devoted to attacks on (inter alia) Mrs. Grundy, Jesuits, vivisection, and modern divorce. Swinburne in 1889 summed up the development with a wicked epigram: "What brought good Wilkie's genius nigh perdition? /Some demon whispered – 'Wilkie, have a mission!'" (Page 1974: 262).

George Meredith in 1870 remained a novelist in search of an audience. *Evan Harrington*, which had been serialized in 1860 in the popular weekly *All the Year Round*, remained his most popular work, though it never achieved the critical regard of *Richard Feverel*. In 1864, after the controversy surrounding *Modern Love*, Chapman and Hall brought out *Emilia in Italy* (later retitled *Sandra Belloni*) which follows a young half-Italian singer who in the 1840s is adopted by the family of a morally dubious English merchant, Samuel Pole; her struggle to pursue a musical career is interwoven with the financial decline of the Pole family. Emilia's mixed ancestry naturally recalls Aurora Leigh, and reflects an increasing fascination among novelists with virtuoso foreign singers and actresses modeled on the likes of Grisi and Rachel (the model for Vashti in *Villette*). Such figures typically serve as moral and cultural foils to English insularity – as in George Eliot's *Daniel Deronda*, for example – and Emilia accentuates by contrast that familiar target of Meredith's irony, middle-class sentimentality. The novel left space for a sequel, *Vittoria*, serialized in the *Fortnightly* in 1866, which follows Emilia's career in Italy as both an opera singer (the title is her stage name) and a participant in Italian resistance to the Austrian occupation (an increasingly prominent fictional motif in the 1860s as both an expression of liberal ideals and a rich field for intrigue and conspiracy). Eager for a larger income, Meredith had begun this novel while still at work on *Rhoda Fleming* (published by Tinsley in 1865), an even more overt appeal to popular taste dealing with that increasingly hackneyed topic, the seduction and betrayal of a poor farmer's daughter by a middle-class rake. He began to find a wider readership in 1871, when *The Adventures of Harry Richmond* was serialized (anonymously) in the *Cornhill*. The novel returns to autobiographical material of father–son relationships, which had figured centrally in *Richard Feveral* and *Evan Harrington*, but this time the comedy of manners is structured more along the lines of a picaresque

Bildungsroman, which is narrated by its hero up to the age of about 30. The young Harry seeks out the charming charlatan of a father who had abandoned him as a child, then suffers through the old man's elaborate, self-defeating schemes to marry Harry to a German princess, while his wealthy grandfather counters with his own designs for Harry, who becomes "a kind of shuttlecock" between them. This crowded adventure, with Meredith's characteristically diffuse, oblique, sometimes disjointed narrative structure, full of abrupt and often unclear shifts in scene and chronology, confounded most reviewers' expectations of the novel form; most called it a romance, or "a sketch in three volumes." But the majority praised its "animation and fullness of life," in R. H. Hutton's phrase, and spoke of Meredith's "singular power and energy" as a distinctive presence in the world of fiction, to be enjoyed and reckoned with. "He holds in literature a place by himself," remarked the *Westminster* (Williams 1971: 156, 160, 164).

Meredith had another, more subtle influence on the literary marketplace in his work as a publisher's reader for Chapman and Hall (who had published *Richard Feverel*). In this important job he had the inevitable lapses of judgment – some colossal, as when he recommended against publishing *East Lynne* – but he also nurtured several important literary careers. In 1869 he read a manuscript entitled *The Poor Man and the Lady*, from a young Dorset architect's assistant named Thomas Hardy. Meredith found the social criticism implicit in the title too heavy-handed, and counseled the aspiring author to write a story with more plot. Hardy pursued the advice with a vengeance and produced *Desperate Remedies*, a full-blown sensation novel with concealed illegitimate children, bigamous marriages, and resort to murder in the inevitably futile effort to conceal a scandalous past. So thoroughly plot-driven is the novel that its 21 chapter titles all take the form "The events of" followed by some interval of time. But though Hardy would later explain that he had put "too crude an interpretation" on Meredith's advice, the novel was published in 1871 by Tinsley (which made its fortune publishing *Lady Audley's Secret*), and launched Hardy's career. The following year Tinsley published *Under the Greenwood Tree*, which began Hardy's series of novels set in what he would famously call Wessex. Subtitled "A Rural Painting of the Dutch School," a favorite realist paradigm for humble settings, the work is set in the village of Mellstock, where the familiar Hardy preoccupation with the erosion of traditional rural society is already in place: the old church orchestra is being replaced by a modern organ. But the novel is perhaps the most cheerful Hardy ever wrote, with little hint of the darkness for which he would become proverbial. In 1873 Tinsley published *A Pair of Blue Eyes*, set in north Cornwall, where a young architect has been commissioned to restore an aging church tower. The action centers around a love triangle, a recurrent structure of Hardy's novels: the architect falls in love with the daughter of the local Vicar, but his humble parentage (he is the son of a mason) is an insuperable obstacle, and she is subsequently wooed by an affluent literary man, who breaks off their engagement when he learns of the earlier affair. In a grotesque irony – the first of many in Hardy's fiction – when the young architect returns from India, where he has made his fortune, he finds himself riding to Cornwall on the same train with his rival, while the baggage van (as they discover) is carrying the body of their common love.

The most important novel of the early 1870s came from the writer by now acknowledged to be the greatest living English novelist. In early 1869, George Eliot began "A Study in Provincial Life," as she would later subtitle it, about a town in the Midlands on the eve of the first Reform Bill. After slow progress for more than a year, she abandoned the project and began a new work, "Miss Brooke," which took fire, and which in May of 1871 she combined with the earlier effort. This fusion (which takes place with chapter 11 of the finished novel) would give her completed work its distinctive parallel plots, organized around three "love problems" exploring the relations between marriage and the aspiration to a vocation, not merely a career but a moral calling. "The home epic" of Victorian England, at once domestic life and the novel form devoted to representing that life, is thus set against heroic aspiration more in keeping with traditional epic, again as both a mode of experience and as a literary genre adequate to its struggles. Daringly, however, George Eliot began her finished work with a brief "Prelude" intimating that her heroine's quest would end in failure. This "melancholy" emphasis, as many readers felt it, underscores the scope of Eliot's outwardly modest aims. Dorothea Brooke, a young woman with the moral fervor of a Saint Theresa, is born into a world bereft of opportunities for "epic life," a world offering "no coherent faith and social order which could perform the function of knowledge for the ardently willing soul" (Eliot 1995c: 3). The failure Eliot represents thus transcends the disappointment of her central character to gather in an entire social order, which seems no longer to provide a medium for genuinely heroic endeavor. The diagnosis recalls that of

Mill's *On Liberty*, among others, but Eliot offers a far more complex representation of society. The central, recurrent burden of her realism – the struggle towards enlarged understanding through the frustration of desire – expands into an anatomy of the moral possibilities of modern life, developed with unparalleled breadth and intricacy in the "great web" that is *Middlemarch*.

The novel was published by Blackwood in the unusual format of eight lengthy parts appearing from December 1871 to December 1872, initially bi-monthly, which allowed reviewers in the monthlies to record their reactions as the novel was unfolding. Its attack on conventional femininity was especially striking, and many observed a newly acerbic note in the narration, particularly in the characterization of Celia Brooke and Rosamond Vincy. As the conservative *Saturday Review* complained, "All the weak and mean and knavish people are blond ... and blue eyes are uniformly disingenuous" (D. Carroll 1971: 319). It naturally took some time to grasp the large parallels that would focus the frictions between moral aspiration and social deference, particularly within the central marriages, first Dorothea and Casaubon and then Lydgate and Rosamond (the third "love problem" of Fred Vincy and Mary Garth struck most as less consequential, if eminently warm and engaging). As the design did unfold, so did the risk of it seeming too schematic: old science versus new science, self-effacing helpmeet versus self-absorbed social climber, and above all the parallel frustrations of vocation in Dorothea and Lydgate. But most readers marveled at the extraordinary richness of detail. "It is not compact, doubtless," Henry James noted, "but when was a panorama compact?" (D. Carroll 1971: 354). As throughout Eliot's career, reviewers praised the depth of her characterization; while acknowledging the breadth of Trollope's canvas, R. H. Hutton remarked, "His characters are carved out of the materials of ordinary society; George Eliot's include many which make ordinary society seem a sort of satire on the life behind it" (302). Therein lies the distinctive social psychology of *Middlemarch*: inner life and ordinary society are mutual foils, and the frictions between them produce not merely a discord but a reciprocal moral anatomy. The egoism that disables higher moral life may be registered in both devotion to and contempt for social obligation, while society in turn too often obstructs or undermines the pursuit of larger goods.

The central device in this anatomy is the narrator, whose insistent presence in framing character and action is the most distinctive formal achievement of the novel. Of course direct, sustained moral address, whether as ironic commentary or as sententious injunction, had characterized Eliot's fiction from the outset (and has always vexed efforts to adapt her novels to the screen), but in *Middlemarch* the narrator's mediation has become newly prominent. Some reviewers complained that the narrator's irony was too often uncharacteristically acrid (as when Rosamond, fearing that Lydgate does not return her affection, "felt as forlorn as Ariadne, – as a charming stage Ariadne left behind with boxes full of costumes and no hope of a coach" [Eliot 1995c: 299]). But such severity is balanced by unexpected appeals to the reader's sympathy, perhaps most famously in explicit defense of the repugnant Casaubon, and more subtly throughout the novel in a virtuoso use of free indirect discourse, as in the riveting moment at the close of chapter 74 when Mrs. Bulstrode consoles her corrupt and disgraced husband:

> They could not yet speak to each other of the shame which she was bearing with him, or of the acts which had brought it down on them. His confession was silent, and her promise of faithfulness was silent. Open-minded as she was, she nevertheless shrank from the words which would have expressed their mutual consciousness as she would have shrunk from flakes of fire. She could not say, "How much is only slander and false suspicion?" and he did not say, "I am innocent." (Eliot 1995c: 750-1)

The narrator's commentary everywhere reflects George Eliot's immersion in contemporary thought, which many readers found intimidating. The otherwise admiring R. H. Hutton complained of "the authoress's excessive, almost morbid, intellectual ability," and nearly every reviewer noticed the prominence of scientific discourse ("too often an echo of Messrs. Darwin and Huxley," in James's view). Some of this flowed from the particulars of Lydgate's medical career, but it was of a piece with a more encompassing modernity, perhaps best evoked by Sidney Colvin: "philosophy which declares the human family is deluded in its higher dreams, dependent upon itself, and bound thereby to a closer if sadder brotherhood; the habit in regarding and meditating physical laws, and the facts of sense and life, which leads up to that philosophy and belongs to it" (D. Carroll 1970: 359, 294, 332). All of George Eliot's works grapple with the moral burdens of life in a universe without traditional faith, but none are so thoroughly devoid of that consolation. As Hutton pointed out, Dorothea undergoes her long night of agonized reflection in chapter 80 without a thought of God. Hutton found this "unnatural," but the force of Dorothea's moral passion, and that of the narrator, seems to have cushioned the blow for most readers. Hutton himself moved from a guarded review of the first book to the conclusion that "Middlemarch bids more than fair to be one of the great books of the world," and to a final judgment that George Eliot was "the greatest English authoress," ranking with Fielding and Scott behind all but her fellow Warwickshire native, Shakespeare (314). Henry James, more succinctly but more suggestively, concluded that *Middlemarch* had surpassed even Fielding: "It sets a limit, we think, to the development of the old-fashioned English novel" (359).

The Persistence of Epic

The major poetic achievements at the end of the 1860s likewise pressed the limits of genre. Morris increasingly turned away from lyric to pursue longer narratives, such as *The Earthly Paradise*, a poem of 42,000 lines published in four parts in 1868 and 1870. It is framed as the story of a group of Norse sailors who have fled from a plague in their homeland in search of a refuge; when they finally discover a city in which to settle, they exchange a round of tales with the inhabitants, with each group delivering a story for each month of the year, yielding a total of 24 narratives (introduced by interpolated lyrics), which are themselves predominantly elegiac reworkings of myth and legend of both Norse and classical origin. As he was working on the poem, Morris first visited Iceland, and for the remainder of his career he was deeply influenced by Icelandic saga.

Browning's new stature was crowned by the reception of *The Ring and the Book*, a work of over 20,000 lines published in four volumes from November 1868 through February of 1869. The poem originated with Browning's 1860 discovery in a Florence bookstall of what he called "The Old Yellow Book," a collection of pamphlets and other documents concerning a sensational murder case in 1698. Count Guido Franceschini had killed his young wife Pompilia Comparini, along with her parents, and defended himself by invoking a husband's honor: the parents had defrauded him by concealing Pompilia's illegitimacy, and Pompilia herself, he claimed, had been the lover of a young cleric named Caponsacchi, with whom she fled from Guido's house in Arezzo. It was the stuff of sensation fiction, but the poem reminds us that Browning was ahead of the novelists. James had credited Collins with introducing into fiction "those most mysterious of mysteries, the mysteries which are at our own doors," but the mysteries of domestic tyranny had been indelibly evoked in "My Last Duchess" a quarter-century earlier. The Duke of Ferrara is the *ne plus ultra* of the despotic husband of late Victorian fiction, conjuring up the nightmarish underside of Victorian domestic ideology, which would have a long afterlife in characters such as James's own Gilbert Osmond in *Portrait of a Lady*. It was Browning's monologue, moreover, which more than any other literary form showed the suggestive possibilities of narrative point of view, and in *The Ring and the Book* he exploited them with unprecedented virtuosity. *The Woman in White* had drawn on the model of written legal testimony to narrate a criminal plot from limited points of view, but Browning's poem recounts the central sequence more than a dozen times, each from the vantage of a different character, including not only the central actors but various mouthpieces of public opinion, the opposed attorneys in the trial, and Pope Innocent XII, the final arbiter of the legal process. Browning thus far more radically probes the fragility of human understanding as it is shaped by individual character, and explores the difficulty of disentangling judgment from desire.

Browning's world, however, is not that of Kurosawa's *Rashomon*. *The Ring and the Book* evokes no impasse of conflicting perspective, no final irreconcilability of the various accounts. Instead, the poem celebrates virtue triumphing over legal and social convention through the power of sympathetic understanding, which is redoubled in the poet's transformation of the bare outlines of the case into "truth of force" (Browning 1961: 1.367), a transformation he models on that of the goldsmith shaping a ring. In part, this final assurance derives from Browning's identification with Caponsacchi's selfless rescue of Pompilia (so Browning presents it, in the face of a good deal of evidence to the contrary). Browning aligns the action with the myth of St. George rescuing a desperate maiden from the clutches of the dragon – even changing the historical date of Pompilia's flight to have it fall on St. George's Day. That myth always had a special resonance for Browning; he saw it borne out in his own courtship of Elizabeth Barrett. Caponsacchi's tributes to Pompilia's purity clearly echo the devotion that Browning felt for his wife, which he expresses more directly in an extended apostrophe, "O lyric love." Yet the dragon gets more than his due; Guido, a rich amalgam of criminal aesthete and common thug, alternatively swaggering, fierce, desperate, and groveling, is the one character given two entire books, within which he speaks 500 lines more than Pompilia and Caponsacchi combined.

Still further, however, Browning's poem remains firmly grounded in a belief that art can discover a truth that eludes other vehicles of human understanding. The narrator echoes the faith of Fra Lippo, here refracted through a more demanding aesthetic, one that insists on the power of obliquity, and the alchemical transfiguration of "fact": "So write a book shall mean beyond the facts, /Suffice the eye and save the soul beside" (Browning 1961: xii.862–3). It is faith in the intimation of ineffable truth that would fan the devotion of the burgeoning Browning societies, which increasingly approached the works of the poet as if sitting at the feet of a sage. In the boldest application of a trope that echoes throughout Browning's writings, the poet's creation becomes not merely a more complete truth than anything the law might offer; it becomes a resurrection – and, by implication, a form of redemption.

In December of 1869, a new installment appeared in the other great serial poem of the Victorian era, *The Idylls of the King*. *The Holy Grail and Other Poems* added four books to the *Idylls* published in 1859: *The Coming of Arthur, The Holy Grail, Pelleas and Ettarre*, and *The Passing of Arthur* (recasting "The Morte d'Arthur" of 1842). While the new volume specified the sequence of all eight books, no single publication contained all together, which compounded the challenge of trying to grasp a design in the poem as a whole – if it was indeed a whole. The various books still struck many readers as disconnected tapestries, "very fine descriptive poetry, and nothing beyond" (Andrew 1993: 27), but *The Holy Grail* in particular encouraged readers to find a unifying structure in an allegorical reading of the poem – "Sense at war with Soul," as Tennyson wrote in his dedication, "To the Queen," added in 1873. Though Tennyson offered fuller glosses of this reading, such as the various knights representing individual passions at war with Arthur as an embodied conscience, it frustrated some readers, who complained of the narrow association of greatness with moral – which is to say, sexual – purity. (Whereas Malory had based the downfall of Camelot in the character of Modred, the offspring of Arthur's incestuous relationship with his half-sister, Tennyson tellingly shifted blame to the adulterous Guinevere.) The association also was confounded by the widely shared judgment that Arthur, as a moral paragon, was the main weakness of the poem. This view was reinforced in 1872, when *Gareth and Lynette* was published, containing that book and *The Last Tournament*, which had been separately published in the *Contemporary Review* a year earlier. The latter book, which has no basis in Malory, offered a portrait of the fallen Lancelot consumed by loathing of his own weakness and treachery, which impressed many readers as a much richer achievement than the character of Arthur. But readers still had no complete edition of the poem (save all but *Balin and Balan*, a gripping account of fratricidal rage added in 1885) until a collected "Imperial Edition" of *Tennyson's Works* published by Strahan in 1872–3.

The earliest readers of *Idylls of the King* thus never encountered the poem for the first time as a sustained narrative. Perhaps for this reason, they offered little attention to that dimension of the poem that has come to preoccupy more recent critics, its evocation of the rise and fall of an empire. Tennyson's dedication, "To the Queen," actually underscores this dimension, attacking arguments that British sovereignty over Canada was not worth the cost: "Is this the tone of empire? here the faith /That made us rulers?" (ll. 18–19; Tennyson 1969). The poem represents one of the most powerful of Victorian meditations on the fragility of civilization itself, carved from a "wilderness" of "wild beasts" into a social order whose transience is underscored from the opening book: "Arthur and his knighthood for a space / Were all one will" ("Coming of Arthur," ll. 514–15). Nearly all critics noted the eminently modern anxiety and skepticism that Tennyson infused into Arthurian legend. R. H. Hutton praised Tennyson for capturing "the common term between the ideas of chivalry and the ideas of an age of hesitating trust, an age of a probing intellect, and a trusting heart" (Jump 1967: 388). But the allegorizing impulse tended to denature the social dimension of the poem. As it turns Arthur's harrowing of Guinevere into her own self-condemnation rather than the public humiliation of a disloyal wife (she is denounced by her "conscience"), so the allegorical reading implies that the rebellion of Mark and his Red Knights, a "Round Table of the North," is the expression of unruly desire rather than the uprising of a subject population ("Last Tournament," l. 78). To be sure, no Victorian poem more insistently aligns desire and social order. Thus Arthur in the opening book longs to be joined with Guinevere:

> Then might we live together as one life,
> And reigning with one will in everything
> Have power on this dark land to lighten it,
> And power of this dead world to make it live.
>
> (ll. 90–3)

His yearning underscores the pervasive Victorian idealizing of marriage as a political microcosm, a model of disparate people meshed into "one will." That investment helps to explain what might seem the exorbitant anxiety aroused by perceptions of marriage under threat.

Poisonous Honey and Fleshly Poetry

Among his brisk survey in "To the Queen" of contemporary threats to England's well-being, Tennyson listed "Art with poisonous honey stol'n from France" (l. 56; Tennyson 1969). The phrase is a hit at Baudelaire's influence on Swinburne and the turmoil over *Poems and Ballads*, which had ebbed by 1872. But many of the issues had been revived in a storm over Dante Gabriel Rossetti's *Poems* of 1870, a volume whose genesis is one of the more macabre in English literature. Rossetti had been writing poetry for more than two decades, but before 1870 he was known almost exclusively as a painter. In 1861 he had published a volume of translations, *The Early Italian Poets*, but when he asked Ruskin to recommend some of his poems to Thackeray at the *Cornhill Magazine* (where *Unto this Last* was appearing), Ruskin found "Jenny" so offensive that he refused the favor. In the following year Rossetti's wife Lizzie Siddal, long in fragile health, died of a laudanum overdose, which left Rossetti distraught with guilt (he had been frequently unfaithful). In a wild gesture of atonement, he placed the only manuscript of his poems in her coffin, and he wrote virtually no more poetry until 1868, when a rekindled passion for William Morris's voluptuous wife Jane (one of Rossetti's favorite models) prompted a burst of new sonnets. But as he pondered publishing a volume, he realized he could not reconstruct much of his older work ("Jenny" in particular, long a favorite, eluded him), and he arranged to have the manuscript exhumed from his wife's grave, where it was recovered from amidst her still-golden hair.

When *Poems* first appeared in 1870, it was widely praised, selling out its first edition of a thousand copies within two weeks and six further printings within a year. The dominant forms – ballad, dramatic monologue, and sonnet – all enjoyed great popularity at the time, and were infused by Rossetti's striking pictorial emphasis, which is epitomized in the opening poem, "The Blessed Damozel." Many critics likened the effect to the detail in his painting, as well as to the poetry of his namesake. Dante's influence is central to the most striking feature of the volume, a sonnet sequence entitled *The House of Life* (in astrology, the chief of the 12 "houses" of heaven). But the sequence reads something like the *Vita Nuova* laid waste by despair. *The House of Life* betrays even less sense of chronology than most sonnet sequences, faithful in this regard to its opening lines:

> A Sonnet is a moment's monument,
>   Memorial from the Soul's eternity
>   To one dead deathless hour.
>   (1.1–3; D. G. Rossetti 1901)

As this trope rebukes a search for narrative line, it also summons up the dominant tension structuring the volume: between the memory of past fulfillment or hope in love and a present desolation. Death is a constant presence in the house of Life, and much of the poem wrestles with the relations between the two – typically in the effort to grasp a soul that survives the loss of the body, if only as an enduring sense of the possibility of love itself that (in the words of the final sonnet) might assuage "vain desire at last and vain regret ... And teach the unforgetful to forget" (101.4). It is tempting to read this struggle autobiographically, as a memorial to Rossetti's agony over his wife's death. But the tension is largely that of "The Blessed Damozel," written when he was barely 20. In effect, the past is enshrined as a heaven which lights up the poet's memory across a gulf of longing that can never be bridged. Rossetti thus magnifies the superimposition of present and past inevitable in any lyric "moment," and thereby creates an often challenging obliquity and obscurity of shifting time frames and pronoun referents. "Love," for example, may variously denote the object of one's desire, the desire itself, a habit of being, and a god. At the same time, this multiple perspective does indeed invest the sonnets with the "arduous fullness" Rossetti ascribes to the form.

Ironically, it was one of Rossetti's very few sonnets celebrating achieved and apparently secure married bliss that became the focal point of controversy. In October of 1871, the *Contemporary Review* published "The Fleshly School of Poetry," by a young journeyman poet and journalist, Robert Buchanan, which tore into Rossetti as the representative of a "school" devoted to "sickening," "shameless" sensuality: "it is neither poetic, nor manly, nor even poetic, to obtrude such things as the themes of whole poems. It is simply nasty" (Buchanan 2002: 1332). Though Buchanan gleaned offensive nuggets from a number of poems, his chief exhibit was the sonnet "Nuptial Sleep," which he characterized as "putting on record for other full-grown men to read, the most secret mysteries of sexual connection, and that with so sickening a desire to reproduce the sensual mood" (1332). It is quite extraordinary notice for a poem (which Buchanan quotes in full) whose most graphic lines are the following:

> Their bosoms sundered, with the opening start
>   Of married flowers to either side outspread
>   From the knit stem; yet still their mouths, burnt red,
> Fawned on each other where they lay apart.

(ll. 5–8)

Buchanan's main target may well have been the more audacious Swinburne, whose name recurs throughout the essay, but the abuse took hold, and his attack soon was seconded by the conservative *Quarterly Review*. The ever-sensitive Rossetti, his health already weakened by dependence on alcohol and chloral, suffered a breakdown the following year, and spent the remaining decade of his life under a cloud.

Surely Rossetti could have laughed off such abuse as a hysterical bit of self-righteous prurience, in which "the desire to reproduce the sensual mood" seems more Buchanan's than his own. But Rossetti – like Swinburne, John Morley, and others who rushed to his defense – recognized in the article something more than personal fixation. Buchanan was attacking an emergent poetry clearly affiliated with radical politics. Rossetti's poems certainly did not engage contemporary politics like Swinburne's, who in *Songs Before Sunrise* (1871) devoted much of a volume to the Italian struggle for independence. But the sonnets Rossetti published in 1869 appeared in the *Fortnightly Review*, the liberal journal edited by John Morley, and seemed to affirm a radical individualism. Buchanan was marshalling suspicion of a poetry that, as he frames it, confounds in its very form the satisfying allegory of *Idylls of the King*. Rossetti's work affirmed "that poetic expression is greater than poetic thought, and by inference that the body is greater than the soul, and sound superior to sense" (Buchanan 2002: 1330). The fleshly body, in other words, became for conservative critics a sign of poetic form unleashed from the constraints of "soul" and "sense" – that by now familiar critical attack on the legacy of romanticism. Tellingly, Buchanan recognized in the Laureate's poetry both inspiration and limit case: Rossetti has transgressed the boundaries of sensualism staked out in "Merlin and Vivien" (the fleshly school "wearisomely expand[s]" that poem's "concentrated epicene force") while *Maud* is the main precedent for a "hysteric tone and overloaded style" that is no longer controlled, as in Tennyson's monologue, by dramatic irony (1330). Once again, suspicion of emergent poetry focuses on its affront to a collective sympathy. Whereas the dramatic principle of Tennysonian monologue and narrative instantiates this norm, "Mr. Rossetti is never dramatic, never impersonal – always attitudinizing, posturing, and describing his own exquisite emotions" (1333).

The objection is a familiar one, which runs back through Arnold's *Preface* to attacks on early Tennyson to the early reception of Wordsworth, but the heresy it denounces seemed to be gaining new force in the "poisonous honey stol'n from France." A still fuller, if subtler, expression of that dangerous allure appeared in 1873, when Pater's *Studies in the History of the Renaissance* was published by Macmillan. The work by a largely unknown writer caused a stir most immediately because of its distinctive style, which nearly every reviewer commented upon. A number of them called it "poetry," and most found it epitomized in the famous meditation on Leonardo's Gioconda:

> The presence that rose thus so strangely beside the waters, is expressive of what in the ways of a thousand years men had come to desire. Hers is the head upon which all "the ends of the world are come," and the eyelids are a little weary. It is a beauty wrought out from within upon the flesh, the deposit, little cell by cell, of strange thoughts and fantastic reveries and exquisite passions ... All the thoughts and experience of the world have etched and moulded there, in that which they have of power to refine and make expressive the outward form, the animalism of Greece, the lust of Rome, the mysticism of the middle age with its spiritual ambition and imaginative loves, the return of the Pagan world, the sins of the Borgias. She is older than the rocks among which she sits; like the vampire, she has been dead many times, and learned the secrets of the grave; and has been a diver in deep seas, and keeps their fallen day about her. ... (Pater 1980: 98–9)

This reverie is, among other things, a stunning tribute to the power of nineteenth-century historicism, with its attention to the cumulative force of the past as a shaping presence in every epoch – in Pater's words, "the idea of humanity as wrought upon by, and summing up in itself, all modes of thought and life" (99). The book's significance in this regard is frequently overwhelmed by the mesmerizing style, which Yeats for one found so fascinating that 60 years later he audaciously chose this same passage as the opening exhibit in his *Oxford Book of Modern Poetry*.

But Pater's style became the focal point of a sharp division over the larger aims of his criticism. Some critics took the book at face value as a historical study, and they so consistently objected to its shakiness in this regard that in later editions Pater re-titled it *The Renaissance: Studies in Art and Poetry*. The more discerning, however, noted a subtle tension between the historical dimension and an aim declared in the "Preface," where Pater defines the task of "the aesthetic critic":

> "To see the object as in itself it really is," has been justly said to be the aim of all true criticism whatever; and in aesthetic criticism the first step towards seeing one's object as it really is, is to know one's impression as it really is, to discriminate it, to realize it distinctly ... What is this song or picture, this engaging personality presented in life or in a book, to me? What effect does it really produce on me? Does it give me pleasure? And if so, what sort or degree of pleasure? How is my nature modified by its presence, and under its influence? The answers to these questions are the original facts with which the aesthetic critic has to do.... (Pater 1980: xix–xx)

While quoting the unnamed Arnold, Pater goes on to subtly undermine his aims. Although Pater contends that the aesthetic critic aims to identity a "virtue" in the aesthetic stimulus "as a chemist notes some natural element," his own procedure confounds the hint of scientific objectivity. Instead, the object under analysis becomes so bound up with the critic's sensibility that the aesthetic critic may seem to be delving into himself more than the world at large. For some readers, who valued Pater's insistence on resisting abstract claims about beauty in pursuit of a concrete, vivid impression, this was satisfaction enough, provocation to see the world with newly attentive eyes. For other reviewers, such as Margaret Oliphant, it reflected the exasperating self-absorption of an epicene elitism, which she attacked in language echoing earlier attacks on Arnold: "the productions of a class removed from ordinary mankind by that ultra-culture and academical contemplation of the world as a place chiefly occupied by other beings equally cultured and refined ... an inner circle of Illuminati ... [who] worship attenuated and refined adumbrations of Art, Philosophy, and Thought" (Seiler 1980: 86). Elitism, however, was as nothing to the hedonistic ethic sketched in the "Conclusion" (drawn from the review of Morris's poetry published five years before). Even John Morley, who had published four of the essays in the *Fortnightly* and reviewed the volume enthusiastically, was careful to distance himself. At Oxford, predictably, much of the reaction was fierce. The volume was denounced from university pulpits, and one of Pater's colleagues at Brasenose College lobbied to have him removed from various tutorial responsibilities. The antagonism was epitomized by George Eliot, for whom Pater's book seemed "quite poisonous in its false principles of criticism and false principles of life" (Seiler 1980: 92). But the poison would spread.

3

The Rise of Mass Culture and the Specter of Decline, 1873–1901

Over the final three decades of the century, Victorian literature grew ever more voluminous, diverse, and fragmented in its audiences. The Education Act of 1870, one outcome of ruling-class worries over the qualifications of voters enfranchised by the Second Reform Bill, was a notable milestone in the expansion of working-class literacy. As the reading public grew along with standards of living, enterprising publishers pursued the new audience with cheaper periodicals and publishing formats, further assisted by advances in printing technology and distribution. The most obvious signs of the growing readership were the mass-circulation daily newspapers, forerunners of the contemporary tabloid, which became for a more elite audience emblems of cultural decline. A more subtle impact came in the expansion of magazines. In 1875 the Newspaper Press Directory listed 643 magazines (quarterly, monthly, and weekly) published in the British Isles; by 1903 the number had more than quadrupled, to 2,531 (Keating 1989: 34). This growth powerfully affected the production of fiction; editors eager to fill expanding page runs offered an unparalleled opportunity for serial publication, and could accommodate narratives of lengths other than the traditional triple-decker format. (The magazine *Tit-Bits* [founded 1881], which sold for ½ pence per number, attracted youthful submissions from, among other aspiring authors, Conrad, Joyce, and Virginia Woolf – all of whom it turned down.) Partly as a result, publication of novels in volume form leveled off over the first half of the period, at about 450 adult novels per year (while juvenile fiction steadily expanded), but then surged in the late 1880s, to the point that by the later 1890s publishers were releasing over 1,600 novels per year (Keating 1989: 36, 32–3).

Along with the growing market for novels came new audiences for a broad range of genres: children's literature, travel, practical guides (including guides to authorship), popular science, memoirs. The conditions also nurtured a new genre, the short story (the name itself was coined in 1884), which was ideally adapted to the new venues and became increasingly important to late-century literary careers, particularly those of Kipling and Conan Doyle. The growing array of publishing outlets complicated relations between writer and publisher, which were further strained by the 1884 founding of the Society of Authors, devoted largely to securing the economic interests of authors. The ratification of international copyright in 1891, after more than a half-century of lobbying, gave further leverage to successful writers, who in the increasingly complex environment came to rely on negotiations entrusted to a new figure on the scene, the literary agent. A resurgence of the English drama from the late 1870s onward was driven largely by more lucrative royalty arrangements for playwrights. At the same time, however, the economic pressures behind mass journalism and the burgeoning market for cheap fiction made such writing seem more brutally commodified than ever before – a situation most memorably chronicled in George Gissing's *New Grub Street* (1891).

This supercharged literary marketplace undermined the consoling fiction of a single reading public united by a common human sympathy, which had been an article of faith for critics throughout the period. Critical invective of the 1860s was a harbinger of more direct attacks on mass culture, as it marked the emergence of something like a poetic avant-garde, which defined its aims by severing poetry, and subsequently art generally, from the moral burdens of middle-class respectability. The best poetry, apologists argued, inevitably would confound or affront a "popular" taste that was derided by association with blushing girls (a rhetorical gesture that obliquely recognized the growing feminization of poetry generally). Controversy over appropriate subject matter thus reflected an increasingly divided readership. Controversial novels were nothing new – witness Gaskell's *Ruth*, for example – but the circulating library system carried such enormous weight with publishers that few novelists had dared to challenge Mudie's stranglehold on literary decorum. That grip began to loosen in the 1880s, as writers increasingly looked to France for various models of a literature bold in its subject matter and arcane in its appeal, and found new publishers such as Vizetelly and Heinemann who were daring enough to publish them (sometimes in the face of prosecution). In June 1894 Mudie and Smith themselves abruptly killed off the three-decker novel by announcing that they would no longer pay more than four shillings for a new title – thereby confirming the six-shilling, single-volume format as the standard for new novels, which notably weakened their influence on the subject matter of fiction. The lure of a distinctly French "realism" in the later 1880s prompted a reaction in behalf of "romance," whose apologists aligned fiction with fantasy and dream rather than fidelity to everyday life. But the dichotomy was vexed and unstable, as the world of dreams led into disturbing byways of the psyche. In the "imperial romance" of H. Rider Haggard, the allure of the colonial frontier captured the fascination of "savage" states of consciousness; closer to home, romance readily led into the precincts of criminality, as in Stevenson's *Dr. Jekyll and Mr. Hyde*. The ostensibly escapist energies of romance thus were harnessed to the work of emergent sciences – an anthropology that underwrote the racial hierarchies of empire and a psychology engaged in discerning the increasingly fine lines between normal and deviant behavior.

Science also came to authorize a sense that humankind generally, and Britain in particular, might be subject to momentous biological and cultural decline, which was increasingly summed up as "degeneration." The sense of a social order under siege from various forces, within and without, is felt across a wide body of late-Victorian literature. Some of this apprehension merely reflected the symbolic weight of the calendar, as the end of Victorian's lengthy reign, and of a century unparalleled in its historical self-consciousness, loomed ever nearer. (Wilde captures the association in *Picture of Dorian Gray*: "*Fin du siècle*," sighs one character, to which Lord Henry responds, "*Fin du globe*.") But there were more substantial grounds for concern. The savage destruction of the Franco–Prussian War and the subsequent Paris Commune of 1870–1 was a jolt to faith in progress founded on the superiority of European civilization. In Britain the economy began to decline in relation to the emergent powers of Germany and the United States, and this coincided with increasing strains on the empire, which had displaced Britain's industrial might as a symbol of national pride. Meanwhile, urban poverty came to be an ever more visible and seemingly intractable problem, which to some was fundamentally biological. Towards the end of the period, pessimists found an especially potent symptom of decay in literature itself, particularly in a body of works that came to be labeled "decadent." Ironically, artists who embraced that label were offering their own resistance to the rise of mass culture, but conservative critics tended to conjoin the two as twin symptoms of the decline of civilization. Attacks on elitist art swelled in fierce denunciations of "new woman" fiction and decadent poetry and art, which were viewed as assaults not merely on society but on nature itself – an association that culminated in the spectacular scandal surrounding Oscar Wilde.

Science, Materialism, and Value

In February 1868, *Macmillan's Magazine* published an arresting image of the world of contemporary physics – in words ostensibly uttered by an ancient philosopher. Tennyson's "Lucretius" envisions "Nature" as endless material flux:

> the flaring atom-streams
> And torrents of her myriad universe
> Ruining along the illimitable inane,
> Fly on to class together again, and make
> Another and another frame of things
> For ever.
>
> (ll. 38–43; Tennyson 1969)

This is the same world that Pater would evoke seven months later in his review of Morris's poetry, later the "Conclusion" to *The Renaissance*: that perpetual movement in which "our life ... is but the concurrence, renewed from moment to moment, of forces parting sooner or later on their ways" (Pater 1980: 187). From that "strange, perpetual, weaving and unweaving of ourselves" Pater derived sanction for a life devoted to aesthetic pleasure. Tennyson, unsurprisingly, points a different moral: Lucretius has embraced a "sweet epicurean life," but in this nightmare vision he finds its "sober, settled" pleasures overthrown by the sensuality that undergirds it: that "worst disease of all, /These prodigies of myriad nakednesses, /And twisted shapes of lust, unspeakable, /Abominable ..." (ll. 155–8). Beyond those Epicurean gods who look down on the world in aesthetic detachment (as in so much of Tennyson's poetry) Lucretius's only divinity is Nature itself, and Nature cannot offer him either reason or means to control his own passions: "some unseen monster plays /His vast and filthy hands upon my will, / Wrenching it backward into his" (ll. 219–21).

Tennyson and Pater suggest the centrality of materialism in late-Victorian moral reflection, and the range of potential responses to it. If science has expelled human beings from their unique place in the cosmos, rendering them one more animal form among many, on what grounds can they claim a special meaning and purpose in human life, and a moral code to govern their actions? Are they, too, destined to fall back on brutish instinct – that prospect that Tennyson had conjured up, but seemingly dispelled, in *In Memoriam*? Or might relinquishing the idea of divinity transfigure our very conception of the material world, freeing human beings to find more secure and compelling fulfillment in the here and now?

Scientists, wittingly or no, pressed these questions with remarkable insistence from the late 1860s onwards. In February 1869 the *Fortnightly* published "On the Physical Basis of Life," in which T. H. Huxley (dubbed "Darwin's bulldog" for his vigorous defenses of evolutionary theory) contended that "all vital action," including the very thoughts he was expressing, were "the result of molecular changes in that matter of life" which he called "protoplasm" (Huxley 1917: iv.154). Huxley, who that same year coined the phrase "agnosticism" to define his own religious position, abjured "materialism" as "grave philosophical error" and insisted "our volition counts for something as a condition of the course of events," but the essay seemed to many to embrace what it disclaimed, and to repudiate the grounds of Christian belief; it excited fierce debate. (The very title of the volume in which Huxley collected the essay, *Lay Sermons* [1870], suggests something of the moral significance he attached to science.) In 1871 Darwin's *Descent of Man* reinforced this skepticism when it made explicit a conclusion readily inferred from *The Origin of Species*, that human beings were not the products of a special creation, but were descended from less complex life forms.

The twin impacts of Darwin and materialism made science an inescapable feature of contemporary reflection on value. Victorian intellectual life had not yet bifurcated into what C. P. Snow would call "the two cultures." Although one can see the stirrings of that division in the founding of more specialized journals (*Mind* and *Nature* both date from the early 1870s), humanists and scientists still were engaged in remarkably sustained and vigorous discussion. A central example was the Metaphysical Society, founded in 1869, which gathered a remarkably diverse group of writers and intellectuals, from Huxley to Gladstone and the Catholic Archbishop Manning, to Ruskin and Tennyson, to debate large questions of value and faith in light of contemporary science.

Skepticism authorized by science took many forms. Pater's aestheticism was one important expression of a naturalistic worldview, in which religion became above all a form of aesthetic experience, whose beauty was most apparent to observers detached from its informing belief. C. Winwood Reade created a stir in 1872 with *The Martyrdom of Man*, in which (without repudiating belief in God) he attacked the desire for immortality as morally degrading, "the belief in property after death." Mill's *Autobiography* (1873) rehearsed his view of religious faith as primarily an obstacle to human progress; he described himself as the rare Briton who lacked religious faith not because he had thrown it off, but because he never had it. Along with the *Autobiography*, the other writing he reserved for posthumous publication was his *Three Essays on Religion* (1874), "Nature," "The Utility of Religion," and "Theism." "Nature" was the most provocative, because it attacked the deeply ingrained habit (then as now) of invoking the "natural" as a moral norm. In one light Mill simply extends Baconian empiricism, under which nature is to be studied as a power to be commanded, not a being to be obeyed. But "Nature" also reiterates a disenchantment of the natural world that was registered at mid-century in something like a figurative crisis. Familiar tropes of nature – as maternal figure, as spiritual guide, as a dwelling place of companionable being – were suddenly giving way, in "Nature" (written in 1854), in Ruskin's analysis of the "pathetic fallacy," Rossetti's "The Woodspurge," and the evolutionary stanzas of *In Memoriam* (which John Morley recalled in reading "Nature"). Even in advance of Darwin, nature seemed newly alien. Mill does not lament the passing of a spiritualized nature; "the natural," he suggests, is not merely a false standard of value, but an obstacle to humanity's highest aspirations, inasmuch as it is associated above all with the body, its pleasures and its fragility. This hardly chimes with his praise of uninhibited self-development in *On Liberty*, but it reflects the markedly ascetic streak in Mill's thought. That tension points in turn to a broader conflict: the challenge of reconciling an ideal of culture with a traditional religious order.

The sheer ferment of reflection on faith and value in the 1870s is captured in a comic novel of ideas by the young W. H. Mallock

(1849–1923), which was serialized in *Belgravia Magazine* in 1877. *The New Republic: or Culture, Faith, and Philosophy in an English Country House*, a *roman-à-clef* in the vein of Thomas Love Peacock, captivated readers with its acerbic, thinly disguised burlesques of contemporary intellectual eminences, grounded in what was evidently personal acquaintance. The work clearly settles some personal scores from Mallock's time at Oxford (he was just five years down from Balliol College). Mr. Rose, who is given the chance to read large swaths of Paterian prose in the "languid monotone" that many contemporaries remarked in Pater, is insinuatingly depicted as an erotomaniac, with a special interest in young men: "I rather look upon life as a chamber, which we decorate as we would decorate the chamber of the woman or the youth that we love" (Mallock 1900: 27–8). Dr. Jenkinson is a foolish mouthpiece of Benjamin Jowett's liberal theology, which is depicted as so thoroughly eclectic and secularized that it hardly deserves the label Christian. When the fierce Mr. Herbert (transparently Ruskin, then serving as Slade Professor of Art at Oxford) addresses him as "a consecrated priest of the mystical Church of Christ," "Dr. Jenkinson wince[s] terribly," and he later offers his evening sermon from the stage of a small theatre, its frieze depicting "a long processions of Fauns and Bacchanals," and its curtain blazoned with "Faust on the Brocken, with a long plume, dancing with the young witch, who could boast of no costume at all" (95).

For all of this wicked fun (some of which had to be toned down for book publication; the portrait of Pater helped to blight his prospects at Oxford), the book in its speculative range is surprisingly faithful to the original *Republic*. As thinkers of widely varied expertise still felt engaged in a common ethical quest, they might well recall Plato's speculations about the nature of an ideal society, and the bedrock of reality on which it rested. Mallock gathered in a very wide swath of contemporary thought: along with Pater, Ruskin, Jowett, Carlyle (Donald Gordon), and Matthew Arnold (Mr. Luke), Mallock gives a large place to science, in the figures of Huxley (Mr. Storks), the young mathematician W. K. Clifford (Mr. Saunders), and the physicist John Tyndall (Mr. Stockton). Clifford, a brilliant young Cambridge graduate with the cockiness of a man in his mid-twenties already Professor of Mathematics at University College, London, was much aggrieved by the continuing incursion of religion into science, particularly the persistence of natural theology. He responded with a barrage of lectures and articles, insisting that "the subject of science is the human universe," and fiercely contested the efforts of James Clerk Maxwell, among others, to find free will and divine order in the material world. The very titles bespeak Clifford's self-assurance: "The Unreasonable," "On the Scientific Basis of Morals," "The Ethics of Belief," "The Ethics of Religion," "Cosmic Emotion." The conservative Mallock skewered him as the village atheist, stridently pressing upon all and sundry "an analysis of all the Christian moral sentiments, in which I trace every one of them to such disgusting or paltry origins as shall rob them all of their pestilent *prestige*" (229).

The Irish physicist John Tyndall, a renowned popularizer of science, was a more genial thinker, but even he inflamed the religious establishment with his presidential address to the British Association at Belfast in 1874. There he offered a sweeping historical survey of the triumph of science over theological obstruction, along with the "confession" that in "Matter," traditionally reviled by theology, he had found "the promise and potency of every form and quality of life" (Tyndall 1905: ii.221). Later at the same gathering, the ever-provocative Huxley offered a lecture on "automatism," pressing beyond Tyndall to suggest that consciousness itself might be understood as nothing more than molecular movement. Such a volley might seem to undermine Huxley's own advocacy of educational reform, but the gesture was largely tactical. It aimed above all to chasten the presumptions of those who would dispute the claims of science, and more narrowly to reinforce utilitarian schemes of education at the expense of the aesthetic. An automaton trained in engineering could perform useful work, but what need had it for poetry?

This question became the locus of an epochal debate between Huxley and Arnold. In 1880, in a lecture opening a new "Scientific College" at Birmingham endowed by Sir Josiah Mason, Huxley attacked "the cultured caste," and the model of classical education on which it was grounded, for its disdain of science. Our "modern Humanists," he argued, have fallen into the very habits that Humanism had swept aside during the Renaissance, finding all truth in received authority, whereas science looks "not to authority, nor to what anybody may have thought or said, but to nature ... and bids the learner seek for truth not among words but among things" (Huxley 1905: 133). Huxley's terms closely echo Bacon's war against Scholasticism (with which he aligns Arnold's "the best that has been thought and said"), but they are harnessed to a newly strenuous ethos of scientific objectivity: "the assertion which outstrips the truth is not only a blunder but a crime" (133). Given this imperative, which reinforces the demands of "the business of life," classical education was for most young men simply "a mistake" (136). Without deprecating "real culture," Huxley urged that culture understood in Arnold's terms as a "criticism of life" could be just as readily attained by an exclusively scientific as by an exclusively literary education.

"Science and Culture" mounts a formidable argument, not only in its concessions to the claims of culture ("Industry is a means and not an end") and to Arnold's own catholicity of thought, but because Huxley's own erudition and richly allusive prose were the products of just the sort of education he celebrates. "Our chief apostle of culture," as Huxley called him, accordingly responded with "Literature and Science," a lecture first delivered at Cambridge in 1882 and later revised for delivery in the United States, where Arnold thought its message particularly relevant. Huxley, he urges, leaves out of education nothing less than "the constitution of human nature" – in particular, the insistent human desire to relate fact and value, to connect that which is "interesting" with that which is good and beautiful (Arnold 1960–7: x.61–3). Arnold's account of science is a caricature – it reduces Darwin, for example, to the "interesting" proposition that "our ancestor was a hairy quadruped furnished with a tail and pointed ears" (x.64) – but his argument foregrounds a therapeutic conception of poetry that Mill had suggested half a century earlier in his praise of Wordsworth. Poetry satisfies an "instinct," a "desire," a "need" (the terms echo insistently) that is ultimately "the instinct of self-preservation in humanity" (x.70–1). The appeal is ultimately to life itself. Great writings throughout history "have a fortifying, and elevating, and quickening, and suggestive power, capable of wonderfully helping us to relate the results of modern science to our need for conduct, our need for beauty" (x.68). "Humane letters" are essential for students, because they "will call out their being at more points, will make them live more" (x.70).

The focal point of this vitalizing power, as Arnold evoked it, is poetry, and his most influential defense of poetry came in "The Study of Poetry" (1880), written as an introduction to a multi-volume anthology, *The English Poets*, edited by T. H. Ward. The proliferation of anthologies in the latter half of the century – most famously, F. T. Palgrave's *Golden Treasury* (1861) – reflected Arnold's desire to consolidate literary value and the sense of a national literature amidst the rise of a mass readership. Arnold accordingly addressed the essay to an implied audience uncertain of the value of poetry, and in need of guidance in appreciating it. He begins by urging that poetry has in effect supplanted religion as a source of human value and consolation. "Our religion has materialized itself in the fact ... and now the fact is failing it. But for poetry the idea is everything ... Poetry attaches its emotion to the idea; the idea *is* the fact. The strongest part of our religion today is its unconscious poetry." Increasingly, mankind will "turn to poetry to interpret life for us, to console us, to sustain us," and with this need readers must learn to distinguish true greatness in poetry – to disentangle a "real estimate" of poetic value from the merely "historical" or "personal" estimate (Arnold 196–77: ix.161). To this end, Arnold instances "touchstones" of the truly great, brief passages or even single lines of poetry that exemplify "the very highest poetical quality," which readers may apply in measuring the worth of poetry generally (ix.168). Like all such appeals, Arnold's judgments reflect a distinctive sensibility, in this case one drawn to a "higher seriousness" that too often sounds like mere solemnity. Thus Dryden and Pope become "classics of our prose" rather than poetry, while the "characteristic" note of Chaucer preposterously becomes, not some portion of the *Canterbury Tales*, but the austere piety of *Troilus and Criseyde*: "O martyr souded to virginitee" (ix.175). Dogmatic as the judgments may be, however, their very rigor seems a measure of Arnold's own hunger for consolation; the peremptory tone obscures profound continuities with Paterian impressionism. Arnold disavows the "abstract" in favor of "concrete examples," and (as in "Science and Literature") he makes no effort to explain the emotional impact of the passages he cites, trusting instead to the reader's own response. But he thereby tacitly appeals to the deeply personal engagement that Pater (echoing the earlier Arnold) likewise had urged: "What is this ... to *me*?" (Pater 1980: xx).

Even as Arnold took up the provocation – or, as he saw it, the presumption – of the scientific humanists, he also continued his own critique of doctrinal religion. On the one hand, he deplored a growing rigidity in a theological establishment that felt itself increasingly under siege. At Oxford, Jowett had been deprived of his salary as Professor of Greek owing to his heterodox views. When the liberal A. P. Stanley, Thomas Arnold's biographer, a distinguished religious historian and the Dean of Westminster, invited a group of biblical scholars to participate in a communion ceremony in Westminster Abbey, there were calls for his excommunication because the group included a Unitarian. In *St Paul and Protestantism* (1870), a brief volume collecting three articles from the *Cornhill*, Arnold undertook to pry St Paul away from Protestant dogma, to make him above all a moral exemplar rather than the metaphysician Arnold saw invoked by theologians, and thus to make faith more available to those of a skeptical frame of mind. This emphasis entailed reading the Bible with special attention to its literary nature, a program that Arnold developed in his next work, *Literature and Dogma* (1873). This was Arnold's most sustained and controversial analysis of religion, much of it a reflection on biblical interpretation in broad accordance with the Higher Criticism. Taking up a leading emphasis of both continental scholars and John Henry Newman – and an issue that continues to vex constitutional debate in America – Arnold argued that the meaning of the Bible necessarily changes over time, and thus not only rewards but in effect enjoins ongoing interpretation. Once again, Arnold worked to separate speculative from moral knowledge, approaching religion from the side of conduct, as a pragmatic issue. Faith, Arnold concluded, is "morality touched by emotion," a mode of understanding which impels believers to translate moral precepts into practice. This evacuation of doctrinal content naturally frustrated many – including T. S. Eliot, who mocked Arnold's "counsel to get all the emotional kick of Christianity one can, without the bother of believing it" (T. S. Eliot 1933: 434). After just two installments, publication of the work in the *Cornhill* was cut short by the editor, Leslie Stephen – himself the free-thinking author of *An Agnostic's Apology* – and the waves of criticism provided Arnold with occasion for a subsequent volume, *God and the Bible* (1876). The Bible read as literature, Arnold concluded, best illustrated the power of religious faith as an experience based in human yearning, whose truth resides in its power to meet these needs.

Ruskin during the 1870s was carrying out his own long-running battle against science in prolific but increasingly eccentric fashion (Mallock's Mr. Herbert urges "utterly stamping out and obliterating every general tendency peculiar to our own time" [Mallock 1900: 132]). His output over the decade is almost dizzying in range – and, many argue, in its incoherence. In November 1875 Ruskin had no fewer than seven books in press. In *Val d'Arno* (1872), he was concerned principally with general relations of art and science; three later volumes set out a quirky attack on what Ruskin regarded as the almost demonic pride of science. *Prosperpina*, *Love's Meine*, and *Deucalion* (all lecture series beginning in 1875) fancifully transformed the world of flowers, birds, and stones, respectively, with chains of figurative association and mythic allusion crowding aside scientific analysis – although *Deucalion* offered an unusually pointed attack on contemporary geology, whose analysis of the physics of glacial activity were defiling his youthful memories of Italy and the Alps. Other volumes emerged from lectures given as the Slade Professor of Art at Oxford, to which Ruskin was appointed in 1870. The position gave him a large and steady audience, drawn not only by his reputation but by his often mesmerizing force as a speaker, which Mallock evoked in *The New Republic*: "that singular voice of his, which would often hold the theatre breathless ... There was something strange and aerial in its exquisite modulations that seemed as if it came from a disconsolate spirit, hovering over the waters of Babylon and remembering Zion" (Mallock 1900: 17). The hint of a prophecy grounded in dispossession and despair is a keen insight. Predictably, the lectures ranged widely, with many different arts – from Greek sculpture to contemporary illustration – serving as springboards to reflection on the moral and social order in which they were produced: "You cannot have a landscape by Turner, without a country for him to paint; you cannot have a portrait by Titian, without a man to be portrayed ... The beginning of art is in getting our country clean, and our people beautiful" (Ruskin 1903–12: xxii.153). Less predictably, the lectures became increasingly disjointed and meandering, overwhelmed by trains of personal association, particularly those that led back to an idyllic childhood. Thus the subtitle of *Proserpina*: "*Studies of Wayside Flowers / While the air was yet pure / Among the Alps, and in the Scotland and England which my Father knew.*" As Ruskin himself recognized, he was hovering on the edge of madness.

The most sustained and moving memorial to this struggle is *Fors Clavigera*, an almost unclassifiable serial publication that appeared monthly from January 1871 until 1878, and continued intermittently thereafter until a final letter at Christmas of 1884. *Letters to the Workingmen and Labourers of Great Britain*, as the work is subtitled, was most obviously a complement to his Oxford lectures, which were addressed to a small elite. But the opening letter presents *Fors* as first and foremost a kind of expiation: obliged, Ruskin puts it, "to endeavour to make our English youth care somewhat for the arts ... I must clear myself from all sense of responsibility for the material distress around me" (Ruskin 1903–12: xxviii.13) – a rationale which might have been addressed to almost any audience. The title itself, moreover, may have been the most gnomic of Ruskin's many and increasingly arcane coinages. In the penultimate letter Ruskin declared, "the entire body of teaching throughout the series ... is one steady assertion of the necessity that educated persons should share their thoughts with the uneducated" (xxix.499), but his title reinforces "Of Kings' Treasuries" in stressing the difficulty of true "discernment" in reading. As he explained it in the second letter, *fors* means chance or accident, but in Ruskin's use it also could mean force, fortune, or fortitude; *clavigera* derives from *clava*, club, and *gero*, to bear, but also could suggest key-bearer (clavis) and nail-bearer (clavus). The title is in Latin, he explained, because "the Letters will be on many things ... and I could not have given an English one that meant so many" (xxviii.27–8). The apology carries on his earlier work's emphasis on education as a mode of initiation into a select community, a note likewise central to his quixotic "Guild of St George," founded about the same time as a collective devoted to the preservation of undeveloped land and England's cultural heritage. At the same time, the serial form itself, with each letter opening "My Friends," clearly appealed to a more encompassing sense of community like that conjured in Dickens's addresses to his readers, and Ruskin struggled against the often vatic or peremptory character of his prose by printing and responding to letters from readers. But the letters remained anchored in his daily life, and as that life grew more turbulent, their details veered between sometimes embarrassingly intimate revelation and increasingly opaque webs of private association. They read as if Ruskin's imaginative fixations, even as they threatened his sanity, also were a bulwark against the nightmares of science and other challenges to his faith in the power of art.

Twilight of the Poetic Titans

Arnold's criticism rarely engaged living poets; in "The Study of Poetry" he stopped short of the "burning ground" of the Romantics, which might engulf his touchstones. But his letters suggest that he found little contemporary poetry to inspirit and rejoice him. Arnold's career in the 1870s was almost entirely devoted to criticism; the only volume of poetry to appear was a selection of his verse published in the Golden Treasury series in 1878. In 1873, Tennyson and Browning had 15 or more productive years ahead of them, but had they died in 1873, their poetic reputations would not be substantially different. With the success of *Idylls of the King* and the Imperial Library edition of his works in 1872–3, Tennyson was a wealthy man, receiving a guaranteed 5,000 pounds per year in royalties from his publisher (equivalent to several million dollars today). With this security, Tennyson during the 1870s turned his energies to drama. In 1874 he began work on *Queen Mary*, based on J. A. Froude's *History of England*. The text was published in 1875, and after extensive cutting, under the advice of Henry Irving, a theatrical version ran for 23 performances the following year, with Irving in the role of King Philip. *Harold* appeared later in 1876, but the tepid response to *Queen Mary* deterred managers from staging it. *Becket*, completed in 1879, was not published until 1884, largely because Irving felt that he couldn't afford a production. When Irving finally did stage the play in 1893, after Tennyson's death, it was a great success (he starred, with Ellen Terry as Rosamund); Irving acted it the night he died (13 October 1905). Two shorter plays, *The Cup* and *The Falcon*, were staged in 1879 and 1881, respectively, and published in a single volume in 1884. *Ballads and Other Poems* (1880), was his first book of non-dramatic poetry for eight years. But much of the new work was elegy for the many friends and contemporaries who were passing away.

Browning was far and away the most prolific of the three poets during the 1870s, but also the most eccentric. After the success of *The Ring and the Book*, he turned out a series of long poems, published almost annually, which prompted increasingly exasperated reviews, and have never won much appreciation. Many of their topics hint at worries over fidelity to the memory of his wife. *Balaustion's Adventures, Including a Transcription from Euripides* (1871), centers on a figure reminiscent of the young Elizabeth Barrett – an association differently reinforced by Browning's "transcript" of Euripides's *Alcestis*, whose title character is a woman who has volunteered to die in the place of her husband, with the fervent condition that he never remarry. In 1871, Browning turned to one of Elizabeth's heroes, Louis Napoleon, who had been deposed with the fall of the Second Empire, which was brought about by the Franco–Prussian War of 1870–1, over which he presided with disastrous incompetence. In *Prince Hohenstiel-Schwangau, Saviour of Society*, the exiled leader offers a lengthy, often incoherent apology for his career from asylum in England – a theme that develops Browning's long-standing fascination with casuistry, but which many reviewers, to Browning's exasperation, overlooked, ignoring the rather glaring irony in the subtitle to read the work as a lament for the Second Empire. *Fifine at the Fair* (1872) records the musings of a latter-day Don Juan in nearly 2,400 lines of Alexandrines as he contemplates the alluring sensuality of the gypsy dancer Fifine. The poem is framed as an afternoon seaside stroll of Don Juan with his eminently respectable wife, Elvire – a juxtaposition that suggests the peculiar appeal of the subject for Browning. Though he called the poem "the most metaphysical and boldest he had written since *Sordello*" (Irvine and Honan 1974: 463), it is deeply engaged by wayward desire. Fifine is a figure of commodified sexuality reminiscent of Rossetti's "Jenny" (Rossetti actually took the poem to be an attack on his own), and her seductive appeal throws into relief the bonds and burdens of married life.

A preoccupation with fidelity likewise shapes *Red Cotton Night-Cap Country* (1873), another poem set in France, whose more than 4,000 lines of blank verse Browning produced in a mere six weeks. The poem recounts the grotesque history of a Norman landowner who had tried to drown himself in the Seine, then burned his hands off, and finally leapt to his death from a tower, apparently in an effort to purge his guilt over an extramarital affair. In the following year, Browning developed the concerns of *Balaustion's Adventure* into *Aristophanes's Apology* (1875), narrated by the now married and mature Balaustion, who relates the Greek comedian's attack on Euripides for trying to find beauty in the sordid – a quest Browning clearly meant to echo his own (Euripides was Browning's favorite Greek author). All this comes as 3,500 lines of argument preliminary to a "transcription," as Browning called it, of Euripdes's *Herakles*, the whole running to nearly 6,000 lines, or nearly half of length of *Idylls of the King*. "What has come to him in these latter days?" puzzled Margaret Oliphant, whose frustration was widely echoed (Litzinger and Smalley 1970: 400). The flood continued with *The Inn Album* later in the same year (1875), which unpacks from a few lines inscribed in its title document 3,000 lines of blank verse concerning a rivalry between two men, one "elder," who are competitors in both cards and seduction, and whose struggle over the same woman ends with the death of both the elder rival and the woman herself. The poem draws on the sensational recent trial of "the Tichborne claimant," in which a man claiming to be the long-lost heir to a peerage and a large fortune mesmerized the public for months. But this hardly seemed material from which to extract either lyric pathos or moral enlightenment, and reviewers were as bewildered as ever. The eminence so long and hardly won was beginning to erode, and in his next volume, *Pachiarotto, and How He Worked in Distemper*,

Browning lashed out at his critics. It was his first collection of shorter poems since *Dramatis Personae*, but the effect is surprisingly single-minded in its attention to the audiences for poetry. The title poem offers a slashing satire in Hudibrastic couplets:

> Was it 'grammar' wherein you would coach me –
> You, – pacing in even that paddock
> Of language allotted you *ad hoc*,
> With a clog at your fetlocks, – you – scorners
> Of me free of all of its corners?
>
> (554–8; Browning 1980)

Only with *Dramatic Idyls* (1879) did Browning after seven volumes finally attract enough readers to warrant a second edition. The six monologues have a picturesque clarity lacking in his recent volumes, with a stronger narrative emphasis than in his earlier collections – a note perhaps signaled (along with a bid for renewed popularity) in Browning's appropriation of the Tennysonian term "idyl."

The vanguard of poetry, then, lay elsewhere. Rossetti's 1870 volume made a deep impression, but he published little new poetry over the next decade, and his influence was most notable in the 1880s, after his death. W. E. Henley (1849–1903), a struggling journalist who spent nearly two years in an Edinburgh hospital trying to save his legs from tubercular arthritis, commemorated the ordeal in a remarkable poetic sequence entitled *In Hospital*, which was distinguished both by formal innovation (unrhymed, rhythmically irregular sonnets) and by a striking naturalistic idiom indebted to novelistic description:

> A square, squat room (a cellar on promotion)
> Drab to the soul, drab to the very daylight;
> Plasters astray in unnatural-looking tinware;
> Scissors and lint and apothecary jars.
>
> ("Waiting," ll. 1–4; Henley 1908)

The same experience animated "Invictus" ("the unconquered") a paean to heroic resolve which famously concludes "I am the master of my fate; /I am the captain of my soul" (ll. 15–16). Those lines, worn away to a brittle platitude, regain something of their original force if we recall the physical agony from which they emerged. Henley began publishing the poems in 1875, but they did not appear in volume form until 1888, and his greater literary impact would come as an editor.

In 1870 Swinburne was in the ascendant, particularly (as Arnold put it in a letter) among "the young men at Oxford and Cambridge" (Hyder 1970:117). But Swinburne's stature quickly began to decline, under the conjoint influence of political disappointment and alcohol. After *Songs Before Sunrise* in 1871, a volume largely dedicated to republican struggle in Italy, events dampened Swinburne's political fervor; Mazzini died in 1872, with Italy unified, but under a conservative monarchy rather than republican government, and the French Republic turned out to be not much of an improvement over the Second Empire. In the wake of these events, Swinburne began pondering two major projects, a long poem on the Tristram legend – designed to counter what he thought the meretricious modernizing of Tennyson's version – and a drama on the life of Mary Queen of Scots. This latter was published in 1874 as *Bothwell* – a mammoth work in 60 scenes with 62 characters. The project reflected Swinburne's increasing turn to critical prose and scholarship. In 1872 he published *Under the Microscope*, a freewheeling, sometimes frenzied response to his critics, which was savage to a degree more reminiscent of the age of Pope. A wide-ranging and prolific critic, Swinburne in 1875 published a monograph on the Elizabethan poet Chapman, along with a volume of critical writings on nineteenth-century writers entitled *Essays and Studies*. In 1875 he also brought out another volume of political poetry, *Songs of Two Nations*, which reprinted two published poems, "A Song of Italy" and "Ode on the Proclamation of the French Republic," and a group of 24 sonnets entitled *Dirae* ("Curses").

Work on the classically inspired *Erectheus: A Tragedy* (1876) seems to have appealed to Swinburne in part for the sheer discipline required (reinforced by the scrutiny of Jowett, now the Master of Balliol). From his undergraduate days, Swinburne had abused alcohol, particularly when he was in London, and by the 1870s it was taking a toll on his poetry. When *Poems and Ballads: Second Series* was published in 1878, critics remarked on a greater decorousness, but also a lack of the passion of its predecessor. It is only a third the length of the first volume, and its most striking lyric, "Ave Atque Vale," an elegy for Baudelaire, had been written a decade earlier. There are remarkably few monologues, and in their place more poetry of landscape, along with a great deal more explicit concern with fellow writers, from elegies on Baudelaire, Gautier, Barry Cornwall, and Francois Villon, to a number of formal experiments in the stanza forms associated with early French and Provencal lyric. Swinburne had long been drawn to forms such as the rondel and ballade as occasions to display his formal virtuosity, but here he followed their conventions more exactly (always more difficult in English, with its relative paucity of rhyme) and in even more demanding forms, such as the sestina and double sestina. The volume also includes ten translations from Villon, "our sad bad mad glad brother," as another poem describes that "prince of all ballad-makers," whom Swinburne felt to be a companion spirit. Such continuities as there are with the first *Poems and Ballads* are muted ones, tellingly signaled by several rows of asterisks in "The Complaint of the Fair Armouress" deleting objectionable subject matter. In the following year, Swinburne largely surrendered control of his affairs to his friend Theodore Watts, who installed him at a suburban villa in Putney, The Pines, where he lived for the remainder of his life. Scholars have long debated the effects of this arrangement on Swinburne's subsequent, quite prolific output – and whether The Pines constituted a haven or a prison (or something of both). In any case, Swinburne by 1878 was no longer a byword for daring modern poetry.

One poet who emerged in the decade would become just that, although not until after World War I, when the bulk of his poetry finally appeared. When *Poems* of Gerard Manley Hopkins was published posthumously in 1918, Hopkins was embraced by T. S. Eliot and others as an honorary Modernist. But this gesture effaced the roots of his achievement in the 1860s. Hopkins matriculated at Balliol in 1863, where he was greatly influenced by the criticism of Ruskin and the emergent aestheticism of Pater (who for a time was his tutor), and harbored ambitions to be both a painter and a poet. "A Vision of the Mermaids," written when he was still a schoolboy, was headed by a Blakean illustration, and evoked a Keatsian sensuous hunger reminiscent of Browning's Bishop of St. Praxed's: "And was as tho' some sapphire molten-blue /Were vein'd and streak'd with dusk-deep lazuli, /Or tender pinks with bloody Tyrian dye" (ll. 47–9; Hopkins 1970). This sensuousness was checked, however, by a deeply ascetic strain, which made Hopkins unusually responsive to Newman and the Oxford movement (the *Apologia* was published in his first year at Oxford), and led him to give up painting as "a strain upon the passions which I should think it unsafe to encounter." "The Habit of Perfection" (1866) evokes a paradoxically sensual allure in renunciation itself:

> Shape nothing lips; be lovely-dumb;
> It is the shut, the curfew sent

From there where all surrenders come
Which only makes you eloquent.

(ll. 5–8)

In 1866 Hopkins, who had been raised an Anglican, was received into the Roman Catholic Church by Newman himself, and in 1868 he entered the Society of Jesus. About this time he tried to burn all of his poetry as a gesture of submission, and he wrote no more until late in 1875, when, with the encouragement of his Rector, he wrote a tribute to five Franciscan nuns who had died in a shipwreck on the Thames.

"The Wreck of the Deutschland," an ode of 35 8-line stanzas, is the central poetic expression of Hopkins's faith, which discovers divine grace at work even in outwardly senseless destruction. Hopkins was especially moved by report of one of the nuns crying out as the ship went down, "O Christ, Christ come quickly": as he recast it, "The cross to her she calls Christ to her, christens her wild-worst Best" (l. 192; Hopkins 1970). But the Jesuit periodical to which he offered the poem declined to print it; the editor, like all of Hopkins's early readers, was bewildered by its stunningly eccentric idiom and form.

I am soft sift
In an hourglass – at the wall
Fast, but mined with a motion, a drift,
And it crowds and it combs to the fall;
I steady as a water in a well, to a poise, to a pane
But roped with, always, all the way down from the tall
Fells or flanks of the voel, a vein
Of the gospel proffer, a pressure, a principle, Christ's gift.

(ll. 25–32)

Alliteration and assonance, often drawing on arcane terms or neologisms ("voel," Welsh for "bare hill"), are so emphatic that they tend to distract from parsing the syntax, which in its turn is so labyrinthine with repetition and displacement of common word order that modifiers are often cut adrift from their antecedents to generate sometimes bewildering ambiguity (what is the object of "roped with"?). Not only word order but parts of speech are dislocated, subtly creating a shadow syntax, with words frequently hovering between verb and adjective ("steady") or noun and verb ("poise"), typically evoking a sense of tautly arrested energy or tense balancing of discordant forces. Above all, the meter is so irregular that it seemed impossible to scan.

This metrical eccentricity was the main burden of Hopkins's reflection on his poetry, which he carried out in correspondence among a small circle of friends. The most important of these was Robert Bridges, a far more conservative poet (rewarded with the Laureateship in 1913), for whom Hopkins worked out an intricate explanation of his seeming perversity. In "Wreck of the Deutschland" the reader must "strongly mark the beats of the measure, according to the number belonging to each of the eight lines of the stanza, as the indentation guides the eye" (2, 3, 4, 3, 5, 5, 4, and 6) "not disguising the rhythm and rhyme, as some readers do ... but laying on the beast too much stress rather than too little, not caring whether one, two, three, or more syllables go to a beat ... letting the scansion run on from one line into the next, without break to the end of the stanza," but also adjusting the strength of the stress in proportion to the number of syllables belonging to it – though how one distinguishes between strong and weak stress, Hopkins conceded, "is better told by the ear than by any instruction in short space given" (Hopkins 1970: 256). More generally, Hopkins worked out an elaborate taxonomy of what he called "sprung rhythm," which further incorporated hyper-metric extensions, additional syllables that he called "outriders," which he illustrated by reference to the opening lines of his sonnet, "The Windhover: To Christ Our Lord":

> I caught this morning morning's minion, king-
>   dom of daylight's dauphin, dapple-dawn-drawn Falcon, in his riding
>   Of the rolling level underneath him steady air, and striding
> High there, how he rang upon the rein of a wimpling wing
> In his ecstasy!
>
> (ll. 1–5)

Although these formulae naturally have preoccupied Hopkins scholars, his own summary explanation appealed to a more intuitive understanding. He used the form, he explained, "because it is nearest to the rhythm of prose, that is the native and natural rhythm of speech, the least forced, the most rhetorical and emphatic of all possible rhythms," combining seemingly incompatible virtues, "markedness of rhythm" and "naturalness of expression" (Hopkins 1970: 257).

Deeply indebted to the discipline of Ignatian meditation, which was central to Hopkins's Jesuit training, Hopkins's poetry returns to a wellspring of romantic lyricism, restoring to the natural world a sacral presence that had been emptied out in much poetry at mid-century. His achievement also underscores how often the force of religious faith and doubt – in this as in most epochs – impelled innovations in poetic form. The skepticism of contemporary science found haunting expression in "The City of Dreadful Night," by the Scottish poet and journalist James Thomson, which appeared in the *National Reformer* in 1874. The journal was a central forum of Victorian free-thinking (a euphemism for religious skepticism or atheism), but Thomson's poem offered far more than a rationalist attack on established religion. In 21 sections of varying length comprising roughly 1100 lines, Thomson evokes a dream world akin to Browning's Childe Roland wandering an urban landscape out of Dante's *Inferno* (which supplies one of Thomson's epigraphs). There is little narrative thread linking the sections; the interest is sustained by the nightmarish vignettes of a city of lost faith, in which gloom is punctuated by fierce moral invective. The effect is in keeping with Thomson's sobriquet "B. V.": "Bysshe Vanolis," which signals his allegiance to Shelley and the German poet Novalis, in a suggestive fusion of lyrical atheistic humanism and overwhelming pessimism. "City" in one light delivers on Clough's call for a poetry of modern urban life, but Thomson's landscape (reminiscent at points of Gustav Dore's illustrated *London* [1874]) is largely phantasmagoric, its anonymous, spectral figures finding fellowship in despair, their voices decrying the moral horror of the city and of a world without purpose, attacking any effort to explain it as a divine order, and seeking (in loosely Swinburnian cadences) for relief only in death:

> We do not ask for longer term of strife,
> > Weakness and weariness and nameless woes;
> We do not claim renewed and endless life
> > When this which is our torment here shall close,
> An everlasting conscious inanition!
> We yearn for speedy death in full fruition,
> > Dateless oblivion and divine repose.
> > > > (xiii.36–42; Thomson 1880)

Yet again Tennyson's Lotos Eaters cast their spell, now with little residue of piety to counter their allure. The traditional solace of the heavens has been dissolved by modern physics, laying waste not only a theology but a traditional poetic figure of beauty and longing:

If we could near them with the flight unflown,
  We should but find them worlds as sad as this,
Of suns all self-consuming like our own
  Enringed by planet worlds as much amiss:
They wax and wane through fusion and confusion;
The spheres eternal are a grand illusion,
  The empyrean is a void abyss.

(xvii.22–8)

The poem closes with a haunting image of a "bronze colossus," a "stupendous, superhuman" image of Melancolia, the presiding spirit of the city:

The moving moon and stars from east to west
  Circle before her in the sea of air;
Shadows and glooms glide round her solemn rest.
  Her subjects often gaze up to her there:
The strong to drink new strength of iron endurance,
The weak new terrors; all renewed assurance
  And confirmation of the old despair.

(xxi.78–84)

Though little read today, Thomson's "Night" would have a powerful impact on late Victorian readers, including a young American insurance agent named Wallace Stevens, who took up some of its concerns and even some of its cadences in a more hopeful poem, "Sunday Morning."

The Decline of the Marriage Plot

The novel in the 1870s remained devoted to representations of domestic life, typically organized around the marriage plot. Increasingly, however, rituals of courtship became objects of irony and suspicion, whether out of a sense that they constrained a more complex representation of domestic life, or because other spheres of experience seemed more compelling. The expanding fiction marketplace of the 1870s was supplied in no small part by long-established novelists whose output was often stunningly prolific. Ainsworth, born in 1805, continued to turn out historical fiction even after the genre lost favor with the reading public; although he published 25 novels between 1860 and his death in 1882, he died impoverished, a far cry from the great success of the late 1830s and 1840s. Mary Elizabeth Braddon, "the Queen of the Circulating Libraries," was consistently popular, and even more prolific. Although she had slipped from the peak of her renown in the mid-1860s, when she could command 2,000 pounds per novel, by 1899 57 of her novels had appeared in inexpensive "yellowback" editions, and she continued writing into the new century (she lived until 1915). Diana Mulock Craik (she married in 1865) never rivaled the immense success of *John Halifax Gentleman*, but her output continued unabated; almost annually a new novel appeared, frequently organized around a topical social issue: married women's property rights, spinsterhood, the "deceased wife's sister" debate, the social roles of women generally (her attitudes were conservative). That byword for decorous femininity, Charlotte Yonge, continued to turn out novels of domestic life emphasizing the challenges confronting women, such as *The Clever Woman in the Family* (1865) and *The Pillars of the House* (1873). Editor of the *Monthly Packet* ("Evening Reading for the Younger Members of the English Church") from 1851 to 1890, Yonge also produced a host of stories and longer tales for children; at her death in 1901 more than 150 volumes of her work had been published. More daring heroines poured from the pen of Rhoda Broughton, who could turn out a novel in six weeks, and continued to publish throughout the century, although her writing naturally came to seem less provocative than it had in the 1860s: as she herself would muse, "I began my career as Zola. I finish it as Miss Yonge" (Sutherland 1989: 89).

In the seven years after *East Lynne*, 15 novels by Mrs. Henry Wood appeared; after 1867, when she took over the editorship of the *Argosy* (a rival to Braddon's *Belgravia*), most of her work appeared there, including 11 full-length novels (which gradually moved away from the sensation mode). "That wicked Ouida," who after her early successes moved to Italy – which only enhanced her mystique – had 10 novels published during the 1870s, and ultimately some 44 novels and story collections. Most of her fiction after the 1860s was set on the continent, but its central characters ranged widely, from poor orphans (*Folle Farine* [1871]) to the Russian and Austro-Hungarian aristocracy (*Wanda* [1883]); she even developed a special niche in reflective canine protagonists: *Puck* (1870), *A Dog of Flanders* (1872). (Such was Ouida's fame that newspapers throughout the English-speaking world in 1907 reported on her financial distress – which was blamed on lavish treatment of her dogs.) Annie Edwardes (1830?–96) specialized in bohemian heroines, somewhat in the vein of Broughton, but in the later 1870s and 1880s she found a sympathetic subject in the rise of higher education for women, which offered settings in which Linton's "Girl of the Period" would soon metamorphose into "the new woman." Broughton was also an important model for Helen Mathers, who in 1875 (at 22) scored a major success with *Comin' Thro' The Rye*, and for the next two decades produced nearly a novel a year, most of them similarly depicting bold, independent heroines with unusual (for the time) sexual frankness.

Margaret Oliphant managed to reconcile prolific output with critical esteem – and became Queen Victoria's favorite novelist. In 1876 she concluded her Chronicles of Carlingford with *Phoebe Junior*, a work reminiscent of the previous title in the series, *Miss Marjoribanks*. Here the young woman who seeks to win over Carlingford society is an outsider, the granddaughter of the humble Tozers who had first appeared in *Salem Chapel*; her ambition is hampered by her grandparents' connections with both dissent and trade. The series clearly owed much to Trollope's Chronicles of Barset – Oliphant even echoed the *Last Chronicle* in having the hero's clergyman father forge a promissory note – but Oliphant hardly required Trollope for inspiration; ultimately she would publish twice as much as her better-known contemporary. Trollope himself had continued with the Palliser novels, bringing Phineas Finn back from his Irish exile in *Phineas Redux* (1874), charting the culmination of Plantagenet Palliser's political career in *The Prime Minster* (1876), and finally the predictably wayward lives of his offspring in *The Duke's Children* (1880). Reviewers increasingly failed to share Trollope's admiration for Palliser, and they were further disappointed by the growing "vulgarity" of his fictional world, in which a caddish adventurer like Lopez in *The Prime Minister* could be mistaken for a gentleman. The *Saturday Review*, whose reviewers had long been among Trollope's supporters, pronounced that he had succumbed to an inevitable "decadence" of artistic power (Smalley 1969: 426)

Trollopean "vulgarity" was most concerted in *The Way We Live Now*, serialized in monthly parts from February 1874 to September 1875, which focuses on a shadowy financier. Financial speculation had been a long-standing preoccupation of Victorian writers; it not only generated distinctive forms of suspense, and could link broad reaches of society when it failed, but it was closely tethered to questions of moral character. In the traditional model of the business partnership, the liability of shareholders was unlimited; in the event of a failure, creditors could seize all of a shareholder's property up to the amount of the company's debt, a draconian condition rationalized on the grounds that "full faith and credit" was a moral as well as a financial commitment. When the Joint Stock Companies Act of 1856 legalized limited liability, under which shareholders were liable only to the value of their shares, many commentators attacked the innovation as undermining individual responsibility and licensing speculation. The 1860s saw a broad range of drama and novels dealing with disastrous speculation – most famously *Our Mutual Friend*, but also notably a number of works by Mrs. J. H. Riddell (1832–1906), who built her career around a remarkable knowledge of City finance, which informs such novels as *The Race for Wealth* (1866) and *The Senior Partner* (1881). The failure of the discount firm Overend & Gurney in July 1865 precipitated a broader financial crisis the following year, and a decade later, even as Trollope's novel was still appearing in serial, the firm of Alexander Collie ceased payments, giving the work added topicality.

Whereas earlier novelistic accounts of financial scandal tended to focus on sheer greed – particularly in association with the railway boom of the 1840s – Trollope's title hints at a more sweeping disaffection: traditional moral norms are giving way on all fronts to a corrosive dishonesty and ruthless self-interest. The attack reflects in part Trollope's personal disappointments in both politics and publishing, but it also registers a transformation in economic life, in which the increasingly global reach of financial markets allowed credit to be manipulated on a scale that makes Thackeray's *Vanity Fair* seem bucolic by comparison. Trollope charts the corruption as an erosion of the standards embodied in the gentleman, a norm incarnated in Roger Carbury, who captures Trollope's distinctly middle-class revision of the ideal. Roger is insistently "old-fashioned," a foil to the way everyone else lives now, and thus one of the very few characters in the novel to resist the blandishments of Melmotte, the rogue financier at the heart of the action. Carbury's essentially feudal ethos is rooted in an idealized conception of a lord's responsibilities. "He owes a duty to those who live on his land. He owes a duty to his country. And, though it may seem fantastic to say so, I think he owes a duty to those who have been before him" (Trollope 1982: ii.473). At the same time, Carbury also believes that "a Man's standing in the world should not depend at all upon his wealth" (i. 49) and he speaks skeptically of land itself: "Land is a luxury, and of all luxuries is the most costly" (i. 47). Far from old-fashioned, this stance was distinctly contemporary, and turned out to be highly prescient, as the British economy from the early 1870s slipped into a long agricultural depression, which eroded the value of landed estates – a development that would make the novelistic depiction of affluent country life increasingly nostalgic. Landowners sought income derived from finance, both through marriage and through the corporate directorships that are a focal point of intrigue in Trollope's novel. The latter offered occupation that was not so directly bound up with buying and selling as to seem "trade," but by the same token often was shrouded in mystery – and thus suspicion – as to the actual sources of income.

The book was prompted, Trollope recalled, by "the commercial profligacy of the age." But it originated as "the Carbury book," centering on the figure with which it opens, the widowed writer Lady Carbury (Roger's cousin). The figure of Melmotte came to prominence only after the work was underway, and partly in response to various international scandals unfolding as Trollope wrote; even the great banquet that Melmotte hosts for the Chinese Emperor is based on an event of 1873. But the financier could easily double the strivings of Lady Carbury within Trollope's broadly Carlylean critique of sham labor. Just as the directors of the "South Central Pacific and Mexican Railway" earn money by floating shares, not by building a railway, so Lady Carbury increasingly turns her energies, not to writing better books, but to flattering potential reviewers. (This did not sit well with reviewers.) And meanwhile her idle, parasitic son, Sir Felix, is as woeful an example of Carlyle's Dandiacal Body as can be found anywhere in Victorian literature. Even Melmotte commands some respect from the narrator for his titanic energies, and the stoicism with which he confronts his doom, but the ironically named Sir Felix is beyond happiness or redemption.

While *The Way We Live Now* echoes the social criticism of Carlyle and Ruskin, in his *Autobiography* Trollope distanced himself from their pessimism. "[T]he loudness and extravagance of their lamentations," he urged, are so at odds with prevailing opinion regarding the rising standards of health, education, and general comfort, "that the general effect of their teaching is the opposite of what they have intended" (Trollope 1980a: 354). Yet the novel may be the bleakest of Trollope's works; it depicts a world in which all forms of value have curdled into the pursuit of money, and few characters withstand the trend. "I don't think I'll marry anybody," concludes Melmotte's daughter Marie. "What's the use? It's only money. Nobody cares for anything else"

(Trollope 1982: ii.402). For Lady Carbury, the one unforgivable sin is "romance": "Love is like any other luxury," she tells her daughter. "You have no right to it unless you can afford it" (ii. 324). Although this cynicism – so reminiscent of Linton's "girl of the period" – finds a mouthpiece in nearly all of Trollope's novels, nowhere else is it so prominent or so little qualified. The emphasis creates a certain dissonance: the novel celebrates true romance in a world where it barely exists, and where even Trollope's moral touchstone, Roger Carbury, disdains it as something of mere externals (i.74). Romance thus becomes aligned with the insubstantiality of Melmotte's figments and fictions. This tension helps to explain Trollope's rather defensive account of the novel as a "satire" whose criticism, like most satires, is exaggerated. Certainly that was the note sounded by most reviews, and though Trollope earned 3,000 pounds for the novel, Chapman and Hall lost money on it. That outcome proved to be another historical milestone: *The Way We Live Now* was the last major novel published in the monthly serial format monthly Dickens and Thackeray.

Another major novel of 1874 evoked an almost antithetical social milieu. *Far from the Madding Crowd* is set in the agricultural districts of south western England, a world which by comparison with modern urban life seemed "immutable": "The Citizen's *Then* is the rustic's *Now*" (Hardy 1960: 140). The setting of the novel, along with the narrator's ironic commentary framing similarly pointed and often wry observation from its humble characters, put many readers in mind of George Eliot, particularly *Adam Bede*; some even speculated that she was the author of the anonymous story, which was serialized in the *Cornhill*. When the real authorship became known, it made Thomas Hardy a novelist to be reckoned with. Critics complained of Hardy's frequently shambling, at times ungrammatical prose style, and of his preternaturally erudite and articulate rustic commentators, who seemed too transparently projections of the novelist (reviewers repeatedly invoked demeaning stereotypes of the rural laborer). But nearly all the reviewers found the fictional world vivid and engrossing, with an impact that often recalled that of travel literature. The work gave metropolitan readers a sense of contact with an exotic realm less than a hundred miles from London, "an almost untouched side of human life" in fiction, as one reviewer remarked (Cox 1970: 35). R. D. Blackmore's *Lorna Doone: A Romance of Exmoor* (1869) had drawn on West Country landscapes, but more as a wild backdrop to historical romance. Hardy, somewhat in the vein of William Barnes's Dorset dialect poems, for the first time turned all of his energies into capturing an entire way of life – not merely "provincial life," but the densely textured reality of an essentially pre-modern agrarian world, which was disappearing even as he wrote.

Hardy frames that world with running commentary on a cosmos that seems indifferent to it – taking up the skeptical strain that animated so much writing of the 1870s. Of all Victorian novelists, Hardy was most attentive to the impact of science on faith, and he embraced the bleakest inferences. Pre-industrial life notoriously offered Hardy an arena in which to dramatize the elemental frustrations of human longing, the clash of disparate desires, the mysterious refusal of others to bend to our wills, the ebbing of passion over time, the continual suffering inflicted by the seemingly random drift and caprice of an unsympathetic natural order, that play of impersonal forces that Hardy so frequently evokes as something like a malicious demiurge, whether it be "Doom" or "Fate" or what his poetry more modestly calls "hap." This ironic perspective is sustained by an unusually pervasive, sometimes quite bold attention to sexual desire as a natural force – a feature of Hardy's novels that would deeply impress D. H. Lawrence. *Far from the Madding Crowd* is built around erotic rivalry, as three very different men are captivated by the beautiful but capricious Bathsheba Evendene. She rebuffs the prosperous, middle-aged Boldwood because "she esteemed and liked him, but she did not want him" (Hardy 1960: 127) – "want" conjuring up both erotic longing and the vulnerability of need. Bathsheba, whose rare independence as a landowner nurtures a willful, sometimes baffling impulsiveness, quickly discovers that she does want Sergeant Troy, even though she may not esteem or even like him. He is a stock figure of stage melodrama, but for Hardy that is much of the point, as Bathsheba succumbs solely to his mesmerizing physical presence. The attraction is most vividly evoked when Troy performs the "sword-exercise," which in Hardy's dazzling description becomes less a display than a kind of ravishment. As the blade whirls around Bathsheba's body, "she was enclosed in a firmament of light, and of sharp hisses, resembling a sky-full of meteors close at hand" (177). The consequent psychic disintegration of Boldwood – for whom Troy becomes "the impersonator of Heaven's persistent irony towards him" (350) – is set off by the stolid Gabriel Oak, Bathsheba's third suitor, whose stoicism makes him uniquely able to transcend self-interest; as the narrator puts it, he "looked upon the horizon of circumstances without any special regard to his own standpoint in the midst" (276).

Erotic rivalry is reconfigured when Troy discovers the death of his former lover, who was pregnant with his child. With a perversity that would become a hallmark of the Hardyesque, Troy falls upon her body in its coffin, in the presence of Bathsheba, then declares that the dead woman "is more to me … than ever you were, are, or can be" (281). It is a characteristically grotesque enactment of one of the most insistent motifs of Hardy's fiction: marriage, trumped by the force of desire, becomes an empty form. Though the culminating marriage of Bathsheba and Gabriel resists this inference, the marriage plot is clearly under siege – a point on which Hardy's novel unexpectedly converges with Trollope's.

As *Far from the Madding Crowd* was appearing in the *Cornhill*, the work of another literary iconoclast began appearing in the *Fortnightly*. George Meredith's *Beauchamp's Career*, his most accessible novel to date, charts the defeat of a protean idealism, "the obverse of Byronism," as the narrator puts it; "melodious lamentations, demoniacal scorn, are quite alien to him. His faith is in working and fighting" (Meredith 1910: i.38–9). Nevil Beauchamp, a throwback to the muscular manhood of the 1850s, is a well-born, ardent young naval officer, who gains rapid promotion and recognition for heroism during the Crimean War, then becomes a passionate wooer of a young French aristocrat engaged to a much older man, but withdraws with the utmost grace and goodwill when he realizes his case is hopeless. On his return to England some years later, he is drawn into Radical politics and stands for Parliament, which predictably enrages the Tory uncle who has raised him, and who proceeds to horsewhip Beauchamp's elderly, eccentric political advisor, the aptly named Dr. Shrapnel (modeled on Carlyle). Much of the second volume of the novel turns on Beauchamp's efforts to elicit an apology for this injustice, which are interwoven with other expressions of his political and emotional commitments. Amid this stress on thwarted idealism, marriage is more a matter of course than of passion, and Beauchamp himself weds, almost in passing, a woman he regards only as a friend. The final note of the novel is savagely ironic, underscoring Meredith's temperamental affinities with Hardy. When Beauchamp dies while saving a child from drowning, his uncle and Shrapnel find themselves together thinking, "This is what we have in exchange for Beauchamp! … the insignificant bit of mudbank life remaining in this world in place of him" (ii.315). The bitter enemies are united in their common failure to grasp the driving force of Beauchamp's career.

A more harrowing account of marriage, set against a more hopeful yet eccentric idealism, shapes George Eliot's *Daniel Deronda*, which was serialized in eight monthly parts beginning in February of 1876. The only one of her novels to be set in the present day, *Deronda* is in some ways George Eliot's version of "the way we live now." In the central figure of Gwendolen Harleth, the vanity of Rosamond Vincy is developed into something a good deal more complex, more susceptible of self-awareness and change, which comes about when Gwendolen recognizes her own status as an extension of male vanity. She is a desirable commodity in a world of elegant but ultimately ruthless sexual exchange. That predicament is brought home when poverty drives her to marry a suavely cruel aristocrat, Grandcourt, who constantly solicits an audience to admire her beauty, but slaps down the faintest sign of independence as a disagreeable "spectacle" (Eliot 1995a: 447). The pressure of the male gaze is redoubled throughout the novel in female characters more overtly dependent on performance, the singer Mirah Cohen and the actress Al-Charisi. As these callings solicit both public regard and payment, they are redolent of prostitution, the seeming antithesis of domestic womanhood. Yet this dichotomy is blurred by Gwendolen's plight, as well as that of Grandcourt's abandoned mistress; their experience corrodes the boundary between affective life and exchange that structures so much of the mid-Victorian novel.

Affluent English society confines Deronda himself in a different manner, which enables a far-reaching critique of Victorian liberalism. Raised as the son of a wealthy aristocrat, Deronda has never known the identity of his real parents, and his estrangement from his privileged milieu nurtures a keen sense of its insularity as well as a sympathy with alien worlds. His guardian Sir Hugo Mallinger has given him the education of an English gentleman; he sends Daniel to Cambridge in pursuit of "a little disinterested culture to make head against cotton and capital, especially in the House" (177) – phrasing which suggests how readily Arnold's criticism could be absorbed into an apology for aristocratic power. Deronda, with a sensibility "enlarged by his early habit of thinking himself imaginatively into the experience of others" (511), struggles towards a more cosmopolitan perspective. In the process, he experiences a crisis of vocation in terms familiar from Arnold's criticism, as a conflict between "many-sided sympathy" and "any persistent course of action" (322, 365–45) – a tension which the novel also insistently genders as a clash between feminine and masculine tendencies.

The resolution of this tension gives the novel its distinctive and controversial shape. In *Middlemarch* large moral quests are defeated by personal weakness and a provincial social order. In *Daniel Deronda*, the conflict between sympathy and action, along with Daniel's crisis of vocation, is resolved with his discovery that he was born a Jew. Eliot had explored a very similar conflict in her verse drama *The Spanish Gypsy* (1867), where a young woman about to be married to a Christian nobleman in fifteenth-century Spain discovers that her father is in fact King of the Gypsies, who insists that she renounce her engagement to lead her nation. In both works, national inheritance is a burden of moral obligation writ large; the past is not "the dead hand" of Casaubon's will but a living claim on one's deepest allegiance. But what in the poem feels a stark dilemma becomes a remarkably unruffled choice for Deronda. His discovery concretizes a visionary realm in the novel evoked by the mystical Mordecai, who has claimed the as-yet-bewildered Deronda as a vessel for the transmission of Jewish culture and belief. Mordecai's faith is gratified when Daniel embraces his calling as a leader of the Jewish people in Palestine. In effect, Deronda is offered in unusually literal terms what Burke had called a "choice of inheritance," able as he is to make his identity a matter not only of blood but of conscious decision – a gesture that seems to reconcile the claims of the self-made man and more traditional networks of kinship.

But that resolution is won at the expense of both Englishness and realism itself. James suggested that *Middlemarch* had reached the limit of "the old-fashioned novel"; *Daniel Deronda* strains that limit. Although the marriage plot seems reaffirmed with Daniel's engagement to Mirah, that gesture marks a transcendence of English life rather than a reaffirmation of it. The novel ends with the characters poised on the threshold of new possibility unimaginable in England itself, rather than (as in *Middlemarch*) finding forms of consolation amid the ruins of larger ambitions. A number of contemporary reviewers recognized the force of romance (which leavens the entire narrative in various invocations of heroes both historical and fictional) but most were displeased by it. Their responses shaped a critical discussion that persisted until quite recently, particularly through the influential formulations of Henry James. Like most early critics, James divided the novel into two "halves," what he called the English and the Jewish, and found the presentation of Gwendolen's world much superior to that surrounding Daniel's discovery of his heritage. But James may also have recognized in the resolution of the novel a compromise of the cosmopolitanism with which Daniel had grappled, and which meant so much to James himself. In the terms of the novel, Daniel cannot be both an Englishman and a Jew. His choice of inheritance passes a grim verdict on the moral claims of Englishness.

In outline Meredith's *The Egoist* (1879) recalls the ordeal of Gwendolen Harcourt and other renderings of domestic tyranny. A young woman engaged to a wealthy man soon feels herself suffocating, trapped in a cage, looking forward to "a life-long imprisonment." Sir Willoughby Patterne, outwardly all that his surname suggests – a handsome, charming baronet, a consummate gentleman in command of a great fortune – turns out to embody a ravening insecurity, which seeks everywhere a mirror to his own vanity. Most suggestively, he epitomizes a subtle contempt informing Victorian idealizations of womanhood, "an infinite grossness in the demand for purity infinite, spotless bloom" (Meredith 1968: 151). But Meredith's novel is, as the subtitle puts it, "A Comedy in Narrative," and few Victorian novels so vividly evoke the power of genre. For Meredith, the focal interest lies in the struggle to "read" other characters, and thereby come to a better grasp of one's own, within the elaborate masks and roles of affluent English life. "Comedy is a game played to throw reflections upon social life, and it deals with human nature in the drawing-room of civilized men and women, where we have no dust of the outer world, no mire, no violent crashes" (33). The rules of the game are exacting. Sir Willoughby lives oblivious to his own self-worship, because none dares to point it out. Once Clara Middleton realizes her predicament, "She could not, as in a dear melodrama, from the aim of a pointed finger denounce him," so strongly is she bound by "the rigor of those laws of decency which are a garment to ladies of pure breeding" (519–20). Melodrama, this suggests, cannot do justice to drawing-room society – the genre is too closely intertwined with more plebeian desires. The nature of the game also explains the lack of outward incident in the novel, which devotes nearly all of three volumes to a few weeks at Patterne Hall, where Clara is staying with her father in anticipation of her marriage, while making increasingly desperate efforts to win a freedom she feels can come only from Sir Willoughby withdrawing his offer of marriage – a gesture which is deeply offensive to the Egoist. By this point in his career Meredith enjoyed a clear *succes d'estime*; not to know him, remarked Margaret Oliphant (one of the more exasperated reviewers of the novel), "is to argue yourself unknown" (I. Williams 1971: 236), and nearly all reviewers pronounced the book the most important novel of the season. But it was a respect without much real affection; nearly all reviewers agreed that Meredith was too clever by half, and that his style (like that of Carlyle, to whom he was frequently compared) was a willful obstacle to wider appreciation. Even W. E. Henley, perhaps his staunchest supporter (who managed to enthuse over the book in three different reviews), called him "the owner and the victim of a monstrous cleverness which will neither be suppressed nor admonished" (I. Williams 1971: 207).

The Aesthetic Movement

The aesthetic movement came to sum up a broad range of phenomena linked by the celebration of beauty in everyday life. Its proximate origin was the rise of Pre-Raphaelite painting; while Ruskin's criticism – particularly his defense of those young artists – was an important influence, his austere moralism always sat uneasily with the likes of Rossetti. In the early 1860s, the Pre-Raphaelite example was extended into the world of interior decoration, particularly with the 1861 founding of Morris, Marshall, Faulkner and Company, whose guiding spirit was William Morris. Unlike earlier design firms, Morris's company set itself against the burgeoning world of machine-made housewares, following Ruskin's celebration of handicraft in the production of stained glass, wallpaper, furniture, fabrics, and other items. These quickly gained a circle of admirers, and reinforced a notion of advanced (and affluent) taste available only to an elite – an association that grated against Morris's increasingly socialist politics. Meanwhile, the "fleshly school" controversy played its part in linking Rossetti's seductive canvases to a cult of the senses that repudiated bourgeois decorum, while Pater's *Renaissance* set forth a model of aesthetic education and critical prose uniquely attuned (so it seemed) to the last refinements of beautiful form. In 1878 Sir Coutts Lindsay opened the Grosvenor Gallery, which offered space to artists who had been refused by the Royal Academy, among them a number of painters affiliated with Pre-Raphaelite style, as well as the American-born, French-trained J. M. W. Whistler. To many cognoscenti Whistler's impressionist canvases had surpassed the work of Burne-Jones, the most influential painter of the mid-1870s, but when Ruskin viewed *Nocturne in Black and Gold* at the Grosvenor in June 1878, he responded in the next issue of *Fors Clavigera* with high dudgeon: "I have seen, and heard, much of Cockney impudence before now; but never expected to hear a coxcomb ask two hundred guineas for flinging a pot of paint in the public's face" (Ruskin 1903: xxix.160). Even 60 years after Keats, "Cockney" still could sting, and Whistler responded by suing Ruskin for libel. The public enjoyed the spectacle of two spokesmen for beauty trading savage personal invective – culminating in a verdict in Whistler's favor, but with the derisory damages of one farthing and no reimbursement for legal costs, which ultimately bankrupted him.

More was at stake, however, than art-world vanity. Ultimately the quarrel turned on the very nature of art. Whistler's canvases were pressing in the direction of a view that Pater had enunciated in an essay on Giorgione published in the *Fortnightly* in October 1877. Complaining of what he called "the false generalization of all art into forms of poetry" – the habit of looking to various works for some quantum of "imaginative thought," while neglecting the formal, sensuous appeal of the work – Pater urged that "a great picture has no more definite message for us than an accidental play and sunlight and shadow for a few moments on the wall or floor" (Pater 1980: 104). More sweepingly, *"All art constantly aspires to the condition of music"* (Pater's uncharacteristic emphasis), that art form in which it is most difficult to disentangle "subject matter" from the form itself. Ironically, this prescription clashed with Pater's own practice; his account of the Mona Lisa, to look no further, is deeply invested in eliciting a "poetry" informing her enigmatic glance. But deprecating the "mere matter" of an artwork undercut the traditional moral burdens of art, freeing the artist to choose almost any subject matter, on the grounds that the "essentially artistic" element is the treatment, the technique. This was dangerous ground, which may explain why Pater withheld "The School of Giorgione" from *The Renaissance* until the third edition of 1888. The celebration of form would become especially notorious in the work of the man who became the most visible icon of the aesthetic movement, indeed who most transformed it into the register of spectacle, Oscar Wilde.

Wilde (1854–1900) was an Irish Protestant born in Dublin, his father a well-known surgeon knighted for his achievements, his mother an author of Irish nationalist verse, which she published over the name "Speranza." After three years at Trinity College in Dublin, Wilde won a scholarship to Magdalen College, Oxford, where he came under the spell of Pater and Ruskin as he developed a reputation as a great talker and wit (shorn of his Irish accent) and as a dandy in his dress. When

Wilde came down from Oxford in 1878, after the triumph of a double First and the Newdigate Prize for poetry, he half-heartedly looked into a number of career paths – as a Fellow at Magdalen, as a journalist, even as the member of an archeological expedition – while living off a rapidly dwindling inheritance. He quickly became known as a man about town in London, cultivating the acquaintance of artists and writers, and of young actresses and society women – most notably Sarah Bernhardt and the young Lily Langtry, then creating a sensation as "the Jersey Lily," and soon to be the mistress of the Prince of Wales. Flattered and amused by Wilde's extravagant, witty devotion, expressed in both flowers and poetry, these prominent women enjoyed his company, and his large figure stood out in any crowd – reinforced by his flamboyant dress, which included knee breeches and a tail coat cut in the outline of a cello.

Aside from the intrinsic pleasures of notoriety – which secured him the acquaintance of the Prince himself – Wilde had the further goal of securing production of a play he had written, *Vera, or the Nihilists*, about an assassination plot on the Czar. He was not successful, but meanwhile he was himself becoming an object of theatrical attention. In December 1877 *The Grasshopper* burlesqued the opening of the Grosvenor Gallery; more substantially, *Where's The Cat?* began a successful run at the Criterion in November of 1880, with Herbert Beerbohm Tree playing the role of a young aesthete in Wilde's highly wrought manner ("I feel like – like a room without a dado"). *Punch* pounced on the new phenomenon, and began a series of caricatures of young aesthetes by George du Maurier, the most famous in the issue of 30 October 1880, with a line Wilde allegedly had uttered while still at Oxford: "I do hope I can live up to my blue china." These images in turn prompted a series of sketches involving two aesthetic types, the poet Maudle and the painter Postlethwaite, which ran almost weekly. The editor of *Punch*, F. C. Burnand, seeing the theatrical possibilities, turned a French comedy into *The Colonel*, with an aesthete named Lambert Stryke distinguished by Wilde's mannerisms, which opened in February 1881. The Prince of Wales persuaded Queen Victoria herself to attend, and a royal command performance was offered at Balmoral.

The reputation quickly grew. In April Gilbert and Sullivan's *Patience* opened at the Opera Comique, and later transferred to the newly built Savoy Theater, which the producer D'Oyly Carte had designed expressly for Gilbert and Sullivan productions. Here Wilde was echoed in the memorable character of Bunthorne, whose lines have become the anthology version of aestheticism: "If you're anxious for to shine in the high aesthetic line, as a man of culture rare" (l. 1: Gilbert 1924). "Line" neatly links theater and career – and for the rest of 1881 Wilde's life would imitate art. In April 1881 David Bogue brought out Wilde's *Poems*, cementing the public image of Wilde as a being of effete, arcane pleasures, and in September 1881 D'Oyly Carte himself, who had opened *Patience* to great success in New York, thought it would be a good idea to put the original on display. He proposed to split with Wilde the profits of a lecture tour of North America, which took Wilde on an exhausting round from New York to San Francisco and back, then north to Montreal and Toronto and back south to Alabama and Georgia, by way of dozens of stopping points, then back to New England and the Canadian maritimes. The tour garnered immense publicity in both Britain and America, enlivened by a host of comic anecdotes – such as Wilde sharing a lunch of whiskies with silver miners in Leadville, Colorado (Ellmann 1988: 204).

But Wilde's fame had more than a hint of danger about it, which would soon color the whole body of literature and art affiliated with aestheticism. Even before Wilde appeared on the scene, the world of "culture" had become associated with effeminacy, first as a sphere of contemplation removed from the world of action, then as an arena of desire that threw off the self-discipline crucial to Victorian masculinity. The objections aroused by the "Conclusion" to Pater's *The Renaissance* – further inflamed by Mallock's mockery in *The New Republic* – led Pater to withdraw it from the second edition of 1877, on the grounds (as he explained when reinstating it for the third) that "it might possibly mislead some of those young men into whose hands it might fall" (Pater 1980: 186n). The danger, as Mallock's satire suggested, was partly same-sex desire, and this association was amplified in the histrionic self-display of Wilde. There was little ground for this identification in Wilde's *Poems*. Predominantly sonnets, mostly devoted to foreign sites or famous historical figures – with a few glances at French models, such as "Impression du Matin" and some longer, weary progresses of a disillusioned soul drifting through exotically colored landscapes – the volume is deeply derivative. *Punch* called it "Swinburne and water," but Keats and water is more like it. Wilde's languid rhythms could hardly be more remote from Swinburne, whose presence is conjured only by occasional vague erotic insinuation, as in the longest poem in the volume, "Charmides": "he whose life had been /A fiery poise of sin, a splendid shame" (ll. 173–4; Wilde 1909). The most incisive review was a witty attack on the floor of the Oxford Union, which voted to reject Wilde's gift of the book on the grounds that the poems in it were mostly not by Wilde at all, but by a host of better-known authors already represented in the Union library. The volume is indeed steeped in echoes of earlier poets, but that derivative character is in keeping with an aura of refined and rarefied pleasure, of an Art fundamentally arcane and esoteric, that was mocked in *Punch*: "How Consummate! How Perfect! How Supreme, Precious and Blessed! Nay, how Utter!" (25 December 1880). By the 1880s, however, unutterable transgression was becoming more insistently linked with the sin that had only recently acquired a name – homosexuality – and something in Wilde's extravagant and mocking wit very early on suggested that this was the terminus of his daring insinuation. Over the course of his career, Wilde's dandyistic performance would give a new meaning to "effeminacy" and become the model of a new form of sexual identity. "The high aesthetic line" came to seem more dangerous than ever.

Aesthetic Poetry

The suspicion aroused by Wilde echoed attacks on Swinburne and "the fleshly school" a decade earlier, where poetic eccentricity also was denounced by affiliation with unmanly sexual interests. Those attacks reverberated in obituary tributes to Rossetti, who died in 1882. Rossetti's two-volume *Poems* of 1881 expanded *The House of Life* to 100 sonnets, but the additions to the 1870 volume did not substantially alter Rossetti's standing, for both admirers and detractors, as a benchmark of poetic daring. In Pater's 1883 account (reprinted in *Appreciations* [1888]), Rossetti's work embodied a unique way of seeing "which recognized no conventional sense of what poetry was called to be" (Pater 1913: 206); it was in this sense "mainly of the esoteric order," but thereby enlarged the very field of poetry (218). J. H. Shairp, however, in the conservative *Contemporary Review* complained of "a morbid and unmanly art and poetry" in which "what is new, rare, or antique, is valued because it is so, and not for any spiritual meaning or intrinsic worth ... Hence comes affectation, and artificial, as opposed to natural and healthy, sentiment." "This worship of sensuous beauty for its own sake," he continued, "is not the growth of a vigorous age, strong in manhood, but is the mark of a late and decadent civilization" (Shairp 1884: 23, 20).

The shadow of "decadence" came to haunt literature over the next two decades, but the worry echoes a recurrent note in this history. It recasts critical resistance throughout the period to poetry that seemed eccentric or narrowly subjective – a stance so powerful that it drives Shairp himself to contend that Shakespeare's sonnets "are not obscure, but transparent" (29). Formerly, however, "morbid and unmanly art" had been attacked principally as a personal or party failing; increasingly it would be seen as a symptom of cultural decline, frequently understood in quasi-biological terms. Some of the harping on manhood may reflect an anxiety that the very field of poetry was becoming increasingly feminized. That prospect had been worried at great length in an 1870 volume, *Poetry of the Period* by Alfred Austin (collecting articles written before the attacks on Rossetti). Tennyson's poetry, Austin explained, could be summed up in a single word, "feminine"; "the most unreasonable of his worshippers would not dare for one moment ... to call him masculine" (Austin 1870: 78). Likewise Swinburne, who has failed to live up to his own celebration of "a masculine strain" (84). In sum, "Scott was manly and masculine; his successors are just as distinctly feminine." By 1880, the ascendance of Swinburne and Rossetti unsettled a more traditional gendering of poetry (perhaps in response, Austin in 1893 would be named Poet Laureate following the death of Tennyson).

With Tennysonian manhood increasingly seen as an ideal either unrealized, nostalgic, or misplaced (although still frequently instanced as a paradigm of healthy moral balance), the often skeptical gaze that women's poetry brought to gender and desire was less easily marginalized. Women poets were increasingly reviewed in leading literary journals such as the *Academy* and the *Athenaeum*, and also served as reviewers themselves – a privilege long accorded them with regard to fiction, but more grudgingly surrendered in the realm of poetry. Much of women's poetry in the 1880s continued to grapple with images of femininity embedded in lyric tradition. Christina Rossetti, who typically approached the issue with teasing obliquity, addressed it more directly in a sonnet sequence entitled *Monna Innominata*, published in *A Pageant and Other Poems* (1881). Here Rossetti imagines the "unnamed ladies" of Italian troubadour poetry, silent objects of masculine praise, offered the chance to speak for themselves, and thus to seem more fully human, relieved from "the exceptional penalty of exceptional honour" (C. Rossetti 1979–90: ii.86). Vitality inheres not in static, single-minded devotion, but in divergence of experience and subtle frustrations of longing, which frequently undercut the clichés of Petrarchan love.

> I wish I could remember, that first day,
>   First hour, first moment of your meeting me,
>   If bright or dim the season, it might be
> Summer or winter for aught I can say;
> So unrecorded did it slip away ...
> (ll. v.–5; Rossetti 1979–90)

Subtle dissonance gave way to more emphatic assertion of feminine independence in another volume of 1881, *Xantippe and Other Verse*, whose anonymous author turned out to be the 19-year-old Amy Levy (1861–89), a student at Newnham College, Cambridge. The title poem is an extended monologue spoken by the wife of Socrates, a byword for shrewishness whom Levy re-imagines as an intellectual woman rebuffed by her husband: "He wished a household vessel" (l. 237). Though the poem recalls the thematic engagements of Barrett Browning, stylistically it owes more to Mrs. Browning's husband – a conjoint influence echoed in a number of monologues by women through the 1880s. Levy's poetry is striking in its union of stylistic variety with a recurrent bleakness unrelieved by religious consolation. Thus what might seem a mere parody of Swinburne, "Felo de Se" (Self-Murder), concludes with a haunting sense of anomie, all the more harrowing for what by comparison with the male poet seems an exhausted understatement:

> I have neither a voice nor hands, nor any friend nor a foe;
> I am I – just a Pulse of Pain – I am I, that is all I know.
> For Life, and the sickness of Life, and Death and desire to die; –
> They have passed away like the Smoke, here is nothing but Pain and I.
> (ll. 25–8)

In "A Minor Poet," the title poem of Levy's 1884 volume, the suicidal speaker feels a moment of relief in surveying a vista of London rooftops, but cannot escape the sense that "Underneath /For all the sunset glory, Pain is king" (ll. 107–8). In the same volume, "Magdalen" is rare among "fallen woman" poems in refusing moral consolation, whether through rebuke of the social order or through appeal to justice in another world. For the dying speaker, "Nothing is known or understood /Save only Pain" (ll. 74–5).

One of Levy's final poems, "A Ballad of Religion and Marriage," captures with edgy playfulness an impatience with the burdens of conventional womanhood:

> Grant in a million years at most,
> Folk shall be neither pairs nor odd –
> Alas! We shan't be there to boast
> 'Marriage has gone the way of God.'
>
> (ll. 29–32)

Levy's restiveness at the burdens of both marriage and the stigmatizing of those "odd" women leading a single life reflected in part her passionate attraction to other women. Unconventional desire is more explicit in the collaborative writings of Katherine Bradley (1846–1914) and Edith Cooper (1862–1913), aunt and niece who wrote under the name "Michael Field" – declaring themselves in an early lyric to be "Against the world … /Poets and lovers ever more" ("It was deep April," ll. 4–6; Field 2000). That note of buoyant fulfillment, a frequent presence in their verse, is a marked contrast to the more somber and perplexed tones of so much poetry of the decade. During the 1880s they published several volumes of poetic drama, which led the aging Robert Browning to seek out the acquaintance of his "two dear Greek woman," as he came to call them. The tag derives from the inspiration for much of their early work; their first volume of lyrics, *Long Ago* (1889), was inspired by Henry Wharton's 1885 edition of Sappho's fragments, which restored the feminine pronoun to the addressee of the poems. Sappho had long figured as a peculiarly fraught emblem of the woman poet, an image of both lyric power and unrequited longing, which drove her to suicide. (Hence, among many other reworkings, Christina Rossetti's wry lyric of 1862, "What Sappho would have said had her leap cured instead of killing her.") Michael Field's Sappho gives expression to a wider range of experience, from a youthful rapture at the glance of the fisherman Phaon ("Dreamless from happy sleep I woke") to a more detached survey of the range of desire:

> Maids, not to you my mind doth change;
> Men I defy, allure, estrange,
> Prostrate, make bond or free:

Soft as the stream beneath the plane
To you I sing my love's refrain;
Between us is no thought of pain,
     Peril, satiety.
          ("Maids, not to you" [ll. 1–7; Field 2000)])

A sometimes fierce eroticism, ("Come, Gorgo, put the rug in place; and passionate recline; /I live to see thee in thy grace, /Dark, virulent, divine") is answered by subtle chastening and refinement, varieties of *askesis* or self-discipline – a structure especially gratifying to Pater, who singled out as his favorite in the volume a poem that opens

When through thy breast wild wrath doth spread
And work the inmost being harm,
Leave thou the fiery word unsaid,
     Guard thee; be calm.
                              (ll. 1–4; Field 2000)

Life-Writing

The early 1880s formed an unusually crowded chapter in the necrology of Victorian literature. George Eliot died in December 1880; Disraeli, Carlyle, and Ainsworth in the following year; Rossetti and Trollope in 1882. Save for the now-obscure and impoverished Ainsworth, their passing occasioned a great deal of reminiscence, of varying forms. It seemed a biographer's field day – but that trope is too jaunty to accord with the burdens attached to Victorian life-writing. The genre was most fully institutionalized in the *Dictionary of National Biography*, launched in 1885 under the general editorship of Leslie Stephen, with the first series completed in 66 volumes in 1900. The *DNB* was the ultimate codification of mid-Victorian individualism, for which biography was a crucial moral vehicle – arguably the most effective genre in stimulating readers to emulation, as Samuel Smiles recognized. But biographers seeking truth often encountered conflicting imperatives. Exemplarity seemed to require a subject largely free of moral blemish ("What a brute you were to tell me to read Keats's letters," Arnold complained to Clough in 1848 [Arnold 1932: 106]), while the hallowing of privacy often drew veils over personal life; it is hard to imagine Boswell's *Life of Johnson* being written in the 1870s. Carlyle himself had felt the pressure much earlier, writing in the late

1830s of Lockhart's mammoth *Life of Scott*, "A Damocles' sword of *Respectability* hangs forever over the poor English life-writer (as it does over poor English Life in general) and reduces him to the verge of paralysis" (Carlyle 1869: iii.154). Carlyle's own biography of the skeptical John Sterling, which tried to rescue that independent, iconoclastic mind from more orthodox religious appropriations, had aroused a good deal of resistance when it appeared in 1851. The more common route was a resolute avoidance of controversy, which turned many mid-Victorian memoirs into monuments of decorous piety. Mary Kingsley's *Life and Letters* of her husband Charles, who died in 1876, gives virtually no hint of his family life, let alone the deep sexual and religious anxieties that energized his writings and also caused recurrent breakdowns.

Politicians posed special challenges and temptations to the biographer, because their lives were thoroughly involved in ongoing, often bitter partisanship – none more than Disraeli. Of his fellow eminences, Disraeli went out with the greatest literary flourish; having recently stepped down as Prime Minister, in 1880 he commanded from Longmans 10,000 pounds for his final novel, *Endymion*. But throughout his career, Disraeli's Jewish ancestry had made him an object of widespread anti-Semitic suspicion – even to many of his allies – as "the Hebrew conjurer," a deft performer whose avowed Christian faith was merely a screen for treacherous loyalties to an alien culture. This rhetoric inflamed the many early memoirs and biographies, which fed on conspiracy theorizing reminiscent of that which had dogged the Tractarians. Even the more dispassionate accounts tended to be openly polemical, stalking horses in ongoing party debates. The exemplary "Victorian" life and letters in six volumes, by two *Times* journalists, W. F. Moneypenny and George Buckle, did not appear until 1920, and even this was largely devoted to championing Disraeli's politics, particularly his imperialism. By contrast, George Otto Trevelyan's biography of his uncle, *Life and Letters of Lord Macaulay* (1876), could more readily call on the rhetoric of early Victorian earnestness (recalling Stanley's *Life of Arnold*) to describe the career of the Whig historian and politician, not least because Macaulay had grown up at the heart of "the Clapham sect," his father a close associate of the great evangelical Wilberforce.

Literary figures typically were less polarizing, but John Forster's biography of Dickens, which appeared in 1872, underscored the peculiar difficulties facing even biographers of the widely loved. The public naturally expected an authorized biography, which Forster, the editor of the *Examiner* and Dickens's close friend and advisor, seemed well equipped to supply. But Dickens was the most public of all Victorian novelists, a status he developed not only through his many appearances and readings, but also through the mode of address in his novels and voluminous journalism, where he cultivated a peculiar sense of intimacy with his readership. Readers liked to feel that they knew Charles Dickens, and as a man not only great but good. This writer who conveyed a heart-wringing sympathy for the poor and downtrodden, who celebrated the small, everyday habits and satisfactions of humble English life, who conveyed compassion for all but the most irredeemable characters of his works: how could such a man not be a moral paragon himself? Forster failed to grasp the weight of these expectations. A notoriously pompous fellow, he frustrated some readers simply through his own thrusting prominence in the story he told: one reviewer called it "The Autobiography of John Forster with Recollections of Charles Dickens." Still, most readers were gripped by the great revelation of the first volume, the difficult home life that culminated in Dickens's employment at the age of 12 in Warren's blacking factory. For many, this movingly confirmed Dickens's heroic self-fashioning, although for some it only underscored his lack of formal education and the enduring taint of vulgarity – always a stigma for unsympathetic readers such as J. F. Stephen. The second volume was more unsettling. Although Forster deftly skirted the controversy surrounding Dickens's very public separation from his wife in 1858, as his financial advisor Forster was privy to a good deal of correspondence showing Dickens's preoccupation with his income, and could not resist printing a great deal of it. Though hardly surprising in the career of a spectacularly self-made man, this emphasis dismayed many readers who wished to believe that great writing is a moral calling unblemished by concern for material gain. Still worse, Forster was unable to grasp the obscure psychological investments motivating the hectic, ultimately self-destructive reading tours of Dickens's final decade, and he left the impression that they were driven almost wholly by greed. The upshot, many critics agreed, was that Dickens's reputation had been unwittingly diminished by a biographer who wrote in a spirit of adulation.

Autobiography offered a more supple vehicle for representing a life and the values to which it was dedicated – as Newman's *Apologia* (1864) and Mill's *Autobiography* (1874) very differently showed. Mill began drafting his work in 1854, feeling "the sacred duty of fixing in my writing, so that it may not die with me, everything that I have in my mind which is capable of assisting the destruction of error and the growth of just feelings and true opinions" (Mill 1963–91: xxvii.644). The result was a tension bordering on paradox, in which Mill sought to submerge the individual in a collective pursuit of enlightenment. His personal history, he declares, is uninteresting as a narrative, and his character in no way exceptional, save for the exemplary significance of "the successive phases of any mind which was always pressing forward" within an age of intellectual transition. This is a startling disclaimer for one of the most famous accounts of human education ever written, which describes Mill learning Greek at three, Latin at the age of seven, logic at 12, and political economy at 13. But the emphasis is in keeping with Mill's political faith, which was grounded in the utilitarian axiom that progress rested in education, not in the exceptional student. Despite the pronounced elitism in Mill's political thought, it was crucial to believe that enlightenment was open to more than a select few.

This emphasis on system – and the good fortune of having been exposed to expert authority – is borne out even in the most intimate section of the narrative, "A Crisis in My Mental History," where Mill famously analyzes a prolonged depression in his early twenties, not as a by-product of sexual frustration, family dynamics, or a young man's insecure place in the world – causes we would be more likely to explore today – but as a direct outgrowth of the precepts of his education. The emphasis on logical analysis, he concluded, had worn away the grounds for feeling any pleasure in its triumph, or indeed in anything – an injury that Mill famously repaired through the reading of Wordsworth, and by a new attention to "the internal culture of the individual." Self-scrutiny thus became an analysis of the limitations of Benthamism itself, and a powerful apology for distinctly aesthetic pleasure. This emphasis helps to explain a remarkable feature of Mill's crisis: no evidence of it is to be found anywhere else – neither in Mill's own contemporary writings nor in other observations of this very visible young public man. It may be, of course, that the ascetic Mill was simply well schooled in the art of self-suppression. But there is more than a hint here that the "Crisis" was largely shaped in retrospect, as something that *ought* to have been triggered by the peculiar emphases of that early education. Autobiography in this light becomes a mode of pointed social and moral criticism, its work closely akin to that of Mill's more explicit and far-reaching revision of utilitarian thought in the essays on Bentham and Coleridge (Loesberg 1977).

The power of life-writing as a mode of critical reflection is one of several neglected confluences between Mill's thought and that of Pater, whose *Study in the History of the Renaissance* was published in 1873. In the essays of this volume, as in his later development of what he called "Imaginary Portraits," individual lives encapsulate epochal cultural change – the emergence of Christianity, the Renaissance, the *Aufklarung* in Germany. Various forms of experience and belief can be evoked with special clarity and poignancy within a single career. Hence Pater's most sustained exploration of aestheticism and religious faith would appear in *Marius the Epicurean* (1885), a *Bildungsroman* set in Antonine Rome. In this regard, both Pater and Mill reflect the enduring force of Carlyle's example – one reminder of how often gulfs of temperament are bridged by the common dilemma of framing new schemes of value in an increasingly secular world. Pater's celebration of art, which would be enormously influential over the remainder of the century, has suffered from being reduced to a stigmatized temperament – a reduction that the terms of his own criticism certainly encouraged. But for all his seeming divergence from Mill, Pater's aestheticism is in important respects a development of the Benthamite insistence on pleasure as the central measure of value. The more substantial opposition between the two comes in Pater's resistance to system and method Pater left logic to Bentham's hedonic calculus, and occupied himself almost exclusively with Mill's "internal culture," in pursuit of an art of living exquisitely.

Autobiography could be woven into a host of different genres, such as Arnold's wry self-references in his criticism. Ruskin's fragmentary *Praeterita* (1900), which grew out of *Fors Clavigera*, suggests the formal range that was possible, as it alternates bluff, tendentious political credo – "I am a Tory of the old school" – with reminiscence of lyrical intensity, summoning up at moments the aura of a prose poem. *Praeterita*, however, reflects not only Ruskin's habitual disdain for his public – which he could afford to affront – but also his increasing oblivion to it; the work was cut short by Ruskin's final descent into madness in 1889. Most writers felt more constrained by norms of decorum, particularly (as Newman testified) a model of reserve that deprecated not only intimate exposure but excessive self-assertion. Newman of course braved such intimacy in his *Apologia*, because his polemical aim required a close interweave of public and private. Only through vindicating his personal character could he give requisite support to his chosen faith.

Sometimes the burden of disclosure was too great. John Addington Symonds in the late 1880s produced a memoir differently bound to exploring the relations between public and private life. It was devoted principally to explaining – primarily to himself and his family (a wife and three children) but also to a broader, potentially sympathetic readership – the nature and burdens of his homosexuality. His executor, Horatio Brown, decided the work could not be published, and it remained in manuscript for nearly a century. A similar reserve burdened Samuel Butler, who from 1873 to 1884 worked at an autobiographical family novel focused on the life of Ernest Pontifex. Pontifex struggles to escape the influence of a brutal, humorless clergyman father closely modeled on Butler's own – who was in turn the son of a famous father, Dr. Samuel Butler, Headmaster of Shrewsbury School and Bishop of Lichfield. Ernest (the name is pointedly ironic) serves as vehicle for bitter, sometimes savage reflection on the psychological legacies of evangelical faith and the stern discipline it so often imposed:

> To parents who wish to lead a quiet life I would say: Tell your children that they are naughty – much naughtier than most children. Point to the young people of some acquaintances as models of perfection and impress your own children with a deep sense of their own inferiority, You carry so many more guns than they do that they cannot fight you. This is called moral influence. (Butler 1966: 57)

Even the iconoclastic Butler lacked the courage to publish so harsh a portrait; it appeared as *The Way of All Flesh* only in 1903, a year after his death.

The burdens of reserve posed a special challenge to women writers. On the one hand, a great deal of women's writing turned on bearing witness to an inner life or domestic world hidden from public view. Hence the force of Jane Eyre's assertion, "Nobody knows how many rebellions besides political rebellions ferment in the masses of life which people earth" (Brontë 1996: 125). Yet such claims frequently were rebuked as a self-defeating betrayal of womanhood itself. This was a widespread response to Caroline Norton, for example, whose pioneering appeals for women's domestic rights were greeted uneasily even by women who shared her views, largely because they so insisted on her personal hardships. Florence Nightingale's bitterly personal invective against the lot of women, *Cassandra*, was written in 1852, but was suppressed throughout her lifetime, in part because it would have tarnished the image of the coolly impassioned Lady with the Lamp (it was published only in 1928).

Harriet Martineau's *Autobiography*, written in 1855 but published posthumously in 1876, anticipates just this suspicion of over-exposure. It opens with an Introduction in the spirit of Mill, explaining her work as a "duty" and an "obligation" to her reformist principles, but one that could be carried out only by suppressing all personal correspondence on the grounds of respect for privacy. While conceding that many writers have prepared their letters for publication, she rejoined, "What were the letters worth, as letters, when these arrangements became known?" (Martineau 1877: i.5). The query redounds uneasily on the autobiographer's own project, but it underscores the reticence that even unconventional women felt obliged to preserve towards the private sphere. Not even this circumspection, however, could save Martineau from Margaret Oliphant's objection that her work was unwomanly, an offense against "good taste, as well as against all family loyalty and the needful and graceful restraints of private life." More often, the memoirs of well-known women defused such objections by being couched as quasi-domestic projects. Thus Oliphant applauded the *Personal Recollections of Mary Somerville* (1871), in part because the famous scientist's life had been dictated to and edited by her daughter – a strategy similar to that employed in Anna Jameson's *Memoir* (1879) and Mary Howitt's *Autobiography* (1889) (Fraser 1997: 184–6).

To such suspicions George Eliot seemed especially vulnerable. At her death she was no longer quite the force she had been a decade earlier, with the publication of *Middlemarch*. Following *Daniel Deronda* in 1876, Eliot devoted herself to a collection of essays published as *Impressions of Theophrastus Such* (1879), a quirky assemblage of "characters" in the tradition of the ancient Greek Theophrastus, coupled with more topical engagements, such as an analysis of anti-Semitism (in "The Modern Hep! Hep! Hep!"), all of this mediated by the (sketchy) title persona. But though the reception of the volume was tepid, Eliot remained a figure of immense authority and esteem, despite the stigma of her relationship with G. H. Lewes. Lewes died in 1878, and soon after the grieving Eliot finished editing his *Problems of Life and Mind* (1874–9) she married the much younger John Cross (thereby eliciting a letter from the brother who had refused all contact with her for 25 years, welcoming her back into the family). When Eliot died, Cross undertook the widow's chore in preparing a memoir, but he could not face the prospect of addressing her unorthodox life. The three-volume life that appeared in 1883 blithely avoided nearly all allusion to any compromising fact – no small achievement in narrating the life of so unconventional a woman.

Carlyle's authorized life was a more inflammatory one, which brought his career back to public attention after a long eclipse, and prompted a fierce debate not only about his character but also about the decorums of biography and the relations of public and private life. Carlyle had bequeathed the task to his long-time admirer and friend, the historian James Anthony Froude, to whom he had granted before his death virtually unchecked access to his personal papers, as well as the letters and journals of his late wife, Jane, which recorded a recurrent, vivaciously bitter sense of neglect by her famous husband. Carlyle himself had drawn extensively on these writings in a memoir of his wife that he composed after her sudden death in 1866, in which he excoriated himself for his failings as a husband, and for obscuring her own literary gifts while he basked in celebrity. The revelations were an affront to biographical tact, in which domestic harmony was a central locus of value, but Froude felt that scrupulous truth-telling was in keeping with the great man's example. In March 1881, just a month after Carlyle's death, his *Reminiscences* were published in two volumes. Initially the outcry centered on Carlyle's acerbic characterizations of public figures, but it soon veered toward the treatment of his wife. Froude was roundly denounced for publishing such intimate details, which in turn undermined the hero-worship they ostensibly furthered. Battered but undaunted, Froude pressed ahead with a four-volume biography, the first two volumes (covering the first half Carlyle's life, up until his move to London) appearing in 1882, and the second half in 1884. Recognizing the frequent pettiness of Carlyle's behavior and the pain he had inflicted on his wife, Froude ended up framing the conflict as an inescapable clash between literary genius and marriage itself. But many readers drew a more despairing inference: if even so great a stoic as Carlyle could not live up to the role of a considerate husband, the very institution of marriage might seem threatened – a view soon to be widely echoed in a variety of forums. The controversy also undermined a familiar idealization of the male writer's life, which had often seemed to confound the dichotomies of public and private life. Writing had seemed a harmonious yet productive withdrawal from the world, its influence akin to that of an idealized femininity. As Froude's biography challenged this fantasy of literature as a special kind of work, it also offered a caustic version of domesticity itself (T. Broughton 1999: 83–112).

The notion of literature as a special calling was more pointedly deflated with the 1883 publication of Anthony Trollope's *Autobiography*, a year after his death, in the midst of the Carlyle controversy. Trollope was not responding to the controversy (he had composed the work in 1875–6) but he framed his own career as exemplary of an earlier era of novel-writing, when titans walked the earth. In one sense the *Autobiography* is a comic pendant to the satire in *The Way We Live Now*: against the idea of literary genius it celebrates honest, disciplined labor, and chronicles in great detail – itemized to pounds, shillings, and pence – the success that Trollope derived from his hard work. What disconcerted many readers, however, was less Trollope's unabashed attention to the bottom line than his concerted demystification of novel-writing itself. Critics had long regretted Trollope's prodigious output, suggesting that it resulted in too much "mechanical" writing, but the *Autobiography* seemed to embrace this characterization. Over against appeals to the novelist's dependence on inspiration, Trollope rejoined "it would not be more absurd if the shoemaker were to wait for inspiration" (Trollope 1980a: 121). The work of the novelist was no more exalted than that of the cobbler, the craft followed "rules of labour similar to those which an artisan or mechanic is forced to obey" (323), which for Trollope amounted to producing 250 words per quarter-hour for two to three hours every day, in all seasons and wherever he might be. Any less disciplined conception grounded in a notion of "genius," Trollope suggests at several points, is simply "unmanly." The very alienation of the writer's labor reaffirms his masculinity, along with a proper separation of public and private spheres. To be sure, Trollope also protests that the novelist's calling remains undervalued, shadowed as it is by the old suspicion that novels at their best "are but innocent" (218). But he answers this with a straightforward moralism: the novelist "must preach his own sermons with the same purpose as the clergyman," and "can make virtue alluring and vice ugly, while he charms his reader instead of wearying him" (223). Appealing to the novels of Edgeworth, Austen, Scott, Thackeray, Dickens, and George Eliot, he asks, can any reader "find a scene, or a passage, or a word that would teach a girl to be immodest, or a man to be dishonest? When men in their pages have been described as dishonest and women as immodest, have they not been punished?" (223).

Morality and the Novel

For the growing number of novelists who felt constrained by the moral strictures of Mudie's and the monthlies, Trollope's apology for the novel seemed simplistic, even fatuous. But the provocation initiated a host of critical exchanges, which called attention to the increasingly protean character of the novel as a form. Trollope's sharpest critic in this vein was Henry James (1843–1917). Born to a wealthy family in New York City, James spent much of his twenties traveling in Europe, and in 1875, shortly after publishing his first novel, *Roderick Hudson*, he decided to settle there – writing to his family "I take possession of the old world – I inhale it – I appropriate it!" (Edel 1977: 429). *Roderick Hudson*, the story of an aspiring sculptor from Northampton, Massachusetts, drawn to Rome to pursue his art, already signals James's departure from the world of Trollope, in a theme that reverberates throughout his career: the allure of a distinctly aesthetic passion that conflicts with more worldly ambitions.

James came to wider notice with another subject, Americans abroad. This reflected an increasing commerce, both economic and romantic, between New World and Old, as leisured Americans ventured to Europe (much like James) as the locus of "culture," a storehouse of history and arts that their own country lacked, and which they frequently absorbed not merely through material appropriation but through social amalgamation, marriage to European aristocrats offering Americans a unique prestige and the noble lineage a vital infusion of money. James's breakthrough came with *Daisy Miller*, a novella serialized in the *Cornhill* in 1878, which describes a young American in Rome left too much to her own devices. The title quickly became shorthand for a social type, "the American girl," an elusive, often dangerous compound of hardy independence and wide-eyed innocence set loose in a world far more complex and treacherous than she recognizes. James's most substantial early work in this vein, *Portrait of a Lady* (1881), recounts the story of Isabel Archer, "a certain young woman affronting her destiny" (James 1966: x–xi). Endowed with an immense fortune by a cousin who wishes her to enjoy a special freedom, Isabel instead becomes trammeled by her wealth. She declines marriage to a wealthy, handsome, liberal-minded English peer precisely because the secure and prominent social standing he offers seems too confining, and instead accepts an American expatriate and connoisseur of shadowy past and dubious means. Gilbert Osmond soon reveals himself to be an unscrupulous adventurer whose connoisseurship recalls that of Browning's Duke of Ferrara (the novel's title subtly gestures to the parallel): artistic pleasure is warped by the lust for social recognition and power, which shackles Isabel's independence in a psychic prison reminiscent of Gwendolen Harleth's.

Portrait of a Lady offers a searching critique of aestheticism as well as transatlantic society, but it also reflects James's own affiliations with French realism, particularly those novelists who worked in the spirit of Flaubert as votaries of art for art. Though James, like nearly all novelists working in England, was less bold in his choice of subject than his French counterparts, he admired the realist commitment to formal design and carefully calibrated effect, frequently calling on tropes of painterly composition to capture their aspirations. English novels, by contrast, seemed mere "baggy monsters." From such a vantage, the art of Trollope (which James professed to admire) was "gross, importunate" in its very abundance (Smalley 1969: 525), enshrining a disdain for artistic design "as a kind of affectation" (Smalley 1969: 525). He took particular umbrage at Trollope's "suicidal satisfaction" in puncturing the novelist's illusion of narrating events that are assumed to be real – perhaps forgetting that few novel-readers are so credulous.

Implicit in this allegiance to form, as in Pater's contemporary appeal to the trope of music as the archetype of all art, is a rebuke to moral constraints on artistic subject matter. James himself made no direct assaults on those strictures, and allowed that Trollope and English novelists generally were "more at home in the moral world" than the French (Smalley 1969: 540). But the aesthetic movement aroused an increasingly visceral opposition in other commentators; as the first flush of novelty passed, and the movement became increasingly visible and far-reaching in its influence, parody gave way to more barbed attacks. In 1884, Vernon Lee turned heads with *Miss Brown*, a novel that reverses the myth of Pygmalion and Galatea: a young painter-poet transforms an orphaned servant-girl into a social and aesthetic sensation, only to have her conclude that he needs to be rescued from the callousness of his aestheticism. Vernon Lee was the pen name of Violet Paget (1856–1935), a precocious art critic and scholar of independent means whose own career in many ways resembled that of the aesthetes she portrayed. She wrote in a variety of genres and mingled in various artistic and intellectual avant-gardes – she was a friend and admirer of Pater – and certainly knew artistic London well enough to produce what amounted to a *roman-à-clef*. The central characters evoke in particular Rossetti and the young Jane Burden, who would marry Morris and become one of Rossetti's favorite models (Lee's hero is mesmerized by Miss Brown's enigmatic beauty), and the novel also includes recognizable portraits of Wilde and Swinburne, among others. The focal point of attack is the credo "Everything is legitimate for the sake of an artistic effect" (Lee 2004: 194), uttered by the protagonist Walter Hamlin, whose "moral nullity" (320) is brought home to Anne Brown when he refuses to rehabilitate the filthy hovels on his country estate, because they form part of a picturesque landscape (244–8).

Miss Brown is a minor novel (James himself, to whom Lee dedicated it, recoiled from what he thought its moral coarseness), but its concerns register some tectonic shifts in late-Victorian society that would become central preoccupations of the novel. Anne Brown herself confronts new intellectual and social possibilities open to affluent young women who no longer felt their destinies so tightly harnessed to marriage, particularly with the opening of university education to women in the late 1870s. "No man that ever breathed," she comes to realize, "could have satisfied cravings which were in reality not after a man, but after a higher life, a more complete activity, a nobler aim" (210). This aspiration for "a higher life" would become a hallmark of the "new woman," who as both social type and novelistic convention became a topic of fierce debate for the remainder of the century. For some women, the world of art, most vividly embodied in the aesthetic movement, offered that reward. But Anne's disillusionment with Hamlin points to an alternate path: alleviating the suffering of the poor.

Urban poverty of course had been a long-standing preoccupation of Victorian writers. But from *Sketches by Boz* through the studies of Mayhew and other "social investigators," humanitarian sympathy frequently warred with sheer fascination at the exotic – a frisson all the more pronounced when the exotic appeared in such proximity to one's own world. The quasi-ethnographic stance is captured in the trope of the narrator as a traveler to an alien, frequently dangerous world in the byways of London. Thus James Greenwood enjoyed great success with a series of studies, such as *The Seven Curses of London* (1869), *In Strange Company* (1873), and *The Wilds of London* (1874), which originated in his persona as "the amateur casual," an investigator into the life of the casual laborer, the most abject of London's poor, who struggled to survive without regular employment or housing. The potential fearfulness of such characters was dampened by the sense – amply conveyed by Dickens – that such poverty was confined to small pockets of the city. But by the late 1870s, public attention was recognizing the huge extent of largely unbroken poverty and desperate housing conditions in the East End. Here was a reality that disarmed the picturesque, and cried out for intervention. As Andrew Mearns proclaimed in his influential pamphlet *The Bitter Cry of Outcast London* (1883), "seething in the very centre of our great cites, concealed by the thinnest crust of civilization and decency, is a vast mass of moral corruption, of heart-breaking misery and absolute godlessness" (Mearns 1883:1). That urgency would be compounded by growing economic depression beginning in 1884, which fueled an increasing sense of desperation among workers, an increasingly vigorous radical politics, including sporadic anarchist bombings, and an acute sense of vulnerability to widespread social unrest, most notably rioting in 8 February, 1886, which panicked much of the West End, and another pitched battle on "Bloody Sunday," 13 November, 1887.

Some of the propertied classes reacted, as Beatrice Webb would later describe it, with "a new consciousness of sin," others with a deep sense of threat, but across the spectrum a new understanding of urban poverty was taking hold. For much of the period the deepest problems of poverty were seen to be a function of moral character, less a matter of abysmal housing and unemployment than of "demoralization." Increasingly, however, the urban environment itself came to seem a moral and physical quagmire, a source of "degeneration" from whose corrupting effect the poor could not rescue themselves unassisted (Stedman Jones 1984: 285–96). Ultimately this shift would motivate greater state intervention, but more immediately it prompted calls for greater contact between rich and poor, which prompted affluent reformists to take up residence in the East End – forming "settlements" of which the most influential would be Toynbee House, founded in 1883. Although "settlement" itself is redolent of a colonial project – extending civilization to benighted regions of the earth – the settlement movement and the aesthetic movement became (as *Miss Brown* suggests) for many cognoscenti twinned forms of rebellion from middle-class respectability. In practice, the two pursuits mingled and overlapped; a great deal of "radical" intelligentsia moved with relative ease between the East End and the Grosvenor Gallery, Whistler and Fabianism (a socialist offshoot of the ethical "Fellowship of the New Life"), and novelists found many engaging subjects in this convergence of distant social spheres and the clash of dissonant styles. Could one reconcile the claims of beauty and realism? Lee's novel reflects an ongoing puritanical mistrust of those who dedicated themselves to beauty. Like a belated Harold Skimpole, the effete dilettante of *Bleak House*, Walter Hamlin's aesthetic sensibility becomes a sign of personal pathology and social disorder, which is registered in his oblivion to the suffering around him. In the intervening decades, however, the likes of Skimpole seemed more difficult to quarantine. The urban poor had become more alien and threatening to an affluent readership, and thus also a more urgent object of representation. At the same time, they offered writers an aesthetic challenge: their lives were an affront to Mudie's sensibilities, but also a provocation to extend the moral boundaries of art while elaborating new senses of social possibility and danger.

The gulf between West End and East End came to prominence in the novel largely through the success of Walter Besant's *All Sorts and Conditions of Men* (1882). Throughout the 1870s, Besant (1836–1901) almost annually had produced a novel in partnership with James Rice, the editor of *Once a Week*. After Rice's death in 1882, Besant on his own scored an enormous success with *All Sorts*, which describes two young people finding a sense of connection to a social world seemingly remote from their own. Harry Le Breton discovers that he is not the orphan of an aristocratic officer, as he had been led to believe, but Harry Goslett, son of a humble sergeant of the line killed in the Indian Mutiny. Angela Marsden Messenger, wealthy brewery heiress, is a young graduate of the recently founded Newnham College, who wishes to pursue a socially productive life, but unlike Dorothea Brooke sees no way to reconcile this ambition with marriage, and thus sets up as a seamstress organizing better working conditions for her sisters in the trade. When their paths converge, they hatch the scheme of a "Palace of Delight," where East End residents might find healthy, uplifting relief from the monotony of their existence.

The impact of Besant's novel was unusually palpable: the dream of a "Palace of Delight" actually came to fruition in a substantial "People's Palace" erected in the Mile End Road in 1887 (and opened by Queen Victoria in the year of her Jubilee). But the book's popularity owed less to its social portrait than to its fundamentally romantic framing. It is a fantasy out of Shakespearian comedy, with two children of wealth assuming new identities and finding happiness denied them in their more privileged world. The novel is more overtly indebted to Dickens, particularly his attack on utilitarian gloom in *Hard Times*, the People's

Palace is a more refined version of Sleary's Circus. The setting is likewise Dickensian, as the disguised protagonists work out their project, and inevitably fall in love, while living in a boarding house filled with variously eccentric inhabitants; the plot even turns up a purloined inheritance that is ultimately restored to the rightful heir. The novel is of its time, however, in the particular emphases of the social agenda, which register the influence of Ruskin, Wilde, and the aesthetic movement: "It will not be mere amusement, but a more concerted training of imagination: there were to be professors of Painting, Drawing, Sculpture, and Design; and lectures in Furniture, Colour, and Architecture," and, with a bow to William Morris, "There shall be no house in the East End," the girl cried, "that shall not have its panels painted by one member of the family, its woodwork carved by another, its furniture designed by a third, its windows planted with flowers by another" (Besant 1997: 74).

Rising political agitation (in which Morris figured prominently), combined with Besant's great success, made the urban poor a staple of novels of the later 1880s, although the forms of engagement ranged widely. In 1884, M. Charlotte Despard (1844–1939), who had turned out romantic novels for Tinsley in the 1870s, produced *A Voice from the Dim Millions, Being the True History of a Working Woman*. Margaret Harkness, writing as "John Law" (1861–1921), wrote a series of more pointedly political novels, of which the best known is *A City Girl* (1887), the story of an East End seamstress that was admired by Friedrich Engels. At times the engagements were pressed to more lurid ends, on the model of Emile Zola in France, who was drawn to lives of the poor as the focal point of a literary program that aligned the writer and the scientist, as two observers scrupulously detached from the objects of their gaze. The novelist on Zola's model regarded human life as simply one part of a natural rather than a moral order – hence the term "naturalism" to describe his program – and he tested this quasi-scientific detachment with accounts of the most sordid details of life among the brutally poor, chronicling the ravages of hunger, drunkenness, and venereal disease. Though English writers rarely approached Zola's extreme, Julia Frankau (1864–1916) caused a small tempest in this vein with *A Babe in Bohemia* (1889), the story of an epileptic girl with venereal disease, who eventually slashes her own throat. Even Henry James was drawn into the vogue of the urban novel, producing *The Princess Cassmassima* (1885), in which rich and poor are drawn into contact as participants in a shadowy anarchist plot. Poverty posed special difficulties to James's imagination, however, as reflected in the very name of his protagonist, Hyacinth Robinson, which ostensibly registers his mixed ancestry as the child of a working-class French mother and a British lord.

The most enduring novels of urban life in the 1880s were written by George Gissing (1857–1903): *Workers In the Dawn* (1880), *The Unclassed* (1884), *Thyrza* (1887), and *The Nether World* (1889). Although Gissing also made forays into sardonic observation of middle-class milieus, in *Isabel Clarendon* (1886), *Demos* (1886), and *A Life's Morning* (1888), he became noted above all for his depictions of the urban working classes. Whereas Besant's social imagination is summed up in the maxim, "All sorts and conditions of men are pretty much alike" (Besant 1997: 179), Gissing's early fiction drew on his own sense of social marginality, enforced by personal experience, which made poverty seem powerfully constitutive of human character. Son of a Wakefield pharmacist, Gissing at 15 won a scholarship to Owens College, Manchester, where he achieved academic distinction before being expelled on the verge of graduation, after being sentenced to a month in prison for stealing from a cloakroom – money he took in order to help a 17-year-old prostitute, Nell Robinson.

Gissing's first novel (whose publication he financed with a small inheritance) is a thinly veiled recounting of his life with Nell, whom he married even as he was describing his protagonist's agony in coping with a drunken, violent, thieving wife who sold herself for liquor. The relationship with his wife may have crystallized a radical ambivalence, in which a deep sympathy for poverty frequently collides with disgust at the degradation of the poor. Poverty in Gissing's novels is often hard to disentangle from vulgarity. His early fiction is full of aspiring writers like Arthur Golding, hero of *Workers in the Dawn*, who dream of lifting themselves and others out of poverty by sheer force of disciplined imagination. This very personal romance of course hews closely to the ideal of Arnoldian culture, which would be widely echoed in the decade, not only in fiction but also in the East End settlement movement. But Gissing's faith in cultural uplift was fragile at best, and in *Demos* he ridicules the aspirations of working-class politics, setting socialism into demeaning contrast with middle-class aestheticism. (The novel drew added topicality from its appearance shortly after the February riots.) In *Thyrza*, the novel's title figure is a hat-maker in Lambeth whose "artist's soul" blossoms in her aspiration to become an opera singer, but at the same time estranges her from the poverty around her, even as the recognition of her talent is fleeting and her happiness elusive. Critics noted the idealizing impulse in the character, so much like the doomed heroines she performs in her operas. In *The Nether World*, Gissing withheld even this consolation. Here the young woman who dreams of escaping her dreary life through a career as an actress is attacked by a rival (on stage and in their manager's affections) and ends up horribly scarred by vitriol.

Reviewers of Gissing, while frequently troubled by the bleak subject matter, typically cleared his novels of the taint of Zola's naturalism; they were not prurient – which is to say, their treatment of sexuality was sufficiently muted and oblique. But another novelist threw down the gauntlet. George Moore (1852–1933), son of an Irish country squire, became Zola's leading apologist in Britain, taking up his example in *A Modern Lover* (1883). The story follows the career of an aspiring artist moving between relationships with an older woman who supports him financially – the better to encourage the (false) view that she is his mistress – and the strong-willed aristocrat he eventually marries, in part because she more aggressively promotes his career. The novel offers engaging insights into the London and Parisian art worlds – one of the models for the protagonist was the painter Alma-Tadema – but most commentary turned on the novel's offhand boldness in treating sexuality, warning Moore that he should "leave off studying Zola" if he wished to develop his talent. The circulating libraries exerted more forceful pressure by ordering only a few dozen copies; when an exasperated Moore asked his publisher to bring out a single volume edition at 6 shillings, Tinsley replied that it would be of no use, since W. H. Smith controlled all the bookstalls, "and what he will not circulate, he will not sell" (Frazier 2000: 93).

Thus began Moore's long battle with Mudie and Smith, which he pursued more aggressively in his next novel, *A Mummer's Wife*, published by Henry Vizetelly, Zola's English publisher. In this story of a Potteries dressmaker, Kate Ede, drawn into adultery by a touring actor, Moore offered something like an English *Madame Bovary*. The book offended not only in its representation of illicit passion, as well as its clinical detailing of both her husband's asthma and her own descent into alcoholism, but in the suggestion that Kate has been drawn to her sorry end by the illusions of romantic fiction – the very life blood of the circulating libraries. Mudie's and Smith's predictably banned the book. But Moore had launched a preemptive assault on the libraries with an article in *Longman's*, "A New Censorship of Literature," and subsequently a pamphlet, *Literature at Nurse*, which echoed defenses of Swinburne nearly two decades earlier, attacking those who would confine the reading of fiction to "young girls and widows of sedentary habits" (Frazier 2000: 114). The familiar gendered appeal was successful; a number of reviewers in the weeklies came to Moore's defense, and the first edition sold out within six weeks, with six further impressions over the next four years. But the resistance to Zolaism was far from over.

Moore's "New Censorship" contributed to a swelling discussion of the moral burdens of fiction, which had been sparked by an 1884 Besant lecture entitled, "The Art of Fiction," and would continue for the next decade. Besant was a driving force in the 1884 founding of the Society of Authors, a guild devoted to enhancing the professional standing and financial rewards of authorship, particularly through the pursuit of international copyright. His lecture at the Royal Institution, soon reprinted in *Longman's*, defends fiction from traditional suspicion and disdain, arguing that it is "an Art in every way worthy to be called the equal of the Arts of Painting, Sculpture, Music, and Poetry," and that, in pointed contrast to Trollope's recent pronouncements, it is "far removed from the mere mechanical arts" and cannot be taught to those not "endowed with the natural and necessary gifts" (Besant 1971: 228). James could hardly disagree with these precepts; the mere discussion of the novel as an artistic form was a welcome approach to French reflection. But James was troubled by Besant's prescriptive moralism, and he responded with his own "Art of Fiction," also published in *Longman's*, which has entirely eclipsed Besant's essay. The novel, James objected, lives upon creative freedom, and its main issues are "questions (in the widest sense) of execution" (James 1971: 254). While it is bound to the representation of life, the result are "as various as the temperament of man," and "successful in proportion as they reveal a particular mind, different from others" (244). Here is the Paterian note that would become central to the rise of Modernism; while still declaring fidelity to external experience, the finished product is valued less for that correspondence than for the distinction of the creative temper at work. Besant had declared that the novelist is bound by personal experience, and should not attempt to venture beyond his own class or familiar geography. This was aggravated by a familiar moralism, which saddled the novelist with "conscious moral purpose." For James, these prescriptions shackled the imagination. "There is no impression of life, no manner of seeing it and feeling it, to which the plan of the novelist may not offer a place" (255), He conceded that "the air of reality (solidity of specification)" was "the supreme virtue of the novel," but that could be produced only though fidelity to one's own impressions: "impressions *are* experience" and therefore he urged the aspiring writer, "Try to be one of the people on whom nothing is lost!" (247).

Romance

James's "The Art of Fiction" would have a major influence on twentieth-century literary criticism, particularly as it gestured toward an idea of organic narrative form that was taken up by the so-called "New Criticism." But its subsequent prominence has obscured a pointed contemporary response, which marks an important divergence within late-Victorian fiction. "A Humble Remonstrance," also published in *Longman's*, took issue with the fundamental axiom of both Besant and James. The novel, this writer insisted, "exists, not by its resemblances to life, which are forced and material ... but by its immeasurable difference from life, which is designed and significant, and is both the method and the meaning of the work" (Stevenson 1971: 261). James, praising a recent novel entitled *Treasure Island*, had been frustrated by the lack of realism, which made it impossible to quarrel with the author: "I have been a child, but I have never been on a quest for buried treasure." There never was such a child, rejoined the new disputant, because every child has experienced just such a world in his dreams. And this is the realm of the novel: "not a transcript of life, to be judged by its exactitude, but a simplification of some side or point of life, to stand or fall by its significant simplicity" (265).

The author of "A Humble Remonstrance" was none other than the author of that children's tale, Robert Louis Stevenson (1850–94), who in explaining the motive behind his famous adventure also grounded the burgeoning popularity of romance in the 1880s. The division of novel and romance is notoriously tendentious, but Stevenson's remonstrance is a useful point of departure, and his own career figures centrally in both Victorian and later discussion of the mode. The dream world of romance gained new allure in the 1880s, in part as a recoil from the increasingly harsh subject matter pursued under the banner of realism. At the same time, romance always had found sympathetic material in the remote and exotic, and in this sense it seemed naturally affiliated with the work of empire. In this guise, romance had been kept alive throughout the period in the form of historical narratives of discovery and conquest. Africa was especially alluring as uncharted territory, and a host of explorers, fortified by the recent discovery of quinine to resist malaria, set off for what Conrad would call "the heart of darkness." David Livingstone's *Missionary Travels* (1857) sold 70,000 copies within a few months of publication, a fame later expanded by Edward Stanley's *How I Found Livingstone* (1872). This and related titles, such as Richard Burton's *Lake Regions of Central Africa* (1860) have been described as "nonfictional quest romances" (Brantlinger), and in form they are closely akin to avowedly fictional tales such as Ballantyne's *Black Ivory: A Tale of Adventure among the Slaves of East Africa* (1873).

Stevenson himself drank deeply of the allure of remote and exotic locations – exotic, at least, from the vantage of the metropolis – but he experienced them from a perspective that set his fiction apart from most of what became known as "imperial romance." Born in Edinburgh to a family of distinguished engineers, Stevenson was diagnosed with consumption at an early age, and spent much of his adult life traveling in search of hospitable climates. Those journeys formed the occasion of his earliest magazine essays, and remained a staple of his career. The income from such writings was small and fitful, however, and by the age of 31, he recounted, "I was head of a family; I had lost my health; I had never paid my way, had never yet made two hundred pounds a year" (Stevenson 1999: 196). He found fame through a gesture of imaginary travel: he and his 12-year-old stepson one afternoon invented the map of a place called Treasure Island, which prompted Stevenson to develop a narrative serialized in a boys' magazine called *Young Folks*. This initial publication, for which Stevenson was paid by the column, yielded only about 30 pounds and negligible attention; only with book publication in 1884 did Stevenson come to the notice of a wider audience.

Stevenson's invalidism nurtured a decidedly ironic understanding of adventure. *Treasure Island*, the quintessential boy's adventure, winks at many of the conventions of the genre. Although it is heavily indebted to earlier tales of Ballantyne, Marryat, and Cooper – as Stevenson readily acknowledged in "My First Book" – Stevenson brought to the genre not only his distinctive style, but an unusually wry self-consciousness about manhood itself, which is the ultimate prize in most adventure fiction. *Treasure Island* predictably celebrates courage, hardy resourcefulness, and something like inspired whim in its boy hero, Jim Hawkins, and it has its share of murderous violence and deftly plotted suspense. But the island itself is uninhabited (save by a marooned pirate), and with no indigenous population to be conquered, Stevenson offers no occasion to trumpet schemes of progress or racial hierarchies. Instead, he subtly anatomizes the complicity of the hero and the outlaw – and of men and boys – in the charismatic figure of Long John Silver, the one-legged leader of the pirates (and the title character in the original version of the story, "The Sea Cook"). One of those rare fictional creations who has entirely transcended his original context, Silver is fascinating largely through the ease with which he moves across the boundaries between outlaw and gentleman – "gentlemen of fortune and gentlemen born," as the pirates would have it – at times making the distinction seem little more than a masquerade. A presence alternately bloodcurdling and weirdly avuncular, Silver incarnates the bourgeois virtues of thrift and self-command alongside the allure of untrammeled aggression, and thus the tension that lies at the heart of adventure – and of the models of "manliness" informing it. "I like that boy, now; I never seen a better boy than that" (Stevenson 1999: 155): it says a great deal about both worlds that Jim Hawkins basks in the praise of a murderous pirate. Jim's moral decisions thus become framed as a choice between surrogate fathers, and Stevenson's fiction would remain far more pointedly engaged by the burdens of male rivalry and emulation than by relations between men and women. The preoccupation no doubt reflects a vexed relationship with his own father, who was deeply frustrated by Stevenson's choice of career and his lapse from the family's strict Calvinist faith. But it also registers a broader cultural anxiety informing late-Victorian adventure, an anxiety that would be anatomized by a young physician in Vienna, Sigmund Freud.

Treasure Island soon inspired a novel more characteristic of the imperial energies of late-Victorian adventure, and a more spectacular literary success. Henry Rider Haggard (1856–1925), a 29-year-old barrister, was among many Londoners discussing Stevenson's novel in the spring of 1885 when his brother challenged him to see if he could do better. Haggard quickly began his own novel for boys, and in six weeks he produced *King Solomon's Mines.* Though Haggard's book also turns on a search for treasure, it is situated on a recognizable imperial frontier, drawing on his own experience in South Africa. Haggard, the unpromising sixth son of a Norfolk landowner, had been shipped off to Africa in 1875 in the entourage of the newly appointed

Lieutenant Governor of Natal, where he witnessed the growing political conflicts among English, Boers, and Zulus, which had been heightened by the discovery of diamonds in the Transvaal in 1867. Whereas Stevenson's tale is narrated by the boy hero, Haggard's narrator is a renowned elephant-hunter, Allan Quatermain, who is enlisted in the search for an Englishman vanished in the interior, in quest of the legendary mines. Quatermain is a landlocked version of the grizzled sea captain, a type of lightly-worn experience also echoed in the trail-guide of American frontier adventure, and as such an ideal vehicle for both Haggard's own experience of southern Africa and his unprepossessing prose. "I am more accustomed to handle a rifle than a pen," Quatermain pronounces at the outset, even as he laments his lack of space for attention to important differences between the Zulu and Kukuana dialects (Haggard 1887: 9–10). Knowledge in this novel is at least proto-ethnographic, and the narrative is deeply engaged by the contact between Europeans and the African peoples they were displacing. The Zulu in particular had made a profound impact on the young Haggard, who was in Africa during the height of the Zulu War in January 1879, when a column of more than a thousand British troops was virtually annihilated in a surprise attack.

Haggard's experience brought home a tension anatomized as early as Tennyson's Cambridge prize poem, "Timbuctoo," which laments that the work of empire, as it pressed to the exotic margins of the earth, was eliminating the very mystery on which the romantic imagination fed. Hence writers tended to push back the frontier by imagining quests to ever more remote interiors – in this case the mines of King Solomon, a locale tellingly remote not only in distance but in time. Partly for this reason, Haggard's novel is remarkably free of the racist aggression that animates so much colonial adventure. It certainly trades on familiar fantasies of European conquest, wherein native populations bow down before god-like Europeans, "overawed by our white appearance and by our magic properties," as Quatermain puts it – the "magic" of Winchester rifles and the forecast of a solar eclipse (Haggard 1887: 120. And the hierarchy of white over black remains firm – frequently enunciated by blacks themselves. But the climactic armed struggle turns on the effort to restore to power a rightful Zulu king exiled by a tyrannical usurper; it is a civil war, not an imperial conquest, and it is evoked with something of the majesty Tennyson had discovered in the Light Brigade, and something of the turbulence of Scott's battlefields. A regiment of Kukuan fighters dubbed "the

Greys" goes forth to defend a hopeless position in a manner redolent of Thermopylae: "They were foredoomed to die, and they knew it"; "It could not be otherwise; they were being condemned, with the wise recklessness of human life that marks the great general" – in this case, the Kukuana warrior Indafoos (196). As the tumult pays tribute to the bravery and dignity of the Kukuan fighters, it is also a foil to consummate British pluck: "Anyway, the slaughter will be awful, and as we have a reputation to keep up, we shall have to be in the thick of it" (181). But the swagger also sets off more calculated humor, a wry self-awareness too often unappreciated in Haggard, as when Quatermain on the verge of battle reflects on the difficulty of arraying himself in an ill-fitting chain mail shirt: "I put it on over all my clothes, which caused it to bulge out in a somewhat ungainly fashion" (182).

The comparative equanimity with which Haggard in this novel evokes race reflects in part a pronounced homoeroticism in late-Victorian adventure. "Women were excluded," Stevenson wrote of *Treasure Island* (193), and he is echoed by Quatermain: "I can safely say there is not a *petticoat* in the whole history" (Haggard 1887: 13). The absence of that distraction – aside from a hint of foiled miscegenation late in the novel – enables the characters to devote a good deal of energy to admiring the heroic male form, particularly those "of great stature and breadth" (48), such as Umbopa recognizes in Sir Henry Curtis. "Kisses and the tender words of women are sweet, but the sound of men's spears and the smell of men's blood, are sweeter far!" (162): this comes from the tyrannical King Twala, but it could be uttered by almost any character. This appeal is conjoined with a fantasy of the unknown African interior as a point of contact with ancient life; the journey into the interior is a journey into the past. That pattern was amplified in *She* (1887), Haggard's most popular work, in which the petticoat becomes a source of terror. English travelers to central Africa encounter a mysterious, godlike white Queen, Ayesha ("She-who-must-be-obeyed"), who for 2,000 years has been pining over the death of her Greek lover, now eerily reincarnated in one of the travelers, his direct descendant. Her powers of "fascination" recall the dangerous compound of beauty and wisdom in Pater's Gioconda and other late-Victorian femmes fatales, but she is a more violent and peremptory being. After killing the African bride of her beloved (herself a paragon of feminine devotion) Ayesha enslaves the men with her glance, but in a display of her powers suddenly reverts to her true age, and withers before their eyes – the threat of a woman's power abruptly curtailed.

Regionalism

As it is associated with simpler or "primitive" ways of life and thought, romance could gather in a broad range of topics and treatments. But the association is profoundly equivocal, turning not only on the nature of the primitive – was it simpler and less troubled or more violent and dangerous? – and also on the relative proximity of that state to the implied reader. In late-Victorian imperial fantasy, the excitement of adventure increasingly registers anxieties over empire itself, as an enterprise that might turn against the conqueror and efface the hierarchies it was designed to enforce, whether through the Briton "going native" or through a more subtle erosion of power due to over-extended resources and demoralizing defeats. The grotesque destruction of General Gordon's garrison at Khartoum in 1884, where the hallowed general's head was displayed on a post, was a special blow to British complacency (even as it made Gordon one of the most famous of Victorian martyrs). Such episodes gave new resonance to the symbolic pattern of *The Moonstone*, in which the spoils of empire came to seem haunted – an association that reverberates throughout late-Victorian ghost stories.

But the primitive also was affiliated with settings closer to home, which could beckon as something of a refuge from perplexities of life in the modern metropolis – even when they were settings for violent conflict. In the 1880s rural life became newly prominent in novel and romance – a phenomenon soon to be labeled regionalism, a tag that in itself reflects a metropolitan perspective (what "region" is more distinctive than Dickens's London?). Of course the interest in provincial settings was hardly new; Maria Edgeworth notably offered *Castle Rackrent* (1800) as "a specimen of manners and characters, which are perhaps unknown in England." More notable in the 1880s, however, is the mingling of such broadly socio-political interest with an appeal to nostalgia for a simpler world, or at least a world of more elemental passion and conflict, such as those expressed in the traditional ballad. Obituaries of George Eliot in 1881 expressed a marked preference for the earlier, pastoral fictions – the world of *Adam Bede* rather than of *Middlemarch*. Stevenson during the last decade of his short career gratified this appeal with Scottish historical settings, although his treatments frequently complicate or undermine the usual consolations of romance. *Kidnapped* (1886), a relatively straightforward adventure clearly indebted to Scott, is set in the aftermath of the uprising of 1745, and (like *Waverly*) brings together a passionate Jacobite and a more pragmatic hero, David Balfour. A sequel, *Catriona*, appeared in 1893; both novels were serialized in magazines aimed at young readers. *The Master of Ballantrae* (1889) is a more somber work, also set in the aftermath of the 1745 uprising, but focusing on the fierce, ultimately fratricidal struggle between rival claimants to the title estate. That familiar structure is enriched by Stevenson's fascination with psychic doubling, here inflected by the world of Scottish folk tale and its uncanny haunting. At the time of his death in 1894, Stevenson was working on four novels set largely in Scotland, of which the most complete is *The Weir of Hermiston* (1896). In a plot tellingly indebted to Stevenson's own life, the protagonist gives up his law studies in revulsion at the legalism of his rigid, embittered father, a Scottish judge, and is exiled to a rural village, where he falls into a dangerous romance with a local girl.

The foremost narrator of rural life in the 1880s, as Stevenson himself had suggested in "A Humble Remonstrance," was Hardy, increasingly regarded as one of the most important novelists in England, but more narrowly as "the historian of Wessex." Following *The Trumpet-Major* of 1880, set in the Napoleonic Wars, Hardy solidified his reputation with three Wessex novels published during the 1880s. *Two on a Tower* (1882) recounts the romantic entanglement of a young astronomer and an older woman of higher social standing. The hero's calling offers especially vivid testimony to Hardy's interest in contemporary science: he aimed, he wrote Edmund Gosse, "to make science, not the mere padding of a romance, but the actual vehicle of romance" (Millgate 1982: 231), and readers frequently single out a passage in which the hero, dangling precariously from a cliff face, ponders the escarpment as a record of eons of geological time. But the remote heavens ultimately matter less as objects of wonder than as diminishments of the earthly lovers, whose romance culminates when the heroine, pregnant by the young astronomer, entraps into marriage the Bishop of Melchester – a resolution that offended many reviewers. The *Woodlanders* (1887) was Hardy's favorite among his novels, and the most popular since *Far from the Madding Crowd* – perhaps because of its forest setting and prominent melodramatic conventions. The hero, Giles Winterborne, resists the love of a peasant girl (who out of desperate poverty sells the one thing that attracts him, her beautiful hair) to pursue a woman of higher standing, Grace Melbury, who in turn obliges her father by marrying a young doctor who turns out to be a philanderer. When Grace and Giles seem finally on the verge of reconciliation at a proverbial cottage in the woods, their happiness is forestalled by Hardyesque catastrophe.

Hardy's most enduring work of the decade was *The Mayor of Casterbridge* (1886), his richest study of character, and a novel in which the action is integrated into a more densely textured Wessex society. Michael Henchard is a hay-trusser who through force of pride and willpower shapes himself into the titular eminence as a successful corn-dealer, only to be destroyed by the very qualities that had secured his success. Henchard's rise and fall capture the volatility of economic life at mid-century, in years straddling the abolition of the Corn Laws in 1846, as well as the sometimes ferocious aggression informing the career of the self-made man, within which the grain market could become an arena of masculine rivalry as fierce and nearly as destructive as a duel by sword. In the relations between Henchard and the Scottish protégé who displaces him, Hardy evokes a rivalry powerfully tinged with homoerotic desire, which is at war with the interests of courtship (the novel opens with Henchard emblematically selling his wife to a stranger); the frustration of that desire ultimately is turned to a concerted self-abasement. It seems as if Henchard wishes to make his own ruin more complete and more purposeful, less a by-product of the vagaries of exchange and something more akin to the working of inexorable fate, which culminates with the conclusion of Henchard's will, expressing the desire for utter oblivion: "that no man remember me." The struggle unfolds in an intricately particularized Casterbridge, modeled on Hardy's native Dorchester, where the marketplace is the focal point of a social order whose entire spectrum Henchard traverses over the course of his struggles as master and man. Yet the novel's symphony of allusions to tragic action does indeed gesture towards transcendence of that setting; Henchard is one of the rare characters in Victorian fiction to attain to something like tragic depth.

The stature accorded to Hardy by the end of the 1880s was frequently grudging. Admiration of his extraordinary descriptive techniques was tempered by frustration at "an almost Olympian ruthlessness towards his own characters" (Cox 1970: 133) and, more frequently, by recoil from the insistent "pessimism" of his work, which grew more troubling as reviewers recognized in it not mere eccentricity but a more programmatic congruence with continental thought, particularly the vogue of Schopenauer. Other contemporaries offered more consoling fare. Hall Caine (1853–1931) first made a mark in 1887 with *The Deemster*, set in eighteenth-century Isle of Man (where Caine spent part of his boyhood) and centered, like so much romance in the 1880s, on masculine rivalry. The rift between the title character (a Manx judge) and his brother, the Bishop of Man, is transmitted to the next generation with murderous results. Caine's romances are well plotted and atmospheric, and he evokes sometimes brutal male aggression with forceful economy, but the frame is ultimately melodramatic, the main emphasis falling on atonement and redemption; the book closes with the Lord's Prayer. The work was a huge success (envious rivals called Caine "the boomster"), which he repeated with a series of historical romances, *The Bondman* (1890), *The Scapegoat* (1891), on Jewish life in Morocco, and, most successfully, *The Manxman* (1894). Caine, the child of a ships' smith who left school at 14, ultimately carved out one of the most lucrative of all Victorian literary careers; his novels, deftly marketed by Heinemann, helped to establish the standard 6s. one-volume format, and he left an estate of a quarter-million pounds.

A more bucolic regionalism emerged in the work of the Scottish writer J. M. Barrie (1860–1937). Born in Kirriemuir, Angus, the ninth child of a handloom weaver and a sternly pious stonemason's daughter, Barrie followed the well-traveled road south after a university scholar-ship to try his hand at English journalism. After producing articles on Scottish subjects in the *St. James Gazette*, he began a series of sketches for the *British Weekly*, a dozen of which were collected in 1888 under the title *Auld Licht Idylls*. The sketches, narrated by the local school-master, are set in Thrums, a village closely modeled on Kirriemuir, where life centers on the waning authority of the Auld Licht commun-ion, product of an epochal sectarian division within the Scotish Kirk in the 1840s. The material was doubly removed from a metropolitan readership, not only in geography but in history: though set in the present, the social details are more obviously those of the generation of Barrie's mother, and presented as a vanishing way of life. The bothies and blackfishes and traveling showmen are inexorably dying out. This emphasis recalls Hardy's fiction, but Barrie's narrator, unlike Hardy's, trades more in wry bemusement at the archaic customs and enthusi-asms than in sympathy with those who sustain them. Among other "scandals in connection with the kirk,"

There was, for instance, the time when Easie Haggart saved the minister. In a fit of temporary mental derangement the misguided man had one

Sabbath day, despite the entreaties of his affrighted spouse, called at the post-office, and was on the point of reading the letter there received, when Essie, who had slipped on her bonnet and followed him, snatched the secular thing from his hands. (Barrie 1913: 67)

As in much regional fiction, the donnée is not far removed from that of Dickens's early sketches, but the archness reflects a greater divide between the author (as well as his audience) and the subject matter. Even after his later rise to fame as a dramatist, Barrie was little appreciated among the rural population he depicted. His metropolitan readers welcomed just such humor and evocative atmosphere; it was an invitation to relatively uncomplicated pleasure (signaled by "Idylls"), which would come to be emulated by other writers, most notably John Watson (writing as "Ian McLaren") and Samuel Crockett. This body of writing became known as the "Kailyard" school, a term bestowed by a disgruntled reviewer (drawing on Burns) who summed up the atmosphere as that of the kailyard or cabbage-patch. In 1889, however, Barrie was greeted as one of two great arrivals on the London literary scene.

The Arrival of Kipling

The other tyro of 1889 was a young journalist of even more remote provenance, whose debut was the most widely heralded since that of the young Dickens, and whose work would become indelibly linked with imperial adventure. Rudyard Kipling (1865–1936) was born in Bombay; sent at the age of six to be schooled in England (like most Anglo-Indians), he endured five years of misery at a boarding house in Southsea, then entered the United Services College in North Devon, an experience commemorated in a novel, *Stalky and Co* (1899). In 1882 he returned to India to become an assistant to the editor of the *Civil and Military Gazette* in Lahore, where in 1884 he began publishing brief stories, which frequently developed out of his news reports. In 1888 a collection of those stories was published in Calcutta as *Plain Tales from the Hills*, to be followed within a year by six shorter volumes of new work published in the new Indian Railway Library series, later collected as *Soldiers Three* and *Wee Willie Winkie*. On top of this prolific output, a collection of ballads, *Departmental Ditties*, was published in 1886 and quickly went into new editions, each expanded in size. Confident of his future as a writer, Kipling left India in March 1889, never to return for more than a brief visit. He arrived in London in October, and the chorus of praise quickly swelled.

Reviewers marveled at both the extraordinary economy of *Plain Tales* (initially confined by space constraints to roughly 2,400 words each) and the vividness of their exotic subject matter. For many, the shadowy world of Anglo-India had become newly substantial. There had been earlier works, of course. Henry Cunningham enjoyed success with *The Chronicles of Dustypore* (1875), its title signaling a Trollopean interest in Anglo-Indian life, and B. M. Croker produced a series of breezy novels depicting romantic intrigue among Anglo-Indians in the 1880s and 1890s. But Kipling's stories were greeted as a revelation. "[T]hey appear to lift the veil from a state of society so immeasurably distant from our own and to offer us glimpses of unknown depths and gulfs of human existence," as T. H. Ward put it in *The Times* (Green 1971: 51). Andrew Lang, in a *Daily News* review of November 1889, found an achievement made to order for his celebration of romance: "*Plain Tales from the Hills* will teach more of India, of our task there, of the various peoples whom we try to rule, than many Blue Books. Here is an unbroken field of actual romance, here are incidents as strange as befall in any city of dream ... and the incidents are true" (Green 1971: 48). This paradoxical response was widely echoed, as if for British readers the "truth" of India had always been a space of fantasy. But the tension hints at Kipling's distinctive achievement. Much of the romance is that of sheer exoticism; many of the early tales are little more than expanded anecdotes, news items framed by a narrator of wonderfully trenchant descriptive powers. At the same time, the "strange" settings are leavened by the humdrum rhythms of Anglo-Indian life seen from an insider's perspective – the rituals of courtship, colonial administration, military life all reduced largely to fatiguing, sometimes mind-numbing routine punctuated by catastrophe. "One of the few advantages India has over England," opens "The Phantom Rickshaw," "is a great Knowability": "After five years' service a man is directly or indirectly acquainted with the two or three hundred Civilians in his Province, all the Messes of ten or twelve Regiments and Batteries, and some fifteen hundred other people of the non-official caste" – until by the end of 20 he knows something about every Englishman in the empire (Kipling 1961: 70). This knowingness is a central feature of Kipling's narrators – one reviewer called his work the romance of professionals – but it is also felt in an oppressive visibility experienced by most of the characters, as if they were living in a small, unusually confining English town. Removed as it is from conventional social vigilance, it is a world more tolerant of sexual lapses – in one preface Kipling felt obliged to stress that Anglo-Indian social life involved more than "playing tennis and breaking the Seventh Commandment" (Gilmour 2002: 51). But romance seems largely routinized, as mere deference to custom or a search for diversion. In Kipling's world, characters show their resourcefulness in wrestling as much with boredom as with fear.

This emphasis was especially noted in Kipling's representation of common soldiers, which was the most consistently praised feature of his work (and one among the three groups into which his early stories were gathered, the others being Anglo-Indian and Native life). Kipling's soldier stories puncture nearly all the triumphalist narratives of the empire. To be sure, the British are superior beings: "God has arranged that a clean-run youth of the British middle classes shall, in the matter of backbone, brains, and bowels, surpass all other youth" (94). But the British army in India is one of "blackguards commanded by gentle-men," trained "to do butcher's work with efficiency and dispatch" (Kipling 1961: 93–4). His soldiers do not march off to brass brands and cheering crowds; they typically have escaped from a dead-end existence in which "the Queen's uniform" commands little respect, and they enlist out of a yearning for employment, to escape from a world of romantic disappointment or boredom or disgrace. They are transformed through a deeply personal dedication; they fight not for England but for "the widder" at Windsor, and above for all the cama-raderie of their fellow soldiers, who will forgive them all save coward-ice. Kipling's stories repeatedly turn on the interplay between their brute animal resilience and their susceptibility to tenderness and loss. The dynamic is most fully developed in the stories collected as *Soldiers Three*, which discovers a microcosm of Victoria's army in the compan-ionship of Ortheris, Learoyd, and Mulvaney, a Cockney, Yorkshireman, and Irishman, respectively. In "On Greenhow Hill," for example, as the three pursue a Native deserter whom they plan to kill, they ponder his motives, imagining "there was a lass tewed wi' it" (Kipling 1961: 118); that thought prompts Learoyd, as he reflects on a landscape reminiscent of the Yorkshire moors, to recall his enlistment after the death of a young woman he loved. "I've been forgetting her ever since," he concludes, but the story itself concludes with an image of Ortheris, who has been listening the while, bringing down the deserter with a single bullet from 700 yards. "He was staring across the valley, with the smile of the artist who looks on the completed work" (128). It is a richly self-reflexive, profoundly ambiguous tribute to Kipling's own confidence in his craft.

Less "knowable," tellingly, are the Indians themselves. To the Anglo-Indian readers for whom the *Plain Tales* were originally written, the "strange" was not the country at large, but its native inhabitants. (This dimension was obscured by Kipling's revisions of the stories for the "Home" audience.) Frequently they are little more than a background of teeming "life," whose very vagueness underscores the sharp divisions enforced by race. When Kipling does probe those divisions by venturing across them, the stories do not question the boundary, but they do bring home its costs, and the violence that enforces it. This is particularly marked in stories of inter-racial desire. In "Lispeth," which opens *Plain Tales*, a beautiful young Hill-girl who has been raised as a Christian falls in love with a wounded Englishman, and nurtures the fantasy – casually encouraged by the Chaplain's wife – that he will return to marry her. When the dream is exploded, she exclaims, "I am going back to my own people. You have killed Lispeth ... There is left only old Jedeh's daughter" (Kipling 1900: 9). The story pivots on a fantasy of the civilizing process, hammered home when Lispeth returns to "her mother's gods" and "her own unclean people" in "the dress of a Hill-girl, infamously dirty." But the complacency with which the Chaplain's wife views the devastation of her false hopes gives a lingering force to her final words: "You are all liars, you English" (9). The lovers of Englishmen who venture "Beyond the Pale," in the title of one story, invariably become martyrs to their own passion and the brute realities of domination. Even "Without Benefit of Clergy," an account of almost complete happiness between Holden and his mistress Ameera "snatched under the shadow of a sword," dwells on the burdens of separation imposed by devotion to "an alien" (a phrase applicable to both lovers), and concludes with Ameera and their beloved son dying of cholera because Holden cannot remove them to the safety of an English refuge.

The Indian mistresses of Kipling's early stories are more vividly drawn than most of the Anglo-Indian women, who are generally relegated to the margins. They are a constant point of reference, but as a world of possibility or distraction or regret set alongside the more pressing claims of male comradeship. "Wot's a woman, or a 'ole bloomin' depot o' women, 'longside the chanst of field-service?"

one of the drummer boys remarks in "The Drums of the Fore and Aft" (Kipling 1961: 98). English women figure most prominently as prospective wives – though marriage itself is a rare event – or as already-married social doyennes whose influence is magnified by the knowability of their small world, and who can serve as all-purpose fixers, as it were, ministering to men in want of a wife or afflicted by more obscure psychic need brought on by the rigors of their job.

The homosocial force of Kipling's fiction, and its attachment to the energies of empire, is vividly captured in "The Man Who Would Be King," the last story he wrote before leaving India, and one of his richest. The narrator is a typically knowing figure, a newspaper editor whose humdrum tasks belie his surprising range of competence and connections within the daily workings of empire – a fantasy of the journalist bleeding into the diplomat and the secret agent, which would be developed not only in *Kim* but throughout twentieth-century political fiction. The editor recounts the story of two "loafers," Dravot and Carnehan, discharged soldiers reduced to blackguards adrift on the colonial frontier, who glimpse in the uncharted regions of Kafiristan a field for their own peculiar sort of knowingness, which is that of military drill: "in any place where they fight a man who knows how to drill men can always be a King" (Kipling 1961: 135). The editor dismisses their scheme as an "idiotic adventure," but it is in essence that of the British Empire. The story invites us to admire a strange kind of genius in the audacity of seeking to subdue an alien nation armed only with ingenuity and a few dozen carbines. The enterprise comes to ruin with the lapse of that most crucial form of discipline, the sexual, when Dravot, drunk on dreams of siring a dynasty, forswears his pact with Carnehan to stay clear of women. When his prospective bride draws blood in recoiling from him, she explodes the god-like aura and authority enforced by the adventurers' mastery of drill and Freemasonry (an apt emblem of the homosocial networks that undergird imperial rule, which in this case enables the two men to display a seeming miraculous insight into ancient symbols). All of this is recounted by Carnehan when he makes his way back to the editor several years later, physically broken and on the verge of madness, carrying in a bag the severed head of his friend and displaying the scars of his own crucifixion. It is a powerfully equivocal image: their brutal subjugation of Kafiristan seems a travesty of Christian sacrifice, yet the story also seems to encourage a view that their ambition was intertwined with devotion to a larger good, which was foiled by the weakness of the would-be deliverers. That clash of interpretations would resonate throughout late-Victorian representations of empire.

Fiction and the Forms of Belief

As writers explored the imperial frontier, as well the margins of the British Isles, they felt themselves delving into the history of conscious-ness itself. This was a view enforced by the evolutionary schemes of emergent social sciences, within which "primitive" social organization was the counterpart of a primitive mentality. The romance of the exotic was thus closely aligned with an interest in psychological states more elemental than, or at least less constrained by, the mental habits enforced by civilization. Andrew Lang, the most vigorous popularizer of romance, argued that the genre appealed to "the old barbarian under our clothes" who could enjoy "a true Zulu love story" (Brantlinger 1988: 232). (Lang was a student of the anthropologist E. B. Tylor, who analyzed what he called "survivals" of primitive thought in modern life.) Through its affiliation with dream states, the romance could thus be an especially apt vehicle for representing and exploring the grounds of belief and the supernatural. Spiritualism had a long his-tory, of course, as a response to doubts about a future life, but even with its decline the interest was reconfigured in more outwardly respectable scientific speculation, which was epitomized in the Society for Psychical Research, founded in 1882. The extraordinary roster of contributors speaks to the urgency of the shared preoccupations, the relatively short life of the society to the emergent fissures within the dream of a single culture.

In this climate, historical romance regained some of its earlier cur-rency as a picturesque frame for exploring religious faith. Hence the striking success of *John Ingelsant: A Romance,* by the unknown J. H. Shorthouse (1834–1903), partner in a Birmingham chemical manu-facturer. Turned down by publishers, who were convinced that the vogue for historical fiction had passed, Shorthouse had his work pri-vately printed in 1880, and a copy made its way to Alexander Macmillan, who agreed to publish it; the work sold 10,000 copies in the following year. The novel's most overt appeal is a richly circumstantial, closely plotted representation of sectarian struggles during the English Civil War and corresponding religious intrigue in Papal Italy. The two worlds are bridged by Shorthouse's singular hero, a superbly disciplined courtier and diplomatist whose gifts as an agent of Jesuit machination bring him into contact with virtually every important social and intellectual figure of the era. Ingelsant embodies a fantasy of historical omnipresence, a more sober anticipation of the likes of Zelig and Forrest Gump, who similarly turn up at seemingly every epochal event of their time, and thereby encapsulate the epoch. Yet the central burden remains Ingelsant's experience of these cultural struggles as a deeply personal spiritual journey, shaped by, as he summarizes it, "the noblest parts of man's nature arrayed against each other ... On the one side obedience and faith, on the other, freedom and the reason" (Shorthouse 1882: ii.344). The novel was so popular in some circles that hostesses forbade discussion of it over dinner.

The techniques of Ingelsant's romance were echoed in fictional experiments of Walter Pater during the same decade, in a genre he would call the "imaginary portrait." Here, too, the enabling structure is an *Universalgeschicte* or "world-history" in miniature, whereby the life of a single character encapsulates an epochal cultural transition, a "renaissance" in Pater's broad sense of the term, a movement (or at least a yearning) toward new vitality and enlightenment from a darkness typically associated with neglected or thwarted desire – on the model of the recovered "Hellenic tradition" in "Winckelmann." Thus "Duke Carl of Rosenmold" becomes a forerunner of the German *Aufklarung*, "Sebastian van Storck" a Spinoza-like figure of speculation in seventeenth-century Holland. These are for the most part brief stories, far less richly circumstantial than Shorthouse's romance, but in *Marius the Epicurean* (1885) Pater developed the paradigm to the length of a two-volume novel, set in Antonine Rome, whose central figure encapsulates the transition between paganism and Christianity. As it discovers a mirror of modern religious experience in the early Christian epoch, Pater's romance hearkens back to the more overtly polemical historical romances of Newman, Wiseman, and Kingsley in the 1850s. But for Pater the central conflict has shifted, momentously, from doctrinal conflict within Christianity to the question of whether a recognizably modern aestheticism can be reconciled with Christian belief – or, more broadly, allegiance to any "system" that locates its authority beyond the visible world. Pater thus in effect recasts Arnold's broad dynamic of Hebraism and Hellenism – obedience and faith versus freedom and reason, in Shorthouse's terms – in a characteristically unsteady equilibrium. While seeming to unfold toward a conversion experience, the volume concludes with the more tentative closure of the *Bildungsroman*, in which the supreme value remains openness to new experience: "obedience" is reconfigured as a fidelity to the ongoing possibility of revelation. Resistant as it is to most conventions of the novel – meditation trumps plot and even dialogue – many were captivated by aesthetic reflection rendered in what Yeats would later call "the only great prose in modern English" (Yeats 1965: 202).

The personal religious crisis was framed in a distinctly realist vein in the work of William Hale White (1831–1913), who wrote as "Mark Rutherford." *The Autobiography of Mark Rutherford* (1881) sketches a milieu reminiscent of Oliphant's *Salem Chapel*, but refuses nearly all the usual consolations of domestic fiction in pursuit of raw fidelity to the agonies of doubt. The child of well-to-do dissenting shopkeepers, "rigid Calvinistic dependents" who intend him for the Dissenting ministry, Rutherford charts his growing alienation from a hidebound and unreflective community (modeled on Hale White's own Bedford, ironically the home of John Bunyan), which only exacerbates an innate tendency to solitude and a somewhat priggish disappointment in other people. That estrangement shapes an unusually austere version of Jesus, as a mirror of "absolute loneliness": "He is not the Saviour for the rich and prosperous," "for they want no Saviour." Christianity itself, he urges, is "essentially the religion of the unknown and of the lonely" – hardly a sentiment a congregation wishes to hear (White 1938: 89). White evokes a remarkable sense of psychological transparency, not only in the outwardly artless prose – "Nothing particular happened to me till I was about fourteen, when I was told it was time I became converted" (55) – but also in the refusal of melodramatic heightening, even when depression leaves him feeling that he is "sinking into a bottomless abyss" (90). Even emotional breakdown is recounted with striking equanimity: "mine is the tale of a commonplace life, perplexed by many problems I have never solved; disturbed by many difficulties I have never surmounted" (45).

The most famous crisis of belief in the Victorian novel appeared in 1888, when *Robert Elsmere* by Mary Augusta Ward ("Mrs. Humphry Ward," 1851–1920) became one of the best-selling works of the era. A review by Gladstone, then Prime Minister, sealed a sense of epochal significance, and the work sold 3,500 copies in a three-volume edition, 38,000 copies in a 6s single-volume edition, and an estimated 100,000 pirated copies in America (where the novel seemed to be arguing for a separation of Church and state) – all this in the first year of publication. In setting the experience within domestic life, Ward recalls novels of the 1840s and 1850s, in which the burdens of religious doubt – whether as skepticism or conversion – were felt most keenly as family ruptures. When Elsmere's conscience compels him to resign his Anglican ministry, his agonies are compounded by the jolt to his pious wife; his scrupulousness seems to attack the core of her faith. The particulars of Elsmere's skepticism recall Carlyle's diagnosis – Elsmere's doubt is directed against particulars of Anglican doctrine, not faith itself – and the apologetic design chimes with Huxley's grateful tribute to *Sartor Resartus*: for Elsmere as for Carlyle, fervent belief becomes compatible with an entire absence of theology. The enormous popularity of the book suggests that many novel readers still hungered for such consolation. (In 1887, Sherlock Holmes's profound unworldliness is brought home by his never having heard of Carlyle.) But the novel offered a more topical appeal: Elsmere (modeled on the Oxford scholar T. H. Green) possesses an eloquence that captivates working men and aristocrats alike, and he works out the moral burdens of his vocation by turning to settlement work in the East End, where he founds a "New Brotherhood of Christ" that continues to thrive after his premature death. "Whatever comes of it," one admirer remarks, "the spirit that is moving here is the same spirit that spread the Church, the spirit that sent Benedictine and Franciscan into the world, that fired the children of Luther, or Calvin, or George Fox" (Ward 1888: ii.407). More than 50 years after *Sartor*, English readers still were moved by the quest for a new mythus.

Ward's may have been the best-selling novel of religious doubt, but the most distinctive and in many ways most influential late-Victorian novel of spiritual crisis appeared in 1883, when *The Story of an African Farm* appeared over the name Ralph Iron. That name was well suited to a story depicting the hard-scrabble farming life of European settlers – German, English, and Boer – on the South African frontier. But the novel turned out to be the work of a young woman named Olive Schreiner (1855–1920), a daughter of German missionaries who grew up in the Cape Colony, and its heroine would become the model for a new genre of fiction, as well as the archetype of a social phenomenon known as "the New Woman." Schreiner's novel also reflects the enduring impact of Carlyle ("Alone he must wander down into the land of Absolute Negation and Denial" [Schreiner 1995: 162]), but that influence is crossed with the strenuous rationalism of Mill and Herbert

Spencer, as two of the main characters struggle to fight free of inherited faith. Waldo Farber, son of the old German overseer of the farm, has been brought up in a German pietism to which he clings through a good deal of suffering, casual cruelty, and his German "aptitude for burrowing" (197), moving from the "old God" of impossible demands to a "new God" of love to "no God" (149) – only to finally arrive at a stoic appreciation of the order of nature and life lived in the present moment. But for most readers his ordeal was overshadowed by a more arresting quester, young Lyndall. She stands apart not only in her social marginality – she is the orphaned cousin of young Em, who stands to inherit the farm that her late English father had left in the custody of his wife, the Boer matriarch Tant' Sannie – but also in her magnetic defiance of conventional womanhood. Like an Emily Brontë trans-planted to the Cape Colony, Lyndall turns her Millian disdain for custom into a withering critique of gender roles. Girls' boarding schools become "machines" to discover "into how little space a human soul can be crushed" (185); the woman who marries without love is no different from a "creature in the street": "They both earn their bread in one way" (190).

Schreiner's social criticism is harnessed to an unusually heterodox narrative form, full of dream vision, shifting perspective, abrupt leaps in temporality, and a bleak conclusion that refuses all the usual con-solations of mid-Victorian fiction. In atmosphere the work rivals Hardy at his most austere, not merely in the setting but in the explo-ration of a profound solitude, in which the cosmos seems a more intimate companion than other human beings. "In the day of their bitterest need all souls are alone," Waldo reflects (Schreiner 1995: 102), and yet he confides to Lyndall that when he herds his sheep "it seems that the stones are really speaking – speaking of the old things" (49). Lyndall herself can finally discover no such consolation. Women require, she insists, "a many-sided, multiform culture" that the world denies them (193), an era "when love is no more bought or sold ... when each woman's life is filled with earnest, independent labour," but she feels herself unable to work for that goal, afflicted by a radical anomie: "I am asleep, swathed, shut up in self; till I have been deliv-ered I will deliver no one" (196), and she is finally unable to work this "deliverance" that comes from within. Her defiance of conven-tion culminates in a sexual relationship with a man (never named) whom she does not love and never marries, and she dies not long after bearing their illegitimate child.

Sex, Science, and Danger

For all its bleakness, Schreiner's novel stirred fervent discussion among "advanced" circles in England, especially London, where sexual politics had assumed an unprecedented prominence and volatility. In Schreiner's novel, all the pieties of gender seem called into question; when the aloof farmhand Gregory Rose dons the guise of a female nurse to tend to Lyndall in her suffering, he seems rescued from a psychic prison. We are worlds removed from the burlesque cross-dressing of Tennyson's *Princess*. A decade later, the crusading journalist W. T. Stead would look back on the novel as "the germ and essence of all the fiction of the Revolt" that would flourish in the interval (Ardis 1990: 63). By the mid-1880s, however, the revolt was well under way in the streets and drawing rooms of London. New consciousness of the East End and the settlement movement was only one form of a new mobility available to affluent women, possibilities already glimpsed but largely muffled in Besant and more fully and sardonically chronicled in *Miss Brown*. The interest in material refinement nurtured by the aesthetic movement was reinforced by the development of department stores in the 1870s, those temples of commodity culture in which shopping as a matter of utilitarian need blurred with ever-more varied appeals to fantasy and the pleasures of "just looking," a pursuit that middle-class women increasingly could indulge unchaperoned. Among those women most accustomed to independence were those who had enjoyed the new access to university education – a privilege feverishly resisted by conservatives, who contended that such study was inimical to feminine biology, and would undermine a woman's reproductive capacity. A more diffuse anxiety was aroused by the prospect that such women simply would not be interested in marriage – a fear informing not only increasingly vivid stereotypes of the "mannish" spinster or the fatal "She-who-must be-obeyed" but also fantasies such as Besant's dystopic 1887 novel, *The Revolt of Man*, in which men struggled to overthrow the effects of the "Great Transition" when women had assumed power.

In August of 1888, the *Daily Telegraph* printed an article by Mona Caird declaring conventional marriage outmoded; it prompted an outpouring of 27,000 letters in the following weeks on the question "Is Marriage a Failure?" Continuing agitation against the Contagious Diseases Acts of the 1860s (which finally were repealed in 1886) publicized an image of man as sexual predator while decrying the double standard of sexual morality enforced by the Acts; the agitation brought many conventional women into political life for the first time, even as it underscored the ongoing prominence of prostitution in the metropolis. That reality was luridly underscored by W. T. Stead, editor of the *Pall Mall Gazette*, who in 1885 launched a series of articles on "The Maiden Tribute of Modern Babylon," which documented the sale of young girls for sex (with horrific narratives of violated innocence that eerily resembled the pornography they denounced). Stead created a firestorm, landing himself in jail but also setting in motion the Criminal Law Amendment Act of 1885, which raised the legal age of consent – and, in an after-thought, appended a provision interdicting "acts of gross indecency between men," the notorious "Labouchere amendment," which would have momentous consequences in the London literary world a decade later. And then on 31 August, 1888, the horribly mutilated body of a prostitute was found in Whitechapel in the East End – the first of five killings by the elusive Jack the Ripper.

This maelstrom of new sexual visibility, confusion, and danger would profoundly shape the literature of the late 1880s and 1890s. The association of romance with "primitive" mentalities and desires, states of mind in which the discipline of civilized existence seemed in abeyance, found a new field within the metropolis, where shocks to decency were increasingly explained in terms of psychological abnormality or deviance. At the same time, an increasing body of reflection, such as that sponsored by the Society for Psychical Research, urged that even normal minds were reservoirs of contending forces, divided between the realms of consciousness and dream. It seemed that the human psyche could best be studied through aberration or abnormality, but the boundary between normal and deviant could be disturbingly insecure, and science itself could seem a willful conjuring of psychic disorder.

The most enduring literary monument to this fascination appeared in January 1886, with the publication of Robert Louis Stevenson's *The Strange Case of Dr. Jekyll and Mr Hyde*. Its origins were far removed from dispassionate investigation; it was designed to appeal to a Christmas market hungry for gothic and sensation fiction, and Stevenson himself called it a "shilling shocker." But the commercial appeal was joined with an exploration of divided selfhood that nearly all readers found mesmerizing. The "case" is at once legal and medical (Wilde quipped that Jekyll and Hyde reads "dangerously like an experiment out of the *Lancet*" [Wilde 1982: 295]). The investigation of a brutal crime gradually comes to disclose Dr. Jekyll's experiments on his own psyche, in the conjuring of a psychic double who clearly embodies an array of repressed or disavowed impulses, and who materializes as a brute capable of horrific acts. The desires are never named – a suggestive vagueness that has exercised many critics – but Stevenson seems as much interested in the social conditions that thwart their open acknowledgment as he is in the mere fact of their existence. The story is set in a world of male professionals, nearly all single men, who live under the pervasive threat of stained reputation – a shadow of scandal that may reflect something of Stevenson's stern upbringing, but also the growing association of London with a world of sexual transgression and danger. The story elicited almost unanimous praise – many marveling at such psychological complexity in such an unlikely format – and the title characters were quickly integrated into both medical and popular literature, where they would become archetypes of both mental disease and the burdens of civilized existence.

A very different but equally enduring scientist entered the world in the following year, with a little-noted short novel published in *Beeton's Christmas Annual* for 1887. In *A Study in Scarlet*, Arthur Conan Doyle (1859–1930), himself a medical doctor by training, introduced the famous detective who trained his powers of deduction and experiment not on his own mind, but on reading the seemingly opaque surfaces of modern life, which under his analysis became strangely transparent. This first appearance of Sherlock Holmes captivated an editor for *Lippincott's Monthly Magazine* in Philadelphia, who signed up Conan Doyle for a second novel, published in the magazine in 1890 as *The Sign of Four*. In the following year, Conan Doyle gave up medicine for writing, seeing a particular financial opportunity in the short story. A serial novel with a detective protagonist might lose any reader who missed an installment, but a recurrent character in a series of stories, he reasoned, might secure a steady audience. Conan Doyle proceeded to write for the new *Strand* magazine a set of stories that would become famous when collected as *The Adventures of Sherlock Holmes* (1892).

"You remind me of Edgar Allan Poe's Dupin," remarks Sherlock Holmes's flatmate and associate, Dr. Watson, in the second chapter of *A Study in Scarlet* (Conan Doyle 1994: 30). In acknowledging this debt to the inventor of the detective story, Conan Doyle also clears space for his own hero. Whereas Dupin was conceived as something like a study in pure ratiocination, Holmes is more vigilantly attentive to social codes. In Holmes's London, "that great cesspool into which all the loungers and idlers of the empire are irresistibly drained" (18), as Watson puts it (himself just returned from service in Afghanistan), we see renewed and amplified the pressures of urbanization in the nineteenth century, which make it essential to "read" the appearances of strangers. "By a man's finger-nails, by his coat-sleeve, by his boots, by his trouser-knees, by the callosities of his forefinger and thumb, by his expression, by his shirt-cuffs – by each of these things a man's calling is plainly revealed" (28). Holmes's powers connect the mundane pressures of bourgeois urban life with the rise of modern criminology, epitomized in the theories of Cesare Lombroso, which attempted to ward off crime by constructing typologies of "deviant" and criminal appearances. To a sufficiently vigilant observer, Holmes believes, "deceit ... was an impossibility"; in this faith Holmes represents yet another Victorian invocation of a moral order that would contain the threats of a world seemingly bereft of divine assistance. In its power to dispel the mysterious, Holmes's analysis paradoxically conjures its own sense of magic or divination – as Watson again wryly points out: "You would certainly have been burned had you lived a few centuries ago" (34). Like the magus of old, moreover, the detective nurtures his powers through a profound social alienation. This is something more than scientific detachment: Holmes "loathed every form of society with his whole Bohemian soul" (33). As the series unfolded, Conan Doyle compounded this estrangement by emphasizing Holmes's anti-social qualities: his use of cocaine, long withdrawals from public contact, and almost neurasthenic sensibility to incursions on his privacy. In these attributes, the great detective came to seem something of a deviant himself.

Sherlock Holmes thus resembles the hero of Oscar Wilde's *The Picture of Dorian Gray* – a conjunction underscored by their common appearance in *Lippincott's Magazine* in 1890 (the editor had signed up the two authors at the same dinner party). Wilde's novella elicits surprising affinities between the detective and the epicure, who marshals a quasi-scientific mode of self-analysis, "vivisecting" his own "Bohemian soul" (Wilde 1987: 204). The novel thus also recalls *Jekyll and Hyde* (as many reviewers noted), all the more as it contains its own doppelgänger, in the picture that mysteriously externalizes the moral life of its subject. Wilde, however, fuses Dorian's aesthetic education with another version of the Pygmalion myth – which in this version is redolent of *Frankenstein*. "The lad was his own creation," thinks Lord

Henry Wotton of his young protégé, but the young Dorian soon outstrips the master in the audacity of his "new hedonism." Lord Henry steers Dorian into a Faustian bargain, whereby a portrait of the beautiful, wealthy young man absorbs the burdens of age and sin, while the young man remains miraculously untouched by time, free to explore ever more esoteric sources of pleasure. The novel is true to aestheticism – again the wellspring is Pater's *Renaissance*, whose insinuating rhetoric Wilde closely echoes – in associating the pursuit of beauty with structures of discipleship, which readily shade into seduction. The aesthetic guide offers initiation into arcane experience, which typically presses against the bounds of conventional morality. But Wilde is far bolder than Pater in suggesting the potentially scandalous character of that pursuit, and in foregrounding the decadent body. Dorian's experience and influence are "poisonous," that very term George Eliot had applied to *The Renaissance*, and he embodies to horrifying effect Lord Henry's maxim, "One could never pay too high a price for any sensation" (204).

Dorian Gray's fate confirms a very familiar moralizing of undisciplined aesthetic pleasure; in effect, the novel recasts Tennyson's "The Palace of Art" as Grand Guignol. The transference of Dorian's corruption to the painting itself also echoes the comforting logic of Holmes and other late-Victorian typologists of deviance, here expressed by the painter, Basil Hallward: "There are no such things as secret vices" (Wilde 1987: 257). Deviance, like murder, will out. But the moral design (which Wilde himself thought too insistent) did not disarm critical outrage at the insinuation of unspeakable acts. Attacks on the "disgusting" and "nauseous" subject matter, which amplified earlier suspicion of Wilde and aestheticism, was fanned by the recent "Cleveland Street affair," the discovery of a male brothel patronized by Lord Arthur Somerset, a member of the Prince of Wales's official household, as well as (so it was rumored) the Prince's eldest son. The *Scots Observer* was hardly alone in linking Wilde to that scandal, lamenting that a man of his talent had chosen "to write for none but outlawed noblemen and perverted telegraph boys" (Wilde 1987: 346). But when the work was expanded and reprinted in volume form the following year, Wilde was nothing abashed. He added a Preface that threw down the gauntlet: "There is no such thing as a moral or immoral book. Books are well written, or badly written. That is all" (3). Pater's aesthete seemed to have passed a moral threshold, and had become the decadent. And art itself seemed more dangerous than ever.

Fictions of the Artist

Dorian Gray is part of a large body of late-century fiction devoted to writers, artists, and performers. Writers needed little persuasion to be interested in writers' lives, but in the early Victorian period the engagement had always been at least faintly apologetic. Dickens in *David Copperfield* had been most engaged by the novelist's achievement of domestic happiness and public recognition – not merely as an entertainer but as a gentleman. Thackeray in *Pendennis* discovered in the bohemian existence of the periodical writer the redeeming virtues of fellowship, loyalty, and hard work – and occasionally talent. But the growing view of art as an arena of distinctive forms of value was reflected in a new version of the artist's life, in which integrity was affirmed through resistance to, even contempt for, respectable morality. Of course that tension had always been a burden for women writers, whose very dedication to their art typically seemed an affront to femininity – witness the struggles of Aurora Leigh. But increasingly the sheer unconventionality of the public woman became the focus of interest; in *Villette* it is Vashti's audacity that fascinates Lucy Snowe, not any apology for her performance. Al-Charisi, Deronda's mother, puts in the starkest terms the clash between domestic womanhood and the artist's life, but we are left merely to imagine the force of her charismatic performance. In the last two decades of the century, the gifts of the virtuoso performer increasingly came to the fore, along with the celebration of genius as something like a secular mystery cult. The actress or musician incarnates the mesmerizing force of art itself as inexplicable power, an "influence," in Wilde's emphasis, that not only entertains, but *fascinates* – eliciting a compound of delight and resistance that suggests not only the moral audacity of art, but also its power to seduce or ravish, to make the audience feel it is surrendering to a power beyond its control.

The performing life that figures centrally in *Daniel Deronda* is fairly muted in this regard – the discipline of Klesmer and Mirah engages Eliot more than their charisma – but even that life is a great distance from the world of melodrama in *Nicholas Nickleby*, for example, where the stage offers wholesome entertainment and a decent income, but hardly a claim to new horizons of experience. That prospect moves front and center in the later works of Henry James. In *The Tragic Muse* (1890) the gifts of a young actress draw a rising young diplomat away from his career, while a young Member of Parliament surrenders his political prospects and his fiancée for the love of painting. (Both men find a sounding board in a character drawn in part from Wilde himself.) In a series of short stories throughout the 1890s ("The Lesson of the Master," "The Figure in the Carpet") James explored varieties of literary influence and discipleship, taking up again the logic of Wilde's novel, but also, more broadly, the ongoing affiliation of aestheticism with forms of initiation into often arcane modes of experience. Such was the allure of the art world that even Kipling, encouraged soon after he arrived in London to try his talents at a novel, produced one about a young painter who loses his sight, *The Light That Failed* (1890). (For most readers the work confirmed that Kipling's genius lay in other genres.) Fascination with the charismatic performer reached a zenith of sorts with George du Maurier's *Trilby* (1894), the tale of a free-living waif in Paris who is miraculously transformed into a ravishing singer – nurtured, it turns out, by literal mesmerism. The novel was an immense success, giving the world not only the name for a style of hat but also a byword for the powerful impresario, the man who could magically transform those under his charge: Svengali. Much of the novel's popularity derived from its idyllic scenes of bohemian life, in which the more sordid aspects are airbrushed by bonhomie, but the novel also registers a collective fascination with forms of arcane or occult "influence" – here focused in the markedly anti-Semitic portrait of Svengali as a master manipulator.

The romance of art and performance naturally was shadowed by more skeptical accounts, both of their moral pretensions and of the very possibility of reconciling aesthetic ideals with the material economies of art and literature, particularly in an age of mass readership. The most withering account of the underbelly of authorship came in Gissing's *New Grub Street* (1891), in which intellectual and artistic pretensions are pulverized by the continuing power of Mudie's Library, and even literary drudgework can barely stave off poverty. The blighted ambitions of Edwin Reardon, an aspiring novelist, and Marian Yule, who helps to edit a literary magazine, are set off by the career of Jasper Milvain, an eager, cynical participant in the "New Journalism," who succeeds by mastering the smart turn of phrase for his equally cynical editors, and makes his way to happiness and prosperity. The more familiar attacks, as we have seen, focused on the character of artists who disdained moral convention, and they ranged from the genial satire of Gilbert and Sullivan, through the more pointed anatomies of

Miss Brown, to an increasingly strident chorus from reviewers, which was epitomized in the response to *Dorian Gray.* Marie Corelli (1855–1924), who rocketed to popularity in the 1890s writing fashionable romances, largely built her immense success on inverting the familiar hierarchies, roundly insisting that true art was popular art, and attacking with might and main all who seemed disdainful of her lowbrow, predominantly suburban readership. The title of *Wormwood* (1890) sums up her view of the likes of Wilde, while *The Sorrows of Satan* (1895) develops an especially vivid fantasy of the source of all this trash: it is nothing less than diabolical temptation. For all its unwitting comedy, the fantasy is faithful to the increasingly vehement, sometimes hysterical tones in which the conflict was perceived. The elite artist was repeatedly described as a symptom of cultural crisis – a condition often summed up as "decadence."

Decadence

"Decadence" became one of the most inflammatory and protean slogans of the Victorian age. The currency of the term was in part a by-product of self-confidence; the very archetype of cultural decline was Rome, and was not Britain the greatest empire since Rome? But over the course of the century decadence seemed an ever more real and disturbing possibility, which preoccupied a broad range of Victorian writers. It haunted Tennyson, most memorably in *Idylls of the King*; Pater, in a predictably different vein, evoked "the delicate sweetness of a refined and comely decadence" (Pater 1980: xxiii), qualities which again trouble the connection between beauty and morality. A host of forces made the prospect of decline seem more than a fanciful analogy. Increasingly aggressive questioning of religious faith seemed to undermine conventional moral sanctions; that erosion seemed reflected in newly provocative forms of social freedom – as registered in the periodic waves of "moral panic" triggered most often by unorthodox sexuality or (what was much the same thing) perceived threats to female purity. Newly bold subject matter in a variety of art forms seemed to further divorce pleasure and morality. The growing power of "the masses," registered in both the ballot box and in the expansion of publishing and entertainment catering to popular tastes, exacerbated anxiety that traditional modes of deference, both social and political, would be overthrown. On the scientific front, the drive towards systematic taxonomies that would define categories and norms of humanity – in terms of race, gender, intelligence, body type, morality, sanity – generated a newly insistent labeling of deviance, which was readily combined with various quasi-evolutionary schemes to produce stories of "degeneration," biological decline or exhaustion. (Many commentators continued to regard evolution as a teleological process, which could be understood in terms of progress and regression.) From the early 1870s an agricultural depression was compounded by a decline in British manufacturing relative to American and German industry. As pride in "the workshop of the world" was increasingly transferred to Britain's imperial might, empire came to seem for many an enervating project, not only in terms of resources committed to maintain unstable dominions, but, as it blurred the boundaries of Britain itself, with increasing numbers of imperial subjects joining a growing tide of immigration (Indian, Jewish, Chinese) into Britain's cities.

These anxieties were most vividly registered in the resurgence of gothic narrative in the latter decades of the century. The prominence of gothic is one facet of the growing late-Victorian preoccupation with the burdens of history – the dark side of an earlier faith in progress, and another means of imposing coherence on sometimes dizzying change. Mid-Victorian schemes of progress typically celebrate a steady march away from the past, a seemingly unbounded expansion of civilized order, an ongoing harmonizing of discordant forces. Within such a world, failings or frustrations tend to be interpreted as the return to an earlier state, or the eruption of a past that has not been left behind, usually because it is aligned with intractable psychic forces antagonistic to civilization itself. Hence the remarkable consistency with which late-Victorian narratives of psychic deviance or division – *Jekyll and Hyde, Dorian Gray, She, The Time Machine, Heart of Darkness* – frame their central conflict as a form of atavism, of return to an earlier, "primitive" state of mind. Gothic gives particularly arresting shape to this threat, which is in essence what Freud called a return of the repressed. And the broad narrative of such regression sometimes seems inescapable, emerging in the most unlikely contexts. The creation of the *New English Dictionary*, for example, the first volume of which appeared in 1888, had been proposed in 1857 as a project that would consolidate the history of the language on scientific principles, and in the process do justice to the extraordinary power many believed was attached to the language and the culture that produced it. Yet the result was to many deeply disturbing: the sheer multifariousness of the language, the mingling of ancient and more recent formations that rebuked any clear scheme of progress or development over time, seemed more "mongrel" than civilized. It was as if science had turned against progress, leading into a confusing past rather than beckoning towards a more hopeful future.

These varied narratives typically bring home a radical questioning of the faith in human freedom and self-determination that underwrites so many early Victorian schemes of value. When Lord Henry thinks of Dorian Gray as "his creation," he recalls the worries of *Great Expectations* a generation earlier, yet Dorian himself seems to embrace the submission to forces beyond his control. Identity itself, as he comes to envision it, is shaped by what became known as "organic memory," a broadly Lamarckian scheme in which biological inheritance incorporates the experience of one's ancestors as well as their physical traits. Decadence in this regard is but one focal point of a broad late-Victorian preoccupation with the limits of human agency, which is most pointed in the impact of evolutionary thought – particularly the psychology of Henry Maudsley, though the impact is reinforced very differently by Freud. It also extends to economic theory, which with the "marginal revolution" of the early 1870s markedly shifts from a focus on production and the disciplines that sustain it, to an analysis of consumption and the desires that direct it. In a more speculative vein, the attenuation of human agency in decadence might seem to encapsulate the transformation of mid-Victorian liberalism into a collectivist political theory in which human welfare increasingly depended on state intervention.

For a small audience, however, "decadence" was something to be embraced and celebrated, precisely because it designated a subversion of the established order, a protest against bourgeois respectability nearly as diffuse and protean as attacks on decadence. If decadence suggested belatedness, as a style it might also signify "the latest" in a more exhilarating sense of the absolutely contemporary. As Gautier put it, in a characteristically exorbitant 1868 Preface to Baudelaire's *Fleurs du Mal*:

> The style inadequately called decadent is nothing but art arrived at the point of extreme maturity yielded by the slanting sun of aged civilizations: an ingenious, complex, learned style, full of shades and of refinements of meaning, constantly pushing back the boundaries of speech, borrowing from every technical vocabulary, taking colours from every palette and notes from every keyboard a style that struggles to express

the most inexpressible thoughts, what is vague and most elusive in the outlines of form, listening to translate the subtle confidences of neurosis, the dying confessions of passion grown depraved, and the strange hallucinations of the obsession that is turning to madness. (Reed 1985: 10)

In France, decadence gained broad currency in the 1880s as a reaction against Zola's naturalism; the unflinching, quasi-scientific recording of society as a natural organism encouraged a return to Baudelaire's celebration of the artificial and exquisite. The major document of these years was the novel that so powerfully influenced Wilde, Huysmans's *Au Rebours* (1884), whose title – "Against the Grain" or "Against Nature" – captures a defining impulse of the perspective. In England the stylistic credo was more immediately translated into a character typology indebted to Huysmans, in which the aestheticist pursuit of beauty and freedom had warped into self-destructive alienation from the world. That type first became visible in the work of George Moore, particularly *A Mere Accident* (1887) and *Confessions of a Young Man* (1888), and assumed its most vivid image in Wilde's Dorian Gray – and later, for many observers, in Wilde himself. Of course the decadent protest was subject to the powerful ambiguity embodied in Wilde's protagonist: what originated as defiance of respectability readily came to seem a surrender of the will to the power of instinct.

"The decadent" thus became a tag encompassing styles, characters, states of mind, and historical figures, typically linking literary innovation with varieties of sexual dissidence. Decadence as a literary movement coincided with a newly visible homosexuality, which found expression in a number of forms – not merely the insinuating obliquity of Pater and Wilde, but in "Uranian" poetry, an idealized "New Comradeship" heavily influenced by Edward Carpenter and the Calamus poems of Walt Whitman, and an emergent sexology, most notably that of Havelock Ellis, who drew heavily on John Addington Symonds's complex (anonymous) analysis of his "sexual inversion" in *A Problem in Modern Ethics* (1891). The New Woman, a companion figure of decadence if not "the decadent," who was typically male, was variously associated with both ungoverned sexual appetite and an utter lack of desire. The influential "little magazines" most closely connected with decadent literature – the *Century Guild Hobby Horse, The Artist, The Yellow Book* – were all associated with the flouting of gender and sexual norms, perhaps most vividly in Aubrey Beardsley's illustrations for the *Yellow Book*.

This welter of what a contemporary called "sexual anarchy" has made the 1890s the most fabled decade in English literary history – a prominence that reflects both its acute historical consciousness and the cult of celebrity that was nourished in its literature. At the same time, chronicles of the "gay" or "yellow" or "decadent" or "queer" 1890s naturally obscure a great variety of cultural energy. Decadence shaped literature concertedly resistant to it, most notably in the careers of Kipling and W. E. Henley, who even at the time were regarded as a "counter-decadence." Beyond these large figures, as we'll see, were a host of literary careers that resist easy placement. Even *The Yellow Book*, a quarterly often taken to be the iconic journal of decadence, was notable for the sheer variety of authors that its publisher, John Lane, recruited: writers particularly associated with decadence, to be sure, such as Arthur Symons, Lionel Johnson, Ernest Dowson, and Beardsley, but also figures who confound such affiliation – Henry James, Arnold Bennett, George Saintsbury, H. G. Wells – and some who explicitly attacked the very concept, such as Hubert Crackenthorpe in "Reticence in Literature." More immediately, an account of the 1890s focused on Wilde tends to obscure the impact of arguably the single most influential writer in the stirring of this great maelstrom, the Norwegian dramatist Henrik Ibsen, who not only provoked fiery debates but helped to solidify the place of the drama at the very center of English cultural life, an eminence it had not held for more than a century.

Drama in the 1880s

Novelists' attention to performing life reflected in part the new prominence of the theater. At the beginning of the decade, laments over the state of the drama echoed those of half a century before. The appearance of the Comédie-Française at Drury Lane in 1879 renewed a widespread sense that England remained a theatrical backwater, prompting Matthew Arnold (who was especially captivated by Sarah Bernhardt's peformances) to call for a national theater supported by state endowment – a proposal that would be realized in the following century. In *English Dramatists of Today* (1882), William Archer complained that "modern Englishmen cannot be got to take the drama seriously" (Archer 1882: 8). But the burden of Archer's complaint marked an important shift: he yearned for a theater of intellectual and moral challenge rather than mere entertainment. "A drama which opens the

slightest intellectual, moral, or political question is certain to fail ...
The public will accept open vice, but it will have nothing to do with a
moral problem" (8–9).

Over the next decade Archer would find a marked transformation.
The reasons were threefold. The first was rapid improvement in the
financial rewards derived from playwriting, as the royalty system
expanded and copyright became more secure. The 1886 Berne treaty
governing European signatories constrained the habitual British recycling of drama from France and Germany, while in 1891 the long-
awaited American copyright agreement finally suppressed transatlantic
piracy. In this more lucrative environment, there was a growth of
smaller theaters in the West End, which had less use for the elaborate
spectacle of earlier Victorian drama, and where more affluent audiences tended to be more responsive to the aspirations of critics like
Archer. Finally, however, there was the impact of Ibsen, who more
than any other playwright conveyed a new sense of the intellectual possibilities of theater.

The thematic fulcrum of a newly vitalized drama was sexual politics.
At the outset of the decade, W. G. Gilbert was the most acerbic commentator on romantic platitudes, frequently underscoring the material
interests they disguised. In *Engaged* (1877), the heroine Belinda
Treherne tells her lover Belawney, "I love you madly, passionately ...
I care to live but in your heart; I breathe but for your love; yet before
I actually consent to take the irreplaceable step that will place me on
the pinnacle of my fondest hopes, you must give me some idea of your
pecuniary position" (Booth 1969: III.335). Farce is ideally suited to
mocking social forms (including theatrical convention), but typically
playwrights in the genre ended up reaffirming familiar passions that
those forms are presumed to obstruct or distort. Gilbert's operettas
with Sullivan would tend in this direction, but his early work retains
the keener satiric edge of the *Bab Ballads*.

Outside the distinctive niche of Gilbert and Sullivan, the dominant
playwrights of the 1880s were Henry Arthur Jones (1851–1929) and
Arthur Pinero (1855–1934), whose works were not radical in either
content or form, but were sufficiently unconventional in their topics
and treatment to unsettle conservative critics. Jones came to wide
notice almost as if in answer to Archer's pleas: "There is a rift in the
clouds, a break of blue in the heavens," remarked G. A. Sala on the
immense critical and commercial success of *The Silver King* (1882),
the story of a young man tricked into believing himself a murderer,

who flees to Nevada and makes a fortune in mining, then returns home in disguise to discover his innocence (Jackson 1982: 5). This melo-drama of a prodigal son charts a well-worn narrative arc – it recalls Tom Taylor's great success in *The Ticket of Leave Man* (1863) – but it impressed critics by foregoing sensation and spectacle in favor of supple, naturalistic dialogue; even Arnold praised it as model for other British playwrights. It may have helped that Jones displayed a persist-ent disdain for Arnold's philistines, particularly tradesmen. This animus surfaced in his next play, *Saints and Sinners* (1884), which took the daring step of introducing religion to the stage, portraying a hypo-critical Dissenting congregation that drives out its minister in punish-ment for his daughter's sexual lapse. In *The Middleman* (1889) Jones returned to a long-standing subject of melodrama, the exploitation of the worker, here resolved when a disaffected potter rediscovers a lost glaze that makes his own fortune.

Pinero pressed the theater into more sustained and (for the time) daring engagement with contemporary sexual ferment. He started as an actor with Henry Irving's company at the Lyceum in the late 1870s, but soon turned to playwriting, where he would be extremely prolific (he had already written 10 plays by 1882, when he turned 27, and had nearly 60 works produced in his lifetime). He was an innovator as a director, printing entire scripts for every performer (rather than the traditional "sides" recording only cues and lines for a single actor) and presiding over unusually demanding rehearsals. Unlike Jones, he made his early reputation with farce rather than melodrama, but his great achievement was to push melodrama into what became known as "the problem play." The problem, in a nutshell, was sexual fidelity and the double standard – an issue that figured centrally in heated debate over the Contagious Diseases Acts, and one that was readily adapted to melodramatic exposure of a hidden past. In 1887, Pinero wrote *The Profligate*, which depicts a man whose stainless wife prompts agonized memory of his own past transgressions, which in the original version tormented him to the point of suicide. Though the ending was sof-tened for its performance in 1889, the play riveted audiences. But two months after its premiere, the Novelty Theatre staged *A Doll's House*, and for a time all of English drama, and a good deal besides, was over-shadowed by Ibsen.

Edmund Gosse had published an account of Ibsen's work as early as 1879, and Archer began translating his plays in 1880, but the Norwegian's lacerating attacks on bourgeois domesticity could not pass muster with the Examiner of Plays. Ironically, that very ban enhanced the impact of Ibsen as a dramatist of dangerous ideas; his works were available only as texts, unmediated by performance. Thus when a license was finally secured for *A Doll's House*, a small, knowing audience was primed for the experience. The play, culminating in Dora's famous slamming of the door on her married life, created a broader sensation, predictably outraging conservative critics. Ibsen, as Archer gloated, became for a time "the most famous man in the English literary world" (Ibsen 1981: ix). The impact grew with productions in 1891 of *Romersholm* and *Hedda Gabler*, and culminated with the production of *Ghosts*, where the smug hypocrisies of middle-class respectability become an inheritance one cannot escape, distilled in the form of hereditary syphilis. The performances at the Independent Theatre Society were restricted to members, but still provoked new crescendos of revulsion: "An open drain; a loathsome sore unbandaged; a dirty act done publicly ...Absolutely loathsome and fetid" (Ibsen 1981: x).

Against such audacity, *The Profligate* seemed tame and simpleminded, but Pinero took up the gauntlet, and in 1893 he produced a work more widely applauded than any other by an English playwright of the past generation, *The Second Mrs. Tanqueray*. The melodramatic origins are still recognizable – the heroine's past returns to haunt her, and the play culminates with her suicide – but the play offers newly complex attention to the burdens of respectability. When her new husband's world recoils from Paula Tanqueray's compromising past – which is part of what he finds alluring about her – she is plunged into numbing social isolation, compounded by her uneasy relations with her husband's austere daughter (who at the outset of the play is on the verge of declaring herself a nun) and by her sense that her husband's devotion is divided between the two women. The play was a huge success, making a star of its lead actress, Mrs. Patrick Campbell, running for 230 performances and taking in a staggering 36,000 pounds at the box office. As a delighted Archer wrote in his review of opening night, taking up that familiar masculine swagger, "don't you feel that if art is not virile it is childish, and that virile art alone is worth living for?" (Jackson 1982: 172–3).

One reviewer complained that *The Second Mrs. Tanqueray* was much too tame, that the self-sacrifice of its heroine perpetuates the myth of natural female innocence and obscures a more fundamental social reality: for most women marriage amounts to a form of prostitution. George Bernard Shaw (1856–1950), an Irish Fabian and unsuccessful novelist, was galvanized by the experience of Ibsen and the encouragement of J. T. Grein at the Independent Theatre to try his own hand as a playwright. His first effort was *Widowers' Houses* (1892), "An Original Didactic Reality Play in Three Acts," as he later subtitled it, in which the familiar financial burdens of middle-class romance disclose larger social truths. Not only is marriage a business transaction, but the incomes of all concerned in this particular courtship derive from slum housing – a state of affairs clearly pressed towards a larger conclusion, that bourgeois comfort derives from systematic exploitation of the poor, or, as Shaw put it, "gentility fattening on the poverty of the slum as flies fatten on filth" (Shaw 1906: xxvi). In *The Philanderer* (1893) Shaw turned his jaundiced eye on an ideal of sexual freedom associated with the "New Woman." Julia Craven, a woman of "advanced views," looks to marriage as a "degrading bargain," but ultimately cannot live up to her own creed; ready to risk all for her lover, she instead falls into conventional, self-abasing feminine dependence, surrendering her own freedom and self-respect in demanding that her passion be reciprocated. Her predicament is summed up by her lover, the philanderer and "Ibsenist philosopher" Charteris: "Advanced people form charming friendships; conventional people marry" (Shaw 1906: 89) – a bit of repartee that suggests Shaw's affinities with his fellow Irishman, Wilde.

But none of this prepared readers for the cool ferocity of *Mrs. Warren's Profession*. When the title role was offered to Mrs. Theodore Wright, an ardent socialist who had originated the role of Mrs. Alving in *Ghosts*, she declared that she could not even speak the part to herself in private, while the intrepid Grein, who had produced *Ghosts*, refused to stage it, as "unfit for women's ears." It would not be staged even privately until 1902; its first public staging came in America in 1905, and it was not publicly staged in England until 1926 – the year after Shaw received the Nobel Prize. This ginger handling is not hard to explain. Shaw wrote it, he explained, "to draw attention to the truth that prostitution is caused, not by female depravity and male licentiousness, but by simply underplaying, undervaluing, and overworking women so shamefully that the poorest of them are forced to resort to prostitution to keep body and soul together" (Shaw 1993–7: i.111). Kitty Warren, who has made a small fortune first as a prostitute and then as the managing director of a well-capitalized chain of European brothels, returns home to be reconciled with her prim, hard-working daughter, a recent Newnham grad starting a career as an actuary. Though ignorant of her own father's identity, Vivie Warren doesn't grasp her mother's profession, but when the truth is revealed, Mrs. Warren, far from being abashed, offers up her career as a model of economic rationality, and derides the "right and proper" as "only a pretence, to keep the cowardly, slavish, common run of people quiet" (Shaw 1906: 240). In a typical Shavian twist, however, Kitty Warren indulges the sentimental faith that she has a special claim on her own daughter's affection, which Vivie coolly rebuffs – not out of offense, but out of her own sense of self-interest. "I am my mother's daughter … I must have work, and I must make more money than I spend." That ambition cannot be reconciled with the role of the dutiful daughter. In her sentimentality, her daughter concludes, Mrs. Warren is "a conventional woman at heart" (Shaw 1906: 244–6).

The New Woman in Fiction

Mrs. Warren's Profession marked a crucial break with earlier British stage treatments of the "fallen" woman: the fulcrum of conflict, and the ultimate burden of moral judgment, is not the woman but society at large. And it was this emphasis that would find wider currency in the "New Woman" novel. "New Woman" fiction flared up with a blaze reminiscent of the vogue for sensation fiction, and excited more vehement debate. The phrase itself only came into use in 1894, in the midst of fierce polemic, which has always made it a slippery tag. There was nothing "new" about unconventional female characters in novels, and works as disparate as *Dombey and Son* and *Daniel Deronda* had anticipated a central burden of New Woman fiction with harrowing portraits of loveless marriage, in which the wife's predicament was likened to prostitution. But in these earlier representations, the suffering was almost invariably contained by deference to the social order at large. Women who never married were failures, objects of either pity (the spinster) or aversion (the fallen woman). Women who did marry but found themselves in a nightmare had no recourse but flight or providential death, and while novelists occasionally offered the latter relief, almost no abuse could sanction a wife's desertion. The liberalized divorce laws of the late 1850s rarely made their presence felt in fiction, such was the idealization of marriage and feminine submission to wifely duty. It was these pieties that the New Woman novel attacked in frequently audacious style.

There were forerunners, of course. From the 1860s onward, female bohemians and aspiring intellectuals garnered increasingly prominent and sympathetic treatment – though they typically represented very different sexual dynamics (in this regard echoing the contrast of spinster and fallen woman). Linton's "Girl of the Period" in the late 1860s had bewailed another rebellion, of crass materialism and self-assertion within fashionable life, an image that probably derived as much from popular fiction – notably that of Ouida and Rhoda Broughton – as from London drawing rooms. Annie Edwardes, whose novels of the 1860s also popularized "fast" young women, soon recognized new fictional possibilities in women's access to higher education, which she captured in *A Blue Stocking* (1877) and *A Girton Girl* (1885). Other varieties of independence came with the rise of both the aesthetic movement and varieties of social engagement in the East End, which were frequently conjoined in representations of newly independent women in the 1880s, such as *All Sorts and Conditions of Men* and *Miss Brown*. Linton herself wrote sympathetically of a young woman's intellectual aspirations in *The Rebel of the Family* (1880), though she eventually turned savagely on what she regarded as the cult of the female undergraduate in *The One Too Many* (1894), addressed to "the sweet girls still left among us." George Meredith's *Diana of the Crossways* (1885) recounts the life of an Irishwoman who separates from her suspicious older husband and carves out an independent life as a novelist and sexual adventurer; the novel, closely modeled on the life of Caroline Norton, was Meredith's greatest commercial success.

In these works, however, intellectual and political aspiration rarely triggered thoroughgoing rebellion against Victorian sexual politics and its central institution, marriage. The New Woman tag was applied to a more radical questioning of the lot of women (although not often working-class women, who were constrained as much by poverty as by sexual politics). The central burden of the attack became the sanctity of marriage, the axiom that women and their sexuality were properly fulfilled only as wives and that no amount of unhappiness could override the force of their vows. In this emphasis, the prototypical "New Woman" novel is Schreiner's *Story of an African Farm*. The energies of that iconoclastic work became widely diffused in the 1880s, as we've noticed, not only in public debate over marriage and sexuality but in the bolder view, set forth by Havelock Ellis in 1888, that "sexual relationships, so long as they do not result in the production of children, are matters in which the community has, as a community, little or no concern" (Cunningham 1978: 45). Surprisingly, however, little of this became an explicit burden in the novel until the very end of the decade – perhaps because authors and publishers were readier to risk opprobrium in the representation of female sexuality than in attacks on male prerogative. But Mona Caird, the moving spirit behind "Is Marriage a Failure?," struck a new note in *The Wing of Azrael* (1889), where the heroine, forced to marry for money, leaves her brutal husband for another man but ultimately stabs him to death, then throws herself off an ocean cliff. The melodrama recalls sensation fiction, but the novel's sympathies are squarely behind the aggrieved protagonist; though the ending is hardly consoling, at least Caird's heroine escapes the madhouse.

From this juncture the collisions of marriage and desire became a central burden of the novel – energized in large part by the controversy over Ibsen, whose rise to prominence coincided with Caird's novel and Pinero's *The Profligate*. Observers were struck by the number of women (frequently unaccompanied by men) attending matinee performances of Ibsen – whose 1892 characterization by the Examiner of Plays offered a virtual template for attacks on the New Woman: "all the characters in Ibsen's plays appear to me to be morally deranged. All the heroines are dissatisfied spinsters who look on marriage as a monopoly, or dissatisfied married women in a chronic state of rebellion against not only the conditions which nature has imposed on their sex, but against all the duties and obligations of mothers and sisters and wives" (Booth 1991: 173). The caricature quickly became a popular icon, a creature of masculine dress and short hair alternately Amazonian or withered in physique, much given to cigarettes and radical thought. But the conclusion of Caird's novel, echoing Schreiner's, pointed to a challenge, at once formal and political, that dogged fictional representations of the New Woman more than their counterparts in the drama. In questioning the authority of marriage, a novelist undercut the sturdiest of Victorian narrative structures, the romance plot. The moral and political ambitions of the New Woman novel are thus registered in a formal tension: if closure is not to be secured through the prospect of marital happiness, where can it be found? Many New Woman novels starkly suggest that the only alternative is death – a prospect that underscores the skeptical logic informing apologies for realism. A faithful rendering of the oppressive social order leaves no plausible avenues of fulfillment open to women who defy it; to believe otherwise is mere fantasy. Of course many novelists, women writers in particular, did yearn to believe otherwise, and this created a marked division within the New Woman novel. Over against realists who struggled, in Hardy's phrase, to represent "the sexual relationship as it is," other writers opened up spaces of romance, even utopia, in order to explore the sexual relationship as it might be – an impulse registered even in the exotic names of so many heroines: Hadria, Gallia, Evadne.

The realistic emphasis is represented preeminently by Hardy, who in an 1890 *New Review* symposium, "Candour in English Fiction," bemoaned the constraints hobbling efforts to represent the clash between sexual desire and social convention. Pressures on writers and publishers had intensified over the latter half of the 1880s, as the "Maiden Babylon" scandal ignited by W. T. Stead gave rise to the National Vigilance Association, which lobbied for the prosecution of Henry Vizetelly, who in 1889 was jailed for publishing a translation of Zola. In *Tess of the D'Urbervilles* (1891) Hardy nonetheless produced his boldest treatment of female sexuality, and the "moral hobgoblins" that haunt it, in the account of a beautiful young working woman whose poverty makes her unusually vulnerable to male fantasy. The novel recasts Hardy's ongoing preoccupation with the incursions of modernity into rural Wessex, in which new technologies (the railway, steam-powered threshing machines) are aligned with an alien social order. This order materializes first in the guise of Alec D'Urberville, a rakish heir of new urban money who has assumed the surname of an extinct country family, and subsequently in the "advanced" thought of another outsider, Angel Clare. Tess Durbeyfield, whose family (descended from the true D'Urbervilles) is on the verge of destitution, becomes pregnant by Alec, but the "cottage girl" declines his offer of marriage – a decision more troubling to her family than the pregnancy itself. After losing her child, she meets Clare, a clergyman's son engaged in a kind of rural slumming, who prides himself on the unorthodox opinions that would sanction his marrying a beautiful milkmaid. Tess's guilty confession of her past predictably exposes his conventionality; he cannot bear that Tess is not the vestal he had imagined, and he abandons her on their wedding night, leaving her no refuge but the predatory Alec – whose own passing spasm of evangelical fervor is one further provocation in Hardy's onslaught against contemporary moralism. In a savage irony, Tess and Angel enjoy a brief spell of fulfillment only after she kills Alec, and her execution becomes a form of martyrdom to the age-old fear of women's sexuality – an effect underscored by the novel's tendentious subtitle, "A Pure Woman." Hardy had protracted struggles with the editor of the *Graphic*, where the novel first appeared in serial, for whom he repeatedly altered and cut sections deemed too sexually daring, but when the novel finally appeared in book form it was highly praised, and ultimately sold more copies than any of Hardy's works to date. The success was enhanced by more hostile reviews early in 1892, as the swell of controversy over sexual boldness in literature prompted several critics to deplore both the morality and the theology of *Tess* – particularly the mordant closing invocation (in the section titled "Fulfillment") of the "President of the Immortals" having finally "ended his sport with Tess" (Hardy 1978: 489).

A less predictable complaint came from another quarter, in the form of feminist resistance to Tess's martyrdom, which provoked efforts to imagine a different outcome. Henrietta Stannard, writing as John Strange Winter, produced in 1894 a riposte entitled *A Blameless Woman*, echoing Hardy's subtitle but sparing her heroine Tess's fate. The effort to envision a fuller female sexuality not shadowed by martyrdom was most notable in the short stories of George Egerton (born Mary Chevelita Dunne, 1859–1945), published in *Keynotes* (1893) and *Discords* (1894) – the former volume thought so important by its publisher, John Lane, that he made it the inaugural volume of a series of the same title, and commissioned illustrations by Aubrey Beardsley. Reviewers were most struck by Egerton's erotic audacity, expressed not only in unusually forthright social acknowledgment of extramarital desire, but also through sustained interior monologue, in which protagonists reflect on "the untamed primitive savage temperament that lurks in the mildest, best woman" and conjure up fantasies that bear witness to it: "on the stage of an ancient theatre …She can see herself with parted lips and panting, rounded breasts, and a dancing devil in each glowing eye, sway voluptuously to the wild music" (Egerton 1983: 60, 58). It was as if the demure Lucy Snowe had come to inhabit the mind of Vashti, whose enigmatic performance had so fascinated the citizens of Villette. Reviewers were appropriately mesmerized: the author of the *Athenaeum's* "Year in Review" for 1893 called Egerton's work "remarkable chiefly on account of the hysterical frankness of its amatory abandonment." But the review also suggested something of the power of form:

> Along with the short story ("poisonous honey stol'n from France") has come a new license in dealing imaginatively with life … Not so many years ago Mr. George Moore was the only novelist in England who insisted on the novelist's right to be true to life … and he was attacked on all sides. Now every literary lady is "realistic." (Ardis 1990: 87)

"Realistic" in this usage carries the French taint of "sexually provocative," but in fact the short story allowed Egerton a peculiar suppleness of structure that could disarm some of the constraints inherent in realism. Her markedly elliptical narration and the more tenuous sense of closure inherent in the form could accommodate a more expansive horizon of possibility for unconventional women than a strict realism might allow.

Still, the burdens of the New Woman struggling with an unsympathetic world more often consist of starkly drawn suffering, even agony. This was particularly noticeable in one of the first great successes in the mode, Sarah Grand's *The Heavenly Twins* (1893). This sprawling novel of some 900 pages loosely intertwines three central plots. The 19-year-old Evadne Frayling has been raised by parents of comically fossilized convention, who believe "that a woman should hold no opinion that is not of masculine origin" (Grand 1893: 5) and that her life will culminate in marriage, in which she will cede all independence of action and thought to her husband. After her arranged marriage to the middle-aged Colonel Colquhoun, she shrinks from the discovery of his past sexual experience, leaves him for a time, carries on long debates about the sexual double standard, finally agrees to return to him on the condition of celibacy, only to fight her own erotic attraction to him until she finally breaks down under the strain. Edith Beale, brought up with similar notions of fulfillment, is less fortunate: she marries an army officer who turns out to have tertiary syphilis, which agonizingly lays waste both Edith and her child. A glimmer of hope resides in the third female protagonist, Angelica Hamilton-Wells, one of the title twins. Her upbringing underscores the misery wrought by the double standards of gender (her gifts as a violinist are suppressed as unladylike), a burden she begins to escape after witnessing the agonies of Edith. That example prompts her to marry a middle-aged man with the proviso that she may do anything she wishes, short of immorality – a license she exploits to dress up in her brother's clothes and make nightly visits to a lonely young man known as the Tenor. The relationship remains platonic, however, and ultimately she returns to her husband, the social order and her own respectability still intact.

The success of *Heavenly Twins*, which sold some 40,000 copies in its first year, encouraged a host of similar works. George Gissing offered a more modulated account in *The Odd Women* (1893), a title that alluded to long-standing discussion of so-called "superfluous" women who never married. The novel focuses on Rhoda Nunn, an ascetic reformer devoted to giving young single women office skills by mastering the recently invented typewriter (the "typewriter-girl," title of an 1894 novel by Grant Allen, became one emblem of newly independent, upwardly aspiring young women). Rhoda is torn between her sense of independence and the courtship of a wealthy young man who seems actually to respect her moral commitments (and who is captivated by the sexuality he senses beneath her austere demeanor). While the novel contains Gissing's usual attention to the material costs of daily life among the shabby genteel, it is more distinctive in its concluding sense of a complex emotional fulfillment outside of marriage, and for its subtle hint of the lesbian desire that often shadowed the term "odd." In the following year, *A Yellow Aster* by Iota (Kathleen Mannigham Caffyn) presented an even more hardily independent but also aggressively sexual heroine, Gwen Waring, who "neither evaded nor shirked conventions, she simply swept them aside, as she did her lovers" (Cunningham 1978: 57). So great is her unconventionality that she marries more out of boredom than desire, in search of a new form of experience, only to discover that her husband – tellingly named Strange – arouses her no more than all of her rejected lovers. He obligingly leaves her, but when he returns she rather mysteriously discovers a new responsiveness and settles into the married state.

Controversy over the New Woman novel culminated in 1895, when three important works developed different aspects of the genre. *Gallia*, by Menie Muriel Dowie, depicts another feminist heroine, her confidence honed by an Oxford education (she is given to bringing up discussions of legalized prostitution in the company of her elderly maiden aunts), who turns her restless intelligence to sustained analysis of her own thwarted desire. She ultimately concludes that it would be "eminently rational" to select a husband on eugenic grounds, in order to produce children who will improve the race, and accordingly embraces the institution on just these dispassionate grounds. In the same month appeared what became for many the quintessential New Woman novel, Grant Allen's *The Woman Who Did*. The crude title distills a central impulse of the genre – and was quickly answered by Lucas Cleeve, *The Woman Who Wouldn't*, and Victoria Cross, *The Woman Who Didn't*. It also captures Allen's psychological coarseness as a novelist. Herminia Barton finds that she can only experience passion outside of marriage, freed from "vile slavery," yet at the same time she delights to "look up to the man," and soon is punished for her independence of mind when her lover dies and their daughter grows up to be eminently conventional.

Her daughter's engagement, "the final crown in her thorn of martyrdom," prompts Herminia to commit suicide with prussic acid.

The crowning provocation was Hardy's *Jude the Obscure*, published in late 1895 in volume form in the first collected edition of Hardy's novels. The travails of Jude Hawley, a young stonemason, link the twin ideals of education and marriage as sources of agonizing, grotesque disappointment. His dream of university education at Christminster (Oxford) is first derailed when he is entrapped in marriage by a young woman who feigns pregnancy, and later laid waste by class prejudice, in a pointed rebuke to Arnoldian celebrations of culture. Escaping from his loveless marriage, the tender-hearted Jude falls in love with his cousin, Sue Bridehead, whose tortuous vacillations over marriage and sexual commitment represent Hardy's most excruciating exploration of the burdens of respectability. Another avowed free-thinker – she echoes a host of late-Victorian apologists for ancient Greece as the grounds of an ethos more healthy and fulfilling than Christianity – Sue nonetheless finds herself recoiling from an attraction to Jude, who seems almost her Shelleyan epipsyche. They resemble "one person split in two," but Sue flees from that affinity into marriage to an elderly schoolmaster whom she finds sexually repugnant (Hardy 1998: 228). When she finally does tear herself away from her husband – who with his own iconoclastic generosity agrees to a divorce – she enjoys sexual fulfillment (and three children) with Jude, but also recoils from marrying him, and when their unorthodox arrangement becomes known, the resultant stigma drives them to increasing desperation. Their struggles climax when Jude's son by his marriage – who bears the grotesque name "Father Time," the harbinger of "the coming wish not to live" – kills himself and the two younger children, "because we are too menny" (336). The horror drives Sue back to her former husband in a spasm of agonized self-abasement, and a drunken, dying Jude back into the arms of his slatternly first wife, who leaves him to die alone, as he whispers verses from *Job* punctuated by distant cheering from the Christminster boat races. Not merely the marriage plot, but virtually every article of late-Victorian idealism, is left in ruins.

The reception of *Jude* was one of the fiercest episodes in late-Victorian debate over the moral burdens of the novel. For some reviewers it confirmed Hardy's standing at the very summit of contemporary novelists, and the *Saturday Review* called it "great," but even his most ardent admirers were staggered by the bleakness of the book, and its almost complete submergence of the comic in the grotesque. His friend Edmund Gosse acknowledged that Hardy's "genius" warranted freedom to choose whatever subject matter he pleased, but did not conceal his disappointment: "We rise from perusal of it stunned with a sense of the hollowness of existence" (Millgate 1982: 370). Other critics were less restrained. The *Pall Mall Gazette* referred to "Jude the Obscene"; Mrs. Oliphant, reviewing the work in conjunction with *The Woman Who Did* as exhibits in "The Anti-Marriage League," huffed that "nothing so thoroughly indecent as the whole history of Jude in his relations with his wife Arabella has ever been put in English print – that is to say, from the hands of a Master" (Cox 1980: 257). The New York *Critic*, decrying "an undercurrent of morbid animality ... which is sickening to an ordinarily decent mind," concluded "we may as well accept a cage full of monkeys as a microcosm of humanity." Hardy, stung by the criticism, never wrote another novel; freed from financial worries, he devoted the last 30 years of his long life to poetry.

Decadent Form

For hostile critics "decadence" was focused in the sexual audacity of the novel and drama (and their presumed counterparts in daily life), but for its apologists it was, as Gautier's lavish tribute suggests, foremost a stylistic agenda, which was first registered in poetry. British poetry of the 1880s took shape against the ebbing influence of the Laureate. Tennyson's authority remained powerful, and he directed it against much that was new in art, most memorably in *Locksley Hall Sixty Years After* (1886). The speaker of the title poem, a pendant to its namesake in the great 1842 volume, again excoriates the corruptions of the age, but this time rails against the degradation of literature:

> Authors – essayist, atheist, novelist, realist, rhymester, play your part,
> Paint the mortal shame of nature with the living hues of Art.

> Rip your brothers' vices open, strip your own foul passions bare;
> Down with Reticence, down with Reverence – forward – naked – let
>   them stare ...

> Set the maiden fancies wallowing in the troughs of Zolaism, –
> Forward, forward, ay and backward, downward too into the abysm.

Do your best to charm the worst, to lower the rising race of men;
Have we risen from out the beast, then back into the beast again?
(ll. 139–48; Tennyson 1969)

The terms of attack are utterly familiar, but so potent was Tennyson's
name that Gladstone felt obliged to rebut the poem's pessimism in an
article in the *Nineteenth Century*. The Laureate had accepted a peerage in 1884, the same year in which he signed a 10-year contract with
Macmillan guaranteeing him royalties of one-third the list price of all
his volumes sold, with a minimum of 1,500 pounds annually. He had
become a name, a monument – of genius, of poetic wisdom and consolation, even of England and its language. (In German émigré farming communities on the American plains, children were christened the
likes of "Alfred Tennyson Penner," as if in fealty to the immigrants'
new tongue.) The volumes that followed – *Tiresias and Other Poems*
(1885), *Locksley Hall Sixty Years After* (1886), and *Demeter and Other
Poems* (1889) sold vigorously, *Demeter* 20,000 copies in the first week –
but these were increasingly slender collections of largely occasional
verse. There were some moving exceptions: the monologues, "The
Ancient Sage" (based on the Chinese philosopher Lao-tze) and
"Demeter and Persephone," and the lyric, "Crossing the Bar," which
so pleased Tennyson that he asked that it be printed at the end of all
his collections – as it has been since his death in 1892.

Demeter and Other Poems was published on 12 December, 1889 –
the same day that Browning's *Asolando* was published. It also turned
out to be the day of Browning's death, in Venice. Matthew Arnold had
died the previous year, in Liverpool, far more widely recognized as a
critic than a poet, particularly for his pointed criticism in the two decades since *Culture and Anarchy* of an emergent mass culture. But
Arnold and Browning, much more than Tennyson, became crucial
points of reference in a new cult of literature – albeit in very different
ways. Arnold's conception of poetry as psychic balm, and culture as a
pursuit of intellectual balance and harmony, became a foil to very different modes of vision. In France, as Arthur Symons would put it, the
brothers Goncourt exemplified an effort to "to specialize vision," to
develop "a special, unique way of seeing things," which Symons defined
against the Arnoldian effort "to see life steadily, and see it whole."
Their vision, he marveled, "has always been somewhat feverish … with
the diseased sharpness of over-excited nerves" (Symons 1999: 1407).
Derived from Baudelaire, this emphasis takes up English rhetoric of

the late 1860s, particularly the controversy surrounding Swinburne and Pater's fascination with medieval faith as "a beautiful disease of the senses," as he put it in his early review of Morris's poetry. But French commentators gave to these psychic states more precise formal counterparts, in both style and poetic structure – in Gautier's terms, "an ingenious, complex, learned style, full of shades and of refinements of meaning, constantly pushing back the boundaries of language, borrowing from every technical vocabulary, taking colours from every palette and notes from every keyboard, a style that struggles to express the most inexpressible thoughts" (Reed 1985: 10).

The honing of "specialized" vision thus impelled a formal refinement and a resistance to vernacular idioms, which encouraged avoidance of blank verse and other narrative forms in pursuit of an elegant miniaturism, in which the grand gave way to the exquisite, the familiar to the arcane, the whole to the fragment. The rise of the short story, though not immediately motivated by this program, could readily participate in it, particularly insofar as it emulated Poe (a central influence on French decadence) in aiming at a single, unified effect unavailable to more sustained narrative. Thus Symons described the Goncourts having "broken the outline of the conventional novel" in order to capture "this and that revealing moment, this or that significant attitude or accident or sensation" (Symons 1999: 1407). But the aims were most readily translated to lyric, in the cultivation of formal elegance and intricacy and muted but nuanced emotional shading. In England this emphasis built on not only the examples of Baudelaire and Verlaine in France, but on a surprisingly energetic wave of formal experiment in poetry of the late 1870s, of which Hopkins's poetry is the most striking example. Coventry Patmore's *The Unknown Eros* (1877) distinctively collected irregular odes on a wide range of topics, and in the same year Edmund Gosse published an article in the *Cornhill*, "A Plea for Certain Exotic Forms of Verse," which looked to French Parnassianism, particularly Theodore de Banville and the lapidary stanzas of Gautier that had inspired him, as a corrective to the lingering formlessness of spasmodic poetry. (An equally powerful but unstated motive was resistance to the seemingly inescapable influences of Tennyson and Browning.) Gosse singled out for criticism Sydney Dobell's "invertebrate rhapsodies ... so amazing in their beauty of detail and total absence of style," and urged a chastening discipline in "exotic" forms such as the villanelle and the ballade, rhyme forms far more difficult in English than in romance languages (Buckley 1945: 83).

His challenge was taken up most extensively by Austin Dobson (1840–1921), but Swinburne's second series of *Poems and Ballads* (1878) provided many examples in this vein, and even W. E. Henley tried his hand in *Bric-A-Brac*, later incorporated in *A Book of Verses* (1888) – a suggestively proto-decadent title in its subordination of passion to intricate ornament.

For all the difficulties of taxonomy, then, "decadent" poetry was distinguished above all by a formal refinement that tended to resist the traditional appeal to general sympathies that would nurture social and psychic harmony. In this context the poetry of Browning had a special resonance. The monologue feeds on the fascination of arcane experience and unconventional psychology, as well as exotic setting and anecdote that, pried free of Browningesque moral frames, could occasion unfamiliar complexes of feeling. This latter emphasis took up Pater's dictum – a frequent refrain during the period – that all art constantly aspires to the condition of music. In Pater's own criticism, the most influential of the 1880s, this aspiration was associated with the pursuit of "refinement," an effort not merely to capture intricate shadings of sensation and feeling, but to elaborate in ever more subtle forms the impressions experienced by encounters with existing art. Paterian aesthetic experience might even seem an effort to sublimate the Browningesque moment, to modulate its exhilaration into a quieter intensity. In this regard Pater's example would chime with Verlaine's "Art Poetique" (1875), which celebrated "la Nuance," "rien que la Nuance" (1. 14; Verlaine 1974). The emphasis on evocative atmosphere was further reinforced by the model of Whistler's distinctly muted impressionist style – an influence registered as early as Wilde's *Poems* of 1882, in such titles as "Impression du Matin."

The influence of Pater and Browning converged in the career of Arthur Symons (1865–1945), the most influential late-Victorian commentator on French poetry, whose formulations became a central reference point in understanding late-Victorian poetry generally. Symons's first book was a study of Browning (1886), which he followed with a volume of poetry, *Night and Day* (1887), dedicated to Pater. From visits to France, Symons drew an increasingly programmatic view of the literary scene there, which he outlined in an influential essay of 1893, "The Decadent Movement in Literature." That movement, as he described it, was divided into "two main branches," Symbolist and Impressionist. The former was dedicated to the pursuit of a moment's rapture, a sense of contact with "the 'soul' of that which can be apprehended only by the soul – the finer sense of things unseen, the deeper meaning of things evident." Impressionist poetry was more content to linger on the externals of the world, particularly that beyond the bounds of traditional decorum, aspiring to "a style which was itself almost sensation," which would preserve "the very heat and motion of life" (Symons 1999: 1406–7).

This rather elastic view of "decadence" accommodated writers as diverse as Pater and Henley, but it clearly fits the poetry of Symons himself, whose early poems pursue a sort of urban pastoral, seeking out material seemingly resistant to lyric decorum. "Pastel," for example, seems written to order for the "Symbolist" effect analyzed in "The Decadent Movement," and thereby anticipates what Ezra Pound would christen "Imagism":

> The light of our cigarettes
>   Went and came in the gloom
>   It was dark in the little room.
>
> Dark, and then, in the dark,
>   Sudden, a flash, a glow,
>   And a hand and a ring I know.
>
> And then, through the dark, a flush
>   Ruddy and vague, the grace –
>   A rose – of her lyric face.
>
> (Symons 1906)

Though the setting is faintly scandalous (a man and a woman smoking cigarettes in a darkened room, presumably outside conventional domesticity), the payoff is a hazy but epiphanic image of "her lyric face" – conjured in the emphatically visual terms signaled by the title, but nonetheless seeming to transcend the outwardly banal moment.

Michael Field's *Sight and Song* (1892) offers another recurrent theme of decadent treatment, focusing on varieties of *ekphrasis*, the poetic evocation of visual form. Their next volume, *Underneath the Bough* (1893), unites a great variety of stanza forms and occasions to an intricate detailing that also anticipates Pound's imagism, as in the brief "Cyclamens," where the poet's sensibility hovers on the verge of complete absorption into the image:

> They are terribly white:
> There is snow on the ground,
> And a moon on the snow at night;
> The sky is cut by the winter light;
> Yet I, who have all these things in ken,
> Am struck to the heart by the chiselled white
> Of this handful of cyclamen.
>
> (Field 2000)

Lionel Johnson (1867–1902) developed a more lurid (perhaps wryly so) conjunction of the mundane and the transcendent in "A Decadent's Lyric":

> Sometimes, in very joy of shame,
> Our flesh becomes one living flame
> And she and I
> No more are separate, but the same.
>
> (ll. 1–4; L. Johnson 1982)

Johnson, who published two volumes of poems (1895 and 1897), was enshrined by Yeats as a figurehead of "The Tragic Generation," a study in failed promise and dissolution, a brilliant classicist (Pater was his tutor at Oxford) who gradually descended into alcoholism, and died at the age of 34 – emblematically, by falling off a barstool. But Johnson's "decadence" in fact was the product of a fiercely moral, at times ascetic, sensibility – he thought *l'art pour l'art* an absurd slogan – in which the ballad meter can become the vehicle of a tense moral agon. Thus in "Dark Angel" the poet wrestles with a desire intensified by interdiction:

> Through thee, the gracious Muses turn
> To Furies, O mine enemy!
> And all the things of beauty burn
> With flames of evil ecstasy.
>
> (ll. 13–16)

In a note redolent of Hopkins, another writer under the sway of Pater, the experience of beauty is enriched by the struggle to resist it.

Johnson's exact contemporary, Ernest Dowson, who likewise died young (at 32), published a single volume of poetry, *Verses* (1896), which contains what may be the iconic poem of English decadence, "Non Sum Qualis Eram Bonae Sub Regno Cynarae" ("I am not what I was under the reign of good Cynara," the opening of Horace's fourth ode). The lyric is exemplary in its interweaving of "high" and "low," with the language of Horace (marker of elite refinement) invoked to describe sex with a prostitute ("surely the kisses of her bought red mouth were sweet"), a partner who arouses a kind of loyalty, but of a markedly tepid, even louche kind, which is registered only in subsequent (inevitable) disappointment. The hint of parody is a frequent byproduct of the intense historical self-consciousness of most decadent poets, but it is checked by the distinctive form, with its repetition of the fourth and sixth lines of each six-line stanza, and the subtle meter, which reflects Dowson's acquaintance with classical prosody but whose rhythm carries its own sense of engagement:

> I have forgot much, Cynara! Gone with the wind,
> Flung roses, roses riotously with the throng,
> Dancing, to put thy pale, lost lilies out of mind;
> But I was sick and desolate of an old passion,
>   Yea, all the time, because the dance was long:
> I have been faithful to thee, Cynara! In my fashion.
>
>   (ll. 23–8; Dowson 1963)

The Poetry of London

The mingling of "high" and "low" in decadent poetry found much of its material in city life. An especially notable impetus and emblem for that poetry was the late-Victorian music hall. The music hall was one by-product of the increasing specialization of the London theater, in which what had begun as singing societies in working-men's clubs (noted in several of Dickens's novels) merged with varieties of the more elaborate spectacle and performance that had been nurtured by theatrical licensing. The halls kept up their association with a predominantly working-class audience, featuring an array of comic song and dance that persisted into the television "variety show," but they also offered a fantasy of aristocratic glamor and spectacle, in part through the elaborate use of mirroring and lights in which the working-class audience could gaze at itself on parade. By the 1880s, larger venues such as the Alhambra and Gaiety in Leicester Square began to attract more affluent single men, drawn not only by the spectacle and the sense of crossing class lines, but also by the upscale prostitutes who increasingly frequented the promenades. One offshoot of this mingling was poetry like that of Johnson and Symons – the latter of whom found in the music hall an evocative world resembling that of Toulouse-Lautrec's canvases, a scene of baffled longing and solitude amidst the crowd, in which the spectator becomes the spectacle:

> My life is like a music-hall,
>   Where, in the impotence of rage,
> Chained by enchantment to my stall
>   I see myself upon the stage
> Dance to amuse a music hall.
>   ("Prologue," 1–5; Symons 1906)

Music-hall ballad and song, however, would shape a poetry aimed at an audience very different from that of Johnson and Symons – a poetry that became the backbone of the "counter-decadence."

The most influential achievement in this regard was the poetry of Kipling, which was centrally engaged by England's imperial mission (as he imagined it). Though his early *Departmental Ditties* drew on a much older tradition of comic narrative, in *Barrack-Room Ballads* (1890) Kipling aligned himself with the common soldier, who sang not of glory but of the rigors of his job, fearful brutality alternating with rounds of boredom occasionally relieved by women and drink, and the hypocrisy of a country that celebrated heroism but treated the working-class soldier with disdain:

> For it's Tommy this an' Tommy that, an' "Chuck him out, the brute!"
> But it's "Savior of 'is country" when the guns begin to shoot;
> An' it's Tommy this an Tommy that, an anything you please;
> An' Tommy ain't a bloomin' fool – you bet that Tommy sees!
>   ("Tommy", ll. 25–32; Kipling 1930)

The ballad form was taken up by a host of other 1890s poets, such as Henry Newbolt, who became famous with an 1897 volume of ballads celebrating naval heroes, *Admirals All*. Kipling was quickly embraced by Henley, then editing the *Scots* (later the *National*) *Observer*, an avowedly "imperial" journal, which printed his ballads before their appearance in an English volume in 1892. Kipling's poems encouraged Henley to compose songs of more fervent and unequivocal patriotism, which culminated in *For England's Sake: Verses in Time of War*, published during the Boer War of 1900, and best known for "*Pro Rege Nostro*":

> Ever the faith endures,
>   England, my England: –
> "Take and break us: we are yours,
>   England, my own!"
>
> (ll. 21–4)

In 1892, Henley published *The Song of the Sword and Other Verses*, dedicated to Kipling, whose title poem indulged an all-too-familiar dream of war as national uplift and purification, here rejuvenated by the fantasies of social Darwinism:

> Sifting the nations,
> The slag from the metal,
> The waste and the weak
> From the fit and the strong;
> Fighting the brute,
> The abysmal fecundity.
>
> (ll. 127–32)

In the following year, however, Henley republished the volume as *London Voluntaries*, a title that not only underscores the allure of the city as a subject, but also hints at the influence of polemics in behalf of decadence. Though "voluntaries" are certainly a more hearty music than nocturnes, the use of musical directions to title individual poems suggests Paterian precepts, and Symons commended them in his "Decadent Movement." *Largo e mesto* unfolds a nightmare vision of the city in which "brave ships, / No more adventurous and fair"

> But infamously enchanted,
> Huddle together in the foul eclipse,
> Or feel their course by inches desperately,
> As through a tangle of alleys murder-haunted,
> From sinister reach to reach out – out – to sea.
>
> (ll. iv.52–6)

Though reminiscent of Thomson's *City of Dreadful Night*, the strikingly irregular verse and atmospheric emphasis again suggest the influence of Impressionism (which Henley fervently admired in the visual arts, particularly in Whistler).

Even Henley's career thus suggests unexpected interweaving of decadence and its ostensible contraries. This blurring of boundaries is even more notable in the neglected career of John Davidson (1857–1909), a Scots journalist who wrote a novel-length burlesque of decadence entitled *Earl Lavender* (1895), but who was best known for his poetry. *In a Music Hall* (1891) suggests a more rhythmically vigorous Symons, and the title of *Fleet Street Eclogues* (1893, 1896), with its oxymoronic suggestion of urban pastoral, echoes the decadent juxtaposition of high and low, classical and contemporary life. But his most popular work was in an emphatically vernacular idiom, most famously "Thirty Bob a Week" from *Ballads and Songs* (1895), which appropriates Kipling's example to another neglected poetic speaker, the lower-middle-class clerk:

> But I don't allow it's luck and all a toss;
>   There's no such thing as being starred and crossed;
> It's just the power of some to be a boss,
>   And the bally power of others to be bossed:
> I face the music, sir; you bet I ain't no cur;
>   Strike me lucky if I don't believe I'm lost!
>
> (ll. 7–12)

The expansion of clerical employment opened up new subject matter for fiction as well, as workers clutching at the fringes of middle-class respectability frequently sought affordable housing in suburbs such as Camberwell, beyond the more confining conditions of London proper. An unexpected success in this line was *Diary of a Nobody* (1892), by George and Weedon Grossmith, first published as a series of sketches in *Punch* in 1888–9. The project began as a send-up of the vogue for diaries and memoirs that Wilde would mock in *The Importance of Being Earnest*, but it resulted in something warmer and more durable than the usual *Punch* series. Charles Pooter, a middle-aged Holloway clerk working at a mercantile firm in the City, became an emblem of lower-middle-class suburbia, whose confining world magnifies both the small pleasures and the constant anxieties of everyday life. A culmination of "the gent" as a comic type, Pooter is a proud but meek man, his excruciating self-consciousness inflamed by routine social gaffes: "I left the room with silent dignity but caught my foot in the mat" (Grossmith 1991: 115). His diary painstakingly records his ongoing agitation over small articles of dress, recognition by his employer, bullying tradesmen, a feckless son, and the planning of modest social gatherings (centered on cards, drinks, bad puns, and *blanc mange*) for a small circle of erratic friends and acquaintances who find his naivety an easy mark for various schemes; even the occasional holiday out of London is anything but an occasion to relax. Yet Pooter is never thoroughly embittered, and the satire is softened both by his resilience and by his devotion to his wife Carrie, who amply returns his awkward but earnest affection.

Though the shock of the East End was no longer quite so vivid, social investigators and novelists both continued to be drawn to the byways of urban life, which continued to seem an alien, often dangerous world. William Booth – founder of the Salvation Army – entitled his book *In Darkest London and the Way Out* (1890) to echo Livingstone's bestseller *In Darkest Africa* (1889), and proposed rescuing the "submerged tenth" by means of "City colonies." The pioneering social survey of Charles Booth, *Life and Labour of the People of London* (which ran to 17 volumes by 1902), charted income distribution across London with new exactitude, while writers developed an ethnographic emphasis more attentive to the force of ethnicity, particularly in response to a growing influx of immigrants to the East End. Jews had long experienced the peculiar pressures of "Englishness," but the Jewish community in London gained new visibility in *Reuben Sachs* (1889), a short novel by Amy Levy exploring the tensions between social ambition and the "tribal" loyalties of the children of affluent, conservative Jewish families. The novel is saturated with racial typology – the protagonist has "unmistakably the figure and movements of a Jew," his opening words reveal "unmistakably the voice of a Jew" (Levy 2006: 59, 57) – and the familiar ethnographic emphasis of urban fiction is so insistent – the social intricacies of "the Community" are "utterly incomprehensible to an outsider" – that Levy's novel was roundly attacked in the Jewish press for recycling anti-Semitic stereotypes. But the work pointedly explores the pressure of competing loyalties, across generations and religious boundaries, and even across class lines within extended families. Like all of Levy's writing, it is especially attentive to the challenges confronting young women, for whom the social disabilities of gender are compounded by the insularity of their upbringing: "it is difficult to conceive an existence, more curiously limited, more completely provincial than hers" (69). (Levy herself could not finally manage the conflicts of her own cosmopolitan existence; eight months after the book was published, at the age of 27, she committed suicide.)

Israel Zangwill, three years Levy's junior, set out to write a corrective of sorts in *Children of the Ghetto* (1892), which was commissioned by the Jewish Publication Society of Philadelphia. It is less a novel than a series of linked sketches and uplifting tales, the opening half focusing on lives of East End poverty among recent immigrants (Zangwill was a child of immigrants, born in Whitechapel), the second depicting affluent, assimilated Jews of the next generation. Throughout Zangwill celebrates the resilience and dignity of Jewish immigrants, and the power of enduring ties to the Ghetto even among those who have left it behind. The work was an immense success, and its sympathetic treatment of a broad cast of characters helped to earn Zangwill the tag "the Dickens of the Ghetto," a label further vindicated by *Ghetto Tragedies* (1893), *King of the Schnorrers* (1894), and *Dreamers of the Ghetto* (1898).

Yeats

The most enduring poetic voice to emerge in the 1880s belonged to one of the most influential chroniclers of late-Victorian literary life, a young Irishman, William Butler Yeats (1865–1939). Born into a well-connected Protestant family, Yeats spent much of his adolescence in London (with summers in his native Sligo). As the son of a painter, Yeats fell under the Pre-Raphaelite spell at an early age, and was deeply influenced by the poetry of Rossetti and Morris, as well as the prose of Pater. A poem, he remarked in youthful fervor, should be "a painted and bepictured argosy" (Ellmann 1978: 139). As a young man grappling with that familiar Victorian dilemma, recoiling from modern skepticism but unsatisfied with the articles of orthodox belief, Yeats found in poetry what he himself called "a new religion": "deprived by Huxley and Tyndall, whom I detested, of the simple-minded religion of my childhood, I had made a new religion, almost an infallible church of poetic tradition, of a fardel of stories, of personages, and of emotions" sanctioned by long tradition (Yeats 1965: 77). Recalling Burne-Jones's rallying cry, "the more materialistic science becomes, the more angels shall I paint," Yeats struggled to disarm those antagonists of imagination he variously called "rationalism," "materialism," and "the dragon of abstraction."

The quest for new forms of belief was hardly confined to Yeats. Cults of mysticism and magic were gaining currency throughout European capitals, all of them nurturing systems of esoteric orders and natural symbolism. Yeats was early drawn to the world of the occult, most durably the Theosophy of Madame Blavatsky, one of the more prominent vogues growing out of the spiritual ferment that also stirred up the Society for Psychical Research. Blavatsky's appeal to a vaguely Buddhist cosmology sustained by arcane tradition would be reinforced by the fascination of the Kabbalah, which was a central interest of "The Hermetic Students of the Golden Dawn," a secret society which Yeats joined in 1890. At the same time, he was enthralled to discover a mystic forbearer in Blake, whose works he helped to edit from 1889 until 1893.

Yeats's imagination, however, was more distinctively energized by the world of Irish folklore, whose motifs were central to his early poetry, as to many participants in what became known as "the Celtic Renaissance". The early monument of this interest is *The Wanderings of Oisin* (1889), where Yeats develops the emphases of Rossetti – and, more remotely, Keats's narratives – in an evocative pictorialism, where images constantly gesture toward symbolic registers that transcend paraphrase. Oisin recounts to St Patrick his "three centuries ... /Of dalliance with a demon thing," Niamh, daughter of the King of the Young, who has enticed him away from the human world. In the second of three parts,

> A lady with soft eyes like funeral tapers,
> And face that seemed wrought out of moonlit vapors,
> And a sad mouth, that fear made tremulous,
> As any ruddy moth, looked down on us;
> And she with a wave-crusted chain was tied
> To two old eagles, full of ancient pride,
> That with dim eyeballs stood on either side.
>
> (ll. ii.69–75; Yeats 1966)

The captive lady seems to represent Ireland under British rule, but the power of the passage resides less in this identification (which eluded most early readers) than in the weirdly evocative local detail, the eyes like funeral tapers and the sad mouth tremulous like a ruddy moth.

Irish motifs and traditional forms had further allure as a means of self-effacement, which might obscure the insecurities of a greatly gifted 23-year-old poet still groping for direction. Yeats desired, as he put it, "once more an art where the artist's handicraft would hide as under those half-anonymous chisels or as we find it in some old Scots ballads," and was drawn to "metrical forms that seemed old enough to have been sung by men half-asleep or riding on a journey" (Yeats 1965: 101, 83). His slender first lyric collection, *Crossways* (1889), amplifies the effect through its reliance on ballad, song, and dialogue. The quest was intensified through Yeats's participation in The Rhymer's Club, a loosely knit group of poets – including Lionel Johnson, Ernest Dowson, John Davidson, Richard LeGallienne, and (less frequently) Symons and Wilde – who in the early 1890s met regularly to discuss poetry. Ironically, however, Yeats's first great lyric came through a loosening of rhythm and more colloquial syntax.

> I will arise and go now, and go to Innisfree,
> And a small cabin build there, of clay and wattles made:
> Nine bean-rows will I have there, a hive for the honey-bee,
> And live alone in the bee-loud glade."
>
> And I shall have some peace there, for peace comes dropping slow,
> Dropping from the veils of the morning to where the cricket sings;
> There midnight's all a-glimmer, and noon a purple glow,
> And evening full of the linnet's wings.
>
> I will arise and go now, for always night and day
> I hear lake water lapping with low sounds by the shore;
> While I stand on the roadway, or on the pavements grey,
> I hear it in the deep heart's core.
>
> ("Innisfree"; Yeats 1966)

Yeats described "Innisfree" (published in *The Rose* [1893]) as a Thoreauvian fantasy of living alone on a small island in Sligo. More recently, critics have read the poem as an imaginative repossession of a conquered island – although that reading is complicated by Yeats's identity as a descendant of the landed Protestant gentry who had spent most of his adult life in London. Certainly after the death of Parnell in 1891 Yeats became increasingly dedicated to the cultural and political independence of his native country. But he would most value in "Innisfree" a more inclusive triumph over "rhetoric," that discursive habit of so much Victorian poetry that Yeats deprecated as "impurities," "curiosities about politics, about science, about history, about religion." "We must create once more the pure work," he resolved (Yeats 1965: 112), and that goal would be central to the rise of literary modernism.

The Scandal of Wilde

During his early career, Wilde had been more a social lion and provo-cateur than a writer; for much of the 1880s he produced little work more durable than reviews. But the 1888 appearance of *The Happy Prince and Other Tales* initiated a remarkably varied and important body of work. "The Portrait of Mr. W. H.," a critical fiction exploring the erotic history informing Shakespeare's sonnets, appeared in 1889, and "The Soul of Man Under Socialism," which idiosyncratically aligns socialism with a radical individualism, appeared in 1891 – the same year four of his articles were collected as *Intentions* (1891). After Pater's writings, *Intentions* represents the most enduring critical volume of the last two decades of the century. Its two most suggestive essays, "The Decay of Lying" and "The Critic as Artist," revived the dialogue form to wittily undermine critical platitudes – that great art is realistic and that the critical endeavour is always subordinate to the artistic. The latter engagement pushes to its horizon the logic of cul-ture developed from Mill through Arnold and Pater. Arnold had argued that critical work may be genuinely creative – "in some epochs no other creation is possible" ("Function of Criticism"); Pater had blurred the distinction between scholarship and creation, while inti-mating that culture might be more fully realized in a sensibility than in a work of art. Wilde insists that the supreme achievement of culture is not art but consciousness – a state of affairs in which the critic, freed from the "one-sidedness" of action, displaces the artist. Though that conclusion chimed with the acute historical consciousness of decadent art, it was more obviously a tacit apology for his own career to date, echoing the Paterian view of Dorian Gray, that human identity is "mul-tiform," and that the richest life is one which multiplies consciousness by cultivating responsiveness to disparate modes of experience.

Increasingly, however, Wilde staked his claim to recognition on the stage. In 1891 he wrote *Salomé*, the greatest work of Symbolist drama in English – though Wilde originally wrote it in French, perhaps to be closer to its central inspirations. In Wilde's version, the death of John the Baptist becomes a deadlock of baffled, mesmerized desire – of Herod and the young Syrian captain enthralled by Salomé, of Salomé attempting in vain to seduce the ascetic Iokanaan (as John is named) – in language that approaches incantation, as of minds in delirium or trance. As Salomé prepares her dance of the seven veils, Herod remarks,

"Ah! Look at the moon! She has become red. She has become red as blood. Ah! The prophet prophesied truly. He prophesied the moon would become red as blood. Did he not prophesy it?" (Wilde 1954: 340). Although Wilde hoped to stage the work in London, the production was blocked by the Examiner of Plays, who invoked an obscure statute forbidding the depiction of biblical characters on stage. Wilde found some consolation, however, not only in praise for the printed version in English, but in a different success on the stage. In February of 1892 *Lady Windermere's Fan: A Play about a Good Woman* opened at the St. James's Theatre. Drawing on the vogue for the problem play, Wilde built his drama around sexual intrigue and hidden pasts on the verge of revelation in a Mayfair drawing room. The title character, heretofore a paragon of virtue, is about to abandon her husband for another man, only to be diverted by an older woman, whose generosity seems out of keeping with her own past. But the play withholds the usual comic culmination of recognition and reconciliation. Lady Windermere never discovers that her deliverer is in fact her ostracized mother ("A Good Woman" hints at the polemical force of Hardy's "A Pure Woman"). Above all, the play captured for the audience Wilde's epigrammatic wit. Though some critics demurred – an envious Henry James pronounced it "infantine" – the play was an enormous success, bringing Wilde financial independence for the first time since he had exhausted his small inheritance.

Two other hits in a similar vein followed in quick succession – *A Woman of No Importance* was produced in April of 1893, *An Ideal Husband* in January 1895. The crowning triumph came just six weeks later, when *The Importance of Being Earnest* opened at the St. James's. As its subtitle suggests, this "trivial comedy for serious people" sends up a host of Victorian platitudes, beginning with the virtues conjured up by "Earnest," that byword of early Victorian morality now utterly foreign to a world given over to pleasure. "What else should bring one anywhere?" Jack remarks (Wilde 1954: 254). In the earlier comedies the pursuit of pleasure risked social ruin, but here desire is insulated from consequence: the characters indulge the appetite not of lechery but of a craving for cucumber sandwiches, the double life not of adultery but an imagined alter ego in "Bunbury" concealing visits to one's young ward in the country. The farce of occluded recognition frees Wilde from the development of character, and gives unparalleled scope to his epigrammatic wit, with its airy inversions of innocence and experience, the platitudes of romantic love, and the social order itself. Thus

Cecily confesses to keeping a diary, "simply a very young girl's record of her own thoughts and impressions, and consequently meant for publication. When it appears in volume form, I hope you will order a copy" (286). To the imposing Lady Bracknell, the discovery of the infant Jack in a handbag recalls the early Victorian fear of social insurrection, displaying "a contempt for the ordinary decencies of family life that reminds one of the worst excesses of the French Revolution" (268). Disapproving of anything that "tampers with natural ignorance," she is relieved that "in England, at any rate, education produces no effect whatsoever. If it did, it would prove a serious danger to the upper classes, and probably lead to acts of violence in Grosvenor Square" (266). Grosvenor Square roared with laughter, and even the usually skeptical *New York Times* pronounced that Wilde had "at last, and with a single stroke, put his enemies at his feet." But the enemies would have the last word. Within three months, Wilde's career was in ruins, destroyed by a scandal more enduring in its literary aftershocks than any other of the era.

Wilde's teasing criticism had articulated an increasingly volatile instability in late-Victorian celebrations of literature and art. The idea of art as embodiment of impersonal beauty immune to moral decorum jostled with an expressivist notion that art was a revelation (however oblique) of potentially disturbing depths in the artist's sensibility. That instability marked the erosion of an earlier conception of popular understanding. The pleasures of difficulty that been vindicated in Browning's long struggle for recognition turned on the idea that obscurity was part and parcel of human truth, the measure of a depth of understanding that, however demanding, was potentially available to all diligent readers. In the wake of Swinburne, however, apologists for new poetic forms increasingly constructed poetry as an arcane or cultic pursuit, fully appreciable only by an elite readership. The popular sympathy rebuked by this view unsurprisingly responded by construing the "depth" of such poetry as an index of perversity. Increasingly, the artist himself was cast as a pathological figure; in 1893 a German critic, Max Nordau, made this case in a volume entitled *Degeneration* (translated into English in early 1895), taking Wilde as a central exhibit.

Wilde's dandyism inflamed the suspicions attached to elite art. Rumors of unorthodox sexuality had dogged him from his earliest renown, and the insinuations became more pointed in response to *The Picture of Dorian Gray*. In 1893, Robert Hichens enjoyed a muted *succès de scandale* with *The Green Carnation*, which described a cult of young men devoted to a famous dramatist ("Esme Amarinth"); Wilde embraced the parody by wearing the title flower as a boutonnière. Despite the dangers signaled by the Cleveland Street scandal, Wilde grew ever bolder in consorting with young working men, most of whom looked to blackmail as a ready source of cash. But his downfall was of aristocratic pedigree. In 1892 he was introduced to an Oxford student, Lord Alfred Douglas, the spoiled, feckless youngest son of the Marquess of Queensberry, who was outraged by his son's ostentatious friendship with a writer of such dubious repute. In late February 1895, inflamed by his son's continual taunts, Queensberry left a card at Wilde's club, addressed "To Oscar Wilde, posing as a somdomite [sic]". With breathtaking audacity, likewise goaded by Lord Alfred, Wilde countered with a suit for libel – a foolhardy gesture, since Queensberry's defense quickly turned up a host of incriminating witnesses, along with Wilde's own deeply equivocal and provocative writing. When Wilde's lawsuit collapsed, the judge passed to the Director of Prosecutions a trove of evidence for prosecuting Wilde under the Labouchere amendment for "acts of gross indecency." Wilde was offered the gentleman's chance to flee the country, a recourse taken by many before him. But he remained to face the charges. His name was quickly removed from the marquees of the theaters where *Earnest* and *An Ideal Husband* were still playing to large houses, and soon the productions were closed down. After a first trial ended with a deadlocked jury, the charges were filed again, and on May 25, Oscar Wilde was convicted and sentenced to two years at hard labour. "The high aesthetic line" had descended to, in the judge's summation, "the centre of a circle of corruption of the most hideous kind among young men." The *News of the World* proclaimed, "The aesthetic cult, in its nasty form, is over" (Ellmann 1988: 477).

Poetry After Wilde

Such stark declarations have provided many an emblematic curtain for literary historians. But the impact of Wilde's downfall was more equivocal. Some aftershocks were immediate and severe. John Lane withdrew Wilde's books from his list, banished Beardsley from his illustration work for *The Yellow Book*, and eventually shut down the journal itself (in June 1897). Even Wilde himself in Reading Gaol for a time embraced the view that he had been insane, submitting a wrenching petition to this effect to the Governor of Reading Gaol, seeking early release. More broadly, the trial marked a culmination of the late-Victorian affiliation of cultural and biological disorder, which had echoed throughout attacks on aestheticism, naturalism, decadence, and the New Woman novel. Indeed, some influential chroniclers, such as Holbrook Jackson, have argued that only with the Wilde scandal did "decadence" become a phenomenon recognized by a truly general public. The verdict confirmed a newly visible and momentous sexual identity – "an unspeakable of the Oscar Wilde sort," as a character in E. M. Forster's *Maurice* (1907) will describe himself (Forster 1972: 159). For many observers this image lent the authority of medicine to an indictment of modern art and writing; for others it would become a rallying point in new programs of self-definition and political emancipation.

Still, a number of literary careers associated with "decadence" continued relatively unaffected by the scandal. The volumes of Dowson and Johnson appeared after Wilde's imprisonment, and Arthur Symons continued as a vigorous polemicist for the latest French literature – although when he published an expanded edition of "The Decadent Movement in Literature" in book form in 1899, he pointedly re-titled it *The Symbolist Movement in Literature*. Max Beerbohm, a young friend of Wilde and chronicler of decadent culture, went on to fame as a caricaturist in both prose and painting, a brilliant parodist, theater critic, and author of the romantic satire *Zuleika Dobson* (1910). Offshoots of the New Woman novel continued to flourish – although increasingly its energies were identified with intellectual careers for women rather than sexual audacity. Mary Cholmondeley enjoyed an international best-seller with *Red Pottage* (1899), a story of two female friends, one who inherits money after struggling as a freelance typist, the other an aspiring novelist whose latest manuscript is burnt by her intolerant brother, a clergyman. Eventually the two women escape the constricting attentions of men and find happiness traveling the world together.

New poets also came to the foreground. After the furor over *Jude the Obscure*, an aggrieved Hardy gave up novel-writing to concentrate on poetry, which had engaged him intermittently since his youth. *Wessex Poems and Other Verses*, published in December 1898 by Harper Brothers, recalls the novels in both subject matter and mood. The poet's stance is habitually retrospective, insisting on the corrosive effects of time – the passing of love, of beauty, of life, even of memory of the dead – and on the varieties of ignorance and avoidance that muffle these harsh realities. As in the novels, Hardy frequently is drawn to a woman's perspective, as a vantage more keenly susceptible to these losses. He also draws heavily on forms of the ballad – that traditional vehicle of thwarted desire – which he melds with a tendentious moralizing likewise familiar from the novels: "Sportsman Time but rears his brood to kill" ("She, to Him I", l. 10; Hardy 1925). Such personifications recall *In Memoriam* and a host of other Victorian lyrics in which the deformation of traditional poetic figures mark an estrangement between human and natural orders. Hardy also captures that clash in his evocation of landscape, which, far from being instinct with companionable spirit, becomes a backdrop to, and subsequently a sardonic memorial of, blasted human hopes. Thus "Neutral Tones" evokes a winter landscape in which the poet recalls meeting his lover, his perspective jaundiced by the passage of time – "The smile on your mouth was the deadest thing /Alive enough to have strength to die" – and concludes,

> Since then, keen lessons that love deceives,
> And wrings with wrong, have shaped to me
> Your face, and the God-curst sun, and a tree,
> And a pond edged with grayish leaves.
>
> (ll. 13–16)

Despite the acerbic tone, such lyrics have an intriguing affinity with the work of Christina Rossetti as they conjure a perspective that seems almost posthumous, a lyric self-detachment *in extremis*, as it were. Clarity of understanding is grounded not merely in retrospect but in a radical alienation, which breaks time itself into a stark divide between a focal moment in the past and a life that seems frozen in a state "after the fact" of disillusion and loss. Hardy gestures towards this condition when he describes "a melancholy satisfaction ... in dying, so to speak, before one is out of the flesh; by which I mean putting on the manners of ghosts, wandering in their haunts, and taking their views of surrounding things" (F. Hardy 1928: 275). This emphasis would culminate in the astonishing series of elegies Hardy wrote after the death of his wife in 1912, when he was in his seventies. But the appeal is clearly in place as early as 1866, when in a monologue a woman complains of those "souls of Now, who would disjoint, /The mind from memory, making Life all aim" ("She, to Him, III"). Poetry thus thrives in its distance from "Life" – at least that immersion in the "Now" that, as another poem has it, is a world of "the self-unseeing." Time dispossesses, but it also enables the peculiar clarity of memory, which seems to reside outside of time.

What surprised most readers of Hardy's poetry (then as now) was its formal range; the sheer variety of stanza structure would prompt Ezra Pound to call Hardy's poetry the culmination of the accentual-syllabic tradition in English poetry that Pound turned against. Within that formal range Hardy also deploys an unusually eclectic vocabulary, ranging the gamut from west-country dialect (the Dorset poetry of William Barnes was an important model) to pointed neologism, which is frequently devoted to capturing negation or deprivation ("unblooms," "unsight," "unhope"). Of course Browning, to whom Hardy was much indebted, had nurtured an appreciation of eccentric perspective conveyed in often arcane syntax and diction, but even Browning was rarely so aggressively estranging as the opening lines of Hardy's volume, a poem entitled "The Temporary The All (Sapphics)":

> Chance and changefulness in my flowering youthtime,
> Set me sun by sun near to one unchosen;
> Wrought us fellowlike, and despite divergence.
>   Fused us in friendship.

Some critics have objected to a supposedly mechanical quality in Hardy's technical virtuosity, as if the forms were mere molds into which he poured words. Hardy himself preferred to stress a "cunning irregularity" in his work, which more sympathetic critics have affiliated with the Gothic aesthetic of Ruskin and Hardy's own early experience as an architect's assistant, in which grotesque juxtaposition within intricate form may be an index of imaginative exuberance – and a call to attention for the reader. But the eccentricities may also underscore a persistently guarded relation to literary authority in a writer who began his career so remote from metropolitan institutions, suffered a good deal under the lash of "taste," and accordingly clung to the integrity of the outsider (T. Armstrong 1993: 30–40). The resistance, however, is richly functional: Hardy's prosody in particular achieves a kind of counterpoint between the outwardly rigorous metrical pattern and the rhythms of colloquial speech, and with that an unusual emotional resonance.

A sensibility in many ways akin to Hardy's found expression in A. E. Housman's *A Shropshire Lad* (1896), the very title hinting at a rural innocence, which is contemplated in retrospect as "the land of lost content." Housman's lyrics are obsessed with baffled desire, which they evoke in terse, subdued, often mordant verse. When ignorance is bliss, 'tis folly to be wise, Thomas Gray remarked of schoolboys at play, but in Housman bliss itself is a kind of folly, and the most fortunate are those who die before their joy does – as in "To an Athlete Dying Young":

> Smart lad, to slip betimes away
> From fields where glory does not stay
> And early though the laurel grows
> It withers quicker than the rose.
>
> (XIX; Housman 1965)

Housman's verse is strikingly narrow in both formal and emotional range. The prosody is derived principally from either ballad or hymn meter – Housman rarely uses lines longer than tetrameter – and an extraordinary number of the poems conclude with a body in the grave. As in Hardy, death is the touchstone of human vanity, but also, more distinctively, something like a refuge from the indignities of time and guilt – a stigma that for Housman was most potently associated with his homosexuality:

> Shot? So quick, so clean an ending?
> Oh, that was right, lad, that was brave;
> Yours was not an ill for mending,
> 'Twas best to take it to the grave.
>
> (XLIV)

Perhaps unsurprisingly, such sentiment was slow to find an appreciative audience, but the volume has never gone out of print.

Housman's volume may have inspired *The Ballad of Reading Gaol*, a poem of 650 lines which appeared anonymously in volume form in 1897. Boldly dedicated to the memory of a cavalry officer executed for the murder of his wife, the poem recounts the man's fate from the vantage of another inmate, in whose eyes the enormity is less the crime – it only exaggerates everyday betrayal – than the punishment, which casts the prisoner beyond the pale of humanity. "All men kill the thing they love," runs the refrain:

> Some love too little, some too long,
> Some sell, and others buy;
> Some do the deed with many tears,
> And some without a sigh:
> For each man kills the thing he loves,
> Yet each man does not die.
>
> (ll. 49–54; Wilde 1909)

The poem resembles Yeats's appropriations of the ballad form more than Kipling's; it is less a means of impersonation than an effort to depersonalize violent desire. And yet a distinctive sensibility can be glimpsed in the agonized imagination of public shame. The volume appeared over the cryptic name "C.3.3." It was the cell number of Oscar Wilde.

Fictions of Decline

The Ballad of Reading Gaol bears witness to the popularity of the ballad form in the 1890s, which typically appealed to those broad public sympathies to which decadent art had been so hostile. But the conviction of Wilde could not banish fears of "degeneration" and cultural decline, a pathology popularly blazoned in Wilde's anathematized body. Literature of the 1890s returns repeatedly to forms of biological disorder, which increasingly were fused with worries over England's place in the world at large. Widespread argument for eugenics or "imperial hygiene," an effort to "improve the race" through regulated breeding, was one response to the worries, which surfaces in a number of New Woman novels. More inchoate versions of the concern animated the emergent genre of speculative fiction, which was preoccupied with invasion by a variety of alien forces. In 1871 the carnage of the Franco–Prussian War had inspired an army engineer, G. T. Chesney, to imagine Britain overrun by Germany and subsequently stripped of its imperial possessions. *The Battle of Dorking* created a sensation – Gladstone himself warned the country against alarmism – and influenced a host of imitations, most memorably *The War of the Worlds* by H. G. Wells. In the interval, writers envisioned a host of adversaries to civilization. Samuel Butler's *Erewhon* (1872) offers a Swiftian fantasy of a society in which illness is a crime, crime a disease, and education turns on the cultivation of irrationality, as in the study of "Hypothetics": "To imagine a set of utterly strange and impossible contingencies, and to require the youths to give intelligent answers to the questions that arise therefrom, is reckoned the fittest conceivable way of preparing them for the actual conduct of their affairs in after life" (Butler 1970: 185–6). *After London* (1885) by Richard Jefferies (1848–87), best known as a naturalist and essayist, imagined England after a mysterious environmental catastrophe ("the event") in which London is reduced to a swamp, the countryside to wilderness, and society has returned to barbarism.

Such works, ironically, could chime with a pastoral impulse, signaled by the subtitle, "Wild England," which suggests that the collapse of civilization might bring a new appreciation of the natural order, which in many ways heralds twentieth-century ecology. Fictions of disaster could thus be closely bound up with utopian fantasy, which also flourished in the 1880s and 1890s. W. H. Hudson's *A Crystal Age* (1887) imagines a future devoted to conservation rather than consumption – to the extent that individual sexuality has been bred out of the species, and reproduction takes place through a single bee-like queen presiding over a communal "house". Most influential among the utopian narratives were Williams Morris's *A Dream of John Ball* (1888) and *News from Nowhere* (1890), in which his socialism found expression in an increasingly tenacious fantasy of England's bucolic countryside – a conjunction that echoes the appeal of regionalist fiction in the last two decades of the century.

Morris's romances participate in a widespread cultural phenomenon at century's end, the construction of "England" as a pastoral world. In effect, the attractions of regionalist literature were invoked to consolidate an image of the nation at large that could be set against fear of decline. The nostalgic appeal of the thatched-roof cottage had figured centrally in earlier medievalist visions, but that appeal was amplified by growing worry over the nature of urban life, where conditions seemed to be physically and morally degrading vast segments of the population. As Britain's manufacturing economy began to lose ground to Germany and America, the "workshop of the world" seemed a less compelling image of national power than Britain's imperial possessions. In this context, rural life had a deeply equivocal appeal. On the one hand, it might build confidence that the British "race" would continue to produce the hardy, healthy specimens who had subdued so much of the world – a confidence that had been deeply shaken by accounts of the urban working classes at home and imperial trauma abroad. At the same time, the countryside would increasingly beckon as a refuge from the metropolis and the burdens of empire. This latter appeal figures centrally in projects as diverse as Ruskin's Guild of St. George, the prose romances of Morris, and the 1895 founding of the National Trust for Places of Historic Interest and National Beauty.

As in earlier regionalist literature, rural life was imagined as a realm especially responsive to the world of dreams and the supernatural, which in turn was affiliated with oral tradition. Andrew Lang, that indefatigable apologist for romance, in 1889 brought out the *Blue Fairy Book*, the first of his many collections of fairy tales distinguished by the colors in their titles. In the following year, Joseph Jacobs's *English Fairy Tales* more closely emulated the work of the Grimms, who at the beginning of the century had sought out folk tradition as a ground for German national identity. (This was an appeal to history closely akin to that animating the *New English Dictionary* and related work in historical philology.) Childhood became an especially rich vehicle for this association – as is tellingly encapsulated in the career of Kenneth Grahame, who moved from writing for the *Yellow Book* and a collection entitled *Pagan Days* (1893) to volumes conjuring idyllic images of childhood for an adult audience, *The Golden Age* (1895) and *Dream Days* (1898). To be sure, literature for boys still drank deeply of imperial fantasy – as reflected in the popularity of Henty – and that topic remained closely bound up with stories of school life, widely understood to be the training ground for imperial rule. (Kipling worked a distinctive variation on the usual patterns in *The Jungle Book* [1894], where the exotic setting becomes a space for negotiating many of the challenges usually associated with school life.) The expansion of secondary education for girls brought about new fictional possibilities, which were developed most notably by L. T. Meade (1854–1915), a prolific novelist and editor of *Atalanta*, a magazine for girls. But the countryside gained a prominence in children's literature even beyond what it had enjoyed in the likes of *The Water Babies* – an emphasis that culminated in the following decade, with the publication of *The Wind in the Willows*, *The Secret Garden*, and *Tales of Peter Rabbit*, and even a vogue for photographs purporting to capture fairies in their native habitat.

The appeal of "faery" also could be turned to the construction of a distinctly Celtic identity – a habit of mind, so most commentators agreed, especially at home in the realm of the supernatural, and one typically opposed to the "Saxon" that most felt predominated in the English imaginary. This had been the burden of Arnold's *On the Study of Celtic Literature* (1867) and a related impulse animated the "Celtic

Revival" from the 1870s onwards. This naturally was most prominent in Ireland, but it also gathered in figures from elsewhere on the "Celtic fringe." Arthur Machen (Arthur Llewellyn Jones, 1863–1947) was a Welsh writer drawn from his earliest work to varieties of magic and the occult. His *Fantastic Tales* appeared in 1890, and his first novel, the fantasy *Great God Pan* (1894), was published in John Lane's Keynotes series. Though Machen was associated with decadence, his work also illustrates its persistence after the fall of Wilde. His greatest work, *The Hill of Dreams*, takes its "Robinson Crusoe of the Soul" into a nightmare realm of delirium; though not published until 1907, it was written between 1895 and 1897. Even more distinctive was Fiona MacLeod, the pseudonym and alter ego of the Scottish author William Sharp (1855–1905). MacLeod, who took shape in the early 1890s, was allegedly a spinster born in the Hebrides and living in Iona, where she produced 16 mythic novels and story collections, as well as a great deal of poetry. *Pharais, A Romance of the Isles* (1894) is exemplary in its celebration of dreamy Celtic consciousness ("Pharais" is Gaelic for "Paradise").

In early 1895, just as Wilde's trials were unfolding, a narrative appeared that depicted evolution itself as an engine of British decline. *The Time Machine*, by the 28-year-old H. G. Wells (1866–1946), envisioned a scientist traveling through the fourth dimension to an England 800,000 years in the future, where he discovers that the human race has diverged into two distinct species: small, gentle, childlike creatures called the Eloi are preyed upon by the subterranean, ape-like Morlocks. The scenario is one of social class transmuted into biological conflict: "the gradual widening of the present merely temporary and social difference between the Capitalist and the Labourer" has inverted the dynamic of power, reducing the Eloi to mere "fatted cattle," who are little more than a food stock for the "ant-like" Morlocks (Wells 2001: 109, 125). It is a horrifying image of degeneration, which underscores the ephemerality of human identity in the face of evolutionary time, and turns upside down Tennysonian consolations of movement toward "a higher race": "I grieved to think how brief the dream of the human intellect had been. It had committed suicide" (141). The fate is all the more harrowing for the suggestion that it was not beyond human control, that the downfall of the Eloi was a by-product of their own complacency in the pursuit of "comfort and ease," where body and mind have no spurs to further exercise: "This ever has been the fate of energy in security; it takes to art and to eroticism, and then come languor and decay" (92). For all his immersion in contemporary science (Wells actually attended Huxley's lectures in South Kensington), he cannot shake the common allure of Lamarckian use-inheritance, whose imagined social imperatives fuel a cultural criticism very much like that aroused by Wilde.

More than any other Victorian author, Wells embraced the radically alienating perspectives on human experience suggested by modern science, which seemed to challenge not only human complacency but the very survival of the species. *The Island of Doctor Moreau* (1896), the most macabre of all his works, warps "the great chain of being" in the account of a demented vivisectionist who surgically alters animals into creatures of recognizably human capacities, which he then brutally suppresses lest they turn against him – a struggle that effaces both the mental and social distinctions between man and beast. Wells's best-known work, *The War of the Worlds* (1897–8), unforgettably envisions south-eastern England invaded by beings from Mars, who – as only gradually dawns on the horrified narrator – are pursuing a new food supply. The horror is subtly drawn out by the markedly understated narration, which owes much to the flat prose of journalistic dispatches – a feature still faintly evident in Orson Welles's more histrionic re-working of the story as a radio play set in New Jersey in 1938, which confirmed the story's power to terrify some 40 years and an ocean away from its original setting.

But the ultimate late-Victorian invasion fantasy was penned by an Irishman, Bram Stoker, the business manager of Henry Irving's Lyceum Theatre. The fantasy of a foreign vampire who ventures to England to suck the blood of the unwary, *Dracula* (1897) has come to seem the ultimate late-Victorian allegory machine, whose eponymous hero could embody virtually any imagined alien threat, from Jews to homosexuals to foreign capital, to a more encompassing "reverse colonization" of England. This protean significance – Dracula's semantic indeterminacy resonating with his physical shape-shifting – owes much to Stoker's dizzying manipulation of perspective. Borrowing from Collins's *The Woman in White*, Stoker develops his narrative through multiple vantage points, captured in juxtaposed letters, journals, newspaper stories, and even recordings on the newly invented phonograph. The structure reinforces a sense of the sheer pervasiveness of Dracula's threat, which materializes in the startling, highly sexualized intimacy of his attacks. The text is very much of its time in making the body itself the locus of a social crisis, but after more than a century the cultural force of that association is undiminished; there have been dozens of film adaptations, and the novel has never been out of print.

The more degrading poverty of urban life continued to attract novelists. W. Somerset Maugham, for example, launched his immensely successful career in 1897 with the Zolaesque *Liza of Lambeth*. The topicality of such settings was enhanced by the outbreak of the Boer War in 1899, when military recruiters were appalled at the physical condition of the urban poor who volunteered for service. The single most unsettling tale of slum life was *Child of the Jago* (1896) by Arthur Morrison (1863–1945), in many respects the most harrowing of all Victorian novels of urban poverty, an *Oliver Twist* without prospect of rescue or redemption. Morrison, who as a young man worked in the People's Palace and as a freelance journalist lived in the Shoreditch neighborhood where the novel is set (his volume of urban sketches, *Tales of Mean Streets*, appeared in 1894), chronicles with painstaking topography a world of perpetual brutality, in which the main source of guidance and value is criminal loyalty. The title character, Dicky Parott, grows up in a world where women fight each other with broken bottles, and his own father is hanged for a murder of revenge. Dicky himself, whose only education is that of a thief for a Fagin-like fence, is predictably a target for rescue by a virtuous slum priest, but he ends up dying in a knife fight, his final claim to distinction his refusal to betray the name of his killer.

The preoccupation with crime took on a new wrinkle in the stories of E. W. Hornung, which centered on the character of Raffles, a gentleman thief or "cracksman" who combines world-class cricket skills with a gift for inventive and lucrative crime. Hornung's stories, collected as *The Amateur Cracksman* (1899) and *Raffles* (1901), develop the intellectual affinities between criminal and gentleman detective that Conan Doyle had exploited, fusing the two figures into what would become an archetype of twentieth-century popular entertainment, the immensely suave "cat burglar" played in film by the likes of Cary Grant. A similar amalgam of characteristics crystallized in the figure of the spy, another late-Victorian character of dubious identity and loyalties. Of course the spy was a figure of long standing in Victorian fiction, whose preoccupation with information and secrecy amplified that of the culture at large. In the earlier part of the period, however, spying typically is a degrading activity, a standing affront to gentlemanly frankness and respect for privacy from which middle-class characters such as Robert Audley recoil (often when they find themselves in the role). By the 1890s, however, the figure had become an icon of masculine omnicompetence and erotic allure.

The more romantic possibilities of espionage fiction were developed by Anthony Hope, whose popular *The Prisoner of Zenda* (1894) recounts the intrigue of an Englishman visiting the kingdom of Ruritania, where he manages to stave off an assassination attempt on the King by posing as the monarch – a formula which has had a long afterlife in both print and film versions. Hope's novel, in effect a masculinized offshoot of the aristocratic romance fantasies of Ouida and Marie Corelli, clearly links the allure of espionage with the growing currency of divided or twinned selfhood – a motif which resonates in works as diverse as *The Picture of Dorian Gray* and Mark Twain's *The Prince and the Pauper*. But it also registers an increasing sense of international rivalry and interconnectedness, with the corresponding anxiety captured throughout late-Victorian fiction over porous borders and internal treachery – threats that enhanced the stature of the agent who could defeat them. Espionage as an invasion fantasy first gained wide popularity in the works of E. P. Oppenheim (1866–1946), beginning with *The Mysterious Mr. Sabin* (1898), the story of a criminal mastermind seeking knowledge that will aid in his planned invasion of England – a design in which he is defeated by a dashing young Englishman, Lord Wolfenden, and by a hardy plot device that had engaged Wilkie Collins 40 years earlier: compromising membership in a secret society's whose orders cannot be defied. Oppenheim's success points the way to the immensely popular writings of John Buchan, Ian Fleming, and John LeCarre, among others.

The most enduring late-Victorian novel of espionage, however, is a work that on its surface has little to do with the topic. Kipling's *Kim* (1901) is outwardly a boy's adventure story, which follows a resourceful Irish orphan in India who throws in his lot with a Nepalese lama searching for enlightenment, and displays his hardy ingenuity in a series of challenges across much of the subcontinent. Like many adventure heroes, Kim is distinguished by his ability to bridge disparate worlds, and to cope with seemingly antagonistic claims on his loyalties. But he is set apart by his power to internalize contrasting identities in a form of psychic hybridity. From his upbringing on the streets, he not only can pass as a native Indian, whether Hindu or Muslim, but he sometimes thinks in "Hindustanee," sometimes in English, and from time to time even finds himself asking "Who is Kim?" (Kipling 1987b: 166), as if he were not sure just what he is or where he belongs. Kim's social dispossession thus becomes a rare gift: precisely because he is raised on the margins of both British and Indian society, he becomes able to move almost effortlessly between them. In this regard he is the most "knowing" of all Kipling's characters, and an ideal participant in "the Great Game," the network of surveillance by which the British and their Indian agents seek to enforce imperial power. Kim thus becomes a central agent in the work of empire, and so, many critics have argued, is the novel itself. Although Kipling is keenly attentive to the dynamics of Foucauldian "knowledge/power," particularly the work of surveying and mapping the countryside, by relegating it to the realm of play he denatures the brute political realities at stake. Still, the dynamic is faithful to a vital equivocation in Kipling's work: from Kim's vantage, the Game is an escape from an Anglo-English life that is arid, confining, almost stifling in its discipline, while India is aligned with freedom, generosity, and beauty, which is epitomized in the people and landscapes he encounters on the Great Trunk Road. He embraces Indian ways not out of self-interest, but out of a more visceral delight in his own talents and in the world around him, whose sheer multifariousness is an ideal space for intrigue. "The game is so large that one sees but little at a time" (217): in this emphasis the world of Kim brings us surprisingly close to postmodern fantasies of interconnectedness, such as Pynchon's *Gravity's Rainbow*.

Of course the trope of the game is also faithful to the high road that led from British elite education to the imperial garrison. Kipling himself charted that path in *Stalky and Co.* (1899), where the public school nurtures in its rebellious hero an audacity and resourcefulness that turn out to be ideal preparation for daring military exploits in India. Stalky thus recalls the "loafers" of "The Man Who Would Be King," but is redeemed by the self-discipline that they cannot maintain. Once again the dream of empire turns on a fantasy of something like perpetual adolescence. Immortalized in the following decade in Barrie's *Peter Pan*, the dream is more hauntingly evoked by the schoolmaster Henry Newbolt, in "Vitai Lampada," in which soldiers are urged on with the refrain, "Play up, and play the game".

Conrad

A far more somber view of empire came from Joseph Conrad (1857–1924), who throughout his writings portrayed Europeans in exotic settings, not in order to celebrate their hardy resourcefulness but to explore moral and epistemological crises precipitated by the loss of familiar frames of reference. In Conrad's fiction boys' adventure and imperial romance are transfigured by a deep suspicion not only of imperial ambition but also of its rationale in visions of human progress, a suspicion reinforced in a narrative technique that would become a hallmark of early Modernism. Uniquely among major British authors of the century, Conrad's works were written in his third language, which he did not begin to learn until adulthood. Born Josef Korzeniewski in a Poland partitioned between Russian and Austrian occupation, Conrad left his homeland at 17 for life as a merchant sailor, which would form the raw material for much of his writing. He first visited England in 1878, but by 1886 he had received his certificate as a master in the British merchant service and become a naturalized British subject. Not until 1894, partly out of difficulty in finding new commands on fully rigged sailing ships – a dying mode of commerce in the age of steam – did Conrad turn to writing as a career. That year he submitted to Fisher Unwin a manuscript he had begun in 1889 (and had rescued from, among other perils, a capsized ship in the Congo). *Almayer's Folly*, which appeared in April 1895, seemed well suited to the hunger for popular romance addressed by Fisher Unwin's "Pseudonym Library," offering readers a story of interracial romance in eastern Borneo. One review expressed hopes that Conrad might become the Kipling of the Malay Archipelago. But the title figure embodies a countervailing disillusion more profound than anything in early Kipling. A Dutch trader who has lost everything in pursuit of wealth, Almayer is left with nothing more than his "Folly," a crumbling mansion in the jungle that stands as an emblem of his ruined hopes.

This dissonance would become a defining note of Conrad's work, in which romantic faith in a host of ideals – progress, solidarity, self-discipline, civilization, reason itself – is confounded or exploded by experience. The disillusionment – a quintessence of the deflationary impulses of realism – is evoked through a host of innovative formal strategies, all of which work to isolate and underscore the working of individual consciousness baffled by circumstance, as characters struggle to register and come to terms with events that elude or confound familiar frames of reference. The most obvious instrument to this end is a recurrent character, Marlow, who recounts episodes from his own career while pondering their elusive meaning. In the process, the familiar seaman's yarn becomes a sounding of moral and epistemological depths. Marlow's narration foregrounds and complicates the distinction between plot and story that is likewise underscored by the detective narrative: his account of a sequence of events is interwoven with, and often interrupted by, a recounting of his quest to understand them – a quest that seems to internalize the struggles of traditional romance. This challenge is crystallized locally in a device christened "delayed decoding": a narrative frequently will recount objects or events that seem only perceived rather than understood, and whose meaning appears only belatedly (Watt 1979). So, for example, as Marlow is voyaging upriver in *Heart of Darkness*, he sees the helmsman clutching what seems to be a cane, only gradually realizing that the man has been impaled on a spear. The emphasis reflects Conrad's affinities with Paterian impressionism, with its stress on fidelity to the impression as the foundation of meaning. In an oft-cited preface to his second novel, *The Nigger of the 'Narcissus'*," Conrad sums up his ambition with the claim, "My task ... is, by the power of the written word to make you hear, to make you feel – it is, before all, to make you *see*" (Watt 1979: 83). This echoes Henry James's insistence on "showing" rather than "telling," which would become an axiom of modernist narration and criticism. But the conjunction between two forms of "seeing," witnessing and understanding, is in Conrad's work typically vexed. For Marlow, "the meaning of an episode," as the narrator in *Heart of Darkness* describes him, "was not inside like a kernel but outside, enveloping the tale which brought it out only as a glow brings out a haze" (Conrad 1988: 9). The various mists and shadows that confront Conrad's characters are not mere obstacles to perception, but – in keeping with the emphases of late-century symbolism – a constituent, inescapable feature of meaning, whose "misty halos" always incorporate the diffractions of the percipient consciousness itself.

Formally Conrad's most complex construction of meaning comes in *Lord Jim* (serialized 1899–1900), where Marlow narrates the story of a young naval officer who inexplicably betrayed every code of the sea by abandoning a ship crowded with civilian passengers. How could "one of us," Marlow insistently wonders, behave thus? The event unsettles Marlow as something more than a personal failure; it seems to confound the moral order that knits together that suggestively indeterminate collective, "us": sailors? Englishmen? Europeans? Human beings? But in his effort to understand Jim, Marlow must try to piece together various second-hand accounts of Jim's career, which takes him from an English vicarage to death in a remote trading village in

Patusan, and the truth Marlow constructs remains partial and provisional, a haze in which the vagaries of Jim's imagined psyche answer in part to the needs of Marlow's.

Conrad's most famous story, *Heart of Darkness* (1899), is more straightforward in the pursuit of knowledge, but more harrowing in its conclusions. It is steeped in Conrad's characteristic rhetoric of obscurity and enigma, but here Marlow's circumspection answers less to the difficulty of his search than to the enormity of his discoveries. His experience originated, Marlow recalls, in a boyhood fantasy of "the glories of exploration," which lingers in the adult – despite the inexorable contraction of uncharted spaces on the globe – and impels him toward what remains the most alluring space of mystery, central Africa. The association fuses the impulse of boys' adventure with the worst depradations of imperialism, for Conrad's tale derived from his experience sailing up the Congo under the reign of the Belgian King Albert, who presided over perhaps the most brutal episode in "the scramble for Africa." Marlow's service in the unnamed trading company that sends him up the Congo is framed as a manifold quest. He sails in pursuit of wealth, of excitement, of knowledge, of "improvement," and yet he encounters a world of disorientation verging on madness, as he follows in the path of Europeans wreaking havoc on the countryside and its inhabitants. What sustains Marlow's quest, and becomes its focal point, is word of a man named Kurtz, a company agent whose fabulous success at plunder has become shrouded in suspicion, with hushed suggestions that his "methods" are "unsound" (Conrad 1988: 61). The reality, predictably, is much worse: the Kurtz who Marlow finally encounters is a dying, barely sane man who has turned into something like a tribal god, presiding over "unspeakable rites" in a compound with a fence surmounted by human skulls.

Kurtz is the *ne plus ultra* of the Victorian fantasy of "going native." Whereas in Tennyson's "Locksley Hall" the "savage woman" fascinates as an image of erotic release, Kurtz's transformation is something more than a failing of self-discipline. "The wilderness [...] had whispered to him things about himself which he did not know" (57) – much as Lord Henry had aroused Dorian Gray – but here the initiation into forbidden experience signals a thoroughgoing atavism, exposing the ravening aggression, one more heart of darkness, at the core of human experience generally. Kurtz thus becomes a demonic emblem of the violence only tenuously sublimated in the cause of civilization, and an especially pointed mockery of the mythology of empire. "All

Europe contributed to the making of Kurtz," Marlow remarks, and Kurtz takes up the banner of progress with a report to "the International Society for the Suppression of Savage Customs." It opens with familiar invocations of the march of mind, and the supremacy of Europeans, who appear to Africans "in the nature of supernatural beings" – only to break off with a concluding scrawl, "Exterminate all the brutes" (51). It is Tennyson's nightmare realized: man has indeed reeled back into the beast. And yet Marlow strangely comes to admire Kurtz, as a man who has grasped his own condition – "his own exalted and incredible degradation." Kurtz's insight into the depths of human depravity gives him in Marlow's eyes a moral authenticity that explodes the polite evasions of bureaucratic rationality, the temporizing, evasive habit of mind that would veil "monstrous passions" and "brutal instincts" with the euphemism "unsound." "Kurtz was a remarkable man," Marlow concludes, "He had something to say ... He had summed up – he had judged." The verdict is pronounced in Kurtz's final words: "The horror! The horror!" (69)

Epilogue

Heart of Darkness was serialized just two years after the very zenith of British imperial fervor, which accompanied the Diamond Jubilee of Victoria in 1897. Describing the Jubilee parade through central London in June, the Daily Mail (voice of the conservative lower middle classes) swelled with pride: "the sun never looked down until yesterday on the embodiment of so much energy and power" (Read 1994: 352). By 1901 the empire covered 12 million square miles, more than one fifth of the world's land surface, and almost as large a fraction of its population, with 400 million people (Read 1994: 350). But even Kipling was unsettled by the Jubilee spectacle of a nation "drunk with sight of power," and offered a cautionary hymn for publication in The Times:

> For heathen heart that puts her trust
> In reeking tube and iron shard,
> All valiant dust that builds on dust,
> And guarding, calls not Thee to guard,
> For frantic boast and foolish word –
> Thy mercy on Thy people, Lord!
>
>   ("Recessional," ll. 25–30)

A less august celebration took place arose on May 19, 1900, when news reached London of the relief of a besieged British garrison at a railway junction, Mafeking, in South Africa. The city was convulsed with frenzy, as torchbearing crowds surged into the streets on what was recalled as "Mafeking Night." "We accepted Waterloo and Trafalgar more calmly," marveled one commentator, reflecting on the outward insignificance of the military triumph (Read 1994: 356). The response suggested less imperial confidence than sheer relief. Britain had been at war for six months against a force of Boer farmers whom they outnumbered seven to one, yet the Boers would sustain a guerilla war for another two years before finally consolidating their independence. In the process, the British lost over 20,000 men to battle and disease, and spent over 200 million pounds – immensely more than they had spent in any previous conflict during the Victorian age. Looking forward at century's end, the skepticism of Thomas Hardy in "The Darkling Thrush" (dated December 1900) seemed newly resonant:

> So little cause for caroling
>   Of such ecstatic sound
> Was written on terrestrial things
>   Afar or nigh around,
> That I could think there trembled through
>   His happy good-night air
> Some blessed Hope, whereof he knew,
>   And I was unaware.
>
> (ll. 25–32; Hardy 1925)

Three weeks into the new century, on 22 January 1901, Queen Victoria died. She had been on the throne for nearly 64 years, and most of her subjects could not remember a time when she was not Queen. Predictably, her death brought with it a widely shared sense of a new beginning, but one filled with trepidation. "Will England last the century?" asked a title in the *Fortnightly*; "What should England do to be saved?" posed another in the *Westminster* (Read 1994: 369). In literary history, Victoria's death, like her ascension to the throne, has become associated with a literary interregnum, as if writers were once again trapped between two worlds, Victorianism dead and Modernism as yet powerless to be born. In part, this is a trick of historical inertia and the coincidence of her death with a new century. Thus Yeats in the Introduction to his *Oxford Book of Modern Verse* (1936) roundly declared:

Then in 1900 everybody got down off his stilts; henceforth nobody
drank absinthe with his black coffee; nobody went mad; nobody committed suicide; nobody joined the Catholic Church ... Victorianism had
been defeated. (Yeats 1936: ix)

As that last sentence suggests, however, for a younger generation,
"Victorianism" could not merely be allowed to pass; it had to be van-
quished. This particular episode in literary history was first scripted by
writers eager to cut their predecessors down to size.

In or about December 1910 human character changed, Virginia
Woolf famously declared (Woolf 1980: i. 320), and historians have
been glad to agree with her – even if not quite certain just what had
happened. Whatever its historical referent, the declaration is one episode in a remarkably widespread program of cultural parricide – or, in
some cases, matricide. In order to become a writer, Woolf declared, she
had to kill the angel in the house. Related senses of constraint or confinement are echoed by writers of remarkably varied ambitions, as if
their own work could not flourish without disabling the pretensions of
their fathers' and grandfathers' generations. Strachey's *Eminent
Victorians* (1918) is the most famous and still one of the most elegant
efforts in this vein. But the broad impulse persisted at least until
World War II, and even became institutionalized in university English
departments, where the Victorians were deemed unworthy of serious
study. (Pioneering efforts in reclamation, such as Evelyn Waugh's early
study of D. G. Rossetti, typically originated outside the academy.)
A broad swath of nineteenth-century fiction – most notably Scott,
Dickens, and the Brontës – was relegated to the realm of adolescent
literature; poetry of the period, particularly under the instruction of
T. S. Eliot, became associated with mawkish, feminine sentimentality;
and women writers (Austen and George Eliot excepted) virtually
disappeared from view.

This revaluation was already underway, however, well before
Victoria's death, and in fact has obscured a host of continuities
between Victorian and Modernist literature. The rise of "New
Criticism" in the study of fiction was built on Henry James's model as
both novelist and critic, particularly as mediated by Percy Lubbock's
The Craft of Fiction (1920). The hallmarks of Modernist fiction – the
rhetorics of obscurity, the emphasis on "showing" rather than "telling"
harnessed to skeptical epistemologies conveyed by increasingly complicated, sometimes elusive narration – are clearly in place in James's and

Conrad's works of the late 1890s. Even "The Oxen of the Sun" episode of *Ulysses*, where the bravura imitations of many centuries of English prose seem designed to subsume the whole of English literature with the achievement of Joyce's novel, draws on the spirit of the 1890s, where "decadent" consciousness is so deeply bound up with an acute historical consciousness expressed through parody. The obliquity of Modernist narration develops out of late-Victorian preoccupation with secrecy and exposure, particularly in representations of desire. "The love that dare not speak its name" in this light informs Modernist axioms about "the literary": true art is subtle, indirect, allusive, "difficult." Long before the contemporary gay rights movement, Wilde had his revenge.

Even in poetry, the ostensibly more radical break heralded by imagism is largely guided by symbolist precepts articulated throughout the 90s. T. S. Eliot paid ample tribute to the impression that Symons's *Symbolist Movement in Literature* (1899) made on him while a student at Harvard. Hence the fairly marked continuities between the poetry of Symons and Michael Field, say, and the early lyrics of Pound. The continuity is even more pronounced in the career of Yeats, who from a relatively early stage in his career aimed to purge his poetry of "rhetoric," or what he elsewhere called "'impurities,' curiosities about science, about politics, about history, about religion" (Yeats 1965: 112) – that discursive dimension characteristic of mid-Victorian poetry in its wrestling with varieties of faith and doubt. Thus he complained of "that brooding over scientific opinion that so often extinguished the central flame in Tennyson" (Kermode 1971: 64). Of course the Victorian poets had developed their own means of disarming rhetoric – or at least of hedging its truth-claims – in a genre that was avowedly rhetorical, the dramatic monologue. That genre offered a model of impersonality, of indirection, of the exploration of psychic and social pathology, and of the many functions of irony; both Eliot and Pound were much influenced by the example of Browning.

Paul Verlaine in conversation with Yeats made a slightly different complaint about *In Memoriam*: Tennyson, he remarked, "is too noble, too Anglais; when he should have been broken-hearted, had many reminiscences" (Yeats 1965: 229). One might rejoin that the sentiment is too *français*, presuming a purity in emotional desolation, which memory somehow corrupts. But it does recognize the central power of nostalgia in Victorian literature. Through much of the twentieth century nostalgia has been a central appeal of that literature, not only as it serves the longing for a vanished time – a central allure in Masterpiece Theater adaptations of Victorian novels – but, more subtly, as Victorian literature itself anatomizes that desire. This was perhaps more apparent to writers in the earlier part of the twentieth century, who repeatedly turned to late-Victorian writers for phrases evocative not merely of loss, but of a haunting sense of diminishment: "Gone with the Wind," "The Days of Wine and Roses," and that riveting moment in O'Neill's *Long Day's Journey into Night*, in which Jamie taunts his disappointed father by reciting from Rossetti's *House of Life*: "Look in my face. My name is Might-Have-Been; /I am also called No More, Too Late, Farewell" (O'Neill 1956: 168). In repudiating the past, these works remind us, we may bind ourselves ever more tightly to it.

Perhaps this appeal will diminish with the passage of time, as the literature of the Victorian age is no longer the work of a parent's or grandparent's generation, but of an ever more remote past. Certainly much recent academic study of Victorian literature has worked to complicate or even to disable sympathetic response, by stressing in its works a strange admixture of the childlike and the brutal, its effusive sentiment seen as an index of blindness or willful evasion, its large affirmations exposed as ruses of power. But the allure of Victorian literature persists in a host of broadly postmodern recuperations, as artists and audiences in a variety of genres and forms seem to be rediscovering in particular the sheer capaciousness of Victorian narrative, and the surprising aesthetic pleasures afforded by the baggy monsters that Modernists disdained. Even without such mediation, however, Victorian writing has retained a remarkable capacity to entertain and to console, even amidst the peculiar horrors of the twentieth century. A teenager in Amsterdam, for example, noted a pleasure that helped to sustain her family while in hiding from the Gestapo. "Daddy," Anne Frank recorded in March of 1944, "read out loud to us from Dickens" (Frank 1995: 206).

Works Cited

Ainsworth, William (1865). *Jack Sheppard: A Romance*. London: Routledge.

Adburghum, Alison (1983). *Silver Fork Society: Fashionable Life and Literature from 1814 to 1840*. London. Constable.

Allen, Grant (1895). *The Woman Who Did*. Boston: Roberts Brothers.

Allott, Miriam (1974). *The Brontës: The Critical Heritage*. London: Routledge & Kegan Paul.

Altick, Richard D. (1957). *The English Common Reader: A Social History of the Mass Reading Public, 1800–1900*. Chicago, IL: University of Chicago Press.

Altick, Richard D. (1991). *The Presence of the Present: Topics of the Day in the Victorian Novel*. Columbus, OH: Ohio State University Press.

Andrew, Aletha (1993). *An Annotated Bibliography and Study of the Contemporary Criticism of Tennyson's Idylls of the King: 1859–1886*. New York: Peter Lang.

Archer, William (1882). *English Dramatists of Today*. London: Sampson Low.

Ardis, Ann (1990). *New Women, New Novels: Feminism and Early Modernism*. New Brunswick: Rutgers University Press.

Armstrong, Tim (ed.) (1993). *Thomas Hardy: Selected Poems*. London: Longman.

Arnold, Matthew (1932). *The Letters of Matthew Arnold to Arthur Hugh Clough*, ed. Howard Foster Lowry. Oxford: Clarendon Press.

Arnold, Matthew (1960–77) *The Complete Prose Works of Matthew Arnold*, 11 vols, ed. R. H. Super. Ann Arbor: University of Michigan Press.

Arnold, Matthew (1979). *The Poems of Matthew Arnold*, 2nd edn, ed. Kenneth and Miriam Allott. Longman: London.

Austin, Alfred (1870). *The Poetry of the Period*. London: Bentley.

[Aytoun, W. E. and Theodore Martin.] (1865). *The Book of Ballads. Ed. By Bon Gautier*. New York: W. J. Widdleston.

Bagehot, Walter (1999). "Wordsworth, Tennyson, and Browning; or, Pure, Ornate, and Grotesque Art in English Poetry," in T. Collins and V. J. Rundle, 1999, pp. 1308–19.

Ballantyne, R. M. (1949). *Coral Island*. London: J. M. Dent.

Barnett, George L. (1971). *Nineteenth-Century British Novelists on the Novel*. New York: Appleton-Century-Crofts.

Barrett Browning, Elizabeth (1890). *Poetical Works*, 6 vols. London: Smith, Elder.

Barrett Browning, Elizabeth (1996). *Aurora Leigh*, ed. Margaret Reynolds. New York: Norton.

Barrie, J. M (1913). *Auld Licht Idylls. The Kirriemuir Edition of the Works of J. M. Barrie*, vol. 3. London: Hodder and Stoughton.

Beer, Gillian (2000). *Darwin's Plots: Evolutionary Narrative in Darwin, George Eliot, and Nineteenth-Century Fiction*, 2nd edn. Cambridge: Cambridge University Press.

Besant, Walter (1971). "The Art of Fiction," in G. L. Barnett, 1971, pp. 228–39.

Besant, Walter (1997). *All Sorts and Conditions of Men*. Oxford: Oxford University Press.

Bevington, Merle Mowbray (1941). *The Saturday Review: Representative Educated Opinion in Victorian England*. New York: Columbia University Press.

Booth, Michael R. (ed.) (1969–76). *English Plays of the Nineteenth Century*, 5 vols. Oxford: Clarendon Press.

Booth, Michael R. (1991). *Theatre in the Victorian Age*. Cambridge: Cambridge University Press.

Braddon, Mary Elizabeth (1998). *Lady Audley's Secret*. London: Penguin.

Brantlinger, Patrick (1988). *Rule of Darkness: British Literature and Imperialism, 1830–1914*. Ithaca, NY: Cornell University Press.

Brontë, Anne (1992). *The Tenant of Wildfell Hall*, ed. Herbert Rosengarten. Oxford: Clarendon Press.

Brontë, Charlotte (1974). *Shirley*. London: Penguin.

Brontë, Charlotte (1979). *Villette*. London: Penguin.

Brontë, Charlotte (1996). *Jane Eyre*. London: Penguin.

Brontë, Emily (1995). *Wuthering Heights*. London: Penguin.

Broughton, Rhoda (1993). *Cometh Up As a Flower*. Stroud: Alan Sutton.

Broughton, Rhoda (1993a). *Not Wisely but Too Well*. Stroud: Alan Sutton.

Broughton, Trev Lynn (1999). *Men of Letters, Writing Lives: Masculinity and Literary Auto/Biography in the Late Victorian Period*. London: Routledge.

Browning, Robert (1961). *The Ring and the Book*. New York: Norton.

Browning, Robert (1970). *Poetical Works, 1833–1864*, ed. Ian Jack. London: Oxford University Press.

Browning, Robert (1981). *Robert Browning: The Poems*, Vol Two, ed. John Pettigrew. New Haven, CT: Yale University Press.

Browning, Robert and Elizabeth Barrett (1969). *The Letters of Robert Browning and Elizabeth Barrett Barrett*, ed. Elvan Kintner. Cambridge, MA: Harvard University Press.

Buchanan, Robert (1999). "The Fleshly School of Poetry: Mr. D. G. Rossetti," in T. Collins and V. Rundle, 1999, pp. 1329–40.

Buckley, Jerome (1945). *William Ernest Henley: A Study in the "Counter-Decadence" of the 'Nineties*. Princeton, NJ: Princeton University Press.

Bulwer-Lytton, Edward (1970). *England and the English*, ed. Standish Meacham. Chicago, IL: University of Chicago Press.

Burns, Wayne (1961). *Charles Reade: A Study in Victorian Authorship*. New York: Bookman Associates.

Butler, Samuel (1966). *The Way of All Flesh*. London: Penguin.

Butler, Samuel (1970). *Erewhon*. London: Penguin.

Buzard, James (2005). *Disorienting Fiction: The Autoethnographic Work of Nineteenth-Century British Novels*. Princeton, NJ: Princeton University Press.

Caine, Hall (1891). *The Deemster*, 2 vols. Leipzig: Heinemann and Balestier.

Caird, Mona (1885). "Is Marriage a Failure?" *Daily Telegraph*.

Carlyle, Thomas (1869). *Critical and Miscellaneous Essays*, 4 vols. Boston: Estes and Lauriat.

Carlyle, Thomas (1908). *Sartor Resartus* and *On Heroes, Hero-Worship, and the Heroic in History* (1840). London: Dent.

Carlyle, Thomas (1970–2006). *The Collected Letters of Thomas and Jane Welsh Carlyle*, gen. ed. Charles Richard Sanders, 35 vols. Durham, NC: Duke University Press.

Carlyle, Thomas (1971). *Carlyle: Selected Writings*, ed. Alan Shelston. London: Penguin.

Carlyle, Thomas (1977). *Past and Present*, ed. Richard D. Altick. New York: New York University Press.

Carlyle, Thomas (1989). *The French Revolution: A History*, 2 vols, ed. K. J. Fielding and David Sorenson. Oxford: Oxford University Press.

Carroll, David (ed.) (1971). *George Eliot: The Critical Heritage*. London: Routledge & Kegan Paul.

Carroll, Lewis (1982). *The Adventures of Alice in Wonderland* and *Through the Looking Glass*. Oxford: Oxford University Press.

Chase, Karen and Michael Levenson (2000). *The Spectacle of Intimacy: A Public Life for the Victorian Family*. Princeton, NJ: Princeton University Press.

Chittick, Kathryn (1990). *Dickens and the 1830s.* Cambridge: Cambridge University Press.

Clough, Arthur Hugh (1951). *The Poems of Arthur Hugh Clough,* ed H. F. Lowry, A. L. P. Norington, and F. L. Mulhauser. Oxford: Clarendon Press.

Clough, Arthur Hugh (1999). "Recent English Poetry," in T. Collins and V. Rundle, 1999, pp. 1254–69.

Collins, Philip (1971). *Dickens: The Critical Heritage* London: Routledge & Kegan Paul.

Collins, Thomas and Vivienne J. Rundle (eds.) (1999). *Broadview Anthology of Victorian Poetry and Poetic Theory.* Peterborough, CA: Broadview.

Collins, Wilkie (1966). *The Moonstone.* London: Penguin.

Collins, Wilkie (1999). *The Woman in White.* London: Penguin.

Conan Doyle, Arthur (1994). *Sherlock Holmes: The Major Stories,* ed. John A. Hodgson. New York: St. Martin's.

Conrad, Joseph (1986). *Lord Jim.* London: Penguin.

Conrad, Joseph (1988). *Heart of Darkness,* ed. Joseph Kimbrough, 3rd edn. New York: Norton.

Corelli, Marie (1996). *The Sorrows of Satan.* Oxford: Oxford University Press.

[Courthope, W. J.] (1874). "Modern Culture." *Quarterly Review* 136 (October 1874): 205–20.

Cox, R. G. (1970). *Thomas Hardy: The Critical Heritage.* London: Routledge & Kegan Paul.

Cronin, Richard, Alison Chapman, and Antony H. Harrison (2002). *A Companion to Victorian Poetry.* Malden, MA: Blackwell.

Cross, Nigel (1985). *The Common Writer.* Cambridge: Cambridge University Press.

Cunningham, Gail (1978). *The New Woman and the Victorian Novel.* London: Macmillan.

Darwin, Charles (1968). *The Origin of Species By Means of Natural Selection.* London: Penguin.

Davidoff, Lenore (1973). *The Best Circles: Women and Society in Victorian England.* Totowa, NJ: Rowman & Littlefield.

Dawson, Carl (1973). *Matthew Arnold, The Poetry: The Critical Heritage.* London: Routledge & Kegan Paul.

Dawson, Carl and John Pfordresher (1979). *Matthew Arnold, Prose Writings: The Critical Heritage.* London: Routledge & Kegan Paul.

Dickens, Charles (1936). *A Tale of Two Cities.* New York: New American Library.

Dickens, Charles (1965). *American Notes.* New York: Fromm International.

Dickens, Charles (1966). *Hard Times,* ed. George Ford and Sylvere Monod. New York: Norton.

Dickens, Charles (1967). *Little Dorrit.* London: Penguin.

Dickens, Charles (1970). *Dombey and Son*. London: Penguin.

Dickens, Charles (1971). *Our Mutual Friend*. London: Penguin.

Dickens, Charles (1974). *The Mystery of Edmund Drood*. London: Penguin.

Dickens, Charles (1978). *Nicholas Nickleby*. London: Penguin.

Dickens, Charles (1982). *Oliver Twist*. Oxford: Oxford University Press.

Dickens, Charles (1985). *David Copperfield*. London: Penguin.

Dickens, Charles (1987). *The Pickwick Papers*. London: Penguin.

Dickens, Charles (1993). *Bleak House*. London: Penguin.

Dickens, Charles (1995). *Sketches by Boz*. London: Penguin.

Dickens, Charles (1996). *Great Expectations*. London: Penguin.

Dickens, Charles (1997). *Barnaby Rudge*. London: Penguin.

Dickens, Charles (1998). *The Old Curiosity Shop*. Oxford: Oxford University Press.

Dickens, Charles (1999). *Martin Chuzzelwit*. London: Penguin.

Dickens, Charles (2006). *A Christmas Carol and Other Christmas Books*. Oxford: Oxford University Press.

Dilke, Charles Wentworth (1868). *Greater Britain: A Record of Travel in English-Speaking Countries*, 2 vols. in 1. London: Macmillan.

Disraeli, Benjamin (1980). *Sybil, or The Two Nations*. London: Penguin.

Disraeli, Benjamin (1983). *Conigsby, or The New Generation*. London: Penguin.

Dodds, John W. (1952). *The Age of Paradox: A Biography of England, 1841–1851*. New York: Rinehart.

Donaldson, Sandra (ed.) (1993). *Elizabeth Barrett Browning: An Annotated Bibliography of the Commentary and Criticism, 1826–1990*. New York: G. K. Hall.

Dostoevsky, Fyodor (1968). *Notes from Underground*, trans. David Magarshack, in *Great Short Works of Fyodor Dostoevsky*. New York: Harper & Row, pp. 263–377.

Dowling, Linda (1986). *Language and Decadence*. Princeton, NJ: Princeton University Press.

Dowson, Ernest (1963). *Poems*, ed. Mark Longaker. Philadelphia, PA: University of Pennsylvania Press.

du Maurier, George (1894). *Trilby*, 2 vols. Leipzig: Bernhard Tauchnitz.

Edel, Leon (1977). *The Life of Henry James*, 2 vols. London: Penguin.

Edgeworth, Maria (1995). *Castle Rackrent*. Oxford: Oxford University Press.

Egerton, George (1983). *Keynotes and Discords*. London: Virago.

Eliot, George (1856). "Ruskin's Modern Painters". *Westminster Review*, NS 9 (April 1856).

Eliot, George (1963). *Essays of George Eliot*, ed. Thomas Pinney. New York: Columbia University Press.

Eliot, George. (1973). *Scenes of Clerical Life*. London: Penguin.

Eliot, George (1979). *The Mill on the Floss*. London: Penguin.
Eliot, George (1980). *Adam Bede*. London: Penguin.
Eliot, George (1980a). *Romola*. London: Penguin.
Eliot, George (1995a). *Daniel Deronda*. London: Penguin.
Eliot, George (1995b). *Felix Holt, The Radical*. London: Penguin.
Eliot, George (1995c). *Middlemarch, A Study of Provincial Life*. London: Penguin.
Eliot, T. S. (1932). *Selected Essays*. London: Faber & Faber.
Ellmann, Richard (1978). *Yeats: The Man and His Masks*. New York: Norton.
Ellmann, Richard (1988). *Oscar Wilde*. New York: Alfred A. Knopf.
Emeljanow, Victor (1987). *Victorian Popular Dramatists*. Boston: Twayne.
Erickson, Lee (1996). *The Economy of Literary Form: English Literature and the Industrialization of Publishing, 1800–1850*. Baltimore, MD: Johns Hopkins University Press.
Erickson, Lee (2002). "The Market," in Cronin, Chapman, and Harrison (eds.), *A Companion to Victorian Poetry*, pp. 245–60.
Feldman, Paula (1999). "The Poet and the Profits: Felicia Hemans and the Literary Marketplace," in Isobel Armstrong and Virginia Blain (eds.), *Women's Poetry: Late Romantic to Late Victorian*. London: Macmillan, pp. 71–101.
Field, Michael (2000). *Music and Silence: The Gamut of Michael Field*, ed. Ivor C. Treby. N.p.: De Blackland Press.
Fitzgerald, Edward (1999). *The Rubaiyyat of Omar Khayyam*, in T. Collins and V. Rundle, eds., 1999, pp. 147–55.
Forster, E. M. (1987). *Maurice*. New York: Norton.
Forster, John (1966). *The Life of Charles Dickens*, 2 vols. London: Dent.
Frank, Anne (1991). *Anne Frank: The Diary of a Young Girl*, trans. Susan Massotty. New York: Anchor.
Fraser, Hilary with David Brown (1997). *English Prose of the Nineteenth Century*. London: Longman.
Frazier, Adrian (2000). *George Moore, 1852–1933*. New Haven, CT: Yale University Press.
Froude, James Anthony (1882). *Thomas Carlyle, A History of the First Forty Years of His Life, 1795–1835*. London: Longman, Green.
Froude, James Anthony (1904). *Thomas Carlyle: A History of His Life in London, 1834–1881*. New York: Scribners.
Gaskell, Elizabeth (1969). *Wives and Daughters*. London: Penguin.
Gaskell, Elizabeth (1970). *Mary Barton: A Tale of Manchester Life*. London: Penguin.
Gaskell, Elizabeth (1970a). *North and South*. London: Penguin.
Gaskell, Elizabeth (1975). *Life of Charlotte Brontë*. London: Penguin.
Gaskell, Elizabeth (1976). *Cranford*. London: Penguin.

Gaskell, Elizabeth (2001). *Ruth*. London: J. M. Dent.

Gilbert, W. S. (1924). *The Bab Ballads* and *Songs of a Savoyard*. London: Macmilllan.

Gill, Stephen (1998). *Wordsworth and the Victorians*. Oxford: Clarendon Press.

Gilmour, David (2002). *The Long Recessional: The Imperial Life of Rudyard Kipling*. New York: Farrar, Strauss, Giroux.

Girouard, Mark (1981). *The Return to Camelot: Chivalry and the English Gentleman*. New Haven, CT: Yale University Press.

Gissing, George (1968). *New Grub Street*. London: Penguin.

Gissing, George (1992). *The Nether World*. Oxford: Oxford University Press.

Gissing, George (2000). *The Odd Women*. Oxford: Oxford University Press.

Grand, Sarah (1893). *The Heavenly Twins*. New York: Cassell.

Gray, Donald J. (1976). *Victorian Literature: Poetry*. New York: Macmillan.

Green, Roger Lancelyn (1971). *Kipling: The Critical Heritage*. London: Routledge & Kegan Paul.

Greenwell, Dora (1867). *Poems*. London: A. Strahan.

[Greg, W. R.] (1851). "English Socialism, and Communistic Association," *Edinburgh Review* 189 (January 1851): 1–17.

Grossmith, George and Weedon Grossmith (1991). *The Diary of a Nobody*. Stroud: Alan Sutton.

Haggard, H. Rider (1886). *King Solomon's Mines*. Leipzig: Bernhard Tauchnitz.

Haggard, H. Rider (1887). *She*, 2 vols. Leipzig: Bernhard Tauchnitz.

Hallam, Arthur Henry (1999). "On Some of the Characteristics of Modern Poetry," in T. Collins and V. Rundle (eds.), 1999, pp. 1190–1205.

Hardy, Florence Emily (1928). *The Early Life of Thomas Hardy*. London: Macmillan.

Hardy, Thomas (1925). *Collected Poems of Thomas Hardy*. New York: Macmillan.

Hardy, Thomas (1960). *Far from the Madding Crowd*. New York: New American Library.

Hardy, Thomas (1978). *Tess of the D'Urbervilles*. London: Penguin.

Hardy, Thomas (1998). *Jude the Obscure*. London: Penguin.

Hardy, Thomas (2001). *The Mayor of Casterbridge*, ed. Phillip Mallett. New York: Norton.

Hardy, Thomas (2006). *The Return of the Native*, ed. Philip Mallett, 2nd edn. New York: Norton.

Hare, Augustus J. C. (1894). *Life and Letters of Maria Edgeworth*, 2 vols. Boston: Mifflin.

Heineman, Helen (1979). *Mrs. Trollope: The Triumphant Feminine in the Nineteenth Century*. Athens, OH: Ohio University Press.

Hemans, Felicia (2002). *Selected Poems, Prose, and Letters*, ed. Gary Kelly. Peterborough: Broadview.

Henley, W. E. (1908). *The Works of W. E. Henley*, 7 vols. London: David Nutt.

Hogan, Robert (1969). *Dion Boucicault*. New York: Twayne.

Hollingsworth, Keith (1963). *The Newgate Novel, 1830–1847*. Detroit, MI: Wayne State University Press.

Hood, Thomas (1976). "The Song of the Shirt," in D. J. Gray, 1976, p. 37.

Hopkins, Gerard Manley (1970). *The Poems of Gerard Manley Hopkins*, 4th edn, ed. W. H. Gardner and N. H. MacKenzie. London: Oxford University Press.

Horne, T. H. (1844). *The New Spirit of the Age*. London: Smith, Elder.

House, Humphrey (1941). *The Dickens World*. Oxford: Oxford University Press.

Housman, A. E. (1965). *The Collected Poems of A. E. Housman*. New York: Holt, Rinehart and Winston.

Howe, Susanne (1966). *Wilhelm Meister and His English Kinsmen*. New York: AMS Press.

Hughes, Thomas (1989). *Tom Brown's Schooldays*. Oxford: Oxford University Press.

Hunt, Peter (1994). *An Introduction to Children's Literature*. Oxford: Oxford University Press.

Huxley, T. H. (1905). *Science and Education*. New York: P. H. Collier.

Huxley, T. H. (1917). *Collected Essays*, 9 vols. New York: Appleton.

Huysmans, Joris-Karl (1959). *Against Nature (A Rebours)*, trans. Robert Baldick. London: Penguin.

Hyder, Clyde K (1970). *Swinburne: The Critical Heritage*. London: Routledge & Kegan Paul.

Ibsen, Henrik (1981). *Four Major Plays*, trans. James McFarlane and Jens Arup. Oxford: Oxford University Press.

Ingelow, Jean (1898). *Poems*. 2 vols. London: Longman, Green.

Irvine, William (1972). *Apes, Angels, and Victorians: The Story of Darwin, Huxley, and Evolution*. New York: McGraw-Hill.

Irvine, William and Park Honan (1974). *The Ring, The Book, and the Poet: A Biography of Robert Browning*. New York: McGraw-Hill.

Jackson, Russell (ed.) (1982). *Plays by Henry Archer Jones*. Cambridge: Cambridge University Press.

James, Henry (1966). *The Portrait of a Lady*. London: Penguin.

James, Henry (1971). "The Art of Fiction," in G. L. Barnett, 1971, pp. 240–55.

James, Henry (1977). *The Princess Casamassima*. London: Penguin.

James, Henry (1979). *The Tragic Muse*. London: Penguin.

James, Louis (1963). *Fiction for the Working Man, 1830–1850*. Oxford: Oxford University Press.

Jeffares, A. Norman and Peter Van de Kemp (2005). *Irish Literature in the Nineteenth Century*, 3 vols. Portland, OR: Irish Academic Press.

Jefferies, Richard (2006). *After London*. Whitefish, MT: Kessinger.

Jenkins, Anthony (1991). *The Making of Victorian Drama*. Cambridge: Cambridge University Press.

Jewsbury, Geraldine Endsor (1845). *Zoe: The History of Two Lives*, 3 vols. London: Chapman and Hall.

Johnson, Edgar (1952). *Charles Dickens: His Tragedy and Triumph*, 2 vols. New York: Simon and Schuster.

Johnson, Lionel (1982). *Collected Poems of Lionel Johnson*, 3rd edn., ed. Ian Fletcher. New York: Garland.

Jump, J. D. (1971). *Tennyson: The Critical Heritage*. London: Routledge & Kegan Paul.

Keating, Peter (1969). *The Haunted Study: A Social History of the English Novel, 1875–1914*. London: Secker & Warburg.

Kermode, Frank (1971). *Romantic Image*. London: Collins.

Kingsley, Charles (1890). *Literary and General Lecture and Essays*. London: Macmillan.

Kingsley, Charles (1902). *The Life and Works of Charles Kingsley*, 19 vols. London: Macmillan.

Kingsley, Charles (1995). *The Water-Babies: A Fairy Tale for a Land-Baby*. Oxford: Oxford University Press.

"Kingsley's *Andromeda*." *Saturday Review* 5 (1858): 594–5.

Kipling, Rudyard (1899). *Stalky and Co*. Leipzig: Bernhard Tauchnitz.

Kipling, Rudyard (1900). *Plain Tales from the Hills*. New York: Regent Press.

Kipling, Rudyard (1930). *Poems, 1886–1929*, 3 vols. Garden City, NY: Doubleday, Doran.

Kipling, Rudyard (1961). *The Best Short Stories of Rudyard Kipling*, ed. Rabdall Jarrell. Garden City, NY: Doubleday.

Kipling, Rudyard (1987a). *Jungle Books*. London: Penguin.

Kipling, Rudyard (1987b). *Kim*. London: Penguin.

Kucich, John (1994). *The Power of Lies: Transgression in Victorian Fiction*. Ithaca, NY: Cornell University Press.

Landon, Letitia Elizabeth (1997). *Selected Writings*, ed. Jerome McGann and Daniel Riess. Peterborough: Broadview.

Lawrence, G. A. (1860). *Guy Livingstone*. Leipzig: Bernhard Tauchnitz.

Lear, Edward (1992). *A Book of Nonsense*. New York: Knopf.

Leary, Patrick (2005). "Googling the Victorians," *Journal of Victorian Culture* 10/1 (spring 2005): 72–86.

Lee, Vernon (2004). *Miss Brown*. Doylestown, PA: Wildside Press.

Le Fanu, Sheridan (1966). *Uncle Silas: A Tale of Bartram-Haugh*. Dover: New York.

Leighton, Angela and Margaret Reynolds (eds.) (1995). *Victorian Women Poets: An Anthology*. Oxford: Blackwell.

ver, Charles (1899). *The Confessions of Harry Lorrequer*, 2 vols. Boston: Little, Brown.

y, Amy (1993). *The Complete Novels and Selected Writings*, ed. Melvin New. Gainesville, FL: University of Florida Press.

Amy (2006). *Reuben Sachs: A Sketch*, ed. Susan David Bernstein. eterborough: Broadview.

Linton, Eliza Lynn (1884). *The Girl of the Period and Other Social Essays*. Leipzig: Bernhard Tauchnitz.

Litzinger, Boyd and Donald Smalley (eds.) (1970). *Browning: The Critical Heritage*. New York: Barnes and Noble.

Livingstone, David (1859). *Missionary Travels and Research in South Africa*. New York: Harper.

Loesberg, Jonathan (1977). *Fictions of Consciousness: Mill, Newman, and the Reading of Victorian Prose*. New Brunswick, NJ: Rutgers University Press.

Lover, Samuel (2001). *Handy Andy: A Tale of Irish Life*. Honolulu: University of Hawaii Press.

Macaulay, Thomas Babington (1842). *Lays of Ancient Rome*. London: Longman, Brown, Green.

Macaulay, Thomas Babington (1873). *Critical, Historical, and Miscellaneous Essays*, 6 vols. New York: Mason, Baker, and Pratt.

Macaulay, Thomas Babington. (1879). *The History of England from the Accession of James I*. New York: Harper Brothers.

McGann. Jerome (1982). "Tennyson and the Histories of Criticism," *Review* 4 (1982): 219–53.

Mallock, W. H. (1900). *The New Republic, or Culture, Faith, and Philosophy in an English Country House*. London: Chatto & Windus.

Mangan, J. A. (1986). *The Games Ethic and Imperialism*. Harmondsworth: Viking.

Mansel, H. J. (1863). "Sensation Novels," *Quarterly Review* 113 (April 1863): 481–514.

Martineau, Harriet (1877). *Harriet Martineau's Autobiography*, 2 vols. London: Smith, Elder.

Martineau, Harriet (1962). *Society in America*, ed. Seymour Martin Lipset. Garden City, NY: Anchor.

Martineau, Harriet (2004). *Illustrations of Political Economy: Selected Tales*, ed. Deborah Ann Logan. Peterborough, Ontario: Broadview.

Mayhew, Henry (1968). *London Labour and the London Poor* (1861–62), 4 vols. New York: Dover.

Mearns, Andrew (1883). *The Bitter Cry of Outcast London*. Boston: Cupples, Upham.

Meredith, George (1910). *Beauchamp's Career*, 2 vols. New York: Chares Scribner.

Meredith, George (1968). *The Egoist*. London: Penguin.

Meredith, George (1971). *The Ordeal of Richard Feverel*. Boston: Houghton Mifflin.

Meredith, George (1976). *Modern Love*, in D. J. Gray, 1976, pp. 517–27.

Mermin, Dorothy (1989). *Elizabeth Barrett Browning: The Origins of a New Poetry*. Chicago, IL: University of Chicago Press.

Mermin, Dorothy (1993). *Godiva's Ride: Women of Letters in England, 1830–1880*. Bloomington: Indiana University Press.

Mill, John Stuart (1963–91). *The Collected Works of John Stuart Mill*, 33 vols, gen ed. John M. Robson. Toronto: University of Toronto Press.

Miller, D. A. (1988). *The Novel and the Police*. Berkeley, CA: University of California Press.

Millgate, Michael (1982). *Thomas Hardy, A Biography*. New York: Random House.

Moore, George (1922). *A Mummer's Wife*. New York: Boni and Liveright.

Morris, William (1883). *The Defense of Guinevere, and Other Poems*. London: Ellis & White,

Morris, William (1890). *The Earthly Paradise*. London: Reeves & Turner.

Morris, William (2003). *News from Nowhere, or An Epoch of Rest*. Oxford: Oxford University Press.

Morrison, Stanley (1896). *A Child of the Jago*. Chicago, IL: Stone.

Mulock Craik, Diana (2005). *John Halifax, Gentleman*, ed. Lynn Alexander. Peterborough, Ontario: Broadview.

Newbolt, Henry (1898). *Admirals All, and Other Verses*. New York: John Lane.

Newman, John Henry (1965). *Prose and Poetry*, ed. Geoffrey Tillotson. Cambridge, MA: Harvard University Press.

Newman, John Henry (1968). *Apologia pro Vita Sua*, ed. David J. DeLaura. New York: Norton, 1968.

Oliphant, Margaret (1867). "Novels," *Blackwood's* 102 (September 1867): 257–80.

Oliphant, Margaret (1870). *Miss Marjoribanks*, 2 vols. Leipzig: Bernhard Tauchnitz.

Oliphant, Margaret (1986). *Salem Chapel*. London: Virago.

Oliphant, Margaret (2002). *Phoebe Junior, A Last Chronicle of Carlingford*, ed. Elizabeth Langland. Peterborough, ON: Broadview.

O'Neill, Eugene (1956). *Long Day's Journey Into Night*. New Haven, CT: Yale University Press.

Ouida [Marie de la Ramee] (1890). *Under Two Flags*. New York: Peter Fenelon Collier.

Page, Norman (1974). *Wilkie Collins: The Critical Heritage*. London: Routledge & Kegan Paul.

Pater, Walter (1912). *Imaginary Portraits*. London: Macmillan.

Pater, Walter (1913). *Appreciations, with an Essay on Style.* London: Macmillan.

Pater, Walter (1918). *Marius the Epicurean,* 2 vols. London: Macmillan.

Pater, Walter (1974). "Poems by William Morris," in *Pre-Raphaelitism: A Collection of Critical Essays,* ed. James Sambrook. Chicago, IL: University of Chicago Press, 1974, pp. 105–17.

Pater, Walter (1980). *The Renaissance: Studies in Art and Poetry,* ed. Donald L. Hill. Berkeley: University of California Press.

Patmore, Coventry (1949). *The Poems of Coventry Patmore.* London: Oxford University Press.

Patten, Robert L. (1978). *Charles Dickens and His Publishers.* Oxford: Clarendon Press.

Peck, John (1988). *War, the Army and Victorian Literature.* New York: St. Martin's.

Pinero, Arthur Wing (1986). *Plays,* ed. George Rowell. Cambridge: Cambridge University Press.

Procter, Adelaide Anne (1871). *The Poems of Adelaide Procter.* Boston: J. R. Osgood.

Pugin, Augustus Welby (1841). *Contrasts, or A parallel between the noble edifices of the middle ages, and corresponding buildings of the present day, shewing the present decay of taste.* London: C. Dolman.

Pykett, Lyn (2005). *Wilkie Collins.* Oxford: Oxford University Press.

Pyle, Andrew (ed.) (1994). *Liberty: Contemporary Responses to John Stuart Mill.* Bristol: Thoemmes Press.

Ray, Gordon (1955). *Thackeray: The Uses of Adversity, 1811–1846.* New York: McGraw-Hill.

Read, Donald (1994). *The Age of Urban Democracy: England 1868–1914.* London: Longman.

Reade, Charles (1864). *Hard Cash: A Matter of Fact Romance,* 3 vols. Leipzig: Bernhard Tauchnitz.

Reade, Charles (1875). *Griffith Gaunt, or Jealousy.* Boston: Osgood.

Reed, John R. (1985). *Decadent Style.* Athens, OH: Ohio University Press.

Rosenberg, John (1961). *The Darkening Glass: A Portrait of Ruskin's Genius.* New York: Columbia University Press.

Rossetti, Christina (1979–90). *The Complete Poems of Christina Rossetti. A Variorum Edition,* ed. R. W. Crump, 3 vols. Baton Rouge: Louisiana State University Press.

Rossetti, Dante Gabriel (1901) *The Collected Works of Dante Gabriel Rossetti,* ed. William M. Rossetti, 2 vols. London: Ellis and Elvey.

Rousseau, Jean Jacques (1953). *The Confessions,* trans. J. M. Cohen. London: Penguin.

Ruskin, John (1903–12). *The Works of John Ruskin,* 39 vols, ed. E. T. Cook and Alexander Wedderburn. New York: Longmans, Green.

St. Clair, William (2004). *The Reading Nation in the Romantic Period*. New York: Cambridge University Press.

Schramm, Jan-Melissa (2000). *Testimony and Advocacy in Victorian Law, Literature, and Theology*. Cambridge: Cambridge University Press.

Schreiner, Olive (1995). *The Story of an African Farm*. London: Penguin.

Seiler, R. H. (1980). *Walter Pater: The Critical Heritage*. London: Routledge & Kegan Paul.

Shairp, J. H. (1882). "Aesthetic Poetry," *Contemporary Review* 42 (July 1882): 17–32.

Shaw, George Bernard (1906). *Plays Pleasant and Unpleasant*, vol. 1. New York: Brentano's.

Shaw, George Bernard (1993–7). *Complete Prefaces*, 3 vols., ed. Dan H. Laurence and Daniel J. Leary. London: Allen Lane.

Shorthouse, J. H. (1882). *John Ingelsant: A Romance*, 2 vols. Leipzig: Bernhard Tauchnitz.

Siegel, Jules Paul (1971). *Thomas Carlyle: The Critical Heritage*. New York: Barnes & Noble.

Sinclair, Catherine (n.d.). *Beatrice*. London: Ward, Lock, and Tyler.

Smalley, Donald (1969). *Trollope: The Critical Heritage*. London: Routledge & Kegan Paul.

Smiles, Samuel. *Self-Help, with illustrations of character, conduct, and perseverance*, ed. Peter W. Sinnema. Oxford: Oxford University Press.

Smith, Alexander (1853). *Poems*. Boston: Ticknor, Reed, and Fields.

Southey, Robert (1829). *Sir Thomas More; or, Colloquies on the Progress and Prospects of Society*. London: John Murray.

Stanley, Arthur Penryn (n.d.). *Life and Correspondence of Thomas Arnold, D.D.* New York: Harper Brothers.

Stead, W. T. (1885). "The Maiden Tribute of Modern Babylon," *Pall Mall Gazette*, No. 6336, Vol XLII (July 6, 1885).

Stedman Jones, Gareth (1984). *Outcast London: A Study in the Relationship between Classes in Victorian Society*. New York: Pantheon.

Stevenson, Robert Louis (1971). "A Humble Remonstrance," in G. L. Barnett, 1971, pp. 256–65.

Stevenson, Robert Louis (1999). *Treasure Island*. New York: Penguin.

Stevenson, Robert Louis (2002). *The Strange Case of Doctor Jekyll and Mr. Hyde*, ed. Martin A. Danahay. Peterborough, Ont: Broadview.

Stoker, Bram. *Dracula* (1898). New York: Norton.

Sutherland, John (1989). *The Stanford Guide to Victorian Fiction*. Stanford: Stanford University Press.

Swinburne, Algernon Charles (1925–27). *The Complete Works of Algernon Charles Swinburne.*, ed. Edmund Gosse and T. J. Wise, 20 vols. London: Heinemann.

Symons, Arthur (1906). *Poems*, 2 vols. London: Heinemann.

Symons, Arthur (1999). "The Decadent Movement in Literature," in T. Collins and V. Rundle, 1999, pp. 1405–13.

Taylor, Henry (1864). *The Poetical Works of Henry Taylor, D.C.L.* Vol. 1: *Philip van Artevelde*. London: Chapman and Hall.

Taylor, Tom (1985). *Plays*, ed. Martin Banham. Cambridge: Cambridge University Press.

Tennyson, Alfred, Lord (1969). *The Poems of Tennyson*, ed. Christopher Ricks. London: Longmans.

Tennyson, Hallam (1897). *Alfred, Lord Tennyson. A Memoir by His Son.* New York: Macmillan.

Thackeray, William Makepeace (1970). *The History of Henry Esmond.* London: Penguin.

Thackeray, William Makepeace (1991). *The History of Pendennis*, ed. Peter L. Shillingsburg. New York: Garland.

Thackeray, William Makepeace (1996). *The Newcomes.* London: Penguin.

Thackeray, William Makepeace (2001). *Vanity Fair, A Novel without a Hero.* London: Penguin.

Thackeray, William Makepeace (n.d.). *Novels by Eminent Hands and Miscellaneous Papers. The Works of William Makepeace Thackeray*, vol X. New York: International Book Company.

Thomson, James (1880). *The City of Dreadful Night.* London: Reeves and Turner.

Thorpe, Michael (1972). *Clough: The Critical Heritage.* London: Routledge & Kegan Paul.

Tillotson, Geoffrey and Donald Hawes (1968). *Thackeray: The Critical Heritage.* London: Routledge & Kegan Paul.

Trollope, Anthony (1973). *Can You Forgive Her?,* Oxford: Oxford University Press.

Trollope, Anthony (1973a). *The Duke's Children.* Oxford: Oxford University Press.

Trollope, Anthony (1973b). *The Eustace Diamonds.* Oxford: Oxford University Press.

Trollope, Anthony (1973c). *Phineas Finn.* Oxford: Oxford University Press.

Trollope, Anthony (1973d). *Phineas Redux.* Oxford: Oxford University Press.

Trollope, Anthony (1973e). *The Prime Minister.* Oxford: Oxford University Press.

Trollope, Anthony (1980). *An Autobiography.* Oxford: Oxford University Press.

Trollope, Anthony (1980a). *Barchester Towers*, 2 vols. in 1. Oxford: Oxford University Press.

Trollope, Anthony (1980b). *Doctor Thorne.* Oxford: Oxford University Press.

Trollope, Anthony (1980c). *Framley Parsonage*. Oxford: Oxford University Press.

Trollope, Anthony (1980d). *The Small House at Allington*. Oxford: Oxford University Press.

Trollope, Anthony (1980e). *The Warden*. Oxford: Oxford University Press.

Trollope, Anthony (1981). *The Last Chronicle of Barset*. Oxford: Oxford University Press.

Trollope, Anthony (1982). *The Way We Live Now*. Oxford: Oxford University Press.

Trollope, Frances (1840). *The Life and Adventures of Michael Armstrong, The Factory Boy*. London: Henry Colburn.

Trollope, Frances (1949). *Domestic Manners of the Americans*, ed. Donald Smalley. New York: Vantage.

Tupper, Martin (1976). *Proverbial Philosophy*, in D. J. Gray, 1976, pp. 386–7.

Tyndall, John (1905). *Fragments of Science*, 2 vols. New York: P. F. Collier.

Verlaine, Paul (1974). *Verlaine: Selected Poems*, trans. Joanna Richardson. London: Penguin.

Ward, Mrs. Humphry (1888). *Robert Elsmere*, 2 vols. London: Macmillan.

Warren, Samuel (1932). *Ten Thousand A-Year*. New York: A. L. Burt.

Watt, Ian (1979). *Conrad in the Nineteenth Century*. Berkeley: University of California Press.

Webster, Augusta (2000). *Augusta Webster: Portraits and Other Poems*, ed. Christine Sutphin. Peterborough, Ontario: Broadview.

Wells, H. G. (1993). *A Critical Edition of The War of the Worlds*, ed. David Y. Hughes and Harry M. Geduld. Bloomington, IN: Indiana University Press.

Wells, H. G. (2001). *The Time Machine: An Invention (1895)*, ed. Nicholas Ruddick. Peterborough, Ontario: Broadview.

Welsh, Alexander (1985). *George Eliot and Blackmail*. Cambridge, MA: Harvard University Press.

White, William Hale (1938). *The Autobiography of Mark Rutherford*. London: Jonathan Cape.

Wilde, Oscar (1909). *The Works of Oscar Wilde*, vol 1, *Poems*. New York: Lamb.

Wilde, Oscar (1954). *Oscar Wilde: Plays*. London: Penguin.

Wilde, Oscar (1982). *The Artist as Critic: Critical Writings of Oscar Wilde*, ed. Richard Elmann. Chicago, IL: University of Chicago Press.

Wilde, Oscar (1987). *The Picture of Dorian Gray (1890)*, ed. Donald L. Lawler. New York: Norton.

Williams, Ioan (1971). *Meredith: The Critical Heritage*. London: Routledge & Kegan Paul.

Wolff, Robert Lee (1977). *Gains and Losses: Novels of Faith and Doubt in Victorian England*. New York: Garland.

Wood, Ellen (2002). *East Lynne*, ed. Andrew Maunder. Peterborough, Ontario: Broadview.

Woolf, Virginia (1953). *The Common Reader: First Series.* New York: Harcourt Brace.

Woolf, Virginia (1974). *The Death of the Moth and Other Essays.* New York, Harcourt Brace Jovanovich.

Woolf, Virginia (1980). *Collected Essays*, 4 vols. London: Hogarth Press.

Yeats, William Butler (1936). *The Oxford Book of Modern Verse, 1892–1935.* New York: Oxford University Press.

Yeats, William Butler (1965). *The Autobiography of William Butler Yeats.* New York: Collier.

Yeats, William Butler (1966). *The Collected Poems of W. B. Yeats.* New York: Macmillan.

Yonge, Charlotte (1997). *The Heir of Redclyffe.* Oxford: Oxford University Press.

Young, G. M. (1964). *Victorian England: Portrait of an Age*, 2nd edn. Oxford: Oxford University Press.

Index

9 780631 220824